2015-2016 EDITION NO SEPARATE POLICY CHAPTERS VERSION

AMERICAN GOVERNMENT

AND POLITICS TODAY

2015-2016 EDITION NO SEPARATE POLICY CHAPTERS VERSION

AMERICAN GOVERNMENT
AND POLITICS TODAY

Lynne E. Ford
College of Charleston

Barbara A. Bardes
University of Cincinnati

Steffen W. Schmidt
Iowa State University

Mack C. Shelley II
Iowa State University

CENGAGE
Learning·

ustralia • Brazil • Mexico • Singapore • United Kingdom • United States

American Government and Politics Today, No Separate Policy Chapters Version, 2015-2016 Edition

Lynne E. Ford, Barbara A. Bardes, Steffen W. Schmidt, Mack D. Shelley II

Product Team Manager: Carolyn Merrill

Associate Product Manager: Scott Greenan

Content Developer: Lauren Athmer, LEAP Publishing, Inc.

Associate Content Developer: Amy Bither

Product Assistant: Abby Hess

Senior Media Developer: Laura Hildebrand

Marketing Manager: Valerie Hartman

Senior Content Project Manager: Rosemary Winfield

Senior Art Director: Linda May

Manufacturing Planner: Fola Orekoya

IP Analyst: Alex Ricciardi

IP Project Manager: Brittani Morgan

Production Service: Integra Software Services Pvt. Ltd

Compositor: Integra Software Services Pvt. Ltd

Text Designer: Studio Montage

Cover Designer: Studio Montage

Cover Image: Blend Images / Mike Kemp / Gerry Images; Jeffrey Coolidge / Photodisc / Getty Images

> For product information and technology assistance, contact us at **Cengage Learning Customer & Sales Support, 1-800-354-9706.**
>
> For permission to use material from this text or product, submit all requests online at **www.cengage.com/permissions.** Further permissions questions can be emailed to **permissionrequest@cengage.com.**

Library of Congress Control Number: 2014955960

Package: 978-1-285-87245-2

Text-only edition: 978-1-305-10881-3

Loose-leaf edition: 978-1-305-63460-2

Cengage Learning
20 Channel Center Street
Boston, MA 02210
USA

Cengage Learning is a leading provider of customized learning solutions with office locations around the globe, including Singapore, the United Kingdom, Australia, Mexico, Brazil, and Japan. Locate your local office at **www.cengage.com/global.**

Cengage Learning products are represented in Canada by Nelson Education, Ltd.

To learn more about Cengage Learning Solutions, visit **www.cengage.com.**

Purchase any of our products at your local college store or at our preferred online store **www.cengagebrain.com.**

Printed in the United States of America

Print Number: 01 Print Year: 2014

Brief Contents

Contents

PART III   PEOPLE AND POLITICS

Chapter 6: Public Opinion and Political Socialization 201

Chapter 7: Interest Groups 232

Chapter 10: The Media and Politics 346

PART IV POLITICAL INSTITUTIONS

Chapter 11: The Congress 379

Chapter 12: The President 418

Chapter 13: The Bureaucracy 454

Chapter 14: The Courts 487

Letter to Instructor

Dear American Politics Instructor:

Americans are often cynical about our national political system. College students in particular are at a loss to know what to do about the polarized politics and policy gridlock occurring within the modern political system, making American Politics a tough course to teach. This edition of *American Government and Politics Today* is designed to help you move your students from the sidelines of politics to full engagement by equipping them with the knowledge and analytical skills needed to shape political decisions at the local, state, and national levels. Based on review feedback, we include a strong emphasis on the power of modern social media and its ability to engage citizens with one another, as well as to connect citizens with political issues and ideas. The solid content on institutions and the processes of government included in previous editions remains. New features such as "Everyday Politics" and "What Would You Do?" will help you bring politics to life in your classroom, while demonstrating to students why politics matters and how it surrounds them each day—at times without their even knowing it. Each chapter has the most up to date data and information, and includes coverage of current issues and controversies that we believe will engage students and hold their interest.

We believe that part of America's cynicism stems from the growing reality of "two Americas": one with opportunity afforded by privilege and wealth and another whose opportunities, rights, and privileges seem stunted by a lack of wealth. Does the promise of America exist for both groups, or only one? How do the 99 percent regain the promise of the American Dream? What role can political engagement play in doing so? Knowledge is power, and in this edition we try to strike a balance between the content and the skill-building necessary for course success, while also presenting students with current controversies in politics and opportunities to engage with those issues. The new **Everyday Politics** feature found in each chapter uses an example from popular culture, such as the movie *Twelve Years a Slave,* to illustrate the realities of a political issue (such as slavery) and how the federal system has addressed or confronted the issue. In the end-of-chapter feature **What Would You Do?** students are presented with a political or judicial issue, and put into the role of active decision-maker. Students must apply material from the chapter to solve a problem or avert a crisis. These active learning opportunities bring the issues that students are confronted with on a daily basis alive and give students the opportunity to apply their knowledge and skills.

New to this Edition

This edition has been substantially revised and updated to include the 2014 national elections. In response to our reviewers, we have added Chapter 10: "The Media and Politics." This chapter puts a strong emphasis on the importance of the Internet and on social media for every aspect of politics. Chapter 9 now combines material on "Campaigns, Voting, and Elections" in a format that will lead the student seamlessly through the electoral process. Many features have been greatly revised for this edition:

- "Everyday Politics" is a new to this edition and focuses on a media resource such as a movie, television drama or sitcom, or website that links to the specific chapter topics. The feature is designed to enhance student interest by linking popular culture connections to political content.
- "You Can Make a Difference" has been revised to create the more active feature, "What Would You Do?" In this feature, students are put in the position of a decision-maker facing an important political dilemma. Students are asked to think critically about the decision, using the knowledge gained from study of the chapter to make an educated decision. The feature "shows" instead of "tells."

Greater attention has been paid to gender issues throughout the text as suggested by reviewers. New material is included on the Equal Pay Act, as well as the Lilly Ledbetter Act, in addition to updated coverage of women's rights and gender equality, gender and racial discrimination, and the pay gap. All tables and figures have been updated and the results of the 2014 election are reported throughout the book.

Recent court decisions that have been made on same sex marriage and campaign financing, as well as foreign policy crises in Ukraine and Syria are integrated into the appropriate chapters in order to ensure that the book addresses the most timely political events and topics.

Mindtap

As an instructor, MindTap is here to simplify your workload, organize and immediately grade your students' assignments, and allow you to customize your course as you see fit. Through deep-seated integration with your Learning Management System, grades are easily exported and analytics are pulled with just the click of a button. MindTap provides you with a platform to easily add in current events videos and RSS feeds from national or local news sources. Looking to include more currency in the course? Add in our KnowNow American Government Blog link for weekly updated news coverage and pedagogy.

Seeing students actively engage with the topics addressed in this book and witnessing an eagerness to learn more about the issues currently facing our nation are some of the most exciting experiences given to any faculty member, particularly when many of students will only take one undergraduate course in political science. It is our hope that the revisions to this text will help you reach many students and transform them into thoughtful and engaged citizens for the rest of their lives.

Sincerely,

Lynne E. Ford
  FordL@cofc.edu
Barbara A. Bardes
  Barbara.Bardes@uc.edu
Steffen W. Schmidt
Mack C. Shelley, II

Letter to Student

Dear Student:

Whether you are a political science major, an international affairs major, or are simply taking this course to fulfill a general requirement, we hope that you will enjoy this book and all of its features. *American Government and Politics Today* is meant to be enjoyed as well as studied. To ensure that the most relevant topics are addressed, the book has been thoroughly revised to include the results of the 2014 national elections, global events and foreign policy, and Supreme Court decisions that affect your life. In every chapter, resources are included to help you go online or use social media to investigate the issues presented in the text that capture your interest. American politics is dynamic and it is our goal to provide you with clear discussions of the institutions of national government and the political processes so that you can be informed and understand the issues as you participate in our political system.

As a student, the federal government may seem remote from your daily life, but that could not be further from the truth! The issues facing the nation today are serious and require your attention, whether it seems that way upon first glance or not. Decisions made in Washington, D.C. and in your state capital can determine, for example, the rate of interest that you will pay on student loans, who must serve in the military, or the level of investment in higher education relative to sustaining pensions and Medicare. You may have heard people talking about the "1 percent" and the "99 percent"—this is a way of capturing the gap between the very rich and everyone else. In what ways does rising wealth inequality matter in America? Is it still possible for everyone to achieve the American Dream? Is political equality possible in the face of economic and social inequality? These are just a few of the questions raised by this text. The promise of America is very much alive, but our future is far from certain. Understanding how politics works and knowing your rights as a citizen are critical to shaping the nation's future. Political questions rarely have simple answers. Political issues invite multiple perspectives that can be shaped as much by gender, race, ethnicity or sexual orientation as by political party or ideology. Throughout this text, we will try to equip you with what you need to develop your own political identity and perspective so that you can fully engage in the national conversation about our shared future.

This edition's interactive features are intended to help you succeed in your coursework as well as to understand the role of politics in the modern world.

- Learning Outcomes: These outcomes begin each chapter and serve as your "take-aways," highlighting the most important content, concepts and skills. This will make it easy to check your own learning as you work through each chapter.

- Margin Definitions: These make it easy to double-check your understanding of key terms within the chapters.

- What If: This chapter-opening feature is designed to get you thinking about why politics and government matters to you and your community.

- Everyday Politics: This new feature will help you see politics and popular culture in a new way.

- What Would You Do?: This chapter-ending feature presents a scenario with *you* as the decision-maker. You will need to know and understand the material before you can apply it to solve the problem or avert a crisis.

- Social Media Margin Questions: Each chapter includes a social media screen capture that poses a critical thinking question. This feature will challenge you to apply chapter content to the real world.

- Chapter Summaries: Revised for this edition, the end-of-chapter summaries link back to a Learning Objective to better test your understanding of the topics at hand.

- Print, Media and Online Resources: Each chapter offers a brief list of additional resources that will allow you to explore further the topics that interest you.

The Benefits of Using Mindtap as a Student

As a student, the benefits of using MindTap with this book are endless. With automatically graded practice quizzes and activities, an easily navigated learning path, and an interactive eBook, you will be able to test yourself in and outside of the classroom with ease. The accessibility of current events coupled with interactive media makes the content fun and engaging. On your computer, phone, or tablet, MindTap is there when you need it, giving you easy access to flashcards, quizzes, readings, and assignments.

Information is power: when you are well informed, you can participate in discussion with your friends, family, and colleagues and debated ideas with confidence. You can influence events rather than watch as a passive bystander. The future of our Republic depends on your full engagement. You are the next generation of leaders and we wish you well.

Sincerely,

Lynne E. Ford
    FordL@cofc.edu
Barbara A. Bardes
    Barbara.Bardes@uc.edu
Steffen W. Schmidt
Mack C. Shelley, II

MindTap™ QUICK START GUIDE

1. To get started, navigate to: www.cengagebrain.com and select "Register a Product".

A new screen will appear prompting you to add a Course Key. A Course Key is a code given to you by your instructor - this is the first of two codes you will need to access MindTap. Every student in your course section should have the same Course Key.

2. Enter the Course Key and click "Register".

If you are accessing MindTap through your school's Learning Management System such as BlackBoard or Desire2Learn, you may be redirected to use your Course Key/Access Code there. Follow the prompts you are given and feel free to contact support if you need assistance.

3. Confirm your course information above, and proceed to the log in portion below.

If you have a CengageBrain username and password, enter it under "Returning Students" and click "Login". If this is your first time, register under "New Students" and click "Create a New Account".

4. Now that you are logged in, you can access the course for free by selecting "Start Free Trial" for 20 days, or enter in your Access Code.

Your Access Code is unique to you and acts as payment for MindTap. You may have received it with your book or purchased separately in the bookstore or at CengageBrain.com. Enter it and click "Register".

NEED HELP?

For CengageBrain Support: Login to **Support.Cengage.com**. Call **866-994-2427** or access our **24/7 Student Chat!** Or access the **First Day of School PowerPoint Presentation** found at cengagebrain.com.

Resources

Students…

Access your American Government and Politics Today resources by visiting

www.cengagebrain.com/shop/isbn/9781285853017

If you purchased MindTap or CourseReader access with your book, enter your access code and click "Register." You can also purchase the book's resources here separately through the "Study Tools" tab or access the free companion website through the "Free Materials" tab.

Instructors…

Access your American Government and Politics Today resources via

www.cengage.com/login.

Log in using your Cengage Learning single sign-on user name and password, or create a new instructor account by clicking on "New Faculty User" and following the instructions.

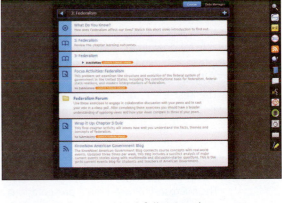

American Government and Politics Today, 2015-2016 Edition—Text Only Edition

ISBN: 9781285860435

This copy of the book does not come bundled with MindTap.

MindTap™
Personal Learning Experience

MindTap for American Government and Politics Today, 2015-2016 Edition

Instant Access Code: 9781285873251

Printed Access Code: 9781285859965

MindTap for **American Government** is a highly personalized, fully online learning experience built upon Cengage Learning content and corre-lating to a core set of learning outcomes. MindTap guides students through the course curriculum via an innovative Learning Path Navigator where they will complete reading assignments, challenge themselves with focus activities, and engage with interactive quizzes. Through a variety of gradable activities, MindTap provides students with opportunities to check themselves for where they need extra help, as well as allowing faculty to measure and assess student progress. Integration with programs like YouTube, Evernote, and Google Drive allows instructors to add and remove content of their choosing with ease, keeping their course current while

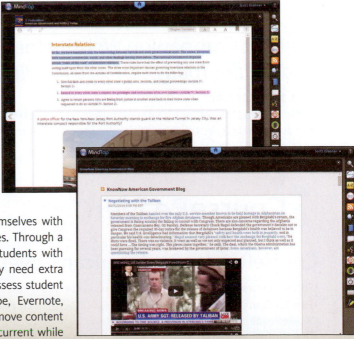

tracking local and global events through RSS feeds. The product can be used fully online with its interactive eBook for *American Government and Politics Today, 2015-2016 Edition*, or in conjunction with the printed text.

Instructor Companion Website for *American Government and Politics Today, 2015-2016 Edition*

ISBN: 9781285872513

This Instructor Companion Website is an all-in-one multimedia online resource for class preparation, presentation, and testing. Accessible through Cengage.com/login with your faculty account, you will find available for download: book-specific Microsoft® PowerPoint® presentations; a Test Bank compatible with multiple learning management systems; an Instructor Manual; Microsoft® PowerPoint® Image Slides; and a JPEG Image Library.

The Test Bank, offered in Blackboard, Moodle, Desire2Learn, Canvas and Angel formats, contains Learning Objective-specific multiple-choice and essay questions for each chapter. Import the test bank into your LMS to edit and manage questions, and to create tests.

The Instructor's Manual contains chapter-specific learning objectives, an outline, key terms with definitions, and a chapter summary. Additionally, the Instructor's Manual features a critical thinking question, lecture launching suggestion, and an in-class activity for each learning objective.

The Microsoft® PowerPoint® presentations are ready-to-use, visual outlines of each chapter. These presentations are easily customized for your lectures and offered along with chapter-specific Microsoft® PowerPoint® Image Slides and JPEG Image Libraries. Access the Instructor Companion Website at www.cengage.com/login.

Cognero for *American Government and Politics Today, 2015-2016 Edition*

ISBN: 9781285873985

Cengage Learning Testing Powered by Cognero is a flexible, online system that allows you to author, edit, and manage test bank content from multiple Cengage Learning solutions, create multiple test versions in an instant and deliver tests from your LMS, your classroom or wherever you want. The test bank for *American Government and Politics Today* contains Learning Objective-specific multiple-choice and essay questions for each chapter.

CENGAGE**brain**.com

Student Companion Website for *American Government and Politics Today, 2015-2016 Edition*

ISBN: 9781285872476

This free companion website for *American Government and Politics Today* is accessible through cengagebrain.com and allows students access to chapter-specific interactive learning tools including flashcards, glossaries, and more.

CourseReader for American Government

ISBN for CourseReader 0-30 Instant Access Code: 9781111479954
ISBN for CourseReader 0-30 Printed Access Code: 9781111479978

CourseReader: American Government allows instructors to create their reader, their way, in just minutes. This affordable, fully customizable online reader provides access to thousands of permissions-cleared readings, articles, primary sources, and audio and video selections from the regularly-updated Gale research library database. This easy-to-use solution allows instructors to search for and select just the material they want for their courses. Each selection opens with a descriptive introduction to provide context and concludes with critical-thinking and multiple-choice questions to reinforce key points. CourseReader is loaded with convenient tools like highlighting, printing, note-taking, and downloadable PDFs and MP3 audio files for each reading. CourseReader is the perfect complement to any Political Science course. It can be bundled with your current textbook, sold alone, or integrated into your learning management system. CourseReader 0-30 allows access to up to 30 selections in the reader. Instructors should contact their Cengage sales representative for details. Students should check with their instructor to see if CourseReader 0-30 is required for their specific course.

Election 2014 Supplement

ISBN: 978-1-305-50018-1
Written by John Clark and Brian Schaffner, this booklet addresses the 2014 congressional and gubernatorial races, with real-time analysis and references.

Acknowledgments

In preparing this edition of *American Government and Politics Today*, we have received superb guidance and cooperation from a skilled team of publishers and editors. We have greatly appreciated the collaboration and encouragement given by Carolyn Merrill, Product Team Manager.

Lauren Athmer, of LEAP Publishing, our developmental editor, deserves our thanks for her many contributions to the project and her well-considered suggestions for improvement. We are also indebted to editorial assistant Abigail Hess for her help.

We would also like to give special thanks to Emily A. Neff-Sharum of University of North Carolina, Pembroke, for authoring this edition's Instructor's Manual, and Heather Ramsier of Valencia College for authoring this edition's Test Bank.

Any errors remain our own. We welcome comments and suggestions from instructors and students alike who are using the book. Their suggestions have helped to strengthen the book and make it more helpful to students and faculty in the changing world of higher education.

Reviewers

We would also like to thank the instructors who have contributed their valuable feedback through reviews of this text:

Tony Cordell, *Marist School*
Charles J. Finocchiaro, *University of South Carolina*
Vinette Meikle Harris, *Houston Community College - Central*
Richard Krupa, *Harper College*
Drew L. Landry, *South Plains College*
Hans E. Schmeisser, *Abraham Baldwin Agricultural College*
Noah Zerbe, *Humboldt State University*
Terri Towner, *Oakland University*
Dr. Elsa Dias, *Pikes Peak Community College*
Heather Ramsier, *Valencia College*
Zack Sullivan, *Inver Hills Community College*
Sharon Sykora, *Slippery Rock University*
Christopher Gilbert, *Gustavus Adolphus College*
Narges Rabii, *Saddleback College*

From previous editions:

Krista Ackermann, *Allan Hancock College*
Martin J. Adamian, *California State University, Los Angeles*
Hugh M. Arnold, *Clayton College and State University, Morrow, Georgia*
William Arp III, *Louisiana State University, Baton Rouge*
Louis Battaglia, *Erie Community College*
David S. Bell, *Eastern Washington University, Cheney*
Teri Bengtson, *Elmhurst College*
Dr. Curtis Berry, *Shippensburg University, Shippensburg, Pennsylvania*
John A. Braithwaite, *Coastline Community College, Fountain Valley, California*
Richard G. Buckner, *Santa Fe Community College, New Mexico*
Kenyon D. Bunch, *Fort Lewis College, Durango, Colorado*
Ralph Bunch, *Portland State University, Oregon*
Dewey Clayton, *University of Louisville, Kentucky*
Frank T. Colon, *Lehigh University, Bethlehem, Pennsylvania*
Frank J. Coppa, *Union County College, Cranford, New Jersey*
Irasema Coronado, *University of Texas at El Paso*
Richard D. Davis, *Brigham Young University, Salt Lake City, Utah*
Ron Deaton, *Prince George's Community College, Largo, Maryland*
Marshall L. DeRosa, *Louisiana State University, Baton Rouge*
Jodi Empol, *Montgomery County Community College, Pennsylvania*

Robert S. Getz, *SUNY–Brockport, New York*
Kristina Gilbert, *Riverside Community College, Riverside, California*
William A. Giles, *Mississippi State University, Starkville, Mississippi*
Paul-Henri Gurian, *University of Georgia*
Willie Hamilton, *Mount San Jacinto College, San Jacinto, California*
Matthew Hansel, *McHenry County College, Crystal Lake, Illinois*
David N. Hartman, *Rancho Santiago College, Santa Ana, California*
Robert M. Herman, *Moorpark College, Moorpark, California*
J. C. Horton, *San Antonio College, Texas*
Alice Jackson, *Morgan State University, Baltimore, Maryland*
Robert Jackson, *Washington State University, Pullman*
John D. Kay, *Santa Barbara City College, California*
Bruce L. Kessler, *Shippensburg University, Shippensburg, Pennsylvania*
Samuel Krislov, *University of Minnesota, Minneapolis, Minnesota*
Terence Lenio, *McHenry County College*
Carl Lieberman, *University of Akron, Ohio*
James J. Lopach, *University of Montana, Missoula, Montana*
Jarol B. Manheim, *George Washington University, District of Columbia*
Steve J. Mazurana, *University of Northern Colorado, Greeley*
Jeanine Neher, *Butte Glen Community College*
Keith Nicholls, *University of South Alabama, Mobile, Alabama*
Stephen Osofsky, *Nassau Community College, Garden City, New York*
Neil A. Pinney, *Western Michigan University, Kalamazoo*
Walter V. Powell, *Slippery Rock University, Slippery Rock, Pennsylvania*
Eleanor A. Schwab, *South Dakota State University, Brookings*
Joseph L. Smith, *Grand Valley State University, Allendale, Michigan*
Michael W. Sonnlietner, *Portland Community College, Oregon*
Mark J. Wattier, *Murray State University, Murray, Kentucky*
Stella Webster, *Wayne County Community College— Downtown, Detroit, Michigan*
Lance Widman, *El Camino College, Torrance, California*
Robert D. Wrinkle, *Pan American University, Edinburg, Texas*

About the Authors

Lynne E. Ford Lynne E. Ford is Associate Vice President for the Academic Experience and professor of political science at the College of Charleston in Charleston, South Carolina. She received her B.A. from The Pennsylvania State University and her M.A. and Ph.D. in government and political behavior from the University of Maryland-College Park. Ford's teaching and research interests include women and politics, elections and voting behavior, political psychology, and civic engagement. She has written and published articles on women in state legislatures, the under-representation of women in political office in the American South, and work-family policy in the United States. She has also authored *Women and Politics: The Pursuit of Equality* and *The Encyclopedia of Women and American Politics*. Ford served as department chair for eight years and she has led a number of campus-wide initiatives including general education reform, faculty compensation, and civic engagement. For the past four years she served as Associate Provost for Curriculum and Academic Administration.

Barbara A. Bardes Barbara A. Bardes is Professor Emerita of Political Science and former Dean of the University of Cincinnati Blue Ash. She received her B.A. and M.A. from Kent State University and her doctorate in Political Science from the University of Cincinnati. She held faculty and administrative positions at Loyola University Chicago before returning to the University of Cincinnati, her hometown, as a college administrator. Bardes has written articles on public opinion and foreign policy, on women and politics, and on assessment of college courses. Her publications include: *Thinking About Public Policy* (with M. Dubnick), *Declarations of Independence: Women and Politics in Nineteenth Century American Fiction* (with S. Gossett), and *Public Opinion: Measuring the American Mind* (with B. Oldendick). Most recently she has been teaching *American Government and Politics* in an online course and testing the *Mindtap* interactive features of this book.

Steffen W. Schmidt Steffen W. Schmidt is a professor of political science at Iowa State University. He grew up in Colombia, South America, and has studied in Colombia, Switzerland, and France. He has a B.A. from Rollins College and obtained his Ph.D. from Columbia University, New York, in public law and government. Schmidt has published fourteen books and over one hundred and thirty articles in scholarly journals and is the recipient of numerous prestigious teaching prizes, including the Amoco Award for Lifetime Career Achievement in Teaching and the Teacher of the Year award. He is a pioneer in the use of web-based and real-time video courses and is a member of the American Political Science Association's section on Computers and Multimedia. He is known as "Dr. Politics" for his extensive commentary on US politics in US and international media. He is a weekly blogger for Gannett, comments on CNN en Español and Univision as well as WNYC, New York. He's on Facebook (SteffenWSchmidt) and Twitter (DrPolitics).

Mack C. Shelley, II Mack C. Shelley, II is a professor of political science and statistics at Iowa State University. After receiving his bachelor's degree from American University in Washington, DC, he went on to graduate studies at the University of Wisconsin at Madison, where he received a master's degree in Economics and a Ph.D. in Political Science. He arrived at Iowa State in 1979. From 1993 to 2002 he served as elected co-editor of the *Policy Studies Journal*. Shelley has also published numerous articles, books, and monographs on public policy, including *The Permanent Majority: The Conservative Coalition In The United States Congress; Biotechnology And The Research Enterprise: A Guide To The Literature (with William F. Woodman and Brian J. Reichel); American Public Policy: The Contemporary Agenda (with Steven G. Koven and Bert E. Swanson); and Quality Research In Literacy And Science Education: International Perspectives And Gold Standards (with Larry Yore and Brian Hand).*

Career Opportunities: Political Science

Introduction

It is no secret that college graduates are facing one of the toughest job markets in the past fifty years. Despite this challenge, those with a college degree have done much better than those without since the 2008 recession. One of the most important decisions a student has to make is the choice of a major; many consider future job possibilities when making that call. A political science degree is incredibly useful for a successful career in many different fields, from lawyer to policy advocate, pollster to humanitarian worker. Employer surveys reveal that the skills that most employers value in successful employees—critical thinking, analytical reasoning, and clarity of verbal and written communication—are precisely the tools that political science courses should be helping you develop. This brief guide is intended to help spark ideas for what kinds of careers you might pursue with a political science degree and the types of activities you can engage in now to help you secure one of those positions after graduation.

Careers in Political Science

LAW AND CRIMINAL JUSTICE

Do you find that your favorite parts of your political science classes are those that deal with the Constitution, t he legal system and the courts? Then a career in law and criminal justice might be right for you. Traditional jobs in the field range from lawyer or judge to police or parole officer. Since 9/11, there has also been tremendous growth in the area of homeland security, which includes jobs in mission support, immigration, travel security, as well as prevention and response.

PUBLIC ADMINISTRATION

The many offices of the federal government combined represent one of the largest employers in the United States. Flip to the bureaucracy chapter of this textbook and consider that each federal department, agency, and bureau you see looks to political science majors for future employees. A partial list of such agencies would include the Department of Education, the Department of Health and Human Services, and the Federal Trade Commission. There are also thousands of staffers who work for members of Congress or the Congressional Budget Office, many of whom were political science majors in college. This does not even begin to account for the multitude of similar jobs in state and local governments that you might consider as well.

CAMPAIGNS, ELECTIONS, AND POLLING

Are campaigns and elections the most exciting part of political science for you? Then you might consider a career in the growing industry based around political campaigns. From volunteering and interning to consulting, marketing and fundraising, there are many opportunities for those who enjoy the competitive and high-stakes electoral arena. For those looking for careers that combine political knowledge with statistical skills, there are careers in public opinion polling. Pollsters work for independent national organizations such as Gallup and YouGov, or as part of news operations and campaigns. For those who are interested in survey methodology there are also a wide variety of non-political career opportunities in marketing and survey design.

INTEREST GROUPS, INTERNATIONAL AND NONGOVERNMENTAL ORGANIZATIONS

Is there a cause that you are especially passionate about? If so, there is a good chance that there are interest groups out there that are working hard to see some progress made on similar issues. Many of the positions that one might find in for-profit companies also exist in their non-profit interest group and nongovernmental organization counterparts, including lobbying and high-level strategizing. Do not forget that there are also quite a few major international organizations—such as the United Nations, the World Health Organization, and the International Monetary Fund, where a degree in political science could be put to good use. While competition for those jobs tends to be fierce, your interest and knowledge about politics and policy will give you an advantage.

FOREIGN SERVICE

Does a career in diplomacy and foreign affairs, complete with the opportunity to live and work abroad, sound exciting for you? Tens of thousands of people work for the State Department, both in Washington D.C. and in consulates throughout the world. They represent the diplomatic interests of the United States abroad. Entrance into the Foreign Service follows a very specific process, starting with the Foreign Service Officers Test—an exam given three times a year that includes sections on American government, history, economics, and world affairs. Being a political science major is a significant help in taking the FSOT.

GRADUATE SCHOOL

While not a career, graduate school may be the appropriate next step for you after completing your undergraduate degree. Following the academic route, being awarded a Ph.D. or Master's degree in political science could open additional doors to a career in academia, as well as many of the professions mentioned earlier. If a career as a researcher in political science interests you, you should speak with your advisors about continuing your education.

Preparing While Still on Campus

INTERNSHIPS

One of the most useful steps you can take while still on campus is to visit your college's career center in regards to an internship in your field of interest. Not only does it give you a chance to experience life in the political science realm, it can lead to job opportunities later down the road and add experience to your resume.

SKILLS

In addition to your political science classes, there are a few skills any number of which will prove useful as a complement to your degree:

Writing: Like anything else, writing improves with practice. Writing is one of those skills that is applicable regardless of where your career might take you. Virtually every occupation relies on an ability to write cleanly, concisely, and persuasively.

Public Speaking: An oft-quoted 1977 survey showed that public speaking was the most commonly cited fear among respondents. And yet oral communication is a vital tool in the modern economy. You can practice this skill in a formal class setting or through extracurricular activities that get you in front of a group.

Quantitative Analysis: As the internet aids in the collection of massive amounts of information, the nation is facing a drastic shortage of people with basic statistical skills to interpret and use this data. A political science degree can go hand-in-hand with courses in introductory statistics.

Foreign Language: One skill that often helps a student or future employee stand out in a crowded job market is the ability to communicate in a language other than English. Solidify or set the foundation for your verbal and written foreign language communication skills while in school.

STUDENT LEADERSHIP

One attribute that many employers look for is "leadership potential" which can be quite tricky to indicate on a resume or cover letter. What can help is a demonstrated record of involvement in clubs and organizations, preferably in a leadership role. While many people think immediately of student government, most student clubs allow you the opportunity to demonstrate your leadership skills.

Conclusion

Hopefully reading this has sparked some ideas on potential future careers. As a next step, visit your college's career placement office, which is a great place to further explore what you have read here. You might also visit your college's alumni office to connect with graduates who are working in your field of interest. Political science opens the door to a lot of exciting careers, have fun exploring the possibilities!

2015-2016 EDITION NO SEPARATE POLICY CHAPTERS VERSION

AMERICAN GOVERNMENT
AND POLITICS TODAY

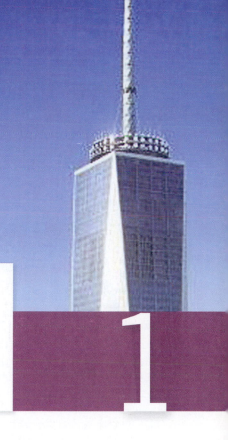

One Republic— Two Americas?

1

In April 2012, One World Trade Center reached a height of 1,271 feet, making it once again the tallest building in New York City. The tower, built at Ground Zero of the September 11, 2001, terrorist attacks, was designed to represent the resilience of the American spirit. The design includes a mast that brings its total height to 1,776 feet.

AFP/Getty Images/Newscom

WATCH & LEARN MindTap™ for American Government

Watch a brief "What Do You Know?" video summarizing The Democratic Republic.

LEARNING OUTCOMES

After reading this chapter, students will be able to:

- **LO1.1:** Define the institution of government and the process of politics.

- **LO1.2:** Identify the political philosophers associated with the "social contract" and explain how this theory shapes our understanding of the purpose of government and the role for individuals and communities in the United States.

- **LO1.3:** Describe the U.S. political culture and identify the set of ideas, values, and ways of thinking about government and politics shared by all.

- **LO1.4:** Compare and contrast types of government systems and identify the source of power in each.

- **LO1.5:** Define political ideology and locate socialism, liberalism, conservatism, and libertarianism along the ideological spectrum.

- **LO1.6:** Apply understanding of the purpose of government and the U.S. political culture to evaluate government's ability to meet new challenges over time.

Taxes Never Increased and Local Services Disappeared?

BACKGROUND

The power to tax and spend is a defining function of government. Taxation is a concurrent power, meaning that the federal, state, and local governments can all collect taxes. Taxes on property, goods and services, and income provide revenue for government to operate. Dating back to the earliest days of the republic, the government's power to tax has provoked strong negative reactions. The Boston Tea Party in 1773, the Whiskey Rebellion in 1794, and California's 1978 Proposition 13, known as the "People's Initiative to Limit Property Taxation," are all examples of popular rebellions. More recently, the Tea Party protests have brought attention to questions about the government's power to tax and the appropriate size and role of government. Many fiscally conservative candidates promise to eliminate tax increases and shrink the size of government. In reality, eliminating tax increases means cutting state and local budgets and eliminating services that people have come to expect. How should communities respond? What happens to schools, roads, police and fire protection, and other public services when local governments can no longer afford to pay for them?

TAXES PAY FOR LOCAL SERVICES WE EXPECT

The tax system allows government to redistribute revenue in a variety of ways. Intergovernmental transfers provide money collected by state and federal governments to local governments, accounting for roughly 40 percent of local operating dollars. Cities and towns make up the rest of their budget through property taxes, local sales taxes, and various user fees. In a recession, people buy fewer goods and services. This means that local governments collect less revenue from sales taxes and need to make up the deficit by other means or cut the budget. Local budget cuts often mean that services to citizens are dramatically reduced or eliminated altogether.

Local governments—counties and cities—usually take responsibility for parks and recreation services, police and fire departments, housing services, emergency medical services, municipal courts, transportation services, and public works (streets, sewers, trash collection, snow removal, and signage).

NO TAXES, NO SERVICES: TOUGH CHOICES

In conservative Colorado Springs, Colorado, home of the "Taxpayer's Bill of Rights," voters rejected a tax increase to restore a budget deficit caused by declining sales tax revenues. The city turned off one-third of its streetlights to save electricity costs. The city also locked public restrooms, reduced bus service, and stopped maintaining the city parks.

In New Jersey, Republican governor Chris Christie cut $3 billion from the state budget in his first two years in office. As a result, Trenton, New Jersey, fired one-third of the police force (103 officers). Between January 2011 and January 2012, gun-related assaults increased by 76 percent, robberies with a firearm increased by 55 percent, car thefts more than doubled, and break-ins more than tripled. The domestic violence unit was eliminated.

In 27 states, municipalities have introduced accident response fees to collect revenue to fund rescue, fire, and ambulance services. Drivers and/or their insurance companies are billed for municipalities' response to traffic accidents. The fees range from about $300 to more than $2,000 per hour per vehicle and are based on the piece of equipment used. Extrication devices, popularly known as "Jaws of Life," are among the most costly. Responding to citizen complaints, many states are reviewing the practice and 13 states have banned the "crash tax."

For Critical Analysis

1. *The U.S. tax system is designed to collect and redistribute revenue. Public goods and services paid for by tax revenue are therefore available to all in most cases (police protection, snow removal) or to those in the community who qualify because of special needs (legal aid to the poor, Medicaid). Some services or facilities are financed with "user fees." In other words, you pay only for what you as an individual use (toll roads, parking meters). Consider the local government services just mentioned. In your view, is it better to pay for each with tax revenue or user fees? What if the services rendered are in response to an accident? How does your answer relate to your perspective on the appropriate role for government?*

2. *We all live in the same country, but will decisions about who has access to public goods and services mean that we are creating two Americas? What kind of country do you want to live in?*

ALTHOUGH IT HAS BECOME POPULAR TO COMPLAIN about government, we could not survive as individuals or as communities without it. The challenge is to become invested enough in the American system and engaged enough in the political process so that the government we have is the government we want and deserve. This is a tremendous challenge, because, until you understand how our system works, "the government" can seem as though it belongs to somebody else; it can seem distant, hard to understand, and difficult to use when there is a problem to solve or there are hard decisions to make. Nevertheless, democracies, especially *this* democracy, derive their powers from the people, and this fact provides each of you with a tremendous opportunity. Individuals and groups of like-minded individuals who participate in the system can create change and shape the government to meet their needs. Those who opt not to pay attention or fail to participate must accept what others decide for them—good or bad.

Complicating matters further is the simple truth that although we all live in the same country and share the same political system, we may experience government differently. This leads us to hold different opinions about how big or small government should be, what kind of role government should play in our individual lives, what kinds of issues are appropriate for policymakers to handle, and what should be left to each of us alone.

At the heart of the debate over health care and health insurance is the question of how best to pay for, and provide access to, health care for every citizen. In 2012, this country's federal, state, and local governments, corporations, and individuals spent $2.8 trillion, or about $8,915 for every person, on health care.[1] Health insurance costs are rising faster than wages or inflation. Costs like this are not sustainable and drain the economy of resources needed elsewhere. The Patient Protection and Affordable Care Act (commonly known as the Affordable Care Act) was signed into law in 2010, although many of its provisions will take more than five years to implement and there have been several delays and extensions granted early in the implementation. The Act is large and complicated because the issue it addresses is large and complicated.

Several aspects of the law are favored by nearly everyone, such as providing access to insurance for people with preexisting conditions or allowing children to stay on their parents' insurance until age 26. The law also requires people to be insured either through their employer or by purchasing insurance, so that the costs and risks are spread across the entire population. Failure to do so results in a penalty. Because young people are typically healthy and rarely incur expensive medical bills, their participation is necessary to offset the costs of caring for others and to maintain the stability of the state and federal health exchanges. As a group, "young invincibles," as they have been labeled by the health insurance industry, have proven difficult to convince of the necessity of health insurance. The law's insurance mandate seems at odds with the value we place on individual responsibility; yet, health care is something everyone requires, and the costs are more manageable if everyone is included.

We resolve these and other conflicting values using the political process, and institutions of government are empowered to make decisions on our behalf. In the case of health care, the conflict has been resolved by the judiciary. The U.S. Supreme Court scheduled an unprecedented six hours of oral arguments over the

LISTEN & LEARN
MindTap® for American Government

Access Read Speaker to listen to Chapter 1.

---

1. Centers for Medicare and Medicaid Services, accessed at www.cms.gov.

course of three days in March 2012. The justices faced a number of critical questions, including whether or not the law's requirement that individuals carry health insurance was within the powers granted to Congress by the Constitution. On June 28, 2012, the Supreme Court issued a 5-4 decision upholding nearly all of the health-care law,[2] including the minimum coverage provision. Chief Justice John Roberts wrote the majority opinion. President Obama called the ruling "a victory for people all over this country whose lives will be more secure," because nearly 30 million Americans who currently lack health insurance will eventually be covered as a result of the law. While in most cases a Supreme Court ruling settles the question, in this case it did not. Republican candidates for Congress in 2012 promised to repeal the law if elected. Although Republicans maintained their majority in the House of Representatives, Democrats controlled the Senate and the White House, leaving multiple legislative attempts at repeal unsuccessful. In September 2013, Senator Ted Cruz (R-TX) controlled the Senate floor for more than 21 hours in what political satirists referred to as a "fauxilibuster" (because a bill was not placed before the body, a true filibuster was not possible). His goal was to attract support to defund implementation of the health-care law. Partisan politics continues to prevent Congress from making performance-enhancing adjustments to the existing law.

Sir Winston Churchill, British prime minister during World War II, once said, "No one pretends that democracy is perfect or all-wise. Indeed, it has been said that democracy is the worst form of government except all those other forms that have been tried from time to time."[3] Our system is not perfect, but it is more open to change than most. This book offers essential tools to learn about American government and politics today so that you are prepared to change this country for the better.

What are your dreams for the future, and what role do you believe the government can and should play in helping you realize your dreams? There was a time when we all aspired to live the "American Dream" and when we believed that government played an essential role in ensuring that the opportunity to achieve the American Dream was available to everyone. Members of each successive generation were confident that if they worked hard and followed the rules, they would live richer and more successful lives than the generation before them. Public policy has historically been an effective tool to promote economic growth, educational equity, homeownership, and job security. Is that still true today?

There are some troubling signs, to be sure. Significant inequality in income and wealth exists in the United States, and rather than shrinking, the gap has widened for your generation and your parents' generation. In 1979, the richest 1 percent accounted for 8 percent of all personal income; by 2012, their share had more than doubled, to 19.3 percent, their largest share since 1928.[4] As the economy began to improve, the greatest gains in income share went to the top 10 percent of earners. Hourly wage workers, notably fast food workers, raised awareness over the recovery gap by participating in a one-day labor walkout and demanding an increase to the $7.25 federal minimum hourly wage. To add momentum to the movement, President Obama signed an Executive Order early in 2014 raising the minimum wage for workers under new federal contracts to $10.10 an hour. The global economic recession, the unemployment rate, rising

---

2. National Federation of Independent Business, et. al. v. Sebelious, Secretary of Health and Human Services, et.al. 567 U.S. (2012)
3. House of Commons speech on November 11, 1947.
4. Facundo Alvaredo, Anthony B. Atkinson, Thomas Piketty, and Emmanuel Saez. 2013. "The Top 1 Percent in International and Historical Perspective." *Journal of Economic Perspectives*, 27(3): 3–20.

Jim West/Alamy

Hundreds rallied near a Detroit, Michigan McDonald's restaurant in support of a strike by fast food workers who were demanding a raise from their current wages of about $7.40 an hour to $15 an hour. Similar strikes for higher wages took place in cities around the country.

home foreclosures, and corporate relocation of jobs overseas all present government with significant challenges. Moreover, people's trust in nearly all institutions (government, media, banks, business, churches, and organized labor) has fallen over the past decade (see Figure 1–1). Native-born citizens know less than ever about the very political system they hope will restore their confidence in the future; one in three failed the civics portion of the naturalization test in a national telephone survey.[5] Can people effectively engage in political activity to change their lives for the better when they know so little about the governmental system?

There are also some hopeful signs. According to the Center for the Study of the American Dream at Xavier University, a majority of Americans surveyed (63 percent) remain confident that they will achieve the American Dream despite the current challenges. More than 75 percent believe they have already achieved some measure of it. Those surveyed defined the American Dream in terms of a good life for their family (45 percent), financial security (34 percent), freedom (32 percent), opportunity (29 percent), the pursuit of happiness (21 percent), a good job (16 percent), and homeownership (7 percent). How does this definition fit with your own? Are you surprised that homeownership is last on the list? How might the mortgage crisis and the persistent economic recession influence how we define our future dreams?

Interestingly, the study found that Latinos and immigrants are most positive about the possibility of achieving the American Dream and are more optimistic about the future of the country than the population as a whole. Finally, a majority of Americans view immigration as an important part of keeping the American Dream alive and believe that immigration continues to be one of America's greatest strengths. In his 2014 State of the Union address, President Obama said, "What I believe unites the people of this nation, regardless of race or region or

5. "U.S. Naturalization Civics Test: National Survey of Native-Born U.S. Citizens, March 2012," conducted by the Center for the Study of the American Dream, Xavier University, accessed at http://www.xavier.edu/americandream/programs/National-Civic-Literacy-Survey.cfm

party, young or old, rich or poor, is the simple, profound belief in opportunity for all—the notion that if you work hard and take responsibility, you can get ahead."[6]

What is the state of America today? Given the economic and educational disparities evident in the United States today, are we one America or two? Are you confident that your life will be better than that of your parents and grandparents? Can the problems we face as a nation today be addressed by the political system? Is the American republic up to today's challenges? These will be central questions in our analysis of American government and politics today.

Politics and Government

■ **LO1.1:** Define the institution of government and the process of politics.

Politics

The process of resolving conflicts and deciding "who gets what, when, and how." More specifically, politics is the struggle over power or influence within organizations or informal groups that can grant or withhold benefits or privileges.

Before we can answer any of these provocative questions, we first have to define some terms. What is politics? **Politics** is the process of resolving conflicts and deciding "who gets what, when, and how."[7] Although politics may be found in many places outside of government (for example, in your family or workplace), for the purposes of this book, we refer to conflicts and decisions found at the federal, state, and local levels regarding the selection of decision makers, the structure of institutions, and the creation of public policy. Politics is particularly intense when decisions are made that hit close to home, such as decisions about how to spend local and state tax dollars. Equally intense are political decisions that yield leaders for our country. Elections at the national and state levels attract the most media attention, but thousands of elected and appointed officials make up the government and render decisions that impact our lives.

Government

The preeminent institution in which decisions are made that resolve conflicts or allocate benefits and privileges. It is unique because it has the ultimate authority within society.

Government is the term used to describe the formal **institutions** through which decisions about the allocation of resources are made and conflicts are resolved. Government can take many forms, come in many sizes, and perform a variety of functions, but at the core, all governments rule. To govern is to rule. Governments can, as a matter of their authority, force you to comply with laws through taxes, fines, and the power to send you to prison, or worse—to death row. The inherent power of government is what led the founders of the United States to impose limitations on the power of government relative to the rights of individuals. Likewise, the power of government leads Americans to be wary of too much government when less will do.

Institutions

An ongoing organization that performs certain functions for society.

Why Is Government Necessary?

■ **LO1.2:** Identify the political philosophers associated with the "social contract" and explain how this theory shapes our understanding of the purpose of government and the role for individuals and communities in the United States.

Americans may not always like government, but they like the absence of government even less. Governments are necessary at a minimum to provide public goods and services that all citizens need but cannot reasonably be expected to provide for themselves. National security and defense are obvious examples. But governments do far more than provide for the common defense. As you will learn in Chapter 2, our founding documents such as the Declaration of Independence and the Constitution are predicated upon and convey through their language a set of shared political values. Government reinforces those values regularly. One of our

---

6. State of the Union Address, January 28, 2014. Accessed at http://www.whitehouse.gov/the-press-office/2014/01/28/president-barack-obamas-state-union-address
7. Harold Lasswell, *Politics: Who Gets What, When, and How* (New York: McGraw-Hill, 1936).

defining values is belief in the rule of law, which means that laws determined through the political process are enforced uniformly and that no individual, regardless of wealth, privilege, or position, is above the law. Government includes a system of justice administered by institutions known as the courts to maintain this important value. We will return to this discussion of fundamental values later in this chapter. In addition to providing public goods and services and reinforcing shared values, governments are necessary to provide security so that liberty may flourish.

Our contemporary understanding of why government is necessary has been shaped by Enlightenment thinkers from seventeenth- and eighteenth-century Europe. During the Age of Enlightenment, also known as the Age of Reason, philosophers and scientists challenged the **divine right of kings** and argued that the world could be vastly improved through the use of human reason, science, and religious tolerance. Essential to this argument was the belief that all individuals were born free and equal, and imbued with natural rights. Individuals were in control of their own destiny, and by working with others, a society could shape a government capable of both asserting and protecting individual rights. English **social contract** theorists such as Thomas Hobbes (1588–1679) and John Locke (1632–1704) were particularly influential in shaping our theory of government. Hobbes was far more pessimistic about human nature than Locke. Hobbes believed that without government and the rule of law, people would revert to a state of nature, and individuals would be left to fight over basic necessities, rendering life "solitary, poor, nasty, brutish, and short."[8] To avoid such a fate, Hobbes argued for a single ruler, a Leviathan, so powerful that the rights of the weak could be protected against intrusion by the strong. By contrast, Locke took basic survival for granted, believing that all humans were endowed with reason—an internal code of conduct. Therefore, individuals are willing to give up a portion of their individual liberty in order to gain the protection of government through the social contract. Government is formed to protect life, liberty, and property; however, if a government compromises its legitimacy by violating the social contract, it is the people's duty to end the abusive government and replace it with a new form.

It is within this theoretical framework that we understand the necessity for government: to provide security, to protect liberty and enforce property rights, and to maintain legitimacy by exercising authority consistent with the fundamental values of those governed. Consent of the governed is the basis for power and legitimacy in American democracy.

Fundamental Values

■ **LO1.3:** Describe the U.S. political culture and identify the set of ideas, values, and ways of thinking about government and politics shared by all.

The authors of the United States Constitution believed that the structures they had created would provide for both democracy and a stable political system. They also believed that the nation could be sustained by its **political culture**. A critical question facing America today is to what extent do all citizens continue to share in a single political culture? Does the widening wealth and income gap threaten to undermine our shared political values as well as our confidence in government? We live under one republic, but are we increasingly two Americas?

Divine Right of Kings
A political and religious doctrine that asserts a monarch's legitimacy is conferred directly by God and as such a king is not subject to any earthly authority, including his people or the church.

Social Contract
A theory of politics that asserts that individuals form political communities by a process of mutual consent, giving up a measure of their individual liberty in order to gain the protection of government.

Political Culture
The set of ideas, values, and ways of thinking about government and politics that is shared by all citizens.

---

8. Thomas Hobbes, *Leviathan: Revised student edition* (Cambridge Texts in the History of Political Thought) Cambridge University Press; Revised Student Edition (August 28, 1996).

Beyond Our Borders

Importing Workers: Challenging Cultures in Europe

One of the most controversial issues in American politics is the debate over what to do about undocumented immigrants who have come to the United States for employment and a better life. An estimated 12 million individuals reside in the United States without legal status. Some conservatives believe that the best solution is deporting the undocumented people to their respective native countries. Others, including President Obama and moderate leaders of both parties, have argued that the United States should recognize its need for workers and implement a system by which individuals can come to this country to work and someday earn a right to citizenship. Immigration is a major source of population growth and cultural change in the United States. The political focus on undocumented immigrants can overshadow the tremendous benefits of immigration. For example, immigrants are among the founders of many prominent American technology companies, such as Google, Yahoo, and eBay.

Nations, especially those in Europe, have long admitted immigrants as unskilled and semi-skilled workers to fuel their economies and increase their populations. Immigrants make up about 12 percent of the population of Germany and 15 percent of that of Austria. Thirty-seven percent of Luxembourg's populace are immigrants; in Switzerland, that figure is around 23 percent. For many decades, Great Britain has allowed individuals who were subjects of the British Commonwealth to enter the country, while France extended legal residency to many French citizens from its former colonies in North Africa. Germany estimates that it will need to attract up to 1.5 million additional skilled workers through immigration to compensate for an aging population.

All nations face a dilemma in how to balance the cultural energy immigrants bring with the tensions associated with integration and assimilation processes. Immigrants may find limits to employment, education, and housing. Nonwhite and Muslim residents claim they are the subject of unwarranted police attention through racial or religious profiling. Clashes sometimes turn violent. Young people rioted in France in the last few years over the lack of employment opportunities for nonwhite French residents, while the Netherlands has seen outbreaks of violence by Muslim residents against other Dutch citizens. Youth riots in Sweden were particularly surprising given the nation's reputation for welcoming the world's refugees, most recently people fleeing the civil war in Syria. Many of these states are

Sergey Brin, co-founder and president of Google, was born in Moscow, Russia. When Brin was six, his family entered the United States with the assistance of HIAS, the Hebrew Immigrant Aid Society. In honor of the 30th anniversary of his family's immigration, Brin gave $1 million to HIAS, which he credits with helping his family escape anti-Semitism in the Soviet Union.

engaged in serious internal discussion about how to socialize new residents to the culture of their new home and how to ensure that immigrants can find economic opportunities for themselves and their children, while at the same time challenging the prejudice and racism sometimes found in the native population.

For Critical Analysis

1. *How can the inevitable tensions created when new ideas and customs confront established cultures be resolved? What role is appropriate for government in this process?*

2. *To what extent should nations ensure that immigrants accept the cultural and political values of their new home? In what specific ways does multiculturalism benefit political, social, and economic development?*

There is considerable consensus among American citizens about concepts basic to the U.S. political system. Given that the population of the United States is made up primarily of immigrants and descendants of immigrants with diverse cultural and political backgrounds, how can we account for this consensus? Primarily, it is the result of **political socialization**—the process by which beliefs and values are transmitted to successive generations. The nation depends on families, schools, houses of worship, and the media to transmit the precepts of our national culture. With fewer people going to church and a widening educational gap that strongly correlates with economic disparities, we may need to reexamine the ways in which our political culture is transmitted. On the other hand, you can find these fundamental values reaffirmed in most major public speeches given by the president and other important officials in American politics. We will return to these important questions throughout the book, but particularly in Chapter 6.

Liberty. As you recall, the advancement and protection of individual liberty is central to the social contract theory of government. **Liberty** is among the natural rights articulated by Locke and later by Thomas Jefferson in the Declaration of Independence ("life, liberty, and the pursuit of happiness"). In the United States, our civil liberties include religious freedom—both the right to believe in whatever religion we choose and freedom from any state-imposed religion. Liberty, as a political value, has two sides to it—one positive (the freedom to) and one negative (the freedom from). The freedom of speech—the right to political expression on all matters, including government actions—is an example of a positive liberty. Freedom of speech is one of our most prized liberties; a democracy could not endure without it. The right to privacy is a more controversial liberty claim. The United States Supreme Court has held that the right to privacy can be derived from other rights that are explicitly stated in the Bill of Rights. The Supreme Court has also held that under the right to privacy, the government cannot ban either abortion[9] or private sexual behavior by consenting adults.[10]

Positive freedoms are not absolute, and individual liberty can be limited, such as in times of war. When Americans perceive serious threats, they have supported government actions to limit individual liberties in the name of national security. Such limits were imposed during the Civil War, World War II, and the McCarthy era of the Cold War. Following the terrorist attacks on the World Trade Center and the Pentagon on September 11, 2001, Congress passed legislation designed to provide greater security at the expense of some civil liberties. In particular, the USA PATRIOT (Uniting and Strengthening America by Providing Appropriate Tools Required to Intercept and Obstruct Terrorism) Act gave law enforcement and intelligence-gathering agencies greater latitude to search out and investigate suspected terrorists.

Political Socialization
The process through which individuals learn a set of political attitudes and form opinions about social issues. Families and the educational system are two of the most important forces in the political socialization process.

Liberty
The greatest freedom of individuals that is consistent with the freedom of other individuals in the society.

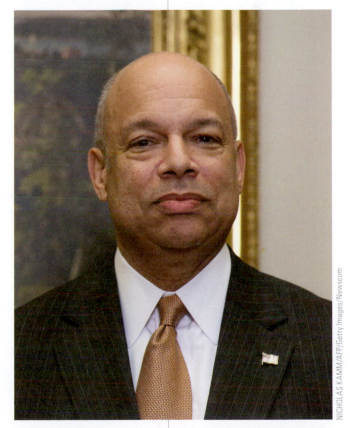

U.S. Homeland Security Secretary Jeh Johnson. Johnson replaced Janet Napolitano in January 2014.

9. *Roe v. Wade*, 410 U.S. 113 (1973).
10. *Lawrence v. Texas*, 539 U.S. 558 (2003).

Confidence in Institutions Declines: How Do We Know?

Figure 1–1 ▶ Confidence in Institutions Declines

Gallup polling shows a loss in faith in institutions in the past 10 years, including steep declines regarding Congress, banks, and the presidency.

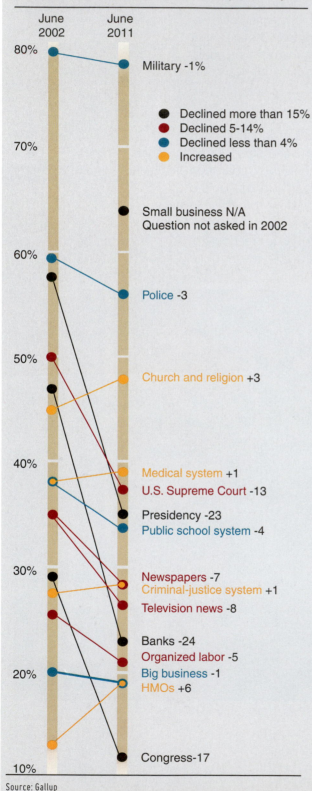

June 2002   June 2011

- 80%
- 70%
- 60%
- 50%
- 40%
- 30%
- 20%
- 10%

Military -1%

● Declined more than 15%
● Declined 5-14%
● Declined less than 4%
● Increased

Small business N/A
Question not asked in 2002

Police -3

Church and religion +3

Medical system +1
U.S. Supreme Court -13
Presidency -23
Public school system -4

Newspapers -7
Criminal-justice system +1
Television news -8

Banks -24
Organized labor -5
Big business -1
HMOs +6

Congress-17

Source: Gallup

Throughout this book, you will find a number of visual features including figures, tables, photographs, and political cartoons. These visual features are carefully selected to present information that is critical to your understanding of the content in each chapter. Therefore, you must study the visuals carefully. In addition, you may be tested on this information.

Figure 1–1 presents Gallup polling data on the public's loss of confidence in major institutions at two points in time. Gallup Poll regularly conducts public opinion polls in more than 140 countries around the world. You will often see these polls referenced in the mass media. Begin by reading the title of the figure and the descriptive information—the caption—right below the title. Together, the title and caption summarize the information that you need in order to understand the graphic. Captions below photographs and cartoons have a similar function. Figure 1–1 shows two points in time, indicating a change in public attitudes. Other ways to show change over time include line graphs.

This figure communicates a lot of information. On the left vertical axis, you will find the scale indicating the percentage of people who express a great deal or quite a lot of confidence in each institution. To display the magnitude of the change (decline or increase) in confidence, the authors have used four colors. The key for the colors is found on the right, near the top. Yellow, for example, represents an increase in confidence. Black indicates the most dramatic loss of confidence in the institution between 2002 and 2011. Read the graphic starting on the left and moving to the right and follow the line connecting the two dots. Like many figures, tables, and photographs, this visual presents you with descriptive data. Descriptive information provides an answer to *what* or *who* questions but does not typically answer *why* or *how* questions. Analysis (determining why or how) is a form of critical thinking. The accompanying text may provide theories or results from other research, and sometimes you will find questions for critical analysis. Synthesizing all of the information to create a new explanation or understanding is the most important skill you can develop in college.

Order and the Rule of Law. As noted earlier, individuals and communities create governments to provide stability and order in their lives. Locke justified the creation of governments as a way to protect every individual's property rights and to organize a system of impartial justice. In the United States, laws passed by local, state, and national governments create order and stability in every aspect of life, ranging from traffic to business to a national defense system. Citizens expect these laws to create a society in which individuals can pursue opportunities and live their lives in peace and prosperity. People also expect the laws to be just and to apply to everyone equally. The goal of maintaining **order** and security, however, can sometimes run counter to the values of liberty and equality.

Order
A state of peace and security. Maintaining order by protecting members of society from violence and criminal activity is the oldest purpose of government.

Individualism. The Declaration of Independence begins with a statement on the importance of the individual in our political culture: "When in the Course of human events, it becomes necessary for one people to dissolve the political bands which have connected them with one another, and to assume among the Powers of the earth, the separate and equal station to which the Laws of Nature and of Nature's God entitle them..." By a "separate and equal station," Jefferson was distinguishing the belief in the rationality and autonomy of individuals from the traditions of aristocracies and other systems in which individuals did not determine their own destiny. Individualism asserts that one of the primary functions of government is to enable individuals' opportunities for personal fulfillment and development. In political terms, individualism limits claims by groups in favor of the individual. Therefore, it should come as no surprise that a universal right to health care is not a part of the United States Constitution.

Equality. Thomas Jefferson wrote in the Declaration of Independence, "We hold these truths to be self-evident, that all men are created equal..." The proper meaning of equality, however, has been disputed by Americans since the Revolution.[11] Much of American history—and world history—is the story of how the value of **equality** has been extended and elaborated.

Equality
As a political value, the idea that all people are of equal worth.

Political equality reflects the value that we place on the individual. At our founding, political leaders excluded some people from the broad understanding of a politically autonomous person. African Americans, women, Native Americans, and most men who did not own property were excluded from the equal extension of political rights. Under a social contract theory of government, individuals must freely enter the compact with others on an equal basis. Although Enlightenment philosophers believed in the inherent equality of all persons, they did not define all individuals as full persons. Recall that the Constitution counted slaves as three-fifths of a person. For a period of our history, a married woman was indivisible from her husband and could not act as a full person.[12] Today, of course, we believe all people are entitled to equal political rights as well as the opportunities for personal development provided by equal access to education and employment. In reality, we still have work to do to be sure that opportunities afforded by society and protected by government can be fully realized by everyone in society.

Recently, some cultural observers and scholars have begun to question whether political and social equality can coexist with economic inequality. In a book titled *Why Nations Fail*, Massachusetts Institute of Technology (MIT)

---

11. Gary B. Nash, *The Unknown American Revolution: The Unruly Birth of Democracy and the Struggle to Create America* (New York: Viking, 2005); and Alfred F. Young, ed., *Beyond the American Revolution: Explorations in the History of American Radicalism* (DeKalb, IL: Northern Illinois University Press, 1993).
12. British Common Law known as "coverture" meant that once married, a woman's identity was "covered" by her husband's, leaving her no independent rights.

OUT OF THE MOUNTAIN OF DESPAIR.
A STONE OF HOPE

Allen Brown/dbimages/Alamy

The Martin Luther

King, Jr., National
Memorial, located on the
national mall in Washington
DC, is administered by the
National Park Service. The
image of Dr. King emerges
from a granite "stone of
hope" surrounded by a
"mountain of despair"
reflecting the steadfast
resolve of an entire
generation to achieve a fair
and honest society.

Property

Anything that is or may be subject
to ownership. As conceived by the
political philosopher John Locke, the
right to property is a natural right
superior to human law (laws made
by government).

economist Daron Acemoglu argues that
"when economic inequality increases, the
people who have become economically more
powerful will often attempt to use that
power in order to gain even more political
power. And once they are able to monopolize political power, they will start using that
for changing the rules in their favor."[13] Many
people point to the Supreme Court's decision in *Citizens United v. Federal Election
Committee*[14] and the growth in Super PAC
spending in federal elections as evidence of
the growing political influence of a few very
wealthy individuals and interests. According
to Alan Krueger, former chairman of
President Obama's Council of Economic
Advisers, the size of the middle class has
steadily declined over the last three decades.
Whereas in 1970 a little over half of all
American households had an income within
50 percent of the median, today the figure is
just over 40 percent. Put differently, the
share of all income accruing to the top
1 percent increased by 13.5 percent from
1979 to 2007. This is the equivalent of shifting $1.1 trillion of annual income to the top
1 percent of families. More troubling, as
income inequality has increased, year to year
and generation to generation, economic
mobility (the opportunity to improve one's
economic standing) has declined. Can the
values of political and social equality with-
stand the significant erosion of economic
equality that has accompanied the great recession? Civil rights and the value of
equality will be discussed further in Chapter 5.

Property.   The value of reducing economic inequality is in conflict with the right
to **property**. This is because reducing economic inequality typically involves the
transfer of property (usually in the form of money) from some people to others.
For many people, liberty and property are closely entwined. A capitalist system is
based on private property rights. Under **capitalism**, property consists not only of
personal possessions but also of wealth-creating assets, such as farms and factories. The investor-owned corporation is in many ways the preeminent capitalist
institution. The funds invested by the owners of a corporation are known as
capital—hence, the very name of the system. Capitalism is also typically characterized by considerable freedom to make binding contracts and by relatively
unconstrained markets for goods, services, and investments. Property—especially
wealth-creating property—can be seen as giving its owner political power and
the liberty to do whatever he or she wants. At the same time, the ownership of

13. Acemoglu, Daron and James Robinson. *Why Nations Fail: Power, Prosperity, and Poverty*. (New York: Crown Publishers, 2012).
14. 558 U.S. 08-205 (2010)

property immediately creates inequality in society. The desire to own property, however, is so widespread among all classes of Americans that egalitarian movements have had a difficult time securing a wide following here.

As with the other values shaping our political culture, even individual property rights are not absolute. **Eminent domain** allows government to take private land for public use in return for just compensation. Weighing the public's interest against the interest of private landowners is a delicate political judgment. Typically, eminent domain is used to acquire land for roads, bridges, and other public works projects. A 2005 Supreme Court ruling, however, allowed the city of New London, Connecticut, to "take" homeowners' property and turn it over to private developers, who built an office park and expensive condominiums.[15] In this atypical case, the majority ruled that economic stimulus and the increase in city tax revenues fulfilled the public use requirement for eminent domain takings. Since the ruling, several state and local governments have passed laws to forbid the kind of takings at issue in this case.

Why Choose Democracy?

■ **LO1.4:** Compare and contrast types of government systems and identify the source of power in each.

Today, 196 nations exist in the world. Nearly all have some form of government that possesses authority and some degree of legitimacy. Governments vary in their structure and how they govern. The crucial question for every nation is who controls the government. The answer could be a small group, one person—perhaps the monarch or a dictator—or no one.

At one extreme is a society governed by a **totalitarian regime**. In such a political system, a small group of leaders or a single individual—a dictator—makes all political decisions for the society. North Korea is an example of a totalitarian state.

Capitalism
An economic system characterized by the private ownership of wealth-creating assets, free markets, and freedom of contract.

Eminent Domain
A power set forth in the Fifth Amendment to the U.S. Constitution that allows government to take private property for public use under the condition that just compensation is offered to the landowner.

Totalitarian Regime
A form of government that controls all aspects of the political and social life of a nation.

STRINGER/Reuters/Corbis

Demonstrators carry placards and hold a Syrian opposition flag during a protest against Syria's President Bashar al-Assad's regime in Kafranbel in Idlib province January 18, 2013.

15. *Kelo v. City of New London*, 545 U.S. 469 (2005).

Citizens are deprived of the freedom to speak, to dissent, to assemble, and to seek solutions to problems. Individual needs, including food, are subsumed by the interests of the ruler and the regime. Famine, widespread malnutrition, and illness exist as a result of the country's "military first" policy. Running afoul of the regime can often mean imprisonment or death. Kim Jong-il was succeeded by his son, Kim Jong-un in 2011, continuing an unbroken 63-year reign that began with Kim Jong-il's father, Kim Il-sung. Under Kim Jong-un's rule, North Korea has inflamed relations with South Korea and the United States by developing and testing short-range ballistic missiles and rockets. Totalitarianism is an extreme form of authoritarianism.

Authoritarianism is also characterized by highly concentrated and centralized power maintained by political repression. Authoritarianism differs from totalitarianism in that only the government is fully controlled by the ruler, leaving social and economic institutions to outside control. The contemporary government of China is often described as authoritarian. China is ruled by a single political party, the Communist Party. Policies are made by Communist Party leaders without input from the general population. The Chinese market economy is expanding rapidly with little government intrusion or regulations, but signs of political dissent are punished severely. Internet access is monitored and political content restricted.

Many terms for describing the distribution of political power are derived from the ancient Greeks, who were the first Western people to study politics systematically. One form of rule by the few was known as **aristocracy**, literally meaning "rule by the best." In practice, this meant rule by leading members of wealthy families who were, in theory, the best educated and dedicated to the good of the state. The ancient Greeks had another term for rule by the few, **oligarchy**, which means rule by a small group for corrupt and self-serving purposes.

The Greek term for rule by the people was **democracy**, which means that the authority of the government is granted to it from the people as a whole. Within the limits of their culture, some of the Greek city-states operated as democracies. Today, in much of the world, the people will not grant legitimacy to a government unless it is based on democratic principles. Mass protests against the Assad regime in Syria as well as unrest in Ukraine are recent examples.

If totalitarianism is control of all aspects of society by the government, **anarchy** is the complete opposite. It means that there is no government at all. Each individual or family in a society decides for itself how it will behave, and there is no institution with the authority to keep order in any way. As you can imagine, examples of anarchy do not last very long. A state of anarchy may characterize a transition between one form of government (often totalitarian or authoritarian and repressive) and one where people want more power but do not yet have political institutions to structure popular participation. The interim period can be chaotic and violent, as in Somalia and to a lesser degree in Tunisia, Egypt, Libya, and Yemen following the Arab Spring rebellions. Entire cities have been destroyed in the Syrian uprising and ensuing civil war, leading to a mass exodus of the population as refugees.

Direct Democracy as a Model

The system of government in the ancient Greek city-state of Athens is usually considered the purest model of **direct democracy**, because the citizens of that community debated and voted directly on all laws, even those put forward by

---

Authoritarianism
A type of regime in which only the government is fully controlled by the ruler. Social and economic institutions exist that are not under the government's control.

Aristocracy
Rule by "the best;" in reality, rule by an upper class.

Oligarchy
Rule by the few in their own interests.

Democracy
A system of government in which political authority is vested in the people. Derived from the Greek words *demos* ("the people") and *kratos* ("authority").

Anarchy
The absence of any form of government or political authority.

Direct Democracy
A system of government in which political decisions are made by the people directly, rather than by their elected representatives; probably attained most easily in small political communities.

the ruling council of the city. The most important feature of Athenian democracy was that the **legislature** was composed of all of the citizens. Women, foreigners, and slaves, however, were excluded because they were not citizens. This form of government required a high level of participation from every citizen; participation was seen as benefiting the individual and the city-state. The Athenians believed that although a high level of participation might lead to instability in government, citizens, if informed about the issues, could be trusted to make wise decisions. Greek philosophers also believed that debating the issues and participating in making the laws was good for the individual's intellectual and personal development.

Direct democracy has also been practiced in Switzerland and in the United States in New England town meetings. At New England town meetings, which can include all of the voters who live in the town, important decisions—such as levying taxes, hiring city officials, and deciding local ordinances—are made by majority vote. Some states provide a modern adaptation of direct democracy for their citizens; representative democracy is supplemented by the **initiative** or the **referendum**—processes by which the people may vote directly on laws or constitutional amendments. The **recall** process, which is available in many states, allows the people to vote to remove an official from state office.

Because of the Internet, Americans have access to more political information than ever before. Voters can go online to examine the record of any candidate. Constituents can contact their congressional representatives and state legislators by sending them email. Individuals can easily find like-minded allies and form political interest groups using social networking sites such as Twitter, Facebook, Google+, and countless others. During the 2008 presidential campaign, the

Legislature
A governmental body primarily responsible for the making of laws.

Initiative
A procedure by which voters can propose a law or a constitutional amendment.

Referendum
An electoral device whereby legislative or constitutional measures are referred by the legislature to the voters for approval or disapproval.

Recall
A procedure allowing the people to vote to dismiss an elected official from state office before his or her term has expired.

Sen. Marco Rubio (R-FL) speaks to the delegation at the Republican National Convention at the 2012 Republican National Convention in Tampa, Florida. Senator Rubio, an emerging leader within the Republican Party, actively uses social media to promote his ideas and issue positions.

Olivier Douliery/MCT/Newscom

Barack Obama @
@BarackObama

Follow

Four more years.
pic.twitter.com/bAJE6Vom

↩ Reply ↻ Retweet ★ Favorite ••• More

Barack Obama/Twitter

Does seeing a more personal side to candidates via their websites or social media accounts make you more likely to vote for them?

Obama campaign pioneered new uses of the Internet to connect supporters, solicit campaign donations, and maintain nearly constant contact between likely voters and the campaign.

In 2012, social media provided voters with new forms of real-time engagement through breaking campaign news, the debates, and election night returns. President Obama's victory Tweet of "Four more years," as shown in the screen capture, set a record for re-Tweets. Facebook motivated people to get to the polls; seeing that friends had already voted worked as a form of peer pressure to do likewise. In the last week of the 2012 campaign, Twitter released a political engagement map that allowed users to track Tweets about specific candidates or issues around the country.

There are limits, however, to how much political business people currently want to conduct using technology, largely because of security concerns. Although Colorado offered its citizens the opportunity to vote online in 2000, the Pentagon canceled a plan for troops overseas to vote online in 2004 due to Internet security concerns. The extent of National Security Agency (NSA) surveillance and spying disclosed by Edward Snowden in documents leaked to *The Guardian* and *The Washington Post*, as well as massive personal data breaches reported by retailers, universities, and states, have increased the American people's skepticism about conducting important transactions online. Several states, however, do allow for voter registration online.

The Limits of Direct Democracy

Although they were aware of the Athenian model, the framers of the U.S. Constitution had grave concerns about the stability and practicality of direct democracy. During America's colonial period, the idea of government based on the consent of the people gained increasing popularity. Such a government was the main aspiration of the American Revolution, the French Revolution in 1789, and many subsequent revolutions. At the time of the American Revolution, however, the masses were still considered to be too uneducated to govern themselves, too prone to the influence of demagogues (political leaders who manipulate popular prejudices), and too likely to subordinate minority rights to the tyranny of the majority.

James Madison defended the new scheme of government set forth in the U.S. Constitution, while warning of the problems inherent in a "pure democracy:"

A common passion or interest will, in almost every case, be felt by a majority of the whole . . . and there is nothing to check the inducements to sacrifice the weaker party or an obnoxious individual. Hence it is that such democracies have ever been spectacles of turbulence and contention, and have ever been found incompatible with personal security or the rights of property; and have in general been as short in their lives as they have been violent in their deaths.[16]

Like other politicians of his time, Madison feared that direct democracy would deteriorate into mob rule. What would keep the majority of the people, if given direct decision-making power, from abusing the rights of minority groups?

did you know?

A 2007 poll of New York University students revealed that 20 percent of them would give up their vote in the next election for an iPod Touch and that half of them would give up their voting privileges for a lifetime for $1 million.

A Democratic Republic

The framers of the U.S. Constitution chose to craft a **republic**. To Americans of the 1700s, the idea of a republic also meant a government based on common beliefs and virtues that would be fostered within small communities. The rulers were to be lay persons—good citizens who would take turns representing their fellow citizens.

The U.S. Constitution created a form of republican government that we now call a **democratic republic**. The people hold the ultimate power over the government through the election process, but policy decisions are made by elected officials. For the founders, even this distance between the people and the government was not sufficient. The Constitution made sure that the Senate and the president would be selected by political elites rather than by the people, although later changes to the Constitution allowed the voters to elect members of the Senate directly.

Despite these limits, the new American system was unique in the amount of power it granted to ordinary citizens. Over the course of the following two centuries, democratic values became increasingly popular, at first in the West and then throughout the rest of the world. The spread of democratic principles gave rise to another name for our system of government—**representative democracy**. The term *representative democracy* has almost the same meaning as *democratic republic*, with one exception. In a republic, not only are the people sovereign, but there is no king. What if a nation develops into a democracy but preserves the monarchy as a largely ceremonial institution? This is exactly what happened in Britain. Not surprisingly, the British found the term *democratic republic* to be unacceptable, and they described their system as a representative democracy instead.

Principles of Democratic Government. All representative democracies rest on the rule of the people as expressed through the election of government officials. In the 1790s in the United States, only free white males were able to vote, and in some states they had to be property owners as well. Women did not receive the right to vote in national elections in the United States until 1920, and the right to vote was not secured in practice in all states by African Americans until the 1960s. Today, **universal suffrage** is the rule.

Because everyone's vote counts equally, the only way to make fair decisions is by some form of **majority** will. But to ensure that **majority rule** does not become oppressive, modern democracies also provide guarantees of minority rights. If political minorities were not protected, the majority might violate the fundamental rights of members of certain groups, especially groups that are unpopular or that differ from the majority population, such as religious or ethnic minorities.

To guarantee the continued existence of a representative democracy, there must be free, competitive elections. Thus, the opposition always has the opportunity to win elective office. For such elections to be totally open, freedom of the press and speech must be preserved so that opposition candidates may present their criticisms of the government.

Republic
A form of government in which sovereignty rests with the people, as opposed to a king or monarch.

Democratic Republic
A republic in which representatives elected by the people make and enforce laws and policies.

Representative Democracy
A form of government in which representatives elected by the people make and enforce laws and policies; may retain the monarchy in a ceremonial role.

Universal Suffrage
The right of all adults to vote for their representatives.

Majority
More than 50 percent.

Majority Rule
A basic principle of democracy asserting that the greatest number of citizens in any political unit should select officials and determine policies.

---

16. James Madison, in Alexander Hamilton, James Madison, and John Jay, *The Federalist Papers*, No. 10 (New York: Mentor Books, 1964), p. 81. See Appendix C of this textbook.

Limited Government
The principle that the powers of government should be limited, usually by institutional checks.

Another key feature of Western representative democracy is the principle of **limited government**. Not only is the government dependent on popular sovereignty, but the powers of the government are also clearly limited, either through a written document or through widely shared beliefs. The U.S. Constitution sets down the fundamental structure of the government and the limits to its activities. Such limits are intended to prevent political decisions based on the ambitions of individuals in government rather than on constitutional principles. Wisely, the founders created constitutional limits on government that actually rely on human nature and ambition. Consider the counsel of Madison in Federalist #51:

> *Ambition must be made to counteract ambition. The interest of the man must be connected with the constitutional rights of the place. It may be a reflection on human nature that such devices should be necessary to control the abuses of government. But what is government itself but the greatest of all reflections on human nature? If men were angels, no government would be necessary. If angels were to govern men, neither external nor internal controls on government would be necessary.*[17]

As neither is the case, constitutional democracy in the United States is based on an intricate set of relationships—federalism, separation of powers, and checks and balances. Each will be discussed in more detail in later chapters.

Who Really Rules in America?

Americans feel free to organize, to call and email their representatives, and to vote candidates in and out of office. We always describe our political system as a democracy or democratic republic. However, do the people of the United States actually hold power today? Political scientists have developed several theories about American democracy, including *majoritarian* theory, *elite* theory, and theories of *pluralism*. Advocates of these theories use them to describe American democracy either as it actually is or as they believe it should be.

Majoritarianism

Majoritarianism
A political theory holding that in a democracy, the government ought to do what the majority of the people want.

Many people think that in a democracy, the government ought to do what the majority of the people want. This simple proposition is the heart of majoritarian theory. As a theory of what democracy should be like, **majoritarianism** is popular in concept among ordinary citizens. Majorities, however, can sometimes mobilize around issues with outcomes harmful to minorities. Even if much of the decision making in American government is done on the basis of majorities, it is rarely unchecked. For example, in 2008 a majority of voters (52 percent) in California approved Proposition 8, amending the state constitution to ban same-sex marriage. This action prompted a flurry of actions in state and federal appellate courts. In 2012, a federal appeals court struck down California's ban. The U.S. Supreme Court declined to review the decision in 2013, effectively ending Proposition 8. Many scholars, however, consider majoritarianism to be a surprisingly poor description of how U.S. democracy actually works. In particular, they point to the low level of turnout for elections.

---

17. James Madison, in Alexander Hamilton, James Madison, and John Jay, *The Federalist Papers*, No. 51 (New York: Mentor Books, 1968). See Appendix C.

Polling data have shown that many Americans are neither particularly interested in politics nor well informed. Few are able to name the persons running for Congress in their districts, and even fewer can discuss the candidates' positions. Despite the court battles and ongoing political rancor over the Affordable Care Act as the enrollment deadline approached in 2014, 42 percent of Americans reported in a Kaiser Health tracking poll that they were unaware of the law.[18]

Elitism

If ordinary citizens do not indicate policy preferences with their votes, then who does? One answer suggests that elites really govern the United States. Rather than opting out of participation, ordinary Americans are excluded. **Elite theory** is usually used simply to describe the American system. Few people today believe it is a good idea for the country to be run by a privileged minority. In the past, however, many people believed that it was appropriate for the country to be run by an elite. Consider the words of Alexander Hamilton, one of the framers of the Constitution:

> All communities divide themselves into the few and the many. The first are the rich and the wellborn, the other the mass of the people... The people are turbulent and changing; they seldom judge or determine right. Give therefore to the first class a distinct, permanent share in the government. They will check the unsteadiness of the second, and as they cannot receive any advantage by a change, they therefore will ever maintain good government.[19]

Some versions of elite theory posit a small, cohesive, elite class that makes almost all of the important decisions for the nation, whereas others suggest that voters choose among competing elites.[20] New members are recruited through the educational system so that the brightest children of the masses allegedly have the opportunity to join the elite stratum. One view suggests that the members of the elite are primarily interested in controlling the political system to protect their own wealth and the capitalist system that produces it.[21] Studies of elite opinion, however, have also suggested that elites are more tolerant of diversity, more willing to defend individual liberties, and more supportive of democratic values than are members of the mass public.

Pluralism

A different school of thought holds that our form of democracy is based on group interests. As early as 1831, French commentator Alexis de Tocqueville noted the American penchant for joining groups: "As soon as the inhabitants of the United States have taken up an opinion or a feeling which they wish to promote in the world, they look out for mutual assistance; and as soon as they have found one another out, they combine. From that moment they are no longer isolated men, but a power seen from afar..."[22]

Elite Theory
A perspective holding that society is ruled by a small number of people who exercise power to further their self-interest.

---

18. Kaiser Health Tracking Poll: April 2013. Accessed at http://kff.org/health-reform/poll-finding/kaiser-health-tracking-poll-april-2013/.
19. Alexander Hamilton, "Speech in the Constitutional Convention on a Plan of Government," in *Writings*, ed. Joanne B. Freeman (New York: Library of America, 2001).
20. Michael Parenti, *Democracy for the Few*, 7th ed. (Belmont, CA: Wadsworth Publishing, 2002).
21. G. William Domhoff, *Who Rules America?* 4th ed. (New York: McGraw-Hill Higher Education, 2002).
22. Alexis de Tocqueville, *Democracy in America*, Volume II, Section 2, Chapter V, "Of the uses which the Americans make of Public Associations" (available in many editions, and as full text in several Web locations).

Politics with a Purpose

When Passions Mobilize

"We the People" has profound meaning in the twenty-first century. A quick internet search reveals literally millions of websites with "citizens against" and just as many more with "citizens for" in their titles.

People organize into groups in order to influence the system and affect changes in public policy. Many groups mobilize to keep watch on government power. Some address specific policy problems—the environment, handgun violence, or urban gas well drilling—while others have bigger issues, such as reducing taxes or the national debt. In recent months, several interest groups have mobilized either against the Obama administration's approach to health care reform and increased government spending or in support of the president's initiatives. While such groups may have ties to a political party or to an existing political organization, many people who join do so out of real passion and may have little political experience. Sometimes, the actions of one person result in the mobilization of hundreds or more fellow citizens.

In October 2013, the United States federal government closed for fifteen days when Congress failed to pass legislation authorizing the government to continue spending money. During the shutdown, approximately 800,000 federal employees were indefinitely furloughed, and another 1.3 million who were deemed "essential" were required to report to work without knowing if they would be paid for their time. The shutdown meant that national parks were closed, research funded by the federal government was suspended, the Internal Revenue Service (IRS) warned of delays in processing tax returns and refunds, and services in the District of Columbia were curtailed. One man, watching the news of the shutdown from his home in South Carolina, grew concerned when a reporter observed how vulnerable the national monuments would be to vandals in their unguarded state. Chris Cox threw his bicycle, lawnmower, and a rake into his truck and drove to Washington. According to news accounts, he patrolled the memorials for several days by bicycle to keep watch over them but when he saw trashcans on the national mall overflowing he changed his focus. "I realized that I could serve my country better as a custodian," he said. Cox spent 10 hours a day as an unofficial, unpaid groundskeeper. Commuters and tourists Tweeted photos of him mowing the grass around the Lincoln Memorial carrying a South Carolina flag, earning him the nickname "Lawnmower Man." Cox called his crusade the "Memorial Militia."

What motivates a person to drive over 500 miles to keep national monuments in good order? "I'm not here to point fingers," he said. "I just want to try to get Americans to rally behind these parks. Forget about the party you're in and who you voted for and come together as Americans and make a difference." What are the issues about which you care most deeply? Chances are good that other similarly motivated individuals would welcome your help!

Source: Susan Bird, "Shutdown's Mystery 'Lawnmower Man' Will use his Reward to Do More Good Deeds," November 18, 2013. Accessed at www.care2.com/

Chris Cox rakes leaves near the Lincoln Memorial in Washington, Wednesday, Oct. 9, 2013, while the federal government was closed.

Pluralism
A theory that views politics as a conflict among interest groups. Political decision making is characterized by bargaining and compromise.

Pluralist theory proposes that even if the average citizen cannot keep up with political issues or cast a deciding vote in any election, the individual's interests will be protected by groups that represent her or him. Theorists who subscribe to **pluralism** see politics as a struggle among groups to gain benefits for their members.

Many political scientists believe that pluralism works very well as a descriptive theory. As a way to defend the practice of democracy in the United States, however, pluralism has problems. Poor citizens are rarely represented by interest groups.

At the same time, rich citizens are often overrepresented, in part because they understand their own interests. As political scientist E. E. Schattschneider observed, "The flaw in the pluralist heaven is that the heavenly chorus sings with a strong upper-class accent."[23] There are also serious doubts as to whether group decision making always reflects the best interests of the nation.

Critics see a danger that groups may become so powerful that all policies become compromises crafted to satisfy the interests of the largest groups. The interests of the public as a whole, then, would not be considered. Critics of pluralism have suggested that a democratic system can be virtually paralyzed by the struggle among interest groups. We will discuss interest groups at greater length in Chapter 7.

Political Ideologies

■ **LO1.5**: Define political ideology and locate socialism, liberalism, conservatism, and libertarianism along the ideological spectrum.

A political **ideology** is a closely linked set of beliefs about politics. Political ideologies offer their adherents well-organized theories that propose goals for the society and the means by which those goals can be achieved. At the core of every political ideology is a set of guiding values. The two ideologies most commonly referred to in discussions of American politics are *liberalism* and *conservatism*. In the scheme of ideologies embraced across the globe, these two, especially as practiced in the United States, are in the middle of the ideological spectrum, as noted in Table 1–1.

The Traditional Political Spectrum

A traditional method of comparing political ideologies is to array them on a continuum from left to right, based primarily on how much power the government should exercise to promote economic equality, as well as the ultimate goals of government activity. Table 1–1 shows how ideologies can be arrayed in a traditional political spectrum. In addition to liberalism and conservatism, the table includes the ideologies of socialism and libertarianism.

did you know?
The phrase "In God We Trust" was made the national motto on July 30, 1956, but had appeared on U.S. coins as early as 1864.

Ideology
A comprehensive set of beliefs about the nature of people and about the role of an institution or government.

Table 1–1 ▶ The Traditional Political Spectrum

	SOCIALISM	LIBERALISM	CONSERVATISM	LIBERTARIANISM
How much power should the government have over the economy?	Active government control of major economic sectors	Positive government action in the economy	Positive government action to support capitalism	Almost no regulation of the economy
What should the government promote?	Economic equality, community	Economic security, equal opportunity, social liberty	Economic liberty, morality, social order	Total economic and social liberty

23. E. E. Schattschneider, *The Semi-Sovereign People* (Hinsdale, IL: The Dryden Press, 1975; originally published in 1960).

Socialism
A political ideology based on strong support for economic and social equality. Socialists traditionally envisioned a society in which major businesses were taken over by the government or by employee cooperatives.

Libertarianism
A political ideology based on skepticism or opposition toward almost all government activities.

Liberalism
A set of beliefs that includes the advocacy of positive government action to improve the welfare of individuals, support for civil rights, and tolerance for political and social change.

Conservatism
A set of beliefs that includes a limited role for the national government in helping individuals, support for traditional values and lifestyles, and a cautious response to change.

Socialism falls on the left side of the spectrum. Socialists play a minor role in the American political arena, although socialist parties and movements are very important in other countries around the world. In the past, socialists typically advocated replacing investor ownership of major businesses with either government ownership or ownership by employee cooperatives. Socialists believed that such steps would break the power of the very rich and lead to an egalitarian society. In more recent times, socialists in Western Europe have advocated more limited programs that redistribute income.

On the right side of the spectrum is **libertarianism**, a philosophy of skepticism toward most government activities. Libertarians strongly support property rights and typically oppose regulation of the economy and redistribution of income. Libertarians support *laissez-faire* capitalism. (*Laissez-faire* is French for "let it be.") Libertarians also tend to oppose government attempts to regulate personal behavior and promote moral values.

In the Middle: Liberalism and Conservatism

The set of beliefs called **liberalism** includes advocacy of government action to improve the welfare of individuals, support for civil rights, and tolerance for social change. American liberals believe that government should take positive action to reduce poverty, to redistribute income from wealthier classes to poorer ones, and to regulate the economy. Those who espouse liberalism may also be more supportive of the rights of historically underrepresented groups including women, the LGBT (lesbian, gay, bisexual, transgender) community, and racial minorities.

The set of beliefs called **conservatism** includes a limited role for the government in helping individuals. Conservatives believe that the private sector can outperform the government in almost any activity. Believing that the individual is primarily responsible for his or her own well-being, conservatives typically oppose government programs to redistribute income. Conservatism may also include support for what conservatives refer to as traditional values regarding individual behavior and the importance of the family. Liberals are often seen as an influential force within the Democratic Party, and conservatives are often regarded as the most influential force in the Republican Party.

The Difficulty of Defining Liberalism and Conservatism

While political candidates and commentators are quick to label candidates and voters as "liberals" and "conservatives," the meanings of these words have evolved over time. Moreover, each term may represent a different set of ideas to the person or group that uses it.

Liberalism. The word *liberal* has an odd history. It comes from the same root as *liberty*, and originally it simply meant "free." In that broad sense, the United States as a whole is a liberal country, and all popular American ideologies are variants of liberalism. In a more restricted definition, a *liberal* was a person who believed in limited government and who opposed religion in politics. A hundred years ago, liberalism referred to a philosophy that in some ways resembled modern-day libertarianism. For that reason, many libertarians today refer to themselves as *classical liberals*.

How did the meaning of the word *liberal* change? In the 1800s, the Democratic Party was seen as the more liberal of the two parties. The Democrats of that time stood for limited government and opposition to moralism in politics. Democrats opposed Republican projects such as building roads, freeing the slaves, and prohibiting the sale of alcoholic beverages. Beginning with Democratic president

Woodrow Wilson (served 1913–1921), however, the party's economic policies began to change. President Franklin Delano Roosevelt won a landslide election in 1932 by pledging to take steps to end the Great Depression. Roosevelt and the Democratic Congress quickly passed several measures that increased federal government intervention in the economy and improved conditions for Americans. By the end of Roosevelt's presidency in 1945, the Democratic Party had established itself as standing for positive government action to help the economy. Although Roosevelt stood for new policies, he kept the old language—as Democrats had long done, he called himself a liberal. We will discuss the history of the two parties in greater detail in Chapter 8.

Outside of the United States and Canada, the meaning of the word *liberal* never changed. For this reason, you might hear a left-of-center European denounce U.S. president Ronald Reagan (served 1981–1989) or British prime minister Margaret Thatcher (served 1979–1990) for their "liberalism," meaning that these two leaders were enthusiastic advocates of *laissez-faire* capitalism and limited government.

Conservatism. The term *conservatism* suffers from similar identity problems. In the United States and Western Europe, conservatives tended to believe in maintaining traditions and opposing change. Conservatives were more likely to support the continuation of the monarchy, for example. At the end of World War II, Senator Robert A. Taft of Ohio was known as "Mr. Conservative," and he steadfastly opposed the Democratic Party's platform of an active government. He was not, however, a spokesperson for conservative or traditional personal values.

Today, conservatism is often considered to have two quite different dimensions. Some self-identified conservatives are "economic conservatives" who believe in less government, support for capitalism and private property, and allowing individuals to pursue their own route to achievement with little government interference. Recent presidential campaigns have seen great efforts to motivate those individuals who might be called "social conservatives" to support Republican candidates. Social conservatives are much less interested in economic issues than in supporting particular social values, including opposition to abortion, support for the death penalty or the right to own firearms, and opposition to gay marriage. Given these two different dimensions of conservatism, it is not surprising that conservatives are not always united in their political preferences. The Tea Party, for example, emerged out of the divisions among conservatives and the Republican Party. Thus, its followers are neither entirely conservative nor exclusively Republican.

Libertarianism. Although libertarians make up a much smaller proportion of the population in the United States than do conservatives or liberals, this ideology shares the more extreme positions of both groups. If the only question is how much power the government should have over the economy, then libertarians can be considered conservatives. However, libertarians advocate the most complete possible freedom in social matters. They oppose government action to promote conservative moral values, although such action is often favored by other groups on the political right. Libertarians' strong support for civil liberties seems to align them more closely with modern liberals than with conservatives. Ron Paul, a congressman from Texas and a candidate for the Republican presidential nomination in 2008 and 2012, is known for his libertarian positions. Although Paul has never won the Republican nomination, he remains popular among college students, most likely because of his positions in favor of personal freedoms, liberalizing drug laws, and bringing home troops serving abroad. His son, Rand Paul, a Republican Senator from Kentucky, also espouses libertarian positions and often aligns with the Tea Party.

The Challenge of Change

■ **LO1.6: Apply understanding of the purpose of government and the U.S. political culture to evaluate government's ability to meet new challenges over time.**

The United States faces enormous internal and external challenges. In the next 50 years, not only will the face of America change as its citizens age, become more diverse, and generate new needs for laws and policies, but the country will also have to contend with a decline in economic dominance in the world. Other nations, including China and India, have much larger populations than the United States and are assuming new roles in the world. The United States and its citizens will need to meet the challenges of a global economy and mitigate the impact of global environmental change. Technology has transformed the way we live, learn, and work. All of these challenges—demographic change, globalization, ubiquitous technology, and environmental change—will impact how the American political system functions in the future.

Demographic Change in a Democratic Republic

The population of the United States is changing in fundamental ways that will impact the political and social system of the nation. Long a nation of growth, the United States has become a middle-aged nation with a low birthrate and an increasing number of older citizens who want the services from government they were promised. Social Security and Medicare are among the few government entitlements remaining, and any suggestion that either program be changed elicits immediate political action by older citizens and their interest groups. In communities where there is a large elderly population whose children are grown and gone, increasing taxes in support of public education is a difficult proposition. Both the aging of the population and its changing ethnic composition will have significant political consequences.

Like other economically advanced countries, the United States has in recent decades experienced falling birthrates and an increase in the number of older citizens. As you can see in Figure 1–2, the proportion of the population most likely to be in the labor force remains relatively stable even as the percentage of the elderly and young increase slightly. According to the projections, by 2050 just over half of the population (54 percent) will fall within prime earning years, while a quarter of the population (those under 20) will be considered dependents and roughly 20 percent will be elderly. The "aging of America" is a weaker phenomenon than in many other wealthy countries, however. Today, the median age of the population is 37.2 in the United States and 40.0 in Europe. By 2050, the median age in the United States is expected to decline slightly to 36.2. In Europe, it is expected to reach 52.7. As is already the case in many European nations, older citizens demand that their need for pensions and health care dominate the political agenda. Young people in the United States, at times apathetic about politics, could

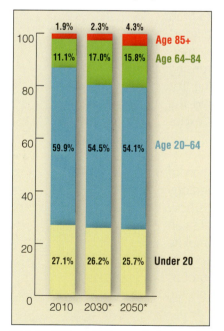

Figure 1–2 ▶ The Aging of America

*Data for 2030 and 2050 are projections.
Source: U.S. Census Bureau (Projections and Distribution of the Total Population by Age for the United States: 2010–2050).

use their vote to reorient the policy agenda. In the 2012 presidential contest, people younger than 30 made up a larger share of the electorate than those 65 and older.

Ethnic Change

As a result of differences in fertility rates and immigration, the ethnic character of the United States is also changing. Non-Hispanic white Americans have a fertility rate of just over 1.8 per two people; African Americans have a fertility rate of 2.1; and Hispanic Americans have a current fertility rate of almost 3.0. Figure 1–3 shows the projected changes in the U.S. ethnic distribution in future years.

A large share of all new immigrants are Hispanic. A **Hispanic** or **Latino** is someone who can claim a heritage from a Spanish-speaking country (other than Spain). Today, most individuals who share this heritage prefer to refer to themselves as Latino rather than Hispanic; however, government agencies such as the Census Bureau use the terms Hispanic and *non-Hispanic white* for their tables. In this book, Hispanic is used when referring to government statistics, while Latino is used in other contexts.

Latinos may come from any of about 20 primarily Spanish-speaking countries, and, as a result, they are a highly diverse population. The three largest Hispanic groups are Mexican Americans at 58.5 percent of all Latinos, Puerto Ricans (all of whom are U.S. citizens) at 9.6 percent of the total, and Cuban Americans at 3.5 percent. The diversity among Hispanic Americans results in differing political behavior; however, the majority of Latino Americans vote Democratic.

Barack Obama captured the majority of the Latino vote in 2008 and in 2012. Between the two presidential elections, the Latino population grew and grew more Democratic, particularly in states like Colorado, New Mexico, and Nevada. Nationally, the Latino share of the electorate rose to 10 percent of the whole, and President Obama attracted 71 percent of their support compared to 27 percent for Governor Romney. Similarly, Obama attracted a higher percentage of votes from African Americans (93 percent) and Asian Americans (73 percent) than did

Hispanic
Someone who can claim a heritage from a Spanish-speaking country other than Spain. This is the term most often used by government agencies to describe this group. Citizens of Spanish-speaking countries do not use this term to describe themselves.

Latino
Preferred term for referring to individuals who claim a heritage from a Spanish-speaking country other than Spain.

Figure 1-3 ▶ **Distribution of U.S. Population by Race and Hispanic Origin, 1980–2075**

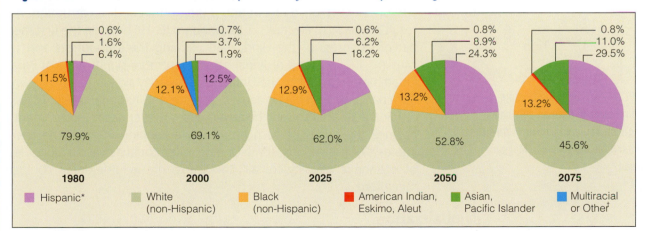

Data for 2025, 2050, and 2075 are projections.
*Persons of Hispanic origin can be of any race.
†The "multiracial or other" category in 2000 is not an official census category but represents all non-Hispanics who chose either "some other race" or two or more races in the 2000 census.
Source: U.S. Bureau of the Census.

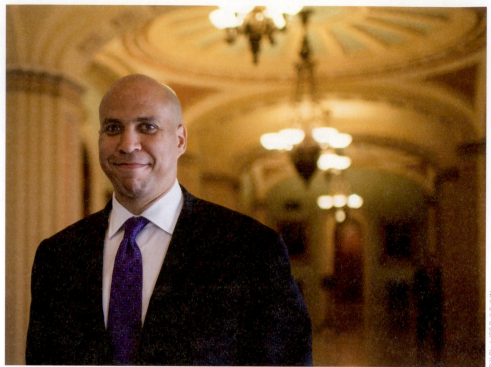

Senator-elect Cory Booker (D-NJ) before being sworn in on the Senate floor on Thursday, Oct. 31, 2013. Booker won a special election to fill the late Sen. Frank Lautenberg's seat. He is the first African American Senator to be elected since Barack Obama in 2004 and the first to represent the state of New Jersey. African American Senators Tim Scott (R-SC) and Mo Cowan (D-MA) were appointed by their respective governors to complete the unfinished terms of senators who resigned.

did you know?

In 2012, New Hampshire became the first state to have an all-woman delegation in Congress. The state also elected a female governor, Maggie Hassan.

the Republican candidate. As the nation's population grows more diverse, political parties and candidates will need to attend carefully to the new demographic reality in America. Republicans, in particular, have signaled their intent to compete for Latino voters, but positions on immigration reform emphasizing border security and enforcement, as well as a significant split within the party over creating a path to citizenship for illegal immigrants, currently makes a shift in support unlikely. Marco Rubio, the Cuban American Republican Senator from Florida and likely future Republican presidential contender, has called changing demographics one of his party's biggest challenges.

The United States is becoming a more ethnically diverse nation in every way. Bobby Jindal, an American of Indian descent, was elected governor of Louisiana (even though he did not represent any major ethnic group in that state) by running on a platform of effective government and promising an end to corruption. As a result of the 2012 elections, Tulsi Gabbard (D-HI) became the first member of Congress of the Hindu faith, joining three Buddhists and two Muslims. The election of Jindal—and even more significantly of Barack Obama as president of the United States—may signal the end of white dominance in political leadership at state and national levels. A multi-ethnic, multiracial society, however, poses challenges to government to balance the needs of each group while keeping in mind the overall interests of the country. If the United States could achieve a higher level of economic equality for all Americans, group differences could be minimized.

Globalization

Globalization of the world economy has advanced rapidly. The power of the American economy and its expansion into other parts of the world spurred similar actions by the European, South American, and Asian nations. Huge international corporations produce and market products throughout the world. American soft drinks are produced and sold in China, while Americans buy clothing manufactured in China or the former states of the Soviet Union. Jobs are outsourced from the United States to India, the Philippines, or Vietnam, while other nations outsource jobs to the United States. Companies such as General Electric (GE) employ design teams that collaborate in the design and production of jet engines, with employees working around the clock, across all time zones.

Globalization brings a multitude of challenges to the United States and all other nations, beginning with the fact that no single government can regulate global corporations. Globalization changes employment patterns, reducing jobs in one nation and increasing employment in another. Products produced in low-wage nations are cheaper to buy in the United States, but the result is little control over quality and consumer safety. If you have an Apple iPhone or iPad, chances are that most of its components were manufactured and assembled overseas—most likely in China. When President Obama asked the late Steve Jobs what it would take to make iPhones in the United States, Jobs simply replied "those jobs aren't coming back."[24] Apple is not alone; nearly all U.S. electronics manufacturers rely on factories overseas.

Another challenge of globalization worthy of careful consideration is global conflict. At one time, stability in the world was accomplished by maintaining relative parity between the world superpowers: the United States and the Soviet Union. With the breakup of the Soviet Union and the populist challenges to authoritarian rule around the globe, the United States often finds itself in a quandary over how to confront aggression. When military intervention is not a viable option, and diplomatic overtures have proven ineffective, what remains for the United States to do? Take, for example, the case of chemical weapons in Syria. As the Syrian crisis escalated and the world grew concerned over the possibility of chemical weapons being used by Syrian president Bashar al-Assad or perhaps falling into the wrong hands, White House correspondent Chuck Todd asked the president if he envisioned using the U.S. military in this situation. The president responded, "I have, at this point, not ordered military engagement in the situation. But the point that you made about chemical and biological weapons is critical . . . We have been very clear to the Assad regime, but also to other players on the ground, that a red line for us is we start seeing a whole bunch of chemical weapons moving around or being utilized. That would change my calculus. That would change my equation."[25] The "red line" became a call to action for those who wanted the United States to militarily remove Assad. President Obama pulled back from plans to conduct an airstrike in retaliation for a chemical-weapons attack on civilians. Instead, he accepted a Russian offer to work jointly to remove the chemical weapons. The failure to act called into question the international credibility of the United States and left the president weakened in other instances of aggression, such as Vladimir Putin's incursion into the Crimean peninsula of Ukraine in March of 2014. Global conflict and instability pose a grave challenge to U.S. foreign policy and our nation's ability to provide leadership in an uncertain world.

The Technology Revolution

Rapidly changing technology has transformed the way we communicate with one another, where and how we work, and even where and how we learn. You may be reading this book electronically, and you may even be completing this

---

24. Charles Duhigg and Keith Bradsher, "How the US Lost out on iPhone Work" *New York Times*, January 21, 2012.
25. Presidential Remarks, August 20, 2012. Accessed at: www.whitehouse.gov/the-press-office/2012/08/20/remarks-president-white-house-press-corps

course online. In 2005, Thomas Friedman wrote a book titled *The World Is Flat*, in which he signaled that globalization and technology are intertwined, each fueling the other. New technologies erase boundaries and connect the previously unconnected, meaning that more people can suddenly compete, connect, and collaborate.[26] In a subsequent book, Friedman observed that when he wrote *The World Is Flat*, "Facebook wasn't even in it...'Twitter' was just a sound, the 'cloud' was something in the sky, '3G' was a parking space, 'applications' were what you sent to colleges, and 'Skype' was a typo."[27] In other words, the world becomes "flatter" every day. What sort of education and training will tomorrow's workforce require? What role will colleges and

Everyday Politics

▶ Between Two Ferns with Zach Galifianakis

Between Two Ferns with Zach Galifianakis is an internet comedy series appearing on the website Funny or Die. Galifianakis is a stand-up comedian and movie actor (most famous for his role in *The Hangover* movie trilogy) who invites celebrity guests to appear on a mock talk-show set. Guests are not told in advance what the interview will include and Galifianakis is known for asking awkward, and in his words, "inappropriate" questions. Guests appearing on the show have included Justin Bieber, Jon Stewart, Samuel L. Jackson, and Jennifer Lawrence.

In March 2014, President Obama was a guest on the show, appearing to promote the Affordable Care Act and to encourage youth to enroll before the March 31 deadline. Galifianakis and the president exchanged banter on a number of topics before arriving at the president's plug for Healthcare.gov. After the show, Obama sent out a Tweet thanking Galifianakis "for sending so many folks to #GetCoveredNow at Healthcare. gov." He signed the tweet "-bo," meaning that he sent it himself. Although the White House promoted the appearance through social media and on its website and blog, the president's appearance attracted critics who claimed he had tarnished the dignity of the office.* Stephen Colbert said that the appearance "set off a firestorm on Fox News and later that day on Fox News..." Mocking Bill O'Reilly's claim that President Lincoln would never have done this, Colbert replied, "It's true. You can't fight that logic. Abe Lincoln would never have done a viral web video." Colbert also noted that all of the attention boosted traffic to Healthcare.gov by 40 percent.

The White House / Twitter

Critical Thinking

1. *Pew Research Center reports that young people (ages 18–24) get the bulk of their news content online (41 percent) or through social networking (34 percent) with far fewer reading a daily newspaper (6 percent).** Was the president right to go where young viewers can be found to promote the Affordable Care Act?*

2. *What conclusions can you draw about American political and popular culture from this episode? Where are there boundaries between politics and daily life? In a political system controlled by the populace, should there be any boundaries?*

*http://www.whitehouse.gov/blog/2014/03/11/watch-president-obama-between-two-ferns-zach-galifianakis

** Pew Research Center for the People & the Press. Accessed at www.people-press.org/2012/09/27/section-1-watching-reading-and-listening-to-the-news-3/.

26. Thomas Friedman, *The World is Flat: A Brief History of the Twenty-first Century*. New York: Ferrar, Straus, and Giroux, 2005.
27. Thomas L. Friedman and Michael Mandelbaum. *That Used to be Us: How America Fell Behind in the World it Invented and How We Can Come Back*. New York: Ferrar, Straus, and Giroux, 2011.

universities play? Will the degree you are earning today enable you to work effectively in a transformed global economy?

Environmental Change

The challenges posed by environmental change are political, technological, and global. The great majority of scientists agree that the climate is changing and global warming is taking place. Many scientists and global organizations are focusing their efforts on measures to reduce humankind's contribution to global warming through carbon emissions and other actions. While the Bush administration balked at joining in the imposition of the measures on all nations until developing nations such as China and India were included, the Obama administration has signaled strong support for an international treaty to reduce global warming.

While many scientists are working on the technologies to slow global warming, others believe that it is more important to concentrate on mitigating the impact of global climate change, whatever the cause. The United States, like many other nations, has a concentration of population on the seacoasts: of the 25 most densely populated U.S. counties, 23 are found along the coast. Scientists estimate that global sea levels rose by seven inches over the twentieth century and subsiding land exacerbates the problem in low-lying coastal areas like New Orleans and the communities surrounding the Chesapeake Bay.[28] In 2012, "Superstorm" Sandy made landfall in New York and New Jersey, killing more than 100 people and displacing thousands from their homes and businesses with an estimated $65 billion in damages. How should policies change in the face of rising seas and more hurricanes and coastal damage? Climate change is predicted to have more immediate and dire consequences on nations in Africa, where droughts could cause millions to starve. Should the United States play a much greater role in ameliorating these disasters and others caused by manmade climate change in the near future, or should our policy priorities focus on technologies to change our lifestyles years from now?

What will all of these changes mean for you, your generation, and the nation? Is the American government nimble enough to recognize the many challenges we will face in the future in time to meet them? What will doing so mean for the commitments we have made to previous generations and the promises we make to one another as a single nation? Can the United States continue to replicate and embrace a single political culture, or have we become two Americas? These and other questions will guide our exploration of American government and politics today.

---

28. United States Environmental Protection Agency. "Climate Impacts on Coastal Areas." Accessed at www.epa.gov/climatechange/impacts-adaptation/coasts.html.

The World Wide Web at 25 Years Old is Ubiquitous: How Do We Know?

Just 25 years ago, the World Wide Web was introduced in a concept paper written by Sir Tim Berners-Lee proposing an "informational management" system. In 1990, Berners-Lee released to the world the code for his system—for free. Today, 87 percent of adults report using the Internet.

Describing the Web as "ubiquitous" indicates the breadth and depth of its influence and presence in our lives. Ubiquitous means: omnipresent, pervasive, permeating, and everywhere.

In 2014, the Pew Research Center marked the twenty-fifth birthday of the Web by undertaking a series of studies about its role in American life and in partnership with Elon University; it will explore emerging trends in digital technology by tapping experts in privacy, cybersecurity, and net neutrality.** Of course you can access all of the surveys, interviews, and research online.

Figure 1—4 and Table 1—2 present data in a graphic format to allow you to assess the dynamic presence of the Web in American life. Figure 1—4 describes how quickly a particular technology was adopted by one-quarter of the population.*** It took just 7 years for the Web to be used by 25 percent of the American population, compared to 46 years for electricity and 26 years for the telephone. What factors might explain the different rates of adoption? Table 1—2 gives you a sense of how difficult it would be for people to give up different types of technology that permeate our lives.**** Interestingly, among Internet users, social media would be the easiest technology to give up. Would you say that is true for you? How well do your opinions match this national sample?

Figure 1-4 ▶ Technology Adoption

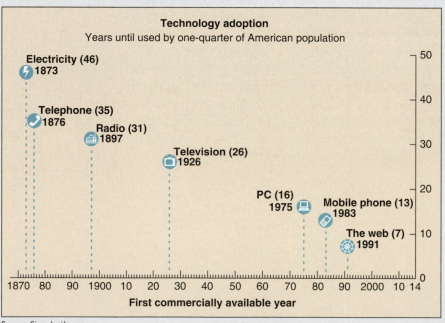

Source: Singularity.com

---

  * Pew Research Center, February 2014, "The Web at 25." Access at: www.pewinternet.org/2014/02/27/the-web-at-25-in-the-u-s/.
  ** Elon University, "Imagining the Internet: A History and Forecast." Access at: http://www.elon.edu/e-web/imagining/.
  *** "Daily Chart," *The Economist*, March 12, 2014.
**** The information was collected by surveying a nationally representative sample of adults by landline and cell phone, in English and in Spanish, over four days in January 2014.

Finally, Figure 1—5 is a reflection of earlier themes in this chapter. U.S. political culture has a strong emphasis on the individual. While a clear majority of people say that the Internet has been a good thing, 90 percent say it has been good for them as an individual while 72 percent say the same is true for society. What might account for that difference? In what ways do individuals benefit from Internet-based technology that might differ from society as a whole?

Table 1–2 ▶ Technology Dependency

How hard would it be to give up these technologies?

% of users of each technology who report how difficult it would be to give up …

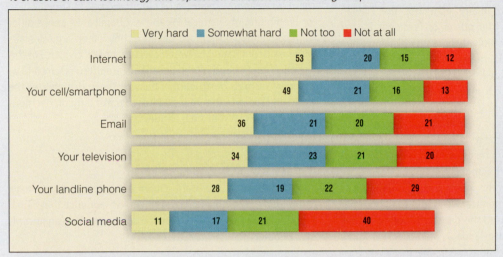

Source: Pew Research Center Internet Project Survey, January 9–12, 2014. N=1,006 adults' N=857 internet users; N=717 landline owners; N=928 cell owners.

Figure 1–5 ▶ Has the Internet Been a Good Thing or a Bad Thing?

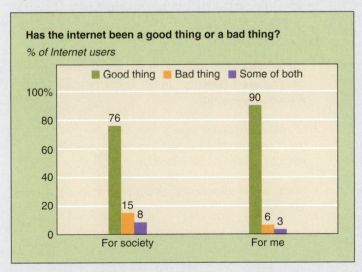

Source: Pew Research Center Internet Project Survey, January 9–12, 2014. N= 857 Internet users.

What Would You Do?

Chemical Weapons and Civil War in Syria

Arab Spring is the term used to describe a series of popular demonstrations, protests, and revolutionary uprisings in six Arab countries beginning in 2010. Regimes were overthrown and dictators forced from power in Tunisia, Egypt, Libya, and Yemen. Protests in Syria began in January 2011 but the "Syrian Revolution" did not result in the ouster of President Bashar al-Assad—it descended into a violent civil war with more than 146,000 deaths and produced a massive civilian refugee crisis. The Syrian regime's allies include Russia and Iran.

The United States watched from a distance until August 21, 2013, when Assad's government gassed to death over a thousand civilians, including hundreds of children, using a gas classified as a weapon of mass destruction (sarin). In reaction, President Obama called on Congress to authorize military intervention, but ultimately asked Congress to wait because he hoped Russia would join with the international community in pushing Assad to give up his chemical weapons. On September 10, 2013, the president addressed the nation: "No one disputes chemical weapons were used in Syria… Moreover, we know that the Assad regime was responsible."* The president concluded his address with the following statement directly reflecting the ideals of our nation: "America is not the world's policeman. Terrible things happen across the globe, and it is beyond our means to right every wrong. But when, with modest effort and risk, we can stop children from being gassed to death, and thereby make our own children safer over the long run, I believe we should act. That's what makes America different. That's what makes us exceptional. With humility, but with resolve, let us never lose sight of that essential truth."

The very next day, *The New York Times* carried an opinion column by Russian President Putin urging the United States to work through the United Nations rather than take unilateral military action.** He characterized the violence in Syria not as a battle for democracy, but as "an armed conflict between government and opposition in a multireligious country." Russia, he claimed, was not protecting the Syrian regime, but rather international law. Putin continued, "I welcome the President's interest in the dialogue with Russia on Syria. We must work together to keep hope alive…" Putin took exception to American exceptionalism: "We are all different, but when we ask for the Lord's blessings, we must not forget that God created us all equal."

An international agreement was eventually reached on the disposal of Syria's chemical weapons. However, by early 2014 only one-third of the stockpile had been destroyed, the Syrian civil war showed no signs of ending, and Bashar al-Assad was preparing for reelection.

Why Should You Care?

The Chemical Weapons Convention (1997) is joined by 189 nations and outlaws the production, stockpiling, and use of chemical weapons. The treaty is monitored by the Organization for Prohibition of Chemical Weapons. Chemical weapons differ from conventional weapons because they kill on a mass scale, with no discrimination between combatant and civilian. For this reason, chemical and biological agents are often referred to as weapons of mass destruction. Their existence destabilizes the world and requires the United States to make difficult decisions about how to confront such dangers.

What Would You Do?

If you had been President Obama, how would you have responded to the clear and overwhelming evidence that Syrian President Assad used a weapon of mass destruction against his own people?

What You Can Do

Over six million people have been displaced within Syria or are trying to escape the violence by leaving Syria. While you are unlikely to influence the outcome of the civil war, you can participate in humanitarian efforts to aid Syrian civilians.

- The United Nations Refugee Agency (UNHCR) is leading the coordinated response of many nations, agencies, and non-governmental organizations (NGOs). You can find ways to assist from the United States on their website: www.unrefugees.org.

- To help students and faculty from Syria, consider adopting the "Commitment to Action," an effort facilitated by the Institute of International Education: www.iie.org.

- Learn world geography: http://maps.nationalgeographic.com/maps.

*"Remarks by the President in Address to the Nation on Syria." September 10, 2013. Accessed at www.whitehouse.gov/the-press-office/2013/09/10/remarks-president-address-nation-syria.

**"A Plea for Caution From Russia." *The New York Times* September 11, 2013. Accessed at www.nytimes.com/2013/09/12/opinion/putin-plea-for-caution-from-russia-on-syria.html.

Purestock/Getty Images

Key Terms

anarchy 14	equality 11	limited government 18	recall 15
aristocracy 14	government 6	majoritarianism 18	referendum 15
authoritarianism 14	Hispanic 25	majority 17	representative democracy 17
capitalism 12	ideology 21	majority rule 17	republic 17
conservatism 22	initiative 15	oligarchy 14	social contract 7
democracy 14	institution 6	order 11	socialism 22
democratic republic 17	latino 25	pluralism 20	totalitarian regime 13
direct democracy 14	legislature 15	political culture 7	universal suffrage 17
divine right of kings 7	liberalism 22	political socialization 9	
elite theory 19	libertarianism 22	politics 6	
eminent domain 13	liberty 9	property 12	

Chapter Summary

■ **LO1.1:** Governments are necessary at a minimum to provide public goods and services that all citizens need but cannot reasonably be expected to provide for themselves. National security and defense are obvious examples. Our founding documents such as the Declaration of Independence and the Constitution are predicated upon and convey through their language a set of shared political values. Government reinforces those values regularly.

■ **LO1.1:** Politics is the process of resolving conflicts and deciding "who gets what, when, and how." Government is the institution within which decisions are made that resolve conflicts or allocate benefits and privileges. It is unique because it has the ultimate authority within society.

■ **LO1.2:** Political philosophers Thomas Hobbes and John Locke believed governments were formed on the basis of consent. Individuals, all equal and endowed with reason, give up a portion of their individual liberty in order to gain the protection of government through the social contract. Government is formed to provide security and protect life, liberty, and property. Consent to be governed can be withdrawn if government becomes too powerful or abuses fundamental political values such as liberty, equality, individualism, the rule of law, and property rights.

■ **LO1.3:** The authors of the United States Constitution believed that the new nation could be sustained by its political culture—the set of ideas, values, and ways of thinking about government and politics that are shared by all citizens. There is considerable consensus among American citizens about concepts basic to the U.S. political system and the fundamental values it embodies, such as liberty, equality, individualism, the rule of law, and property rights. These agreements define our political

culture and are transmitted to successive generations through the process of political socialization.

■ **LO1.4:** Governments can vary in form depending on who controls the government. In a democracy, authority is held by the people as a whole. In totalitarian and authoritarian regimes, control is exercised by a single individual or a small group. Greek terms are often used to indicate how widely power is distributed. An aristocracy is "rule by the best," while an oligarchy is "rule by a few," and democracy is understood as "rule by the people." The United States is a representative democracy, where the people elect representatives to make the decisions.

■ **LO1.4:** Theories of American democracy include majoritarianism, in which the government does what the majority wants; elite theory, in which the real power lies with one or more elites; and pluralist theory, in which organized interest groups contest for power.

■ **LO1.5:** Popular political ideologies can be arrayed from left (liberal) to right (conservative). We can also analyze economic liberalism and conservatism separately from cultural liberalism and conservatism. Other ideologies on the left (communism) and the right (fascism), however, also exist in the world.

■ **LO1.6:** The United States faces significant change and challenges ahead. Among these are demographic changes in the nation, the impact of economic globalization and the spread of global conflict, technology innovations, and the threats posed by environmental change. This is set against a backdrop of rising economic inequality that may undermine the opportunity for social mobility and progress in ways we have not experienced as a people before.

Selected Print, Media, and Online Resources

PRINT RESOURCES

Acemoglu, Daron, and James Robinson. *Why Nations Fail: The Origins of Power, Prosperity, and Poverty.* New York: Crown Publishers, 2012. The authors, one an economist and the other a political scientist, argue that nations thrive when they develop inclusive political and economic institutions and fail when institutions concentrate power and opportunity in the hands of only a few. Economic growth cannot be sustained in countries with limited political participation, nor can open political systems be maintained when large economic inequalities exist.

Friedman, Thomas L., and Michael Mandelbaum. *That Used to Be Us: How America Fell Behind in the World It Invented and How We Can Come Back.* New York: Farrar, Straus, and Giroux, 2011. Friedman and Mandelbaum argue that America faces four challenges on which our future depends: globalization, the information technology revolution, chronic deficits, and excessive energy consumption. Drawing on America's core values and from hundreds of examples, the authors argue that the country can regain its footing.

McCall, Leslie. *The Undeserving Rich: American Beliefs about Inequality, Opportunity, and Redistribution.* New York: Cambridge University Press, 2013. An evidence-based examination of the public's knowledge of growing income inequality, the strongly held belief that equality of opportunity is the best counter to income inequality, and deep ambivalence over public policies emphasizing income redistribution.

Obama, Barack. *Dreams from My Father: A Story of Race and Inheritance.* New York: Three Rivers Press, 2004. President Obama's best-selling autobiography ends before his rise to national prominence. He describes the sense of isolation he felt due to his unusual background and his attempts to come to grips with his multiethnic identity.

Packer, George. *The Unwinding: An Inner History of the New America.* New York: Farrar, Straus and Giroux, 2013. A narrative tale of America's "unwinding" told through the lives of everyday Americans and cultural icons with a focus on economic transformation, decline of political institutions, and fraying of the social contract.

MEDIA RESOURCES

All Things Considered—A daily broadcast of National Public Radio (NPR) that provides extensive coverage of political, economic, and social news stories.

American Experience—A Public Broadcasting Service (PBS) documentary series highlighting the people and stories that have shaped America's past and present. Many of the films are available online: www.pbs.org/wgbh/americanexperience/films/.

ONLINE RESOURCES

American Conservative Union—information about conservative positions: www.conservative.org

Americans for Democratic Action—home of one of the nation's oldest liberal political organizations: www.adaction.org

Bureau of the Census—a wealth of information about the changing face of America: www.census.gov

Center for the Study of the American Dream—located at Xavier University, a research center dedicated to the study of the American Dream: past, present, and future: www.xavier.edu/americandream/

Pew Research Center—a nonpartisan repository for facts on the issues, attitudes, and trends shaping American and the world, Pew is a research center and does not take positions on policy: www.pewresearch.org

University of Michigan—a basic "front door" to almost all U.S. government Web sites: www.lib.umich.edu/govdocs/govweb.html

U.S. Government—access to federal government offices and agencies: www.usa.gov

Master the concept of The Democratic Republic with MindTap™ for American Government

REVIEW MindTap™ for American Government
Access Key Term Flashcards for Chapter 1.

TEST YOURSELF MindTap™ for American Government
Take the Wrap It Up Quiz for Chapter 1.

STAY CURRENT MindTap™ for American Government
Access the KnowNow blog and customized RSS for updates on current events.

STAY FOCUSED MindTap™ for American Government
Complete The Focus Activities for The Democratic Republic.

The Constitution

2

An Occupy Wall Street protestor holds his copy of the Constitution at a rally in Union Square, New York City.

Ramin Talaie/Corbis News/Corbis

 WATCH & LEARN MindTap® **for American Government**

Watch a brief "What Do You Know?" video summarizing The Constitution.

LEARNING OUTCOMES

After reading this chapter, students will be able to:

- **LO2.1:** Explain the theoretical and historical factors that influenced the writers of the U.S. Constitution.

- **LO2.2:** Describe the structure of the Articles of Confederation, and explain why the confederation failed.

- **LO2.3:** Identify and explain the compromises made by the delegates to come to agreement on the U.S. Constitution.

- **LO2.4:** Explain the rationale for, and give examples of the separation of powers and the checks and balances in the U.S. Constitution.

- **LO2.5:** Explain why some states and their citizens especially wanted the Constitution to include a bill of rights.

- **LO2.6:** Demonstrate understanding of the formal and informal processes for amending the U.S. Constitution.

The Constitution Had Banned Slavery Outright?

BACKGROUND

In the earliest days of the Virginia colony, about half of the immigrants were indentured servants, meaning that at some point they could pay enough or fulfill the terms of their contract to be freed. Many African Americans fell into this category. By the 1650s, however, great plantations had formed in the southern states and they needed agricultural labor. In 1654, a Virginia court found that John Casor, an African American, was a "property," owned for life by another black colonist. Shortly after this case, law established that the children of slaves were also property. What these decisions meant was that former African American indentured servants in some states were now regarded as property, while indentured servants in other states such as Massachusetts and Connecticut could buy their freedom. As the agricultural needs of the country grew, so did the trade in slaves. By the end of the Revolutionary War, the new nation had nearly 650,000 slaves.

WHAT TO DO ABOUT THE SLAVERY ISSUE?

One of the most hotly debated issues at the Constitutional Convention concerned slavery. Most northern colonies had already abolished slavery, and the argument over the morality of owning human property was well known. Given the language of the Declaration of Independence ("All men are created equal…that they are endowed by their Creator with certain unalienable rights, that among them are life, liberty, and the pursuit of happiness…"), why did the writers of the U.S. Constitution have so much difficulty with the issue of slavery? As you will learn in this chapter, the Constitutional Convention eventually agreed to two huge compromises to gain approval of the final document: Slaves would count as only three-fifths of a person for purposes of representation and the slave trade could not be banned until after 1808. The debate over slavery—or, more specifically, over how the founders dealt with it—continues to this day. Some contend that those delegates who opposed slavery should have made greater efforts to ban it completely.*

DID THE FOUNDERS HAVE NO OTHER CHOICE?

Some historians argue that the founders had no choice. The South was an important part of the economy, and the southern states depended on slave labor for their agricultural production. Virginia, perhaps the most powerful of the southern states, counted nearly 300,000 slaves in its population in 1790; North Carolina, South Carolina, and Maryland each counted about 100,000 in that census. Although political leaders from Virginia, such as George Washington, had serious doubts about slavery, the delegates from those states may never have agreed to the Constitution if slavery had been threatened—meaning that these states would not have joined the new nation. The founders believed, as James Madison said, "Great as the evil is, a dismemberment of the Union would be worse… If those states should disunite from the other states…they might solicit and obtain aid from foreign powers."** Benjamin Franklin, then president of the Pennsylvania Society for the Abolition of Slavery, also feared that without a slavery compromise, delegates from the South would abandon the convention.

CRITICS ARGUE THAT ETHICS SHOULD HAVE PREVAILED

Critics of the founders' actions nonetheless believe that any compromise on slavery implicitly acknowledged the validity of the institution in 1860. According to these critics, the delegates who opposed slavery had a moral obligation to make greater efforts to ban it. At the time, many delegates felt that slavery would eventually end. Would the southern states actually have left the Union if slavery were banned? Would they have tried to form a separate nation? If slavery had been banned in 1789 or shortly thereafter, would the southern states have adapted to a paid labor system rather than expanded the slave population to 4 million by 1860? Sixty years later, the South's dependence on slavery was confronted by the antislavery movement in the North, leading to the Civil War and the decades of discrimination against African Americans that followed the war.

*See *A Slaveholder's Union: Slavery, Politics, and the Constitution in the Early American Republic* by George William Van Cleve, Chicago: University of Chicago Press, reprint edition, 2011, for a focus on how deeply slavery influenced the writing of the Constitution.

** Speech before the Virginia ratifying convention on June 17, 1788, as cited in Bruno Leone, ed., *The Creation of the Constitution* (San Diego, CA: Greenhaven Press, 1995), p. 159.

For Critical Analysis

1. *Do you think that antislavery delegates to the convention should have insisted on ending slavery throughout the new nation?*

2. *Do you think the nation would have survived without the southern states?*

3. *How would our nation be different if slavery had been abolished in 1789?*

NO MATTER WHICH POLITICAL PARTY occupies the White House or holds a majority in the Congress, the opposition is likely to claim, sooner or later, that some action taken or law passed violates the Constitution. Groups ranging from the Tea Party to the Occupy movement rally under the banner of the Constitution. Why is this *old* document such a symbol to Americans? Why hasn't it been changed more drastically or replaced completely since 1789? You may think that the Constitution is not relevant to your life or to modern times, but it continues to define the structure of the national and state governments and to regulate the relationship between the government and each individual citizen.

The Constitution of the United States is a product of the historical period in which it was written, a product of the colonists' experiences with government. Many of its provisions were grounded in the political philosophy of the time, including the writings of Thomas Hobbes and John Locke. The delegates to the Constitutional Convention in 1787 brought with them two important sets of influences: their political culture and their political experience. In the years between the first settlements in the New World and the writing of the Constitution, Americans had developed a political philosophy about how people should be governed and had tried out several forms of government. These experiences gave the founders the tools with which they constructed the Constitution. Milestones in the nation's early political history are shown in Table 2–1.

LISTEN & LEARN
MindTap™ for American Government

Access Read Speaker to listen to Chapter 2.

Table 2–1 ▶ Milestones in Early U.S. Political History

YEAR	EVENT
1607	Jamestown established; Virginia Company lands settlers.
1620	Mayflower Compact signed.
1630	Massachusetts Bay Colony set up.
1639	Fundamental Orders of Connecticut adopted.
1641	Massachusetts Body of Liberties adopted.
1682	Pennsylvania Frame of Government passed.
1701	Pennsylvania Charter of Privileges written.
1732	Last of the 13 colonies (Georgia) established.
1756	French and Indian War declared.
1765	Stamp Act; Stamp Act Congress meets.
1774	First Continental Congress.
1775	Second Continental Congress; Revolutionary War begins.
1776	Declaration of Independence signed.
1777	Articles of Confederation drafted.
1781	Last state (Maryland) signs Articles of Confederation.
1783	"Critical period" in U.S. history begins; weak national government until 1789.
1786	Shays's Rebellion.
1787	Constitutional Convention.
1788	Ratification of Constitution.
1791	Ratification of Bill of Rights.

The Colonial Background

■ **LO2.1:** Explain the theoretical and historical factors that influenced the writers of the U.S. Constitution.

In 1607, the English government sent a group of farmers to establish a trading post, Jamestown, in what is now Virginia. The Virginia Company of London was the first to establish a permanent English colony in the Americas. The king of England gave the backers of this colony a charter granting them "full power and authority" to make laws "for the good and welfare" of the settlement. The colonists at Jamestown instituted a **representative assembly**, setting a precedent in government that was to be observed in later colonial adventures.

> Jamestown was not an immediate success. Of the 105 people who landed, 67 died within the first year. But 800 new arrivals in 1609 added to their numbers. By the spring of the next year, frontier hazards had cut their numbers to 60. This period is sometimes referred to as the "starving time" for Virginia, brought about by a severe drought in the Jamestown area, which lasted from 1607 to 1612.

Separatists, the *Mayflower*, and the Compact

The first New England colony was established in 1620. A group of religious separatists who wished to break with the Church of England came over on the ship *Mayflower* to the New World, landing at Plymouth (Massachusetts). Before going onshore, the adult males—women were not considered to have any political status—drew up the Mayflower Compact, which was signed by 41 of the 44 men aboard the ship on November 21, 1620. This group was outside the jurisdiction of the Virginia Company of London, which had chartered its settlement in Virginia, not Massachusetts. The separatist leaders feared that some of the *Mayflower* passengers might conclude that they were no longer under any obligations of civil obedience. Therefore, some form of public authority was imperative. As William Bradford (one of the separatist leaders) recalled in his accounts, there were "discontented and mutinous speeches that some of the strangers amongst them had let fall from them in the ship; That when they

Representative Assembly
A legislature composed of individuals who represent the population.

The signing of the compact aboard the *Mayflower*. In 1620, the Mayflower Compact was signed by almost all of the men aboard the *Mayflower* just before they disembarked at Plymouth, Massachusetts. It stated, "We...covenant and combine ourselves togeather into a civil body politick...; and by virtue hearof to enacte, constitute, and frame such just and equal laws...as shall be thought [necessary] for the generall good of the Colonie."

Library of Congress Prints and Photographs Division [LC-USZ61-206]

came a shore they would use their owne libertie; for none had power to command them."[1]

The compact was a political statement in which the signers agreed to create and submit to the authority of a government, pending the receipt of a royal charter. The Mayflower Compact's historical and political significance is twofold: It depended on the consent of the affected individuals, and it served as a prototype for similar compacts in American history. According to Samuel Eliot Morison, the compact proved the determination of the English immigrants to live under the rule of law, based on the *consent of the people*.[2]

More Colonies, More Government

Another outpost in New England was set up by the Massachusetts Bay Colony in 1630. Then followed other settlements in New England, which became Rhode Island, Connecticut, and New Hampshire, among others. By 1732, the last of the 13 colonies, Georgia, was established. During the colonial period, Americans developed a concept of limited government, which followed from the establishment of the first colonies under Crown charters. Theoretically, London governed the colonies. In practice, owing partly to the colonies' distance from London, the colonists exercised a large measure of self-government. The colonists were able to make their own laws, as in the Fundamental Orders of Connecticut in 1639. In 1641, the Massachusetts Body of Liberties supported the protection of individual rights and was made a part of colonial law. In 1682, the Pennsylvania Frame of Government was passed. Along with the Pennsylvania Charter of Privileges of 1701, it foreshadowed our modern Constitution and Bill of Rights. All of this legislation enabled the colonists to acquire crucial political experience.

British Restrictions and Colonial Grievances

The conflict between Britain and the American colonies began in the 1760s when the British government decided to raise revenues by imposing taxes on the American colonies. Policy advisers to Britain's young King George III, who ascended to the throne in 1760, decided that it was only logical to require the American colonists to help pay the costs for their defense during the French and Indian War (1756–1763). The colonists, who had grown accustomed to a large degree of self-government and independence from the British Crown, viewed the matter differently.

In 1764, the British Parliament passed the Sugar Act. Many colonists were unwilling to pay the tax imposed by the act. Further regulatory legislation was to come. In 1765, Parliament passed the Stamp Act, providing for internal taxation—or, as the colonists' Stamp Act Congress, assembled in 1765, called it, "taxation without representation." The colonists boycotted the purchase of English commodities in return. The success of the boycott (the Stamp Act was repealed a year later) generated a feeling of unity within the colonies.

The British, however, continued to try to raise revenues in the colonies. When Parliament passed duties (taxes) on glass, lead, paint, and other items in 1767, the colonists again boycotted British goods. The colonists' fury over taxation climaxed in the Boston Tea Party, when colonists disguised themselves as Native

King George III (1738–1820) was king of Great Britain and Ireland from 1760 until his death on January 29, 1820. Under George III, the British Parliament attempted to tax the American colonies. Ultimately, exasperated at repeated attempts at taxation, the colonies proclaimed their independence on July 4, 1776.

---

1. John Camp, *Out of the Wilderness: The Emergence of an American Identity in Colonial New England* (Middleton, CT: Wesleyan University Press, 1990).

2. See Morison's "The Mayflower Compact," in Daniel J. Boorstin, ed., *An American Primer* (Chicago: University of Chicago Press, 1966), p. 18.

Americans of the Mohawk tribe and dumped close to 350 chests of British tea into Boston Harbor as a gesture of protest. In retaliation, Parliament passed the Coercive Acts (the "Intolerable Acts") in 1774, which closed Boston Harbor and placed the government of Massachusetts under direct British control. The colonists were outraged—and they responded.

The Colonial Response

New York, Pennsylvania, and Rhode Island proposed the convening of a colonial congress. The Massachusetts House of Representatives requested that all colonies hold conventions to select delegates to be sent to Philadelphia for such a congress.

The First Continental Congress

The First Continental Congress was held at Carpenters' Hall on September 5, 1774. It was a gathering of delegates from 12 of the 13 colonies (delegates from Georgia did not attend until 1775). At that meeting, there was little talk of independence. The Congress passed a resolution requesting that the colonies send a petition to King George III expressing their grievances. Resolutions were also passed requiring that the colonies raise their own troops and boycott British trade. The British government condemned the Congress's actions, treating them as open acts of rebellion.

The delegates to the First Continental Congress declared that in every county and city, a committee was to be formed whose mission was to spy on the conduct of friends and neighbors and to report to the press any violators of the trade ban. The formation of these committees was an act of cooperation among the colonies, which represented a step toward the creation of a national government.

The Second Continental Congress

By the time the Second Continental Congress met in May 1775 (this time all of the colonies were represented), fighting had already broken out between the British and the colonists. One of the main actions of the Second Continental Congress was to establish an army, naming George Washington as commander in chief. The participants in that Congress still attempted to reach a peaceful settlement with the British Parliament. One declaration of the Congress stated explicitly that "we have not raised armies with ambitious designs of separating from Great Britain, and establishing independent states." But by the beginning of 1776, military encounters had become increasingly frequent.

Public debate was acrimonious. Then Thomas Paine's *Common Sense* appeared in Philadelphia bookstores. The pamphlet was a colonial best seller. (By today's standards, a book would have to sell between 9 and 11 million copies in its first year of publication to equal the success of *Common Sense*.) Many agreed that Paine did make common sense when he argued that

> *a government of our own is our natural right: and when a man seriously reflects on the precariousness of human affairs, he will become convinced, that it is infinitely wiser and safer, to form a constitution of our own in a cool and deliberate manner, while we have it in our power, than to trust such an interesting event to time and chance.*[3]

Students of Paine's pamphlet point out that his arguments were not new—they were common in tavern debates throughout the land. Rather, it was the near poetry of his words—which were at the same time as plain as the alphabet—that struck his readers.

---

3.   *The Political Writings of Thomas Paine*, Vol. 1 (Boston: J. P. Mendum Investigator Office, 1870), p. 46.

Declaring Independence

On April 6, 1776, the Second Continental Congress voted for free trade at all American ports with all countries except Britain. This act could be interpreted as an implicit declaration of independence. The next month, the Congress suggested that each of the colonies establish a state government unconnected to Britain. Finally, in July, the colonists declared their independence from Britain.

The Resolution of Independence

On July 2, the Resolution of Independence was adopted by the Second Continental Congress:

> *RESOLVED, That these United Colonies are, and of right ought to be free and independent States, that they are absolved from allegiance to the British Crown, and that all political connection between them and the state of Great Britain is, and ought to be, totally dissolved.*

The actual Resolution of Independence was not legally significant. On the one hand, it was not judicially enforceable, for it established no legal rights or duties. On the other hand, the colonies were already, in their own judgment, self-governing and independent of Britain. Rather, the Resolution of Independence and the subsequent Declaration of Independence were necessary to establish the legitimacy of the new nation in the eyes of foreign governments, as well as in the eyes of the colonists. What the new nation needed most were supplies for its armies and a commitment of foreign military aid. Unless it appeared to the world as a political entity separate and independent from Britain, no foreign government would enter into a contract with its leaders.

July 4, 1776—The Declaration of Independence

By June 1776, Thomas Jefferson (at the age of 33) was writing drafts of the Declaration of Independence in the second-floor parlor of a bricklayer's house in Philadelphia. On adoption of the Resolution of Independence, Jefferson argued that a declaration clearly putting forth the causes that compelled the colonies to separate from Britain was necessary. The Second Congress assigned the task to him, and he completed his work on the declaration, which enumerated the colonists' major grievances against Britain. Some of his work was amended to gain unanimous acceptance (for example, his condemnation of the slave trade was eliminated to satisfy Georgia and North Carolina), but the bulk of it was passed intact on July 4, 1776. On July 19, the modified draft became "the unanimous declaration of the thirteen United States of America." On August 2, it was signed by the members of the Second Continental Congress.

Universal Truths. The Declaration of Independence has become one of the world's most famous and significant documents. The words opening the second paragraph of the Declaration are known most widely:

> *We hold these Truths to be self-evident, that all Men are created equal, that they are endowed by their Creator with certain unalienable Rights, that among these are Life, Liberty, and the Pursuit of Happiness—That to secure these Rights, Governments are instituted among Men, deriving their just Powers from the Consent of the Governed, that whenever any Form of Government becomes destructive of these Ends, it is the Right of the People to alter or abolish it, and to institute new Government.*

Natural Rights
Rights held to be inherent in natural law, not dependent on governments. John Locke stated that natural law, being superior to human law, specifies certain rights of "life, liberty, and property." These rights, altered to become "life, liberty, and the pursuit of happiness," are asserted in the Declaration of Independence.

Social Contract
A voluntary agreement among individuals to secure their rights and welfare by creating a government and abiding by its rules.

Natural Rights and a Social Contract. The assumption that people have **natural rights** ("unalienable Rights"), including the rights to "Life, Liberty, and the Pursuit of Happiness," was a revolutionary concept at that time. Its use by Jefferson reveals the influence of the English philosopher John Locke (1632–1704), whose writings were familiar to educated American colonists.[4] In his *Two Treatises on Government*, published in 1690, Locke had argued that all people possess certain natural rights, including the rights to life, liberty, and property, and that the primary purpose of government was to protect these rights. Furthermore, government was established by the people through a **social contract**—an agreement among the people to form a government and abide by its rules. As you read earlier, such contracts, or compacts, were not new to Americans. The Mayflower Compact was the first of several documents that established governments or governing rules based on the consent of the governed. In citing the "pursuit of happiness" instead of "property" as a right, Jefferson clearly meant to go beyond Locke's thinking.

After setting forth these basic principles of government, the Declaration of Independence goes on to justify the colonists' revolt against Britain. Much of the remainder of the document is a list of what "He" (King George III) had done to deprive the colonists of their rights. (See Appendix A at the end of this book for the complete text of the Declaration of Independence.)

Once it had fulfilled its purpose of legitimating the American Revolution, the Declaration of Independence was all but forgotten for many years. According to scholar Pauline Maier, the Declaration did not become enshrined as what she calls "American Scripture" until the 1800s.[5]

The Rise of Republicanism

Although the colonists had formally declared independence from Britain, the fight to gain actual independence continued for five more years—until British general Charles Cornwallis surrendered at Yorktown in 1781. In 1783, after Britain formally recognized the independent status of the United States in the Treaty of Paris, Washington disbanded the army. During these years of military struggles, the states faced the additional challenge of creating a system of self-government for an independent United States.

Some colonists had demanded that independence be preceded by the formation of a strong central government. But others, who called themselves Republicans, were against a strong central government. They opposed monarchy, executive authority, and virtually any form of restraint on the power of local groups.

From 1776 to 1780, all of the states adopted written constitutions. Eleven of the constitutions were completely new. Two of them—those of Connecticut and Rhode Island—were old royal charters with minor modifications. Republican sentiment led to increased power for the legislatures. In Pennsylvania and Georgia, **unicameral** (one-body) **legislatures** were unchecked by executive or judicial authority. Basically, the Republicans attempted to maintain the politics of 1776. In almost all states, the legislature was predominant.

Unicameral Legislatures
A legislature with only one legislative chamber, as opposed to a bicameral (two-chamber) legislature, such as the U.S. Congress. Today, Nebraska is the only state in the Union with a unicameral legislature.

---

4. Not all scholars believe that Jefferson was truly influenced by Locke. For example, Jay Fliegelman states that "Jefferson's fascination with Homer, Ossian, Patrick Henry, and the violin is of greater significance than his indebtedness to Locke," in Jay Fliegelman, *Declaring Independence: Jefferson, Natural Language, and the Culture of Performance* (Palo Alto, CA: Stanford University Press, 1993).

5. See Pauline Maier, *American Scripture: Making the Declaration of Independence* (New York: Knopf, 1997).

The Articles of Confederation: The First Form of Government

■ **LO2.2:** Describe the structure of the Articles of Confederation, and explain why the confederation failed.

The fear of a powerful central government led to the passage of the Articles of Confederation, which created a weak central government. The term **confederation** is important; it means a voluntary association of *independent* **states**, in which the member states agree to only limited restraints on their freedom of action. As a result, confederations seldom have an effective executive authority.

In June 1776, the Second Continental Congress began the process of drafting what would become the Articles of Confederation. The final form of the Articles was achieved by November 15, 1777. It was not until March 1, 1781, however, that the last state, Maryland, agreed to ratify what was called the Articles of Confederation and Perpetual Union. Well before the final ratification of the Articles, however, many of them were implemented: The Continental Congress and the 13 states conducted American military, economic, and political affairs according to the standards and the form specified by the Articles.[6]

Under the Articles, the 13 original colonies, now states, established on March 1, 1781, a government of the states—the Congress of the Confederation. The Congress was a unicameral assembly of so-called ambassadors from each state, with each state possessing a single vote. Each year, the Congress would choose one of its members as its president (that is, presiding officer), but the Articles did not provide for a president of the United States.

The Congress was authorized in Article X to appoint an executive committee of the states "to execute in the recess of Congress, such of the powers of Congress as the United States, in Congress assembled, by the consent of nine [of the 13] states, shall from time to time think expedient to vest with them." The Congress was also allowed to appoint other committees and civil officers necessary for managing the general affairs of the United States. In addition, the Congress could regulate foreign affairs and establish coinage and weights and measures, but it lacked an independent source of revenue and the necessary executive machinery to enforce its decisions throughout the land. Article II of the Articles of Confederation guaranteed that each state would retain its sovereignty. Figure 2–1 illustrates the structure of the government under the Articles of Confederation; Table 2–2 summarizes the powers—and the lack of powers—of Congress under the Articles of Confederation.

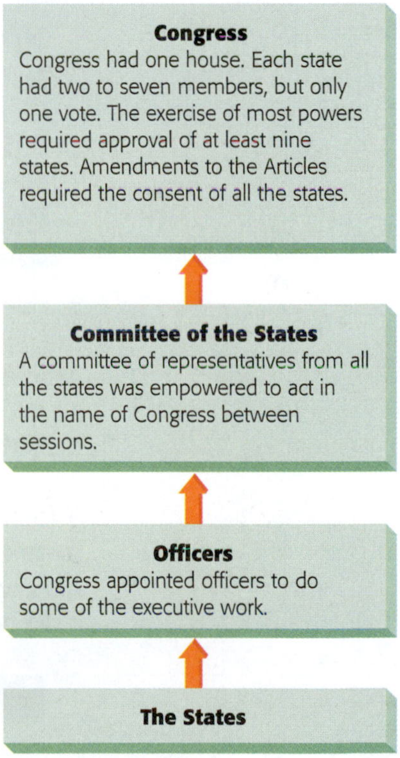

Accomplishments under the Articles

The new government made some accomplishments during its eight years of existence under the Articles of Confederation. Certain states' claims to western lands were settled. Maryland had objected to the claims of the Carolinas, Connecticut, Georgia, Massachusetts, New York, and Virginia. It was only after these states consented to give up their land claims to the United States as a whole that Maryland signed the Articles of Confederation. Another accomplishment under the

Confederation
A political system in which states or regional governments retain ultimate authority except for those powers they expressly delegate to a central government. A voluntary association of independent states, in which the member states agree to limited restraints on their freedom of action.

States
A group of people occupying a specific area and organized under one government; may be either a nation or a subunit of a nation.

Figure 2–1 ▶ The Confederal Government Structure under the Articles of Confederation

Congress
Congress had one house. Each state had two to seven members, but only one vote. The exercise of most powers required approval of at least nine states. Amendments to the Articles required the consent of all the states.

Committee of the States
A committee of representatives from all the states was empowered to act in the name of Congress between sessions.

Officers
Congress appointed officers to do some of the executive work.

The States

---

6. Robert W. Hoffert, *A Politics of Tensions: The Articles of Confederation and American Political Ideas* (Niwot, CO: University Press of Colorado, 1992).

Table 2–2 ▶ Powers of the Congress of the Confederation

CONGRESS HAD POWER TO	CONGRESS LACKED POWER TO
Declare war and make peace.	Provide for effective treaty-making power and control foreign relations; it could not compel states to respect treaties.
Enter into treaties and alliances.	Regulate interstate and foreign commerce; it left each state free to set up its own tariff system.
Establish and control armed forces.	Compel states to meet military quotas; it could not draft soldiers or demand revenue to support an army or navy.
Requisition men and revenues from states.	Collect taxes directly from the people; it had to rely on states to collect and forward taxes.
Regulate coinage.	Compel states to pay their share of government costs.
Borrow funds and issue bills of credit.	Provide and maintain a sound monetary system or issue paper money; this was left up to the states, and monies in circulation differed tremendously in value.
Fix uniform standards of weight and measurement.	
Create admiralty courts.	
Create a postal system.	
Regulate Indian affairs.	
Guarantee citizens of each state the rights and privileges of citizens in the several states when in another state.	Establish an enforcement division to ensure those rights.
Adjudicate disputes between states on state petition.	

Articles was the passage of the Northwest Ordinance of 1787, which established a basic pattern of government for new territories north of the Ohio River. All in all, the Articles represented the first real pooling of resources by the American states.

Weaknesses of the Articles

Despite these accomplishments, the Articles of Confederation had many defects. Although Congress had the legal right to declare war and to conduct foreign policy, it did not have the right to demand revenues from the states. It could only *ask* for them. Additionally, the actions of Congress required the consent of nine states. Any amendments to the Articles required the unanimous consent of the Congress and confirmation by every state legislature. Furthermore, the Articles did not create a national system of courts.

Basically, the functioning of the government under the Articles depended on the goodwill of the states. Article III of the Articles simply established a "league of friendship" among the states—no national government was intended.

did you know?

The Articles of Confederation specified that Canada could be admitted to the Confederation if it ever wished to join.

The most fundamental weakness of the Articles, and the most basic cause of their eventual replacement by the Constitution, was the lack of power to raise funds for the militia. The Articles contained no language giving Congress coercive power to raise revenues (by levying taxes) to provide adequate support for the military forces controlled by Congress. When states refused to send revenues to support the government (*not one state* met the financial requests made by Congress under the Articles), Congress resorted to selling off western lands to speculators or issuing bonds that sold for less than their face value. Due to a lack of resources, the Continental Congress was forced to disband the army, even in the face of serious Spanish and British military threats.

Shays's Rebellion and the Need for Revision of the Articles

Because of the weaknesses of the Articles of Confederation, the central government could do little to maintain peace and order in the new nation. The states bickered among themselves and increasingly taxed each other's goods. At times they prevented trade altogether. By 1784, the country faced a serious economic depression. Banks were calling in old loans and refusing to give new ones. People who could not pay their debts were often thrown into prison.

By 1786, in Concord, Massachusetts, three times as many people were in prison for debt as for all other crimes combined. In Worcester County, Massachusetts, the ratio was even higher—20 to 1. Most of the prisoners were small farmers who could not pay their debts because of the economic chaos.

In August 1786, mobs of musket-bearing farmers led by former Revolutionary War captain Daniel Shays seized county courthouses and disrupted the trials of debtors in Springfield, Massachusetts. Shays and his men then launched an attack on the federal arsenal at Springfield, but they were repulsed. Shays's Rebellion demonstrated that the central government could not protect the citizenry from armed rebellion or provide adequately for the public welfare. The rebellion spurred the nation's political leaders to action. As John Jay wrote to Thomas Jefferson,

> *Changes are Necessary, but what they ought to be, what they will be, and how and when to be produced, are arduous Questions. I feel for the Cause of Liberty.... If it should not take Root in this Soil[,] Little Pains will be taken to cultivate it in any other.*[7]

did you know?

Daniel Shays incurred the debts that led to Shays's Rebellion because he never received pay for serving in the Revolutionary War.

Drafting the Constitution

Concerned about the economic turmoil in the young nation, five states called for a meeting to be held at Annapolis, Maryland, on September 11, 1786—ostensibly to discuss commercial problems only. It was evident to those in attendance (including Alexander Hamilton and James Madison) that the national government had serious weaknesses that had to be addressed if it were to survive. Among the important problems to be solved were the relationship between the states and the central government, the powers of the national legislature, the need for executive leadership, and the establishment of policies for economic stability.

Those attending the meeting prepared a petition to the Continental Congress for a general convention to meet in Philadelphia in May 1787 "to consider the

---

7. Excerpt from a letter from John Jay to Thomas Jefferson written in October 1786, as reproduced in Winthrop D. Jordan et al., *The United States*, combined ed., 6th ed. (Englewood Cliffs, NJ: Prentice Hall, 1987), p. 135.

exigencies of the union." Congress approved the convention in February 1787. When those who favored a weak central government realized that the Philadelphia meeting would in fact take place, they endorsed the convention. They made sure, however, that the convention would be summoned "for the sole and express purpose of revising the Articles of Confederation." Those in favor of a stronger national government had different ideas.

The designated date for the opening of the convention at Philadelphia, now known as the Constitutional Convention, was May 14, 1787. Because few of the delegates had actually arrived in Philadelphia by that time, however, the convention was not formally opened in the East Room of the Pennsylvania State House until May 25.[8] Fifty-five of the 74 delegates chosen for the convention actually attended, and only about 40 played active roles at the convention. Rhode Island was the only state that refused to send delegates.

Who Were the Delegates?

Who were the 55 delegates to the Constitutional Convention? They certainly did not represent a cross section of American society in the 1700s. Indeed, most were members of the upper class. Consider the following facts:

1. Thirty-three were members of the legal profession.
2. Three were physicians.
3. Almost 50 percent were college graduates.
4. Seven were former chief executives of their respective states.
5. Six were owners of large plantations.
6. Eight were important businesspersons.

They were also relatively young by today's standards: James Madison was 36, Alexander Hamilton was only 32, and Jonathan Dayton of New Jersey was 26. The venerable Benjamin Franklin, however, was 81 and had to be carried in on a portable chair. Not counting Franklin, the average age was just over 42. What almost all of them shared, however, was prior experience in political office or military service. Most of them were elected members of their own states' legislatures. George Washington, the esteemed commander of the Revolutionary War troops, was named to chair the meeting. There were, however, no women or minorities among this group. Women could not vote anywhere in the confederacy and, while free African Americans played an important part in some northern states, they were certainly not likely to be political leaders.[9]

The Working Environment

The conditions under which the delegates worked were far from ideal and were made even worse by the necessity of maintaining total secrecy. The framers of the Constitution believed that if public debate took place on particular positions, delegates would have a more difficult time compromising or backing down to reach agreement. Consequently, the windows were usually shut in the East Room of the State House. Summer quickly arrived, and the air became heavy, humid, and hot by noon of each day.

---

8. The State House was later named Independence Hall. This was the same room in which the Declaration of Independence had been signed 11 years earlier.

9. For a detailed look at the delegates and their lively debates, see Carol Berkin, *A Brilliant Solution: Inventing the American Constitution* (New York: Harcourt, 2002).

Politics with a Purpose

How to Form a More Perfect Union?

"We the People of the United States, in Order to form a more perfect Union, establish Justice, insure domestic Tranquility, provide for the common defense, promote the general Welfare, and secure the Blessings of Liberty to ourselves and our Posterity, do ordain and establish this Constitution for the United States of America." What did the framers of the Constitution mean by "a more perfect union"? Why was establishing justice and insuring domestic tranquility at the top of their list? The framers were reacting to the then-current problems created by the Articles of Confederation.

Adopted in 1781, the Articles of Confederation governed the emerging nation until our existing Constitution replaced it in 1787. Although the central government had very little power, the Articles held competing and disparate interests together for the first years of the nation's independence.

Whether to amend or replace the Articles of Confederation was a dispute between those who enjoyed power under the Articles and those who found their weaknesses too dangerous and unprofitable. Under the Articles, the Congress had very little power. It could not regulate commerce or foreign trade nor levy taxes, and it had to depend on the states to begin to pay down the war debt. To deal with the difficulty of deficits without power to tax, Congress simply printed more money, which led to inflation, a lack of trust in the printed currency, and reliance on gold and silver.[*]

Members of Congress, as well as those whose economic interests were hurt by the economic instability, were frustrated. In addition to the aforementioned problems, the national government could not effectively regulate trade (all 13 states could negotiate separate trading arrangements with each other and with foreign governments). For people such as seaport merchants, large plantation owners, and commercial farmers who depended on trade, this was a trying and unstable situation.[**]

On the other hand, some people did approve of the Articles. Smaller farmers and those who lived inland depended less on trade and were more likely to believe the state governments were sufficient to solve their problems. Like Thomas Jefferson and Patrick Henry, many feared a strong national government and preferred a less active government that would keep taxes low and provide debt relief. With the success of the Articles in creating the Northwest Territory, a contingent in state governments was suspicious of national encroachment on their power.

So, why would states give up the enormous power they enjoyed under the Articles of Confederation? Initially, they did not. As early as 1786, calls were made to reform the Articles, and it was through crises such as Shays's Rebellion that those favoring a stronger national government were able to organize to form a Constitutional Convention. Meeting in 1787, they deliberated for months to draft a document that was acceptable to the participants. The new Constitution was ratified in July 1788 a promise of greater protection of civil liberties, and lobbying efforts modern politicians would recognize.[***]

[*] www.loc.gov/rr/program/bib/ourdocs/articles.html, accessed September 22, 2008.
[**] Keith L. Dougherty, *Collective Action under the Articles of Confederation*, New York: Cambridge University Press, 2011.
[***] Lee Epstein and Thomas G. Walker, *Constitutional Law for a Changing America: Institutional Powers and Constraints*, 8th ed., New York: Sage Press, 2014.

Factions among the Delegates

What we know about the actual daily work of the convention comes from the detailed personal journal kept by James Madison. A majority of the delegates were strong nationalists—they wanted a central government with real power, unlike the central government under the Articles of Confederation. George Washington and Benjamin Franklin preferred limited national authority based on a separation of powers. They were apparently willing to accept any type of national government, however, as long as the other delegates approved it. A few advocates of a strong central government, led by Gouverneur Morris of Pennsylvania and John Rutledge of South Carolina, distrusted the ability of the common people to engage in self-government.

Among the nationalists, several went so far as to support monarchy. This group included Alexander Hamilton, who was chiefly responsible for the Annapolis Convention's call for the Constitutional Convention.

Still another faction consisted of nationalists who were less democratic in nature and who would support a central government only if it was founded on very narrowly defined republican principles. Many of the other delegates from Connecticut, Delaware, Maryland, New Hampshire, and New Jersey were concerned about only one thing—claims to western lands. As long as those lands became the common property of all of the states, they were willing to support a central government.

Finally, there was a group of delegates who were totally against a national authority. Two of the three delegates from New York quit the convention when they saw the nationalist direction of its proceedings.

Politicking and Compromises

■ **LO2.3:** Identify and explain the compromises made by the delegates to come to agreement on the U.S. Constitution.

The debates at the convention started on the first day. James Madison had spent months reviewing European political theory. When his Virginia delegation arrived ahead of most of the others, it got to work immediately. By the time George Washington opened the convention, Governor Edmund Randolph of Virginia was prepared to present 15 resolutions, which set the agenda for the remainder of the convention—even though, in principle, the delegates had been sent to Philadelphia for the sole purpose of amending the Articles of Confederation. They had not been sent to write a new constitution.

The Virginia Plan. Randolph's 15 resolutions proposed an entirely new national government under a constitution. It was, however, a plan that favored the large states, including Virginia. Basically, it called for the following:

Bicameral Legislature
A legislature made up of two parts, called chambers. The U.S. Congress, composed of the House of Representatives and the Senate, is a bicameral legislature.

1. A **bicameral** (two-chamber) **legislature**, with the lower chamber chosen by the people and the smaller upper chamber chosen by the lower chamber from nominees selected by state legislatures. The number of representatives would be proportional to a state's population, thus greatly favoring the states with larger populations, including slaves, of course. The legislature could void any state laws.
2. The creation of an unspecified national executive, elected by the legislature.
3. The creation of a national judiciary, appointed by the legislature.

It did not take long for the smaller states to realize they would fare poorly under the Virginia plan, which would enable Virginia, Massachusetts, and Pennsylvania to form a majority in the national legislature. The debate on the plan dragged on for many weeks. It was time for the small states to come up with their own plan.

The New Jersey Plan. On June 15, lawyer William Paterson of New Jersey offered an alternative plan. After all, argued Paterson, under the Articles of Confederation, all states had equality; therefore, the convention had no power to change this arrangement. He proposed the following:

1. The fundamental principle of the Articles of Confederation—one state, one vote—would be retained.
2. Congress would be able to regulate trade and impose taxes.

3. All acts of Congress would be the supreme law of the land.
4. Several people would be elected by Congress to form an executive office.
5. The executive office would appoint a Supreme Court.

Basically, the New Jersey plan was simply an amendment of the Articles of Confederation. Its only notable feature was its reference to the **supremacy doctrine**, which was later included in the Constitution.

The "Great Compromise."

The delegates were at an impasse. Most wanted a strong national government and were unwilling even to consider the New Jersey plan, but when the Virginia plan was brought up again, the small states threatened to leave. The issues involved in the debate included how states and their residents would be represented. Small states feared that the Virginia plan with its powerful national government would pass laws that would disadvantage smaller states. The larger states, aware that they would be the economic force in the new nation, absolutely opposed a government in which smaller states had the balance of power. Roger Sherman of Connecticut proposed a solution that gave power to both the small states and the larger states. On July 16, the **Great Compromise** was put forward for debate:

1. A bicameral legislature in which the lower chamber, the House of Representatives, would be apportioned according to the number of free inhabitants in each state, plus three-fifths of the slaves.
2. An upper chamber, the Senate, which would have two members from each state elected by the state legislatures.

This plan, also called the Connecticut Compromise because of the role of the Connecticut delegates in the proposal, broke the deadlock. It did exact a political price from the larger states, however, because it permitted each state to have equal representation in the Senate. Having two senators represent each state in effect diluted the voting power of citizens living in more heavily populated states and gave the smaller states disproportionate political powers. But the Connecticut

Supremacy Doctrine
A doctrine that asserts the priority of national law over state laws. This principle is rooted in Article VI of the Constitution, which provides that the Constitution, the laws passed by the national government under its constitutional powers, and all treaties constitute the supreme law of the land.

Great Compromise
The compromise between the New Jersey and Virginia plans that created one chamber of the Congress based on population and one chamber representing each state equally; also called the Connecticut Compromise.

George Washington presided over the Constitutional Convention of 1787. Although the convention was supposed to start on May 14, 1787, few of the delegates had actually arrived in Philadelphia by that date. The convention formally opened in the East Room of the Pennsylvania State House (later named Independence Hall) on May 25. Only Rhode Island did not send any delegates.

Compromise resolved the large-state–small-state controversy. In addition, the Senate acted as part of a checks-and-balances system against the House, which many feared would be dominated by, and responsive to, the masses. Another important piece of the debate, however, needed a resolution: How were slaves to be counted in determining the number of members of Congress allotted to a state?

The Three-Fifths Compromise. Part of the Connecticut Compromise dealt with this problem. Slavery was still legal in many northern states, but it was concentrated in the South. Many delegates were opposed to slavery and wanted it banned entirely in the United States. The South wanted slaves to be counted along with free persons in determining representation in Congress. Delegates from the northern states objected. Sherman's three-fifths proposal was a compromise between northerners who did not want the slaves counted at all and southerners who wanted them counted in the same way as free whites. Sherman's Connecticut plan spoke of three-fifths of "all other persons" (and that is the language of the Constitution itself). It is not hard to figure out, though, who those other persons were.

The Three-Fifths Compromise illustrates the power of the southern states at the convention.[10] The three-fifths rule meant that the House of Representatives and the electoral college would be apportioned in part on the basis of *property*—specifically, property in slaves. Modern commentators have asserted that the three-fifths rule valued African Americans only three-fifths as much as whites. Actually, the additional southern representatives elected because of the three-fifths rule did not represent the slaves at all. Rather, these extra representatives were a gift to the slave owners—the additional representatives enhanced the power of the South in Congress.

The Three-Fifths Compromise did not completely settle the slavery issue. There was also the question of the slave trade. Eventually, the delegates agreed

did you know?

During the four centuries of slave trading, an estimated 10 million to 11 million Africans were transported to North and South America—and that only 6 percent of these slaves were imported into the United States.

A slave auction in the South, about 1850.

A slave auction in the Deep South, c.1850 (coloured engraving), American School, (19th century)/ Private Collection/Peter Newark American Pictures/The Bridgeman Art Library

10. See Garry Wills, *"Negro President": Jefferson and the Slave Power* (New York: Houghton Mifflin, 2003).

that Congress could not ban the importation of slaves until after 1808. The compromise meant that the matter of slavery was never addressed directly. The South won 20 years of unrestricted slave trade and a requirement that escaped slaves in free states be returned to their owners in slave states.

Other Issues. The South also worried that the northern majority in Congress would pass legislation that was unfavorable to its economic interests. Because the South depended on agricultural exports, it feared the imposition of export taxes. In return for acceding to the northern demand that Congress be able to regulate commerce among the states and with other nations, the South obtained a promise that export taxes would not be imposed. As a result, the United States is among the few countries that do not tax their exports.

There were other disagreements. The delegates could not decide whether to establish only a Supreme Court or to create lower courts as well. They deferred the issue by mandating a Supreme Court and allowing Congress to establish lower courts. They also disagreed over whether the president or the Senate would choose the Supreme Court justices. A compromise was reached with the agreement that the president would nominate the justices and the Senate would confirm the nominations. These compromises, as well as others, resulted from the recognition that if one group of states refused to ratify the Constitution, it was doomed.

Working toward Final Agreement

■ **LO2.4:** Explain the rationale for, and give examples of the separation of powers and the checks and balances in the U.S. Constitution.

The Connecticut Compromise was reached by mid-July. The makeup of the executive branch and the judiciary, however, was left unsettled. The remaining work of the convention was turned over to a five-man Committee of Detail, which presented a rough draft of the Constitution on August 6. It made the executive and judicial branches subordinate to the legislative branch.

The Madisonian Model—Separation of Powers. The major issue of **separation of powers** had not yet been resolved. The delegates were concerned with structuring the government to prevent the imposition of tyranny—either by the majority or by a minority. Madison proposed a governmental scheme—sometimes called the **Madisonian model**—to achieve this: the executive, legislative, and judicial powers of government were to be separated so that no one branch had enough power to dominate the others, nor could any one person hold office in two different branches of the government at the same time. The separation of powers was by function, as well as by personnel, with Congress passing laws, the president enforcing and administering laws, and the courts interpreting laws in individual circumstances.

Each of the three branches of government would be independent of the others, but they would have to share power to govern. According to Madison, in Federalist #51 (see Appendix C), "the great security against a gradual concentration of the several powers in the same department consists in giving to those who administer each department the necessary constitutional means and personal motives to resist encroachments of the others."

The Madisonian Model—Checks and Balances. The "constitutional means" Madison referred to is a system of **checks and balances** through which each branch of the government can check the actions of the others. For example, Congress can enact laws, but the president has veto power over congressional acts.

Separation of Powers
The principle of dividing governmental powers among different branches of government.

Madisonian Model
A structure of government proposed by James Madison in which the powers of the government are separated into three branches: executive, legislative, and judicial.

Checks and Balances
A major principle of the American system of government whereby each branch of the government can check the actions of the others.

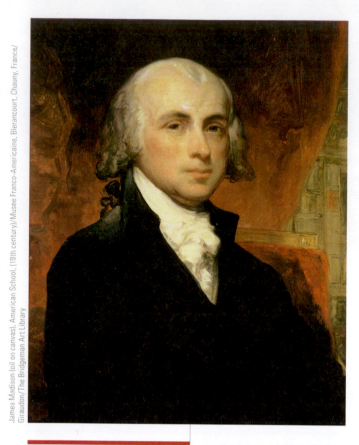

James Madison (1751–1836) earned the title "master builder of the Constitution" because of his persuasive logic during the Constitutional Convention. His contributions to the *Federalist Papers* showed him to be a brilliant political thinker and writer.

Electoral College

A group of persons called electors selected by the voters in each state and the District of Columbia; this group officially elects the president and vice president of the United States. The number of electors in each state is equal to the number of each state's representatives in both chambers of Congress.

Federal System

A system of government in which power is divided between a central government and regional, or subdivisional, governments. Each level must have some domain in which its policies are dominant and some genuine political or constitutional guarantee of its authority.

The Supreme Court has the power to declare acts of Congress and of the executive unconstitutional, but the president appoints the justices of the Supreme Court, with the advice and consent of the Senate. (The Supreme Court's power to declare acts unconstitutional was not mentioned in the Constitution, although arguably the framers assumed that the Court would have this power—see the discussion of judicial review later in this chapter.) Figure 2–2 outlines these checks and balances.

Madison's ideas of separation of powers and checks and balances were not new. The influential French political thinker Baron de Montesquieu (1689–1755) had explored these concepts in his book *The Spirit of the Laws*, published in 1748. Montesquieu not only discussed the "three sorts of powers" (executive, legislative, and judicial) that were necessarily exercised by any government, but also gave examples of how, in some nations, certain checks on these powers had arisen and had been effective in preventing tyranny.

In the years since the Constitution was ratified, the checks and balances built into it have evolved into a sometimes complex give-and-take among the branches of government. Generally, for nearly every check that one branch has over another, the branch that has been checked has devised a means of circumventing the check. For example, suppose that the president checks Congress by vetoing a bill. Congress can override the presidential veto by a two-thirds vote. Additionally, Congress holds the "power of the purse." If it disagrees with a program endorsed by the executive branch, it can simply refuse to appropriate the funds necessary to operate that program. Similarly, the president can impose a countercheck on Congress if the Senate refuses to confirm a presidential appointment, such as a judicial appointment. The president can simply wait until Congress is in recess and then make what is called a "recess appointment," which does not require the Senate's approval. Recess appointments last until the end of the next session of the Congress.

The Executive. Some delegates favored a plural executive made up of representatives from the various regions. This was abandoned in favor of a single chief executive. Some argued that Congress should choose the executive. To make the presidency completely independent of the proposed Congress, however, an electoral college was adopted. Without question, the **electoral college** created a cumbersome presidential election process (see Chapter 9). The process even made it possible for a candidate who came in second in the popular vote to become president by being the top vote-getter in the electoral college, which happened in 2000 and in three prior contests. The electoral college insulated the president, however, from direct popular control. The seven-year single term that some of the delegates had proposed was replaced by a four-year term and the possibility of reelection.

A Federal Republic. The Constitution creates a **federal system** of government that divides the sovereign powers of the nation between the states and the national government. This structure allows for states to make their own laws

Figure 2-2 ▶ Checks and Balances

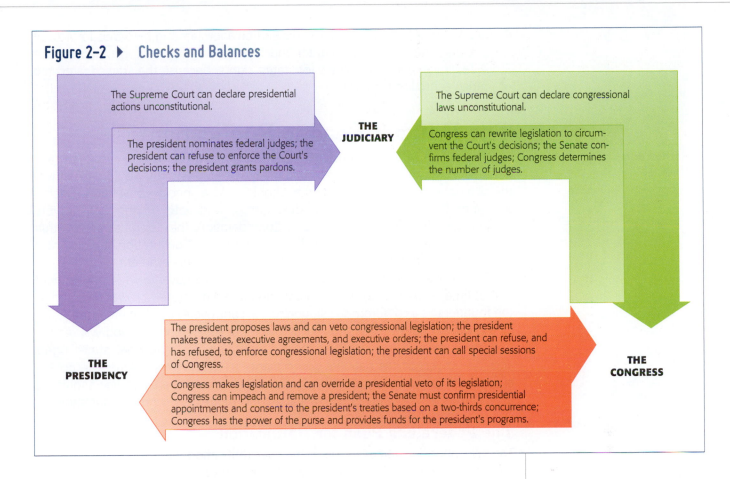

THE JUDICIARY

The Supreme Court can declare presidential actions unconstitutional.

The president nominates federal judges; the president can refuse to enforce the Court's decisions; the president grants pardons.

The Supreme Court can declare congressional laws unconstitutional.

Congress can rewrite legislation to circumvent the Court's decisions; the Senate confirms federal judges; Congress determines the number of judges.

THE PRESIDENCY

THE CONGRESS

The president proposes laws and can veto congressional legislation; the president makes treaties, executive agreements, and executive orders; the president can refuse, and has refused, to enforce congressional legislation; the president can call special sessions of Congress.

Congress makes legislation and can override a presidential veto of its legislation; Congress can impeach and remove a president; the Senate must confirm presidential appointments and consent to the president's treaties based on a two-thirds concurrence; Congress has the power of the purse and provides funds for the president's programs.

about many of the issues of direct concern for their citizens while granting the national government far more power over the states and their citizens than under the Articles of Confederacy. As you will read in Chapter 3, the Constitution expressly granted certain powers to the national government.

For example, the national government was given the power to regulate commerce among the states. The Constitution also declared that the president is the nation's chief executive and the commander in chief of the armed forces. Additionally, the Constitution made it clear that laws made by the national government take priority over conflicting state laws. At the same time, the Constitution provided for extensive states' rights, including the right to control commerce within state borders and to exercise those governing powers that were not delegated to the national government.

The Final Document

On September 17, 1787, the Constitution was approved by 39 delegates. Of the 55 who had originally attended, only 42 remained and three refused to sign the Constitution.

The Constitution that was to be ratified established the following fundamental principles:

1. Popular sovereignty, or control by the people.
2. A republican government in which the people choose representatives to make decisions for them.
3. Limited government with written laws, in contrast to the powerful British government against which the colonists had rebelled.

4. Separation of powers, with checks and balances among branches to prevent any one branch from gaining too much power.
5. A federal system that allows for states' rights, because the states feared too much centralized control.

The Difficult Road to Ratification

Ratification
Formal approval.

The founders knew that **ratification** of the Constitution was far from certain. Because it was almost guaranteed that many state legislatures would not ratify it, the delegates agreed that each state should hold a special convention. Elected delegates to these conventions would discuss and vote on the Constitution. Further departing from the Articles of Confederation, the delegates agreed that as soon as nine states (rather than all 13) approved the Constitution, it would take effect, and Congress could begin to organize the new government.

The federal system created by the founders was a novel form of government at that time—no other country in the world had such a system. It was invented by the founders as a compromise solution to the controversy over whether the states or the central government should have ultimate sovereignty. As you will read in Chapter 3, the debate over where the line should be drawn between states' rights and the powers of the national government has characterized American politics ever since. The founders did not go into detail about where this line should be drawn, thus leaving it up to scholars and court judges to divine their intentions.

The Federalists Push for Ratification

Federalists
The name given to one who was in favor of the adoption of the U.S. Constitution and the creation of a federal union with a strong central government.

Anti-Federalists
An individual who opposed the ratification of the new Constitution in 1787. The Anti-Federalists were opposed to a strong central government.

The two opposing forces in the battle over ratification were the Federalists and the Anti-Federalists. The **Federalists**—those in favor of a strong central government and the new Constitution—had an advantage over their opponents, called the **Anti-Federalists**, who wanted to prevent the Constitution as drafted from being ratified. In the first place, the Federalists had assumed a positive name, leaving their opposition the negative label of *Anti*-Federalist.[11] More important, the Federalists had attended the Constitutional Convention and knew of all the deliberations that had taken place. Their opponents had no such knowledge, because those deliberations had not been open to the public. Thus, the Anti-Federalists were at a disadvantage in terms of information about the document. The Federalists also had time, power, and money on their side. Those who had access to the best communications were Federalists—mostly wealthy bankers, lawyers, plantation owners, and merchants living in urban areas, where communications were better. The Federalist campaign was organized relatively quickly and effectively to elect Federalists as delegates to the state ratifying conventions.

The Anti-Federalists, however, had at least one strong point in their favor: They stood for the status quo. In general, the greater burden is always placed on those advocating change.

The *Federalist Papers*. In New York, opponents of the Constitution were quick to attack it. Alexander Hamilton answered their attacks in newspaper columns over the signature "Caesar." When the Caesar letters had little effect, Hamilton switched to the pseudonym Publius and secured two collaborators—John Jay and James Madison. In a very short time, those three political figures

---

11. There is some irony here. At the Constitutional Convention, those opposed to a strong central government pushed for a federal system because such a system would allow the states to retain some of their sovereign rights (see Chapter 3). The label *Anti-Federalists* thus contradicted their essential views.

wrote a series of 85 essays in defense of the Constitution and of a republican form of government.

These widely read essays, called the *Federalist Papers*, appeared in New York newspapers from October 1787 to August 1788 and were reprinted in the newspapers of other states. Although we do not know for certain who wrote every one, it is apparent that Hamilton was responsible for about two-thirds of the essays. These included the most important ones, which interpreted the Constitution, explained the various powers of the three branches, and presented a theory of *judicial review*—to be discussed later in this chapter. Madison's Federalist #10 (see Appendix C), however, is considered a classic in political theory; it deals with the nature of groups—or factions, as he called them. Despite the rapidity with which the *Federalist Papers* were written, they are considered by many to be perhaps the best example of political theorizing ever produced in the United States.[12]

The Anti-Federalist Response. The Anti-Federalists used such pseudonyms as Montezuma and Philadelphiensis in their replies. Many of their attacks on the Constitution were also brilliant. The Anti-Federalists claimed that the Constitution was written by aristocrats and would lead to aristocratic tyranny. More important, the Anti-Federalists believed that the Constitution would create an overbearing and overburdening central government hostile to personal liberty. (The Constitution said nothing about freedom of the press, freedom of religion, or any other individual liberty.) They wanted to include a list of guaranteed liberties, or a bill of rights. Finally, the Anti-Federalists decried the weakened power of the states.

The Anti-Federalists cannot be dismissed as unpatriotic extremists. They included such patriots as Patrick Henry and Samuel Adams. They were arguing what had been the most prevalent contemporary opinion. This view derived from the French political philosopher Montesquieu, who believed that liberty was safe only in relatively small societies governed by direct democracy or by a large legislature with small districts. The Madisonian view favoring a large republic, particularly as expressed in Federalist #10 and #51 (see Appendix C), was actually the more *un*popular view at the time. Madison was probably convincing because citizens were already persuaded that a strong national government was necessary to combat foreign enemies and to prevent domestic insurrections. Still, some researchers believe it was mainly the bitter experiences with the Articles of Confederation, rather than Madison's arguments, that persuaded the state conventions to ratify the Constitution.[13]

The March to the Finish

The struggle for ratification continued. Strong majorities were procured in Delaware, Pennsylvania, New Jersey, Georgia, and Connecticut. After a bitter struggle in Massachusetts, that state ratified the Constitution by a narrow margin on February 6, 1788. By the spring, Maryland and South Carolina had ratified by sizable majorities. Then on June 21, New Hampshire became the ninth state to ratify the Constitution. Although the Constitution was formally in effect, this meant little without Virginia and New York—the latter did not ratify for another month (see Table 2–3).

---

12. Some scholars believe that the *Federalist Papers* played only a minor role in securing ratification of the Constitution. Even if this is true, they still have lasting value as an authoritative explanation of the Constitution.

13. Of particular interest is the view of the Anti-Federalist position contained in Herbert J. Storing, *What the Anti-Federalists Were For* (Chicago: University of Chicago Press, 1981). Storing also edited seven volumes of the Anti-Federalist writings, *The Complete Anti-Federalist* (Chicago: University of Chicago Press, 1981). See also Josephine F. Pacheco, *Antifederalism: The Legacy of George Mason* (Fairfax, VA: George Mason University Press, 1992).

Table 2-3 ▶   Ratification of the Constitution

STATE	DATE	VOTE FOR—AGAINST
Delaware	Dec. 7, 1787	30—0
Pennsylvania	Dec. 12, 1787	43—23
New Jersey	Dec. 18, 1787	38—0
Georgia	Jan. 2, 1788	26—0
Connecticut	Jan. 9, 1788	128—40
Massachusetts	Feb. 6, 1788	187—168
Maryland	Apr. 28, 1788	63—11
South Carolina	May 23, 1788	149—73
New Hampshire	June 21, 1788	57—46
Virginia	June 25, 1788	89—79
New York	July 26, 1788	30—27
North Carolina	Nov. 21, 1789*	194—77
Rhode Island	May 29, 1790	34—32

*Ratification was originally defeated on August 4, 1788, by a vote of 84–184.

Did the Majority of Americans Support the Constitution?

In 1913, historian Charles Beard published *An Economic Interpretation of the Constitution of the United States*.[14] This book launched a debate that has continued ever since—the debate over whether the Constitution was supported by a majority of Americans.

Beard's Thesis. Beard's central thesis was that the Constitution had been produced primarily by wealthy property owners who desired a stronger government able to protect their property rights. Beard also claimed that the Constitution had been imposed by undemocratic methods to prevent democratic majorities from exercising real power. He pointed out that there was never any popular vote on whether to hold a constitutional convention in the first place.

Furthermore, even if such a vote had been taken, state laws generally restricted voting rights to property-owning white males, meaning that most people in the country (white males without property, women, Native Americans, and slaves) were not eligible to vote. Finally, Beard pointed out that even the word *democracy* was distasteful to the founders. The term was often used by conservatives to smear their opponents.

State Ratifying Conventions. As for the various state ratifying conventions, the delegates had been selected by only 150,000 of the approximately 4 million citizens. That does not seem very democratic—at least not by today's standards. Some historians have suggested that if a Gallup poll could have been taken at that time, the Anti-Federalists would probably have outnumbered the Federalists.[15]

14. Charles A. Beard, *An Economic Interpretation of the Constitution of the United States* (New York: MacMillan, 1913; New York: Free Press, 1986).
15. Jim Powell, "James Madison—Checks and Balances to Limit Government Power," *The Freeman*, March 1996, p. 178.

Beyond Our Borders

What Makes a Constitution?

When Americans think of the Constitution, most visualize an old handwritten document that is protected in our National Archives. They may also reflect on its basic principles—checks and balances, separation of powers, the Bill of Rights—that structure how the national government carries out its work. The United States Constitution, however, was written more than 200 years ago for a relatively small, mostly rural nation. The struggle to write a constitution continues for nations such as Egypt, which has approved two different constitutions within the last few years.

WHAT SHOULD BE INCLUDED?

In February 2012, after the overthrow of the repressive Mubarak government, associate justice of the Supreme Court Ruth Bader Ginsburg visited Egypt and gave an interview broadcast on YouTube. Ginsburg's remarks were criticized by some because she suggested that the Egyptians not use our constitution as a model. While she praised many aspects of the American document, she recommended that the Egyptians look at newer charters such as that of South Africa, the Canadian charter of rights and freedoms, and the Kenyan constitution.

What kinds of models is the justice suggesting? What provisions are included in these new constitutions that make them more appropriate to a nation like Egypt? At the time of her visit, the Egyptian people who had just ended a repressive military regime were engaged in the creation of a new constitution. President Morsi immediately implemented the new Constitution in 2012. In less than one year, however, protests against the new government erupted. Many Egyptians believed that the Morsi constitution was leading to more Islamist control of society. The military took power in August, 2013. A referendum on amendments to the constitution was approved in January 2014. Like other nations writing constitutions after World War II, the Egyptian people must deal with deep religious divisions and serious economic woes. Justice Ginsburg called attention to the South African constitution's bill of rights. It is, in comparison to the U.S. Constitution, very inclusive and modern in its interpretation of human rights. All of the political rights included in the American model are there but, in addition, citizens are guaranteed the freedom to travel; the right to housing; the right to basic education; the right to food, water, and social assistance from the government; and the right to unionize. The government may not discriminate on the basis of race, gender, sex, pregnancy, religion, ethnic or social origin, sexual orientation, and so on.

IS IT A REAL CONSTITUTION?

During the Cold War between the United States and the Soviet Union, the Soviet republics held elections and called themselves

Women wait outside a polling station in Cairo, Egypt, in December 2012. They were among the millions who turned out to vote on the first post-Mubarak constitution.

(Continued)

(Continued)

democratic nations. They all had written constitutions to which they strictly adhered. The elections were not contested, and no opposition candidates or political parties emerged. Newspapers and other media were strictly controlled, as was any access to external information. Today, all of the former Soviet republics have new constitutions, and many are democracies with the same freedoms as other nations in Western Europe or the United States.

Similarly, the People's Republic of North Korea has a fairly new constitution (1998) and claims to be democratic. The military and the premier, Kim Jong-un, however, direct all aspects of life there, including limiting the frequencies available on radios and televisions to those approved by the government. So, it seems that just having a written document outlining the structures of government and freedoms of the people may not be enough to guarantee any form of democratic government, at least in the sense that we know it. As Justice Ginsburg put it, "The spirit of liberty has to be in the population."* In the United States, the Constitution has lasted, in part, because the people have continued to share the values of those who wrote the document and to transmit

those ideas to their children and to those who immigrated to the United States since its founding.

If you would like to read the constitution of any country in the world, go to confinder.richmond.edu. Another site, constitutionmaking.org, provides resources to constitution-makers.

For Critical Analysis

1. *Do you think the United States could have survived without a written constitution?*

2. *How important is it for the people of a nation to have approved their constitution?*

3. *How can you tell if a nation is following the letter and the spirit of its constitution?*

* "Ruth Bader Ginsburg Talks Constitution, Women and Liberty on Egyptian TV," www.Huffingtonpost.com/2012/02/01. February 1, 2012.

Support Was Probably Widespread. Much has also been made of the various machinations used by the Federalists to ensure the Constitution's ratification (and they did resort to a variety of devious tactics, including purchasing at least one printing press to prevent the publication of Anti-Federalist sentiments). Yet the perception that a strong central government was necessary to keep order and protect the public welfare appears to have been fairly pervasive among all classes—rich and poor alike.

Further, although the need for strong government was a major argument in favor of adopting the Constitution, even the Federalists sought to craft a limited government. Compared with constitutions adopted by other nations in later years, the U.S. Constitution, through its checks and balances, favors limited government over "energetic" government to a marked degree.

did you know?

Not all of the states had ratified the Constitution by April 30, 1789, when George Washington became president of the United States of America.

The Bill of Rights

■ **LO2.5:** Explain why some states and their citizens especially wanted the Constitution to include a bill of rights.

The U.S. Constitution would not have been ratified in several important states if the Federalists had not assured the states that amendments to the Constitution would be passed to protect individual liberties against incursions by the national government. The idea of including certain rights in the Constitution had been discussed in the convention. There were those who believed that including these rights was simply unnecessary, whereas others suggested that carefully articulating certain rights might encourage the new national government to abuse any that were not specifically defined. Some rights, including the prohibition of *ex post facto lawmaking*, were included in the document. *Ex post facto lawmaking* is passing laws that make one liable for an act that has already taken place. Also prohibited were *bills of attainder*, through which a legislature could pass judgment on someone without legal process. Many of the recommendations of the state ratifying conventions, however, included specific rights that were considered later by James Madison as he labored to draft what became the Bill of Rights.

A "Bill of Limits"

Although called the Bill of Rights, essentially the first 10 amendments to the Constitution were a "bill of limits," because the amendments limited the powers of the national government over the rights and liberties of individuals.

Madison had to cull through more than 200 state recommendations.[16] It was no small task, and in retrospect he chose remarkably well. One of the

Everyday Politics

 ## Personhood and States' Rights: *12 Years a Slave*

The 2013 Best Picture Academy Award winner, *12 Years a Slave*, tells the compelling story of Solomon Northup, a free black man who was kidnapped and sold into slavery. His tale illustrates some of the flaws and consequences of the United States Constitution. In 1841, Northup was a free black man working and living with his family in New York. Northup was kidnapped in Washington, DC, and sold into slavery. For twelve years, Northup experienced the horrors of slave life; he kept his true identity a secret for fear of extreme punishment or even death at the hands of his various masters. Eventually, he was able to get word of his misfortune and whereabouts to his family and friends in New York, who then rescued him. Northup attempted to bring his kidnappers to justice, but despite his status as a free-born man, the American judicial system worked against him. He remained free, but so did his captors. We believe this to be true because the film is based on Northup's own memoir, *Twelve Years a Slave*, published after his ordeal but lost from public view until 1968.

Solomon Northup was a highly regarded craftsman with a family and the rights of a citizen in New York State, where he was born and lived. Upon his kidnapping and transport to Louisiana, he became "property," available to be sold from one person to another for profit. He had no rights or recourse. The Constitution was no help to him because at the time, it was silent on the issue of slavery. In the state of Louisiana, where Northup eventually ended up working on plantations, he could claim no rights under the U.S. or the state constitutions. Federalism assured Louisiana of its right to slavery and to its own legal code. The true end of slavery did not come with the Civil War, but with the adoption of the Thirteenth, Fourteenth, and Fifteenth Amendments, which abolished slavery, granted protections to all persons under the law, and granted the right to vote to the formerly enslaved Americans.

Critical Thinking

1. *How would Northup's life in Louisiana have been different if he had been granted the rights in the first ten amendments of the Constitution?*

2. *Why do you think the Congress could abolish the importation of more slaves in 1808 but permit the continued practice of slavery at the state level?*

---

16. For details on these recommendations, including their sources, see Leonard W. Levy, *Origins of the Bill of Rights* (New Haven, CT: Yale University Press, 1999).

rights appropriate for constitutional protection that he left out was equal protection under the laws—but that was not commonly regarded as a basic right at that time. Not until 1868 did the states ratify an amendment guaranteeing that no state shall deny equal protection to any person. (The Supreme Court has since applied this guarantee to certain actions of the federal government as well.)

The final number of amendments that Madison and a specially appointed committee came up with was 17. Congress tightened the language somewhat and eliminated five of the amendments. Of the remaining 12, two—dealing with the apportionment of representatives and the compensation of the members of Congress—were not ratified immediately by the states. Eventually, Supreme Court decisions led to reform of the apportionment process. The amendment on the compensation of members of Congress was ratified 203 years later—in 1992!

No Explicit Limits on State Government Powers

On December 15, 1791, the national Bill of Rights was adopted when Virginia agreed to ratify the 10 amendments. On ratification, the Bill of Rights became part of the U.S. Constitution. The basic structure of American government had already been established. Now the fundamental rights and liberties of individuals were protected, at least in theory, at the national level. The proposed amendment that Madison characterized as "the most valuable amendment in the whole lot"—which would have prohibited the states from infringing on the freedoms of conscience, press, and jury trial—had been eliminated by the Senate. Thus, the Bill of Rights as adopted did not limit state power, and individual citizens had to rely on the guarantees contained in a particular state constitution or state bill of rights. The country had to wait until the violence of the Civil War before significant limitations on state power in the form of the Fourteenth Amendment became part of the national Constitution.

did you know?

About 11,000 amendments have been proposed to the Constitution. Five hundred of those have been to change the electoral college process used to elect the president.

Altering the Constitution: The Formal Amendment Process

■ **LO2.6:** Demonstrate understanding of the formal and informal processes for amending the U.S. Constitution.

The U.S. Constitution consists of 7,000 words and is shorter than any state constitution except that of Vermont, which has 6,880 words. One of the reasons the U.S. Constitution is relatively short is that the founders intended it to be only a framework for the new government, to be interpreted by succeeding generations. The formal amending procedure does not allow for changes to be made easily, which has kept it short. Article V of the Constitution outlines the ways in which amendments may be proposed and ratified (see Figure 2–3).

Two formal methods of proposing an amendment to the Constitution are available: (1) a two-thirds vote in each chamber of Congress or (2) a national convention that is called by Congress at the request of two-thirds of the state legislatures (the second method has never been used).

Ratification can occur by one of two methods: (1) by a positive vote in three-fourths of the legislatures of the various states or (2) by special conventions called in the states and a positive vote in three-fourths of them. The second method has been used only once, to repeal Prohibition (the ban on the production and sale of alcoholic beverages). That situation was exceptional because it involved an amendment (the Twenty-first) to repeal an amendment (the Eighteenth, which had created Prohibition). State conventions were necessary for repeal of the Eighteenth Amendment, because the "pro-dry" legislatures in the most conservative states would never have passed the repeal. (Note that Congress determines the method of ratification to be used by all states for each proposed constitutional amendment.)

Many Amendments Are Proposed; Few Are Accepted

Congress has considered more than 11,000 amendments to the Constitution. Many proposed amendments have been advanced to address highly specific problems. An argument against such narrow amendments has been that amendments ought to embody broad principles, in the way that the existing Constitution does. For that reason, many people have opposed such narrow amendments as one to prohibit the burning or defacing of the American flag.

Only 33 amendments have been submitted to the states after having been approved by the required two-thirds vote in each chamber of Congress, and only 27 have been ratified—see Table 2–4. (The full, annotated text of the U.S. Constitution, including its amendments, is presented in Appendix B at the end of this book.) It should be clear that the amendment process is much more difficult than a graphic depiction such as Figure 2–3 can indicate. Because of competing social and economic interests, the requirement that two-thirds of both the House and Senate approve the amendments is difficult to achieve. Thirty-four senators, representing only 17 sparsely populated states, could block any amendment. For example, the Republican-controlled House approved the Balanced Budget Amendment within the first 100 days of the 104th Congress in 1995, but it was defeated in the Senate by one vote.

Figure 2–3 ▶ The Formal Constitutional Amending Process

There are two ways of proposing amendments to the U.S. Constitution and two ways of ratifying proposed amendments. Among the four possibilities, the usual route has been proposal by Congress and ratification by state legislatures.

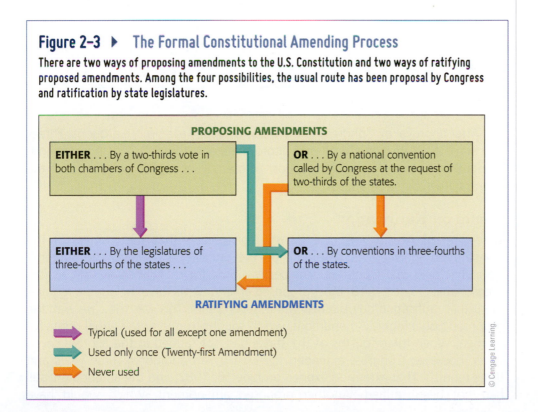

© Cengage Learning.

Table 2-4 ▶ Amendments to the Constitution

AMENDMENT	SUBJECT	YEAR ADOPTED	TIME REQUIRED FOR RATIFICATION
First to Tenth	The Bill of Rights	1791	2 years, 2 months, 20 days
Eleventh	Immunity of states from certain suits	1795	11 months, 3 days
Twelfth	Changes in electoral college procedure	1804	6 months, 3 days
Thirteenth	Prohibition of slavery	1865	10 months, 3 days
Fourteenth	Citizenship, due process, and equal protection	1868	2 years, 26 days
Fifteenth	No denial of vote because of race, color, or previous condition of servitude	1870	11 months, 8 days
Sixteenth	Power of Congress to tax income	1913	3 years, 6 months, 22 days
Seventeenth	Direct election of U.S. senators	1913	10 months, 26 days
Eighteenth	National (liquor) prohibition	1919	1 year, 29 days
Nineteenth	Women's right to vote	1920	1 year, 2 months, 14 days
Twentieth	Change of dates for congressional and presidential terms	1933	10 months, 21 days
Twenty-first	Repeal of the Eighteenth Amendment	1933	9 months, 15 days
Twenty-second	Limit on presidential tenure	1951	3 years, 11 months, 3 days
Twenty-third	District of Columbia electoral vote	1961	9 months, 13 days
Twenty-fourth	Prohibition of tax payment as a qualification to vote in federal elections	1964	1 year, 4 months, 9 days
Twenty-fifth	Procedures for determining presidential disability and presidential succession and for filling a vice presidential vacancy	1967	1 year, 7 months, 4 days
Twenty-sixth	Prohibition of setting minimum voting age above 18 in any election	1971	3 months, 7 days
Twenty-seventh	Prohibition of Congress's voting itself a raise that takes effect before the next election	1992	203 years

After approval by Congress, the process becomes even more arduous. Three-fourths of the state legislatures must approve the amendment. Only those amendments that have wide popular support across parties and in all regions of the country are likely to be approved.

Limits on Ratification

A reading of Article V of the Constitution reveals that the framers of the Constitution specified no time limit on the ratification process. The Supreme Court has held that Congress can specify a time for ratification as long as it is "reasonable." Since 1919, most proposed amendments have included a requirement that ratification be obtained within seven years. This was the case with the proposed Equal Rights Amendment, which sought to guarantee equal rights for women. When three-fourths of the states had not ratified in the allotted seven years, however, Congress extended the limit by an additional three years and three months. That extension expired on June 30, 1982, and the amendment still had not been ratified. Another proposed amendment, which would have guaranteed congressional representation to the District of Columbia, fell far short of the 38 state ratifications needed before its August 22, 1985, deadline.

On May 7, 1992, Michigan became the 38th state to ratify the Twenty-seventh Amendment (on congressional compensation)—one of the two "lost" amendments of the 12 that originally were sent to the states in 1789. Because most of the amendments proposed in recent years have been given a time limit of only seven years by Congress, it was questionable for a time whether the amendment would take effect even if the necessary number of states ratified it. Hundreds of years is apparently not too great a lapse in time, because the amendment was certified as legitimate by archivist Don Wilson of the National Archives on May 18, 1992.

The National Convention Provision

The Constitution provides that a national convention requested by the legislatures of two-thirds of the states can propose a constitutional amendment. Congress has received approximately 400 convention applications since the Constitution was ratified; every state has applied at least once. Fewer than 20 applications were submitted during the Constitution's first hundred years, but more than 150 have been filed in the last two decades. No national convention has been held since 1787, and most national political and judicial leaders are uneasy about the prospect of convening a body that conceivably could do as the Constitutional Convention did—create a new form of government. The state legislative bodies that originate national convention applications, however, do not appear to be uncomfortable with such a constitutional modification process; more than 230 state constitutional conventions have been held.

Informal Methods of Constitutional Change

Formal amendments are one way of changing our Constitution, and, as is obvious from their small number, they have been resorted to infrequently and are very difficult to pass and ratify. If we don't include the first 10 amendments (the Bill of Rights), which were adopted soon after the ratification of the Constitution, only 17 formal alterations have been made to the Constitution in the more than 200 years of its existence.

Just looking at the small number of amendments vastly understates the ability of the Constitution to adjust to changing times. The brevity and ambiguity of the original document have permitted great alterations in the Constitution by way of varying interpretations over time. As the United States grew, both in population and territory, new social and political realities emerged. Congress, presidents, and the courts found it necessary to interpret the Constitution's provisions in light of these new realities. The Constitution has proved to be a remarkably flexible document, adapting itself repeatedly to new events and concerns. The National Constitution Center website, as shown in the screen capture, offers the full text of the Constitution, with opportunities to explore specific topics and issues.

Congressional Legislation

The Constitution gives Congress broad powers to carry out its duties as the nation's legislative body. For example, Article I, Section 8 of the Constitution gives Congress the power to regulate foreign and interstate commerce. Although the Constitution has no clear definition of foreign commerce or interstate commerce, Congress has

National Constitution Center

Would the Founders find it acceptable that we continue to use the same core Constitution today?

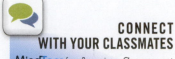

cited the *commerce clause* as the basis for passing thousands of laws that have defined the meaning of foreign and interstate commerce.

Similarly, Article III, Section 1 states that the national judiciary shall consist of one supreme court and "such inferior courts, as Congress may from time to time ordain and establish." Through a series of acts, Congress has used this broad provision to establish the federal court system of today, which includes the Supreme Court, the courts of appeal, and district courts. This provision allows Congress to create a court such as the Foreign Intelligence Surveillance Act (FISA) court to review requests for wiretapping suspected terrorists.

In addition, Congress has frequently delegated to federal agencies the legislative power to write regulations. These regulations, numbering in the tens of thousands, become law unless challenged in the court system. Nowhere does the Constitution outline this delegation of legislative authority.

Presidential Actions

Even though the Constitution does not expressly authorize the president to propose bills or even budgets to Congress, presidents since the time of Woodrow Wilson's administration (1913–1921) have proposed hundreds of bills to Congress each year.[17] Presidents have also relied on their Article II authority as commander in chief of the nation's armed forces to send American troops abroad into combat, although the Constitution provides that only Congress has the power to declare war.

The president's powers in wartime have waxed and waned through the course of American history. President Abraham Lincoln instituted a draft and suspended several civil liberties during the Civil War. During World War II, President Franklin Roosevelt approved the internment of thousands of Japanese American citizens. President George W. Bush significantly expanded presidential power in the wake of the terrorist attacks of 2001, especially in regard to the handling of individuals who could be defined as "enemy combatants." The creation of the detention facility at Guantánamo Bay, Cuba, made it possible for those prisoners to be held and interrogated by the military under the full control of the executive branch. After 2010, when President Obama faced a divided Congress, he too began to use executive power more liberally. Obama created the DREAM Act, which allows the children of unauthorized immigrants to stay in the country if they are attending college or in the military. He also raised the minimum wage for federal employees without the authorization of Congress. Presidents have also conducted foreign affairs by the use of executive agreements, which are legally binding documents made between the president and a foreign head of state. The Constitution does not mention such agreements.

Judicial Review

Another way of changing the Constitution—or of making it more flexible—is through the power of judicial review. Judicial review refers to the power of U.S. courts to examine the constitutionality of actions undertaken by the legislative and executive branches of government. A state court, for example, may rule that a statute enacted by the state legislature is unconstitutional. Federal courts (and ultimately, the United States Supreme Court) may rule unconstitutional not only

---

17. Note, though, that the Constitution, in Article II, Section 3, does state that the president "shall from time to time…recommend to [Congress's] consideration such measures as he shall judge necessary and expedient." Some scholars interpret this phrase to mean that the president has the constitutional authority to propose bills and budgets to Congress for consideration.

acts of Congress and decisions of the national executive branch but also state statutes, state executive actions, and even provisions of state constitutions.

Not a Novel Concept. The Constitution does not specifically mention the power of judicial review. Those in attendance at the Constitutional Convention, however, probably expected that the courts would have some authority to review the legality of acts by the executive and legislative branches, because, under the common-law tradition inherited from England, courts exercised this authority. Alexander Hamilton, in Federalist #78, explicitly outlined the concept of judicial review. Whether the power of judicial review can be justified constitutionally is a question that has been subject to some debate, particularly in recent years. For now, suffice it to say that in 1803, the Supreme Court claimed this power for itself in *Marbury v. Madison*, in which the Court ruled that a particular provision of an act of Congress was unconstitutional.[18]

Allows the Court to Adapt the Constitution. Through the process of judicial review, the Supreme Court adapts the Constitution to modern situations. Electronic technology, for example, did not exist when the Constitution was ratified. Nonetheless, the Supreme Court has used the Fourth Amendment guarantees against unreasonable searches and seizures to place limits on the use of wiretapping and other electronic eavesdropping methods by government officials. The Court has needed to decide whether antiterrorism laws passed by Congress or state legislatures, or executive orders declared by the president, violate the Fourth Amendment or other constitutional provisions. Additionally, the Supreme Court has changed its interpretation of the Constitution in accordance with changing values. It ruled in 1896 that "separate-but-equal" public facilities for African Americans were constitutional; but by 1954, the times had changed, and the Supreme Court reversed that decision.[19] Woodrow Wilson summarized the Supreme Court's work when he described it as "a constitutional convention in continuous session." Basically, the law is what the Supreme Court says it is at any given time.

Interpretation, Custom, and Usage

The Constitution has also been changed through interpretation by both Congress and the president. Originally, the president had a staff consisting of personal secretaries and a few others. Today, because Congress delegates specific tasks to the president and the chief executive assumes political leadership, the executive office staff alone has increased to several thousand persons. The executive branch provides legislative leadership far beyond the expectations of the founders.

Changes in the ways of doing political business have also altered the Constitution. The Constitution does not mention political parties, yet these informal, "extraconstitutional" organizations make the nominations for offices, run the campaigns, organize the members of Congress, and in fact change the election system from time to time. The emergence and evolution of the party system, for example, has changed the way the president is elected. The entire nominating process with its use of primary elections and caucuses to choose delegates to the

did you know?

The states have still not ratified an amendment (introduced by Congress in 1810) barring U.S. citizens from accepting titles or nobility from foreign governments.

---

18. 5 U.S. 137 (1803). See Chapter 15 for a further discussion of the *Marbury v. Madison* case.
19. *Brown v. Board of Education of Topeka*, 347 U.S. 483 (1954).

party's nominating convention is the creation of the two major political parties. The president is then selected by the electors who are, in fact, chosen by the parties and are pledged to a party's candidate.

A recent book by Bruce Ackerman argues that the rise of political parties and growth of the executive represent the failure of the Founding Fathers to understand how the government would develop over time. He proposes that the only reason that the system has maintained its checks is the development of the Supreme Court into the guarantor of our rights and liberties.[20] Perhaps most striking, the Constitution has been adapted from serving the needs of a small, rural republic to providing a framework of government for an industrial giant with vast geographic, natural, and human resources.

---

20. Bruce Ackerman, *The Failure of the Founding Fathers: Jefferson, Marshall, and the Rise of Presidential Democracy* (Cambridge, MA: The Belknap Press, 2005).

What Would You Do?

Abolishing the Electoral College

The U.S. Constitution is an enduring document that has survived more than 200 years of turbulent history. It is also, however, a changing document. Twenty-seven amendments have been added to the original Constitution. How can you, as an individual, actively influence the debate over the electoral college and whether it should be abolished?

Why Should You Care?

The laws of the nation have a direct impact on your life, and none more so than the Constitution—the supreme law of the land. The most important issues in society are often settled by the Constitution. In the years since our nation's founding, there have been a number of cases in which individuals chosen as electors did not vote for the individual who won the presidential election in their state. These are known as "faithless electors."

There is also the matter of over-representation. The population of North Dakota, which is the least-populated state in the country, is represented by three electoral votes; it has one representative and two senators. In a large state, such as Florida, the voters are represented by 29 electors. In North Dakota, each elector represents around 200,000 voters. In Florida, each elector represents 655,000 voters.

What Would You Do?

As a member of the House of Representatives from a mid-sized state that receives a lot of attention during the presidential election as a swing state, would you vote to eliminate the electoral college and replace it with a popular election?

What You *Can* Do

Do you feel that your vote makes a difference? Many voters are beginning to feel disenfranchised by the political process, especially during presidential elections. The effects of the electoral college contributes to this issue. After the most recent presidential election, a 2012 poll found that 60 percent of Americans favored replacing the electoral college with a direct election.*

The Every Vote Counts Amendment proposes to abolish the electoral college and would provide for the direct popular election of the president. If you would like to further investigate Every Vote Counts, go to **www.washingtonwatch.com**, a forum for monitoring proposed legislation in Washington, DC. Visit the Take Action box, where you can comment on the amendment, alert your friends and colleagues about the issue, and write your representative in Congress.

---

*The Quinnipiac University Poll. December 6, 2012.

Purestock/Getty Images

Key Terms

Anti-Federalist 54	Federalist 54	ratification 54	state 43
bicameral legislature 48	federal system 52	representative assembly 38	supremacy doctrine49
checks and balances 51	Great Compromise 49	separation of powers 51	unicameral legislature 42
confederation 43	Madisonian model 51	social contract 42	
electoral college 52	natural rights 42		

Chapter Summary

■ **LO2.1:** The first permanent English colonies were established at Jamestown in 1607 and Plymouth in 1620. The Mayflower Compact created the first formal government for the British colonists. By the mid-1700s, other British colonies had been established along the Atlantic seaboard from Georgia to Maine.

■ **LO2.1:** In 1763, the British tried to impose a series of taxes and legislative acts on their increasingly independent-minded colonies. The colonists responded with boycotts of British products and protests. Representatives of the colonies formed the First Continental Congress in 1774. The delegates sent a petition to the British king expressing their grievances. The Second Continental Congress established an army in 1775 to defend the colonists against attacks by British soldiers.

■ **LO2.1:** On July 4, 1776, the Second Continental Congress approved the Declaration of Independence. Perhaps the most revolutionary aspects of the Declaration were its assumptions that people have natural rights to life, liberty, and the pursuit of happiness; that governments derive their power from the consent of the governed; and that people have a right to overthrow oppressive governments.

■ **LO2.1:** Based on their understanding of natural rights and the social contract, as well as their experience with an oppressive British regime, all of the colonies adopted written constitutions during the Revolutionary War. Most of these gave great power to their legislatures and restrained the power of the executive.

■ **LO2.2:** At the end of the Revolutionary War, the states had signed the Articles of Confederation, creating a weak central government with few powers. In this government, each state had one vote and there was no executive. The Congress had no power to raise revenue and virtually no way to amend the Articles. The Articles proved to be unworkable because the national government had no way to ensure compliance by the states with such measures as securing tax revenues.

■ **LO2.3:** General dissatisfaction with the Articles of Confederation prompted the call for a convention at Philadelphia in 1787.

Although the delegates ostensibly convened to amend the Articles, the discussions soon focused on creating a constitution for a new form of government. The Virginia plan and the New Jersey plan did not garner widespread support. The Great Compromise offered by Connecticut helped to break the large-state/small-state disputes dividing the delegates. The Three-Fifths Compromise, which counted slaves as three-fifths of a person for purposes of representation, was adopted to keep the southern states from leaving the union.

■ **LO2.4:** The final version of the Constitution provided for the separation of powers, checks and balances, and a federal form of government. The principles of separation of powers and checks and balances were intended to prevent any one branch of the government from becoming too powerful. Each branch of government needs to cooperate with the other branches for the government to be effective.

■ **LO2.5:** Fears of a strong central government prompted the addition of the Bill of Rights to the Constitution. The Bill of Rights secured for Americans a wide variety of freedoms, including the freedoms of religion, speech, and assembly. It was initially applied only to the federal government, but amendments to the Constitution following the Civil War made it clear that the Bill of Rights would apply to the states as well.

■ **LO2.6:** An amendment to the Constitution may be proposed either by a two-thirds vote in each house of Congress or by a national convention called by Congress at the request of two-thirds of the state legislatures. Ratification can occur either by a positive vote in three-fourths of the legislatures of the various states or by a positive vote in three-fourths of special conventions called in the states for the specific purpose of ratifying the proposed amendment. The process for amending the Constitution was made very difficult to ensure that most of the states and the majority of both houses agree to the proposed change. Informal methods of constitutional change include congressional legislation, presidential actions, judicial review, and changing interpretations of the Constitution.

Selected Print, Media, and Online Resources

PRINT RESOURCES

Armitage, David. *The Declaration of Independence: A Global History.* Cambridge, MA: Harvard University Press, 2007. The author examines the history of the Declaration of Independence and then looks at its impact on the peoples and governments of other nations.

Breyer, Stephen G. *Active Liberty: Interpreting Our Democratic Constitution.* New York: Knopf, 2005. Supreme Court Justice Stephen Breyer offers his thoughts on the Constitution as a living document. He argues that the genius of the Constitution rests in the adaptability of its great principles to cope with current problems.

Bernstein, R. B. *The Founding Fathers Reconsidered.* New York: Oxford University Press, 2011. The author, based on extensive research, presents portraits of the founding fathers as real people with flaws, ambitions, rivalries, and ideas of how to build a new nation.

Hamilton, Alexander, et al. *The Federalist: The Famous Papers on the Principles of American Government.* Benjamin F. Wright, ed. New York: Friedman/Fairfax Publishing, 2002. This is an updated version of the papers written by Alexander Hamilton, James Madison, and John Jay and published in the *New York Packet*, in support of the ratification of the Constitution.

Meacham, Jon. *Jefferson: The Pursuit of Power.* New York: Random House, 2012. Meacham presents a biography of Jefferson as a premier politician, power broker, strategist and managerial president moving the young nation forward.

MEDIA RESOURCES

12 Years a Slave—This 2013 film portrays the true story of Solomon Northup, a free African American who is kidnapped and sold into slavery in the 1830s.

In the Beginning—A 1987 Bill Moyers TV program that features discussions with three prominent historians about the roots of the Constitution and its impact on our society.

Good Night and Good Luck—In this 2005 feature film, George Clooney plays the famous journalist Edward R. Murrow, who works to discredit the tactics of Senator Joseph McCarthy in the 1950s. As McCarthy tries to ferret out and punish communist sympathizers, Murrow defends aspects of the Bill of Rights: freedom of press, of speech, and of the right to associate with others.

John Adams—An Emmy award-winning mini-series focuses on John Adams role in starting the Revolutionary War and ends with his actions as the first Vice President of the United States. The series aired in 2008.

Thomas Jefferson—A 1996 documentary by acclaimed director Ken Burns. The film covers Jefferson's entire life, including his writing of the Declaration of Independence, his presidency, and his later years in Virginia. Historians and writers interviewed include Daniel Boorstin, Garry Wills, Gore Vidal, and John Hope Franklin.

ONLINE RESOURCES

Avalon Project—provides digital documents relevant to law, history, and diplomacy including James Madison's notes on the Constitutional Convention debates, taken from his daily journal: www.yale.edu/lawweb/avalon/

Emory University School of Law—collects U.S. founding documents, including the Declaration of Independence, scanned originals of the U.S. Constitution, and the *Federalist Papers*: www.law.emory.edu/erd/docs/federalist

FindLaw.com—comprehensive resource for legal information: www.findlaw.com/casecode/state.html

National Constitution Center—offers information on the Constitution—including its history, current debates over constitutional provisions, and news articles: www.constitutioncenter.org

University of Oklahoma Law Center—houses several U.S. historical documents online: www.law.ou.edu/hist

Master the concepts of The Constitution with MindTap™ for American Government

REVIEW MindTap™ for American Government
Access Key Term Flashcards for Chapter 2.

STAY CURRENT MindTap™ for American Government
Access the KnowNow blog and customized RSS for updates on current events.

TEST YOURSELF MindTap™ for American Government
Take the Wrap It Up Quiz for Chapter 2.

STAY FOCUSED MindTap™ for American Government
Complete the Focus Activities for The Constitution.

Federalism

3

Demonstrators hold an anti-gay marriage rally inside the Utah State Capitol on January 28, 2014 in Salt Lake City, Utah. A federal judge ruled unconstitutional a voter-approved ban on same-sex marriage in the state of Utah. In June 2014, the United States Court of Appeals for the 10th Circuit in Denver became the first federal appeals court in the nation to declare that same-sex couples have a "fundamental right" to wed, making it very likely that the same-sex marriage question will move from the states to the U.S. Supreme Court.

George Frey/Getty Images

 WATCH & LEARN MindTap™ **for American Government**

Watch a brief "What Do You Know?" video summarizing Federalism.

LEARNING OUTCOMES

After reading this chapter, students will be able to:

■ **LO3.1:** Define federalism and contrast the federal system of government with the unitary and confederal systems in explaining where governmental power lies.

■ **LO3.2:** Identify two advantages and two disadvantages of the U.S. federal system.

■ **LO3.3:** Locate the sources of federalism in the U.S. Constitution; using the terms *vertical control* and *horizontal control*, explain how the founders intended federalism and separation of powers to limit the expansion of national power.

■ **LO3.4:** Explain the historical evolution of federalism as a result of the Marshall Court, the Civil War, the New Deal, civil rights, and federal grant-making.

■ **LO3.5:** Evaluate immigration policy as a challenge to modern federalism.

What if?

One State's Same-Sex Marriages Had to Be Recognized Nationwide?

BACKGROUND

The full faith and credit clause of the Constitution requires states to recognize that a couple married in Iowa is also married when they move to Delaware. But what if one state recognizes same-sex marriages and the other does not?

All matters involving marriage, divorce, and the custody of children have traditionally been handled through state laws. However, the Supreme Court has overturned state laws that forbid marriages between persons of separate races (*Loving v. Virginia*, 1967) and laws that regulate sexual conduct between consenting adults in the privacy of their own dwelling (*Lawrence v. Texas*, 2003).

Without the benefit of state-sanctioned marriage, gay couples confront many legal barriers regarding health benefits, care for an ill partner, fostering or adoption of children, and disposition of an estate. Currently seventeen states and the District of Columbia issue marriage licenses to same-sex couples. Thirty-three states prohibit same-sex marriage by statute, by constitutional amendment, or both. Under the U.S. Constitution, which state laws will prevail—those that allow same-sex marriage or those that prohibit such unions? Does the full faith and credit clause of the Constitution apply in the case of same-sex marriage?

FEDERAL LAW INTERVENES

Prior to 1996, the federal government left the definition of marriage to the states, and any union recognized by a single state was also recognized by the United States government. The Defense of Marriage Act (DOMA) enacted in 1996 specifically defines marriage as a union of one man and one woman and allows state governments to ignore same-sex marriages performed in other states. In June 2013, the U.S. Supreme Court ruled (5-4) that same-sex couples in states permitting same-sex marriage could not be denied federal benefits, thereby striking down part, but not all, of DOMA's restrictions. "The federal statute is invalid, for no legitimate purpose overcomes the purpose and effect to disparage and to injure those whom the State, by its marriage laws, sought to protect in personhood and dignity," Justice Anthony Kennedy wrote in the majority opinion. "By seeking to displace this protection and treating those persons as living in marriages less respected than others, the federal statute is in violation of the Fifth Amendment." Importantly, this case was decided very narrowly under the Fifth Amendment's due process clause. The court did not change the status of same-sex marriage in every state, nor did it require states that define marriage as exclusive to one man and one woman to change that definition. What if they had selected a different constitutional basis for the decision—full faith and credit or a more expansive equal protection argument? Either might result in a requirement that all states legalize same-sex marriage and recognize same-sex marriages performed in another state.

HOW LIKELY IS CHANGE?

Since the Defense of Marriage Act became law, public opinion regarding gay marriage has shifted dramatically. A recent Gallup poll found that, if given the opportunity to vote on a law legalizing same-sex marriage in all fifty states, 52 percent would vote in favor of the law while 43 percent would vote against it.* President Obama opposed same-sex marriage when first elected, but in an interview televised in May 2012, he announced that his position had evolved and he publicly endorsed same-sex marriage. Recent polls confirm the same type of attitude change in the public. Do these shifts mean that DOMA will be repealed or that the U.S. Supreme Court will declare the entire law unconstitutional? No, but already the federal government has backed away from DOMA. Federal benefits of all types have been extended to same-sex partners; these include: Social Security benefits, access to military housing, family and medical leave protections, and tax advantages. Within the states, challenges of statutory prohibitions on gay marriage are on the rise.

* Gallup Politics poll conducted by telephone July 10–14, 2013, among a random sample of 2,027 adults age 18 and older, living in the United States. Accessed at: http://www.gallup.com/poll/163730/back-law-legalize-gay-marriage-states.aspx

For Critical Analysis

1. A federal system allows a degree of consistency across states but also variation between states on some issues. Given the political, moral, and social issues presented by same-sex marriage, do you believe this is a question best settled by federal law or by individual states? Why?

2. Now that federal benefits have been extended to all persons in same-sex marriages, regardless of where live, will states feel pressure to change their laws to support marriage equality? Why or why not?

THE UNITED STATES IS, as the name implies, a union of states. Unlike in many other nations, the national government does not have all of the authority in the system; rights and powers are reserved to the states by the Tenth Amendment. But the situation is even more complicated because there are more than 89,000 separate governmental units in the United States (see Table 3–1). Distributing authority across multiple levels and throughout many units of government is one of the ways the power of government over individuals is limited, although you can see how it might be interpreted differently.

Visitors from France or Spain are often awestruck by the complexity of our system of government. Consider that a criminal action can be defined by state law, national law, or both. Thus, a criminal suspect can be prosecuted in the state court system or in the federal court system (or both). Think about a routine task such as getting a driver's license. Each state has separate requirements for the driving test, the written test, the number of years between renewals, and the cost for the license. In 2005, Congress passed the REAL ID Act requiring states to include a specified set of information on the license so that it can be used as an identity card for travel and entrance to secure facilities, but the act was opposed by several states that insisted on maintaining their own requirements. If the licenses issued by those states do not meet the new requirements, the IDs will not be accepted at airports for travel. The U.S. Department of Homeland Security announced that implementation and a one-year period of deferred enforcement began in January 2014. The U.S. Department of Homeland Security reported that only twenty-two states were in compliance. The period of full implementation now extends through 2016. Opposition to creating a national identity card remains strong across the political spectrum.

Relations between central governments and local units are structured in various ways around the world. Federalism is one of these ways. Understanding **federalism** and how it differs from other forms of government is important to understanding the American political system. The impact of policies on the individual would be substantially different if we did not have a federal form of government in which governmental authority is divided between the central government and various subunits.

LISTEN & LEARN

MindTap™ for American Government

Access Read Speaker to listen to Chapter 3.

Federalism
A system of government in which power is divided by a written constitution between a central government and regional or subdivisional governments. Each level must have some domain in which its policies are dominant and some genuine constitutional guarantee of its authority.

Table 3-1 ▶ Governmental Units in the United States

With more than 89,000 separate governmental units in the United States today, it is no wonder that intergovernmental relations in this country are so complicated. Actually, the number of school districts has decreased over time, but the number of special districts created for single purposes, such as flood control, has increased from only about 8,000 during World War II to more than 37,000 today.

Federal government	1
State governments	50
Local governments	89,476
Counties	3,033
Municipalities (mainly cities or towns)	19,492
Townships (less extensive powers)	16,519
Special districts (water, sewer, and so on)	37,381
School districts	13,051
TOTAL UNITS	89,527

Source: U.S. Census Bureau, 2012 Statistical Abstract, Table 428, 2007 data.

Three Systems of Government

■ **LO3.1:** Define federalism and contrast the federal system of government with the unitary and confederal systems in explaining where governmental power lies.

Today, there are 196 independent nations in the world. Each of these countries has its own system of government. Relations between central governments and local units typically fit one of three models: (1) the unitary system, (2) the confederal system, or (3) the federal system.

A Unitary System

Unitary System
A centralized governmental system in which local or subdivisional governments exercise only those powers given to them by the central government.

A **unitary system** of government assigns ultimate governmental authority to the national, or central, government; subnational governments exercise only the powers the central government chooses to delegate. The central government can also withdraw powers previously delegated to local or regional governments. American colonists lived under Great Britain's unitary system, and this experience no doubt contributed to their fear of recreating an unchecked centralized power. The majority of countries today operate under a unitary form of government.

A Confederal System

Confederal System
A system consisting of a league of independent states, each having essentially sovereign powers. The central government created by such a league has only limited powers over the states.

You were introduced to the elements of a **confederal system** of government in Chapter 2, when we examined the Articles of Confederation. A confederation is the opposite of a unitary governing system. It is a league of independent states in which a central government or administration handles only those matters of common concern expressly delegated to it by the member states. The central government has no ability to make laws directly applicable to member states unless the members explicitly support such laws. The United States under the Articles of Confederation was a confederal system. Very few examples of confederal systems are found today; however, Switzerland is one modern example.

A Federal System

The federal system lies between the unitary and confederal forms of government. In a federal system, authority is divided, usually by a written constitution, between a central government and regional, or subdivisional, governments (often called constituent governments). The central government and the constituent governments both act directly on the people through laws and through the actions of elected and appointed governmental officials. Within each government's sphere of authority, in theory, each is supreme. Thus, a federal system differs sharply from a unitary one, in which the central government is supreme and the constituent governments derive their authority from it. Australia, Brazil, Canada, Germany, India, and Mexico are examples of other nations with federal systems (see Figure 3–1 for a comparison of the three systems).

did you know?

According to the U.S. Census, there were 89,055 units of government in 2012, a significant decline from 1942, when there were 155,116 governmental bodies.

Why Federalism?

■ **LO3.2:** Identify two advantages and two disadvantages of the U.S. federal system.

How best to distribute power in the new government was a question that consumed the founders. Too much power concentrated in any one place posed an unacceptable risk to liberty, but the experience of too little coordinated authority under the Articles of Confederation was sobering. Although not everyone agreed,

Figure 3-1 ▶   **The Flow of Power in the Three Systems of Government**

In a unitary system, power flows from the central government to the local and state governments. In a confederal system, power flows in the opposite direction—from the state governments to the central government. In a federal system, the flow of power, in principle, goes both ways.

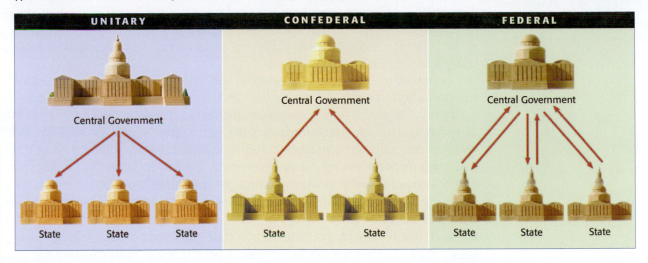

federalism provided a means to ensure stability while empowering the states to govern in areas closest to the everyday lives of citizens.

A Practical Constitutional Solution

At the Constitutional Convention in Philadelphia, advocates of a strong national government debated states' rights proponents. This debate continued throughout the ratifying conventions in the several states. The resulting federal system was therefore one of many compromises.[1] Supporters of the new Constitution were political pragmatists—they realized that without a federal arrangement, the new Constitution would not be ratified. Federalism retained state traditions and local power while establishing a strong national government capable of handling common problems.

Even if colonial leaders had agreed on the desirability of a unitary system, size and regional isolation would have made such a system difficult in practice. At the time of the Constitutional Convention, the 13 colonies were much larger geographically than England or France. Slow travel and communication contributed to the feeling of isolation in many regions within the colonies. It could take several weeks for all of the colonies to be informed about a particular political decision. A federal form of government that delegates certain functions to the states or provinces made sense. Finally, federalism brings government closer to the people. Not only can local or state governments adopt policies that speak specifically to local or regional needs, the people in those communities have more immediate access public officials. Alexis de Tocqueville marveled at the stability of public life in America. Government authority shared between the central government and the many states allows the people to exert direct influence over political decisions and indeed to seek political office themselves. There are more than 500,000 elected positions in the United States and 96 percent of those are at the state or local level.[2]

---

1. For a contemporary interpretation of this compromise and how the division of power between the national government and the states has changed, see Edward A. Purcell, *Originalism, Federalism and the American Constitutional Enterprise: A Historical Inquiry* (New Haven, CT: Yale University Press, 2007).
2. Christopher R. Berry and Jacob E. Gersen. June 2007. "The Fiscal Consequences of Electoral Institutions." The Law School, The University of Chicago, The Chicago Working Paper Series Index: www.law.uchicago.edu/Lawecon/index.html.

**COMPARE
WITH YOUR PEERS**
MindTap for American Government

Access the Federalism Forum:
Polling Activity—State Income Tax.

Benefits for the United States. In the United States, federalism has yielded many benefits. State governments long have been a training ground for future national leaders. Many presidents first made their political mark as governors. The states have been testing grounds for new government initiatives. As United States Supreme Court Justice Louis Brandeis once observed: "It is one of the happy incidents of the federal system that a single courageous state may, if its citizens choose, serve as a laboratory and try novel social and economic experiments without risk to the rest of the country."[3]

Examples of programs pioneered at the state level include unemployment compensation, begun in Wisconsin, and air pollution control, initiated in California. Statewide health care plans pioneered in Hawaii and Massachusetts provided models for the Affordable Care Act. Today, states are experimenting with policies initiating education reforms, legalizing recreational marijuana use, and implementing environmental protection measures. States in the West are highly attuned to water politics and drought conditions that impact local economies. The states have employed a variety of different strategies for dealing with the recession and home mortgage crisis—both national problems, but experienced differently across the states. Some states focused on attracting new industries, while others invested in education and training opportunities for their residents. Indeed, states have widely different schemes for financing government and provision of public services. As shown in Figure 3–2, seven states do not have an income tax (making them magnets for retirees) and five states do not have a sales tax.

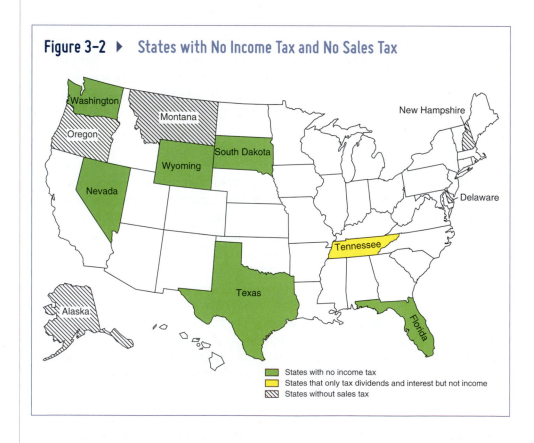

Figure 3–2 ▸ States with No Income Tax and No Sales Tax

Legend:
- States with no income tax
- States that only tax dividends and interest but not income
- States without sales tax

---

3. *New State Ice Co. v. Liebmann*, 285 U.S. 262 (1932).

Allowance for Many Political Subcultures. The American way of life is characterized by many political subcultures, which divide along the lines of race and ethnic origin, region, wealth, education, and the influence of religion. Regions of the country trend toward conservative or liberal politics, depending on the relative balance of these influences. When the Constitution was written, the diversity of the 13 "states" was seen as an obstacle to the survival of the nation. How could the large, rural, slaveholding states ever coexist with states where slavery was illegal? What would prevent a coalition of the larger states from imposing unfair laws on smaller states and minority groups? In Federalist #51 (see Appendix C), Madison argued that adopting a federal system would protect the people from the absolute power of the national government and the will of an unjust majority. He put it this way:

> In the compound republic of America, the power surrendered by the people is first divided between two distinct governments, and then the portion allotted to each subdivided among distinct and separate departments. Hence a double security arises to the rights of the people. The different governments will control each other, at the same time that each will be controlled by itself.

Had the United States developed into a unitary system, various political subcultures certainly would have been less able to influence government behavior than they have been, and continue to, in our federal system. It is also quite possible that the nation would not have survived, because flourishing political subcultures contribute to the overall political stability of the nation. Ted Cruz, the popular conservative Republican senator from Texas, for example, would likely be unelectable in New York. Political subcultures both reflect and contribute to the overall diversity of the United States.

Political scientist Daniel Elazar claimed that one of federalism's greatest virtues is that it encourages the development of distinct political subcultures. These political subcultures reflect differing demands and preferences for government. Federalism, he argues, allows for "a unique combination of governmental strength, political flexibility, and individual liberty."[4] The existence of political subcultures allows a wider variety of interests to influence government. As a result, political subcultures have proven instrumental in driving reform even at the national level, as shown by the differing state approaches to such issues as same-sex marriage, gun laws, and marijuana policy. Handgun regulation runs the gamut from forbidding the ownership of handguns in the city of Chicago to allowing the open carrying of weapons in the state of Virginia. In 2014, Colorado and Washington became the first states in the country to enact a state-legal system of marijuana cultivation and sales to adults 21 years of age and older. Twenty states allow legal use of marijuana for medical purposes under a variety of restrictions and regulations.

Arguments against Federalism. Some see federalism as a way for powerful state and local interests to block progress and to impede national plans. Smaller political units are more likely to be dominated by a single political interest or group, and at times in our history this influence has limited rights for minority groups. (This was essentially the argument that Madison put forth in Federalist #10, provided in Appendix C.) Alternatively, progressive dominant factions in states have pressured the national government for change in many areas, such as the environment, same-sex marriage, and nutrition labels on food.

did you know?

The state of Alaska is 429 times larger than the state of Rhode Island, but Rhode Island's population is larger than Alaska's.

---

4. Daniel Elazar, *American Federalism: A View from the States*, 2nd ed. (New York: Crowell, 1972).

Critics of federalism also argue that too many Americans suffer as a result of the inequalities that exist across the states. Individual states differ markedly in educational spending and achievement, crime and crime prevention, and even the safety of their buildings. States also differ considerably on women's rights, specifically regarding support for equal pay and free access to safe, legal abortion. Not surprisingly, these critics argue for increased federal legislation and oversight. This involves creating national educational standards, national building code standards, national expenditure minimums for crime control, and so on. The Affordable Care Act expanded the number of people who qualify for Medicaid. Typically, the federal government only covers about half of the cost of Medicaid, but under the new healthcare law the federal government agreed to cover the full cost for the first three years. Under the law, all states were initially required to expand Medicaid coverage under threat of losing the federal contribution for all Medicaid. The Supreme Court ruled that the states could not be coerced to participate and thus Medicaid expansion became optional; around half of the states opted out.[5] In those states, the income cutoff to be eligible for Medicaid is generally much lower than what was set in the Affordable Care Act, so fewer people will qualify. Many of the states choosing not to take the federal money to expand Medicaid are led by Republican governors who oppose the Affordable Care Act.

Others see dangers in the expansion of national powers at the expense of the states. President Ronald Reagan (served 1981–1989) said, "The Founding Fathers saw the federalist system as constructed something like a masonry wall. The States are the bricks, the national government is the mortar… Unfortunately, over the years, many people have increasingly come to believe that Washington is the whole wall."[6]

Budtender Rob Johnston
helps a customer on the first
day of legal recreational
marijuana sales in Denver,
Colorado, January, 1, 2014.

Joe Amon/The Denver Post/Getty Images

5. *National Federation of Independent Business v. Sebelius*, 567 U.S. ___ (2012).
6. Text of the address by the president to the National Conference of State Legislatures, Atlanta, Georgia (Washington, DC: The White House, Office of the Press Secretary, July 30, 1981), as quoted in Edward Millican, *One United People: The Federalist Papers and the National Idea* (Lexington, KY: The University Press of Kentucky, 1990).

The Constitutional Basis for American Federalism

■ **LO3.3:** Locate the sources of federalism in the U.S. Constitution; using the terms *vertical control* and *horizontal control*, explain how the founders intended federalism and separation of powers to limit the expansion of national power.

The term *federal system* is not found in the U.S. Constitution. Nor is it possible to find a systematic division of governmental authority between the national and state governments in that document. Rather, the Constitution sets out different

Everyday Politics

John Adams

John Adams became the second president of the United States (served 1797–1801) after serving two terms as vice president during George Washington's administration. The television mini-series *John Adams* is based on historian David McCollough's Pulitzer Prize winning book of the same title. Starring Paul Giamatti as John Adams, the seven-part series aired on HBO in the spring of 2008. It depicts Adams' political life and highlights the role he played in the nation's founding. The show won thirteen Emmy awards, more than any other miniseries in history.

John Adams was born in Braintree, Massachusetts, in 1735, to a family steeped in political engagement. His cousin, Samuel Adams, was a leader in the Sons of Liberty and a prominent figure in the American Revolution. John was educated at Harvard College and trained in the law. The miniseries opens with Adams being asked to defend Captain Thomas Preston and his "Redcoat" soldiers following the Boston Massacre in 1770. Boston was in turmoil following the British imposition of a variety of taxes designed to raise revenue from the colonies. Adams was a principled man and accepted the case because he believed every man deserved a fair trial even though he plainly struggled with the tension between his duty to judicial principle and his allegiance with the colonies as war seemed inevitable. Adams was elected to the Continental Congress as a delegate from Massachusetts; in that body he argued passionately for the values of liberty contained in the Declaration of Independence, which he helped Thomas Jefferson to write.

Once the war began, Adams was sent to Europe to join Benjamin Franklin in his efforts to convince France to join with the colonies as an ally against Britain. Adams did not share Franklin's knack for diplomatic tact and he was soon redirected to secure a war loan from the Dutch. Upon the conclusion of the war, Adams was appointed the first U.S. ambassador to the United Kingdom.

In 1789, Adams returned to the United States to become vice president, although he found the role frustrating. He was a staunch opponent of slavery and unlike many of his contemporaries never owned a slave himself. Adams' relationship with his wife, Abigail Adams is evidence that he valued the opinions and perspectives of women as well. Adams was a strong Federalist but his presidency was weakened substantially when he signed the controversial Alien and Sedition Acts. These acts were intended to silence opposition to the Federalists, but they were so unpopular (and unconstitutional) that they bore a large portion of the blame for the downfall of the Federalist Party.

Critical Thinking

1. *Federalist philosophies of government prevailed in designing the United States government, but the founders' strong commitment to liberty and independence limited the ultimate power of the national government. Identify the tensions between the desire for stability and order and the commitment to liberty in the John Adams story. What would you say was his greatest contribution to defining American federalism?*

2. *If John Adams were to return as an observer of twenty-first century American government, which aspect of modern politics and government do you believe would most horrify him and of which would he be most proud?*

types of powers. These powers can be classified as (1) the powers of the national government, (2) the powers of the states, and (3) prohibited powers. The Constitution also makes it clear that if a state or local law conflicts with a national law, the national law will prevail.

Powers of the National Government

The powers delegated to the national government include both expressed and implied powers, as well as the special category of inherent powers. Most of the powers expressly delegated to the national government are found in Article I, Section 8, of the Constitution. These enumerated powers include coining money, setting standards for weights and measures, making uniform naturalization laws, admitting new states, establishing post offices, and declaring war. Another important enumerated power is the power to regulate commerce among the states—a topic we deal with later in this chapter.

The Necessary and Proper Clause.
The implied powers of the national government are also based on Article I, Section 8, which states that Congress shall have the power

> [t]o make all Laws which shall be necessary and proper for carrying into Execution the foregoing Powers, and all other Powers vested by this Constitution in the Government of the United States, or in any Department or Officer thereof.

Elastic Clause or Necessary and Proper Clause
The clause in Article I, Section 8, that grants Congress the power to do whatever is necessary to execute its specifically delegated powers.

This clause is sometimes called the **elastic clause**, or **necessary and proper clause**, because it provides flexibility to the U.S. constitutional system. It gives Congress all of those powers that can be reasonably inferred but that are not expressly stated in the brief wording of the Constitution. The clause was first used in the Supreme Court decision of *McCulloch v. Maryland* (discussed later in this chapter) to develop the concept of implied powers.[7] Through this concept, the national government has succeeded in strengthening the scope of its authority to meet the numerous problems that the framers of the Constitution did not, and could not, anticipate.

Inherent Powers.
A special category of national powers that is not implied by the necessary and proper clause are the inherent powers of the national government. These powers derive from the fact that the United States is a sovereign power among nations, and so its national government must be the only government that deals with other nations. Under international law, it is assumed that all nation-states, regardless of their size or power, have an *inherent* right to ensure their own survival. To do this, each nation must have the ability to act in its own interest among and with the community of nations.

Note that no specific clause in the Constitution says anything about the acquisition of additional land. Nonetheless, through inherent powers, the federal government made the Louisiana Purchase in 1803 and then went on to acquire Florida, Texas, Oregon, Alaska, Hawaii, and other lands. The United States grew from a mere 13 states to 50 states, plus several "territories."

The national government has these inherent powers whether or not they have been enumerated in the Constitution. Some constitutional scholars categorize inherent powers as a third type of power, completely distinct from the delegated powers (both expressed and implied) of the national government.

---

7. 4 Wheaton 316 (1819).

Politics with a Purpose

States Learning from Each Other

When you move, it is a challenge to locate the goods and services you need in a new town. If you attend college out of state, you may wonder if you are eligible to vote and, if you are, how to register. Or, if you wish to vote by absentee ballot in your hometown, how do you get one? Federalism is responsible for many of the differences in the answers to these questions and countless others that exist across cities and states.

The nature of power held by national, state, and local governments has changed over time. State governments, rather than the federal government, increasingly have been asked to solve the problems of their citizens' education, health care, clean air, and safe streets, to name a few. How do states accomplish these tasks? Do they decide independently, or can they work cooperatively to learn from each other how best to solve policy problems?

One way that states can cope with these challenges is through associations and organizations designed to share policy ideas and provide members with support. For example, the State Legislative Leaders Foundation hosts educational programs so that leaders can learn from experts and each other. Other examples are mayors' groups (the United States Conference of Mayors), governors' associations (National Governors Association), and groups for state government officials (Council of State Governments). * These organizations provide networking opportunities for officials to learn from each other. In addition, they provide information on how students can get involved with state government and become part of the policy innovation process. Legislative internships are available in all states and many states also sponsor mock student legislatures that recommend policy initiatives to the legislature itself.**

Sharing experiences across states has led to policy innovation and diffusion. Policy entrepreneurs find new solutions to problems. States and localities adopt these policies, adapt them to their needs, and share information and ideas.

* http://usmayors.org, www.nga.org, www.csg.org
** For information on state internships, go to National Council of State Legislatures and search for internships at www.ncsl.org.

Powers of the State Governments

The Tenth Amendment states that the powers not delegated to the United States by the Constitution, nor prohibited by it to the states, are reserved to the states, or to the people. These are the reserved powers that the national government cannot deny to the states. States had all the power when the Constitution was written, so it is not surprising that these reserved powers are not more clearly specified, but it does lead to questions about whether a certain power is delegated to the national government or reserved to the states. State powers include each state's right to regulate commerce within its borders and to provide for a state militia. States also have the reserved power to make laws on all matters not prohibited to the states by the U.S. Constitution or state constitutions and not expressly, or by implication, delegated to the national government. Furthermore, the states have **police power**— the authority to legislate for the protection of the health, morals, safety, and welfare of the people. Their police power enables states to pass laws governing such activities as crimes, marriage, contracts, education, intrastate transportation, and land use.

The ambiguity of the Tenth Amendment has allowed the reserved powers of the states to be defined differently at different times in our history. When widespread support for increased regulation by the national government exists, the Tenth Amendment tends to recede into the background. When the tide turns the other way (in favor of states' rights), the Tenth Amendment is resurrected to justify arguments supporting increased states' rights. The current climate, reflected in Congress and in decisions rendered by the U.S. Supreme Court, favors state prerogatives.

Police Power
The authority to legislate for the protection of the health, morals, safety, and welfare of the people. In the United States, most police power is reserved to the states.

Concurrent Powers

In certain areas, the states share **concurrent powers** not specifically listed in the Constitution with the national government. An example is the power to tax. The types of taxation are divided between the levels of government. For example, states may not levy a tariff (a set of taxes on imported goods); only the national government may do this. Neither government may tax the facilities of the other. If the state governments did not have the power to tax, they could not operate independent of the federal government.

Other concurrent powers include the power to borrow funds, to establish courts, and to charter banks and corporations. To a limited extent, the national government exercises police power, and to the extent that it does, police power is also a concurrent power. Concurrent powers exercised by the states are normally limited to the geographic area of each state and to those functions *not* granted by the Constitution exclusively to the national government (such as the coinage of money and the negotiation of treaties).

did you know?

Under Article I, Section 10, of the Constitution, no state is allowed to enter into any treaty, alliance, or confederation.

Prohibited Powers

The Constitution prohibits or denies several powers to the national government. The national government may not impose taxes on goods sold to other countries (exports). Moreover, any power not granted expressly or implicitly to the federal government by the Constitution is prohibited to it. The states are also denied certain powers. No state is allowed to enter into a treaty on its own with another country.

The Supremacy Clause

The supremacy of the national constitution over subnational laws and actions is established in the **supremacy clause** of the Constitution. The supremacy clause (Article VI, Clause 2) states the following:

> *This Constitution, and the Laws of the United States which shall be made in Pursuance thereof; and all Treaties made…under the Authority of the United States, shall be the supreme Law of the Land; and the Judges in every State shall be bound thereby, any Thing in the Constitution or Laws of any State to the Contrary notwithstanding.*

In other words, states cannot use their reserved or concurrent powers to prevent or undermine national policies. All national and state officers, including judges, are bound by oath to support the Constitution. Hence, any legitimate exercise of national governmental power supersedes any conflicting state action.[8] Of course, deciding whether a conflict actually exists is a judicial matter, as shown in the case of *McCulloch v. Maryland*.

National government legislation in a concurrent area is said to preempt (take precedence over) conflicting state or local laws or regulations in that area. One of the ways in which the national government has extended its powers is through the preemption of state and local laws by national legislation. In the first decade of the twentieth century, fewer than 20 national laws preempted laws and regulations issued by state and local governments. By the beginning of the twenty-first century, the number had risen to nearly 120.

Some political scientists believe that national supremacy is critical for the longevity and smooth functioning of a federal system. Nonetheless, the application

---

8. An example of this is President Dwight Eisenhower's disciplining of Arkansas Governor Orval Faubus in 1957 by federalizing the National Guard to enforce the court-ordered desegregation of Little Rock High School.

of this principle has been a continuous source of conflict. The most extreme example of this conflict was the Civil War.

Vertical and Horizontal Checks and Balances

Recall from Chapter 2 that one of the goals of the founders was to prevent the national government from becoming too powerful. For that reason, they divided the government into three branches—legislative, executive, and judicial. They also created a system of checks and balances that allowed each branch to check the actions of the others. Separation of powers functions as a **horizontal control** when branches of government on the same level (state or national) check one another against the expansion of power. Federalism is also an important form of checks and balances and it is known as a **vertical control** because the checks and balances involve power-sharing relationships between the states and the national government.

For example, the reserved powers of the states act as a check on the national government. Additionally, the states' interests are represented in the national legislature (Congress), and the citizens of the various states determine who will head the executive branch (the presidency). Finally, national programs and policies are administered by the states. This gives the states considerable control over the ultimate shape of those programs and policies. For example, the states are playing a major role in implementing the Affordable Care Act.

The national government, in turn, can check state policies by exercising its constitutional powers under the clauses just discussed, as well as under the commerce clause (to be examined later). Furthermore, the national government can influence state policies indirectly through federal grants or the federal budget process.

Horizontal Control
A check against the expansion of government power that relies on checks and balances between branches of government on the same level.

Vertical Control
A structural check against the accumulation of too much power in any one level of government (national or state).

Interstate Relations

So far, we have examined only the relationship between central and state governmental units. The states, however, have constant commercial, social, and other dealings among themselves. The U.S. Constitution imposes certain "rules of the road" on interstate relations. These rules have prevented any one state from setting itself apart from the other states. The three most important clauses governing interstate relations in the Constitution, all derived from the Articles of Confederation, require each state to do the following:

1. Give full faith and credit to every other state's public acts, records, and judicial proceedings (Article IV, Section 1).
2. Extend to every other state's citizens the privileges and immunities of its own citizens (Article IV, Section 2).
3. Agree to return persons who are fleeing from justice in another state back to their home state when requested to do so (Article IV, Section 2).

The Full Faith and Credit Clause. This provision of the Constitution protects the rights of citizens as they move from state to state. It provides that "full faith and credit shall be given in each State to the public Acts, Records and judicial Proceedings of every other State." This clause applies only to civil matters. It ensures that rights established under deeds, wills, contracts, and the like will be honored by any other states. It also ensures that any judicial decision with respect to such property rights will be honored, as well as enforced, in all states. The **full faith and credit clause** has contributed to the unity of American citizens, particularly as we have become a more mobile society. One issue that remains undecided is whether this clause will be applied to same-sex marriages. Until Section 3

Full Faith and Credit Clause
This section of the Constitution requires states to recognize one another's laws and court decisions. It ensures that rights established under deeds, wills, contracts, and other civil matters in one state will be honored by other states.

of the Defense of Marriage Act (DOMA) was ruled unconstitutional in 2013, DOMA barred same-sex married couples from being recognized as "spouses" for purposes of federal laws and benefits.[9] As discussed previously, same-sex couples married in a state where such unions are legal are eligible for all of the federal rights and benefits accruing to any other married persons. Court challenges in states where gay marriage is not legal will likely result in a U.S. Supreme Court review.

Privileges and Immunities. **Privileges and immunities** are defined as special rights and exceptions provided by law. Under Article IV, "The Citizens of each State shall be entitled to all Privileges and Immunities of Citizens in the several States." This clause indicates that states are obligated to extend to citizens of other states protection of the laws, the right to work, access to courts, and other privileges they grant their own citizens. If you are a student from Iowa attending college in Ohio, you have the same rights as Ohioans to protest a traffic ticket, to buy a car, to hold a job, and to travel freely throughout the state.

Interstate Extradition. The Constitution clearly addressed the issue of how states should cooperate in catching criminals. Article IV, Section 2, states that "[a] person charged in any State with Treason, Felony, or another Crime who shall flee from Justice and be found in another State, shall on Demand of the executive Authority of the State from which he fled, be delivered up, to be removed to the State having jurisdiction of the Crime." While the language is clear, a federal judge will not order such an action. It is the moral duty of the governor to **extradite** the accused. From time to time, the governor of a state may refuse to do so, either because he or she does not believe in capital punishment, which might be ordered upon conviction, or because the accused has lived a law-abiding life for many years outside the state in which the crime was committed.

Additionally, states may enter into agreements called **interstate compacts**, if consented to by Congress. In reality, congressional consent is necessary only if such a compact increases the power of the contracting states relative to other states (or to the national government). Typical examples of interstate compacts are the establishment of the Port Authority of New York and New Jersey by an interstate compact between those two states in 1921 and the regulation of the production of crude oil and natural gas by the Interstate Oil and Gas Compact of 1935. Regional compacts between states on higher education, climate change, and economic development exist to promote collaboration and to provide resources for innovation. Compacts allow states work together to address challenges that cross state boundaries. A slightly different form of collaboration can be found in the Common Core State Standards Initiative. The initiative is sponsored by the National Governors Association and the Council of Chief State School Officers, two organizations with a vested interest in raising the quality of educational outcomes. Members of the Common Core State Standards Initiative have agreed to adopt consistent education standards in the areas of math and English language arts to ensure that students are prepared for college or careers no later than the end of high school. Not everyone agrees with this coordinated approach. South Carolina Governor Nikki Haley, for example, argued her state should not "relinquish control of education to the federal government; neither should we cede it to the consensus of other states."[10] Nevertheless, South Carolina adopted the Common Core State Standards.

Privileges and Immunities
Special rights and exceptions provided by law. States may not discriminate against one another's citizens.

Extradite
To surrender an accused or convicted criminal to the authorities of the state from which he or she has fled; to return a fugitive criminal to the jurisdiction of the accusing state.

Interstate Compacts
An agreement between two or more states. Agreements on minor matters are made without congressional consent, but any compact that tends to increase the power of the contracting states relative to other states or relative to the national government generally requires the consent of Congress. Such compacts serve as a means by which states can solve regional problems.

---

9. *United States v. Windsor*, 570 U.S. ____ (2013).
10. Stephanie Banchero "School-standards pushback," *The Wall Street Journal*, published May 8, 2012. Accessed at online.wsj. com/news/articles/SB10001424052702303630404577390431072241906.

Beyond Our Borders

Federalism, Fracking, and European Energy Independence

In the United States, the Constitution defines the federal system by laying out the division of powers and authority between the 50 states and the national government. The European Union (EU) is an economic and political union of 28 member states. In many ways, although the sub-governments are not contained within one nation, the EU functions as a federalist system. Energy independence is a goal for both the United States and the European Union. Just as the United States is dependent on foreign oil for about 40 percent of its supply, much of Europe relies on Russian natural gas that flows through pipelines in Ukraine. Global conflict or unrest in the countries that provide oil and gas threaten energy supplies and lead political leaders to look for alternative sources of energy.

Hydraulic fracturing, popularly known as "fracking," is a drilling process designed to extract natural gas from shale rock layers deep within the earth. Water, sand and chemicals are injected into the rock at high pressure, allowing the gas to flow out to the head of the well. Horizontal drilling techniques allow oil and gas companies to extract natural gas without necessarily disturbing communities at the surface. Royalty payments from gas companies that extract shale gas have been an economic boom to many rural communities in the Midwest. The increased supply of gas derived from shale has increased the nation's energy security, but not without cost and controversy.

Environmentalists note that fracking uses huge amounts of water that must be transported to the fracking site, at significant environmental cost. Potentially carcinogenic chemicals used may escape during the process and contaminate groundwater sources around the fracking site. Methane and other gases are released in the process and contribute to smog and climate change. Finally, fracking may lead to an increase in earthquakes. State legislators and regulators want to protect the environment and public health, but they also recognize the benefits from the revenue the industry brings to state and local economies. Most natural gas-producing states have some form of severance tax that is imposed on resources removed from the ground. The National Council of State Legislatures (NCSL) estimated state revenue as a result of taxes on the oil and gas industry at $18.6 billion.

Fracking is much more prevalent in the United States than in European states. Many Europeans regard the economic boom produced by fracking with trepidation. U.S. natural gas prices, however, have fallen to as little as a quarter of those in Europe as a result of shale gas. The 2014 conflict in Ukraine refocused attention on energy security. When Russia cut off the supply of natural gas to Ukraine in 2006 and 2009, prices rose throughout the EU. Yet, efforts to develop shale gas industries have proceeded slowly; there is no commercial shale gas production anywhere in

Europe today. Poland, the European country that has been most active in shale gas, has only drilled about 50 exploratory wells to date. Environmental concerns are only part of the explanation. In the United States, property holders own the rights to the minerals under their property, whereas in Europe the subsoil is the property of the state. There is no individual economic incentive for European landowners to promote fracking.

A protester blocks access to a drilling site in southern England as part of a campaign against the controversial "fracking" process used in shale gas exploration.

For Critical Analysis

1. *All nations have an interest in promoting security through energy independence. How might EU states overcome the lack of individual economic incentives to promote shale gas exploration?*

2. *How can nations balance the serious environmental concerns associated with fracking with the need to produce a greater share of their energy supply? Are regulations and policies in this area best handled by states or by the central government? Explain.*

Defining Constitutional Powers— The Early Years

■ **LO3.4:** Explain the historical evolution of federalism as a result of the Marshall Court, the Civil War, the New Deal, civil rights, and federal grant-making.

To be effective and to endure, constitutional language must have some degree of ambiguity. Certainly, the powers delegated to the national government and the powers reserved to the states contain elements of ambiguity, thus leaving the door open for different interpretations of federalism. Disputes over the boundaries of national versus state powers have characterized this nation from the beginning. In the early 1800s, the most significant disputes arose over differing interpretations of the implied powers of the national government under the necessary and proper clause and over the respective powers of the national government and the states to regulate commerce.

Although political bodies at all levels of government play important roles in the process of settling such disputes, ultimately the Supreme Court casts the final vote. From 1801 to 1835, the Supreme Court was headed by Chief Justice John Marshall, a Federalist who advocated a strong central government. Two cases decided by the Marshall Court are considered milestones in defining the boundaries between federal and state power: *McCulloch v. Maryland*[11] and *Gibbons v. Ogden*.[12]

McCulloch v. Maryland (1819)

Nowhere in the U.S. Constitution does it state that Congress has the power to create a national bank, although it does have the express power to regulate currency. Twice in the history of the nation Congress has chartered banks—the First and Second Banks of the United States—and provided part of their initial capital; thus, they were national banks. The government of Maryland, which intended to regulate its own banks and did not want competition from a national bank, imposed a tax on the Second Bank's Baltimore branch in an attempt to put that branch out of business. The branch's cashier, James William McCulloch, refused to pay the Maryland tax. When Maryland took McCulloch to its state court, the state of Maryland won. The national government appealed the case to the Supreme Court.

The Constitutional Questions. The questions before the Supreme Court were of monumental proportions. The very heart of national power under the Constitution, as well as the relationship between the national government and the states, was at issue. Congress has the authority to make all laws that are "necessary and proper" for the execution of Congress's expressed powers. Strict Constitution constructionists looked at the word *necessary* and contended that the national government had only those powers *indispensable* to the exercise of its designated powers. To them, chartering a bank and contributing capital to it were not necessary, for example, to coin money and regulate its value.

Loose constructionists disagreed. They believed that the word *necessary* could not be looked at in its strictest sense. As Alexander Hamilton once said, "It is essential to the being of the national government that so erroneous a conception of the meaning of the word *necessary* be exploded." The important issue was, if the national bank was constitutional, could the state tax it?

---

11. 4 Wheaton 316 (1819).
12. 9 Wheaton 1 (1824).

Marshall's Decision. Three days after hearing the case, Chief Justice John Marshall announced the Court's decision. It is true, Marshall said, that Congress's power to establish a national bank was not expressed in the Constitution. He went on to say, however, that if establishing such a national bank aided the government in the exercise of its designated powers, then the authority to set up such a bank could be implied. To Marshall, the necessary and proper clause embraced "all means which are appropriate: to carry out the 'legitimate ends' of the Constitution." Only when such actions are forbidden by the letter and spirit of the Constitution are they thereby unconstitutional. There was nothing in the Constitution, according to Marshall, "which excludes incidental or implied powers; and which requires that everything granted shall be expressly and minutely described." It would be impossible to spell out every action that Congress might legitimately take—the Constitution "would be enormously long and could scarcely be embraced by the human mind."

In perhaps the single most famous sentence ever uttered by a Supreme Court justice, Marshall said, "[W]e must never forget it is a constitution we are expounding." In other words, the Constitution is a living instrument that has to be interpreted to meet the practical needs of government. Having established this doctrine of implied powers, Marshall then answered the other important question before the Court and established the doctrine of national supremacy. Marshall stated that no state could use its taxing power to tax an arm of the national government. If it could, "the declaration that the Constitution...shall be the supreme law of the land, is an empty and unmeaning declamation."

Marshall's decision enabled the national government to grow and to meet problems that the Constitution's framers were unable to foresee. Today, practically every expressed power of the national government has been expanded in one way or another by use of the necessary and proper clause.

Gibbons v. Ogden (1824)

One of the most important parts of the Constitution included in Article I, Section 8, is the so-called **commerce clause**, in which Congress is given the power "[t]o regulate Commerce with foreign Nations, and among the several States, and with the Indian Tribes." What exactly does "to regulate commerce" mean? What does "commerce" entail? The issue here is essentially the same as that raised by *McCulloch v. Maryland*: How strict an interpretation should be given to a constitutional phrase? As might be expected given his Federalist loyalties, Marshall used a liberal approach in interpreting the commerce clause in *Gibbons v. Ogden*.

The Background of the Case. Robert Fulton and Robert Livingston secured a monopoly on steam navigation on New York waters from the New York legislature in 1803. They licensed Aaron Ogden to operate steam-powered ferryboats between New York and New Jersey. Thomas Gibbons, who had obtained a license from the U.S. government to operate boats in interstate waters, decided to compete with Ogden, but he did so without New York's permission. Ogden sued Gibbons. The New York state courts prohibited Gibbons from operating in New York waters. Gibbons appealed to the Supreme Court.

Several issues were before the Court in this case. The first was how the term *commerce* should be defined. New York's highest court had defined the term narrowly to mean only the shipment of goods, or the interchange of commodities, not navigation or the transport of people. The second was whether the national government's power to regulate interstate commerce extended to commerce

---

did you know?

The Liberty Bell cracked when it was rung at the funeral of John Marshall in 1835.

Commerce Clause
The section of the Constitution in which Congress is given the power to regulate trade among the states and with foreign countries.

within a state (*intra*state commerce) or was limited strictly to commerce among the states (*inter*state commerce). The third was whether the power to regulate interstate commerce was a concurrent power (as the New York court had concluded), meaning a power that could be exercised by both state and national governments, or an exclusive national power. Clearly, if such powers were concurrent, many instances of laws that conflicted with each other would occur.

Marshall's Ruling. Marshall defined commerce as all commercial interaction—all business dealings—including navigation and the transport of people. Marshall used this opportunity not only to expand the definition of commerce but also to validate and increase the power of the national legislature to regulate commerce. Marshall wrote: "What is this power? It is the power...to prescribe the rule by which commerce is to be governed. This power, like all others vested in Congress, is complete in itself." Marshall also held that the commerce power of the national government could be exercised in state jurisdictions, even though it cannot reach solely intrastate commerce. Finally, Marshall emphasized that the power to regulate interstate commerce was an exclusive national power. Because Gibbons was duly authorized by the national government to navigate in interstate waters, he could not be prohibited from doing so by a state court.

Marshall's expansive interpretation of the commerce clause in *Gibbons v. Ogden* allowed the national government to exercise increasing authority over all areas of economic affairs throughout the land. In the 1930s and subsequent decades, the commerce clause became the primary constitutional basis for national government regulation.

States' Rights and the Resort to Civil War

In both cases, the Supreme Court expanded and codified national power over state's rights. The question of slavery that led to the Civil War was also a dispute over national government supremacy versus the rights of the separate states.

President Lincoln meets with some of his generals and other troops on October 3, 1862. While many believe that the Civil War was fought over the issue of slavery, others point out that it was really a battle over the supremacy of the national government. In any event, once the North won the war, what happened to the size and power of our national government?

© Bettmann/CORBIS

Essentially, the Civil War brought to an ultimate and violent climax the ideological debate that had been outlined by the Federalist and Anti-Federalist parties even before the Constitution was ratified.

The Shift Back to States' Rights

While John Marshall was chief justice of the Supreme Court he did much to increase the power of the national government and to reduce that of the states. During the Jacksonian era (1829–1837), however, a shift back to states' rights began. The question of the regulation of commerce became one of the major issues in federal–state relations. When Congress passed a tariff in 1828, South Carolina unsuccessfully attempted to nullify the tariff (render it void), claiming that in cases of conflict between a state and the national government, the state should have the ultimate authority over its citizens.

Over the next three decades, the North and South became even more sharply divided over tariffs that mostly benefited northern industries and the issue of slavery. On December 20, 1860, South Carolina formally repealed its ratification of the Constitution and withdrew from the Union. On February 4, 1861, representatives from six southern states met at Montgomery, Alabama, to form a new government called the Confederate States of America.

War and the Growth of the National Government

The ultimate defeat of the South in 1865 permanently ended any idea that a state could successfully claim the right to secede, or withdraw, from the Union. Contrary to the southern states' intention, the Civil War resulted in an increase in the national government's political power.

The War Effort. Thousands of new employees were hired to run the Union war effort and to deal with the social and economic problems that had to be handled in the aftermath of war. A billion-dollar national government budget was passed for the first time in 1865 to cover the increased government expenditures. The first (temporary) income tax was imposed on citizens to help pay for the war. This tax and the increased national government spending were precursors to the expanded future role of the national government in the American federal system. Civil liberties were curtailed in the Union and in the Confederacy in the name of the wartime emergency. The distribution of pensions and widows' benefits also boosted the national government's social role. Many scholars contend that the North's victory set the nation on the path to a modern industrial economy and society.

The Civil War Amendments. The expansion of the national government's authority during the Civil War was reflected in the passage of the Civil War Amendments to the Constitution. Before the war, legislation with regard to slavery was some of the most controversial ever to come before Congress. In fact, in the 1830s, Congress prohibited the submission of antislavery petitions. When new states were admitted into the Union, the primary decision was whether slavery would be allowed. Immediately after the Civil War, at a time when former officers of the Confederacy were barred from voting, the three Civil War Amendments were passed. The Thirteenth Amendment, ratified in 1865, did more than interfere with slavery—it abolished the institution altogether. By abolishing slavery, the amendment also in effect abolished the rule by which three-fifths of the slaves

did you know?

Only after the Civil War did people commonly refer to the United States as "it" instead of "they."

were counted when apportioning seats in the House of Representatives (see Chapter 2). African Americans were now counted in full.

The Fourteenth Amendment (1868) defined who was a citizen of each state. It sought to guarantee equal rights under state law, stating that

> [no] State [shall] deprive any person of life, liberty, or property, without due process of law; nor deny to any person within its jurisdiction the equal protection of the laws.

For a brief time after the ratification of these amendments, the rights of African Americans in the South were protected by the local officials appointed by the Union forces. Within two decades, the Fourteenth Amendment lost much of its power as states reinstituted separate conditions for the former slaves. Decades later, the courts interpreted these words to mean that the national Bill of Rights applied to state governments (see Chapter 4). The Fourteenth Amendment also confirmed the abolition of the three-fifths rule. Finally, the Fifteenth Amendment (1870) gave African Americans the right to vote in all elections, including state elections, although a century would pass before that right was enforced.

The Continuing Dispute over the Division of Power

Although the outcome of the Civil War firmly established the supremacy of the national government and put to rest the idea that a state could secede from the Union, the war by no means ended the debate over the division of powers between the national government and the states. The debate over the division of powers in our federal system can be viewed as progressing through at least two general stages since the Civil War: dual federalism and cooperative federalism.

Dual Federalism and the Retreat of National Authority

Dual Federalism
A system in which the states and the national government each remains supreme within its own sphere. The doctrine looks on nation and state as coequal sovereign powers. Neither the state government nor the national government should interfere in the other's sphere.

During the decades following the Civil War, the prevailing model was what political scientists have called **dual federalism**—a doctrine that emphasizes a distinction between federal and state spheres of government authority. Dual federalism is commonly depicted as a layer cake, because the state governments and the national government are viewed as separate entities, like separate layers in a cake. The national government is the top layer of the cake; the state government is the bottom layer. Nevertheless, the two layers are physically separate. They do not mix. For the most part, advocates of dual federalism believed that the state and national governments should not exercise authority in the same areas.

A Return to Normal Conditions.
The doctrine of dual federalism represented a revival of states' rights following the expansion of national authority during the Civil War. Dual federalism, after all, was a fairly accurate model of the prewar consensus on state–national relations. For many people, it therefore represented a return to normalcy. The national income tax, used to fund the war effort and the reconstruction of the South, was ended in 1872. The most significant step to reverse the wartime expansion of national power, however, took place in 1877, when President Rutherford B. Hayes withdrew the last federal troops from the South. This meant that the national government was no longer in a position to regulate state actions that affected African Americans. While the black population was now free, it was again subject to the authority of southern whites.

The Role of the Supreme Court. The Civil War crisis drastically reduced the influence of the United States Supreme Court. In the pre-war *Dred Scott* decision, the Court had attempted to abolish the power of the national government to restrict slavery in the territories.[13] In so doing, the Court placed itself on the losing side of the impending conflict. After the war, Congress took the unprecedented step of exempting the entire process of the South's reconstruction from judicial review. The Court had little choice but to acquiesce.

In time, the Supreme Court reestablished itself as the legitimate constitutional interpreter. Its decisions tended to support dual federalism, defend states' rights, and limit the powers of the national government. In 1895, for example, the Court ruled that a national income tax was unconstitutional.[14] In subsequent years, the Court gradually backed away from this decision and eventually might have overturned it. In 1913, however, the Sixteenth Amendment explicitly authorized a national income tax.

For the Court, dual federalism meant that the national government could intervene in state activities through grants and subsidies, but for the most part, it was barred from regulating matters that the Court considered to be purely local. The Court generally limited the exercise of police power to the states. In 1918, the Court ruled that a 1916 national law banning child labor was unconstitutional because it attempted to regulate a local problem.[15] In effect, the Court placed severe limits on the ability of Congress to legislate under the commerce clause of the Constitution.

© Bettmann/CORBIS

President Franklin Delano Roosevelt (served 1933–1945). Roosevelt's national approach to addressing the effects of the Great Depression was overwhelmingly popular, although many of his specific initiatives were controversial. How did the Great Depression change the political beliefs of many ordinary Americans?

The New Deal and Cooperative Federalism

The doctrine of dual federalism receded into the background in the 1930s as the nation attempted to deal with the Great Depression. President Franklin D. Roosevelt was inaugurated on March 4, 1933. In the previous year, nearly 1,500 banks had failed (and 4,000 more would fail in 1933). Thirty-two thousand businesses had closed down, and almost one-fourth of the labor force was unemployed. The public expected the national government to do something about the disastrous state of the economy. But for the first three years of the Great Depression (1930–1932), the national government did very little.

The "New Deal." President Herbert Hoover (served 1929–1933) clung to the doctrine of dual federalism and insisted that unemployment and poverty were local issues. The states, not the national government, had the sole responsibility for combating the effects of unemployment and providing relief to the poor. Roosevelt, however, did not feel bound by this doctrine, and his new Democratic administration energetically intervened in the economy. Roosevelt's "New Deal" included large-scale emergency antipoverty programs. In addition, the New Deal introduced major new laws regulating economic activity, such as the National Industrial Recovery Act of 1933, which established the National Recovery

---

13. *Dred Scott v. Sanford*, 19 Howard 393 (1857).
14. *Pollock v. Farmers' Loan & Trust Co.*, 157 U.S. 429 (1895); *Pollock v. Farmers' Loan & Trust Co.*, 158 U.S. 601 (1895).
15. *Hammer v. Dagenhart*, 247 U.S. 251 (1918). This decision was overruled in *United States v. Darby*, 312 U.S. 100 (1940).

Administration (NRA). The NRA, initially the centerpiece of the New Deal, provided codes for every industry to restrict competition and regulate labor relations.

The End of Dual Federalism. Roosevelt's expansion of national authority was challenged by the Supreme Court, which continued to adhere to the doctrine of dual federalism. In 1935, the Court ruled that the NRA program was unconstitutional.[16] The NRA had turned out to be largely unworkable and was unpopular. The Court, however, rejected the program on the ground that it regulated intrastate, not interstate, commerce. This position appeared to rule out any alternative recovery plans that might be better designed. Subsequently, the Court struck down the Agricultural Adjustment Act, the Bituminous Coal Act, a railroad retirement plan, legislation to protect farm mortgages, and a municipal bankruptcy act.

In 1937, Roosevelt proposed legislation that would allow him to add up to six new justices to the Supreme Court. Presumably, the new justices would be more amenable to the exercise of national power than were the existing members. Roosevelt's move was widely seen as an assault on the Constitution. Congressional Democrats refused to support the measure, and it failed. Nevertheless, the "court-packing scheme" had its intended effect. Although the membership of the Court did not change, after 1937 the Court ceased its attempts to limit the national government's powers under the commerce clause. For the next half-century, the commerce clause would provide Congress with an unlimited justification for regulating the economic life of the country.

Cooperative Federalism. Some political scientists have described the era since 1937 as characterized by **cooperative federalism**, in which the states and the national government cooperate to solve complex common problems. Roosevelt's New Deal programs, for example, often involved joint action between the national government and the states. The pattern of national–state relationships during these years created a new metaphor for federalism—that of a marble cake. Unlike a layer cake, in a marble cake the two types of cake are intermingled, and any bite contains cake of both flavors. Cooperative federalism in practice often meant that the federal government provided the funding and set the terms for a policy solution at the national level, but left implementation to the states. Examples of this arrangement might include Aid to Families with Dependent Children (AFDC), a form of financial assistance to families in effect from 1935 to 1996, funded by the federal government but administered by the states. Another example might be the interstate highway system. A series of national laws beginning in 1916 provided coordination and funding to establish the vast network of interconnected highways that allow citizens to travel freely and efficiently throughout the country. Interstate highways and their rights of way are owned by the state in which they were built and maintenance is the responsibility of the state department of transportation.

Cooperative Federalism
The theory that the states and the national government should cooperate in solving problems.

did you know?
The Morrill Act of 1862, providing for land grants to states to create public institutions of higher education, was the first example of the federal government providing grants to the states.

Methods of Implementing Cooperative Federalism

Even before the Constitution was adopted, the national government gave grants to the states in the form of land to finance education. The national government also provided land grants for canals, railroads, and roads. In the 20th century, federal grants increased significantly, especially during Roosevelt's administration during the Great Depression and again during the 1960s, when the dollar amount

16. *Schechter Poultry Corp. v. United States*, 295 U.S. 495 (1935).

of grants quadrupled. These funds were used for improvements in education, pollution control, recreation, and highways. With this increase in grants, however, came a bewildering number of restrictions and regulations. In the aggregate today, states depend on federal funding for over 35 percent of their income.

Categorical Grants. Before the 1960s, most **categorical grants** by the national government were formula grants. These grants take their name from the method used to allocate funds. They fund state programs using a formula based on such variables as the state's needs, population, or willingness to come up with matching funds. Beginning in the 1960s, the national government began increasingly to offer program grants. This funding requires states to apply for grants for specific programs. The applications are evaluated by the national government, and the applications may compete with one another. Program grants give the national government a much greater degree of control over state activities than formula grants.

> **Categorical Grants**
> Federal grants to states or local governments that are for specific programs or projects.

By 1985, categorical grants amounted to more than $100 billion per year. They were spread out across 400 separate programs, but the largest five accounted for more than 50 percent of the revenues spent. These five programs involved Medicaid (health care for the poor), highway construction, unemployment benefits, housing assistance, and welfare programs to assist mothers with dependent children and people with disabilities. In fiscal year 2011, the federal government provided $607 billion in grants to state and local governments. Those funds accounted for 17 percent of federal outlays, 4 percent of gross domestic product (GDP), and a quarter of spending by state and local governments that year.[17]

Why have federal grants to the states increased so much? One reason is that Congress has devolved control of some programs to the states while continuing to provide a major part of the funding for them. This allows states to customize implementation of national programs, thereby increasing the overall effectiveness and improving economic efficiencies. Also, Congress continues to use grants as an incentive to persuade states and cities to adopt and operate programs reflecting federal policy priorities. For example, following the September 11, 2001 terrorist attacks, the federal government created new grants to support state and urban security strategies. In 2013, the federal government transferred over $350 million dollars to states to "to address the identified planning, organization, equipment, training, and exercise needs to prevent, protect against, mitigate, respond to, and recover from acts of terrorism and other catastrophic events."[18] Other grants use the broad federal tax base to redistribute resources among communities and individuals. Finally, grants can help foster policy experimentation at the state and local levels that might be lost in a single national program.

Feeling the Pressure—The Strings Attached to Federal Grants. No dollars sent to the states are completely free of strings, however; all funds come with requirements that must be met by the states. Often, through the use of grants, the national government has been able to exercise substantial control over matters that traditionally have been under the purview of state governments. When the federal government gives federal funds for highway improvements, for example, it may condition the funds on the state's cooperation with a federal policy. This is exactly what the federal government did in the 1980s and 1990s to force the states to raise their minimum drinking age to 21.

---

17. Congressional Budget Office, "Federal Grants to State and Local Governments," Report. March 5, 2013.
18. Homeland Security Grant Program, Federal Emergency Management Agency. Accessed at www.fema.gov/fy-2013-homeland-security-grant-program-hsgp-0.

Such carrot-and-stick tactics inevitably include some kind of consequence if a state does not agree to the entire bargain. For example, the No Child Left Behind (NCLB) Act promised billions of dollars to the states to bolster their education budgets. The funds would only be delivered, however, if states agreed to hold schools accountable to new federal achievement benchmarks on standardized tests designed by the federal government.

Block Grants. **Block grants** lessen the restrictions on federal grants given to state and local governments by grouping several categorical grants under one broad heading. Governors and mayors generally prefer block grants because such grants give the states more flexibility in how the money is spent.

One major set of block grants provides aid to state welfare programs. The Personal Responsibility and Work Opportunity Reconciliation Act of 1996 ended the AFDC program. The Temporary Assistance for Needy Families (TANF) program that replaced AFDC provided a welfare block grant to each state. Each grant has an annual cap. According to some, this is one of the most successful block grant programs. Although state governments prefer block grants, Congress generally favors categorical grants, because the expenditures can be targeted according to congressional priorities.

Federal Mandates. For years, the federal government has passed legislation requiring that states act to achieve particular national goals—improve environmental conditions and the civil rights of certain groups, for example. Since the 1970s, the national government has enacted literally hundreds of **federal mandates** requiring the states to take some action in areas ranging from the way voters are registered, to ocean-dumping restrictions, to the education of persons with disabilities. The Unfunded Mandates Reform Act of 1995 requires the Congressional Budget Office to identify mandates that cost state and local governments more than $50 million to implement. The Congressional Budget Office (CBO) is tasked with estimating the cost of mandates that would apply to state, local, and tribal governments or to the private sector. Their reports demonstrate that public laws generally contain fewer intergovernmental mandates than private-sector mandates. The National Conference of State Legislatures (NCSL) also closely monitors federal mandates.

One way in which the national government has moderated the burden of federal mandates is by granting *waivers*, which allow individual states to try out innovative approaches to carrying out the mandates. For example, Oregon received a waiver to experiment with a new method of rationing health care services under the federally mandated Medicaid program.

The Politics of Federalism

The allocation of powers between the national and state governments continues to be a major issue. The devastation caused by Hurricane Katrina in Louisiana unleashed a heated debate about federalism, as Americans disagreed on which level of government should be held accountable for inadequate preparations and the failures in providing aid afterward. Some 1,300 people died as a result of the storm, while property damage totaled tens of billions of dollars. Many Americans felt that the federal government's response to Katrina was woefully inadequate. Much of their criticism centered on the failures of the Federal Emergency Management Agency (FEMA) in the aftermath of Katrina.

Block Grants
Federal programs that provide funds to state and local governments for general functional areas, such as criminal justice or mental health programs.

Federal Mandates
Requirements in federal legislation that force states and municipalities to comply with certain rules.

did you know?

State government spending in fiscal year 2012 exceeded $1.4 trillion, the majority of which will be directed to five areas: education (38 percent), health care (16 percent), transportation (5 percent), prisons (5 percent), and assistance to the poor (1 percent).

FEMA, the government agency responsible for coordinating disaster preparedness and relief efforts, was disorganized and slow to respond in the days following the storm. On their arrival in the Gulf Coast, FEMA officials often acted counterproductively—on some occasions denying the delivery of storm aid that their agency had not authorized. Some claimed that state and local politicians—including Louisiana Governor Kathleen Blanco and New Orleans Mayor Ray Nagin—were not adequately prepared for the storm. Local officials knew the region and its residents best, yet they failed to make proper provisions for evacuating vulnerable residents.

Although the loss of life and damage to property was significantly lower, Hurricane Sandy confronted major coastal cities in the Northeast and the federal government with the same challenges in the week leading up to the 2012 national election. Storm surge flooded New York City streets, tunnels, and subway lines and cut power in and around the city. New Jersey sustained major damage to its coastal cities and beach communities. Damage amounted to $65 billion. The powerful late-season storm ignited political debate over the storm's link to climate change. Congress ultimately authorized nearly $60 billion in emergency relief for the affected states, but not without heated debate over the role and responsibilities of government related to weather disasters. The New York and New Jersey Port Authority Tweeted updates throughout the storm, to keep residents up to date on the latest news, but despite the instantaneous nature of social media, residents who depended on such sources of news were often too late to act after seeing images of current devastation.

Port Authority NY&NJ/Twitter

Does seeing a more personal side to candidates via their websites or social media accounts make you more likely to vote for them?

What Has National Authority Accomplished?

Generally speaking, conservatives have favored the states and liberals have favored the national government. One reason is that throughout American history, the expansion of national authority has typically been an engine of social change.

Leonard Zhukovsky/Shutterstock.com

Destroyed beach houses in the aftermath of Hurricane Sandy on November 11, 2012 in Far Rockaway, New York. Politicians debated whether this late-season storm was a result of climate change, but ultimately Congress approved more than $60 billion in emergency relief for the region.

Far more than the states, the national government has been willing to alter the status quo. The expansion of national authority during the Civil War freed the slaves—a major social revolution. During the New Deal, the expansion of national authority meant unprecedented levels of government intervention in the economy. In both the Civil War and New Deal eras, support for states' rights was a method of opposing these changes and supporting the status quo.

Civil Rights and the War on Poverty. Another example of the use of national power to change society was the presidency of Lyndon B. Johnson (1963–1969). Johnson oversaw the greatest expansion of national authority since the New Deal. Under Johnson, a series of civil rights acts forced the states to grant African Americans equal treatment under the law. Crucially, these acts included the abolition of all measures designed to prevent African Americans from voting. Johnson's Great Society and War on Poverty programs resulted in major increases in spending by the national government. As before, states' rights were invoked to support the status quo—states' rights meant no action on civil rights and no increase in anti-poverty spending.

Why Would the States Favor the Status Quo? When state governments have authority in a particular field, great variations may occur from state to state in how the issues are handled. Inevitably, some states will be more conservative than others. Therefore, bringing national authority to bear on a particular issue may impose national standards on states that, for whatever reason, have not adopted such standards. One example is the voting rights legislation passed under President Johnson. By the 1960s, there was a national consensus that all citizens, regardless of race, should have the right to vote. A majority of the white electorate in former Confederate states, however, did not share this view. National legislation was necessary to impose the national consensus on the recalcitrant states.

Another factor that may make the states more receptive to limited government, especially on economic issues, is competition among the states. It is widely believed that major corporations are more likely to establish new operations in states with a "favorable business climate." Such a climate may mean low taxes and therefore relatively more limited social services. If states compete with one another to offer the best business climate, the competition may force down taxes all around. Competition of this type also may dissuade states from implementing environmental regulations that restrict certain business activities. Those who deplore the effect of such competition often refer to it as a "race to the bottom." National legislation, in contrast, is not constrained by interstate competition.

A final factor that may encourage the states to favor the status quo is the relative power of local economic interests. A large corporation in a small state, for example, may have a substantial amount of political influence. These local economic interests may have less influence at the national level. This observation echoes Madison's point in Federalist #10 (see Appendix C of this text). Madison argued that a large federal republic would be less subject to the danger of factions than a small state.

At times, states can be seen pushing the national agenda along—often in progressive directions. Two examples are same-sex marriage and decriminalizing marijuana. The Controlled Substance Act passed by Congress in 1970 makes growing, possessing, and selling marijuana illegal. Sixteen states, however, have passed laws decriminalizing marijuana. Typically, decriminalization means no prison time or criminal record for first-time possession of a small amount for personal consumption. The conduct is treated like a minor traffic violation. Twenty states plus the District of Columbia have enacted laws that allow people to use medical marijuana with a doctor's recommendation. Two of those states (Colorado and Washington) have legalized marijuana for recreational use. All of these state actions remain illegal under the Controlled Substance Act, yet the Department of Justice has elected to allow states significant leeway in this area as long as they effectively enforce their own regulations and minors are protected. States are also flexing their muscles relative to the federal regulations promulgated under the commerce clause. The Montana Firearms Freedom Act, for example declares that guns that are manufactured in Montana and remain within the state are not subject to federal regulations, including registration requirements. Other states have adopted "light bulb freedom" laws that would allow the intrastate manufacture and sale of incandescent bulbs contrary to the federal law requiring a switch to compact fluorescent bulbs. Fox News covered this topic regularly in its nightly news segments.

Federalism Becomes a Partisan Issue

The **devolution** of power from the national government to the states has become a major ideological theme for the Republican Party. Republicans believe that the increased size and scope of the federal government—which began with the New Deal programs of Franklin Roosevelt and continued unabated through Lyndon Johnson's Great Society programs and beyond—pose a threat to individual liberty and to the power of the states. As the Republicans became more conservative in their views regarding the extent of national government power, Democrats have become more liberal and supportive of that power.

The "New Federalism." The architects of Lyndon Johnson's War on Poverty were reluctant to let state governments have a role in the new programs. This reluctance was a response to the resistance of many southern states to African

Devolution
The transfer of powers from a national or central government to a state or local government.

Nick Anderson/The Cartoonist Group
cartoonistgroup.com

Cartoonist Nick Anderson succinctly captures the inherent political tensions involved in the federal system.

American civil rights. The Johnson administration did not trust the states to administer antipoverty programs in an impartial and efficient manner.

Republican president Richard Nixon (served 1969–1974), who succeeded Johnson in office, saw political opportunity in the Democrats' suspicion of state governments. Nixon advocated what he called a "New Federalism" that would devolve authority from the national government to the states. In part, the New Federalism involved the conversion of categorical grants into block grants, thereby giving state governments greater flexibility in spending. A second part of Nixon's New Federalism was revenue sharing. Under the revenue-sharing plan, the national government provided direct, unconditional financial support to state and local governments.

Republican President Ronald Reagan was also a strong advocate of new federalism, but some of his policies withdrew certain financial support from the states. Reagan was more successful than Nixon in obtaining block grants, but Reagan's block grants, unlike Nixon's, were less generous to the states than the categorical grants they replaced. Under Reagan, revenue sharing was eliminated.

New Judicial Federalism. In cases where a state's constitution may provide more civil rights and liberties than the minimum standard found in the U.S. Constitution, the U.S. Supreme Court has permitted state judges to base their rulings on their state constitution in a practice known as **new judicial federalism**. It reflects a dual-federalism perspective in that states are, if not coequal sovereigns with the federal government, at least sovereign within their own constitutional spheres. This tradition is attributed to Justice William Brennan's call for state courts to step into the breach left by the U.S. Supreme Court's allegedly unsatisfactory protection of individual rights and civil liberties. Scholars have noted the application of this form of federalism in state court rulings on constitutionality of same-sex marriage laws.

New Judicial Federalism
The increased reliance of state courts of last resort on state constitutions rather than on the federal Constitution for the protection of individual rights.

Federalism in the Twenty-First Century. Today, federalism (in the sense of limited national authority) continues to be an important element in conservative ideology. At this point, however, it is not clear whether competing theories of federalism truly divide the Republicans from the Democrats in practice. Consider that under Democratic president Bill Clinton (served 1993–2001), Congress replaced AFDC with the TANF block grants. This change was part of the Welfare Reform Act of 1996, which was perhaps the most significant domestic policy initiative of Clinton's administration. In contrast, a major domestic initiative of Republican president George W. Bush was increased federal funding and control of education—long a preserve of state and local governments. The Affordable Care Act, as the policy was originally designed, included a significant role for states to create and operate health exchanges to enroll individuals in a variety of health insurance options.

Also, in some circumstances, liberals today may benefit from states' rights understood as policy innovation opportunities. States have been incubators for sustainability and green energy initiatives, states primarily in the West have been leaders in developing death with dignity or assisted suicide laws, while still others have legalized marijuana.

Conservatives today also remain active in limiting the scope of federal power. One example is opposition to the Affordable Care Act, particularly the expansion of coverage under Medicaid and the mandate for coverage. The Tea Party emerged in part as a reaction to increased government spending at the start of the 2008 recession.

Federalism and the Supreme Court Today

The United States Supreme Court, which normally has the final say on constitutional issues, necessarily plays a significant role in determining the line between federal and state powers. Consider the decisions rendered by Chief Justice Marshall in the cases discussed earlier. Since the 1930s, Marshall's broad interpretation of the commerce clause has made it possible for the national government to justify its regulation of virtually any activity, even when an activity would appear to be purely local in character.

Since the 1990s, however, the Supreme Court has been gradually tailoring the national government's powers under the commerce clause. The Court also has given increased emphasis to state powers under the Tenth and Eleventh Amendments to the Constitution. At the same time, other recent rulings have sent contradictory messages with regard to states' rights and the federal government's power.

Reining In the Commerce Power

In a widely publicized 1995 case, *United States v. Lopez*, the Supreme Court held that Congress had exceeded its constitutional authority under the commerce clause when it passed the Gun-Free School Zones Act in 1990.[19] The Court stated that the act, which banned the possession of guns within 1,000 feet of any school, was unconstitutional because it attempted to regulate an area that had "nothing to do with commerce, or any sort of economic enterprise." This marked the first time in 60 years that the Supreme Court had placed a limit on the national government's authority under the commerce clause.

In 2000, in *United States v. Morrison*, the Court held that Congress had overreached its authority under the commerce clause when it passed the Violence against Women Act in 1994.[20] The Court invalidated a key section of the act that provided a federal remedy for gender-motivated violence, such as rape. The Court noted that in enacting this law, Congress had extensively documented that violence against women had an adverse "aggregate" effect on interstate commerce: It deterred potential victims from traveling, from engaging in employment, and from transacting business in interstate commerce. It also diminished national productivity and increased medical and other costs. Nonetheless, the Court held that evidence of an aggregate effect on commerce was not enough to justify national regulation of noneconomic, violent criminal conduct.

One of the central questions in the 2012 challenge to the Affordable Care Act also concerns the commerce power. The most controversial provision of the law, known as the individual mandate, requires individuals to have health insurance either through an employer or by purchasing it through the market. The federal government has argued that Congress is authorized to enact the individual mandate under two provisions of Article I, Section 8, of the U.S. Constitution—its power to regulate commerce and its power to tax. The government argues that health care falls under the heading of commerce because the health care law addresses a pressing national problem that is economic in nature. Opponents of the law say that the requirement to buy a product or service is unprecedented, regulates inactivity rather than activity, and opens the door to allowing Congress unlimited power to intrude on individual freedom. In the decision issued on June 28, 2012, the Supreme Court upheld the law but did so under Congress's

---

19. 514 U.S. 549 (1995).
20. 529 U.S. 598 (2000).

taxing authority and not the commerce clause. Chief Justice Roberts, writing for the 5-4 majority, said the individual mandate "cannot be upheld as an exercise of Congress's power under the commerce clause," which allows Congress to regulate interstate commerce but "not to order individuals to engage in it." He continued, "In this case, however, it is reasonable to construe what Congress has done as increasing taxes on those who have a certain amount of income, but choose to go without health insurance. Such legislation is within Congress's power to tax."[21]

State Sovereignty and the Eleventh Amendment

In recent years, the Supreme Court has issued a series of decisions that bolstered the authority of state governments under the Eleventh Amendment to the Constitution. As interpreted by the Court, that amendment in most circumstances precludes lawsuits against state governments for violations of rights established by federal laws unless the states consent to be sued. For example, in a 1999 case, *Alden v. Maine*, the Court held that Maine state employees could not sue the state for violating the overtime pay requirements of a federal act.[22] According to the Court, state immunity from such lawsuits "is a fundamental aspect of the sovereignty which [the states] enjoyed before the ratification of the Constitution, and which they retain today."

In 2000, in *Kimel v. Florida Board of Regents*, the Court held that the Eleventh Amendment precluded employees of a state university from suing the state to enforce a federal statute prohibiting age-based discrimination.[23] In 2003, however, in *Nevada v. Hibbs*, the Court ruled that state employers must abide by the federal Family and Medical Leave Act (FMLA).[24] The reasoning was that the FMLA seeks to outlaw gender bias, and government actions that may discriminate on the basis of gender must receive a "heightened review status" compared with actions that may discriminate on the basis of age or disability. Also, in 2004, the Court ruled that the Eleventh Amendment could not shield states from suits by individuals with disabilities who had been denied access to courtrooms located on the upper floors of buildings.[25]

Tenth Amendment Issues

The Tenth Amendment states: "The powers not delegated to the United States by the Constitution, nor prohibited by it to the States, are reserved to the States respectively, or to the people." In 1992, the Court held that requirements imposed on the state of New York under a federal act regulating low-level radioactive waste were inconsistent with the Tenth Amendment and thus unconstitutional. According to the Court, the act's "take title" provision, which required states to accept ownership of waste or regulate waste following Congress's instructions, exceeded the enumerated powers of Congress. Although Congress can regulate the handling of such waste, "it may not conscript state governments as its agents" in an attempt to enforce a program of federal regulation.[26]

In 1997, the Court revisited this Tenth Amendment issue. In *Printz v. United States*, the Court struck down the provisions of the federal Brady Handgun

21. Robert Barnes, "Supreme Court upholds Obama's health-care law," *The Washington Post*, published June 28, 2012. Accessed at www.washingtonpost.com/politics/supreme-court-to-rule-thursday-on-health-care-law/2012/06/28/gJQAarRm8V_story.htm
22. 527 U.S. 706 (1999).
23. 528 U.S. 62 (2000).
24. 538 U.S. 721 (2003).
25. *Tennessee v. Lane*, 541 U.S. 509 (2004).
26. *New York v. United States*, 505 U.S. 144 (1992).

Violence Prevention Act of 1993 that required state employees to check the backgrounds of prospective handgun purchasers.[27] Said the Court:

> [T]he federal government may neither issue directives requiring the States to address particular problems, nor command the States' officers, or those of their political subdivisions, to administer or enforce a federal regulatory program.

Other Federalism Cases

■ **LO3.5:** Evaluate immigration policy as a challenge to modern federalism.

In recent years, the Supreme Court has sent mixed messages in federalism cases. At times the Court has favored states' rights, whereas on other occasions it has backed the federal government's position.

The Supreme Court argued in 2005 that the federal government's power to seize and destroy illegal drugs trumped California's law legalizing the use of marijuana for medical treatment.[28] Yet, less than a year later, the Court favored states' rights in another case rife with federalism issues, *Gonzales v. Oregon*.[29] After a lengthy legal battle, the Court upheld Oregon's controversial "Death with Dignity" law, which allows patients with terminal illnesses to choose to end their lives early and thus alleviate suffering. More recently the Court was presented with the issue of immigration. Control of the country's borders would normally fall within the federal government's jurisdiction; however, the state of Arizona argued that the federal government was not doing enough to control illegal immigration and adopted a controversial new law in 2010. When the Court ruled on the constitutionality of the law in 2012, justices said that a state cannot act to undermine federal authority in immigration law and sided with the administration.

The federal government has provided states with financial resources through direct transfer and various forms of grants-in-aid that have enabled states to experiment with innovative solutions to problems and to address the needs of each state's residents. However, as the global recession continues to erode the financial viability of states and the federal government has fewer resources to share, how will federalism fare? If the federal government has fewer "carrots" in the form of financial incentives for state policy behavior, will it resort to "sticks" in the form of more unfunded mandates with stiff penalties for noncompliance? How will the arguments over the best way to provide all citizens with access to affordable health care shape the relationship between the federal government and the states?

did you know?

About 63 percent of undocumented immigrants have been living in the United States for 10 years or longer.

---

27. 521 U.S. 898 (1997).
28. *Gonzales v. Raich*, 545 U.S. 1 (2005).
29. 546 U.S. 243 (2006).

What Would You Do?

Federalism and State Immigration Policy

Until very recently, immigration policy was widely viewed as falling within the purview of the federal government. Regulating the border would also seem to fall to the federal government because it involves more than one state as well as the United States. Citing inaction or ineffective action by the federal government, however, six states have enacted their own immigration laws that are more restrictive than federal statute requires (as indicated in red and orange on the map).

U.S. federal law requires all immigrants over the age of 14 who remain in the United States for more than 30 days to register with the U.S. government and to have registration documents in their possession at all times. In 2010, Arizona adopted a more restrictive law that makes it a misdemeanor crime for an immigrant to be in Arizona without required documents. The law also requires state law enforcement personnel to attempt to determine an individual's immigration status during a stop, detention, or arrest when "reasonable suspicion" exists that the individual is an illegal immigrant. State and local officials are prohibited from restricting enforcement of immigration law and

stiff penalties are imposed on anyone found to be sheltering, hiring, or transporting illegal immigrants. This approach has been labeled "attrition through enforcement."

On June 25, 2012, the U.S. Supreme Court issued a split decision, upholding part of the Arizona law and rejecting other provisions on the grounds that they interfered with the federal government's role in setting immigration policy. The court unanimously affirmed the law's requirement that police check the immigration status of people they detain and suspect to be in the country illegally, emphasizing that state law enforcement officials already possessed the discretion to ask about immigration status. The same ruling, however, rejected parts of the Arizona law that it said undermine federal law. Justice Anthony Kennedy, writing for the majority, also indicated that the court would entertain future challenges to the "show me your papers" provision if there is evidence of illegal racial or ethnic profiling after the law is implemented.

At the federal level, the Obama administration has seemingly adopted contradictory approaches to unauthorized

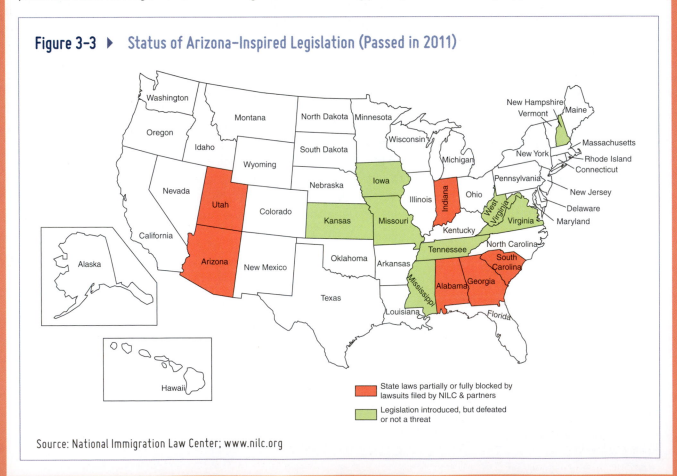

Figure 3-3 ▶ **Status of Arizona–Inspired Legislation (Passed in 2011)**

State laws partially or fully blocked by lawsuits filed by NILC & partners

Legislation introduced, but defeated or not a threat

Source: National Immigration Law Center; www.nilc.org

immigrants. In 2013, the Deferred Action for Childhood Arrivals program was created to halt deportation of young people brought to the United States by their parents when they were minors (under 16) and who meet certain criteria (have lived in the U.S. continuously, are enrolled in school or have graduated from high school, have not been convicted of a felony, and are younger than 30 years old). Nevertheless, the Obama administration has deported more unauthorized immigrants annually than did the George W. Bush administration. President Obama has defended his administration's actions by saying that his hands are tied by the law. Until Congress produces effective immigration reform, deportations must continue. However, under pressure from the Latino community as 2014 mid-term elections neared, the president directed Homeland Security Secretary Jeh Johnson to review America's deportation program, with an eye toward finding more humane ways to enforce the law without contravening it.

Why Should You Care?

Civil rights groups claim that the Arizona law and others like it will promote a form of "racial profiling"—the arrest and detention of individuals just because they look like foreigners. In Alabama, for example, state officials were embarrassed when foreign executives from Mercedes-Benz and Honda were stopped and detained in two separate incidents. The laws have a "chilling effect" on immigrant populations, even among those who are here legally or have become naturalized citizens. Farmers in Georgia and Alabama report that the new immigration laws are depriving them of a stable and experienced workforce, resulting in spoiled crops and higher food prices. Employers and public schools including colleges and universities are now required to document lawful presence for all employees and students. For the first time since the Depression, more Mexicans are leaving the United States than entering it. While illegal immigration causes problems in society, legal immigration is an important positive force for dynamic social and economic change in the country.

What Would You Do?

If you were the governor of a state with a significant population of unauthorized immigrants, would you move to enact state policies or would you rely on the federal government to enact national immigration reform?

What You *Can* Do

Research the immigration policies of your state. Investigate the policies in place on your own campus regarding undocumented immigrants. Think carefully about the implications of policies that promote "attrition by enforcement" for your daily life and for those around you. Will you or someone you know be more likely to be stopped or questioned by law enforcement officials as a result of these laws? Will you be required to provide identity documentation—recall our earlier discussion of opposition to REAL ID Act? Think carefully about how immigration policies relate to building diverse societies and to the value of tolerance on your own campus. Is this another force contributing to the creation of two Americas? Regardless of which side of this issue you may find yourself on, organizations can provide information and a way for you to get involved.

To find a local immigration reform organization, contact FAIR, the Federation for American Immigration Reform (www.fairus.org/action/local-group).

To learn about national legislative initiatives on immigration, contact the Immigration Policy Center (www.immigrationpolicy.org/issues/reform).

To learn about state laws regarding immigration, visit the National Council of State Legislatures Immigration Resource page (www.ncsl.org/research/immigration.aspx).

Purestock/Getty Images

Key Terms

block grants 92	**devolution** 95	**federal mandate** 92	**police power** 79
categorical grants 91	**dual federalism** 88	**full faith and credit clause** 81	**privileges and immunities** 82
commerce clause 85	**elastic clause, or necessary and proper clause** 78		
concurrent powers 80		**horizontal control** 81	**supremacy clause** 80
confederal system 72	**extradite** 82	**interstate compact** 82	**unitary system** 72
cooperative federalism 90	**federalism** 71	**new judicial federalism** 96	**vertical control** 81

Chapter Summary

■ **LO3.1:** There are three basic models for ordering relations between central governments and local units: (1) a unitary system (in which ultimate power is held by the national government), (2) a confederal system (in which ultimate power is retained by the states), and (3) a federal system (in which governmental powers are divided between the national government and the states).

■ **LO3.2:** Among the advantages of federalism are that distributed decision making is effective in large geographic areas, it promotes the development and sustainability of many subcultures within the states, it allows states to serve as incubators for new policies and processes, and it limits the influence of any one group or set of interests. Among the disadvantages of federalism are that powerful states or states controlled by minority interests can limit progress or undermine the rights of minority groups. Federalism also results in inequities across states in terms of policies and spending on services like education or crime prevention.

■ **LO3.3:** The Constitution expressly delegated certain powers to the national government in Article I, Section 8. In addition to these expressed powers, the national government has implied and inherent powers. Implied powers are those that are reasonably necessary to carry out the powers expressly delegated to the national government. Inherent powers are those held by the national government by virtue of its being a sovereign state with the right to preserve itself. The supremacy clause of the Constitution states that the Constitution, congressional laws, and national treaties are the supreme law of the land. States cannot use their reserved or concurrent powers to override national policies. Vertical checks and balances allow states to influence the national government and vice versa. Horizontal checks and balances provide another form of check and balance in that governments on the same level—either state or national—may check one another.

■ **LO3.3:** The Tenth Amendment to the Constitution states that powers not delegated to the United States by the Constitution, nor prohibited by it to the states, are reserved to the states, or to the people. In certain areas, the Constitution provides for concurrent powers, such as the power to tax, which are powers that are held jointly by the national and state governments. The Constitution also denies certain powers to both the national government and the states.

■ **LO3.4:** Two landmark Supreme Court cases expanded the constitutional powers of the national government. Chief Justice John Marshall's expansive interpretation of the necessary and proper clause of the Constitution in *McCulloch v. Maryland* (1819) permitted the "necessary and proper" clause to be used to enhance the power of the national government. Additionally, his decision made it clear that no state could tax a national institution. Marshall's broad interpretation of the commerce clause in *Gibbons v. Ogden* (1824) further extended the constitutional regulatory powers of the national government.

■ **LO3.4:** The controversy over slavery that led to the Civil War took the form of a fight over national government supremacy versus the rights of the separate states. Ultimately, the South's desire for increased states' rights and the subsequent Civil War resulted in an increase in the political power of the national government.

■ **LO3.4:** Since the Civil War, federalism has evolved through at least two general phases: dual federalism and cooperative federalism. In dual federalism, each of the states and the federal government remain supreme within their own spheres. The era since the Great Depression has sometimes been labeled one of cooperative federalism, in which states and the national government cooperate in solving complex common problems.

■ **LO3.4, LO3.5:** The United States Supreme Court plays a significant role in determining the line between state and federal powers. Since the 1990s, the Court has been nipping at the national government's powers under the commerce clause and has given increased emphasis to state powers under the Tenth and Eleventh Amendments to the Constitution. New challenges to the balance of power between the federal and state governments come from the prolonged economic recession that has limited the federal government's ability to transfer funds to states to promote policy innovation and from controversial social issues on which public opinion varies widely by state, including same-sex marriage, medical marijuana, and immigration policy.

Selected Print, Media, and Online Resources

PRINT RESOURCES

Hamilton, Alexander, James Madison and John Jay. *The Federalist Papers.* Clinton Rossiter, Editor. Signet Classics, 2003. These essays remain an authoritative exposition of the founders' views on federalism.

Manna, Paul. *School's In: Federalism and the National Education Agenda.* Washington, DC: Georgetown University Press, 2006. The author examines the changing relationship between the federal government and the states with regard to our public education system.

Nugent, John D. *Safeguarding Federalism: How States Protect Their Interests in National Policymaking.* Norman, OK: University of Oklahoma Press, 2009. Tracing the history of federalism, the author proposes that federalism is a vital force in American politics. He shows how the states protect their interest in policy innovation through a number of tactics, including influencing federal legislation.

MEDIA RESOURCES

City of Hope—A 1991 movie by John Sayles. The film is a story of life, work, race, and politics in a modern New Jersey city. An African American alderman is one of the several major characters.

The Civil War—The PBS documentary series that made director Ken Burns famous. First shown in 1990, it marked a revolution in documentary technique. Photographs, letters, eyewitness memoirs, and music are used to bring the war to life. The DVD version was released in 2002.

McCulloch v. Maryland and Gibbons v. Ogden—These programs are part of the series *Equal Justice under Law: Landmark Cases in Supreme Court History.* They provide more details on cases that defined our federal system.

The Wire—An HBO series set in Baltimore, Maryland highlighting issues of state and local collaboration and competition when addressing the illegal drug trade.

When the Levees Broke: A Requiem in Four Acts—A 2006 documentary by Spike Lee that critically examines the federal, state, and local government response to Hurricane Katrina.

ONLINE RESOURCES

Brookings—policy analyses and recommendations on a variety of issues, including federalism: www.brookings.edu

Catalog of Federal Domestic Assistance—complete listing of the federal grants that may be distributed to states and local governments: www.cfda.gov

Cato Institute—a libertarian approach to issues relating to federalism: www.cato.org

The Constitution Society—links to U.S. state constitutions, the *Federalist Papers*, and international federations, such as the European Union: www.constitution.org

Council of State Governments—information on state responses to federalism issues: www.csg.org

Emory University Law School—access to the *Federalist Papers*—the founders' views on federalism—and other historical documents: http://els449.law.emory.edu/index.php?id=3130

National Council of State Legislatures—research and resources on issues important to states: http://www.ncsl.org/

National Governors Association—information on issues facing state governments and federal–state relations: www.nga.org

Master the concepts of Federalism with MindTap™ for American Government

REVIEW MindTap™ **for American Government**
Access Key Term Flashcards for Chapter 3.

STAY CURRENT MindTap™ **for American Government**
Access the KnowNow blog and customized RSS for updates on current events.

TEST YOURSELF MindTap™ **for American Government**
Take the Wrap It Up Quiz for Chapter 3.

STAY FOCUSED MindTap™ **for American Government**
Complete the Focus Activities for Federalism.

4 Civil Liberties

LEARNING OUTCOMES

After reading this chapter, students will be able to:

- **LO4.1:** Identify the protection of civil liberties in the Bill of Rights, and explain how these protections against government interference were applied to the states.

- **LO4.2:** Give examples of how the Bill of Rights protects freedom of religion while maintaining a separation between the state and religion, thereby limiting the direct influence of religion in public life.

- **LO4.3:** Locate the protections of political expression and dissent in the Constitution, and explain why freedom of expression is critical to people's participation in politics.

- **LO4.4:** Discuss the constitutional protection of privacy rights in personal and public life and evaluate the threats to privacy rights posed by technology and security interests.

- **LO4.5:** Identify the rights of the accused and discuss the role of the Supreme Court in defining criminal due process rights over time.

- **LO4.6:** Evaluate modern threats to civil liberties posed by spy technology, the transfer of personal information through social media, and heightened security concerns following the September 11, 2001 terrorist attacks.

Marchers demonstrate for jobs, peace, and housing at this Martin Luther King, Jr. holiday celebration.

© Jim West Alamy

WATCH & LEARN MindTap™ **for American Government**

Watch a brief "What Do You Know?" video summarizing Civil Liberties.

What if?

Roe v. Wade Were Overturned?

BACKGROUND

The Bill of Rights and other provisions of the U.S. Constitution are the ultimate protections of our civil rights and liberties. But how do these rights work in practice? How do we determine what our rights are in any given situation? One way is through judicial review, the power of the United States Supreme Court or other courts to declare laws and other acts of government unconstitutional. Supreme Court cases are often hotly contested, and the decision in the 1973 case *Roe v. Wade* is one of the most contentious ever handed down. In the *Roe v. Wade* case, the Court declared that a woman's constitutionally protected right to privacy includes the right to have an abortion. The Court concluded that the states cannot restrict a woman's right to an abortion during the first three months of pregnancy. Forty years later, however, the debate over the legality of abortion still rages in the United States.

WHAT IF *ROE V. WADE* WERE OVERTURNED?

If the Supreme Court overturned *Roe v. Wade*, the authority to regulate abortion would fall again to the states. Before the case, each state decided whether abortion would be legal within its borders. State legislatures made the laws that covered abortion. Some critics of the constitutional merits of *Roe v. Wade* have argued that allowing the Supreme Court to decide the legality of abortion nationwide is undemocratic because the justices are not elected officials. In contrast, if state legislatures regained the power to create abortion policy, the resulting laws would more closely reflect the majority opinion of each state's voters rather than a national consensus. Researchers find that public opinion regarding abortion has been remarkably stable since the *Roe v. Wade* ruling. Since 1975, Gallup has asked "Should abortion be legal in certain circumstances?" In 1975, 54 percent said yes—the same percentage replying in the affirmative in 2013. Most Americans do not want *Roe* overturned, but they are willing to put significant restrictions on abortion procedures.

THE POSSIBILITY OF STATE BANS ON ABORTION

Simply overturning *Roe v. Wade* would not make abortion in the United States illegal overnight. In many states, abortion rights are very popular, and the legislatures in those states would not consider measures to ban abortion or to further restrict access to abortion. Some states have laws that would protect abortion rights even if *Roe v. Wade* were overturned. Access to abortions would likely continue in the West Coast states and in much of the Northeast. In much of the South and the Midwest, however, abortion could be seriously restricted or even banned.

STATE CHALLENGES TO *ROE V. WADE*

Texas is the latest state to adopt more stringent regulations on abortion. A statute signed into law by Governor Rick Perry in 2013 includes a ban on abortion procedures at 20 weeks post-fertilization and articulates a compelling state interest to protect fetuses from pain. The law requires that a doctor who performs abortions have admitting privileges at a nearby hospital, and mandates that clinics meet the same standards as other surgical health-care facilities in the state. This last provision has cut the number of clinics providing abortion services in half, with more likely to close because they cannot meet the criteria for surgical centers under the law leaving only 6 in the state. Opposition to the bill came from some within the Texas legislature. Wendy Davis filibustered the bill in an attempt to delay a vote long enough for the legislative session to end. Governor Perry called a second special session and the bill passed. Davis is a Democratic candidate for governor in 2014.

Regardless of the composition of the Supreme Court, the primary holding in *Roe* is vulnerable due to restrictions imposed by the states. In 2013, 22 states enacted 70 restrictions on abortions, according to the Guttmacher Institute. Under the Affordable Care Act, no private insurer is required to cover abortion services except for the exceptions permissible under the Hyde Amendment, which restricts federal funding for abortions of pregnancy resulting from incest and rape.

For Critical Analysis

1. *Why do you think that abortion remains a contentious topic more than 40 years after the* Roe v. Wade *decision?*

2. *Is privacy still at the heart of current challenges to* Roe? *Why or why not?*

LISTEN & LEARN

MindTap for American Government

Access Read Speaker to listen to Chapter 4.

Civil Liberties
Those personal freedoms that are protected for all individuals. Civil liberties typically involve restraining the government's actions against individuals.

did you know?

One of the proposed initial constitutional amendments—"No State shall infringe the equal rights of conscience, nor the freedom of speech, nor of the press, nor of the right of trial by jury in criminal cases"—was never sent to the states for approval because the states' rights advocates in the first Congress defeated it.

"THE LAND OF THE FREE." Liberty and freedom are fundamental to our understanding of what it means to be an American. Up until this point, when we have talked about liberty or limited government, it has been in the context of the structure and functions of government. **Civil liberties**, on the other hand, are express limits on government's ability to interfere in our individual lives and our ability to exercise popular sovereignty. Without the ability to speak or act freely in politics—especially the ability to express dissenting ideas—we could not claim to be a democracy. Pluralism, the belief that diverse opinions and competing ideas strengthen society, applies to government as well. Because governments small and large might be tempted to quiet dissenting voices, civil liberties exist to put limits on government's power. Civil liberties also include due process considerations, particularly for those accused of a crime. In our system, we embrace the presumption of innocence and criminal due process protections seek to equalize the power of the individual accused and the government as accuser. The Fourth Amendment protection against unreasonable search and seizure is vital to everyone.

The Bill of Rights articulate many of the civil liberties limitations on the national government. These limits were later applied to prevent state government restrictions of civil liberties. Liberty and freedom are not absolute rights, however, and this chapter explores the ways in which competing liberties and competing political values are resolved by the political system—most often by the U.S. Supreme Court. Our understanding of personal freedoms evolves over time and in reaction to changes in society and the world. Terrorists significantly altered the American view of civil liberties relative to the desire for national security protections. Digital technology has expanded avenues for political expression and action, but it also subjects each of us to increased surveillance and challenges long-held notions of privacy rights.

Civil Liberties and the Bill of Rights

■ **LO4.1:** Identify the protection of civil liberties in the Bill of Rights, and explain how these protections against government interference were applied to the states.

Civil liberties are constitutionally guaranteed protections *against* government interference or abuse. The First Amendment reads "Congress shall make no law..." meaning that government's actions are restricted when it comes to free speech, religious liberties, and the press. Civil rights, addressed in the next chapter, are different. Civil rights require government to *take action* to protect individuals and their rights. Civil liberties impose limits and civil rights impose positive obligations on government. Adding the Bill of Rights was necessary to gain ratification of the Constitution in several states. Although several state constitutions contained civil liberties guarantees, the proposed federal constitution did not. Thus, the Federalists promised to take up amendments to the constitution aimed at limiting government's ability to violate individual liberty. Twelve amendments were proposed and ten were ratified as the Bill of Rights.

The Bill of Rights is relatively brief. The framers set forth broad guidelines, leaving it up to the courts to interpret these constitutional mandates and apply them to specific situations. Thus, judicial interpretations shape the true nature of the civil liberties and rights that we possess. Because judicial interpretations change over time, so do our rights. Conflicts over the meaning of such simple phrases as *freedom of religion* and *freedom of the press* remain unresolved. One important conflict was over the issue of whether the Bill of Rights limited the powers of state governments as well as those of the national government.

Extending the Bill of Rights to State Governments

Many citizens do not realize that, as originally intended, the Bill of Rights limited only the powers of the national government. At the time the Bill of Rights was ratified, the potential of state governments to curb civil liberties caused little concern. State governments were closer to home and easier to control and most state constitutions already had bills of rights. Rather, the fear was of the potential tyranny of the national government. The Bill of Rights begins with, "Congress shall make no law . . ." It says nothing about *states* making laws.

In 1833, in *Barron v. Baltimore*, the United States Supreme Court held that the Bill of Rights did not apply to state laws.[1] The issue was whether a property owner could sue the city of Baltimore for recovery of his losses under the Fifth Amendment to the Constitution. Chief Justice Marshall spoke for a united court, declaring that the Supreme Court could not hear the case because the amendments were meant only to limit the national government.

State bills of rights were similar to the national one. Furthermore, each state's judicial system interpreted the rights differently. Citizens in different states effectively had different sets of civil rights. Remember that the Thirteenth, Fourteenth, and Fifteenth Amendments were passed after the Civil War to guarantee equal rights to the former slaves and free black Americans, regardless of where they lived. It was not until after the Fourteenth Amendment was ratified in 1868 that civil liberties guaranteed by the national Constitution began to be applied to the states. Section 1 of that amendment provides, in part, as follows:

> No State shall . . . deprive any person of life, liberty, or property, without due process of law.

Incorporation of the Fourteenth Amendment

There was no question that the Fourteenth Amendment applied to state governments. For decades, however, the courts were reluctant to define the liberties spelled out in the national Bill of Rights as constituting "due process of law," which was protected under the Fourteenth Amendment. In 1925, in *Gitlow v. New York*, the United States Supreme Court held that the Fourteenth Amendment applied the First Amendment, freedom of speech, to the states.[2]

Gradually, but never completely, the Supreme Court accepted the **incorporation theory**—the view that most of the protections of the Bill of Rights are incorporated into the Fourteenth Amendment's protection against state government actions. Table 4–1 shows the rights that the Court has incorporated into the Fourteenth Amendment and the case in which it first applied each protection. The later Supreme Court decisions listed in Table 4–1 require the 50 states to accept for their citizens most of the rights and freedoms that are set forth in the U.S. Bill of Rights.

Incorporation Theory
The view that most of the protections of the Bill of Rights apply to state governments through the Fourteenth Amendment's due process clause.

---

1. 7 Peters 243 (1833).
2. 68 U.S. 652 (1925).

Table 4-1 ▶   Incorporating the Bill of Rights into the Fourteenth Amendment

YEAR	ISSUE	AMENDMENT INVOLVED	COURT CASE
1925	Freedom of speech	I	*Gitlow v. New York*, 268 U.S. 652
1931	Freedom of the press	I	*Near v. Minnesota*, 283 U.S. 697
1932	Right to a lawyer in capital punishment cases	VI	*Powell v. Alabama*, 287 U.S. 45
1937	Freedom of assembly and right to petition	I	*De Jonge v. Oregon*, 299 U.S. 353
1940	Freedom of religion	I	*Cantwell v. Connecticut*, 310 U.S. 296
1947	Separation of church and state	I	*Everson v. Board of Education*, 330 U.S. 1
1948	Right to a public trial	VI	*In re Oliver*, 333 U.S. 257
1949	No unreasonable searches and seizures	IV	*Wolf v. Colorado*, 338 U.S. 25
1961	Exclusionary rule	IV	*Mapp v. Ohio*, 367 U.S. 643
1962	No cruel and unusual punishment	VIII	*Robinson v. California*, 370 U.S. 660
1963	Right to a lawyer in all criminal felony cases	VI	*Gideon v. Wainwright*, 372 U.S. 335
1964	No compulsory self-incrimination	V	*Malloy v. Hogan*, 378 U.S. 1
1965	Right to privacy	I, III, IV, V, IX	*Griswold v. Connecticut*, 381 U.S. 479
1966	Right to an impartial jury	VI	*Parker v. Gladden*, 385 U.S. 363
1967	Right to a speedy trial	VI	*Klopfer v. North Carolina*, 386 U.S. 213
1969	No double jeopardy	V	*Benton v. Maryland*, 395 U.S. 784

Freedom of Religion

■ **LO4.2:** Give examples of how the Bill of Rights protects freedom of religion while maintaining a separation between the state and religion, thereby limiting the direct influence of religion in public life.

In the United States, freedom of religion consists of two main principles as presented in the First Amendment. The **establishment clause** prohibits the establishment of a church that is officially supported by the national government, thus guaranteeing a division between church and state. The *free exercise clause* constrains the national government from prohibiting individuals from practicing the religion of their choice. These two precepts can inherently be in tension with one another, however. Public universities must allow religious groups to form on campus under the free exercise clause, but the decision to fund the activities of religious student groups is much more complicated and depends on a number of factors relative to the establishment clause. In the most recent Supreme Court decision on this issue, the majority stipulated that the university may not "silence the expression of selected viewpoints" in making funding decisions.[3]

The Separation of Church and State— The Establishment Clause

The First Amendment to the Constitution states, in part, that "Congress shall make no law respecting an establishment of religion." In the words of Thomas Jefferson, the establishment clause was designed to create a "wall of separation of Church and State."[4]

Establishment Clause
The part of the First Amendment prohibiting the establishment of a church officially supported by the national government. It is applied to questions of state and local government aid to religious organizations and schools, the legality of allowing or requiring school prayers, and the teaching of evolution versus intelligent design.

3. *Rosenberger v. University of Virginia*, 515 U.S. 819 (1995).
4. "Jefferson's Letter to the Danbury Baptists, The Final Letter, as Sent," January 1, 1802, The Library of Congress, Washington, DC.

Perhaps Jefferson was thinking about the religious intolerance that characterized the first colonies. Many of the American colonies were founded by groups that were pursuing religious freedom for their own particular denomination. Nonetheless, the early colonists were quite intolerant of religious beliefs that differed from their own. Established churches, meaning state-protected denominations, existed within 9 of the original 13 colonies.

As interpreted by the United States Supreme Court, the establishment clause in the First Amendment means at least the following:

Neither a state nor the federal government can set up a church. Neither can pass laws which aid one religion, aid all religions, or prefer one religion over another. Neither can force nor influence a person to go to or to remain away from church against his will or force him to profess a belief or disbelief in any religion. No person can be punished for entertaining or professing religious beliefs or disbeliefs, for church attendance or nonattendance. No tax in any amount, large or small, can be levied to support any religious activities or institutions, whatever they may be called, or whatever form they may adopt to teach or practice religion. Neither a state nor the federal government can, openly or secretly, participate in the affairs of any religious organizations or groups and vice versa.[5]

The establishment clause is applied to conflicts over state and local government aid to religious organizations and schools, school prayer, evolution versus intelligent design, posting the Ten Commandments in schools or public places, and discrimination against religious groups in publicly operated institutions. The establishment clause's mandate that government can neither promote nor discriminate against religious beliefs raises particularly complex questions.

Aid to Church-Related Schools. Throughout the United States, all property owners except religious, educational, fraternal, literary, scientific, and similar nonprofit institutions must pay property taxes. A large part of the proceeds of such

Journal-Courier/Valerie Berta/The Image Works

Students bow in prayer outside Jacksonville High School, an Illinois public school. Issues related to prayer are far from settled. These students are participating in See You at the Pole, an event held each September when Christian students meet at the flag pole (symbolic of government) outside their school and share a prayer before school starts.

5. *Everson v. Board of Education,* 330 U.S. 1 (1947).

taxes goes to support public schools. But not all children attend public schools. Fully 12 percent of school-aged children attend private schools, of which 85 percent have religious affiliations. The Court has tried to draw a fine line between permissible public aid to students in church-related schools and impermissible public aid to religion. These issues have arisen most often at the elementary and secondary levels.

In 1971, in *Lemon v. Kurtzman*, the Court ruled that direct state aid could not be used to subsidize religious instruction.[6] The Court in the *Lemon* case gave its most general statement on the constitutionality of government aid to religious schools, stating that the aid had to be secular (nonreligious) in aim, that it could not have the primary effect of advancing or inhibiting religion, and that the government must avoid "an excessive government entanglement with religion." The three phrases above became known as the "three-part *Lemon* test" which has been applied in most of the cases under the establishment clause since 1971. The interpretation of the test, however, has varied over the years.

In several cases, the Supreme Court has held that state programs helping church-related schools are unconstitutional. The Court also has denied state reimbursements to religious schools for field trips and for developing achievement tests. In a series of other cases, however, the Supreme Court has allowed states to use tax funds for lunches, textbooks, diagnostic services for speech and hearing problems, state-required standardized tests, computers, and transportation for students attending church-operated elementary and secondary schools. In some cases, the Court argued that state aid was intended to directly assist the individual child, and in other cases, such as bus transportation, the Court acknowledged the state's goals for public safety.

A Change in the Court's Position. Today's Supreme Court has shown a greater willingness to allow the use of public funds for programs in religious schools. In 1985, in *Aguilar v. Felton*, the Supreme Court ruled that state programs providing special educational services for disadvantaged students attending religious schools violated the establishment clause.[7] In 1997, however, when the Supreme Court revisited this decision, the Court reversed its position. In *Agostini v. Felton*, the Court held that *Aguilar* was "no longer good law."[8] What happened to cause the Court to change its mind? Justice Sandra Day O'Connor answered that: What had changed since *Aguilar* was "our understanding" of the establishment clause. Between 1985 and 1997, the Court's makeup had also changed significantly. Six of the nine justices who participated in the 1997 decision were appointed after the 1985 *Aguilar* decision.

School Vouchers. Questions about the use of public funds for church-related schools are likely to continue as state legislators search for new ways to improve the educational system. An issue that has come to the forefront is school vouchers. In a voucher system, educational vouchers (state-issued credits) can be used to "purchase" education at any school, public or private. In other words, the public money follows the individual student wherever he or she may enroll. Proponents of these programs argue that vouchers allow low-income students to escape poorly performing public schools, while opponents warn that vouchers take money away from public schools that are already underfunded.

6. 403 U.S. 602 (1971).
7. 473 U.S. 402 (1985).
8. 521 U.S. 203 (1997).

School districts in thirteen states and the District of Columbia provide state-funded vouchers to qualifying students. The courts reviewed a case involving Ohio's voucher program in which some $10 million in public funds was spent annually to send 4,300 Cleveland students to 51 private schools, all but five of which were Catholic schools. The case presented a straightforward constitutional question: Is it a violation of separation of church and state for public tax money to be used to pay for religious education?

In 2002, the Supreme Court held that the Cleveland voucher program was constitutional.[9] The Court concluded, by a 5-4 vote, that Cleveland's use of tax-payer-paid school vouchers to send children to private schools was constitutional. The Court's majority reasoned that the program did not unconstitutionally entangle church and state, because families theoretically could use the vouchers for their children to attend religious schools, secular private academies, suburban public schools, or charter schools, even though few public schools had agreed to accept vouchers. The Court's decision raised a further question—whether religious and private schools that accept government vouchers must comply with disability and civil rights laws, as public schools are required to do. Past decisions by the Supreme Court and recent guidance from the Department of Justice suggest that voucher programs must be administered in nondiscriminatory ways.

Despite the United States Supreme Court's decision upholding the Cleveland voucher program, in 2006 the Florida Supreme Court declared Florida's voucher program unconstitutional. The Florida court held that its state constitution bars public funding from being diverted to private schools that are not subject to the uniformity requirements of the state's public school system. The state of Arizona has taken a different approach, passing legislation to allow parents to reduce their state taxes by the amount of tuition paid to a private school. In 2011, the Supreme Court ruled that, because the money was paid directly from the individual to the school and the government did not support the private school, the law could not be challenged by other taxpayers.[10] In 2014, around 82,000 children received school vouchers; however, many of these programs were still being legally contested in state courts.

The Issue of School Prayer—*Engel v. Vitale*. Do the states have the right to promote religion in general, without making any attempt to establish a particular religion? That is the question raised by school prayer and was the issue in 1962 in *Engel v. Vitale*, the so-called Regents' Prayer case in New York.[11] The State Board of Regents of New York had suggested that a prayer be spoken aloud in the public schools at the beginning of each day. The recommended prayer was as follows:

Almighty God, we acknowledge our dependence upon Thee, And we beg Thy blessings upon us, our parents, our teachers, and our Country.

Following implementation, parents of several students challenged the action of the regents, maintaining that it violated the establishment clause of the First Amendment. At trial, the parents lost. The Supreme Court, however, ruled that the regents' action was unconstitutional because "the constitutional prohibition against laws respecting an establishment of a religion must mean at least that in this country it is no part of the business of government to compose official prayers for any group of the American people to recite as part of a religious program carried on by any government." The Court's conclusion was based in part on the

9. *Zelman v. Simmons-Harris*, 536 U.S. 639 (2002).
10. *Arizona School Tuition Organization v. Winn*. 09-987 (2011).
11. 370 U.S. 421 (1962).

"historical fact that governmentally established religions and religious persecutions go hand in hand." In *Abington School District v. Schempp*, the Supreme Court outlawed officially sponsored daily readings of the Bible and recitation of the Lord's Prayer in public schools.[12]

The Debate over School Prayer Continues.

Although the Supreme Court has ruled repeatedly against officially sponsored prayer and Bible-reading sessions in public schools, other means for bringing some form of religious expression into public education have been attempted. In 1983, the Tennessee legislature passed a bill requiring public school classes to begin each day with a minute of silence. Alabama had a similar law. In 1985, in *Wallace v. Jaffree*, the Supreme Court struck down as unconstitutional the Alabama law authorizing one minute of silence for prayer or meditation in all public schools.[13] Applying the three-part *Lemon* test, the Court concluded that the law violated the establishment clause because it was "an endorsement of religion lacking any clearly secular purpose."

Since then, the lower courts have interpreted the Supreme Court's decision to mean that states can require a moment of silence in the schools as long as they make it clear that the purpose of the law is secular, not religious. Opponents argue that it is an opportunity for prayer in disguise.

Prayer Outside the Classroom.

The courts have also dealt with cases involving prayer in public schools outside the classroom, particularly during graduation ceremonies. In 1992, in *Lee v. Weisman*, the United States Supreme Court held that it was unconstitutional for a school to invite a rabbi to deliver a nonsectarian prayer at graduation.[14] The Court said nothing about *students* organizing and leading prayers at graduation ceremonies and other school events, however, and these issues continue to come before the courts. A particularly contentious question in the last few years has been the constitutionality of student-initiated prayers before sporting events, such as football games. In 2000, the Supreme Court held that while school prayer at graduation did not violate the establishment clause, students could not use a school's public-address system to lead prayers at sporting events.[15]

Despite the Court's ruling, students at schools in several states (particularly those in the South) continue to pray over public-address systems prior to sporting events. In other areas, the Court's ruling is skirted by avoiding the use of the public-address system. In North Carolina, a pregame prayer was broadcast over a local radio station and heard by fans who took radios to the game for that purpose. Regardless of the Court's current interpretation, practices related to prayer outside of the formal school setting vary widely but generally conform to community norms. Only when an individual or group objects is the question subject to the courts' interpretation again.

The Ten Commandments.

A related church–state issue is whether the Ten Commandments may be displayed in public schools—or on any public property. Supporters of the movement to display the Ten Commandments argue that they embody American values and that they constitute a part of the official and permanent history of American government.

Opponents of such laws claim that they are an unconstitutional government entanglement with the religious life of citizens. Still, various Ten Commandments installations have been found to be constitutional. For example, the Supreme

---

12. 374 U.S. 203 (1963).
13. 472 U.S. 38 (1985).
14. 505 U.S. 577 (1992).
15. *Santa Fe Independent School District v. Doe*, 530 U.S. 290 (2000).

Court ruled in 2005 that a granite monument on the grounds of the Texas state capitol that contained the commandments was constitutional because the monument as a whole was secular in nature.[16] In another 2005 ruling, however, the Court ordered that displays of the Ten Commandments in front of two Kentucky county courthouses had to be removed because they were overtly religious.[17]

Forbidding the Teaching of Evolution. For many decades, certain religious groups, particularly in southern states, have opposed the teaching of evolution in the schools. To these groups, evolutionary theory directly counters their religious belief that human beings did not evolve, but were created fully formed, as described in the biblical story of creation. State and local attempts to forbid the teaching of evolution, however, have not passed constitutional muster in the eyes of the United States Supreme Court. In 1968, the Court held in *Epperson v. Arkansas* that an Arkansas law prohibiting the teaching of evolution violated the establishment clause because it imposed religious beliefs on students.[18] The Louisiana legislature passed a law requiring the teaching of the biblical story of the creation alongside the teaching of evolution. In 1987, in *Edwards v. Aguillard*, the Supreme Court declared that this law was unconstitutional, in part because it had as its primary purpose the promotion of a particular religious belief.[19]

Nonetheless, state and local groups around the country continue their efforts against the teaching of evolution. The Cobb County school system in Georgia attempted to include a disclaimer in its biology textbooks that proclaims, "Evolution is a theory, not a fact, regarding the origin of living things." A federal judge later ruled that it must be removed. Other school districts have considered teaching "intelligent design" as an alternative explanation of the origin of life. Proponents of intelligent design contend that evolutionary theory has gaps that can be explained only by the existence of an intelligent creative force (God). Intelligent design, at its essence, proposes an original creator, which is a religious belief that cannot be taught in public schools.

Religious Speech. Another controversy in the area of church–state relations concerns religious speech in public schools or universities. In *Rosenberger v. University of Virginia*, the issue was whether the University of Virginia violated the establishment clause when it refused to fund publication costs related to a Christian magazine, *Wide Awake*, but granted funds collected from student activity fees to more than 100 other student organizations.[20] The university argued that providing funding violated the Establishment Clause while Robert Rosenberger and other founders of *Wide Awake* argued under a Free Speech claim that the magazine was designed to promote discussion. The Supreme Court ruled that the university's policy unconstitutionally discriminated against religious speech and that the university may not "silence the expression of selected viewpoints." The Court pointed out that the funds came from student fees, not general taxes, and were used for the "neutral" payment of bills for student groups.

Later, the Supreme Court reviewed a case involving a similar claim of discrimination against a religious group, the Good News Club. The club offers religious instruction to young schoolchildren. The club sued the school board of a public

did you know?

The Pew Research Center found that 33 percent of American adults reject evolution, believing instead that "humans and other living things have existed in their present form since the beginning of time."

---

16. *Van Orden v. Perry*, 125 S. Ct. 2854 (2005).
17. *McCreary County v. American Civil Liberties Union*, 125 S. Ct. 2722 (2005).
18. 393 U.S. 97 (1968).
19. 482 U.S. 578 (1987).
20. 515 U.S. 819 (1995).

mak/Alamy

This steel beam structure was discovered at ground zero following the collapse of the World Trade Center on September 11, 2001. Resembling a cross, the structure became a memorial and place for reflection during the clean-up and reconstruction. The structure is now housed in the National September 11 Memorial Museum.

Free Exercise Clause
The provision of the First Amendment guaranteeing the free exercise of religion.

school in Milford, New York, when the board refused to allow the club to meet on school property after the school day ended. The club argued that the school board's refusal to allow the club to meet on school property, when other groups—such as the Girl Scouts and the 4-H Club—were permitted to do so, amounted to discrimination on the basis of religion. Ultimately, the Supreme Court agreed, ruling in *Good News Club v. Milford Central School* that the Milford school board's decision violated the establishment clause.[21]

Public Expression of Religion. What kinds of religious expression are protected in public displays? The World Trade Center cross is a configuration of steel beams found in the rubble after the September 11, 2001 terrorist attacks collapsed both towers. The proportions resemble a Christian cross and once found the cross became a make-shift memorial and site of reflection. The cross has been installed in the National September 11 Memorial Museum, prompting objections from the group American Atheists. Members of the group are filing a lawsuit arguing that the cross does not belong in a private museum situated on property leased from the government. "It's necessary to fight this because this is inequality on government property," said American Atheists president David Silverman. "If you take the religion away from the cross, you've got scrap metal," Silverman said. "Just like all the other scrap metal that fell on the cross. The only reason that this cross is special is because it is religious."[22]

The Free Exercise Clause

The First Amendment constrains Congress from prohibiting the free exercise of religion. Does this **free exercise clause** mean that no type of religious practice can be prohibited or restricted by government? Certainly, a person can hold any religious belief that he or she wants, or have no religious beliefs. When, however, religious *practices* work against public policy and the public welfare, the government can act. For example, regardless of a child's or parent's religious beliefs, the government can require certain types of vaccinations. The sale and use of some controlled substances for religious purposes has been held illegal, because a religion cannot make legal what would otherwise be illegal.

The extent to which government can regulate religious practices has always been a subject of controversy. In 1990, in *Oregon v. Smith*, the U.S. Supreme Court ruled that the state of Oregon could deny unemployment benefits to two drug counselors who had been fired for using peyote, an illegal drug, in their religious services.[23] The counselors had argued that using peyote was part of the practice of a Native American religion. Many criticized the decision, decrying the increased regulation of religious practices.

21. 533 U.S. 98 (2001).
22. Scott Stump, "World Trade Center Cross Fight Continues as Atheist Group Appeals Ruling," TODAY News, March 6, 2014. Accessed at www.today.com/news/world-trade-center-cross-fight-continues-athiest-group-appeals-ruling-2D79328902.
23. 494 U.S. 872 (1990).

The Religious Freedom Restoration Act. In 1993, Congress responded to the public's criticism by passing the Religious Freedom Restoration Act (RFRA). One of the specific purposes of the act was to overturn the Supreme Court's decision in *Oregon v. Smith*. The act required national, state, and local governments to "accommodate religious conduct" unless the government could show a *compelling* reason not to do so. Moreover, if the government did regulate a religious practice, it had to use the least restrictive means possible.

Some people believed that the RFRA went too far in the other direction—it accommodated practices that were contrary to the public policies of state governments. Proponents of states' rights complained that the act intruded into an area traditionally governed by state laws, not by the national government. In 1997, in *City of Boerne v. Flores*, the Supreme Court agreed and held that Congress had exceeded its constitutional authority with the RFRA.[24] According to the Court, the act's "sweeping coverage ensures its intrusion at every level of government, displacing laws and prohibiting official actions of almost every description and regardless of subject matter." In response to this ruling, 31 states have adopted Religious Freedom Restoration Acts that apply to state and municipalities.

The Arizona legislature passed a bill in 2014 that would have allowed business to deny services to lesbian, gay, bisexual, or transgender (LGBT) customers. Governor Jan Brewer vetoed the law, but that hardly settled the question. Opponents of this and similar bills (pending or adopted) in other states view it as legalizing discrimination. Supporters argue that they should not be compelled by the state to promote views inconsistent with their personal religious beliefs. These divergent opinions were reflected by media Tweets announcing the governor's veto—*The Washington Post* referred to it as an anti-gay bill while *The Wall Street Journal* (a more conservative publication) termed it a religious freedom bill. Most of the cases in this area have arisen when vendors have refused to sell wedding cakes, flowers, or photography services to same-sex couples getting married. A similar religious exemption battle is raging over the Affordable Care Act's contraception mandate. The Supreme Court heard two cases (*Sebelius v. Hobby Lobby* and *Conestoga Wood Specialties Corp. v. Sebelius*) in which a company claimed its objection to providing mandated contraception coverage stemmed from the owners' religious beliefs. In *Burwell v. Hobby Lobby*, decided by a 5-4 vote in June 2014, the Supreme Court ruled that requiring "closely held" corporations to pay for insurance coverage for contraception violated the Religious Freedom Restoration Act of 1993. Justice Ruth Bader Ginsberg read her dissent from the bench, indicating her strong disagreement with the holding in the majority opinion.

Washington Post/WSJ

How reliable is it to depend on media alerts that are headlines only, without text included?

Freedom of Expression

■ **LO4.3:** Locate the protections of political expression and dissent in the Constitution, and explain why freedom of expression is critical to people's participation in politics.

Perhaps the most frequently invoked freedom that Americans have is the right to free speech and a free press without government interference. Citizens have the right to have a say, and all of us have the right

---

24. 521 U.S. 507 (1997).

to hear what others say. For the most part, Americans can criticize public officials and their actions without fear of reprisal by any branch of government.

No Prior Restraint

Prior Restraint
Restraining an action before the activity has actually occurred. When expression is involved, this means censorship.

Restraining an activity before that activity has actually occurred is called **prior restraint**. When expression is involved, prior restraint means censorship, as opposed to subsequent punishment. Prior restraint of expression would require, for example, that a permit be obtained before a speech could be made, a newspaper article published, a movie shown, or an art exhibition opened. Most, if not all, Supreme Court justices have been very critical of governmental action that imposes prior restraint on expression. The Court clearly displayed this attitude in *Nebraska Press Association v. Stuart*, a case decided in 1976:

> *A prior restraint on expression comes to this Court with a "heavy presumption" against its constitutionality . . . The government thus carries a heavy burden of showing justification for the enforcement of such a restraint.*[25]

One of the most famous cases concerning prior restraint was *New York Times v. United States* in 1971, the so-called Pentagon Papers case.[26] The *Times* and *The Washington Post* were about to publish the Pentagon Papers, an elaborate secret history of the U.S. government's involvement in the Vietnam War (1964–1975) released by Daniel Ellsberg, an employee of the RAND corporation. The government wanted a court order to bar publication of the documents, arguing that national security was threatened and that the documents had been stolen. The documents contained evidence that the U.S. government knew that the Vietnam War was likely "unwinnable" and that continuing the war would result in many more causalities than reported. The newspapers argued that the public had a right to know the information contained in the papers, even if it embarrassed the government, and that the press had the right to inform the public. The Supreme Court ruled 6-3 in favor of the newspapers' right to publish the information. This case affirmed the no-prior-restraint doctrine.

WikiLeaks, Edward Snowden, and Classified Information on the Internet

In recent years, an organization known as WikiLeaks, led by Australian Julian Assange, has released thousands of documents online leaked from governments around the world. Most documents had been "classified" by the respective governments as too sensitive to be made public. U.S. military and diplomatic documents were leaked by Chelsea Manning (born Bradley Manning), an Army intelligence officer with access to intelligence data bases. Manning was convicted in 2013 on espionage charges and is currently serving a 35-year sentence. Assange, indicted on unrelated crimes, was granted political asylum by Ecuador, where he continues to reside. Most recently, Edward Snowden, a computer specialist formerly employed by the Central Intelligence Agency (CIA) and a private contractor doing work for the National Security Agency (NSA), leaked thousands of documents detailing the NSA's international Internet surveillance initiatives and a collection of telephone metadata to *The Guardian* and *The Washington Post*. In June 2013, the U.S. government charged Snowden with espionage and revoked his U.S. passport. At the time, Snowden was in flight from Hong Kong to Ecuador

---

25. 427 U.S. 539 (1976). See also *Near v. Minnesota*, 283 U.S. 697 (1931).
26. 403 U.S. 713 (1971).

FLORIAN SCHUH/AFP/Getty Images/Newscom

A supporter of the Anonymous group wearing a Guy Fawkes mask holds up a placard featuring a photo of U.S. intelligence leaker Edward Snowden during a rally in front of Berlin's landmark Brandenburg Gate on November 5, 2013.

with a one-night layover planned in Moscow. Without a passport, he could not continue his travel and remained stranded in the Moscow airport until Russia offered him temporary asylum for one year. Snowden is considered a fugitive from justice by the U.S. government, but a hero and patriot by others. Snowden claims that the only motive for his leaks was to "inform the public as to that which is done in their name and that which is done against them."[27] All of these leaks raise questions about the public's right (and possible need) to know what its government is doing, as well as issues of privacy and national security.

The Protection of Symbolic Speech

Not all expression is in words or in writing. Articles of clothing, gestures, movements, and other forms of expressive conduct are considered **symbolic speech**. Such speech is given substantial protection today by our courts. In a landmark decision issued in 1969, *Tinker v. Des Moines School District*, the United States Supreme Court held that the wearing of black armbands by students in protest against the Vietnam War was a form of speech protected by the First Amendment.[28] The case arose after a school administrator in Des Moines, Iowa, issued a regulation prohibiting students in the Des Moines School District from wearing the armbands. The Supreme Court reasoned that the school district was unable to show that the wearing of the armbands had disrupted normal school activities. Furthermore, the school district's policy was discriminatory, as it banned only certain forms of symbolic speech (the black armbands) and not others (such as lapel crosses and fraternity rings).

   In 1989, in *Texas v. Johnson*, the Supreme Court ruled that state laws that prohibited the burning of the American flag as part of a peaceful protest also violated the freedom of expression protected by the First Amendment.[29] Congress responded by passing the Flag Protection Act

Symbolic Speech
Nonverbal expression of beliefs, which is given substantial protection by the courts.

did you know?
Eighty-four percent of Americans 18–30 years old believe that high school students should be able to exercise the same First Amendment rights as adults, an opinion shared by 75 percent of all Americans.

27. Glenn Greenwald, Ewen MacAskill, and Laura Poitras. "Edward Snowden: the Whistleblower Behind the NSA Surveillance Revelations." *The Guardian*, June 11, 2013. Accessed at www.theguardian.com/world/2013/jun/09/edward-snowden-nsa-whistleblower-surveillance
28. 393 U.S. 503 (1969).
29. 488 U.S. 884 (1989).

Everyday Politics

 ## The Fifth Estate

The Fifth Estate is a 2013 film primarily based on Daniel Domscheit-Berg's book *Inside WikiLeaks: My Time with Julian Assange and the World's Most Dangerous Website*, published in 2011. The book's author was Julian Assange's partner in developing WikiLeaks, an online platform allowing whistleblowers to anonymously leak documents, identities, diplomatic correspondence, military information, and data. In the film, Assange (Benedict Cumberbatch) and Daniel Domscheit-Berg (Daniel Brühl) are online activists dedicated to uncovering and exposing the secrets and corrupt dealings of corporations and governments around the world.

The relationship between Julian and Daniel is at first a partnership, but as WikiLeaks grows and Assange exercises more control over decisions about which information is made public and seems to show less concern about the anonymity of sources, Domscheit-Berg begins to distance himself from the project. Tensions climax over the material leaked by Bradley Manning (now Chelsea Manning), which included classified information related to the Iraq and Afghanistan wars and over 250,000 encrypted U.S. diplomatic cables. Manning's leaks are widely acknowledged to have produced a "chilling effect" on U.S. foreign policy by hampering diplomats' ability to collect and share securely information gathered throughout the world.

Prior to the film's release, WikiLeaks posted a version of the screenplay for *The Fifth Estate* along with a 4,000 word memo in which Assange describes the film as "irresponsible, counterproductive, and harmful." After leaking the script, WikiLeaks tweeted: "As WikiLeaks was never consulted about the Dreamworks/Disney film on us, we've given our advice for free: It's bad." Director Bill Condon has said his film hopes to "explore the complexities and challenges of transparency in the information age and, we hope, enliven and enrich the conversations WikiLeaks has already provoked."*

* Ben Child, "WikiLeaks posts The Fifth Estate script and labels the film 'irresponsible.'" *The Guardian*, September 20, 2013. Accessed at www.theguardian.com/film/2013/sep/20/wikileaks-fifth-estate-julian-assange-benedict-cumberbatch.

For Critical Analysis

1. *Is there a role for secrecy in a free society?*

2. *Julian Assange is a complicated figure in this story. Allusions to a troubled childhood and possible cult involvement permeate the story. Are his motives less trustworthy as a result? Is WikiLeaks the world's most dangerous website, as Domscheit-Berg claims, or is it a critical outlet for whistleblowers around the world?*

---

of 1989, which was ruled unconstitutional by the Supreme Court in June 1990.[30] Congress and President George H. W. Bush immediately pledged to work for a constitutional amendment to "protect our flag"—which has yet to be successful.

In 2003, however, the Supreme Court held that a Virginia statute prohibiting the burning of a cross with "an intent to intimidate" did not violate the First Amendment. The Court concluded that a burning cross is an instrument of racial terror so threatening that it does not warrant protection as a form of free expression.[31]

The Protection of Commercial Speech

Commercial speech is defined as advertising statements. Can advertisers use their First Amendment rights to prevent restrictions on the content of commercial advertising? Until the 1970s, the Supreme Court held that such speech was not

Commercial Speech
Advertising statements, which increasingly have been given First Amendment protection.

---

30. *United States v. Eichman*, 496 U.S. 310 (1990).
31. *Virginia v. Black*, 538 U.S. 343 (2003).

protected at all by the First Amendment. By the mid-1970s, however, more commercial speech had been brought under First Amendment protection. According to Justice Harry A. Blackmun, "Advertising, however tasteless and excessive it sometimes may seem, is nonetheless dissemination of information as to who is producing and selling what product for what reason and at what price."[32] Nevertheless, the Supreme Court will consider a restriction on commercial speech valid as long as it (1) seeks to implement a substantial government interest, (2) directly advances that interest, and (3) goes no further than necessary to accomplish its objective. An advertisement that makes totally false claims can be restricted.

Political campaign advertising crosses the boundaries between individual free speech and commercial speech. For many years, federal law has prohibited businesses, labor unions, and other organizations from engaging directly in political advertising, but corporations and other groups were allowed to create political action committees to engage in regulated activities. In recent years, new organizational forms were created to campaign for issues. Nonprofit organizations, however, were strictly prohibited from directly campaigning for candidates. In 2009, the Supreme Court overturned decades of law on this issue, declaring in *Citizens United v. FEC* that corporations and other associations were "persons" in terms of the law and had free speech rights. According to the majority decision, Citizens United, an incorporated nonprofit group, was unfairly denied the right to pay for broadcasting a movie about Senator Hillary Clinton, which was intended to harm her presidential campaign. President Obama asked Congress to rewrite the campaign finance laws to restrict such forms of political advertising, but it has not successfully done so.[33]

Permitted Restrictions on Expression

At various times, restrictions on expression have been permitted. After the terrorist attacks of September 11, 2001, periods of perceived foreign threats to the government sometimes lead to more repression of speech that is thought to be dangerous to the nation. The Supreme Court changes its view of what might be dangerous speech depending on the times.

Clear and Present Danger. When a person's remarks create a clear and present danger to peace or public order, they can be curtailed constitutionally. Justice Oliver Wendell Holmes used this reasoning in 1919 when examining the case of a socialist who had been convicted for violating the Espionage Act by distributing a leaflet that opposed the military draft. Holmes stated:

> The question in every case is whether the words are used in such circumstances and are of such a nature as to create a clear and present danger that they will bring about the substantive evils that Congress has a right to prevent. It is a question of proximity and degree.[34]

According to the **clear and present danger test**, expression may be restricted if evidence exists that such expression would cause a condition, actual or imminent, that Congress has the power to prevent. Commenting on this test, Justice Louis D. Brandeis in 1920 said, "Correctly applied, it will reserve the right of free speech...from suppression by tyrannists, well-meaning majorities, and from abuse by irresponsible, fanatical minorities."[35]

Clear and Present Danger Test
The test proposed by Justice Oliver Wendell Holmes for determining when government may restrict free speech. Restrictions are permissible, he argued, only when speech creates a *clear and present danger* to the public order.

32. *Virginia State Board of Pharmacy v. Virginia Citizens Consumer Council, Inc.*, 425 U.S. 748 (1976).
33. *Citizens United v. Federal Election Commission*, 558 U.S. (2010).
34. *Schenck v. United States*, 249 U.S. 47 (1919).
35. *Schaefer v. United States*, 251 U.S. 466 (1920).

In 2002, a student who held this banner outside his school in Alaska was suspended for supporting drug use with his "speech." The Supreme Court upheld the principal's decision in the 2007 case *Morse v. Frederick*, saying that public schools are able to regulate what students say about promoting illegal drug use. Do you think banning such speech is a violation of students' free speech rights? Should colleges be able to implement such a ban as well?

Clay Good/Zuma Press

Modifications to the Clear and Present Danger Rule.

Since the clear and present danger rule was first enunciated, the United States Supreme Court has modified it. In 1925, when many Americans feared the increasing power of communist and other left-wing parties in Europe, the Supreme Court heard the case *Gitlow v. New York*.[36] In its opinion, the Court introduced the *bad-tendency rule*. According to this rule, speech or other First Amendment freedoms may be curtailed if a possibility exists that such expression might lead to some "evil." In the *Gitlow* case, a member of a left-wing group was convicted of violating New York State's criminal anarchy statute when he published and distributed a pamphlet urging the violent overthrow of the U.S. government. In its majority opinion, the Supreme Court held that although the First Amendment afforded protection against state incursions on freedom of expression, Gitlow could be punished legally because his expression would tend to bring about evils that the state had a right to prevent. If distributed now, Gitlow's publication would likely have been treated as protected political speech.

The Supreme Court again modified the clear and present danger test in a 1951 case, *Dennis v. United States*.[37] During the early years of the Cold War, Americans were anxious about the activities of communists and the Soviet Union within the United States. Congress passed several laws that essentially outlawed the Communist Party of the United States and made its activities illegal. Twelve members of the American Communist Party were convicted of violating a statute that made it a crime to conspire to teach, advocate, or organize the violent overthrow of any government in the United States. The Supreme Court affirmed the convictions, significantly modifying the clear and present danger test in the process. The Court applied a *grave and probable danger rule*. Under this rule, "the gravity of the 'evil' discounted by its improbability justifies such invasion of free

36. 268 U.S. 652 (1925).
37. 341 U.S. 494 (1951).

speech as is necessary to avoid the danger." This rule gave much less protection to free speech than did the clear and present danger test.

Six years after the *Dennis* case, the Supreme Court heard another case in which members of the Communist Party in California were accused of teaching and advocating the overthrow of the government of the United States. The ruling of the Court greatly reduced the scope of the law passed by Congress. In *Yates v. United States*, the Court held that there was a difference between "advocacy and teaching of forcible overthrow as an abstract principle" and actually proposing concrete action.[38] The Court overturned the convictions of the party leaders because they were engaging in speech rather than action. This was the beginning of a series of cases that eventually found the original congressional legislation to be unconstitutional because it violated the First and Fourth Amendments.

Some claim that the United States did not achieve true freedom of political speech until 1969, when, in *Brandenburg v. Ohio*, the Supreme Court overturned the conviction of a Ku Klux Klan leader for violating a state statute.[39] The statute prohibited anyone from advocating "the duty, necessity, or propriety of sabotage, violence, or unlawful methods of terrorism as a means of accomplishing industrial or political reform." The Court held that free speech does not permit a state "to forbid or proscribe advocacy of the use of force or of law violation except where such advocacy is directed to inciting or producing imminent lawless actions and is likely to incite or produce such action." The incitement test enunciated by the Court in this case is a difficult one for prosecutors to meet. As a result, the Court's decision significantly broadened the protection given to advocacy speech.

These rulings are several decades old but the principles remain intact. Consider these examples of political speech and expression—are they protected by the First Amendment? In July 2010, an evangelical Christian pastor named Terry Jones threatened to set fire to 200 copies of the Quran on the anniversary of the September 11, 2001 terrorist attacks. Although he did not carry out the act, the threat alone resulted in violent protests in the Middle East and Asia, leading to several deaths. A year later, he put the Quran on trial, found it guilty of crimes against humanity, and burned the book in his church sanctuary. Again, violent reactions in Afghanistan and elsewhere resulted in multiple injuries and deaths. American politicians from both parties condemned the actions as unnecessary provocations. General David Petraeus, then the commander of international forces in Afghanistan, cautioned that Jones's actions would endanger U.S. military forces stationed in Islamic regions around the world.

At events and funerals for U.S. soldiers killed in Iraq and Afghanistan, religious extremists from Westboro Baptist Church in Topeka Kansas picket with signs that say "God hates fags," "God hates America," and "Thank God for dead soldiers." The pickets are intended to attract attention to their anti-gay agenda. Westboro Baptist Church was founded by the late Fred Phelps and the congregation consists mainly of his extended family. In 2006, Westboro Baptist Church picketed the funeral of Marine Lance Corporal Matthew Snyder killed in Iraq with signs reading "You're Going to Hell," "Semper Fi Fags," and "God Hates You." Snyder's family filed a lawsuit accusing the church and its founders of defamation, invasion of privacy, and the intentional infliction of emotional distress. A U.S. District Court awarded the family $5 million in damages, but the U.S. Court of Appeals for the Fourth Circuit held that the judgment violated the First Amendment's protections on religious expression. The question, "does the First Amendment protect protesters

38. 354 U.S. 298 (1957).
39. 395 U.S. 444 (1969).

at a funeral from liability for intentionally inflicting emotional distress on the family of the deceased?" was argued before the U.S. Supreme Court. In an 8-1 decision, the Court ruled in favor of Westboro and Fred Phelps. Chief Justice Roberts, writing for the majority, said in part, the protection of the First Amendment "cannot be overcome by a jury finding that the picketing was outrageous."[40] Samuel Alito cast the lone dissenting vote, writing "In order to have a society in which public issues can be openly and vigorously debated, it is not necessary to allow the brutalization of innocent victims like the petitioner." In response, several states passed laws limiting pickets at funerals. In 2012, President Obama signed into law a bill restricting demonstrations at military funerals with regard to time and place.

Just prior to the 2004 election, President George W. Bush was campaigning in Jacksonville, Oregon and chose to eat dinner on a restaurant patio located near a protest zone previously identified by the local sheriff. Although there was a high fence surrounding the dining area, loud chants objecting to Bush's policies on the environment and the war could easily be heard. After a while, Secret Service agents ordered local law enforcement to move the protesters further away while the president's supporters were allowed to remain on their designated street corner. Moss's claim that agents violated his free speech rights goes to the heart of free expression protections in the First Amendment—government cannot treat demonstrators differently based on *what* they are saying. The ACLU of Oregon, speaking in support of Moss said, "If safety were the issue, the protesters would have been moved immediately after Bush decided to dine on the patio, not 15 minutes into his noisy meal."[41] The Court, however, disagreed. Although the unanimous decision stressed that the Constitution does not allow government to treat protesters differently from supporters based on their message, the justices emphasized the assassination threat in giving the Secret Service discretion to react in the moment.

Unprotected Speech: Obscenity

Many state and federal statutes make it a crime to disseminate obscene materials. Generally, the courts have not been willing to extend constitutional protections of free speech to what they consider to be obscene materials. But what is obscenity? Justice Potter Stewart once stated, in *Jacobellis v. Ohio*, a 1964 case, that even though he could not define *obscenity*, "I know it when I see it."[42] The problem is that even if it were agreed on, the definition of *obscenity* changes with the times. The works of Mark Twain and Edgar Rice Burroughs at times have been considered obscene.

Definitional Problems.   The Supreme Court has grappled at times with the difficulty of specifying an operationally effective definition of *obscenity*. In 1973, in *Miller v. California*, Chief Justice Warren Burger created a formal list of requirements that must be met for material to be considered legally obscene.[43] Material is obscene if (1) the average person finds that it violates contemporary community standards; (2) the work taken as a whole appeals to a prurient interest in sex; (3) the work shows patently offensive sexual conduct; and (4) the work lacks serious redeeming literary, artistic, political, or scientific merit. The problem is that one person's prurient interest is another person's medical interest or artistic

---

40. *Snyder v. Phelps*, 562 U.S. _____ (2011).
41. Robert Barnes, "for Michael 'Mookie' Moss, case against Secret Service is matter of free speech." *The Washington Post*, March 16, 2014. Accessed at http://www.washingtonpost.com/politics/for-michael-mookie-moss-case-against-secret-service-is-matter-of-free-speech/2014/03/16/4f3c04c0-abab-11e3-adbc-888c8010c799_story.html
42. 378 U.S. 184 (1964).
43. 413 U.S. 5 (1973).

pleasure. The Court went on to state that the definition of *prurient interest* would be determined by the community's standards. The Court avoided presenting a definition of *obscenity*, leaving this determination to local and state authorities. Consequently, the *Miller* case has been applied in a widely inconsistent manner.

Protecting Children. The Supreme Court has upheld state laws making it illegal to sell materials showing sexual performances by minors. In 1990, in *Osborne v. Ohio*, the Court ruled that states can outlaw the possession of child pornography in the home.[44] The Court reasoned that the ban on private possession is justified because owning the material perpetuates commercial demand for it and for the exploitation of the children involved. At the federal level, the Child Protection Act of 1984 made it a crime to receive knowingly through the mails sexually explicit depictions of children.

Pornography on the Internet. A significant problem facing Americans and lawmakers today is how to control obscenity and child pornography disseminated via the Internet. In 1996, Congress first attempted to protect minors from pornographic materials on the Internet by passing the Communications Decency Act (CDA). This made it a crime to make available to minors online any "obscene or indecent" message that "depicts or describes, in terms patently offensive as measured by contemporary community standards, sexual or excretory activities or organs." It was immediately challenged as an unconstitutional infringement on free speech. The Supreme Court held that the act imposed unconstitutional restraints on free speech and was therefore invalid.[45] In the eyes of the Court, the terms *indecent* and *patently offensive* covered large amounts of nonpornographic material with serious educational or other value. Later attempts by Congress to curb pornography on the Internet also encountered stumbling blocks. The Child Online Protection Act (COPA) of 1998 banned the distribution of material "harmful to minors" without an age-verification system to separate adult and minor users. In 2002, the Supreme Court upheld a lower court injunction suspending the COPA, and in 2004, the Court again upheld the suspension of the law on the ground that it was probably unconstitutional.[46] In 2000, Congress enacted the Children's Internet Protection Act (CIPA), which requires public schools and libraries to install filtering software to prevent children from viewing websites with "adult" content.

Should "Virtual" Pornography Be Deemed a Crime? In 2001, the Supreme Court agreed to review a case challenging the constitutionality of the Child Pornography Prevention Act (CPPA) of 1996. This act made it illegal to distribute or possess "any visual depiction, including any photograph, film, video, picture, or computer or computer-generated image or picture" that "is, or appears to be, of a minor engaging in sexually explicit conduct." The Free Speech Coalition, an adult-entertainment trade association, filed suit alleging that the *appears to be* and *conveys the impression* provisions are overbroad, and thus restrain works otherwise protected by the First Amendment. The Supreme Court, in a 6-3 decision, agreed that the two provisions were overbroad and therefore unconstitutional, noting further that the CPPA prohibits speech that records no crime and creates no victims by its production.[47]

Is there a way for government to prevent the sharing of child pornography on the Internet without violating free express values? Possession and distribution of

---

44. 495 U.S. 103 (1990).
45. *Reno v. American Civil Liberties Union*, 521 U.S. 844 (1997).
46. *Ashcroft v. American Civil Liberties Union*, 542 U.S. 656 (2004).
47. *Ashcroft v. Free Speech Coalition*, 535 U.S. 234 (2002).

child pornography has gone underground. A Justice Department study reported that 21 million unique computer I.P. addresses were identified and tracked sharing child pornography files in 2009, more than 9 million of them in the United States. In 2011, authorities in the United States turned over 22 million images of children actively being abused to make child pornography to the National Center for Missing and Exploited Children to try and identify the victims. According to the International Center for Missing and Exploited Children, these images are crime scene photos of child abuse, not child pornography. Robust enforcement of existing laws has moved child pornography off of easily accessible websites and into password-protected private chat rooms, a world sometimes referred to as the "dark web."[48]

Unprotected Speech: Slander

Defamation of Character
Wrongfully hurting a person's good reputation. The law imposes a general duty on all persons to refrain from making false, defamatory statements about others.

Individuals are protected from **defamation of character**, which is defined as wrongfully hurting a person's good reputation. The law imposes a general duty on all persons to refrain from making false, defamatory statements about others. Breaching this duty orally is the wrongdoing called *slander*. Breaching it in writing is the wrongdoing called *libel*, which we discuss later. The government does not bring charges of slander or libel. Rather, the defamed person may bring a civil suit for damages.

Slander
The public uttering of a false statement that harms the good reputation of another. The statement must be made to, or within the hearing of, persons other than the defamed party.

Legally, **slander** is the public uttering of a false statement that harms the good reputation of another. Slanderous public uttering means that the defamatory statements are made to, or within the hearing of, persons other than the defamed party. If one person calls another dishonest, manipulative, and incompetent to his or her face when no one else is around, that does not constitute slander. The message is not communicated to a third party. If, however, a third party accidentally overhears defamatory statements, the courts have generally held that this constitutes a public uttering and therefore slander, which is prohibited.

did you know?

The American Civil Liberties Union (ACLU) opposes hate speech codes at public universities and calls them government censorship. Instead they argue that more speech and open dialogue is the best antidote to offensive words aimed at individuals or groups based on race, gender, ethnicity, religion or sexual orientation.

Campus Speech

In recent years, students have been facing free-speech challenges on campuses. One issue has to do with whether a student should have to subsidize, through student activity fees, organizations that promote causes that the student finds objectionable.

Student Activity Fees. In 2000, this question came before the United States Supreme Court in a case brought by several University of Wisconsin students. The students argued that their mandatory student activity fees—which helped to fund liberal causes with which they disagreed, including gay rights—violated their First Amendment rights of free speech, free association, and free exercise of religion. They contended that they should have the right to choose whether to fund organizations that promoted political and ideological views that were offensive to their personal beliefs. To the surprise of many, the Supreme Court rejected the students' claim and ruled in favor of the university. The Court stated that "the university may determine that its mission is well served if students have the means to engage in dynamic discussions of philosophical, religious, scientific, social, and political subjects in their extracurricular life. If the university reaches this conclusion, it is entitled to impose a mandatory fee to sustain an open dialogue to these ends."[49]

---

48. Nicholas Kristoff, "He Was Supposed to Take a Photo." *The New York Times*, March 22, 2014. Accessed at www.nytimes.com/2014/03/23/opinion/sunday/kristof-he-was-supposed-to-take-a-photo.html
49. *Board of Regents of the University of Wisconsin System v. Southworth*, 529 U.S. 217 (2000).

Campus Speech and Behavior Codes. Another issue is the legitimacy of campus speech and behavior codes. Some state universities have established codes that challenge the boundaries of the protection of free speech provided by the First Amendment. These codes are designed to prohibit so-called hate speech—abusive speech attacking persons on the basis of their ethnicity, race, or other criteria. A University of Michigan code banned "any behavior, verbal or physical, that stigmatizes or victimizes an individual on the basis of race, ethnicity, religion, sex, sexual orientation, creed, national origin, ancestry, age, marital status, handicap" or Vietnam-veteran status. A federal court found that the code violated students' First Amendment rights.[50]

Although the courts generally have held, as in the University of Michigan case, that campus speech codes are unconstitutional restrictions on the right to free speech, such codes continue to exist. Whether hostile speech should be banned on high school campuses has also become an issue. In view of school shootings and other violent behavior in the schools, school officials have become concerned about speech that consists of bullying, veiled threats, or that could lead to violence. Some schools have even prohibited students from wearing clothing, such as T-shirts bearing verbal messages (such as sexist or racist comments) or symbolic messages (such as the Confederate flag), that might generate "ill will or hatred." Defenders of campus speech codes argue that they are necessary to prevent violence and to promote equality among different cultural, ethnic, and racial groups on campus and greater sensitivity to the needs and feelings of others in the educational environment.

Other universities have created "free speech zones" in an attempt to balance the competing interests. On September 17, 2013 (Constitution Day), Robert Van Tuinen, a student at Modesto Junior College in California was distributing free copies of the U.S. Constitution when he was stopped by campus police and advised that he was in violation of campus policy. The Student Development Office confirmed that distribution of materials could only take place within the

ZUMA Press, Inc. /Alamy

A "designated free speech area" in Modesto California raises questions about our First Amendment Rights. Should speech be limited to a designated zone on a campus where the exchange of ideas is central to the educational mission? Does your campus have a "designated free speech area"?

50. *Doe v. University of Michigan*, 721 F. Supp. 852 (1989).

"free speech zone." The free speech zone is small and must be scheduled well in advance. The Foundation for Individual Rights in Education (FIRE) filed a First Amendment lawsuit on the student's behalf. The resulting settlement expanded Modesto Junior College's policy to allow free speech in open areas across campus and the institution agreed to pay Van Tuinen $50,000.[51]

Hate Speech on the Internet

Extreme hate speech appears on the Internet, including racist materials and denials of the Holocaust (the murder of millions of Jews by the Nazis during World War II). Can the federal government restrict this type of speech? Should it? Content restrictions can be difficult to enforce. Even if Congress succeeded in passing a law prohibiting particular speech on the Internet, an army of "Internet watchers" would be needed to enforce it. Also, what if other countries attempt to impose their laws that restrict speech on U.S. websites? This is not a theoretical issue. In 2000, a French court found Yahoo in violation of French laws banning the display of Nazi memorabilia. In 2001, however, a U.S. district court held that this ruling could not be enforced against Yahoo in the United States.[52]

Freedom of the Press

Freedom of the press can be regarded as a special instance of freedom of speech. At the time of the framing of the Constitution, the press meant only newspapers, magazines, and books. As technology has advanced, the laws touching on freedom of the press have been modified. What can and cannot be printed still occupies an important place in constitutional law, however.

Defamation in Writing

Libel
A written defamation of a person's character, reputation, business, or property rights.

Libel is defamation in writing (or in pictures, signs, films, or any other communication that has the potentially harmful qualities of written or printed words). As with slander, libel occurs only if the defamatory statements are observed by a third party. If one person writes a private letter to another person wrongfully accusing him or her of embezzling funds, that does not constitute libel. The courts have generally held that dictating a letter to an assistant constitutes communication of the letter's contents to a third party, and therefore, if defamation has occurred, the wrongdoer can be sued.

A 1964 case, *New York Times Co. v. Sullivan*, explored an important question regarding libelous statements made about public officials.[53] The Supreme Court held that only when a statement against a public official was made with **actual malice**—with either knowledge of its falsity or a reckless disregard of the truth—could damages be obtained.

Actual Malice
Either knowledge of a defamatory statement's falsity or a reckless disregard for the truth.

Public Figures
An order issued by a judge restricting the publication of news about a trial or a pretrial hearing to protect the accused's right to a fair trial.

The standard set by the Court in the case has since been applied to **public figures** generally. Public figures include not only public officials but also public employees who exercise substantial governmental power and any persons who are generally in the limelight. Statements made about public figures, especially when they are made through a public medium, usually are related to matters of general public interest. Furthermore, public figures typically have some access to a public medium for answering disparaging falsehoods about themselves,

51. Foundation for Individual Rights in Education, "Victory: Modesto Junior College Settles Student's First Amendment Lawsuit," February 25, 2014. Accessed at: www.thefire.org/victory-modesto-junior-college-settles-students-first-amendment-lawsuit/
52. *Yahoo!, Inc. v. La Ligue Contre le Racisme et l'Antisemitisme,* 169 F. Supp. 2d 1181 (N.D. Cal. 2001).
53. 376 U.S. 254 (1964).

whereas private individuals do not. For these reasons, public figures must prove that the statements were made with actual malice in defamation cases. Fifty years later, the principles Justice Brennan drew upon in crafting the majority opinion are still vital to a free society. Brennan argued that "debate on public issues should be uninhibited, robust, and wide-open, and that it may well include vehement, caustic, and sometimes unpleasantly sharp attacks on government and public officials."[54]

A Free Press versus a Fair Trial: Gag Orders

Another major issue concerns media coverage of criminal trials. The Sixth Amendment guarantees the right of criminal suspects to a fair trial—the accused have rights. The First Amendment guarantees freedom of the press. What if the two rights appear to be in conflict? Which one prevails?

Jurors may be influenced by reading news stories about the trial in which they are participating. In the 1970s, judges increasingly issued **gag orders**, which restricted the publication of news about a trial in progress or even a pretrial hearing. In a landmark 1976 case, *Nebraska Press Association v. Stuart*, the Supreme Court unanimously ruled that a Nebraska judge's gag order had violated the First Amendment's guarantee of freedom of the press.[55] Chief Justice Warren Burger indicated that even pervasive adverse pretrial publicity did not necessarily lead to an unfair trial, and that prior restraints on publication were not justified. Some justices even went so far as to suggest that gag orders are never justified.

Despite the *Nebraska Press Association* ruling, the Court has upheld certain types of gag orders. In *Gannett Co. v. De Pasquale* in 1979, the highest court held that if a judge found a reasonable probability that news publicity would harm a defendant's right to a fair trial, the court could impose a gag rule: "Members of the public have no constitutional right under the Sixth and Fourteenth Amendments to attend criminal trials."[56]

The *Nebraska* and *Gannett* cases, however, involved pretrial hearings. Could a judge impose a gag order on an entire trial, including pretrial hearings? In 1980, in *Richmond Newspapers, Inc. v. Virginia*, the Court ruled that actual trials must be open to the public except under unusual circumstances.[57]

In February 2012, 17-year old African American Trayvon Martin was shot and killed by George Zimmerman. Zimmerman was acting as a neighborhood watch captain in Sanford, Florida and had reported Martin to a 911 operator as "a suspicious person" in the neighborhood. The exact circumstances surrounding the altercation were subject to intense scrutiny and disagreement once the case went to trial. The incident attracted international attention, comments from President Obama, and extensive media attention. Zimmerman claimed that he acted in self-defense under Florida's "stand your ground" law. He and his attorneys actively solicited public support and financial contributions using social media and with a dedicated website. Prosecutors sought a gag order, claiming that the website and intense social media campaign could influence potential jurors in the racially charged case. The judge disagreed and refused to grant the order. Prosecutors returned three times to request that parties to the case be prevented from speaking directly to the press or to the public through social media. No gag order was

Gag Orders
An order issued by a judge restricting the publication of news about a trial or a pretrial hearing to protect the accused's right to a fair trial.

---

54. Roy S. Gutterman, "The Landmark Libel Case, Times v. Sullivan, Still Resonates 50 Years Later," *Forbes*, March 5, 2014. Accessed at www.forbes.com/sites/realspin/2014/03/05/the-landmark-libel-case-times-v-sullivan-still-resonates-50-years-later/
55. 427 U.S. 539 (1976).
56. 443 U.S. 368 (1979).
57. 448 U.S. 555 (1980).

ever issued. Zimmerman was eventually acquitted. The pervasive nature of online communication and the sheer number of 24-hour cable news outlets raise questions about whether gag orders are even possible today.

Information companies, such as Google and Verizon, had been operating under a federal gag order of sorts that prevented the companies from informing clients when a government agency subpoenaed data records. This practice was exposed in the information leaked by Edward Snowden. In January 2014, the Obama administration announced surveillance reforms that have eased these restrictions. Tech companies are now in the position of having to convince business clients and private consumers that they can be trusted with private data and information. Google reacted by creating a video using toy figurines and a game board to explain how it responds to search warrants for client email and other online data. Other companies have adopted the practice of releasing regular government transparency reports detailing the types of user data requests they received from the U.S. government.

Google/YouTube

Films, Radio, and TV

As noted, only in a few cases has the Supreme Court upheld prior restraint of published materials. The Court's reluctance to accept prior restraint is less evident with respect to motion pictures. In the first half of the twentieth century, films were routinely submitted to local censorship boards. In 1968, the Supreme Court ruled that a film can be banned only under a law that provides for a prompt hearing at which the film is shown to be obscene. Today, few local censorship boards exist. Instead, the film industry regulates itself primarily through the industry's rating system. Video posted to YouTube is not subject to a rating system. YouTube users can flag any video as containing pornography, mature content or graphic violence, depicting illegal acts or being racially or ethnically offensive. A video is removed only if a review by the company's customer support department agrees that it is inappropriate, or that the video is on its face in violation of the site's terms of use.

did you know?

Over 6 billion hours of video are watched each month on YouTube—that's almost an hour for every person on Earth—and 80 percent of YouTube traffic comes from outside the United States.

Radio and television broadcasting has the least First Amendment protection. In 1934, the national government established the Federal Communications Commission (FCC) to regulate electromagnetic wave frequencies. The government's position has been that the airwaves and all frequencies that travel through the air belong to the people of the United States. Thus, no broadcaster can monopolize these frequencies nor can they be abused. The FCC is the authority that regulates the use of the airwaves and grants licenses to broadcast television, radio, satellite transmission, etc. Based on a case decided by the Supreme Court in 1978, the FCC can impose sanctions on radio or TV stations that broadcast "filthy words," even if the words are not legally obscene.[58]

In determining which type of communication enjoys the greatest protection, the Court favors mediums that are broadly available, accessed by all types of people, and used to engage in political discourse. Print media and the Internet are both cheap and readily accessible to all who want to share information or persuade others of their position. Broadcast media—primarily TV, but also radio—remains more closely regulated because it is a "scarce" resource. The profusion of cable networks and Internet companies like Netflix who create original programming challenge this longstanding approach.

58. *FCC v. Pacifica Foundation*, 438 U.S. 726 (1978).The phrase "filthy words" refers to a monologue by comedian George Carlin, which became the subject of the court case.

The Right to Assemble and to Petition the Government

The First Amendment prohibits Congress from making any law that abridges "the right of the people peaceably to assemble, and to petition the Government for a redress of grievances." Inherent in such a right is the ability of private citizens to communicate their ideas on public issues to government officials, as well as to other individuals. Indeed, the amendment also protects the right of individuals to join interest groups and lobby the government. The Supreme Court has often put this freedom on a par with freedom of speech and freedom of the press. Nonetheless, it has allowed municipalities to require permits for parades, sound trucks, and demonstrations so that public officials can control traffic or prevent demonstrations from turning into riots.

The freedom to demonstrate became a major issue in 1977 when the American Nazi Party sought to march through Skokie, Illinois, a largely Jewish suburb where many Holocaust survivors resided. The Supreme Court let stand a lower court's ruling that the city of Skokie had violated the Nazis' First Amendment guarantees by denying them a permit to march.[59]

This chapter has already reviewed several recent cases involving the right to assemble and protest. Others include a Massachusetts law forbidding abortion opponents from entering a 35-foot buffer zone in front of entrances to facilities where abortions are performed. The law is aimed at preventing conflicts among abortion protestors and counselors, clients, and escorts at abortion clinics. It was challenged by Eleanor McCullen, a woman who regularly stands outside a Planned Parenthood clinic in Boston and attempts to persuade young women entering the site against having an abortion. McCullen contends the ban on approaching and speaking to people within the buffer zone is an unconstitutional violation of the free speech rights protected by the First Amendment. Massachusetts claims the current law strikes the right balance among legitimate, but competing interests.

59. *Smith v. Collin*, 439 U.S. 916 (1978).

In a 9-0 ruling in June 2014, the Supreme Court struck down the Massachusetts law, saying it was too broad. "A painted line on the sidewalk is easy to enforce, but the prime objective of the First Amendment is not efficiency," Chief Justice Roberts wrote. Roberts said that the state has other means to prevent harassment of women entering the clinic.[60]

Ironically, in 1949 Congress passed a law regarding how close protesters could get to the U.S. Supreme Court, saying "It is unlawful to parade, stand, or move in processions or assemblages in the Supreme Court Building or grounds, or to display in the Building and grounds a flag, banner, or device designed or adapted to bring into public notice a party, organization, or movement." In 2013, U.S. District Judge Beryl Howell wrote, "It cannot possibly be consistent with the First Amendment for the government to so broadly prohibit expression in virtually any form in front of a courthouse, even the Supreme Court." The protest restrictions have been challenged on behalf of Occupy DC protesters who were arrested when they attempted to protest on the broad plaza in front of the Supreme Court. The ACLU argues that the courthouse steps are an extension of the town square—a place to air grievances with the judicial system.[61]

Online Assembly

An important question today is whether individuals should have the right to "assemble" online to advocate violence against certain groups (such as physicians who perform abortions) or advocate values that are opposed to our democracy (such as terrorism). While some online advocacy groups promote interests consistent with American political values, other groups aim to destroy those values. Whether First Amendment freedoms should be sacrificed in the interests of national security is a question that will be debated for some time.

Apart from advocating violence or the overthrow of democracy, there are a number of new tools available online to create and send petitions of all sorts— Change.org and iPetition, for example. The White House website includes a page titled "We the People: Your Voice in Government" which is dedicated to providing a means for individuals to create a petition or to sign an open petition on an issue they care deeply about.[62] When the number of signatures on a petition reach a threshold, the administration posts a response. The content of issue petitions is wide ranging—from asking that all single-stall restrooms be made unisex to reforming the postal service.

More Liberties under Scrutiny: Matters of Privacy

■ **LO4.4:** Discuss the constitutional protection of privacy rights in personal and public life and evaluate the threats to privacy rights posed by technology and security interests.

No explicit reference is made anywhere in the Constitution to a person's right to privacy. Until the second half of the twentieth century, the courts did not take a very positive approach toward the right to privacy. During Prohibition, suspected bootleggers' telephones were tapped routinely, and the information obtained was used as a legal basis for prosecution. In *Olmstead v. United States* in 1928, the

60. Adam Liptak and John Schwartz, "Court Rejects Zone to Buffer Abortion Clinic." *The New York Times*, June 26, 2014. Accessed at www.nytimes.com/2014/06/27/us/supreme-court-abortion-clinic-protests.html
61. Robert Barnes, "A Question of Where Protesters Take a Stand" *The Washington Post*, February 16, 2014. Accessed at http://www.washingtonpost.com/politics/a-question-of-where-protesters-take-a-stand/2014/02/16/1bc57ee0-9720-11e3-afce-3e7c922ef31e_story.html
62. We the People: Your Voice in Government https://petitions.whitehouse.gov/

Supreme Court upheld such an invasion of privacy.[63] Justice Louis Brandeis strongly dissented from the majority decision in this case. He argued that the framers of the Constitution gave every citizen the right to be left alone. He called such a right "the most comprehensive of rights and the right most valued by civilized men."

In the 1960s, the highest court began to modify the majority view. In 1965, in *Griswold v. Connecticut*, the Supreme Court overturned a Connecticut law that effectively prohibited the use of contraceptives, holding that the law violated the right to privacy.[64] Justice William O. Douglas formulated a unique way of reading this right into the Bill of Rights. He claimed that the First, Third, Fourth, Fifth, and Ninth Amendments created "penumbras [shadows], formed by emanations [things sent out from] those guarantees that help give them life and substance," and he went on to describe zones of privacy that are guaranteed by these rights. When we read the Ninth Amendment, we can see the foundation for his reasoning: "The enumeration in the Constitution, of certain rights, shall not be construed to deny or disparage [belittle] others retained by the people." In other words, just because the Constitution, including its amendments, does not specifically talk about the right to privacy does not mean that this right is denied to the people.

Some of today's most controversial issues relate to the erosion of privacy rights in the information age. Could we be giving away our right to privacy with the volume of personal data we give away online? Other issues concern abortion and the "right to die." The Supreme Court seems content to allow states to take the lead in these areas at the moment. Since the terrorist attacks of September 11, 2001, Americans have faced another crucial question regarding privacy rights: To what extent should Americans sacrifice privacy rights in the interests of national security? To what degree are we prepared to live in a surveillance society in order to feel protected?

Information Privacy

An important privacy issue, created in part by new technology, is the amassing of information on individuals by government agencies and private businesses, such as marketing firms, grocery stores, and casinos. Personal information on the average American citizen is filed away in dozens of agencies—such as the Social Security Administration and the Internal Revenue Service. Because of the threat of indiscriminate use of private information by unauthorized individuals, Congress passed the Privacy Act in 1974. This was the first law regulating the use of federal government information about private individuals. Under the Privacy Act, every citizen has the right to obtain copies of personal records collected by federal agencies and to correct inaccuracies in such records. However, this applies only to government agencies and has no bearing on records collected by private organization or companies. Other laws are designed to protect the privacy of certain types of information, such as health care records (Health Insurance Portability and Accountability Act, HIPAA).

The ease with which personal information can be obtained by using the Internet for marketing and other purposes has led to unique privacy issues. Maybe privacy is something that individuals define for themselves. Portraits on public websites such as Facebook, LinkedIn, or other networking sites are created by the user and can protect personal data or make certain facts *very public*. The person who submits the information gets to decide. Whether privacy rights can survive in an information age is a question that Americans and their leaders continue to confront.

---

63. 277 U.S. 438 (1928). This decision was overruled later in *Katz v. United States*, 389 U.S. 347 (1967).
64. 381 U.S. 479 (1965).

Beyond Our Borders

Satellite Sentinel Project

Actor George Clooney often finds himself the subject of paparazzi attention. The Satellite Sentinel Project is an attempt to redirect this attention to the conflict and humanitarian crisis in Sudan. The projects tag line is, "The world is watching because you are watching."*

The civil war between the north and south in Sudan concluded with a peace agreement in 2005. That conflict, the longest in African history, has also been characterized as the second deadliest global conflict after World War II. Following South Sudan's independence from Sudan as the result of a referendum vote in July 2011, the region has descended into violence, with ongoing deadly border clashes amid a standoff over oil. Sudan Armed Forces (SAF) bomb oil fields in South Sudan; southern militias from the Sudan People's Liberation Army (SPLA) attack oil fields in the North. Civilians are caught in the crossfire. Aid agencies are unable to get into the region and thousands are seeking to escape. Food relief has become an acute casualty of the conflict.

Sudanese President Omar al-Bashir has been charged with war crimes in connection with armed conflicts between the independent state of South Sudan and Sudan that have killed as many as 400,000 people in the western region of Darfur alone. He is alleged to be responsible for the aerial bombing campaign directed at moving indigenous ethnic groups out of the Nuba Mountains. President al-Bashir's military campaign in the Nuba Mountains has been termed "Starvation Warfare" by Clooney.

Clooney, along with other celebrities including Matt Damon and Brad Pitt, founded Not On Our Watch, a registered nonprofit whose mission is "to focus global attention and resources towards putting an end to mass atrocities around the world." Drawing upon the powerful voices of artists, activists, and cultural leaders, Not On Our Watch generates lifesaving humanitarian assistance and protection for the vulnerable, marginalized, and displaced."** Sudan is on the organization's watch list and Clooney has made several trips to Sudan, often with John Prendergast, human rights activist and former Director for African Affairs at the National Security Council. Prendergast is co-founder of the Enough Project, an initiative to end genocide and crimes against humanity. The Enough Project is affiliated with the Center for American Progress.***

Not On Our Watch and the Enough Project have partnered with Harvard Humanitarian Initiative to use sophisticated private satellite technology to spy on combatants in an active conflict zone with the ultimate goal of protecting civilians.**** The images are analyzed and made public on the project's website, thereby letting combatants know the world is watching.

As Clooney said, "We are the antigenocide paparazzi...if you know your actions are going to be covered you tend to behave much differently than when you operate in a vacuum."***** Satellite time is expensive but DigitalGlobe agreed to donate the images for the start-up of the project. Four staff and a half-dozen student interns with the Harvard Humanitarian Initiative aggregate the images and coordinate the analysis, searching for clues of impending violence. Soon after the Satellite Sentinel Project began, the Harvard team detected SAF troops gathering near the village of Kurmuk and posted the report and images to the website. As a result, more than 1,500 villagers fled to Ethiopia, leaving fewer targets for the SAF. The SAF has changed its tactics to conduct attacks at night or under heavy cloud cover, cloaking weapons under brush or tarps to make them harder to detect in satellite images.

For Critical Analysis

1. Satellite surveillance in the "right hands" can promote humanitarian values like those described above, but what about satellite surveillance in the "wrong hands?" Which civil liberties are at stake as the number of government and commercial satellites overhead increase?

2. Celebrities use their star-power to redirect our attention from them to issues they believe are important. In doing so, they prioritize some crises over others. A free press is an essential civil liberty, but how can we ensure that we are informed about a wide range of issues and not just those attracting the camera's attention at the moment?

* Satellite Sentinel Project http://www.satsentinel.org/
** Not on Our Watch http://notonourwatchproject.org/who_we_are and Enough Project http://www.enoughproject.org/
*** Michael Blanding, "Inside Harvard's Spy Lab." The Boston Globe Magazine, April 29, 2012. Accessed at www.bostonglobe.com/magazine/2012/04/28/inside-george-clooney-harvard-spy-lab/RB6fK8MUYkBn3RvWFZpPqO/story.html?camp=pm
**** Mark Benjamin, "Clooney's 'Antigenocide Paparazzi: Watching Sudan." Time, December 28, 2010. Accessed at http://content.time.com/time/magazine/article/0,9171,2040211,00.htmlatsentinel.org/
***** Michael Blanding, "Inside Harvard's Spy Lab." The Boston Globe Magazine, April 29, 2012. Accessed at www.bostonglobe.com/magazine/2012/04/28/inside-george-clooney-harvard-spy-lab/RB6fK8MUYkBn3RvWFZpPqO/story.html?camp=pm

Privacy Rights and Abortion

Historically, abortion was not a criminal offense before the first movement of the fetus in the uterus, usually between the 16th and 18th weeks of pregnancy. By 1973, however, performing an abortion at any time during pregnancy was a criminal offense in a majority of the states.

Roe v. Wade. In 1973, in *Roe v. Wade,* the United States Supreme Court accepted the argument that the laws against abortion violated "Jane Roe's" right to privacy under the Constitution.[65] The Court held that during the first trimester (three months) of pregnancy, abortion was an issue solely between a woman and her physician. The state could not limit abortions except to require that they be performed by licensed physicians. During the second trimester, to protect the health of the mother, the state was allowed to specify the conditions under which an abortion could be performed. During the final trimester, the state could regulate or even outlaw abortions, except when necessary to preserve the life or health of the woman.

After *Roe,* the Supreme Court issued decisions in several cases defining and redefining the boundaries of state regulation of abortion. During the 1980s, the Court twice struck down laws that required a woman who wished to have an abortion to undergo counseling designed to discourage abortions. In the late 1980s and early 1990s, however, the Court took a more conservative approach. In *Webster v. Reproductive Health Services* (1989), the Court upheld a Missouri statute that, among other things, banned the use of public hospitals or other taxpayer-supported facilities for performing abortions.[66] In *Planned Parenthood v. Casey* in 1992, the Court upheld a Pennsylvania law that required preabortion counseling; a waiting period of 24 hours; and, for girls under the age of 18, parental or judicial permission.[67] The final decision was a 5-4 vote; Sandra Day O'Connor wrote the opinion. While the opinion explicitly upheld *Roe,* it changed the grounds on which the states can regulate abortion. The Court found that states could not place an "undue burden" on a woman who sought an abortion. In this case, the Court found that spousal notification was such a burden. Because many other conditions were upheld, abortions continue to be more difficult to obtain in some states than others.

The Controversy Continues. Abortion continues to be a divisive issue. "Right-to-life" forces continue to push for laws banning abortion, endorse political candidates who support their views, and organize protests. Because of several episodes of violence attending protests at abortion clinics, in 1994 Congress passed the Freedom of Access to Clinic Entrances Act. The act prohibits protesters from blocking entrances to such clinics. The Supreme Court ruled in 1993 that such protesters can be prosecuted under laws governing racketeering, and in 1998 a federal court in Illinois convicted right-to-life protesters under these laws. In 1997, the Supreme Court upheld the constitutionality of prohibiting protesters from entering a 15-foot "buffer zone" around abortion clinics and from giving unwanted counseling to those entering the clinics.[68] In 2006, however, the Supreme Court unanimously reversed its earlier decision that anti-abortion protesters could be prosecuted under laws governing racketeering.[69]

---

65. 410 U.S.113 (1973). Jane Roe was not the real name of the woman in this case. It is a common legal pseudonym used to protect a person's privacy.
66. 492 U.S. 490 (1989).
67. 505 U.S. 833 (1992).
68. *Schenck v. Pro Choice Network,* 519 U.S. 357 (1997).
69. *Scheidler v. National Organization for Women,* 126 S. Ct. 1264 (2006).

In a 2000 decision, the Court upheld a Colorado law requiring demonstrators to stay at least eight feet away from people entering and leaving clinics unless people consent to be approached. The Court concluded that the law's restrictions on speech-related conduct did not violate the free speech rights of abortion protesters.[70]

That same year, the Supreme Court reviewed a Nebraska law banning "partial-birth" abortions. Similar laws had been passed by at least 27 states. A partial-birth abortion is a procedure that can be used during the second trimester of pregnancy. Abortion rights advocates claim that in limited circumstances the procedure is the safest way to perform an abortion, and that the government should never outlaw specific medical procedures. Opponents argue that the procedure has no medical merit and that it ends the life of a fetus that might be able to live outside the womb. The Supreme Court invalidated the Nebraska law on the grounds that, as written, the law could be used to ban other abortion procedures, and it contained no provisions for protecting the health of the pregnant woman.[71] In 2003, legislation similar to the Nebraska statute was passed by the U.S. Congress and signed into law by President George W. Bush. It was immediately challenged in court. In 2007, the Supreme Court heard several challenges to the partial-birth abortion law and upheld the constitutionality of that legislation, saying that the law was specific enough that it did not "impose an undue burden" on women seeking an abortion.[72]

The abortion debate is now driven entirely driven by state legislative action restricting access to abortion and the emphasis on privacy articulated in *Roe* has all but disappeared. More abortion restrictions were adopted by the states in the period between 2011 and 2013 than the entire the entire previous decade. Nearly half of the laws—45 percent—fell into three categories: targeted regulations of abortion providers, bans on abortions after 20 weeks, and restrictions on medical abortions.[73] In 2013, 56 percent of women in the United States lived in one of 27 states characterized as hostile to abortion. A Texas law barring doctors from withdrawing "life-sustaining treatment" to pregnant women led a Fort Worth hospital to keep a pregnant, brain-dead woman on life support for two months against the wishes of her husband and family. The hospital claimed the law required that they maintain the woman on life support until a cesarean section could be performed and the fetus delivered even though when she was admitted to the hospital she was only 14 weeks pregnant and tests showed the fetus suffered from abnormalities. On January 24, 2014, a state district judge ordered the hospital to comply with the family's wishes. The judge's ruling said the law did not apply in this case because the woman was legally dead.[74]

Privacy Rights and the "Right to Die"

A 1976 case was one of the first publicized right-to-die cases.[75] The parents of Karen Ann Quinlan, a young woman who had been in a coma for nearly a year and who had been kept alive during that time by a respirator, wanted her respirator removed. In 1976, the New Jersey Supreme Court ruled that the right to privacy includes the right of a patient to refuse treatment and that patients who are

---

70. *Hill v. Colorado*, 530 U.S. 703 (2000).
71. *Stenberg v. Carhart*, 530 U.S. 914 (2000).
72. *Gonzales v. Carhart*, 550 U.S. (2007) and *Gonzales v. Planned Parenthood*, 550 U.S. (2007).
73. Guttmacher Institute, "More State Abortion Restrictions Were Enacted in 2011–2013 Than in the Entire Previous Decade." January 2, 2014. Accessed at www.guttmacher.org/media/inthenews/2014/01/02/index.html
74. Fernandez, "Texas Woman is Taken Off Life Support After Order." *The New York Times*, January 26, 2014. Accessed at www.nytimes.com/2014/01/27/us/texas-hospital-to-end-life-support-for-pregnant-brain-dead-woman.html
75. *In re Quinlan*, 70 N.J. 10 (1976).

unable to speak can exercise that right through a family member or guardian. In 1990, the Supreme Court took up the issue. In *Cruzan v. Director, Missouri Department of Health*, the Court stated that a patient's life-sustaining treatment can be withdrawn at the request of a family member only if "clear and convincing evidence" exists that the patient did not want such treatment.[76]

What if No Living Will Exists? Since the *Quinlan* decision, most states have enacted laws permitting people to designate their wishes concerning life-sustaining procedures in "living wills" or durable health-care powers of attorney. These laws and the *Cruzan* decision have resolved the right-to-die controversy for situations in which the patient has drafted a living will. Disputes are still possible if there is no living will.

Physician-Assisted Suicide. In the 1990s, another issue surfaced: Do privacy rights include the right of terminally ill people to end their lives through physician-assisted suicide? Until 1996, the courts consistently upheld state laws that prohibited this practice, either through specific statutes or under their general homicide statutes. In 1996, after two federal appellate courts ruled that state laws banning assisted suicide were unconstitutional, the issue reached the United States Supreme Court. In 1997, in *Washington v. Glucksberg*, the Court stated, clearly and categorically, that the liberty interest protected by the Constitution does not include a right to commit suicide, with or without assistance.[77] In effect, the Supreme Court left the decision in the hands of the states. Since then, assisted suicide has been allowed in only one state—Oregon. In 2006, the Supreme Court upheld Oregon's physician-assisted suicide law against a challenge from the Bush administration.[78]

Assistance with end of life choices is now legal in five states. Preferring "death with dignity" or "aid in dying," proponents of laws allowing terminally ill patients to choose assistance in dying eschew the term "assisted suicide." In a Gallup Poll conducted in 2013, 70 percent of respondents agreed that when patients and their families wanted it, doctors should be allowed to "end the patient's life by some painless means." Opponents say that actively ending a life, no matter how frail a person is, is a moral violation and that patients might be pushed to die early for the convenience of others.

Privacy Rights versus Security Issues

As former Supreme Court justice Thurgood Marshall once said, "Grave threats to liberty often come in times of urgency, when constitutional rights seem too extravagant to endure." Not surprisingly, antiterrorist legislation since the attacks on September 11, 2001 has eroded certain basic rights, in particular the Fourth Amendment protections against unreasonable searches and seizures. Several tools previously used against certain types of criminal suspects (for instance, "roving wiretaps" and National Security Letters) have been authorized for use against a broader array of terror suspects. Many civil liberties organizations argue that abuses of the Fourth Amendment are ongoing.

While it has been possible for a law enforcement agency to gain court permission to wiretap a telephone almost since telephones were invented, a roving wiretap allows an agency to tap all forms of communication used by the named person, including cell phones and email, and it applies across legal jurisdictions. Previously, roving wiretaps could only be requested for persons suspected of one of a small

---

76. 497 U.S. 261 (1990).
77. 521 U.S. 702 (1997).
78. *Gonzales v. Oregon*, 126 S. Ct. 904 (2006).

number of serious crimes. Now, if persons are suspected of planning a terrorist attack, they can be monitored no matter what form of electronic communication they use. Such roving wiretaps appear to contravene the Supreme Court's interpretation of the Fourth Amendment, which requires a judicial warrant to describe the *place* to be searched, not just the person, although the Court has not banned them to date. One of the goals of the framers was to avoid *general* searches.

The USA PATRIOT Act. Much of the government's failure to anticipate the attacks of September 11, 2001 has been attributed to a lack of cooperation among government agencies. At that time, barriers prevented information sharing between the law enforcement and intelligence arms of the government. A major objective of the PATRIOT Act was to eliminate those barriers. Lawmakers claimed that the Act would improve lines of communication between agencies such as the Federal Bureau of Investigation (FBI) and the Central Intelligence Agency (CIA), thereby allowing the government to better anticipate terrorist plots. With improved communication, various agencies could more effectively coordinate their efforts in combating terrorism.

did you know?

The USA PATRIOT Act, enacted following the September 11 terrorist attacks, stands for Uniting and Strengthening America by Providing Appropriate Tools Required to Intercept and Obstruct Terrorism Act of 2001.

In addition, the PATRIOT Act eased restrictions on the government's ability to investigate and arrest suspected terrorists. Because of the secretive nature of terrorist groups, supporters of the Act argue that the government must have greater latitude in pursuing leads on potential terrorist activity. After receiving approval of the Foreign Intelligence Surveillance Court (FISA), the act authorizes law enforcement officials to secretly search a suspected terrorist's home. It also allows the government to monitor a suspect's Internet activities, phone conversations, financial records, and book purchases. Although a number of these search and surveillance tactics have long been a part of criminal investigations, the PATRIOT Act expanded their scope to include individuals as terrorist suspects even if they are not agents of a foreign government.

Civil Liberties Concerns. Proponents of the PATRIOT Act insist that ordinary, law-abiding citizens have nothing to fear from the government's increased search and surveillance powers. Groups such as the ACLU have objected to the Act, however, arguing that it poses a grave threat to constitutionally guaranteed rights and liberties. Under the PATRIOT Act, FBI agents are required to certify the need for search warrants to the FISA Court. Rarely are such requests rejected.

In the last few years, the FBI began using the National Security Letter (NSL) to avoid the procedures required by the FISA Court. The NSL allows the FBI to get records of telephone calls, subscriber information, and other transactions, although it does not give the FBI access to the content of the calls. However, as Congress tightened the requirements for warrants under the PATRIOT Act, the FBI evidently began to use the NSLs as a shortcut. While the use of NSLs has been legal for more than 20 years, recent massive use of this technique has led Congress to consider further restrictions in order to preserve the rights of U.S. citizens.

Opponents of the PATRIOT Act fear that these expanded powers of investigation might be used to silence government critics or to threaten members of interest groups who oppose government polices today or in the future. Congress debated these issues in 2005 and then renewed most of the provisions in 2006. It has been renewed again as recently as 2011, over the objections of many civil liberties organizations. One of the most controversial aspects of the PATRIOT Act permits the government to eavesdrop on telephone calls with a warrant from the FISA Court. In 2005, it became known that the Bush administration was eavesdropping on U.S. telephone calls without a warrant if the caller was from outside the United States.

Congress passed the FISA Amendments Act in June 2008, which regulates such calls and gives immunity from prosecution to telecommunications companies.

The incredible growth of modern wireless technology is an opportunity and a challenge for law enforcement officials, but it also carries potential threats to civil liberties. Modern wireless technology makes it possible to track offenders more easily, but is such tracking legal? Most wireless devices—smartphones, tablets, netbooks—contain wireless receivers that connect with the Internet, and most include a GPS transmitter. If you lose your telephone, you can call your service provider and be told approximately where it is because it is signaling a nearby tower or satellite. Is this an invasion of your privacy?

As a result of Edward Snowden's leak of top-secret documents, we now know about the NSA's secret operation to mine phone and Internet data. Moreover, intelligence alliances such as "Five Eyes"(involving the United States, Australia, Canada, New Zealand, and the United Kingdom) funnel massive amounts of data to the NSA. Barton Gellman of *The Washington Post* summarized the value of Snowden's information: "Taken together, the revelations have brought to light a global surveillance system that cast off many of its historical restraints after the attacks on September 11, 2001. Secret legal authorities empowered the NSA to sweep in telephone, Internet, and location records of whole populations."[79] President Obama assured the public that there is "no spying on Americans." In January 2014 the nation learned that the NSA had implanted software in nearly 100,000 computers around the world, thereby allowing the United States to conduct surveillance and create a digital highway for launching cyberattacks. In that same week, President Obama announced that he would accept a series of recommendations for reforms to NSA practices forwarded from an advisory panel. U.S. technology company executives worry that some of the techniques developed by the agency to find flaws in computer systems undermine global confidence in a range of American-made information products like laptop computers and cloud services. Our total dependence on the Internet and its infrastructure for everything—from our social network to finding the weather or traffic reports to looking for the best deal on a purchase—brings a new set of privacy challenges. Your location is signaled by your wireless device, as is that of your friends as you tweet. Unless the individual puts extensive privacy controls into place, purchase records are sent to advertisers, and Facebook data are sent to friends and to friends of friends and to marketers, leading some to claim that in our data-saturated economy, privacy has become a luxury good.[80] Julia Angwin, a senior reporter for ProPublica, cautions that accessing information, communication, and goods on the Internet for free is not really free—we pay for it with our personal data, which is "spliced and diced and bought and sold." Your Google search results depend on the data provided in the past. Personal data can be used to charge people different prices for goods without their knowledge. Rolling back this information give-away will not be easy. With so much of the information given freely by each of us, can we really claim a presumption of privacy? What will happen to your privacy rights in the next few years as you move into the workforce? Can information freely shared prevent you from getting a job? Civil liberty protections are vital to our political system, but the application of these privacy issues to your personal future are well worth considering.

79. Barton Gellman, "Edward Snowden, after months of NSA revelations, says his mission's accomplished." *The Washington Post*, December 23, 2013. Accessed at www.washingtonpost.com/world/national-security/edward-snowden-after-months-of-nsa-revelations-says-his-missions-accomplished/2013/12/23/49fc36de-6c1c-11e3-a523-fe73f0ff6b8d_story.html

80. Julia Angwin, "Has Privacy Become a Luxury Good?" *The New York Times*, March 3, 2014. Accessed at www.nytimes.com/2014/03/04/opinion/has-privacy-become-a-luxury-good.html

The Great Balancing Act: The Rights of the Accused versus the Rights of Society

■ **LO4.5:** Identify the rights of the accused and discuss the role of the Supreme Court in defining criminal due process rights over time.

The United States has one of the highest murder rates in the industrialized world. It is not surprising, therefore, that many citizens have extremely strong opinions about the rights of those accused of crimes. When an accused person, especially one who has confessed to some criminal act, is set free because of an apparent legal technicality, many people opine that the rights of the accused are given more weight than the rights of society and of potential or actual victims. Why, then, give criminal suspects rights? The answer is partly to avoid convicting innocent people, but mostly because all criminal suspects have the right to due process of law and fair treatment. Due process rights are intended to prevent government from abusing its considerable power relative to an individual accused of a crime.

The courts and the police must constantly engage in a balancing act of competing rights. At the basis of all discussions about the appropriate balance is the U.S. Bill of Rights. The Fourth, Fifth, Sixth, and Eighth Amendments deal specifically with the rights of criminal defendants.

The basic rights of criminal defendants are outlined in Table 4–2. When appropriate, the specific constitutional provision or amendment on which a right is based is also given.

Table 4–2 ▶ Basic Rights of Criminal Defendants

LIMITS ON THE CONDUCT OF POLICE OFFICERS AND PROSECUTORS
No unreasonable or unwarranted searches and seizures (Amend. IV)
No arrest except on probable cause (Amend. IV)
No coerced confessions or illegal interrogation (Amend. V)
No entrapment
On questioning, a suspect must be informed of her or his rights
DEFENDANT'S PRETRIAL RIGHTS
Writ of *habeas corpus* (Article I, Section 9)
Prompt arraignment (Amend. VI)
Legal counsel (Amend. VI)
Reasonable bail (Amend. VIII)
To be informed of charges (Amend. VI)
To remain silent (Amend. V)
TRIAL RIGHTS
Speedy and public trial before a jury (Amend. VI)
Impartial jury selected from a cross section of the community (Amend. VI)
Trial atmosphere free of prejudice, fear, and outside interference
No compulsory self-incrimination (Amend. V)
Adequate counsel (Amend. VI)
No cruel and unusual punishment (Amend. VIII)
Appeal of convictions
No double jeopardy (Amend. V)

Extending the Rights of the Accused

■ **LO4.6:** Evaluate modern threats to civil liberties posed by spy technology, the transfer of personal information through social media, and heightened security concerns following the September 11, 2001 terrorist attacks.

During the 1960s, the Supreme Court, under Chief Justice Earl Warren, significantly expanded the rights of accused persons. In *Gideon v. Wainwright*, a case decided in 1963, the Court held that if a person is accused of a felony and cannot afford an attorney, an attorney must be made available to the accused person at the government's expense.[81] This case was particularly interesting because Gideon, who was arrested for stealing a small amount of money from a vending machine, was not considered a dangerous man, nor was his intellect in any way impaired. Gideon pursued his own appeal to the Supreme Court because he believed that every accused person who might face prison should be represented.[82] Although the Sixth Amendment to the Constitution provides for the right to counsel, the Supreme Court had established a precedent 21 years earlier in *Betts v. Brady*, when it held that only criminal defendants in capital (death penalty) cases automatically had a right to legal counsel.[83]

Miranda v. Arizona. In 1966, the Court issued its decision in *Miranda v. Arizona*.[84] The case involved Ernesto Miranda, who was arrested and charged with the kidnapping and rape of a young woman. After two hours of questioning, Miranda confessed and was later convicted. Miranda's lawyer appealed his conviction, arguing that the police had never informed Miranda that he had a right to remain silent and a right to be represented by counsel. The Court, in ruling in Miranda's favor, enunciated the *Miranda* rights that are now familiar to nearly all Americans:

> *Prior to any questioning, the person must be warned that he has a right to remain silent, that any statement he does make may be used against him, and that he has a right to the presence of an attorney, either retained or appointed.*

Two years after the Supreme Court's *Miranda* decision, Congress passed the Omnibus Crime Control and Safe Streets Act of 1968. Section 3501 of the act reinstated a rule that had been in effect for 180 years before *Miranda*—that statements by defendants can be used against them if the statements were made voluntarily. The Justice Department immediately disavowed Section 3501 as unconstitutional and has continued to hold this position. As a result, Section 3501, although it was never repealed, has never been enforced. In 2000, in a surprise move, a federal appellate court held that the all-but-forgotten provision was enforceable, but the Supreme Court held that the *Miranda* warnings were constitutionally based and could not be overruled by a legislative act.[85]

Exceptions to the Miranda Rule. As part of a continuing attempt to balance the rights of accused persons against the rights of society, the Supreme Court has made several exceptions to the *Miranda* rule. In 1984, for example, the Court recognized a "public-safety" exception to the rule. The need to protect the public warranted the admissibility of statements made by the defendant (in this case, indicating where he had placed a gun) as evidence in a trial, even though the defendant had not been informed of his *Miranda* rights.

81. 372 U.S. 335 (1963).
82. Anthony Lewis, *Gideon's Trumpet* (New York: Vintage, 1964).
83. 316 U.S. 455 (1942).
84. 384 U.S. 436 (1966).
85. *Dickerson v. United States*, 530 U.S. 428 (2000).

In 1985, the Court further held that a confession need not be excluded even though the police failed to inform a suspect in custody that his attorney had tried to reach him by telephone. In an important 1991 decision, the Court stated that a suspect's conviction will not be automatically overturned if the suspect was coerced into making a confession. If the other evidence admitted at trial is strong enough to justify the conviction without the confession, then the fact that the confession was obtained illegally in effect can be ignored. In yet another case, in 1994, the Supreme Court ruled that suspects must unequivocally and assertively state their right to counsel in order to stop police questioning. Saying "Maybe I should talk to a lawyer" during an interrogation after being taken into custody is not enough. The Court held that police officers are not required to decipher the suspect's intentions in such situations. Most recently, the *Miranda* protections were further narrowed when the Court found that a suspect must expressly announce his or her desire to remain silent, not just sit silently during questioning.

Video Recording of Interrogations. In view of the numerous exceptions, there are no guarantees that the *Miranda* rule will survive indefinitely. Increasingly, though, law enforcement personnel are using digital cameras to record interrogations. According to some scholars, the recording of *all* custodial interrogations would satisfy the Fifth Amendment's prohibition against coercion and in the process render the *Miranda* warnings unnecessary. Others argue, however, that recorded interrogations can be misleading.

The Exclusionary Rule

Exclusionary Rule
A policy forbidding the admission at trial of illegally seized evidence.

At least since 1914, judicial policy has prohibited the admission of illegally seized evidence at trials in federal courts. This is the so-called **exclusionary rule**. Improperly obtained evidence, no matter how telling, cannot be used by prosecutors. This includes evidence obtained by police in violation of a suspect's *Miranda* rights or of the Fourth Amendment. The Fourth Amendment protects against unreasonable searches and seizures and provides that a judge may issue a search warrant to a police officer only on *probable cause* (a demonstration of facts that permit a reasonable belief that a crime has been committed). The question that must be determined by the courts is what constitutes an unreasonable search and seizure.

The reasoning behind the exclusionary rule is that it forces police officers to gather evidence properly, in which case their due diligence will be rewarded by a conviction. Nevertheless, the exclusionary rule has always had critics who argue that it permits guilty persons to be freed because of innocent errors.

This rule was first extended to state court proceedings in a 1961 United States Supreme Court decision, *Mapp v. Ohio*.[86] In this case, the Court overturned the conviction of Dollree Mapp for the possession of obscene materials. Police found pornographic books in her apartment after searching it without a search warrant and despite her refusal to let them in.

Over the last several decades, the Supreme Court has diminished the scope of the exclusionary rule by creating some exceptions to its applicability. In 1984, the Court held that illegally obtained evidence could be admitted at trial if law enforcement personnel could prove that they would have obtained the evidence legally anyway. The same year, the Court held that a police officer who used a technically incorrect search warrant form to obtain evidence had acted in good faith and therefore the evidence was admissible at trial. The Court thus created the "good faith" exception to the exclusionary rule.

86. 367 U.S. 643 (1961).

CHAPTER 4 • CIVIL LIBERTIES

The Death Penalty

Capital punishment remains one of the most debated aspects of our criminal justice system. Those in favor of the death penalty maintain that it serves as a deterrent to serious crime and satisfies society's need for justice and fair play. Those opposed to the death penalty do not believe it has any deterrent value and hold that it constitutes a barbaric act in an otherwise civilized society.

Cruel and Unusual Punishment?

The Eighth Amendment prohibits cruel and unusual punishment. Throughout history, "cruel and unusual" referred to punishments that were more serious than the crimes—the phrase referred to torture and to executions that prolonged the agony of dying. The Supreme Court never interpreted "cruel and unusual" to prohibit all forms of capital punishment in all circumstances. Indeed, several states had imposed the death penalty for a variety of crimes and allowed juries to decide when the condemned could be sentenced to death. Many believed, however, that the imposition of the death penalty was random and arbitrary, and in 1972 the Supreme Court agreed in *Furman v. Georgia*.[87]

The decision stated that the death penalty, as then applied, violated the Eighth and Fourteenth Amendments. The Court ruled that capital punishment is not necessarily cruel and unusual if the criminal has killed or attempted to kill someone. In its opinion, the Court invited the states to enact more precise laws so that the death penalty would be applied more consistently. By 1976, 25 states had adopted a two-stage, or *bifurcated*, procedure for capital cases. In the first stage, a jury determines the guilt or innocence of the defendant for a crime that has been determined by statute to be punishable by death. If the defendant is found guilty, the jury reconvenes in the second stage and considers all relevant evidence to decide whether the death sentence is, in fact, warranted.

In *Gregg v. Georgia*, the Supreme Court ruled in favor of Georgia's bifurcated process, holding that the state's legislative guidelines had removed the ability of a jury to "wantonly and freakishly impose the death penalty."[88] The Court upheld similar procedures in Texas and Florida, establishing a procedure for all states to follow that would ensure them protection from lawsuits based on Eighth Amendment grounds. On January 17, 1977, Gary Mark Gilmore became the first American to be executed (by Utah) under the new laws.

The Death Penalty Today

Today, 32 states (see Figure 4–1), the military, and the federal government have capital punishment laws based on the guidelines established by the *Gregg* case. State governments are responsible for almost all executions in this country. The execution of Timothy McVeigh in 2001 marked the first death sentence carried out by the federal government since 1963. Only two more have followed. At this time, about 3,095 prisoners are on death row across the nation. The population on death row has been on the decline since 2003. Although California has the largest death row population of any state, Texas has the highest execution rate. The South as a region has executed 1,120 people since 1976; in the Northeast, only 4 people have been put to death over the same time period.[89]

CONNECT WITH YOUR CLASSMATES
MindTap for American Government

Access the Civil Liberties Forum: Discussion—Eighth Amendment Rights.

did you know?

According to the Death Penalty Information center, women represent about 2 percent of death row inmates and 13 women have been executed since 1976.

---

87. 408 U.S. 238 (1972).
88. 428 U.S. 153 (1976).
89. Death Penalty Information Center, Executions by Region. Accessed at www.deathpenaltyinfo.org/number-executions-state-and-region-1976

Politics with a Purpose

The Innocence Project

As long as the United States has imposed capital punishment on convicted felons, there have been claims of innocence by those sentenced to die. Although police officers and judges have always known that sometimes the innocent are falsely accused and convicted, they also believe that most of the individuals were correctly prosecuted and convicted of their crimes. As most Americans know from popular television series such as *CSI* and *Bones*, new scientific techniques make it possible to recover biological and chemical evidence that was previously inaccessible. Most important of these new tools is the use of DNA. DNA molecules contain all of the information about a person's or an animal's genetic makeup and are almost unique to each individual. The importance of DNA to criminal investigations is that DNA molecules found on a strand of hair or saliva on a handkerchief can be tested many years after they were deposited on that object.

In the early 1990s, law students at the Benjamin N. Cardozo School of Law at Yeshiva University began theorizing that DNA found in old evidence records could be used to establish the innocence of individuals wrongfully convicted of crimes. Led by Barry C. Scheck and Peter J. Neufeld, the students and faculty founded the Innocence Project, which is dedicated to helping exonerate innocent people and improving the legal system to avoid wrongful convictions. To date, more than 312 people in 36 states have been exonerated through DNA evidence. One third of the people exonerated by DNA testing were arrested between the ages of 14 and 22.

The Innocence Project identifies a number of reasons why wrongful convictions occur. Witnesses may identify the wrong person as the suspect; individuals who are arrested may feel strongly pressured to make a confession, especially if the prosecution offers a plea bargain for a lesser sentence; forensic science may be faulty in a particular location; the police may have acted out of discriminatory motives or failed to complete an investigation; informants may have given false information; or the defendant's free (or hired) counsel may be incompetent.* The Innocence Project's work has spread throughout the United States and to some foreign countries. Law students provide most of the volunteer investigations into possible cases of wrongful conviction, with guidance from their faculty. Students also research the laws governing criminal procedure in their own state and then lobby for changes to reduce the chance of wrongful convictions. In 2010, former Ohio Governor Ted Strickland signed into law a bill that was

Dewey Bozella, an aspiring boxer, served twenty-six years in prison for a murder he did not commit. He was exonerated by Project Innocence in 2011. What safeguards can be put in place to reduce the number of wrongful convictions?

researched by a student of the Innocence Project at the University of Cincinnati law school. The new legislation requires preservation of DNA evidence forever in serious crimes, strengthens the requirements for police lineups, and gives incentives for the video recording of interrogations in most serious crimes. The legislation is considered groundbreaking for preserving evidence that might prevent wrongful convictions.

If you are interested in taking part in the Innocence Project or finding a center near you, log on to the national website, www.innocenceproject.org, and look for the list of state organizations through the Innocence Network, www.innocencenetwork.org. You can learn a great deal about wrongful convictions from the organization's site and explore changes in the law that may prevent the miscarriage of justice.

* Barry Scheck, Peter Neufeld, and Jim Dwyer, *Actual Innocence: When Justice Goes Wrong and How to Make It Right*, New York: New American Library, 2003.

Figure 4-1 ▶ **Executions by State: 1977–2013**

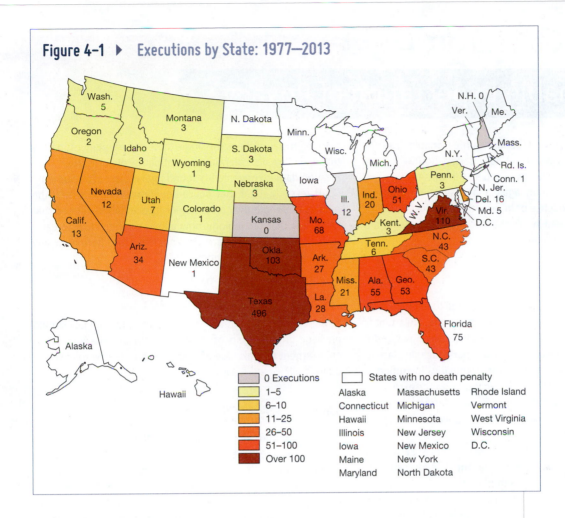

	0 Executions		States with no death penalty
	1–5	Alaska	Massachusetts	Rhode Island
	6–10	Connecticut	Michigan	Vermont
	11–25	Hawaii	Minnesota	West Virginia
	26–50	Illinois	New Jersey	Wisconsin
	51–100	Iowa	New Mexico	D.C.
	Over 100	Maine	New York	
		Maryland	North Dakota	

The most recent controversy over the death penalty concerns the method by which the punishment is carried out. Most states that have the death penalty use a lethal injection to cause the convicted person's death. A combination of three different drugs are injected intravenously. Several cases have been appealed to the Supreme Court on the basis that this method can cause extreme pain and thus violates the Constitution's ban on cruel and unusual punishment. The Court has upheld the three-drug method, most recently in April 2008, although the justices wrote seven opinions in the case, indicating a lack of consensus among them.[90]

Some believe that the declining number of executions reflects the waning support among Americans for the imposition of the death penalty. In 1994, polls indicated that 80 percent of Americans supported the death penalty. Gallup polling recorded the lowest support for the death penalty in forty years in their 2013 survey; just 60 percent indicated support. The current era of lower support may be tied to death penalty moratoriums in several states beginning around 2000 after several death-row inmates were later proven innocent of the crimes of which they were convicted (see Politics with a Purpose). Since 2006, six states have repealed death penalty laws outright.

90. *Baze v. Rees*, 553 U.S. 35 (2008).

What Would You Do?

A Reasonable Expectation of Privacy

The Fourth Amendment protects from unreasonable searches and seizures and draws important boundaries about where we enjoy a reasonable expectation of privacy. In those places, we enjoy heightened protection against a zealous government intent on gathering evidence or information. Yet, just like all of the civil liberties reviewed in this chapter, these boundaries are subject to review and revision.

Why Should You Care?

If law enforcement can demonstrate to a judge that it has credible information that you have committed a crime, a warrant is issued. This allows police to search the place described in the warrant and collect evidence. The exclusionary rule is in place to prevent police from going beyond the boundaries identified in the warrant. But of course there are exceptions to the exclusionary rule—circumstances that even without a warrant, evidence may be collected and used against you—if the officers acted in "good faith"* or if the police might have found the evidence through other legal means.** Warrantless searches are also valid in cases where the individual has no reasonable expectation of privacy—in a public place, for example, or even in your trash. But what about your cell phone, your email, and your Facebook page? What about the information you supply freely when you use a search engine like Google or shop online through Amazon? Most Americans lock their digital devices with an access code, password protect their email accounts, and use privacy settings to restrict access to postings on Facebook. Do these actions protect your privacy?

Recent court rulings suggest that the courts are trying to balance the legitimate needs of law enforcement and individual privacy rights. In some cases, you do not enjoy a reasonable expectation of privacy when using digital devices or social media. In 2010, the New York Supreme Court ruled that an individual had no reasonable expectation of privacy in what she posted to her Facebook pages because the very nature and purpose of social networking sites is to share information with others.*** In another instance, the government argued that consumers knowingly give up location information every time they make a call or send a text message. Location data could be useful to police in establishing a record of a suspect's whereabouts, but it can also establish a record of people's habits and preferences. Finally, the police have identified the smartphone as perhaps the single most important investigatory tool. Calls, emails, calendar appointments, pictures, texts, and location data is conveniently found in one place. The Supreme Court recently ruled that police need a warrant to search the phones of people they arrest. Chief Justice Roberts stated that "[t]he fact that technology now allows an individual to carry such information in his hand does not make the information any less worthy of the protection…"****

What Would You Do?

As a member of Congress, would you vote that the law should privilege privacy rights of individuals over the interests of law enforcement to make use of evidence collected by following a digital trail?

What You *Can* Do

As a college student, you make use of digital technology every day. Do you ever give a thought to the information trail left behind? How much privacy do you believe you have when you surf the web in the university library or text a friend to meet you across town? This is an area of civil liberties that is evolving rapidly. It is difficult to predict with any accuracy where your privacy is secure and where your willingness to freely divulge information compromises your expectation of privacy.

- You can learn more about civil liberties and the Internet at the Center for Internet and Society at Stanford Law School: http://cyberlaw.stanford.edu/our-work/topics/civil-liberties.

- The American Civil Liberties Union (ACLU) is a strong advocate for privacy rights and maintaining the protections of the Fourth Amendment: https://www.aclu.org/blog/tag/search-and-seizure.

- The United States Courts website provides legal background on the development of search and seizure precedent: https://www.aclu.org/blog/tag/search-and-seizure.

* *U.S. v Leon*, 468 US 897 (1984).
** *Segura v U.S.*, 468 US 796 (1984).
*** *Romano v Steelcase, Inc.*, 2010 NY Slip Op 32645U.
**** *Riley v California*, 573 U. S. _____(2014)

Key Terms

actual malice 126
civil liberties 106
clear and present
   danger test 119
commercial speech 118

defamation of character 124
establishment clause 108
exclusionary rule 140
free exercise clause 114

gag order 127
incorporation theory 107
libel 126
prior restraint 116

public figure 126
slander 124
symbolic speech 117

Chapter Summary

■ **LO4.1:** Originally, the Bill of Rights limited only the power of the national government, not that of the states. Gradually and selectively, however, the Supreme Court accepted the incorporation theory, under which no state can violate most provisions of the Bill of Rights.

■ **LO4.2:** The First Amendment protects against government interference with freedom of religion by requiring a separation of church and state (under the establishment clause) and by guaranteeing the free exercise of religion. Controversial issues that arise under the establishment clause include aid to church-related schools, school prayer, evolution versus intelligent design, school vouchers, posting the Ten Commandments in public places, and discrimination against religious speech. The government can interfere with the free exercise of religion only when religious practices work against public policy or the public welfare. The government cannot sponsor or support any specific religious belief.

■ **LO4.3:** The First Amendment protects against government interference with freedom of speech, which includes symbolic speech (expressive conduct). The Supreme Court has been especially critical of government actions that impose prior restraint on expression. Commercial speech (advertising) by businesses has received limited First Amendment protection. Restrictions on expression are permitted when the expression creates a clear and present danger to the peace or public order. Speech that has not received First Amendment protection includes expression that is judged to be obscene or slanderous.

■ **LO4.3:** The First Amendment protects against government interference with the freedom of the press, which can be regarded as a special instance of freedom of speech. Libelous statements are not protected by the freedom of the press. Publication of news about a criminal trial may be restricted by a gag order in some circumstances.

■ **LO4.3:** The First Amendment protects the right to assemble peaceably and to petition the government. Permits may be required for parades, sound trucks, and demonstrations to maintain the public order, and a permit may be denied to protect the public safety.

■ **LO4.4:** Under the Ninth Amendment, rights not specifically mentioned in the Constitution are not necessarily denied to the people. Among these unspecified rights is a right to privacy, which has been inferred from the First, Third, Fourth, Fifth, and Ninth Amendments. Major privacy issues today include electronic access to personal data and government surveillance programs. Abortion rights and end-of-life decisions also involve privacy claims.

■ **LO4.5:** The Constitution includes protections for the rights of persons accused of crimes. Under the Fourth Amendment, no one may be subject to an unreasonable search or seizure or be arrested except on probable cause. Under the Fifth Amendment, an accused person has the right to remain silent. Under the Sixth Amendment, an accused person must be informed of the reason for his or her arrest. The accused also has the right to adequate counsel, even if he or she cannot afford an attorney, and the right to a prompt arraignment and a speedy and public trial before an impartial jury selected from a cross section of the community. The exclusionary rule forbids the admission in court of illegally seized evidence. Under the Eighth Amendment, cruel and unusual punishment is prohibited.

■ **LO4.6:** Civil liberties are not absolute and the interpretation of the protections against government interference with individual rights is subject to the context of the times. Spy technology, personal information freely disclosed through social media, and heightened geopolitical security concerns present the Supreme Court and society with new challenges.

Selected Print, Media, and Online Resources

PRINT RESOURCES

Herman, Susan N. *Taking Liberties: The War on Terror and the Erosion of American Democracy.* New York: Oxford University Press, 2011. The president of the ACLU analyzes the long- and short-term effects of the USA Patriot Act and the new legal practices that have reduced personal liberty.

Lewis, Anthony. *Freedom for the Thought We Hate: Tales of the First Amendment.* New York: Basic Books, 2008. Pulitzer Prize–winning journalist Anthony Lewis writes eloquently on the value of free expression and the resulting need for "activist judges." He provides a series of engaging stories of how the courts came to give real life to the First Amendment.

Lewis, Anthony. *Gideon's Trumpet.* New York: Vintage, 1964. This classic work discusses the background and facts of *Gideon v. Wainwright*, the 1963 Supreme Court case in which the Court held that the state must make an attorney available for any person accused of a felony who cannot afford a lawyer.

Thompson–Cannino, Jennifer, Ronald Cotton, and Erin Roneo. *Picking Cotton: Our Memoir of Injustice and Redemption.* New York: St. Martin's Press, 2009. Jennifer Thompson was raped at knifepoint, but escaped and identified her attacker as Ronald Cotton. Convicted and sent to prison, Cotton maintained his innocence. DNA evidence ultimately proved him right and he was released after 10 years. Thompson and Cotton work together on issues of justice, innocence, and memory.

MEDIA RESOURCES

Constitution USA with Peter Sagal—Over the course of the four-hour PBS series first airing in 2013, Sagal travels cross country on a customized red, white, and blue Harley-Davidson to find out where the Constitution lives, how it works, and how it unites us as a nation. Episode 2, "It's a Free Country," specifically examines the Bill of Rights in everyday life.

Conviction: The Incredible True Story of Betty Anne Waters—A 2010 movie starring Hilary Swank and Sam Rockwell. A working mother puts herself through law school in an effort to represent her brother, who has been wrongfully convicted of murder and has exhausted his chances to appeal his conviction through public defenders.

Gideon's Trumpet—An excellent 1980 movie about the *Gideon v. Wainwright* case. Henry Fonda plays the role of the convicted petty thief Clarence Earl Gideon.

The Lord Is Not on Trial Here Today—A Peabody Award–winning documentary that tells the compelling personal story of Vashti McCollum, and how her efforts to protect her 10-year-old son led to one of the most important and landmark First Amendment cases in U.S. Supreme Court history—the case that established the separation of church and state in public schools.

ONLINE RESOURCES

American Civil Liberties Union (ACLU) —the nation's leading civil liberties organization provides an extensive array of information and links concerning civil rights issues: www.aclu.org

The American Library Association—information on free-speech issues, especially issues of free speech on the Internet: www.ala.org

Center for Democracy and Technology—nonprofit institute that monitors threats to the freedom of the Internet, provides a wealth of information about issues involving the Bill of Rights, and focuses on how developments in communications technology are affecting the constitutional liberties of Americans: www.cdt.org

Death Penalty Information Center—national nonprofit organization serving the media and the public with analysis and information on issues concerning capital punishment: www.deathpenaltyinfo.org

Electronic Privacy Information Center—information on digital privacy issues: www.epic.org/privacy

Foundation for Individual Rights in Education (FIRE) —tracks the rights to free speech, press, religion, and assembly at the nation's colleges and universities; find a rating for your own university's speech and conduct codes: www.thefire.org

Freedom Forum—nonpartisan foundation dedicated to free press, free speech, and free spirit for all people; includes history of flag protection and the First Amendment, as well as the status of the proposed flag amendment in Congress: www.freedomforum.org

Legal Information Institute at Cornell University Law School—searchable database of historic Supreme Court decisions: www.law.cornell.edu/supct/search/

The Oyez Project—provides summaries and the full text of Supreme Court decisions concerning constitutional law, plus a virtual tour of the Supreme Court: www.oyez.org

Master the concepts of Civil Liberties with MindTap™ for American Government

 REVIEW MindTap™ for American Government
Access Key Term Flashcards for Chapter 4.

 STAY CURRENT MindTap™ for American Government
Access the KnowNow blog and customized RSS for updates on current events.

 TEST YOURSELF MindTap™ for American Government
Take the Wrap It Up Quiz for Chapter 4.

 STAY FOCUSED MindTap™ for American Government
Complete the Focus Activities for Civil Liberties.

5 Civil Rights

LEARNING OUTCOMES

After reading this chapter, students will be able to:

- **LO5.1:** Define civil rights and locate in the U.S. Constitution the obligation on government to guarantee all citizens equal protection of the law.

- **LO5.2:** Explain why discrimination against individuals and groups exists in the United States today.

- **LO5.3:** Assess the limits of state and federal law in guaranteeing equality to all people.

- **LO5.4:** Explain why the U.S. Supreme Court plays such an important role relative to civil rights and identify at least two significant Supreme Court decisions that advanced civil rights in the United States.

- **LO5.5:** Identify and explain three significant events related to each of the campaigns for civil rights undertaken by African Americans, women, the Latino community, persons with disabilities, and the LGBTQ community.

- **LO5.6:** Define the goal of affirmative action and explain why this approach is controversial in the United States.

WATCH & LEARN MindTap™ for American Government

Watch a brief "What Do You Know?" video summarizing Civil Rights.

Birthright Citizenship Were Repealed?

BACKGROUND

The Fourteenth Amendment (1868) confers citizenship on "all persons born or naturalized in the United States, and subject to the jurisdiction thereof" and was adopted as a repudiation of the U.S. Supreme Court's *Dred Scott* ruling that people of African descent could *never* be American citizens. As a concept, birthright citizenship has its origins in English common law. Until recently, the idea of repealing birthright citizenship had been largely relegated to advocates of severe restrictions on immigration. However, a group of Republican state and national lawmakers have introduced legislation to repeal birthright citizenship. Several well-known legislators are among the supporters of the repeal, including Senators John McCain, Mitch McConnell, Lindsey Graham, Jeff Sessions, and Jon Kyl.

PAST CHALLENGES

In 1882, the Chinese Exclusion Act (along with other state and federal laws) denied Chinese and other Asians the right to own property, to marry, to return to the United States once they left the country, and to become U.S. citizens. In the case *U.S. v. Wong Kim Ark*, the Supreme Court took up the issue of birthright citizenship. The case involved a man born in San Francisco to Chinese parents who later returned to China. When Wong left the United States to visit his parents, he was denied reentry. The government claimed that Wong had no right to birthright citizenship under the Fourteenth Amendment because his parents remained "subjects of the emperor of China" even while living in California when he was born. In a 7-2 decision, the majority said "The amendment, in clear words and in manifest intent, includes the children born within the territory of the United States of all other persons, of whatever race or color, domiciled within the United States." This case remains the ruling precedent for challenges to birthright citizenship.

A POLITICAL STRATEGY FOR REPEAL

The process for amending the U.S. Constitution is intentionally difficult, requiring the support of two-thirds of both houses of Congress and three-fourths of the state legislatures. Those advocating the repeal of birthright citizenship avoid this path and have instead proposed a two-pronged strategy. At the federal level, a bill has been introduced to reinterpret the "subject to the jurisdiction thereof" language in the Fourteenth Amendment so that noncitizens and illegal immigrants are not covered. Thus, a student who comes to the United States to attend college would not be "subject to the jurisdiction thereof" for the purposes of citizenship, and any children born to that student would not be citizens of the United States. At the state level, several states working together propose to create two types of birth certificates—one for children born to citizens of the United States and one for those born to noncitizens. Neither of these strategies is likely to pass the test of constitutionality, given the precedent set in *Wong*. Further, a repeal of birthright citizenship is not likely to reduce illegal immigration, because most undocumented immigrants are motivated by jobs. Countries without birthright citizenship have not eliminated illegal immigration.

For Critical Analysis

1. *In the media, children born to noncitizens are sometimes referred to as "anchor babies" because they presumably tie their parents to this country. This is a misnomer, however, because only the child born here is a citizen. Why do you think opposition exists to granting citizenship to children born to noncitizen parents?*

2. *Is the concept of birthright citizenship consistent with the values of America? What would be gained and lost by the nation if birthright citizenship were repealed?*

did you know?

At the time of the American Revolution, African Americans made up nearly 25 percent of the American population of about three million.

Civil Rights

All rights rooted in the Fourteenth Amendment's guarantee of equal protection under the law.

■ **LO5.1:** Define civil rights and locate in the U.S. Constitution the obligation on government to guarantee all citizens equal protection of the law.

DESPITE THE WORDS set forth in the Declaration of Independence that "all Men are created equal," the United States has a long history of discrimination based on race, gender, national origin, religion, and sexual orientation, among others. The majority of the population had few rights at the nation's founding. The framers of the Constitution permitted slavery to continue, thus excluding slaves from the political process. Women also were excluded for the most part, as were Native Americans, African Americans who were not slaves, and white men who did not own property. To the nation's founders, equality required a degree of independent thinking and the capacity for rational action, which they believed members of these groups did not possess. Today we believe that all people are entitled to equal political rights as well as the opportunities for personal development provided by equal access to education and employment. Thus, the story of civil rights in the United States is the struggle to reconcile our ideals as a nation with the realities of discrimination individuals and groups still encounter in daily life.

Equality is at the heart of the concept of civil rights. Generally, the term **civil rights** refers to the rights of all Americans to equal treatment under the law, as provided for by the Fourteenth Amendment to the Constitution and by subsequent acts of Congress. Although the terms *civil rights* and *civil liberties* are sometimes used interchangeably, scholars make a distinction between the two. Civil liberties are limitations on government; they specify what the government *cannot* do. Civil rights, in contrast, specify what the government *must* do to ensure equal protection and freedom from discrimination.

The history of civil rights in America is the story of the struggle of various groups to be free from discriminatory treatment. Ending slavery was a necessary but not sufficient prerequisite to advancing civil rights in America. In this chapter, we first look at two movements with significant consequences: the civil rights movement of the 1950s and 1960s and the women's movement, which began in the mid-1800s and continues today. Each of these movements resulted in legislation that secured important basic rights for all Americans—the right to vote and the right to equal protection under the laws. Each demonstrates how individuals working alone and with others in groups can effect significant change. Today's civil rights activists draw on insights and strategies from these earlier movements in making new claims for political and social equality. We then explore a question with serious implications for today's voters and policymakers: What should the government's responsibility be when equal protection under the law is not enough to ensure truly equal opportunities for Americans? Can political and social equality exist in the face of a widening economic gap?

African Americans and the Consequences of Slavery in the United States

■ **LO5.2:** Explain why discrimination against individuals and groups exists in the United States today.

Before 1863, the Constitution protected slavery and made equality impossible. African American leader Frederick Douglass pointed out that "Liberty and Slavery—opposite as Heaven and Hell—are both in the Constitution." Abraham Lincoln stated sarcastically, "All men are created equal, except Negroes."

The constitutionality of slavery was confirmed just a few years before the outbreak of the Civil War in the infamous *Dred Scott v. Sandford* case of 1857. The Supreme Court held that slaves were property, not citizens of the United States, and were not entitled to the rights and privileges of citizenship.[1] The Court also ruled that the Missouri Compromise (1820), which banned slavery in the territories north of 36°30' latitude (the southern border of Missouri), was unconstitutional. The *Dred Scott* decision had grave consequences. Most observers contend that the ruling contributed to making the Civil War inevitable.

> ## did you know?
> June 19th, known as Juneteenth or Freedom Day, celebrates the day in 1865 that slaves in Galveston, Texas, found out they were free three years after Lincoln signed the Emancipation Proclamation.

Ending Servitude

With the Emancipation Proclamation in 1863 and ratification of the Thirteenth, Fourteenth, and Fifteenth Amendments during the Reconstruction period following the Civil War, constitutional inequality for African American males ended.

The Thirteenth Amendment (1865) states that neither slavery nor involuntary servitude shall exist within the United States. The Fourteenth Amendment (1868) says that *all* persons born or naturalized in the United States are citizens of the United States. It states, furthermore, that "[n]o State shall make or enforce any law which shall abridge the privileges or immunities of citizens of the United States; nor shall any State deprive any person of life, liberty, or property, without due process of law; nor deny to any person within its jurisdiction the equal protection of the laws." Note the use of the terms *citizen* and *person*. Citizens have political rights, such as the right to vote and run for political office. Citizens also have certain privileges or immunities (see Chapter 4). All *persons*, however, including noncitizens, have a right to due process of law and equal protection under the law.

The Fifteenth Amendment (1870) reads: "The right of citizens of the United States to vote shall not be denied or abridged by the United States or by any State on account of race, color, or previous condition of servitude." Activists in the women's suffrage movements brought pressure on Congress to include in the Fourteenth and Fifteenth Amendments a prohibition against discrimination based on sex, but with no success.

The Civil Rights Acts of 1865 to 1875

At the end of the Civil War, President Lincoln's Republican Party controlled the national government and most state governments, and the so-called radical Republicans, with their strong antislavery stance, controlled the party. From 1865 to 1875, the Republican majority in Congress succeeded in passing a series of civil rights acts that were aimed at enforcing the Thirteenth, Fourteenth, and Fifteenth Amendments even as legislatures in the southern states moved quickly to pass laws (known as **Black Codes**) intended to limit the civil rights of African Americans and regulate their labor in ways that closely resembled slavery. South Carolina's Black Code (1865) stated that "all persons of color who make contracts for service or labor, shall be known as servants, and those with whom they contract, shall be known as masters."[2] Following the assassination of President Lincoln on April 15, 1865, Andrew Johnson assumed the presidency and presided over the initial period of Reconstruction. Johnson, a Southerner and former

Black Codes
Laws passed by southern states immediately after the Civil War denying most legal rights to freed slaves.

---

1. 19 Howard 393 (1857).
2. "Acts of the General Assembly of the State of South Carolina Passed at the Sessions of 1864–65," pp. 291–304.

Ku Klux Klan members, late 1860s–70s (engraving) (b/w photo), American School, (19th century)/Private Collection/The Stapleton Collection/The Bridgeman Art Library

slave owner, was viewed by radical Republicans as too conciliatory toward southern states.

Following the 1866 elections, in which southern states were not allowed to vote, an emboldened radical Republican majority in Congress moved to take control of Reconstruction. The first Civil Rights Act in the Reconstruction period was passed in 1866 over the veto of President Johnson. That act extended citizenship to anyone born in the United States and gave African Americans full equality before the law. It gave the president authority to enforce the law with military force. Johnson characterized the law as an invasion by federal authority of the rights of the states. It was considered to be unconstitutional, but the ratification of the Fourteenth Amendment two years later ended that concern.

Among the six other civil rights acts passed after the Civil War, one of the most important was the Enforcement Act of 1879, which set out specific criminal sanctions for interfering with the right to vote as protected by the Fifteenth Amendment and by the Civil Rights Act of 1866. Equally important was the Civil Rights Act of 1872, known as the Anti-Ku Klux Klan Act. This act made it a federal crime for anyone to use law or custom to deprive an individual of his or her rights, privileges, and immunities secured by the Constitution or by any federal law.

The last of these early civil rights acts, the Second Civil Rights Act, was passed in 1875. It declared that everyone is entitled to full and equal enjoyment of public accommodations, theaters, and other places of amusement, and it imposed penalties for violators. What is most important about all of the civil rights acts was the belief that congressional power applied to official or government action or to private action. If a state government did not secure rights, then the federal government could do so. Thus, Congress could legislate directly against individuals who were violating the constitutional rights of others. As we will see, these acts were quickly rendered ineffective by law and by custom. They became important in the civil rights struggles of the 1960s, however, 100 years after their passage.

An engraving of Ku Klux Klan members active in the late 1860s as Southerners rebelled against northern influence during Reconstruction.

Jim Crow Laws
Laws enacted by southern states that enforced segregation in schools, in transportation, and in public accommodations.

The Limitations of the Civil Rights Laws

■ **LO5.3:** Assess the limits of state and federal law in guaranteeing equality to all people.

The Reconstruction statutes, or civil rights acts, ultimately did little to secure equality for African Americans. Both the *Civil Rights Cases* and *Plessy v. Ferguson* effectively nullified these acts. Rutherford B. Hayes's election in 1877 marked an end to the progressive advance of rights for African Americans during Reconstruction. He withdrew federal forces from states in the former Confederacy. Without direct oversight, southern and border states created a variety of seemingly race-neutral legal barriers that in reality prevented African Americans from exercising their right to vote, while also adopting policies of racial segregation known as **Jim Crow laws**.

The Civil Rights Cases. The Supreme Court invalidated the 1875 Civil Rights Act when it held, in the *Civil Rights Cases* of 1883, that the enforcement clause of the Fourteenth Amendment (which states that "[n]o State shall make or enforce any law which shall abridge the privileges or immunities of citizens") was limited to correcting actions by states in their *official* acts; thus, the discriminatory acts of private citizens were not illegal.[3] ("Individual invasion of individual rights is not the subject matter of the Amendment.") The 1883 Supreme Court decision removed the federal government as a forceful advocate for advancing civil rights in all aspects of daily human interaction, and it was met with widespread approval throughout most of the United States.

Twenty years after the Civil War, the white majority was all too ready to forget about the three Civil War amendments and the civil rights legislation of the 1860s and 1870s. The other civil rights laws that the Court did not specifically invalidate became effectively null without any mechanisms of enforcement, although they were never repealed by Congress. At the same time, many former proslavery secessionists had regained political power in the southern states.

Plessy v. Ferguson: Separate-but-Equal.

A key decision during this period concerned Homer Plessy, a Louisiana resident who was one-eighth African American. In 1892, he boarded a train in New Orleans. The conductor made him leave the car, which was restricted to whites, and directed him to a car for non-whites. At that time, Louisiana had a statute providing for separate railway cars for whites and African Americans.

Plessy went to court, claiming that such a statute was contrary to the Fourteenth Amendment's equal protection clause. In 1896, the Supreme Court rejected Plessy's contention. The Court concluded that the Fourteenth Amendment "could not have been intended to abolish distinctions based upon color, or to enforce social…equality." The Court stated that segregation alone did not violate the Constitution: "Laws permitting, and even requiring, their separation in places where they are liable to be brought into contact do not necessarily imply the inferiority of either race to the other."[4] With this case, the Court announced the **separate-but-equal doctrine**.

Plessy v. Ferguson became the judicial cornerstone of racial discrimination throughout the United States. Even though *Plessy* upheld segregated facilities in railway cars only, it was assumed that the Supreme Court was upholding segregation everywhere as long as the separate facilities were equal. The result was a system of racial segregation, particularly in the South—supported by laws collectively known as Jim Crow laws—that required separate drinking fountains; separate seats in theaters, restaurants, and hotels; separate public toilets; and separate waiting rooms for the two races. "Separate" was indeed the rule, but "equal" was never enforced, nor was it a reality.

Voting Barriers.

The brief enfranchisement of African Americans ended after 1877, when the federal troops that occupied the South during the Reconstruction era were withdrawn. Southern politicians regained control of state governments and, using everything except race as a formal criterion, passed laws that effectively deprived African Americans of the right to vote. By claiming that political parties were private organizations, the Democratic Party was allowed to restrict black voters from participating in its primaries. Because most southern states were dominated by the Democratic Party, the primary prohibition effectively disenfranchised blacks altogether. The **white primary** was upheld by the Supreme Court until 1944 when, in *Smith v. Allwright*, the Court ruled it a violation of the Fifteenth Amendment.[5]

Separate-but-Equal Doctrine
The 1896 doctrine holding that separate-but-equal facilities do not violate the equal protection clause.

White Primary
A state primary election that restricts voting to whites only; outlawed by the Supreme Court in 1944.

---

3. 109 U.S. 3 (1883).
4. *Plessy v. Ferguson*, 163 U.S. 537 (1896).
5. 321 U.S. 649 (1944).

Grandfather Clause
A device used by southern states to disenfranchise African Americans. It restricted voting to those whose grandfathers had voted before 1867.

Poll Taxes
A special tax that must be paid as a qualification for voting. The Twenty-fourth Amendment to the Constitution outlawed the poll tax in national elections, and in 1966, the Supreme Court declared it unconstitutional in all elections.

Literacy Tests
A test administered as a precondition for voting, often used to prevent African Americans from exercising their right to vote.

Another barrier to African American voting was the **grandfather clause**, which restricted voting to those who could prove that their grandfathers had voted before 1867. **Poll taxes** required the payment of a fee to vote; thus, poor African Americans—and poor whites—who could not afford to pay the tax were excluded from voting. Not until the Twenty-fourth Amendment was ratified in 1964 was the poll tax eliminated. **Literacy tests** were also used to deny the vote to African Americans. Such tests asked potential voters to read, recite, or interpret complicated texts, such as a section of the state constitution, to the satisfaction of local registrars—who were, of course, never satisfied with the responses of African Americans. Each of these barriers to voting was, on its face, race-neutral. Each was vigorously enforced disproportionately against African Americans by government agents and a system of racial intimidation.

Southern states, counties, and towns also passed ordinances and laws to maintain a segregated society and to control the movements and activities of African American residents. In Florida, no "negro, mulatto, or person of color" was permitted to own or carry a weapon, including a knife, without a license. This law did not apply to white residents. Other laws set curfews for African Americans, set limits on the businesses they could own or run and on their rights to assembly, and required the newly freed men and women to find employment quickly or risk penalties. The penalty sometimes meant that the men would be forced into labor at very low wages. Denied the right to register and vote, black citizens were also effectively barred from public office and jury service.

Extralegal Methods of Enforcing White Supremacy. The second-class status of African Americans was also a matter of social custom, especially in the South. In their interactions with southern whites, African Americans were expected to observe an informal but detailed code of behavior that confirmed their inferiority. The most serious violation of the informal code was "familiarity" toward a white woman by an African American man or boy. The code was backed up by the common practice of *lynching*—mob action to murder an accused

These segregated drinking fountains were common in southern states in the late 1800s and during the first half of the 20th century. What landmark Supreme Court case made such segregated facilities legal?

FOR COLORED ONLY

Bettmann/Corbis

individual, usually by hanging and sometimes accompanied by torture. Lynching was illegal, but southern authorities rarely prosecuted these cases, and white juries would not convict. African American women were instrumental in anti-lynching campaigns, beginning in the 1890s with the work of Ida B. Wells-Barnett. As the owner and editor of *The Free Speech*, a Memphis newspaper, she called attention to the brutality of lynching and argued in editorials that lynching was a strategy to eliminate prosperous, politically active African Americans.

African Americans outside the South were subject to a second kind of violence—race riots. In the early twentieth century, race riots were typically initiated by whites. Frequently, the riots were caused by competition for employment. For example, several serious riots occurred during World War II (1939–1945), when labor shortages forced northern employers to hire more black workers.

The End of the Separate-but-Equal Doctrine

■ **LO5.4:** Explain why the U.S. Supreme Court plays such an important role relative to civil rights and identify at least two significant Supreme Court decisions that advanced civil rights in the United States.

The successful attack on the separate-but-equal doctrine began with a series of lawsuits in the 1930s that sought to admit African Americans to state professional schools. In 1909, influential African Americans and progressive whites, including W.E.B. Dubois and Oswald Garrison Villard, joined to form the National Association for the Advancement of Colored People (NAACP) with the express intention of targeting the separate-but-equal doctrine. Although all southern states maintained a segregated system of elementary and secondary schools as well as colleges and universities, very few offered professional education for African Americans. Thus, the NAACP elected to begin its challenge with law schools, believing in part that it would be too expensive for states to establish an entirely separate system of black professional schools, leaving integration as the best option. To pursue this strategy, the NAACP established the Legal Defense and Education Fund (LDF). As a result of several LDF challenges, law schools in Maryland, Missouri, Oklahoma, and Texas were forced to change their policies regarding admittance or matriculation of law school students, paving the way for *Brown v. Board of Education* (1954).

By 1950, the Supreme Court had ruled that African Americans who were admitted to a state university could not be assigned to separate sections of classrooms, libraries, and cafeterias. In 1951, Oliver Brown attempted to enroll his eight-year-old daughter, Linda Carol Brown, in the third grade of his all-white neighborhood school seven blocks from their home. (The alternative was to have her travel by bus to the segregated school across town.) Although Kansas law did not require schools to be segregated by race, in practice there were separate schools for white and black children. When Linda was denied admission to the all-white school, the Topeka NAACP urged Brown to join a lawsuit against the Topeka Board of Education.

Brown v. Board of Education of Topeka.[6] This case established that segregation of races in public schools violates the equal protection clause of the Fourteenth Amendment. First argued in 1952 by NAACP Legal Defense Fund attorney Thurgood Marshall (appointed as the first African American to the U.S. Supreme Court in 1967), the votes were almost evenly split to uphold or strike

---

6. 347 U.S. 483 (1954).

These three lawyers successfully argued in favor of desegregation of the schools in the famous *Brown v. Board of Education of Topeka* case. On the left is George E. C. Hayes; on the right is James Nabrit, Jr.; and in the center is Thurgood Marshall, who later became the first African American Supreme Court justice.

Bettmann/Corbis

down *separate but equal*; Chief Justice Fred Vinson held the swing vote. In 1953, Vinson died, and President Dwight Eisenhower appointed Earl Warren to replace him. *Brown* was reargued, and Warren wrote a unanimous decision to strike down *separate but equal*, arguing that "separate" is inherently unequal.

"With All Deliberate Speed." The following year, in *Brown v. Board of Education* (sometimes called the second *Brown* decision), the Court declared that lower courts needed to ensure that African Americans would be admitted to schools on a nondiscriminatory basis "with all deliberate speed."[7] The district courts were to consider devices in their desegregation orders that might include "the school transportation system, personnel, [and] revision of school districts and attendance areas into compact units to achieve a system of determining admission to the public schools on a nonracial basis."

This legal strategy was only one of many African Americans found successful in their struggle for civil rights, and many difficult days lay ahead. The success of civil rights groups in *Brown* was a flashpoint, sparking an enormous backlash among segregationists. They defied the Court, closed public schools rather than integrate them, and vowed to maintain inequality in other areas such as voting. Violence and sometimes death for civil rights activists followed.

Reactions to School Integration

The white South did not let the Supreme Court ruling go unchallenged. Governor Orval Faubus of Arkansas used the state's National Guard to block the integration of Central High School in Little Rock in September 1957. The federal court demanded that the troops be withdrawn. Finally, President Dwight Eisenhower

---

7. 349 U.S. 294 (1955).

had to federalize the Arkansas National Guard and send in the U.S. Army's 101st Airborne Division to quell the violence. Central High was integrated.

The universities in the South, however, remained segregated. When James Meredith, an African American student, attempted to enroll at the University of Mississippi in 1962, violence flared there, as it had in Little Rock. The white riot was so intense that President John Kennedy was forced to send in 30,000 U.S. combat troops, a larger force than the one then stationed in Korea. There were 375 military and civilian injuries, many from gunfire, and two bystanders were killed. Ultimately, peace was restored, and Meredith began attending classes.[8]

An Integrationist Attempt at a Cure: Busing

In most parts of the United States, residential concentrations by race have made it difficult to achieve racial balance in schools. This concentration results in **de facto segregation**, as distinct from **de jure segregation**, which results from laws or administrative decisions.

Court-Ordered Busing. One solution to both *de facto* and *de jure* segregation seemed to be transporting some African American schoolchildren to white schools and some white schoolchildren to African American schools. The courts ordered school districts to engage in such **busing** across neighborhoods. Busing led to violence in some northern cities, such as in south Boston, where African American students were bused into blue-collar Irish Catholic neighborhoods. In the mid-1970s, almost 50 percent of African Americans interviewed were opposed to busing, and approximately three-fourths of the whites interviewed held the same opinion.

The End of Integration?. During the 1980s and the early 1990s, the Supreme Court began to back away from its earlier commitment to busing and other methods of desegregation. By the late 1990s and early 2000s, the federal courts were increasingly unwilling to uphold race-conscious policies designed to further school integration and diversity. In 2001, a federal appellate court held that the Charlotte-Mecklenburg school district in North Carolina had achieved the goal of integration, meaning that race-based admission quotas could no longer be imposed constitutionally.[9]

The Resurgence of Minority Schools. Today, schools around the country are becoming segregated again, in large part because changing population demographics result in increased *de facto* segregation. Even as African American and Latino students are becoming more isolated, the typical white child is in a school that is more diverse in large part due to the substantial decline in the number and proportion of white students in the population relative to the increase of nonwhites. In Latino and African American populations, two of every five students attend a school with more than 90 percent minority enrollment. Public school segregation is most severe in the western states and in New York. In California, the nation's most multiracial state, half of African Americans and Asians attend segregated schools, as do one-quarter of Latino and Native American students.[10] Sixty years after *Brown*, about half of New York state's public school

De Facto **Segregation**
Racial segregation that occurs because of past social and economic conditions and residential racial patterns.

De Jure **Segregation**
Racial segregation that occurs because of laws or administrative decisions by public agencies.

Busing
In the context of civil rights, the transportation of public school students from areas where they live to schools in other areas to eliminate school segregation based on residential racial patterns.

did you know?

The F.W. Woolworth building in Greensboro, North Carolina, the site of the 1960 lunch counter sit-ins, is now the International Civil Rights Center and Museum; the original portion of the lunch counter and stools where the four students sat has never been moved from its original footprint.

---

8. William Doyle, *An American Insurrection: James Meredith and the Battle of Oxford, Mississippi, 1962* (New York: Anchor, 2003).
9. *Belk v. Charlotte-Mecklenburg Board of Education*, 269 F.3d 305 (4th Cir. 2001).
10. Gary Orfield, *Reviving the Goal of an Integrated Society: A 21st Century Challenge* (Los Angeles, CA: The Civil Rights Project/ Proyecto Derechos Civiles at UCLA, 2009).

students are white, but during the 2010 school year the average black student in New York went to a school where 17.7 percent of the students were white.[11] Most non-white schools are segregated by poverty as well as race. A majority of the nation's dropouts come from nonwhite public schools, leading to large numbers of virtually unemployable young people of color. The Bureau of Labor Statistics reported that in November 2008, the month President Obama was elected, the unemployment rate for African American adult and teen males was nearly twice that for white males—a remarkably persistent gap evident in Figure 5–1.

Generally, Americans are now taking another look at what desegregation means. In 2007, the Supreme Court handed down a decision that would dramatically change the way school districts across the country assigned students to schools. In cases brought by white parents in Seattle and Louisville, the Court, by a narrow 5-4 margin, found that using race to determine which schools students could attend was a violation of the Fourteenth Amendment. White children could not be denied admission to magnet schools or other schools designed to have racially balanced populations on account of their race. Justice Anthony Kennedy was the swing vote in this case. Although he agreed with four justices in striking down voluntary plans that assigned students to schools solely on the basis of race, he also agreed with other justices in holding that integrated education was a compelling educational goal that could be pursued through other methods.[12]

An alternative solution (now implemented in more than 60 school districts across the country) is to integrate schools on the basis of income. A more advantaged school environment translates into higher achievement levels. On the National Assessment of Educational Progress given to all fourth-graders in math, for example, low-income students attending more affluent schools scored

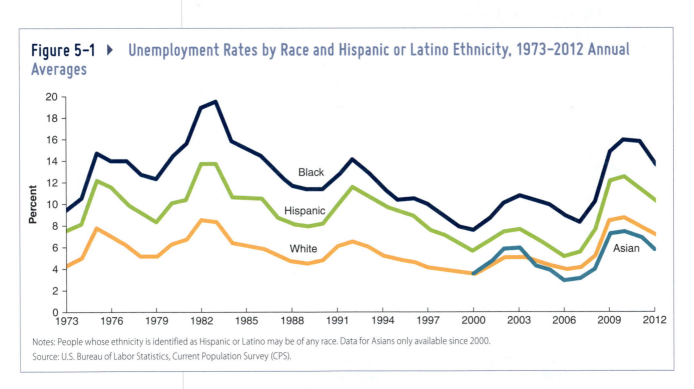

Figure 5–1 ▶   Unemployment Rates by Race and Hispanic or Latino Ethnicity, 1973–2012 Annual Averages

Notes: People whose ethnicity is identified as Hispanic or Latino may be of any race. Data for Asians only available since 2000.

Source: U.S. Bureau of Labor Statistics, Current Population Survey (CPS).

11. John Kucsera and Garry Orfeld, "New York State's Extreme School Segregation: Inequality, Inaction, and a Damaged Future," UCLA Civil Rights Project Report, March 26, 2014. Accessed at http://civilrightsproject.ucla.edu/research/k-12-education/integration-and-diversity/ny-norflet-report-placeholder/Kucsera-New-York-Extreme-Segregation-2014.pdf

12. *Parents Involved v. Seattle School District No. 1*, 550 U.S (2007) and *Meredith v. Jefferson County Board of Education*, 550 U.S. (2007).

almost two years ahead of low-income students attending high-poverty schools. Today more than 3.2 million students live in school districts with some form of socioeconomic integration in place.[13]

The Civil Rights Movement

■ **LO5.5:** Identify and explain three significant events related to each of the campaigns for civil rights undertaken by African Americans, women, the Latino community, persons with disabilities, and the LGBTQ community.

The *Brown* decision applied only to public schools. Not much else in the structure of existing segregation was affected. In December 1955, a 43-year-old African American woman, Rosa Parks, boarded a public bus in Montgomery, Alabama. When the bus became crowded and several white people stepped aboard, Parks was asked to move to the rear of the bus (the "colored" section). She refused, was arrested, and was fined $10, but that was not the end of the matter. For an entire year, African Americans boycotted the Montgomery bus line. The protest was headed by a 27-year-old Baptist minister, Dr. Martin Luther King, Jr. During the protest period, he went to jail and his house was bombed. In the face of overwhelming odds, the protesters won. In 1956, a federal district court issued an injunction prohibiting the segregation of buses in Montgomery. The era of civil rights protests had begun.

King's Philosophy of Nonviolence

The following year, in 1957, King formed the Southern Christian Leadership Conference (SCLC). King advocated nonviolent **civil disobedience** as a means to achieve racial justice. King's philosophy of civil disobedience was influenced, in part, by the life and teachings of Mahatma Gandhi (1869–1948). Gandhi led resistance to the British colonial system in India from 1919 to 1947, using demonstrations and marches, as well as nonviolent, public disobedience to unjust laws. King's followers successfully used these methods to gain wider public acceptance of their cause.

Civil Disobedience
A nonviolent, public refusal to obey allegedly unjust laws.

Nonviolent Demonstrations. African Americans and sympathetic whites engaged in sit-ins, freedom rides, and freedom marches. Groups including the NAACP, the Congress of Racial Equality (CORE), and the Student Nonviolent Coordinating Committee (SNCC) organized and supported these actions. In the beginning, such demonstrations were often met with violence, and the contrasting image of nonviolent African Americans and violent, hostile whites created strong public support for the civil rights movement. In 1960, when African Americans in Greensboro, North Carolina, were refused service at a Woolworth's lunch counter, they organized a sit-in that was aided day after day by sympathetic whites and other African Americans. Enraged customers threw ketchup on the protesters. Some spat in their faces. The sit-in movement continued to grow, however. Within six months of the first sit-in at the Greensboro Woolworth's, hundreds of lunch counters throughout the South were serving African Americans.

The sit-in technique also was successfully used to integrate interstate buses and their terminals, as well as railroads engaged in interstate transportation. Although buses and railroads engaged in interstate transportation were prohibited by law from segregating African Americans from whites, they stopped doing so only after the sit-in protests.

---

13. Richard D. Kahlenberg, "Can Separate Be Equal?" *The American Prospect*, September 16, 2009.

Marches and Demonstrations. One of the most famous of the violence-plagued protests occurred in Birmingham, Alabama, in 1963, when Police Commissioner Eugene "Bull" Connor unleashed police dogs and used electric cattle prods against protesters. People viewed the event with indignation and horror. King was thrown in jail. The media coverage of the Birmingham protest and the violent response by the city government played a key role in ending Jim Crow laws in the United States. The ultimate result was the most important civil rights act in the nation's history, the Civil Rights Act of 1964.

In August 1963, African American leaders A. Philip Randolph and Bayard Rustin organized a massive March on Washington for Jobs and Freedom. Before nearly a quarter-million white and African American spectators and millions watching on television, King told the world: "I have a dream that my four little children will one day live in a nation where they will not be judged by the color of their skin but by the content of their character."

Another Approach—Black Power

Not all African Americans agreed with King's philosophy of nonviolence or with the idea that King's strong Christian background represented the core spirituality of African Americans. Black Muslims and other African American separatists advocated a more militant stance and argued that desegregation should not result in cultural assimilation. During the 1950s and 1960s, when King was spearheading nonviolent protests and demonstrations to achieve civil rights for African Americans, Black Power leaders insisted that African Americans should "fight back" instead of turning the other cheek. Some argued that without the fear generated by black militants, a "moderate" such as King would not have garnered such widespread support from white America.

Malcolm Little (who became Malcolm X after joining the Black Muslims in 1952) and other leaders in the Black Power movement believed that African Americans fell into two groups: "Uncle Toms," who peaceably accommodated the white establishment, and "New Negroes," who took pride in their color and culture and who demanded racial separation as well as power. Malcolm X was assassinated in 1965, but he became an important reference point for a new generation of African Americans and a symbol of African American identity.

The Black Power salute was a human rights protest and one of the most overtly political statements in the 110 year history of the civil rights movement.

World History Archive/Image Asset Management Ltd./Alamy

The Escalation of the Civil Rights Movement

■ **LO5.3:** Assess the limits of state and federal law in guaranteeing equality to all people.

Police dog attacks, cattle prods, high-pressure water hoses, beatings, bombings, the March on Washington, and black militancy—all of these events and developments led to an environment in which Congress felt compelled to act on behalf of African Americans.

Modern Civil Rights Legislation

Equality before the law became "an idea whose time has come," in the words of then Republican Senate Minority Leader Everett Dirksen. The legislation passed during the Eisenhower administration was relatively symbolic. The Civil Rights Act of 1957 established the Civil Rights Commission and a new Civil Rights Division within the Department of Justice. The Civil Rights Act of 1960 was passed to protect voting rights. Whenever a pattern or practice of discrimination was documented, the Justice Department, on behalf of the voter, could bring suit, even against a state. This act, though, wielded little enforcement power and was relatively ineffective.

The 1960 presidential election pitted Vice President Richard Nixon against Senator John F. Kennedy. Kennedy sought the support of African American leaders, promising to introduce tougher civil rights legislation. When Martin Luther King, Jr., was imprisoned in Georgia after participating in a sit-in in Atlanta, Kennedy called Mrs. King to express his support, and his brother, Robert, made calls to expedite King's release. President Kennedy's civil rights legislation was stalled in the Senate in 1963, however, and his assassination ended the effort in his name. When Lyndon B. Johnson became president in 1963, he committed himself to passing civil rights bills, and the 1964 act was the result.

The Civil Rights Act of 1964. The Civil Rights Act of 1964, the most far-reaching bill on civil rights in modern times, forbade discrimination on the basis of race, color, religion, gender, and national origin. The major provisions of the act were as follows:

1. It outlawed arbitrary discrimination in voter registration.
2. It barred discrimination in public accommodations, such as hotels and restaurants, whose operations affect interstate commerce.
3. It authorized the federal government to sue to desegregate public schools and facilities.
4. It expanded the power of the Civil Rights Commission and extended its life.
5. It provided for the withholding of federal funds from programs administered in a discriminatory manner.
6. It established the right to equality of opportunity in employment.

Title VII of the Civil Rights Act of 1964 is the cornerstone of employment-discrimination law. It prohibits discrimination in employment based on race, color, religion, sex, or national origin. Under Title VII, executive orders were issued that banned employment discrimination by firms that received any federal funding. The act created a five-member commission, the Equal Employment Opportunity Commission (EEOC), to administer Title VII.

The EEOC can issue interpretive guidelines and regulations, but these do not have the force of law. Rather, they give notice of the commission's enforcement policy. The EEOC also has investigatory powers. It has broad authority to require the production of documentary evidence, to hold hearings, and to **subpoena** and examine witnesses under oath.

The equal employment provisions have been strengthened several times since its first passage. In 1965, President Johnson signed an Executive Order (11246) that prohibited any discrimination in employment by any employer who received federal funds, contracts, or subcontracts. It also required all such employers to

Subpoena
A legal writ requiring a person's appearance in court to give testimony.

establish *affirmative action plans*, discussed later in this chapter. A revision of that order extended the requirement for an affirmative action plan to public institutions and medical and health facilities with more than 50 employees. In 1972, the Equal Employment Opportunity Act extended the provisions prohibiting discrimination in employment to the employees of state and local governments and most other not-for-profit institutions.

The Voting Rights Act of 1965. As late as 1960, only 29.1 percent of African Americans of voting age were registered in southern states, in stark contrast to 61.1 percent of whites. The Voting Rights Act of 1965 addressed this issue. The act had two major provisions. The first one outlawed discriminatory voter-registration tests. The second authorized federal registration of voters and federally administered voting procedures in any political subdivision or state that discriminated electorally against a particular group. In part, the act provided that certain political subdivisions could not change their voting procedures and election laws without federal approval. The act targeted counties, mostly in the South, in which less than 50 percent of the eligible population was registered to vote. Federal voter registrars were sent to these areas to register African Americans who had been kept from voting by local registrars. Within one week after the act was passed, 45 federal examiners were sent to the South. A massive voter-registration drive drew thousands of civil rights activists, many of whom were white college students, to the South over the summer. This effort resulted in a dramatic increase in the proportion of African Americans registered to vote.

Urban Riots. Even as the civil rights movement earned its greatest victories, a series of riots swept through African American inner-city neighborhoods. These urban riots were different in character from the race riots described earlier in this chapter. The riots in the first half of the twentieth century were street battles between whites and blacks. The urban riots of the late 1960s and early 1970s, however, were not directed against individual whites—in some instances, whites actually participated in small numbers. The riots were primarily civil insurrections, although these disorders were accompanied by large-scale looting of stores. Inhabitants of the affected neighborhoods attributed the riots to racial discrimination.[14] The riots dissipated much of the goodwill toward the civil rights movement that had been built up earlier in the decade among northern whites. Together with widespread student demonstrations against the Vietnam War (1964–1975), the riots pushed many Americans toward conservatism.

The Civil Rights Act of 1968 and Other Housing Reform Legislation. Martin Luther King, Jr., was assassinated on April 4, 1968. Despite King's message of peace, his death was followed by far-reaching rioting. Nine days after King's death, President Johnson signed the Civil Rights Act of 1968, which forbade discrimination in most housing and provided penalties for those attempting to interfere with individual civil rights (protecting civil rights workers,

---

14. Angus Campbell and Howard Schuman, ICPSR 3500: Racial Attitudes in Fifteen American Cities, 1968 (Ann Arbor, MI: Inter-University Consortium for Political and Social Research, 1997). Campbell and Schuman's survey documents both white participation in and the attitudes of the inhabitants of affected neighborhoods. This survey is available online at www.grinnell.edu/academic/data/sociology/minorityresearch/raceatt1968.

among others). Subsequent legislation added enforcement provisions to the federal government's rules against discriminatory mortgage lending practices. Today, all lenders must report to the federal government the race, gender, and income of all mortgage loan seekers, along with the final decision on their loan applications.

Consequences of Civil Rights Legislation

As a result of the Voting Rights Act of 1965 and its amendments, as well as the large-scale voter-registration drives in the South, the number of African Americans registered to vote climbed dramatically. Subsequent amendments to the act extended its protections to other minorities, including Latinos, Asian Americans, Native Americans, and Native Alaskans. To further protect the voting rights of minorities, the law now provides that states must make bilingual ballots available in counties where 5 percent or more of the population speaks a language other than English.

President Lyndon B. Johnson is shown signing the Civil Rights Act of 1968. What are some of the provisions of that far-reaching law?

Some of the provisions in the Voting Rights Act of 1965 were due to "sunset" (expire) in 2007. In July 2006, President George W. Bush signed a 25-year extension of these provisions, following heated congressional debate in which many members, particularly those representing the states and counties still monitored by the Justice Department, argued that the act was no longer needed. In 2013, the U.S. Supreme Court issued a 5-4 decision declaring Section 4 of the Voting Rights Act unconstitutional. Section 4 contains the "coverage formula" that determines which states must receive preclearance from the Justice Department or a federal court in Washington before making any changes to their voting laws. At the time of the Court's ruling, nine states were subject to the preclearance requirement: Alabama, Alaska, Arizona, Georgia, Louisiana, Mississippi, South Carolina, Texas and Virginia. Some counties and townships in other states were also covered. These states and counties were identified in the 1965 law on the basis of past discriminatory acts and the consequences of those acts on minority voting rights. Congress last reviewed the basis for preclearance in 2006, but did not make any changes to the formula. Chief Justice Roberts, writing for the majority in *Shelby County v. Holder*, said "Our country has changed. While any racial discrimination in voting is too much, Congress must ensure that the legislation it passes to remedy that problem speaks to current conditions."[15] Although the Court did not strike Section 5 of the Voting Rights Act (the "preclearance requirement"), without a way to identify which states and localities are subject to prior review, it is largely unenforceable. Justice Ruth Bader Ginsberg summarized her dissenting opinion from the bench to indicate the strength of her disagreement with the majority. She stated that the legacy of Dr. Martin Luther King, Jr., and the nation's commitment to justice had been "disserved by the decision."[16]

15. 570 U.S. ___ (2013).
16. Adam Liptak, "Supreme Court Invalidates key Part of Voting Rights Act," *The New York Times*, June 25, 2013. Accessed at http://www.nytimes.com/2013/06/26/us/supreme-court-ruling.html?pagewanted=all

Although the Supreme Court specifically invited Congress to create a new formula for identifying areas of the country where voting rights should be carefully scrutinized, few believe that Congress will immediately do so. Seven of the nine preclearance states have enacted new voting restrictions since the Supreme Court's ruling. Some of the changes were under review or had been recently rejected by the Justice Department at the time of the ruling. Just two months after the *Shelby* decision, North Carolina passed a new photo ID requirement, eliminated same-day voter registration, ended a program that allowed high school students to pre-register to vote at age 16, and reduced the number of early voting days. North Carolina led the nation in African American turnout in the 2012 election with over 80 percent of eligible black voters participating.[17] A study by Dartmouth University scholars found that the changes in North Carolina will have a disproportionate effect on African American voters.[18] In Texas, a voter ID law previously called "the most stringent in the country" by a federal court will now go into effect along with redistricting maps rejected by the same court for protecting white incumbents while altering districts with minority incumbents.[19] Several other states have similar laws ready to go into effect with the next election. The *Shelby* ruling does not remove federal scrutiny entirely, but challenges to these and other changes will now occur after the fact and based on evidence of voter disenfranchisement. Thirty-four states have passed laws requiring identification at the polls, and most require a state-issued photo ID. Pivotal swing states under Republican control are embracing significant new electoral restrictions on registering and voting that go beyond the voter identification requirements. Republicans in Ohio and Wisconsin adopted measures limiting the time polls are open, in particular cutting into the weekend voting favored by low-income voters and blacks, who sometimes caravan from churches to polls on the Sunday before the election. Proponents of these new state initiatives argue that they are designed to prevent voter fraud, but most studies find that voter fraud in the United States is rare.[20]

Political Representation by African Americans.   The movement of African American citizens into high elected office has been steady, if exceedingly slow. African American representatives hold 43 of the 435 seats in the House of Representatives (9.5 percent) and two of 100 seats in the Senate in the 113th Congress. South Carolina Republican Tim Scott was appointed to fill the Senate seat following Senator Jim Demint's resignation and was elected to a full term in 2014. Cory Booker, former Democratic mayor of Newark, won a special election in 2013 to fill the seat of Frank Lautenberg who passed away. He was also elected to full term in the 2014 election marking the first time ever that two African Americans have been elected to the Senate in the same election. In Utah, voters elected Mia Love to a seat in the House of Representatives making her the first African American Republican woman elected to the House. The 2014 midterm elections added three black Democratic women bringing the total in the House to 18. African American state legislators hold just over 8 percent of seats across

17. Leoneda Inge, "North Carolia Black Turnout Tops in US." North Carolina Public Radio. May 10, 2013. Accessed at http://wunc.org/post/north-carolina-black-voter-turnout-tops-us

18. Michael C. Herron and Daniel A. Smith, "Race, *Shelby County*, and the Voter Information Verification Act" February 12, 2014. Accessed at http://www.dartmouth.edu/~herron/HerronSmithNorthCarolina.pdf

19. Kara Brandeisky and Mike Tigas, "Everything That's Happened Since Supreme Court Ruled on Voting Rights Act," PROPUBLICA, November 1, 2013. Accessed at http://www.propublica.org/article/voting-rights-by-state-map.

20. Wendy R. Weiser and Lawrence Norden, "Voting Law Changes in 2012." Brennan Center for Justice at New York University School of Law, accessed at: http://brennan.3cdn.net/92635ddafbc09e8d88_i3m6bjdeh.pdf

the nation. In 2008, Karen Bass was selected as the first female African American assembly speaker in California. At the local level, the Joint Center for Political and Economic Studies estimated that black elected officials held over 5,700 offices in 2002. In a decisive victory, Barack Obama was elected the first African American president on November 4, 2008. Gwen Ifill called his election a breakthrough for black politicians and predicted that his victory would usher in a new age of black political leadership.[21]

To the befuddlement of researchers, Ifill's projected "new age" has not materialized. Why, for example, do so few black House members run for the Senate? Nearly half of the current U.S. Senate is made up of members who previously served in the House, but not one African American House member has ever been elected to a Senate seat. Bruce Oppenheimer, a political scientist at Vanderbilt University, identified a number of possible reasons. First, most African American House members represent districts in large states where competition for Senate seats is fierce and their name recognition might be low because they represent a small share of the overall population. They are also likely to represent heavily Democratic, liberal districts, which compromises their statewide appeal. Finally, African Americans House members tend to come from less-affluent districts, thus limiting their initial fundraising base for a Senate campaign.[22] Carol Mosely Braun, the first African American woman elected to the Senate, echoes this point. "Without strong fundraising potential," African American politicians "may fail to convince party leaders they can win."[23] Nevertheless, Braun remains optimistic that gains in political representation will continue even in the face of structural barriers because President Obama's election and the success of other African Americans in prominent political roles (Condoleezza Rice and Eric Holder, for example) will serve to normalize black leadership for voters in statewide or national contests. Although Barack Obama was reelected in 2012, he lost among white voters by a margin greater than any victor in American history. This is compelling evidence that there is still a racial divide in American politics.

The U.S. Census and Civil Rights. The census, which calls for a count of the country's population every 10 years (last occurring in 2010), is the basis for virtually all demographic information used by policymakers, educators, and community leaders. The census is used for determining representation for the purposes of redistricting. In this sense, the census data also provide an important tool for enforcing the Voting Rights Act, which forbids drawing districts with the intention of diluting the concentration and thus the political power of minority voters. Census data are also used to allocate federal dollars in support of community development, education, crime prevention, and transportation. For these reasons, civil rights leaders urged full participation from within their communities. Being counted in the census equates to political and community empowerment.

did you know?

During the Mississippi Summer Project in 1964, organized by students to register African American voters, there were 1,000 students and voters arrested, 80 beaten, 35 shot, and 6 murdered; 30 buildings were bombed and 25 churches burned.

21. Gwen Ifill, *The Breakthrough: Politics and Race in the Age of Obama*. New York: Anchor Books, 2009.
22. Bruce I. Oppenheimer, Gbemende Johnson, and Jennifer Selin. "The House as a Stepping Stone to the Senate: Why Do So Few African-American House Members Run?" Paper presented at Conference on Legislative Elections, Process, and Policy: The Influence of Bicameralism, Vanderbilt University 2009. Accessed at http://www.vanderbilt.edu/csdi/archived/ Bicameralism%20papers/stepping%20stone.pdf
23. Jamelle Bouie, "The Other Glass Ceiling," *The American Prospect*, March 14, 2012. Accessed at http://prospect.org/article/ other-glass-ceiling.

Lingering Social and Economic Disparities. According to Joyce Ladner of the Brookings Institution, one of the difficulties with the race-based civil rights agenda of the 1950s and 1960s is that it did not envision remedies for cross-racial problems. How should the nation address problems such as poverty and urban violence that affect underclasses in all racial groups? In 1967, when Martin Luther King, Jr., proposed a Poor People's Campaign, he recognized that a civil rights coalition based entirely on race would not be sufficient to address the problem of poverty among whites as well as blacks. During his 1984 and 1988 presidential campaigns, African American Jesse Jackson also acknowledged the inadequacy of a race-based model of civil rights when he attempted to form a "Rainbow Coalition" of minorities, women, and other underrepresented groups, including the poor.[24]

Race-Conscious or Post-Racial Society? Whether we are talking about college attendance, media stereotyping, racial profiling, or academic achievement, the black experience is different from the white one. As a result, African Americans view the nation and many specific issues differently than their white counterparts do.[25] In survey after survey, when blacks are asked whether they have achieved racial equality, few believe that they have. In contrast, whites are five times more likely than blacks to believe that racial equality has been achieved.[26] As a candidate for the Democratic nomination for president, Barack Obama directly addressed race in America in his "A More Perfect Union" speech delivered in Philadelphia in March 2008.[27] Since taking office, however, President Obama has been criticized by some within the civil rights community for not making the goal of racial equality a higher priority within his administration.

The president addressed racial profiling in ways no previous president could when one of the nation's preeminent African American scholars, Harvard Professor Henry Louis Gates, was arrested in his own home and charged with disorderly conduct for displaying "loud and tumultuous behavior" when he was asked by Cambridge police for identification to prove that he was indeed the homeowner. Police said they were responding to a call from a neighbor who reported seeing "two black men with backpacks" trying to enter the house. Professor Gates had returned home from a trip to China to find his front door stuck; he and the taxi driver were trying to get it open. The president, asked at a news conference to comment on the incident, said, "What I think we know, separate and apart from this incident, is that there's a long history in this country of African Americans and Latinos being stopped by law enforcement disproportionately. That's just a fact."[28]

In February of 2012, when unarmed 17-year-old African American Trayvon Martin was fatally shot by George Zimmerman, a 28-year-old community watch coordinator in the gated Florida community where the shooting took place, President Obama spoke in highly personal terms in acknowledging the racial overtones of the incident: "Obviously, this is a tragedy; we all have to do some soul searching to find out why something like this happened. But my main message is to the parents of Trayvon Martin. You know, if I had a son, he'd look like Trayvon. And, you know, I think they are right to expect that all of us as Americans are going to take this with the seriousness it deserves and that we're going to get to

24. Joyce A. Ladner, "A New Civil Rights Agenda," *The Brookings Review*, Vol. 18, No. 2, Spring 2000, pp. 26–28.
25. Lawrence D. Bobo et al., "Through the Eyes of Black America," *Public Perspective*, May/June 2001, p. 13.
26. Lawrence D. Bobo et al., "Through the Eyes of Black America," *Public Perspective*, May/June 2001, p. 13, p. 15, Figure 2.
27. Barack Obama, "A More Perfect Union," Transcript of speech delivered, March 18, 2008, at the Constitution Center in Philadelphia, PA. http://www.npr.org/templates/story/story.php?storyId=88478467
28. "Obama Addresses Race and Gates Incident," *Washington Post*, July 23, 2009.

This cartoon highlights the issue of racial profiling; however, as you know from the description of the incident in the text, Professor Gates was confronted and later arrested in his home during daylight hours. Why would the cartoonist draw this scene at night? How is the fact that neighborhood racial segregation is still prevalent in the United States related to this incident and the way it has been portrayed by the cartoonist?

the bottom of exactly what happened."[29] Despite the civil rights movement, civil rights legislation, and the election of the first black president, many African Americans continue to feel a sense of injustice in matters of race, and this feeling is often not apparent to, or appreciated by, the majority of white America.

Women's Campaign for Equal Rights

Like African Americans and other minorities, women also have had to make a claim for equality. Political citizenship requires personal autonomy (the ability to think and act for oneself), but the prevailing opinion about women was that they were not endowed with reason. During the first phase of this campaign, the primary political goal of women was to obtain the right to vote.

Early Women's Political Movements

The first political cause in which women became actively engaged was the movement to abolish slavery. When the World Antislavery Convention was held in London in 1840, women delegates were barred from active participation. Partly in response to this rebuff, two American delegates, Lucretia Mott and Elizabeth Cady Stanton, returned from that meeting with plans to work for women's rights in the United States.

In 1848, Mott and Stanton organized the first women's rights convention in Seneca Falls, New York. The 300 people who attended the two-day event debated a wide variety of issues important for expanding women's social, civil, and religious rights, including access to education and employment, marriage and divorce reform, and most controversial of all, **suffrage**. Attendees approved a Declaration of Sentiments modeled in word and spirit on the Declaration of Independence: "We hold these truths to be self-evident: that all men and *women* are created

Suffrage
The right to vote; the franchise.

29. Michael D. Shear, "Obama Speaks Out on Trayvon Martin Killing," *The New York Times*. March 23, 2012.

equal." Groups that supported women's rights held similar conventions in cities in the Midwest and East.

With the outbreak of the Civil War, advocates of women's rights were urged to put their support behind the war effort and women in the North and South dedicated themselves to their respective causes. In 1866 the American Equal Rights Association (AERA) was formed to advance the cause of universal suffrage, but tensions arose immediately between those whose first priority was black male suffrage and those who were dedicated first to women's suffrage. The failure to include women in the Fifteenth Amendment resulted in the dissolution of the AERA and the formation of two rival women's suffrage organizations.

Women's Suffrage Associations

Susan B. Anthony and Elizabeth Cady Stanton formed the National Woman Suffrage Association (NWSA) in 1869 and dedicated themselves almost exclusively to advancing women's suffrage at the federal level by way of a constitutional amendment. In their view, women's suffrage was a means to achieve major improvements in the economic and social situation of women in the United States. Unlike Anthony and Stanton, Lucy Stone, a key founder of the American Woman Suffrage Association (AWSA), continued to support the Fifteenth Amendment (restricted to males) but vowed to support a Sixteenth Amendment dedicated to women's suffrage. The AWSA primarily focused its efforts on the states.

In the November election of 1872, several women attempted to vote under the revolutionary legal reasoning that the Fourteenth Amendment extended citizenship rights to all persons, and voting was among the privilege and immunities of citizenship. In Missouri, Virginia Minor cast her vote and was arrested for illegal voting. In the case of *Minor v. Happersett*, the U.S. Supreme Court ruled that since the federal Constitution did not explicitly grant women the right to vote, the states were free to decide who had the privilege of voting. For suffragists, this left two options—an amendment to the U.S. Constitution or a state-by-state campaign.

For the next 20 years, the two organizations worked along similar paths to educate the public and legislators, testifying before legislative committees, giving public speeches, and conducting public referendum campaigns on women's suffrage with varying degrees of success, as indicated by the map in Figure 5–2. Organizations such as the Women's Christian Temperance Union (WCTU) joined the campaign for suffrage, arguing that only women could be counted on to cast the votes necessary to prohibit the sale and consumption of alcohol. The combination of efforts yielded the movement's first successes. The western territory of Wyoming granted women the right to vote in 1869, and several state legislatures in other regions (outside the South) took up legislation granting women the vote. Political scientist Lee Ann Banaszak calculated that between 1870 and 1890, an average of four states a year took up the question of women's suffrage.[30] In 1890, the two organizations joined forces, creating the National American Woman Suffrage Association (NAWSA), with only one goal—the enfranchisement of women—and continued lobbying in the states and western territories.

Opposition to women's suffrage came from a number of sources, including the liquor industry, big business, and the church. Brewers and distillers were interested in preventing prohibition, and thus hoped to keep women from the

---

30. Lynne E. Ford, *Women and Politics: The Pursuit of Equality.* (Boston: Cengage Learning Wadsworth, 2011).

Figure 5-2 ▸ The Suffrage Map, Early August, 1920

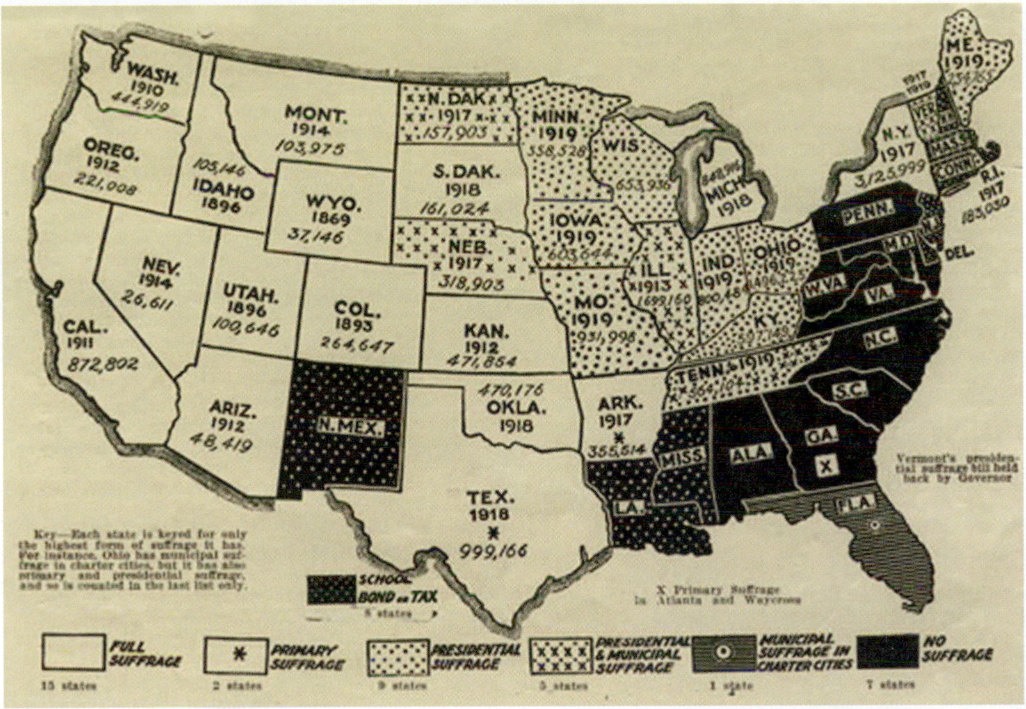

Marjorie Shuler. Courtesy of the Tennessee State Library and Archives

Source: From "Out of Subjection into Freedom" by Mavrjorie Shuler, published in *The Woman Citizen*, p. 360, September 4, 1920.

voting booth. Industry was interested in limiting the reach of progressive policy to set wages and improve working conditions (both areas where female activists were heavily involved), and the church opposed suffrage primarily on ideological grounds. However, beginning in about 1880, the most persistent opponents of the suffrage cause emerged: other women. Suffragists at first dismissed the "antis" but later came to understand that they were a powerful, well-organized force dedicated to protecting traditional gender roles as well as women's social and economic privileges as they understood them.[31]

At the turn of the century, an impatient new generation of women introduced direct protest tactics they had observed while working alongside Emmeline Pankhurst in the British suffrage campaign. Harriot Stanton Blatch (Elizabeth Cady Stanton's daughter), Alice Paul, and Lucy Burns urged NAWSA to return to a federal amendment strategy. The new suffragists, as they were called, intended to *demand* their right to vote. They scheduled a massive parade in Washington, DC, for March 3, 1913, to coincide with Woodrow Wilson's inauguration as president, scheduled for the next day. Alice Paul believed that Congress would only be persuaded to move the suffrage amendment forward if prodded to do so by the president. The parade attracted 8,000 marchers and more than half a million spectators.

Alice Paul continued to agitate for women's suffrage in ways that embarrassed NAWSA's leadership. She organized "Silent Sentinels" to stand in front of the White House with banners reading, "Mr. President, What Will You Do for

31. Susan E. Marshall, *Splintered Sisterhood: Gender and Class in the Campaign Against Women's Suffrage* (Madison, WI: University of Wisconsin Press, 1997).

Silent Sentinels posted in front of the White House gates. The women were often attacked by onlookers and arrested, but the protests continued. Long prison terms were imposed in an attempt to scare women away. Women who could not personally stand on the picket line sent money to support the families of those who were jailed. Women in jail organized hunger strikes, only to be force-fed through the nose.

Library of Congress, Prints & Photographs Division, LC-US262-31799

Table 5–1 ▶ WOMEN'S VOTING RIGHTS AROUND THE WORLD, Selected Countries and Year Women's Suffrage was Granted

Year	Country
1893	New Zealand
1902	Austria
1913	Norway
1918	Canada
1919	Germany
1920	United States
1928	United Kingdom
1930	Turkey
1934	Cuba
1939	El Salvador
1944	France
1945	Japan
1947	Mexico
1948	Israel
1949	China
1950	India
1956	Egypt
1961	Rwanda
1964	Afghanistan
1965	Sudan
1971	Switzerland
1974	Jordan
1980	Iraq
1994	South Africa
2005	Kuwait
2015*	Saudi Arabia

* projected, next municipal elections scheduled for 2015
Source: Center for the American Woman and Politics

Woman Suffrage?" These women were the first picketers ever to appear before the White House. When the United States joined the war against Germany in 1917, women were urged to set aside their goals in favor of the overall war effort. Paul refused and formed the National Woman's Party (NWP) to bring even greater attention to women's disenfranchisement.

Meanwhile, NAWSA members, under the leadership of Carrie Chapman Catt, were pursuing the "winning plan," which entailed a two-pronged lobbying strategy focused on both federal and state legislators. In the end, scholars agree that it was the combination of patient lobbying by NAWSA members and the more militant tactics of the NWP that resulted in Congress passing the suffrage amendment in May 1919. In Tennessee, the last state required to win ratification, the amendment passed by one vote on August 26, 1920. The Nineteenth Amendment reads: "The right of citizens of the United States to vote shall not be denied or abridged by the United States or by any State on account of sex."

The United States was neither the first nor the last to give women the vote. New Zealand introduced universal suffrage in 1893, while Kuwait allowed women to vote and seek public office for the first time in 2005. In 2011, King Abdullah of Saudi Arabia granted women the right to vote and run in future municipal elections, next scheduled for 2015 (see Table 5–1).

The Second Wave Women's Movement

■ **LO5.4:** Explain why the U.S. Supreme Court plays such an important role relative to civil rights and identify at least two significant Supreme Court decisions that advanced civil rights in the United States.

After gaining the right to vote in 1920, women did not flock to the polls in large numbers, nor did many of the thousands of women who had lobbied for and against suffrage seek political office. There was little by way of an organized women's movement again until the second wave began in the 1960s. The civil rights movement of that decade resulted in a growing awareness of rights for all groups, including women. Women's

Beyond Our Borders

The Campaign for Women's Rights around the World

President Jimmy Carter (served 1977–1981) believes that the most serious and unaddressed worldwide challenge is the deprivation and abuse of women and girls.* He is not alone—Hillary Rodham Clinton calls advancing the rights of women and girls "the great unfinished business of the twenty-first century."** Although women's rights have emerged as a high-priority global issue, progress has been slow. The campaign for women's rights in countries where cultural or legal practices perpetuate the inequality of women is especially difficult. December 2014 marks the 35th anniversary of the United Nations' adoption of the Convention on the Elimination of All Forms of Discrimination against Women (CEDAW), an international treaty to promote the adoption of national laws, policies, and practices to ensure that women and girls live free from violence, have access to high-quality education, and have the right to participate fully in the economic, political, and social sectors of their society. Although the treaty has been ratified by 186 countries, the United States is one of only seven nations that have not ratified. International agreements such as CEDAW convey a set of universal ethical standards and global norms regarding human rights.

THE PROBLEM OF VIOLENCE

Most people consider the right to be free from violence as one of the most basic human rights. Women's rights advocates point out that this right is threatened in societies that do not accept the premise that men and women are equal. Some parts of India implicitly tolerate the practice of dowry killing. (A dowry is a sum of money given to a husband by the bride's family.) In a number of cases, husbands, dissatisfied with the size of dowries, have killed their wives in order to remarry for a "better deal"—a crime rarely prosecuted.

THE SITUATION IN AFGHANISTAN

A startling 2001 documentary repeatedly aired on CNN called *Behind the Veil* introduced many Americans to women's rights issues abroad. A courageous female reporter had secretly filmed Afghan women being beaten in the streets, killed in public for trivial offenses, and subjugated in extreme ways. Women's rights became a major issue in our foreign policy. Americans learned that Afghan girls were barred from schools, and by law women were not allowed to work. Women who had lost their husbands during Afghanistan's civil wars were forced into begging and prostitution. Women had no access to medical care. Any woman found with an unrelated man could be executed by stoning, and many were.

Iraqi Girls wait for the start of class at the Eastern Secondary School in Baghdad. The role of women in the new Iraq remains uncertain. What negative consequences could result if discriminatory laws forced Iraqi women—among the region's most educated—to retreat to their homes?

ACTIVISTS FOR EDUCATION

Malala Yousafzai is a Pakistani teenager and education activist. From a very young age, Malala was willing to risk her own life to promote education for girls. A blogger for BBC, she attracted the attention of a documentary film-maker and multiple international media outlets for her work. On October 9, 2012, Malala was riding the bus home from school when a gunman boarded, asked the children to identify her, then shot Malala in the head. Amazingly, she survived, but even as Malala fought for her life, the Taliban repeated its threats to kill her. The attempt on her life sparked international outrage and action. The United Nations launched "I am Malala," a campaign to enroll all children in school by 2015. "Girl Rising" is another international project promoting girls education. The documentary profiles life in the developing world—ordinary girls who confront challenges and overcome nearly impossible odds to pursue their dreams. Prize-winning authors put the girls' stories into words, and renowned actors give them voice.***

NATION BUILDING AND WOMEN'S RIGHTS: POST-CONFLICT CHALLENGES

After the collapse of the Taliban regime, the United States and its allies were able to influence the status of Afghan women. The draft constitution of Afghanistan, adopted in 2004, gave women equality before the law and 20 percent of the seats in the National Assembly. In 2014, women hold 28 percent of the legislative seats. Much of the country, however, remains outside the control of the national government. Women continue to face abuse, including arson attacks on girls' schools, forced marriages, and reimposition of the all-covering burqa garment.

Women in Iraq had enjoyed greater equality than women in most Arab nations. In line with the secular ideology of the Baath Party, Saddam Hussein's government tended to treat men and women alike. A problem for the U.S.-led Coalition Provisional Authority (CPA) that governed Iraq until June 2004 was ensuring that women did not lose ground under the new regime. The interim Iraqi constitution, adopted in March 2004, allotted 25 percent of the seats in the parliament to women. In 2014, women occupied 82 of 325 seats in parliament, or 25.2 percent (considerably higher than the 18 percent held by women in the United States).

For Critical Analysis

1. *Is it fair or appropriate for one country to judge the cultural practices of another? Why or why not?*

2. *Why is education so critical to the success of women and girls?*

* Jimmy Carter, A Call to Action: Women, Religion, Violence and Power. New York, NY: Simon and Schuster, 2014.
** Hillary Rodham Clinton, "Helping Women Isn't Just a 'Nice' Thing to Do," Keynote Address, Women in the World Conference, April 5, 2013. Accessed atwww.thedailybeast.com/witw/articles/2013/04/05/hillary-clinton-helping-women-isn-t-just-a-nice-thing-to-do.html.
*** Girl Rising accessed at http://girlrising.com/.

increased participation in the workforce and the publication of Betty Friedan's *The Feminine Mystique* in 1963 focused national attention on the unequal status of women in American life.

In 1966, Betty Friedan and others dissatisfied with existing women's organizations, and especially with the failure of the Equal Employment Opportunity Commission to address discrimination against women, formed the National Organization for Women (NOW). NOW immediately adopted a blanket resolution designed "to bring women into full participation in the mainstream of American society *now*, exercising all the privileges and responsibilities thereof in truly equal partnership with men."

The second wave gained additional impetus from young women who entered politics to support the civil rights movement or to oppose the Vietnam War. Many found that despite the egalitarian principles of these movements, women remained in second-class positions. In the late 1960s, "women's liberation" organizations began to spring up on college campuses and women organized "consciousness-raising groups," in which they discussed how gender affected their lives. The new women's movement emerged as a major social force by 1970.

Historian Nancy Cott contends that the word *feminism* first began to be used around 1910.[32] At that time, **feminism** meant, as it does today, political, social, and economic equality for women. It is difficult to measure the support for feminism at present because the word means different things to different people. When the dictionary definition of *feminist*—"someone who supports political, economic, and social equality for women"—was read to respondents in a survey, 67 percent labeled themselves as feminists.[33] In the absence of such prompting, however, the term *feminist* (like the term *liberal*) implies radicalism to many people, who therefore shy away from it. Young women have launched a third wave of feminism, embracing a multitude of perspectives on what it means to be a feminist woman.[34]

Feminism
The philosophy of political, economic, and social equality for women and the gender consciousness sufficient to mobilize women for change.

32. Nancy F. Cott, The *Grounding of Modern Feminism* (New Haven, CT: Yale University Press, 1987).
33. Nancy E. McGlen and Karen O'Connor, *Women, Politics, and American Society*, 4th ed. (Upper Saddle River, NJ: Prentice Hall, 2004).
34. See, for example, Jessica Valenti, *Full Frontal Feminism: A Young Woman's Guide to Why Feminism Matters* (Emeryville, CA: Seal Press, 2007); and Jennifer Baumgardner and Amy Richards, *Manifesta: Young Women, Feminism, and the Future* (New York: Farrar, Straus and Giroux, 2000).

The Equal Rights Amendment. NOW leaders and other women's rights advocates sought to eradicate gender inequality through a constitutional amendment. The proposed Equal Rights Amendment (ERA), first introduced in Congress in 1923 by leaders of the National Woman's Party, states: "Equality of rights under the law shall not be denied or abridged by the United States or by any state on account of sex." For decades the amendment was not even given a hearing in Congress, but finally it was approved by both chambers and sent to the state legislatures for ratification in 1972.

As was noted in Chapter 2, any constitutional amendment must be ratified by the legislatures (or conventions) in three-fourths of the states. Since the early twentieth century, most proposed amendments have required that ratification occur within seven years of Congress's adoption of the amendment. Although states competed to be the first to ratify the ERA, by 1977 only 35 of the necessary 38 states had ratified the amendment. Congress granted a rare extension, but the remaining three states could not be added by the 1982 deadline, even though the ERA was supported by numerous national party platforms, six presidents, and both chambers of Congress.

As with the antisuffrage efforts, the staunchest opponents to the ERA were other women. Many women perceived the goals pursued by feminists as a threat to their way of life. At the head of the countermovement was Republican Phyllis Schlafly and her conservative organization, Eagle Forum. Eagle Forum's "Stop ERA" campaign found significant support among fundamentalist religious groups and other conservative organizations; it was a major force in blocking the ratification of the ERA. Twenty-one states have appended amendments similar to the ERA to their own constitutions.

Three-State Strategy. Had the ERA been ratified by 38 states, it would have become the Twenty-seventh Amendment to the Constitution. Instead, that place is occupied by the "Madison Amendment" governing congressional pay raises, first sent to the states in 1789 and not ratified until 1992. ERA supporters argue that acceptance of the Madison Amendment means that Congress has the power to maintain the legal viability of the ERA and the existing 35 state ratifications. This would leave supporters just three states shy of achieving final ratification. The legal rationale for the three-state strategy was developed by three law students in a law review article published in 1997.[35] Support for constitutional equality remains high in the United States; however, mobilizing support for ratification of the ERA in the future may prove difficult. A 2001 poll found that although 96 percent of those polled supported constitutional equality for women and men, 72 percent mistakenly believed that the U.S. Constitution already includes the Equal Rights Amendment.[36]

Challenging Gender Discrimination in the Courts and Legislatures. With the failure of the ERA, feminists turned their attention to national and state laws that would guarantee the equality of women. In 1978, the Civil Rights Act of 1964 was amended by the Pregnancy Discrimination Act, which prohibits discrimination in employment against pregnant women. In addition, Title IX of the Education Amendments was passed in 1972; it bans sex discrimination at all levels and in all

---

Seventy-two years passed between the time the Declaration of Independence was signed in 1776 and women first demanded the vote at the Seneca Falls Convention in 1848; it took another 72 years for women to win suffrage via the Nineteenth Amendment, ratified in 1920, and it took another 72 years before more than two women were elected to serve in the U.S. Senate at the same time (1992).

---

35. Allison Held, Sheryl Herndon, and Danielle Stager, "The Equal Rights Amendment: Why the ERA Remains Legally Viable and Properly Before the States." *William & Mary Journal of Women and the Law*, Spring 1997, pp. 113–136.
36. *The ERA Campaign*, Issue #5, July 2001, accessed at http://eracampaignweb.kishosting.com/newsletter5.html.

aspects of education and deals with issues of sexual harassment, pregnancy, parental status, and marital status. Although Title IX is best known for increasing women's access to sports, its impact toward equalizing admissions to professional programs, financial aid, and educational facilities has more practical significance. Prior to Title IX, women's entrance into professional programs in law, medicine, science, and engineering was limited by quotas. In 1996, the Supreme Court held that the state-financed Virginia Military Institute's policy of accepting only males violated the equal protection clause; this finding led to the admission of women at The Citadel, the state-financed military college in South Carolina, as well.[37]

Gender Discrimination
Any practice, policy, or procedure that denies equality of treatment to an individual or to a group because of gender.

Women's rights organizations challenged discriminatory statutes and policies in the federal courts, contending that **gender discrimination** violated the Fourteenth Amendment's equal protection clause. Since the 1970s, the Supreme Court has tended to scrutinize gender classifications closely and has invalidated a number of such statutes and policies. In 1977, the Court held that police and fire-fighting units cannot establish arbitrary rules, such as height and weight requirements, that tend to keep women from joining those occupations.[38] In 1983, the Court ruled that life insurance companies cannot charge different rates for women and men.[39]

In 1994, Congress repealed the "risk rule" barring women from all combat situations. As a result, over 90 percent of positions in the military were opened to women. The navy opened service on submarines to women in 2012. While women have not been "assigned" to direct combat units, the wars in Iraq and Afghanistan stretched the limits of that law, and more women were "attached" to front-line units in combat support positions. Generally, the public supports increasing women's combat role; a poll found that 53 percent of those polled would favor permitting women to "join combat units, where they would be directly involved in the ground fighting." Thus in 2013, Defense Secretary Leon Panetta and the Chairman of the Joint Chiefs of Starr, General Martin Dempsey, announced the rescission of the combat exclusion for women. "Women have shown great courage and sacrifice on and off the battlefield, contributed in unprecedented ways to the military's mission and proven their ability to serve in an expanding number of roles," Secretary of Defense Leon E. Panetta said. "The Department's goal in rescinding the rule is to ensure that the mission is met with the best-qualified and most capable people, regardless of gender."[40] Women make up roughly 15 percent of the 1.4 million active duty personnel in the U.S. military. Each branch of the military has been directed to create a plan to integrate women into the remaining restricted fields following a set of principles developed by the Joint Chiefs of Staff. Secretary Panetta set a deadline of January 1, 2016 for the process of full integration to be complete.

did you know?

Congresswoman Tammy Duckworth, elected to the House of Representatives in 2012, is the first female double amputee from the Iraq War.

Women in Politics Today

Today, women make up just 20 percent of the U.S. Congress. The United States is ranked 83rd among 190 nations by the Inter-Parliamentary Union based on the proportion of seats held by women in the lower house. Rwanda ranks first—in that nation, women hold 56 percent of seats in the Lower House.[41] The efforts of women's rights

37. *United States v. Virginia*, 518 U.S. 515 (1996).
38. *Dothard v. Rawlinson*, 433 U.S. 321 (1977).
39. *Arizona v. Norris*, 463 U.S. 1073 (1983).
40. "Defense Department Rescinds Direct Combat Exclusion Rule." U.S. Department of Defense News Release January 24, 2014. Accessed at http://www.defense.gov/Releases/Release.aspx?ReleaseID=15784
41. Inter-Parliamentary Union, "Women in National Parliaments," accessed at http://www.ipu.org/wmn-e/classif.htm.

advocates have helped increase the number of women holding political offices at all levels of government. In 2007, Nancy Pelosi of California became the first female Speaker of the House, the most powerful member of the majority party and second in the line of succession to the presidency.

Although no woman has yet been nominated for president by a major political party, in 1984 Geraldine Ferraro became the Democratic nominee for vice president. In 2008 Hillary Rodham Clinton, senator from New York, became one of two final contenders for the presidential nomination of the Democratic Party, but ultimately lost to Barack Obama. In a surprise move, Senator John McCain chose the Alaskan governor, Sarah Palin, for his running mate. However, only one woman was a candidate for the 2012 Republican presidential nomination. Congresswoman Michelle Bachman announced her campaign in June 2011 but withdrew from the race after placing last in the Iowa caucuses in January 2012. Former Secretary of State Hillary Clinton is widely expected to announce that she will seek the presidential nomination of her party in 2016.

In recent presidential administrations, women have been more visible in cabinet posts. President Bill Clinton (served 1993–2001) appointed four women to his cabinet, more than any previous president. Madeleine Albright was appointed to serve as secretary of state, a first for a woman. President George W. Bush also appointed several women to cabinet positions, including Condoleezza Rice as his secretary of state in 2005. President Obama has appointed a number of women to high-ranking positions within his first and second administrations. Valerie Jarrett serves as his senior advisor, his closest aid. Women serve as cabinet secretaries in the Departments of Interior, Commerce, and Health and Human Services. In the area of foreign policy, Susan Rice is national security advisor and Samantha Power serves as ambassador to the United Nations. Upon the retirement of Ben Bernanke, President Obama appointed (and the Senate confirmed) Janet Yellen as the first woman chair of the Board of Governors of the Federal Reserve System. Yellen served as vice-chair for four years prior to taking the helm of the nation's central banking system in February 2014.

Martin H. Simon/ABC/Getty Images

The 113th Congress includes twenty women in the U.S. Senate—the most in history. *ABC World News* anchor Diane Sawyer gathered nearly all the women for an interview in the historic Kennedy Caucus Room in January 2013, just before the start of the new congressional term.

Increasing numbers of women sit on federal judicial benches. President Ronald Reagan (served 1981–1989) was credited with a historic first when he appointed Sandra Day O'Connor to the Supreme Court in 1981. President Clinton appointed a second woman, Ruth Bader Ginsburg, to the Court. O'Connor retired from the Court in 2006. In 2009 President Obama appointed Federal Appeals Court Judge Sonia Sotomayor to fill the vacancy created by Justice David Souter's retirement. Justice Sotomayor is the first Latina to serve on the U.S. Supreme Court. In April 2010, Justice John Paul Stevens announced his retirement, giving President Obama the chance to make a second appointment to the Court. He selected Elena Kagan, the solicitor general of the United States, to fill the vacancy, thus increasing the number of women currently sitting on the Supreme Court to three. President Obama is credited with diversifying the federal bench in numerous ways, appointing record numbers of women and minorities as well as three openly gay judges.

Gender-Based Discrimination in the Workplace

Traditional cultural beliefs concerning the proper role of women in society continue to be evident not only in the political arena but also in the workplace. Since the 1960s, however, women have gained substantial protection against discrimination through laws mandating equal employment opportunities and equal pay.

Title VII of the Civil Rights Act of 1964

Title VII of the Civil Rights Act of 1964 prohibits gender discrimination in employment and has been used to strike down employment policies that discriminate against employees on the basis of gender. Even so-called protective policies violate Title VII if they have a discriminatory effect. In 1991, for example, the Supreme Court held that a fetal protection policy established by Johnson Controls, Inc., the country's largest producer of automobile batteries, violated Title VII. The policy required all women of childbearing age working in jobs that entailed periodic exposure to lead or other hazardous materials to prove that they were infertile or to transfer to other positions. The same requirement was not applied to men. Women who agreed to transfer often had to accept cuts in pay and reduced job responsibilities. The Court concluded that women who are "as capable of doing their jobs as their male counterparts may not be forced to choose between having a child and having a job."[42]

Sexual Harassment

Sexual Harassment
Unwanted physical or verbal conduct or abuse of a sexual nature that interferes with a recipient's job performance, creates a hostile work environment, or carries with it an implicit or explicit threat of adverse employment consequences.

The Supreme Court has also held that Title VII's prohibition of gender-based discrimination extends to **sexual harassment** in the workplace. Sexual harassment occurs when job opportunities, promotions, salary increases, and the like are given in return for sexual favors. A special form of sexual harassment, called hostile-environment harassment, occurs when an employee is subjected to sexual conduct or comments that interfere with the employee's job performance or are so pervasive or severe as to create an intimidating, hostile, or offensive environment.

---

42. *United Automobile Workers v. Johnson Controls, Inc.*, 499 U.S. 187 (1991).

In two 1998 cases, the Supreme Court clarified the responsibilities of employers in preventing sexual harassment. The Court ruled that employers must take reasonable care to prevent and promptly correct any sexually harassing behavior. Claims by the employer that it was unaware of the situation or that the victim suffered no tangible job consequences do not reduce liability.[43] In another 1998 case, *Oncale v. Sundowner Offshore Services, Inc.*, the Supreme Court ruled that Title VII protection extends to same-sex harassment.[44]

Wage Discrimination

Women constitute the majority of U.S. workers today. Although Title VII and other legislation have mandated equal employment opportunities for men and women, women continue to earn less, on average, than men do.

The Equal Pay Act of 1963. The issue of women's wages was first addressed during World War II (1939–1945), when the War Labor Board issued an "equal pay for women" policy to ensure that salaries remained high when men returned from war and reclaimed their jobs. The board's authority ended with the war. Although it was supported by the next three presidential administrations, the Equal Pay Act was not enacted until 1963 as an amendment to the Fair Labor Standards Act of 1938.

The Equal Pay Act requires employers to provide equal pay for substantially equal work. In other words, males cannot legally be paid more than females who perform essentially the same job. The Equal Pay Act did not address occupational segregation, the fact that certain types of jobs traditionally held by women pay lower wages than the jobs usually held by men. For example, more women than men are salesclerks and nurses, whereas more men than women are construction workers and truck drivers. Even if all clerks performing substantially similar jobs for a company earned the same salaries, they typically would still be earning less than the company's truck drivers.

When Congress passed the Equal Pay Act in 1963, a woman, on average, made 59 cents for every dollar earned by a man. Figures recently released by the U.S. Department of Labor suggest that women now earn 81 cents for every dollar that men earn, statistically unchanged from the two prior years. The wage gap is greater for minority women. In some areas, the wage gap is widening. According to the results of a General Accounting Office survey, female managers in 10 industries made less money relative to male managers in 2000 than they did in 1995.[45] A study by the American Association of University Women (AAUW) on the gender pay gap for college graduates found that after one year out of college, women working full time earn only 80 percent as much as their male peers, even among those men and women graduating with the same major and entering the same occupation. The same study found that women earn only 69 percent of men's wages after ten years out of college.[46]

The first bill President Obama signed after taking office in 2009 was the Lilly Ledbetter Fair Pay Act. The law is an example of congressional action undertaken specifically to overturn a decision by the U.S. Supreme Court. Lilly Ledbetter, an employee of Goodyear Tire and Rubber for 19 years, discovered that she was a victim of gender pay discrimination by an anonymous tip when she retired

---

43. 524 U.S. 725 (1998) and 524 U.S. 742 (1998).
44. 523 U.S. 75 (1998).
45. The results of this survey are online at www.gao.gov/audit.htm. To view a copy of the results, enter "GAO-02-156" in the search box. In 2004, the name of this agency was changed to the "Government Accountability Office."
46. Judy Goldberg Dey and Catherine Hill, "Behind the Pay Gap," AAUW Educational Foundation, April 2007.

Figure 5–3 ▶ **Women's Earnings as a Percentage of Men's Earnings in the Past 12 Months by State and Puerto Rico: 2013**

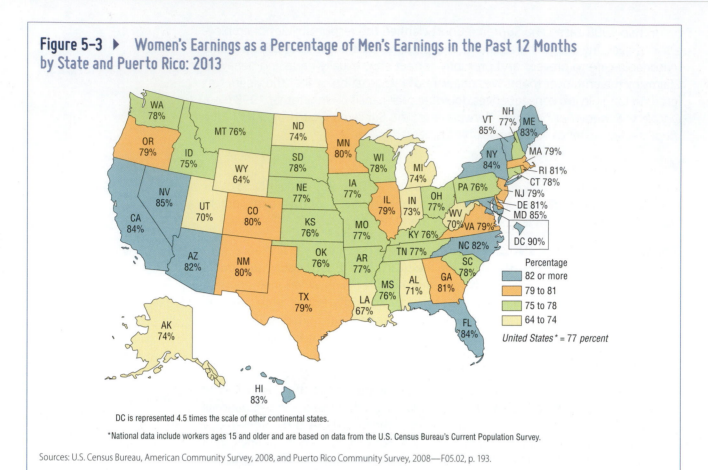

DC is represented 4.5 times the scale of other continental states.

*National data include workers ages 15 and older and are based on data from the U.S. Census Bureau's Current Population Survey.

Sources: U.S. Census Bureau, American Community Survey, 2008, and Puerto Rico Community Survey, 2008—F05.02, p. 193.

in 1998. She filed a complaint under Title VII, but in a 5-4 ruling the U.S. Supreme Court held that race and gender discrimination claims must be made within 180 days of the employer's discriminatory act.[47] As Justice Ginsburg noted in her dissenting opinion, pay disparities often occur in small increments and over time, making them difficult to discover. The Ledbetter Act amends Title VII of the Civil Rights Act of 1964 by stating that the 180-day statute of limitations for filing an equal pay lawsuit regarding pay discrimination resets with each new discriminatory paycheck. It does not, however, provide any additional tools to combat wage discrimination or enforce provisions already in effect. Equal Pay Day, typically celebrated in April, indicates how far into the year women must work to "catch up" to men's wages from the previous year. It is an occasion to call attention to the wage gap and to examine progress toward closing the wage gap between women and men (see Figure 5–3). The earlier in April that Equal Pay Day is celebrated, the less poorly women are being compensated relative to men. For example, Equal Pay Day was celebrated on April 17, 2012 and the following two years on April 8 (2013 and 2014), indicating a slight improvement in women's wages relative to men's.

On Equal Pay Day 2014, President Obama signed an Executive Order prohibiting federal contractors from retaliating against employees who choose to discuss their compensation. It does not compel workers to discuss pay, nor does it require employers to publish or otherwise disseminate pay data, but it is one

---

47. *Ledbetter v. Goodyear Tire & Rubber Co.*, 550 U.S. 618 (2007).

small step toward greater pay transparency, which provides workers a means for discovering violations of equal pay laws. Using a Presidential Memorandum, President Obama instructed the secretary of labor to establish new regulations requiring federal contractors to submit summary data on compensation paid to their employees, including data by sex and race, to the Department of Labor. Meanwhile, Senate Republicans blocked debate over the Paycheck Fairness Act, setting up an election-year fight between the parties over whose policies are friendlier to women.

In his 2014 State of the Union address, President Obama called on Congress to pass the Paycheck Fairness Act—a revision to the Equal Pay Act of 1963. Among other things, the Paycheck Fairness Act would prohibit employers from retaliating against workers for asking questions about salary and require that employers prove that pay disparities are because of skill and background, rather than gender. It also establishes a program through the Department of Labor to train women and girls on negotiating skills. This bill has been introduced in several previous sessions of Congress. The president received a bipartisan standing ovation, when he said, "A woman deserves equal pay for equal work. She deserves to have a baby without sacrificing her job. A mother deserves a day off to care for a sick child or sick parent without running into hardship—and you know what, a father does, too. It's time to do away with workplace policies that belong in a *Mad Men* episode."[48] Despite its active stance on the issue, the White House received criticism for its *Mad Men* Tweet in support of equal pay in 2014.

Economic equality is important to both men and women. President Obama has asked Congress to raise the federal minimum wage for all workers from $7.25 per hour to $10.10 per hour by 2015. Women account for 55 percent of minimum wage workers and are largely concentrated in low-wage sectors. Estimates from the President's Council of Economic Advisers suggest that increasing the minimum wage to $10.10 an hour and indexing it to inflation could close about 5 percent of the gender wage gap. Using his executive authority, the president used an executive order to increase the minimum wage for workers on government contracts. Although the increase will not take effect immediately, data suggest it will have an impact. A National Employment Law Project survey of contractors who manufacture military uniforms, provide food and janitorial services in federal agencies, and truck goods found that 75 percent of them earn less than $10 per hour. One in five was dependent on Medicaid for health care, and 14 percent used food stamps.

While women have made significant progress in the last decade toward equality in politics, education, and the workplace, traditional gender role expectations regarding children and family and the assignment of a disproportionate share of family responsibilities to women make achieving true equality a persistent challenge.

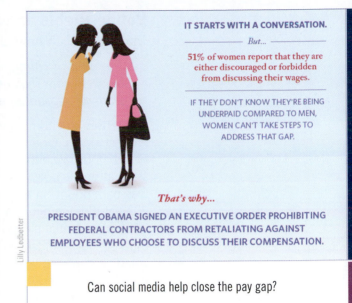

IT STARTS WITH A CONVERSATION.

— *But...* —

51% of women report that they are either discouraged or forbidden from discussing their wages.

IF THEY DON'T KNOW THEY'RE BEING UNDERPAID COMPARED TO MEN, WOMEN CAN'T TAKE STEPS TO ADDRESS THAT GAP.

That's why...

PRESIDENT OBAMA SIGNED AN EXECUTIVE ORDER PROHIBITING FEDERAL CONTRACTORS FROM RETALIATING AGAINST EMPLOYEES WHO CHOOSE TO DISCUSS THEIR COMPENSATION.

Lilly Ledbetter

Can social media help close the pay gap?

48. Nia-Malika Henderson, "Obama, Democrats put spotlight on gender pay gap. Will it matter?" *The Washington Post*, January 29, 2014. Accessed at http://www.washingtonpost.com/blogs/she-the-people/wp/2014/01/29/obama-democrats-put-spotlight-on-gender-pay-gap-will-it-matter/

Voting Rights and the Young

The Twenty-sixth Amendment to the Constitution, ratified on July 1, 1971, reads:

> The right of citizens of the United States, who are eighteen years of age or older, to vote shall not be denied or abridged by the United States or by any State on account of age.

Before this amendment was ratified, the age at which citizens could vote was 21 in most states. One of the arguments used for granting the right to 18-year-olds was that, because they could be drafted to fight in the country's wars, they had a stake in public policy. At the time, the example of the Vietnam War (1964–1975) was paramount. In the first election following ratification, 58 percent of 18- to 20-year-olds were registered to vote, and 48.4 percent reported voting. But by the 2000 presidential election, of the 11.5 million U.S. residents in the 18-to-20 age bracket, 50.7 percent were registered, and 41 percent reported that they had voted. In contrast, voter turnout among Americans aged 65 or older is very high, usually between 60 and 70 percent. People younger than 30 made up a larger share of the electorate in the 2012 presidential election than those 65 and older. Likewise, the share of the vote accounted for by those age 18 to 29 in 2012 rose from 18 to 19 percent.

CONNECT WITH YOUR CLASSMATES

MindTap for American Government

Access the Civil Liberties Forum: Discussion—Minority Rights Protection.

Immigration, Latinos, and Civil Rights

■ **LO5.5:** Identify and explain three significant events related to each of the campaigns for civil rights undertaken by African Americans, women, the Latino community, persons with disabilities, and the LGBTQ community.

Time and again, this nation has been challenged, changed, and culturally enriched by immigrant groups. Immigrants have faced challenges associated with living in a new and different political and cultural environment, overcoming language barriers, and often having to deal with discrimination in one form or another. The civil rights legislation passed during and since the 1960s has done much to counter the effects of prejudice against immigrant groups by ensuring that they obtain equal rights under the law.

One of the questions facing Americans and their political leaders today concerns the effect of immigration on American politics and government. This is especially true with regard to the Hispanic American or Latino community. With the influx of individuals from Latin American countries growing exponentially, issues related to immigration and Hispanic Americans will continue to gain greater attention in years to come. While those in the Latino community did not have to mount a separate campaign to gain access to constitutional suffrage like African Americans and women, they nonetheless have been subject to public and private forms of discrimination.

Mexican American Civil Rights

The history of Mexican Americans spans more than 400 years and varies by region in the United States. Many of the most important challenges to discrimination took place in Texas and California and parallel the claims to rights made by African Americans and women. Mexican American children were forced to attend segregated schools, referred to as "Mexican schools," in California. In a case that preceded *Brown v. Board of Education*, the U.S. Court of Appeals for the Ninth Circuit ruled in 1947 that segregated schools were unconstitutional. In this narrow decision, the court found that while California law provided for separate education for "children of Chinese, Japanese, or Mongolian parentage," the law did not include children of Mexican descent, and therefore it was unlawful to segregate them.[49] California governor Earl Warren, who would later be appointed chief justice of the U.S. Supreme Court and preside over *Brown,* signed a law in 1947 repealing all school segregation statutes.

In 1954, an agricultural worker, Pete Hernandez, was convicted of murder by an all-white jury in Texas. Hernandez maintained that juries could not be impartial unless they included members of other races. The U.S. Supreme Court ruled in *Hernandez v. Texas* that Mexican Americans and other racial groups were entitled to equal protection under the Fourteenth Amendment.[50] The Court ordered that Mr. Hernandez be retried with a jury composed without regard to race or ethnicity.

In the realm of voting rights, Mexican Americans were covered under the 1965 Voting Rights Act, but unlike African Americans, they did not enjoy the singular focus of federal registration oversight. Poll taxes (until ended by the Twenty-fourth Amendment in 1964) limited Mexican Americans' electoral participation, particularly in Texas and California. Political organizing in the 1960s and 1970s by groups such as the La Raza Unida Party, founded in Texas but active in other regions, increased minority representation at the local level. Although Mexican Americans potentially constitute a very large voting bloc, they tend to have low voter turnout rates, which scholars attribute to lower income and education rates as well as recent concerns over immigration status.

The Chicano movement is often characterized as an extension of the Mexican American civil rights movement; it focused on land rights, farmworkers' rights, education, and voting rights, as well as the eradication of ethnic stereotypes and promotion of a positive group consciousness. At first a label with negative connotations, in the 1960s "Chicano" became associated with ethnic pride and self-determination. Movement leaders such as Cesar Chavez and Dolores Huerta were instrumental in founding a number of organizations that, in addition to focusing on labor rights, offered members of the community language classes, assistance in obtaining citizenship, and advocacy for Spanish language rights. The Chicano movement has galvanized and trained successive generations of community and political activists. Recent campaigns have focused on the plight of immigrant workers in low-wage jobs: janitors, truck drivers, domestic workers, and the like.

The Continued Influx of Immigrants

Every year, about 1 million people immigrate to this country, and those born on foreign soil now constitute more than 12 percent of the U.S. population—twice the percentage of 30 years ago.

Since 1977, more than 80 percent of immigrants have come from Latin America or Asia. Latinos have overtaken African Americans as the nation's largest minority. In 2011, 16 percent of the U.S. population identified itself as Hispanic or Latino, 13 percent as African American or black, and 5 percent as Asian. Non-Latino white Americans made up about 66 percent of the population (see Figure 5–4). If current immigration rates continue, minority groups collectively will

---

49. *Mendez v. Westminster School District,* 64 F. Supp. 544 (C.D. Cal. 1946), aff'd, 161 F. 2d 744 (9th Cir. 1947) (en banc).
50. *Hernandez v. Texas,* 347 U.S. 475 (1954).

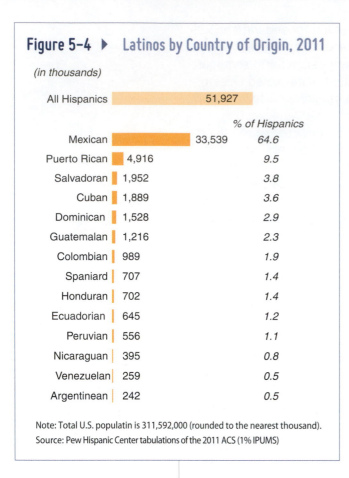

Figure 5–4 ▶   Latinos by Country of Origin, 2011

(in thousands)

		% of Hispanics
All Hispanics	51,927	
Mexican	33,539	*64.6*
Puerto Rican	4,916	*9.5*
Salvadoran	1,952	*3.8*
Cuban	1,889	*3.6*
Dominican	1,528	*2.9*
Guatemalan	1,216	*2.3*
Colombian	989	*1.9*
Spaniard	707	*1.4*
Honduran	702	*1.4*
Ecuadorian	645	*1.2*
Peruvian	556	*1.1*
Nicaraguan	395	*0.8*
Venezuelan	259	*0.5*
Argentinean	242	*0.5*

Note: Total U.S. populatin is 311,592,000 (rounded to the nearest thousand).

Source: Pew Hispanic Center tabulations of the 2011 ACS (1% IPUMS)

constitute the "majority" of Americans by the year 2042, according to estimates by the U.S. Census Bureau. If Latinos, African Americans, and Asians were to form coalitions, they could increase their political strength dramatically and would have the numerical strength to make significant changes. However, as noted in earlier discussions of civil rights campaigns and social movements, coalitions are difficult to form when common interests are not immediately obvious.

Illegal Immigration

Recently, the issue of illegal immigration has become both a hot political issue and a serious policy concern. As many as 12 million undocumented aliens reside and work in the United States. Immigrants typically come to the United States to work, and their labor continues to be in high demand, particularly in construction and farming.

One civil rights question that often surfaces is whether the government should provide services to those who enter the country illegally. Residents of southwestern states complain about the need to shore up border control and perceive that undocumented immigrants place a burden on government-provided social services and the health care industry. Some schools have become crowded with the children of undocumented immigrants. Often, these children require greater attention because of their inability to speak English, although many are themselves native-born U.S. citizens.

On April 23, 2010, Arizona governor Jan Brewer signed a highly controversial bill on immigration designed to identify, prosecute, and deport illegal immigrants. The law made the failure to carry immigration documents a crime and gave the police broad powers to detain anyone *suspected of* being in the country illegally. Governor Brewer said the law "represents another tool for our state to use as we work to solve a crisis we did not create and the federal government has refused to fix." On June 25, 2012, the U.S. Supreme Court issued a split decision, upholding part of the Arizona law while rejecting other provisions on the grounds that they interfered with the federal government's role in setting immigration policy. The court unanimously affirmed the law's requirement that police check the immigration status of people they detain and suspect to be in the country illegally, emphasizing that state law enforcement officials already possessed the discretion to ask about immigration status. The court rejected other portions of the law that criminalized activities such as seeking employment. Leaders in the Latino community maintain that the law will increase racial and ethnic profiling and create a climate of fear among residents of the state. Justice Anthony Kennedy, writing for the majority, left the door open to reconsidering the Arizona law if after implementation there is evidence that it leads to illegal racial and ethnic profiling.

The Arizona law offers an opportunity to examine generational differences in attitudes about immigration. A Brookings Institution report found that Arizona has the largest "cultural generation gap" between older Americans, who are largely white (83 percent), and children under 18, who are increasingly members of minorities (57 percent).[51] This gap fuels conflict over policy issues such as immigration and funding allocations for education and health care. Because older people are more likely to vote and less likely to be connected to the perspectives of youth, the gap also has the potential to further alienate young people from direct political participation. A recent poll found that Americans 45 and older were more likely than young people to favor restricting immigration, a finding attributed to the multicultural environment young people today inhabit.

Citizenship. Members of Congress from both parties have proposed legislation that would either immediately or gradually extend citizenship to undocumented immigrants now residing in the United States. Although not all Americans agree that citizenship should be extended to illegal immigrants, the greater Latino community in the U.S. has taken up the cause. Protests and marches calling for citizenship occurred in 2006, with more than a million individuals participating in demonstrations on May 1, 2006, alone. The citizenship question will be an important political topic for the foreseeable future.

One expedited path to citizenship for immigrants with permanent resident status and permission to work (green card holders) is through military service. Noncitizens have served in the military since the Revolutionary War, and today about 29,000 noncitizens serve in uniform. Service members are eligible for expedited citizenship under a July 2002 executive order, an opportunity realized by nearly 43,000 men and women since September 11, 2001.[52]

Accommodating Diversity with Bilingual Education. The continuous influx of immigrants into this country presents another ongoing challenge—how to overcome language barriers. Bilingual education programs, first introduced in the 1960s, teach children in their native language while also teaching them English. Congress authorized bilingual education programs in 1968 when it passed the Bilingual Education Act, which was intended primarily to help Hispanic children learn English. In a 1974 case, *Lau v. Nichols*, the Supreme Court bolstered the claim that children have a right to bilingual education.[53] In that case, the Court ordered a California school district to provide special programs for Chinese students with language difficulties if a substantial number of these children attended school in the district. Bilingual programs, however, have more recently come under attack. In 1998, California residents passed a ballot initiative that called for the end of bilingual education programs in that state. The law allowed schools to implement English-immersion programs instead. In these programs, students are given intensive instruction in English for a limited period of time and then placed in regular classrooms. The law was immediately challenged in court on the grounds that it unconstitutionally discriminated against non-English-speaking groups. A federal district court concluded that the new law did not violate the equal protection clause and allowed the law to stand, thus ending bilingual education efforts in California.

---

51. William H. Frey, *The State of Metropolitan America* (Washington, DC: Brookings Institution, 2010).
52. Department of Defense, MAVNI Fact Sheet, accessed at http://www.defense.gov/news/mavni-fact-sheet.pdf
53. 414 U.S. 563 (1974).

Affirmative Action

■ **LO5.6:** Define the goal of affirmative action and explain why this approach is controversial in the United States.

The Civil Rights Act of 1964 prohibited discrimination against any person on the basis of race, color, national origin, religion, or gender. It also established the right to equal opportunity in employment. A basic problem remained, however: Minority groups and women, because of past discrimination, often lacked the education and skills to compete effectively in the marketplace. In 1965, the federal government attempted to remedy this problem by implementing the concept of affirmative action. **Affirmative action** policies attempt to "level the playing field" by giving special preferences in educational admissions and employment decisions to groups that have been discriminated against in the past.

In 1965, President Johnson ordered that affirmative action policies be undertaken to remedy the effects of past discrimination. All government agencies, including those of state and local governments, were required to implement such policies. Additionally, affirmative action requirements were applied to companies that sell goods or services to the federal government and to institutions that receive federal funds. They were also required whenever an employer had been ordered to develop such a plan by a court or by the Equal Employment Opportunity Commission because of evidence of past discrimination. Finally, labor unions that had been found to discriminate against women or minorities in the past were required to establish and follow affirmative action plans.

The *Bakke* Case

The first Supreme Court case addressing the constitutionality of affirmative action plans examined a program implemented by the University of California at Davis. Allan Bakke, a white student who had been denied admission to the medical school, discovered that his academic record was better than those of some of the minority applicants who had been admitted to the program. He sued the University of California regents, alleging **reverse discrimination**. The UC Davis Medical School had held 16 places out of 100 for educationally "disadvantaged students" each year, and admitted to using race as a criterion for these 16 admissions. Bakke claimed that his exclusion from medical school violated his rights under the Fourteenth Amendment's provision for equal protection of the laws. The trial court agreed. On appeal, the California Supreme Court agreed also. Finally, the regents of the university appealed to the United States Supreme Court.

In 1978, the Supreme Court handed down its decision in *Regents of the University of California v. Bakke*.[54] The Court did not rule against affirmative action programs. It held that Bakke must be admitted to the UC Davis Medical School because its admissions policy had used race as the sole criterion for the 16 "minority" positions. Justice Lewis Powell, speaking for the Court, indicated that while race can be considered "as a factor" among others in admissions (and presumably hiring) decisions, race cannot be the sole factor. So, affirmative action programs, but not specific quota systems, were upheld as constitutional.

Affirmative Action
A policy in educational admissions or job hiring that gives special attention or compensatory treatment to traditionally disadvantaged groups in an effort to overcome present effects of past discrimination.

Reverse Discrimination
The charge that an affirmative action program discriminates against those who do not have minority status.

---

54. 438 U.S. 265 (1978).

Politics with a Purpose

Race @ College—A New Wave of Student Activism

Following California's lead, several states have amended their constitutions to prohibit public universities from using race as a factor in admissions decisions. Minority populations are growing nationwide, but shrinking on college campuses. What would it mean to live in a post-racial society? The election of Barack Obama as president signalled a seismic shift in racial attitudes to some; others believe that racism has shape-shifted into less obvious forms of discrimination and prejudice. Students on several U.S. campuses have pushed back against the veneer of campus diversity to highlight their feelings of isolation in the face of declining minority enrollments and call out the "microaggressions" they experience every day on campus. Microaggressions are the subtle ways that racial, ethnic, gender and other stereotypes find their way into conversations, comments, and questions that cause minority students to stop and wonder, "what did that mean?"

In a nod to the famous Langston Hughes poem "I, Too," students at Harvard have created the "I, too, am Harvard" (#itooamharvard) campaign that includes a play performed on campus written and directed by Kimiko Matsuda-Lawrence, a Harvard sophomore.[*] The play is based on interviews with 40 Harvard students who identify as black or multi-racial. To promote the play, another student took pictures of students holding signs displaying humiliating remarks made by peers such as "You are really articulate for a black girl" and "Are you all so fast because you spend so much time running from the cops?" Other statements were messages to the university community—"The lack of diversity in this classroom does NOT make me the voice of all black people." The photographs were published on tumblr, picked up by Buzzfeed, and within a day spread to other campuses and around the world.

Students at the University of Michigan launched a social media campaign called "Being Black at the University of Michigan" (#BBUM) in 2013 in reaction to a fraternity party inviting "rappers, twerkers, gangsters" and others "back to da hood again." Although the party never happened, its promotion exposed simmering racial tensions on campus and highlighted the decline in black undergraduate enrollment since Proposal 2 was adopted in 2006.[**] Law students at UCLA created the "33/1100" campaign, highlighting the small number of black students in law classes. Gerloni Cotton helped organize the event because she was often the only black woman in a class of 100 students. When issues of race came up in class, she felt called upon to speak to them. "On one hand I felt isolated, but on the other I felt highlighted—invisible but hypervisible," she said.[***]

"The Black Bruins [spoken word] by Sy Stokes," a video posted to YouTube in November 2013, went viral in a matter of days.[****] Sy Stokes, a student at UCLA, created the spoken word performance to demonstrate how small the black population at UCLA is (roughly 4 percent) and put the administration on notice for falling retention rates for black males in particular. The statistics are startling—in fall 2012, a total of 660 graduate and undergraduate African American males were enrolled at UCLA and 65 percent of them were undergraduate athletes. Stokes also reported that the number of UCLA national championships exceed the number of black male freshmen enrolled. "When every black student in class feels like Rosa Parks on the bus," "when the university refuses to come to our defense," when "our faces are just used to cover up from the public what's really inside," it is clear that UCLA's administration has failed its black community, the students say. The administration claims to share the students' frustrations, but acknowledge that UCLA must do a better job of living up to its commitment to diversity.

[*] Bethonie Butler, "I, Too, am Harvard: Black Students Show How They Belong." *The Washington Post*, March 4, 2014. Accessed at www.washingtonpost.com/blogs/she-the-people/wp/2014/03/05/i-too-am-harvard-black-students-show-they-belong/

[**] Tanzina Vega, "Colorblind Notion Aside, Colleges Grapple with Racial Tension." *The New York Times*, February 24, 2014. Accessed at www.nytimes.com/2014/02/25/us/colorblind-notion-aside-colleges-grapple-with-racial-tension.html?_r=0

[***] Samantha Tomilowitz and Sam Hoff, "UCLA Students Protest Lack of Diversity." *Daily Bruin*, February 10, 2014.

[****] The Black Bruins [spoken word] by Sy Stokes, accessed at www.youtube.com/watch?v=BEO3H5BOlFk

The *Bakke* decision did not end the controversy over affirmative action programs. At issue in the current debate over affirmative action programs is whether favoring one group violates the equal protection clause of the Fourteenth Amendment to the Constitution as it applies to all other groups.

Further Limits on Affirmative Action

Several cases decided during the 1980s and 1990s placed further limits on affirmative action programs by subjecting any federal, state, or local affirmative action program that uses racial or ethnic classifications as the basis for making decisions to "strict scrutiny" by the courts (to be constitutional, a discriminatory law or action must be narrowly tailored to meet a *compelling* government interest).[55] Yet, in two cases involving the University of Michigan, the Supreme Court indicated that limited affirmative action programs continue to be acceptable and that diversity is a legitimate goal. The Court struck down the affirmative action plan used for undergraduate admissions at the university, which automatically awarded a substantial number of points to applicants based on minority status.[56] At the same time, it approved the admissions plan used by the law school, which took race into consideration as part of a complete examination of each applicant's background.[57]

The Supreme Court again narrowed the scope in which race can be used as one of a number of factors in college admissions in *Fisher v. University of Texas at Austin* (2013).[58] The University of Texas adopted the admissions plan at issue in the case soon after the 2003 ruling in the case of *Grutter v. Bollinger* said that race could be taken into account as one of the factors in helping to achieve racial diversity. In 1997, the Texas legislature passed a law requiring the University of Texas to admit all high school seniors who ranked in the top 10 percent of their high school class. When the University of Texas identified racial and ethnic disparities between the entering class and the state's population, however, it altered its race-neutral admissions policy. For Texas applicants not in the top ten percent of their class, the university considered race as one of several factors in the admission decision. Abigail Noel Fisher, a student who was not automatically admitted under the top ten percent rule and was not admitted to the Texas campus, argued that she was denied admission on account of her race while minority students with lower grade point averages than hers were admitted under the diversity plan. The district court and the Fifth Circuit Court of Appeals both sided with the University of Texas at Austin, but in a 7-1 decision the U.S. Supreme Court said that the lower courts erred in not applying the standard of "strict judicial scrutiny" to the university's admissions policy. Any policy that takes race into account must be "precisely tailored to serve a compelling governmental interest." University of Texas officials had argued that their policy's use of race was narrowly tailored to pursue greater diversity. (Justice Elena Kagan recused herself because of her involvement in the case while working in the solicitor general's office.)

State Ballot Initiatives

A ballot initiative passed by California voters in 1996 amended that state's constitution to end all state-sponsored affirmative action programs. The law was challenged immediately by civil rights groups and others, who argued that it violated the Fourteenth Amendment by denying racial minorities and women the equal protection of the laws. In 1997, however, a federal appellate court upheld the constitutionality of the amendment. Thus, affirmative action is now illegal in California in all state-sponsored institutions, including state agencies

---

55. 515 U.S. 200 (1995).
56. *Gratz v. Bollinger*, 539 U.S. 244 (2003).
57. *Grutter v. Bollinger*, 539 U.S. 306 (2003).
58. *Fisher v. University of Texas at Austin*, 570 U.S. ___ (2013).

and educational institutions. In 1998, Washington voters also approved a law banning affirmative action in that state. In 2006, voters in Michigan adopted Proposal 2 (also known as the Michigan Civil Rights Initiative) effectively ending affirmative action by public institutions based on race, color, sex or religion. At the University of Michigan, the proportion of African American students fell from 7 percent in 2006 to 4.6 percent in 2014. Student activists argue that it is a result of Prop 2. University officials have not been able to take race into account in admission decisions or in awarding financial aid packages. Michigan Attorney General Bill Schuette argues that the ban was passed by 58 percent of Michigan voters and therefore represents the will of the citizenry. In *Schuette v. Coalition to Defend Affirmative Action*, decided in April 2014, the Supreme Court upheld the Michigan ban by a 6-2 vote, ruling that policies affecting minorities that do not involve intentional discrimination should be decided at the ballot box rather than in the courtroom.[59] The Court's decision leaves in place state constitutional actions in Arizona, Nebraska, Oklahoma, California and Washington and could serve as an invitation to other states to enact similar bans.

Making Amends for Past Discrimination through Reparations

While affirmative action programs attempt to remedy past discrimination by "leveling the playing field," reparations are a way of apologizing for past discriminatory actions and providing compensation. The legal philosophy of **reparation** requires that victims of a harm be replenished by those who inflicted the harm. In criminal courts, for example, defendants are sometimes sentenced to perform community service or provide restitution to the victim in lieu of jail time. When reparation is used relative to a class of people who experienced discrimination, such as descendants of former slaves or Japanese Americans who were interned during World War II, restitution is made by the government. In 1988, Congress passed legislation that apologized for and admitted that wartime government action against Japanese Americans was based on racial prejudice and war hysteria. Over $1.6 billion has been disbursed to Japanese Americans who were themselves interned or to their heirs.

Proposals for similar forms of restitution for the descendants of slaves in the United States have been under discussion for some time, with little consensus around the issue. On July 29, 2008, the House passed a resolution (with 120 co-sponsors from both parties) apologizing to African Americans for the institution of slavery, Jim Crow laws, and other practices that have denied people equal opportunity under the law. Democrat Steve Cohen from Tennessee introduced the resolution, saying,"… only a great country can recognize and admit its mistakes and then travel forth to create indeed a more perfect union."[60] The Senate followed with a similar resolution of apology the following summer. The resolutions did not contain any mention of financial compensation for descendants of slaves.

When President Obama signed into law the 2010 Defense Appropriations Act on December 19, 2009, it included a footnote, entitled Section 8113,

Reparation
Compensation, monetary or nonmonetary (e.g., formal apology), to make amends for a past transgression or harm.

---

59. Amy Howe, "Divided Court upholds Michigan's ban on affirmative action: In Plain English," SCOTUSblog, April 23, 2014. Accessed at www.scotusblog.com/2014/04/divided-court-upholds-michigans-ban-on-affirmative-action-in-plain-english/
60. "Congress Apologizes for Slavery, Jim Crow," National Public Radio, July 30, 2008.

Asians in America have experienced a long history of discrimination. In 1922, for example, the Supreme Court ruled that Asians were not white and therefore were not entitled to full citizenship rights (*Ozawa v. U.S.*, 1922). Following the Japanese attack on Pearl Harbor in 1941, Executive Order 9066 required the exclusion of all people of Japanese ancestry (including U.S. citizens) from the Pacific coast. Approximately 110,000 people were forcibly relocated to internment camps. In 1944, the Supreme Court upheld the constitutionality of the war relocation camps (*Korematsu v. U.S.*), citing national security concerns during a time of war.

Library of Congress

otherwise known as an "apology to Native Peoples of the United States." The passage of the apology resolution went largely unnoticed but served as the culmination of a five-year attempt by Senator Sam Brownback of Kansas to convince Congress to adopt a formal apology for the government's past treatment of Native Americans. The condensed resolution conveys the nation's regret "for the many instances of violence, maltreatment, and neglect inflicted on Native Peoples by citizens of the United States," as the condensed resolution states. The resolution was not accompanied by monetary reparations or funds for new programs.

Special Protection for Older Americans

Age discrimination is potentially the most widespread form of discrimination, because anyone—regardless of race, color, national origin, or gender—could be a victim at some point in life. In an attempt to protect older employees from such discriminatory practices, Congress passed the Age Discrimination in Employment Act (ADEA) in 1967. The act, which applies to employers, employment agencies, and labor organizations and covers individuals over the age of 40, prohibits discrimination against individuals on the basis of age unless age is shown to be a bona fide occupational qualification reasonably necessary to the normal operation of the particular business. To succeed in a suit for age discrimination, an employee must prove that the employer's action, such as a decision to fire the employee, was motivated, at least in part, by age bias. Even if an older worker is replaced by a younger worker who is also over the age of 40, the older worker is entitled to bring a suit under the ADEA.[61] Most states have their

---

61. *O'Connor v. Consolidated Coin Caterers Corp.*, 517 U.S. 308 (1996).

own prohibitions against age discrimination in employment, and some are stronger than the federal provisions.

Securing Rights for Persons with Disabilities

Persons with disabilities did not fall under the protective umbrella of the Civil Rights Act of 1964. In 1973, however, Congress passed the Rehabilitation Act, which prohibited discrimination against persons with disabilities in programs receiving federal aid. A 1978 amendment to the act established the Architectural and Transportation Barriers Compliance Board. Regulations for ramps, elevators, and the like in all federal buildings were implemented. Congress passed the Education for All Handicapped Children Act in 1975, guaranteeing that all children with disabilities will receive an "appropriate" education. The most significant federal legislation to protect the rights of persons with disabilities, however, is the Americans with Disabilities Act (ADA), which Congress passed in 1990.

The Americans with Disabilities Act of 1990

The ADA requires that all public buildings and public services be accessible to persons with disabilities. It also mandates that employers must reasonably accommodate the needs of workers or potential workers with disabilities. Physical access means ramps; handrails; wheelchair-accessible restrooms, counters, drinking fountains, telephones, and doorways; and easily accessible mass transit. In addition, other steps must be taken to comply with the act. Car rental companies must provide cars with hand controls for disabled drivers. Telephone companies are required to have operators to pass on messages from speech-impaired persons who use telephones with keyboards.

Pamela Moore/E+/Getty Images

The Americans with Disabilities Act (ADA) requires that all public buildings and public services be available to persons with disabilities. Colleges and universities must enable physical access to facilities and educational programs by providing appropriate accommodations.

The ADA requires employers to "reasonably accommodate" the needs of persons with disabilities unless to do so would cause the employer to suffer an "undue hardship." The ADA defines persons with disabilities as persons who have physical or mental impairments that "substantially limit" their everyday activities. Health conditions that have been considered disabilities under federal law include blindness, alcoholism, heart disease, cancer, muscular dystrophy, cerebral palsy, paraplegia, diabetes, acquired immune deficiency syndrome (AIDS), and infection with the human immunodeficiency virus (HIV) that causes AIDS. The Affordable Care Act contains a number of provisions that apply to people living with disabilities. For example, insurance companies are no longer able to deny coverage to people with preexisting conditions, such as a disability.

The ADA does not require that *unqualified* applicants with disabilities be hired or retained. If a job applicant or an employee with a disability, with reasonable accommodation, can perform essential job functions, however, then the employer must make the accommodation. Required accommodations may include installing ramps for a wheelchair, establishing more flexible working hours, creating or modifying job assignments, and creating or improving training materials and procedures.

Limiting the Scope and Applicability of the ADA

Beginning in 1999, the Supreme Court has issued a series of decisions that limit the scope of the ADA. In 1999, the Court held in *Sutton v. United Airlines, Inc.*[62] that a condition (in this case, severe nearsightedness) that can be corrected with medication or a corrective device (in this case, eyeglasses) is not considered a disability under the ADA. In other words, the determination of whether a person is substantially limited in a major life activity is based on how the person functions when taking medication or using corrective devices, not on how the person functions without these measures. Since then, the courts have held that plaintiffs with bipolar disorder, epilepsy, diabetes, and other conditions do not fall under the ADA's protections if the conditions can be corrected with medication or corrective devices. The Supreme Court has also limited the applicability of the ADA by holding that lawsuits under the ADA cannot be brought against state government employers.[63]

The Rights and Status of Gays and Lesbians

■ **LO5.5:** Identify and explain three significant events related to each of the campaigns for civil rights undertaken by African Americans, women, the Latino community, persons with disabilities, and the LGBTQ community.

On June 27, 1969, patrons of the Stonewall Inn, a New York City bar popular with gays and lesbians, responded to a police raid by throwing beer cans and bottles because they were angry at what they felt was unrelenting police harassment. In the ensuing riot, which lasted two nights, hundreds of gays and lesbians fought with police. Before Stonewall, the stigma attached to homosexuality and the resulting fear of exposure had tended to keep most gays and lesbians quiescent. In the months immediately after Stonewall, however, "gay power" graffiti began to appear in New York City. The Gay Liberation Front and the Gay Activist Alliance were formed, and similar groups sprang up in other parts of the country. Thus, Stonewall has been called "the shot heard round the homosexual world."

---

62. 527 U.S. 471 (1999).
63. *Board of Trustees of the University of Alabama v. Garrett*, 531 U.S. 356 (2001).

Growth in the Gay and Lesbian Rights Movement

The Stonewall incident marked the beginning of the movement for gay and lesbian rights. Since then, gays and lesbians have formed thousands of organizations to exert pressure on legislatures, the media, schools, churches, and other organizations to recognize their right to equal treatment.

To a great extent, lesbian and gay groups have succeeded in changing public opinion—and state and local laws—relating to their status and rights. Nevertheless, they continue to struggle against age-old biases against homosexuality, often rooted in deeply held religious beliefs, which allow discrimination to persist. In a widely publicized case involving the Boy Scouts of America, a troop in New Jersey refused to allow gay activist James Dale to be a Scout leader. In 2000, the case came before the Supreme Court, which held that, as a private organization, the Boy Scouts had the right to determine the requirements for becoming a Scout leader.[64] In 1998, a student at the University of Wyoming named Matthew Shepard was brutally beaten, tortured, tied to a fence post, and left to die near Laramie, Wyoming, because he was believed to be gay. His killers could not be charged with a **hate crime** because at the time, the state law did not recognize sexual orientation as a protected class. In 2009, Congress passed the Matthew Shepard Act, expanding the 1969 federal hate crime law to include crimes motivated by the victim's actual or perceived gender, sexual orientation, gender identity, or disability.[65]

State and Local Laws Targeting Gays and Lesbians

Before the Stonewall incident, 49 states had sodomy laws that made various sexual acts, including homosexual acts, illegal (Illinois, which had repealed its sodomy law in 1962, was the only exception). During the 1970s and 1980s, more than half of these laws were either repealed or struck down by the courts. In 2003, the Court reversed an earlier antisodomy position[66] with its decision in *Lawrence v. Texas*.[67] The Court held that laws against sodomy violate the due process clause of the Fourteenth Amendment, stating: "The liberty protected by the Constitution allows homosexual persons the right to choose to enter upon relationships in the confines of their homes and their own private lives and still retain their dignity as free persons." The result of *Lawrence v. Texas* was to invalidate all remaining sodomy laws throughout the country.

Today, 20 states and the District of Columbia have laws protecting lesbians and gays against discrimination in employment, housing, public accommodations, and credit. Several laws at the national level have also been changed over the past two decades. Among other things, the government has lifted a ban on hiring gays and lesbians and voided a 1952 law prohibiting gays and lesbians from immigrating to the United States.

Gays and Lesbians in the Military

The U.S. Department of Defense traditionally has viewed homosexuality as incompatible with military service. In 1993 President Clinton announced a new policy, generally characterized as "don't ask, don't tell" (DADT). Enlistees would not be asked about their sexual orientation, and gays and lesbians would be allowed to serve in the military so long as they did not declare that they were gay or lesbian or commit homosexual acts. Military officials endorsed the new policy (after opposing it initially), but supporters of gay rights were not enthusiastic.

did you know?

Boys Scouts of America dropped the ban on gay scouts as of January 1, 2014, but openly gay scout leaders are still banned.

Hate Crime
A crime motivated by racial, sexual, or other prejudice, typically one involving violence.

64. *Boy Scouts of America v. Dale*, 530 U.S. 640 (2000).
65. "Obama Signs Measure to Widen Hate Crimes Law," *PBS NewsHour*, October 28, 2009.
66. *Bowers v. Hardwick*, 478 U.S. 186 (1986).
67. 539 U.S. 558 (2003).

Everyday Politics

 ## Queen Latifah Performs Mass Wedding at the Grammys

The 2013 Grammy Awards featured more than music awards—33 couples were married in a mass wedding officiated by performing artist Queen Latifah, as artists Macklemore and Ryan Lewis performed their hit song "Same Love." The song, featuring vocals by Mary Lambert, talks about gay and lesbian rights and has become a civil rights anthem of sorts for same-sex marriage advocates. The second verse singles out his fellow hip-hop and rap artists for criticism:

If I was gay, I would think hip-hop hates me
Have you read the YouTube comments lately?
"Man, that's gay" gets dropped on the daily
We become so numb to what we're saying
A culture founded from oppression
Yet we don't have acceptance for 'em
Call each other faggots behind the keys of a message board
A word rooted in hate, yet our genre still ignores it
Gay is synonymous with the lesser
It's the same hate that's caused wars from religion
Gender to skin color, the complexion of your pigment
The same fight that led people to walk outs and sit ins
It's human rights for everybody, there is no difference!
Live on and be yourself

Those married in the mass ceremony represented a diverse group of gay, straight, young, and old couples. The California Family Code identifies a number of positions authorized to officiate a marriage. Queen Latifah was deputized as a commissioner by the State of California for the ceremony. Each couple obtained a marriage license from the county clerk's office prior to the event; once these documents were signed by Queen Latifah, the couples were legally married in California. Same-sex couples from states where gay marriage remains illegal would not be legally married in their home state.

Social media captured the excitement of those at the Grammy's and the 28 million viewers. Wanda Sykes posted on her Twitter page: "Congrats to all the lovely couples" and Ellen DeGeneres's Twitter page had the tweet: "#SameLove was incredible."

Conservative critics blasted the Grammys and called the mass wedding a stunt. Rush Limbaugh called the production despicable and criticized the lyrics of "Same Love" as an attack on right-wing conservatives and Christians. Others called the program divisive. National Academy of Recording Arts and Sciences president Neil Portnow disagreed: "I think it was as elegant and meaningful and powerful as we wanted it to be."*

* Kirthana Ramisetti, "Grammys 2014: Rush Limbaugh, conservative pundits angered by same-sex marriages during Macklemore and Ryan Lewis performance." *Daily News*, January 28, 2014. Accessed at www.nydailynews.com/entertainment/music-arts/conservatives-blast-grammys-wedding-ceremony-article-1.1593880

Critical Thinking

1. *Producers of the 2013 Grammys attempted to make a statement about the fundamental right to marry. Do you view marriage equality as a human rights issue? Why or why not?*

2. *If a musician promotes an opinion on social issues, are you more interested in listening to his or her music? Does the answer depend on whether you agree or disagree with the artist's opinion?*

As a presidential candidate, Barack Obama promised to help bring an end to the "don't ask, don't tell" policy. In March of 2009, Secretary of Defense Robert M. Gates announced a number of interim steps designed to make it more difficult for the military to discharge openly gay men and women. In December 2010, a bill to repeal DADT was enacted, with the caveat that the policy would remain in place until the president, the secretary of defense, and the chairman of the Joint Chiefs of Staff certified that repeal would not harm military readiness, followed by a 60-day waiting period. The certification was sent to Congress on July 22, 2011, making the date of the law's repeal September 20, 2011. Following the repeal, discharged servicemen and servicewomen were permitted to reenlist, and several have successfully done so.

Same-Sex Marriages

One of the most sensitive political issues with respect to the rights of gay and lesbian couples is whether they should be allowed to marry, as heterosexual couples are.

Defense of Marriage Act. The controversy over this issue was fueled in 1993, when the Hawaii Supreme Court ruled that denying marriage licenses to gay couples might violate the equal protection clause of the Hawaii constitution.[68] In the wake of this event, some state legislators grew concerned that they might have to treat gay men or lesbians who were legally married in another state as married couples in their state as well. Opponents of gay rights pushed for state laws banning same-sex marriages, and the majority of states enacted such laws or adopted constitutional amendments. At the federal level, Congress passed the Defense of Marriage Act of 1996 (DOMA), which bans federal recognition of lesbian and gay couples and allows state governments to ignore same-sex marriages performed in other states.

The controversy over gay marriages was fueled again by developments in the state of Vermont. In 1999, the Vermont Supreme Court ruled that gay couples are entitled to the same benefits of marriage as opposite-sex couples.[69] Subsequently, in April 2000, the Vermont legislature passed a law permitting gay and lesbian couples to form "civil unions." The law entitled partners forming civil unions to receive some 300 state benefits available to married couples, including the rights to inherit a partner's property and to decide on medical treatment for an incapacitated partner. In 2005, Connecticut became the second state to adopt civil unions. Neither law entitled partners to receive any benefits allowed to married couples under federal law, such as spousal Social Security benefits.

In 2013, the U.S. Supreme Court declared unconstitutional Section 3 of the law preventing the federal government from recognizing same-sex marriages for the purpose of federal laws or programs even when those couples were legally married in their home state. Justice Anthony Kennedy, writing for the majority in a 5-4 decision, said that the act wrote inequality into federal law and violated the Fifth Amendment's protection of equal liberty. "DOMA's principal effect is to identify a subset of state-sanctioned marriages and make them unequal," he wrote.[70] The decision in *United States v. Windsor* (2013) was issued on June 26, 2013. Almost immediately the federal government changed policy to extend the federal benefits and privileges of marriage to same-sex couples regardless of the law in their home state. Attorney General Eric Holder, the first African American attorney general, has embraced the expansion of civil rights for the LGBTQ community. The government estimates that more than 1,100 federal regulations, rights and laws touch on, or are

---

68. *Baehr v. Lewin*, 852 P.2d 44 (Hawaii 1993).
69. *Baker v. Vermont*, 744 A.2d 864 (Vt. 1999).
70. *United States v. Windsor*, 570 U.S. ____ (2013).

affected by, marital status. In court cases and criminal investigations, for example, same-sex couples are now covered under spousal privilege—the rule that says spouses cannot be forced to testify against each other. The Bureau of Prisons will extend the same visitation rights to married same-sex couples that it does to opposite-sex couples. The Justice Department will also recognize same-sex couples when determining eligibility for programs like the September 11th Victim Compensation Fund, which pays people who were injured or made sick by the 2001 terrorist attacks. Same-sex spouses of police killed in the line of duty will also be eligible for federal benefits. The Department of Defense changed its definition of marriage and spouse such that same-sex couples are now eligible for all federal military benefits, including access to base housing, health and survivor benefits, and family separation allowances. Service members who are stationed in one of the 37 states where same-sex marriage is illegal will be offered up to 10 days of leave so they can travel to one of the 17 states, plus the District of Columbia, that grant same-sex marriage licenses.

Although the *Windsor* decision did not strike down prohibitions on same-sex marriages across the country, federal judges use the reasoning to expand equal treatment of gays and lesbians in other areas of life. In January 2014, the U.S. Court of Appeals for the Ninth Circuit held that gays and lesbians cannot be excluded from juries on the basis of their sexual orientation. Judge Stephen Reinhardt, writing for the unanimous three-judge panel, said that "the Supreme Court's decision was premised on the idea of equal dignity for all, a dignity enhanced by 'responsibilities, as well as rights.'"[71]

State Recognition of Gay Marriages. Massachusetts was the first state to recognize gay marriage. In November 2003, the Massachusetts Supreme Judicial Court ruled that same-sex couples have a right to civil marriage under the Massachusetts state constitution and that civil unions would not suffice.[72] In 2005, the Massachusetts legislature voted down a proposed ballot initiative that would have amended the state constitution to explicitly state that marriage could only be between one man and one woman (but would have extended civil union status to same-sex couples). Although the highest courts in several states had upheld bans on gay marriage, in 2008 the Supreme Court of California ruled that the state was required to recognize gay marriages. In reaction, opponents immediately prepared petitions to put a constitutional amendment on the ballot in November of 2008 to outlaw such marriages. The campaign for and against Proposition 8, which would ban gay marriages in California, cost at least $74 million and was funded by contributions from almost every state. Ultimately, Proposition 8 was approved by a margin of 4 percent. The 18,000 marriages that took place between the California Supreme Court decision and the approval of Proposition 8 remained valid. On August 4, 2010, a federal judge declared California's ban on same-sex marriage unconstitutional, saying that no legitimate state interest justified treating gay and lesbian couples differently from others. The ruling was the first in the country to strike down a marriage ban on federal constitutional grounds rather than on the basis of a state constitution. On the same day the U.S. Supreme Court released the *Windsor* decision, it also ruled that the private-party sponsors of Proposition 8 did not have standing to appeal an adverse federal court ruling. *Hollingsworth v. Perry* (2013) cleared the way for same-sex marriages to resume in California. On October 6, 2014, the Supreme Court said that it would not review a series of U.S. appeals court decisions that struck down

71. "The Expanding Power of U.S. v Windsor" *The New York Times*, January 26, 2014. Accessed at http://www.nytimes.com/2014/01/27/opinion/the-expanding-power-of-us-v-windsor.html
72. *Goodridge v. Department of Public Health*, 798 N.E.2d 941 (Mass. 2003).

Del Martin (L) and Phyllis Lyon (R) are married by San Francisco mayor Gavin Newsom in a private ceremony at San Francisco City Hall on June 16, 2008. Martin and Lyon, a couple since 1953, were active in the gay rights and women's rights movements. Del Martin died on August 27, 2008.

state bans. Thus the most essential questions about same-sex marriage—whether the Constitution's guarantee of equal protection under the law prevents states from defining marriage to exclude same-sex couples and whether a state can revoke same-sex marriage through referendum—remain undecided by the U.S. Supreme Court.

After a period of public opposition to same-sex marriage, President Obama announced an evolution in his thinking in a nationally televised interview in May 2012, saying that he believes same-sex couples should be allowed to marry. His view is supported by a majority of Americans, according to poll data. Polls conducted immediately following the president's statement also found that opposition to gay marriage fell by 11 percentage points among African Americans.

As of November 2014, more than 30 states, the District of Columbia, and 8 Native American Tribal jurisdictions allow and fully recognize same-sex marriage. In several other states judicial action that would overturn a state-imposed ban on same-sex marriages is pending and in still other states active challenges to state-wide bans on gay marriage have not yet been decided by a court. The shift in public opinion favoring gay marriage has been rapid and broad. Same-sex marriage is currently accepted nationwide in 16 countries. While international public opinion, like that of the United States, has become more tolerant overall, there are some notable exceptions. Ugandan President Yoweri Museveni signed a bill criminalizing homosexuality in February 2014. Nigeria banned same-sex unions and arrests people it suspects of being gay. Russia passed a law banning advocacy of gay rights—specifically the propaganda of nontraditional sexual relations to minors. The United Nations estimates that 78 nations ban homosexuality, and seven countries allow the death penalty for those convicted of having consensual homosexual relationships.[73] Homosexuality is defined as a crime in several nations the U.S. considers allies (Saudi Arabia and India are two examples), but to date no punitive sanctions have been imposed. The 2014 Winter Olympic Games held in Sochi Russia focused the world's attention on international anti-gay laws and practices—albeit briefly.

---

73. Somini Sengupta, "Considering what Can Actually Be Done About Gay Rights Violations." *The New York Times*, March 2, 2014.

What Would You Do?

Dealing With Discrimination

You may think that you know what "discrimination" means while applying for or working at a job. But do you understand how it applies to your life? To "discriminate" means to treat differently or less favorably, and discrimination can happen anywhere. Discrimination can come from friends, teachers, coaches, co-workers, managers, and business owners and can be based on race, color, gender, religion, age, sexual orientation, or disability. Tests while applying for a job may have a discriminatory effect on being hired (tests of strength, for example, must be directly related to the requirements of the job). Genetic information, now more widely available, might some day be used by employers in making hiring decisions. Increasingly, evidence shows that employers make use of online sites such as Facebook, tumblr, blogs, and personal websites to learn more about applicants. While doing so may leave employers subject to "failure to hire" lawsuits if information gathered online is used to discriminate illegally, you should be very aware of how you present yourself online. Agencies at the state and federal government examine the fairness and validity of criteria used in screening job applicants and, as a result, ways of addressing the problem of discrimination are available.

Why Should You Care?

Some people may think that discrimination is only a problem for members of racial or ethnic minorities. Actually, almost everyone can be affected. In some instances, white men have experienced "reverse discrimination"—and have obtained redress for it. Also, discrimination against women is common, and women constitute half the population. Therefore, knowledge of how to proceed when you suspect discrimination is another useful tool to have when living in the modern world.

Another form of discrimination is evident in the wage gap. The Bureau of Labor Statistics reports that the median weekly wage for all full-time working women was $706 in 2013, while the median weekly wage for men was $860—that is $0.82 for women per dollar earned by men. A Pew Research report puts the rate at closer to $0.84 for women per dollar earned by men. The statistic most often quoted in the press is $0.77 for women per dollar earned by men. This variation suggests two important facts—the wage gap is real and its root cause is complicated. Salaries for men and women are most equal when their life circumstances are most nearly the same—for most people that will be the college years before you begin full-time work and before you create a family. "After we control for hours, occupation, college major, and other factors associated with pay, the pay gap shrinks but does not disappear. About one-third of the gap cannot be explained by any of the factors commonly understood to affect earnings," the report states.

What Would You Do?

As the U.S. Secretary of Labor charged with overseeing the workforce and enforcing laws related to the work and the workplace, would you concentrate on enforcing the laws and policies already in existence to fight discrimination or would you pursue new policy approaches?

When the U.S. Supreme Court used a narrow interpretation of the statute to rule against Lilly Ledbetter's claim of pay discrimination, Congress passed the Lilly Ledbetter Fair Pay Act in January 2009.

Bill Clark/Roll Call/Getty Images

What You *Can* Do

If you believe that you have been discriminated against by a potential employer, consider the following steps:

- Evaluate your own capabilities, and determine if you are truly qualified for the position.
- Analyze why you were turned down. Would others agree that you have been the object of discrimination, or would they uphold the employer's claim?

If you still believe that you have been treated unfairly, you have recourse to several agencies and services. You should first speak to the personnel director of the company and explain that you believe you have not been evaluated adequately. If asked, explain your concerns clearly and provide detailed examples of behavior you believe is discriminatory.

If you believe you are wrongly paid less than a co-worker, consider the following steps:

- Read *Graduating to a Pay Gap: The Earnings of Men and Women One Year After College Graduation* to familiarize yourself with the problem and with the considerations that likely went into setting your salary—degree, major, prior experience, hours worked, position responsibilities, etc.
- Salary data is difficult to obtain. Ask your co-workers to share their wage or salary information and they may be willing to do so because an equitable workplace is a better environment for everyone.
- Approach this task like a research project. Gather all of the evidence necessary to make a good argument and schedule an appointment with your supervisor or hiring manager. Lay out the facts and recommend a remedy.

Find *Graduating to a Pay Gap: The Earnings of Men and Women One Year After College Graduation* at www.aauw.org/research/graduating-to-a-pay-gap/

Purestock/Getty Images

Key Terms

affirmative action 184	*de jure* **segregation** 157	**literacy test** 154	**sexual harassment** 176
Black Codes 151	**feminism** 172	**poll tax** 154	**subpoena** 162
busing 157	**gender discrimination** 174	**reparation** 187	**suffrage** 167
civil disobedience 159	**grandfather clause** 154	**reverse discrimination** 184	**white primary** 153
civil rights 150	**hate crime** 191	**separate-but-equal doctrine** 153	
de facto **segregation** 157	**Jim Crow laws** 152		

Chapter Summary

■ **LO5.1:** The term *civil rights* refers to the rights of all Americans to equal treatment under the law, as provided for by the Fourteenth Amendment to the Constitution and by subsequent acts of Congress. Although the terms *civil rights* and *civil liberties* are sometimes used interchangeably, scholars make a distinction between the two. Civil liberties are limitations on government; they specify what the government *cannot* do. Civil rights, in contrast, specify what the government *must* do—to ensure equal protection and freedom from discrimination.

■ **LO5.2:** The story of civil rights in the United States is the struggle to reconcile our ideals as a nation with the realities of discrimination individuals and groups may still encounter in daily life. To the nation's founders, political equality

required a degree of independent thinking and a capacity for rational action that at the time they believed were limited to a very few white males. Therefore, other groups and individuals were systematically excluded, not only from the exercise of political rights, but also from access to education and employment. Today we believe that all people are entitled to equal political rights as well as to the opportunities for personal development provided by equal access to education and employment. However, the roots of past discrimination live on in today's discriminatory practices, including racial profiling, the wage gap, the achievement gap in schools, and the "glass ceiling," which prevents women from rising to the top in business and professional firms.

■ **LO5.3:** Although the government has the power to assert rights and the obligation to protect civil rights, it does not always do so. Individuals and groups then organize to bring pressure on government to act. The civil rights movement started with the struggle by African Americans for equality. Before the Civil War, most African Americans were slaves, and slavery was protected by the Constitution and the Supreme Court. Constitutional amendments after the Civil War legally ended slavery, and African Americans gained citizenship, the right to vote, and other rights through legislation. This legal protection was rendered meaningless in practice by the 1880s, however, and politically and socially, African American inequality continued. Legal guarantees mean little when people's attitudes and practices remain discriminatory.

■ **LO5.3:** Legal segregation was declared unconstitutional by the Supreme Court in *Brown v. Board of Education of Topeka* (1954), in which the Court stated that separation implied inferiority. In *Brown v. Board of Education* (1955), the Supreme Court ordered federal courts to ensure that public schools were desegregated "with all deliberate speed." Also in 1955, the modern civil rights movement began with a boycott of segregated public transportation in Montgomery, Alabama. Of particular impact was the Civil Rights Act of 1964, which banned discrimination on the basis of race, color, religion, sex, or national origin in employment and public accommodations. The act created the Equal Employment Opportunity Commission to administer the legislation's provisions.

■ **LO5.3:** The Voting Rights Act of 1965 outlawed discriminatory voter-registration tests and authorized federal registration of persons and federally administered procedures in any state or political subdivision evidencing electoral discrimination or low registration rates. The Voting Rights Act and other protective legislation passed during and since the 1960s apply not only to African Americans but to other ethnic groups as well. Minorities have been increasingly represented in national and state politics, although they have yet to gain representation proportionate to their numbers in the U.S. population. Lingering social and economic disparities have led to a new civil rights agenda—one focusing less on racial differences and more on economic differences.

■ **LO5.4:** The Supreme Court is in the best position within the framework of American government to interpret the values and ideals contained in the founding documents and ensure those ideas are reflected in policy and practice. The Court is often in a good position to pull the public along as more progressive ideas are percolating throughout society by issuing rulings that speed up the timetable for social change, as it did in *Brown v. Board of Education* (desegregating schools) and *United States v. Virginia* (opening VMI, the state military college, to women).

■ **LO5.5:** In the early history of the United States, women were considered citizens, but by and large they had no political rights because they were largely viewed as dependents.

After the first women's rights convention in 1848, the campaign for suffrage gained momentum, yet not until 1920, when the Nineteenth Amendment was ratified, did women finally obtain the right to vote. The second wave of the women's movement began in the 1960s and the National Organization for Women (NOW) was formed in 1966 to bring about complete equality for women in all walks of life. Efforts to secure the ratification of the Equal Rights Amendment failed. Women continue to fight gender discrimination in employment. Federal government efforts to eliminate gender discrimination in the workplace include Title VII of the Civil Rights Act of 1964, which prohibits, among other things, gender-based discrimination, including sexual harassment on the job. Wage discrimination also continues to be a problem for women, as does the glass ceiling. Women make up just 17 percent of the U.S. Congress.

■ **LO5.5:** America has always been a land of immigrants and will continue to be so. Today, more than one million immigrants enter the United States each year, and more than 12 percent of the U.S. population consists of foreign-born persons. Demographers estimate that the foreign-born will account for 15 percent of the nation sometime between 2020 and 2025. In particular, the Latino community in the United States has experienced explosive growth. In recent years, undocumented immigration has surfaced as a significant issue for border states and the nation. Indeed, one of the pressing concerns facing today's politicians at the state and federal level is how U.S. immigration policy should be reformed.

■ **LO5.5:** The Rehabilitation Act of 1973 prohibited discrimination against persons with disabilities in programs receiving federal aid. Regulations implementing the act provide for ramps, elevators, and the like in federal buildings. The Americans with Disabilities Act of 1990 prohibits job discrimination against persons with physical and mental disabilities, requiring that positive steps be taken to comply with the act. The act also requires expanded access to public facilities, including transportation, and to services offered by such private concerns as car rental and telephone companies.

■ **LO5.5:** Gay and lesbian rights groups work to promote laws protecting gays and lesbians from discrimination and to repeal anti-gay laws. After 1969, sodomy laws, which criminalized specific sexual practices, were repealed or struck down by the courts in all but 18 states, and in 2003 a Supreme Court decision effectively invalidated all remaining sodomy laws nationwide. Gays and lesbians are no longer barred from federal employment or from immigrating to this country. Twenty states and the District of Columbia outlaw discrimination based on sexual orientation. Hate crimes based on sexual orientation or gender identity are punishable by federal law under the Matthew Shepard Act of 2009. The Obama administration issued an order extending benefits to partners of federal employees; President Obama, in a change of position, announced his support for same-sex marriage in May 2012. The military's "don't ask, don't tell" policy was repealed effective September 20, 2011.

■ **LO5.6:** Affirmative action programs have been controversial because of charges that they can lead to reverse discrimination against majority groups or even other minority groups. Supreme Court decisions have limited affirmative action programs, and voters in California, Michigan and Washington passed initiatives banning state-sponsored affirmative action in those states.

Selected Print, Media, and Online Resources

PRINT RESOURCES

Kristoff, Nicholas D., and Sheryl WuDunn. *Half the Sky: Turning Oppression into Opportunity for Women Worldwide.* New York: Alfred Knopf, 2009. Written by two Pulitzer Prize–winning journalists, this book demonstrates that the key to solving global poverty is to improve the lives of women around the globe. The book profiles women throughout Asia and Africa who have not only coped with unimaginable forms of brutal discrimination, but created opportunities for survival for themselves and other women.

Liptak, Adam. *To Have and To Hold: The Supreme Court and the Battle for Same-Sex Marriage.* Kindle Single, 2013. Liptak, a Supreme Court reporter for *The New York Times*, puts the historic *Windsor* decision in social and political context.

Moore, Wes. *The Other Wes Moore: One Name, Two Fates.* New York: Random House, 2010. This memoir tells the story of two boys, both named Wes Moore, who grew up in Baltimore, Maryland, within a few blocks of one another; one became a Rhodes Scholar and one is serving a life sentence in the Jessup Correctional Institution.

Morin, Jose Luis. *Latino/a Rights and Justice in the United States: Perspectives and Approaches.* Durham, NJ: Carolina Academic Press, 2009. This book offers a thorough overview of the history and modern incarnation of Latino/a civil rights and experiences within the U.S. justice system. Case studies and a focus on taking action complement the legal analysis.

Sue, Derald Wing. *Microaggressions in Everyday Life: Race, Gender, and Sexual Orientation.* Hoboken, NJ: John Wiley & Sons, 2010. Dr. Sue, a psychology professor at Columbia University, analyzes the unintended slights that take their toll on the people of color, women, gays, transgendered people and other groups.

MEDIA RESOURCES

Chisholm '72: Unbought and Unbossed—A documentary about the career of Congresswoman Shirley Chisholm, the first black woman to run for president of the United States. Includes archival footage and contemporary interviews.

Eyes on the Prize: America's Civil Rights Movement 1954–1985—A 14-part *American Experience* documentary (first aired on public television) that features both movement leaders and the stories of average Americans through contemporary interviews and historical footage.

Fight in the Fields: Cesar Chavez and the Farmworkers' Struggle—A 1997 film documenting the first successful drive to organize farmworkers in the United States; described as a social history with Chavez as a central figure, the documentary draws from archival footage, newsreels, and present-day interviews.

Lioness—A documentary film about a group of female army support soldiers who were a part of the first program in American history to send women into direct ground combat against insurgents in Iraq.

Miss Representation—A documentary exploring how the media's misrepresentations of women have led to the underrepresentation of women in positions of power and influence.

Borderland—A National Public Radio (NPR) series exploring the 2,248 mile border between the United States and Mexico and the lives and stories of the people who cross.

ONLINE RESOURCES

National Immigration Forum—established in 1982, the National Immigration Forum is the leading immigrant advocacy organization in the country, with a mission to advocate for the value of immigrants and immigration to the nation: www.immigrationforum.org/

Pew Hispanic Center—founded in 2001, the Pew Hispanic Center is a nonpartisan research organization that seeks to improve understanding of the U.S. Hispanic population and to chronicle Latinos' growing impact on the nation: www.pewhispanic.org/

Reporting Civil Rights—an anthology of the reporters and journalism of the American civil rights movement hosted by Library of America: www.reportingcivilrights.loa.org/

The Great Divide—a *New York Times* blog series on inequality in the United States and around the world, and its implications for economics, politics, society and culture; moderated by Joseph E. Stiglitz, a Nobel laureate in economics: http://opinionator.blogs.nytimes.com/category/the-great-divide/

Women's Rights National Historical Park—operated by the National Park Service, the park preserves the sites associated with the first women's rights convention in 1848: www.nps.gov/wori/index.htm

Master the concept of Civil Rights with MindTap™ for American Government

 REVIEW MindTap™ **for American Government**
Access Key Term Flashcards for Chapter 5.

 TEST YOURSELF MindTap™ **for American Government**
Take the Wrap It Up Quiz for Chapter 5.

 STAY CURRENT MindTap™ **for American Government**
Access the KnowNow blog and customized RSS for updates on current events.

 STAY FOCUSED MindTap™ **for American Government**
Complete the Focus Activities for Civil Rights.

Public Opinion and Political Socialization

6

President Barack Obama greets students from Medina Elementary School on February 17, 2012, in Medina, WA.

White House Photo/Alamy

WATCH & LEARN MindTap° for American Government

Watch a brief "What Do You Know?" video summarizing Public Opinion and Political Socialization.

LEARNING OUTCOMES

After reading this chapter, students will be able to:

- **LO6.1:** Define public opinion and identify at least two ways public opinion impacts government actions.

- **LO6.2:** Evaluate how the political socialization process shapes political attitudes, opinions, and behavior; explain the impact of demographic characteristics on political behavior.

- **LO6.3:** Describe three forms of social media and explain how social media can shape political decisions or events.

- **LO6.4:** Assess the impact that world opinion of the United States has on the government's domestic and foreign policy decisions.

- **LO6.5:** Identify three factors that might distort public opinion results collected through opinion polling.

What if?

Young People Were Required to Serve?

BACKGROUND

What if the United States adopted a policy that required all persons between the ages of 18 and 22 residing in the country to engage in domestic or military service for a period of at least 18 months? Would this create a stronger bond between young citizens and the nation? How might 18 months of service socialize new generations to politics and political activity?

Young people typically know less about politics, express less interest in politics, and vote less often than their elders. But that can change! In 2012, people under 30 made up a larger share of the electorate than those 65 and older. Thus, young citizens have tremendous potential to shape politics and policy *if* they get involved.

SERVICE AS POLITICAL SOCIALIZATION

The United States has a long history of citizens rendering service to their communities, including the Civilian Conservation Corps, the Peace Corps, and Volunteers in Service to America (VISTA). Teach for America recruits college graduates and trains them to teach in America's most challenged schools. During the Clinton administration, AmeriCorps, a large-scale national service program designed to place young people in service positions in communities across the country, was established. The Obama administration has significantly expanded both the AmeriCorps and VISTA programs. New initiatives include STEM AmeriCorps (designed to mobilize professionals in Science, Technology, Engineering, and Mathematics fields to inspire young people to excel) and FEMACorps (a new 1,600 member AmeriCorps program solely devoted to disaster response and recovery).

Would young people be willing to serve their country? This chapter reviews the process of becoming socialized into civic and political life and, as a result, how we develop and express political opinions. Forces such as the family, schools, faith communities, the media, and peers all shape how we understand public life. Likewise, direct personal experience with politics is a developmental force. From national surveys of first-year college students, we know that roughly a third of all students believe that it is important to keep up with political affairs and that roughly a third report a very good chance that they will participate in community service or volunteer work while in college. These individuals are also more likely to remain engaged with their communities after they graduate from college. Those who oppose national service do so for a variety of reasons, including the disruption to education and career, as well as the belief that individual liberty would be violated.

TOWARD A NATIONAL POLICY

What would the nation gain from a service requirement? The U.S. military has been an all-volunteer force since the repeal of the draft in 1973. Representative Charles B. Rangel, a veteran of the Korean conflict, argued in a 2002 *New York Times* op-ed essay that the draft should be reinstated to promote the philosophy of shared sacrifice and enforce a greater appreciation of the consequences of war. At any given time in the past decade, less than 1 percent of the American population has been on active military duty, compared with 9 percent of Americans who were in uniform during World War II. When President Bill Clinton proposed AmeriCorps, he said "Citizen service bridges isolated individuals, local communities, the national community, and ultimately, the community of all people." AmeriCorps members serve in communities across the United States for one or two years in return for an educational stipend.* The nation benefits from a diverse group of committed individuals performing public work that needs doing. Critics charge that national service amounts to forced voluntarism and that the compulsory nature undermines the benefits for individuals and communities. Without any form of compulsory service, about 25 percent of Americans volunteer at least once a year.

---

* William J. Clinton, "The Duties of Democracy," in E. J. Dionne et. al., eds. *United We Serve: National Service and the Future of Citizenship* (Washington, DC: Brookings Institution, 2003).

For Critical Analysis

1. *Do you believe a national service requirement would improve young people's connection to politics, to their community, and to the country? Why or why not?*

2. *You have no doubt heard the phrase, "with rights come responsibilities." What responsibilities do you have as a resident of your community, of your state, and of the nation?*

IN A DEMOCRACY, the people express their opinions in many different ways. First and foremost, they express their views in political campaigns and vote for the individuals who will represent their views in government. Between elections, individuals express their opinions in many ways, ranging from writing to the editor to calling their senator's office to responding to a blog. Public opinion is expressed and conveyed to public officials through polls, which are reported daily in the media. Sometimes public opinion is expressed through mass demonstrations, rallies, or protests.

In 2003, when President George W. Bush asked Congress to authorize the use of force against Iraq, 72 percent of the public approved. At that time, more than 80 percent of Americans either believed or considered it possible that Saddam Hussein was building an arsenal of biological and other extremely dangerous weapons. By 2005, support for the use of troops in Iraq had declined to 39 percent and, by mid-2007, had fallen to 36 percent. Senator Barack Obama made withdrawal of American troops from Iraq a priority of his campaign and claimed that if he had been in the Senate at that time, he would not have supported the authorization of the use of force. Senator Hillary Clinton, who had voted for the resolution, no longer supported the Iraqi campaign and claimed that she had been misled at the time of the debate. The approval rating of President Bush, inevitably connected with the unpopular war, fell to 30 percent or less. In the past, public opinion has had a dramatic impact on presidents. In 1968, President Lyndon B. Johnson did not run for reelection because of the intense and negative public reaction to the war in Vietnam. In 1974, President Richard Nixon resigned in the wake of a scandal when it was obvious that public opinion no longer supported him. Although President Obama promised to make health-care reform a top legislative priority, vacillating public opinion made it difficult to pressure even members of his own party in Congress to act. His approval ratings heading into the 2012 campaign were closely tied to the public's perception of the state of the economy, and particularly the unemployment rate. Following a number of foreign policy challenges in Syria and Ukraine, as well as the difficulties with online health insurance enrollment under the Affordable Care Act, President Obama's favorability ratings fell below 40 percent. The U.S. Congress started 2014 with the support of just 13 percent of the public. Thus, the extent to which public opinion affects policymaking is not always clear and scholars must deal with many uncertainties when analyzing its impact.

Defining Public Opinion

■ **LO6.1:** Define public opinion and identify at least two ways public opinion impacts government actions.

Among the many different publics, no single public opinion exists. In a nation of more than 300 million people, innumerable gradations of opinion on an issue may exist. Thus, we define **public opinion** as the aggregate of individual attitudes or beliefs shared by some portion of the adult population.

Public opinion is distributed among several different positions, and the distribution of opinion tells us how divided the public is on an issue and whether compromise is possible. When a large proportion of the American public appears to express the same view on an issue, a **consensus** exists, at least at the moment the poll was taken. Figure 6–1 shows a pattern of opinion that might be called consensual. In this situation, 97 percent of adults polled by Gallup for the Lumina Foundation say education beyond high school is important. Issues on which the

LISTEN & LEARN

MindTap for American Government

Access Read Speaker to listen to Chapter 6.

Public Opinion
The aggregate of individual attitudes or beliefs shared by some portion of the adult population.

Consensus
General agreement among the citizenry on an issue.

Figure 6–1 ▶ Consensus Opinion

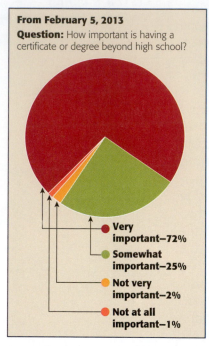

From February 5, 2013
Question: How important is having a certificate or degree beyond high school?

● **Very important—72%**
● **Somewhat important—25%**
● **Not very important—2%**
● **Not at all important—1%**

Source: Gallup-Lumina Foundation Poll Access: http://www.luminafoundation.org/publications/Americas_Call_for_Higher_Education_Redesign.pdf

Figure 6–2 ▶ Divisive Opinion

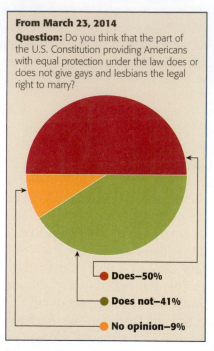

From March 23, 2014
Question: Do you think that the part of the U.S. Constitution providing Americans with equal protection under the law does or does not give gays and lesbians the legal right to marry?

● **Does—50%**
● **Does not—41%**
● **No opinion—9%**

Source: Washington Post-ABCNews National Poll Access: http://www.washingtonpost.com/page/2010-2019/WashingtonPost/2014/03/05/National-Politics/Polling/release_301.xml

Figure 6–3 ▶ Nonopinion

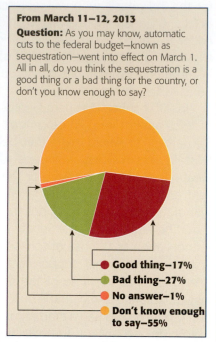

From March 11–12, 2013
Question: As you may know, automatic cuts to the federal budget—known as sequestration—went into effect on March 1. All in all, do you think the sequestration is a good thing or a bad thing for the country, or don't you know enough to say?

● **Good thing—17%**
● **Bad thing—27%**
● **No answer—1%**
● **Don't know enough to say—55%**

Source: Gallup Poll Access: http://www.gallup.com/poll/161732/half-no-view-effect-sequestration.aspx

Divisive Opinion
Public opinion that is polarized between two quite different positions.

Nonopinion
The lack of an opinion on an issue or policy among the majority.

public holds widely differing attitudes result in **divisive opinion** (see Figure 6–2). In a Washington Post-ABC News poll, Americans were asked if they believe the Constitution's guarantee of equal protection of the laws gives gays and lesbians the right to marry. Half of the public now believes that it does, while 41 percent disagree and 9 percent have yet to form an opinion. Sometimes, a poll shows a distribution of opinion indicating that most Americans either have no information about the issue or are not interested enough to formulate a position. This is referred to as **nonopinion** (see Figure 6–3). In April 2013, the Gallup polling organization asked adults whether they believed the automatic budget cuts (sequestration) was a good or bad idea. While 17 percent said the cuts were a good thing for the country and 27 percent thought they were a bad thing, the majority (55 percent) admitted that they did not know enough to say one way or the other. Politicians may believe that the public's lack of knowledge about an issue gives them more room to maneuver, or they may be wary of taking any action for fear that opinion will crystallize after a crisis.

Public Opinion and Policymaking

Sometimes public officials have a difficult time discerning the public's opinion on a specific issue from the public's expression of general anger or dissatisfaction. The Tea Party protests present just such a dilemma. Rallies began in early 2009 to express opposition to the TARP (Troubled Asset Relief Program) bailout bill passed by Congress. Drawing on themes from the Revolutionary War era and the Boston Tea Party in particular, the protesters often arrived dressed as Patriots and holding handmade placards with anti-tax slogans. Organizers have utilized social networking sites and the Internet to call for Tea Party meetings and protests in communities large and small. They have demonstrated against health-care reform and increased government spending. Several rallies were held around the country on April 15th—widely known as tax day. This coalition of disparate groups acting under a single moniker is not "for" or "against" any single policy or program, but is rather an expression of negative opinion directed at incumbents of both parties. As a result, public officials and candidates are having a difficult time responding.

If public opinion is important for democracy, are policymakers really responsive to public opinion? A study by political scientists Benjamin I. Page and Robert Y. Shapiro suggests that the national government is very responsive to the public's demands for action.[1] In looking at changes in public opinion poll results over time, research demonstrates that when the public supports a policy change, the following occurs: Policy changes in a direction consistent with the change in public opinion 43 percent of the time, policy changes in a direction opposite to the change in opinion 22 percent of the time, and policy does not change at all 33 percent of the time. When public opinion changes dramatically—say, by 20 percentage points rather than by just 6 or 7 percentage points—government policy is more likely to follow changing public attitudes.

Public opinion also serves to limit government. Consider the highly controversial issue of abortion. Most Americans are moderates on this issue; they do not approve of abortion as a means of birth control, but they do feel that it should be available. Yet, sizable groups express very intense feelings for and against legalized abortion. Given this distribution of opinion, most officials would rather not try to change policy to favor either of the extreme positions. To do so would clearly violate the opinion of the majority of Americans. In this case, public opinion does not make public policy; rather, it restrains officials from taking truly unpopular actions. In this sense, public opinion plays a vital role in the American system.

How Public Opinion Is Formed: Political Socialization

■ **LO6.2:** Evaluate how the political socialization process shapes political attitudes, opinions, and behavior; explain the impact of demographic characteristics on political behavior.

Most Americans are willing to express opinions on political issues when asked. How do people acquire these opinions and attitudes? Typically, views that are expressed as political opinions are acquired through the process of **political socialization**. People acquire their political attitudes, often including their party identification, through relationships with their families, friends, and coworkers.

Political Socialization
The process by which people acquire political beliefs and attitudes.

Models of Political Socialization

Scholars have long believed that the most important early sources of political socialization are found in the family and the schools. Children learn their parents' views on politics and on political leaders through observation and approval seeking. When parents are strong supporters of a political party, children are very likely to identify with that same party. If parents are alienated from the political system or totally disinterested in politics, children will tend to hold the same attitudes.

---

1. See the extensive work of Page and Shapiro in Benjamin I. Page and Robert Y. Shapiro, *The Rational Public: Fifty Years of Trends in Americans' Policy Preferences* (Chicago: University of Chicago Press, 1992).

Other researchers claim that political attitudes (not party identification) are influenced much more heavily by genetics than by parental or environmental socialization.[2] Perhaps most interestingly, in explaining differences in people's tendencies to possess political opinions at all regardless of their ideology, the researchers find that genetics explains one-third of the differences among people, and shared environment is completely inconsequential. Thinking about how nature (genetics) might shape political attitudes is a relatively new area of research, but it complements the nurture approach taken by generations of political socialization researchers, helping to provide answers to longstanding puzzles.

More sources of information about politics are available to Americans today and especially to young people. Although their basic outlook on the political system may be formed by genetics and early family influences, young people are exposed to other sources of information about issues and values through social media and popular culture. It is not unusual for young adults to hold very different views on issues. The exposure of younger Americans to many sources of ideas may also underlie their more progressive views on such issues as immigration and gay rights.

The Family and the Social Environment

Not only do our parents' political attitudes and actions affect our opinions, but family also links us to other factors that affect opinion, such as race, social class, educational environment, and religious beliefs.

Studies suggest that the influence of parents is due to communication and receptivity. Parents communicate their feelings and preferences to children constantly. Because children have such a strong desire for parental approval, they are very receptive to their parents' views. Children are less likely to influence their parents, because parents expect deference from their children.[3]

Other studies show that if children are exposed to political ideas at school and in the media, they will share these ideas with their parents, giving parents what some scholars call a "second chance" at political socialization. Children can also expose their parents to new media, such as the Internet, Facebook, and Twitter.[4] The demographics of Facebook users show a 25 percent decline in use among 13–17 year olds coupled with significant increases in the 55-and-up age group (80 percent increase).[5]

Education as a Source of Political Socialization.

From the early days of the republic, schools were perceived to be important transmitters of political information and attitudes. Children in primary grades learn about their country mostly in patriotic ways. They learn about pilgrims, the flag, some of the nation's presidents, and how to celebrate national holidays. Without much explicit instruction, children easily adopt democratic decision-making tools such as "taking a vote" and democratic procedures such as "the majority wins." In the middle grades, children learn more historical facts and come to understand the structure and

2. John Alford, Carolyn Funk, and John R. Hibbing, "Are Political Orientations Genetically Transmitted?" *American Political Science Review*, vol. 99, no. 2 (May, 2005).

3. Barbara A. Bardes and Robert W. Oldendick, *Public Opinion: Measuring the American Mind*, 3rd ed. (Belmont, CA: Wadsworth Publishing, 2006), p. 73.

4. For a pioneering study in this area, see Michael McDevitt and Steven H. Chaffee, "Second Chance Political Socialization: 'Trickle-up' Effects of Children on Parents," in Thomas J. Johnson et al., eds., *Engaging the Public: How Government and the Media Can Reinvigorate American Democracy* (Lanham, MD: Rowman & Littlefield, 1998), pp. 57–66.

5. James Brumley, "Facebook Users are Getting Older… And That's a Good Thing" Investor Place, February 4, 2014. Accessed at http://investorplace.com/2014/02/facebook-users-demographics/#.U0FsYFe9Z8E

Politics with a Purpose

First Lady Michelle Obama— Let's Move!

The First Lady of the United States does not have a formal constitutional role within government, but she is a very powerful force in shaping public opinion and social norms. The title was first used when Dolley Madison was eulogized as "America's First lady." Historically, First Ladies have served as the official hostess in the White House and played a supportive role both socially and politically. Today's presidential spouse is much more likely to play a public role of her own design. Michelle Obama graduated from Princeton and earned her law degree at Harvard. Her resume includes practicing law and working with the city of Chicago in launching the youth mentorship program, Public Allies. In the years prior to Barack Obama's election as president in 2008, she served as vice president of community and external affairs for the University of Chicago Hospitals. The Obamas are raising their two daughters, Malia and Sasha, in the White House. They are also the first African American First Family to occupy the White House. The choices made as individuals and as a family are carefully scrutinized by the public. In many ways, the First Family is integral to opinion formation and political socialization. Michelle Obama has adopted a public agenda related to promoting healthy habits and the well-being of children. Soon after the Obamas moved into the White House, she planted a vegetable garden on the South Lawn with more than 55 varieties of fruits and vegetables. The produce is used in preparing meals in the White House and a portion is donated to a local soup kitchen.

In 2010, the First Lady launched the project, Let's Move!, aimed at ending the epidemic of childhood obesity through healthier eating and increased physical activity. Nearly one in three children today are overweight or obese; the numbers are even higher in African American and Hispanic communities, where nearly 40 percent of kids are overweight. Children who are overweight or obese at ages 3 to 5 years old are five times as likely to be overweight or obese as adults. Let's Move! is a comprehensive public health campaign designed to educate people about the causes and consequences of childhood obesity and help everyone make better choices. Nutritional education is combined with practical strategies such as "Supermarket 101" that urges parents to fill the cart with ingredients for healthy meals rather than snack foods. "Chefs Move to Schools" is run through the Department of Agriculture and encourages chefs to adopt a local school. Schools across the country have planted gardens and brought kids into the planning and preparation of healthier school lunches.

Let's Move! urges kids to get at least one hour of physical exercise a day. Let's Move! and NFL's Play 60 program have partnered to promote youth fitness programs of all kinds. Let's Move! involves local governments and nonprofits, school districts, and celebrities. A robust social media campaign invites Americans to contribute to the Let's Move! blog, post to Facebook, and submit YouTube videos. #Letsmove, The Let's Move! Twitter feed, offers advice on eating healthy and features posts by the First Lady, encouraging the youth to think about the right nutrition and amount of physical activity needed to stay healthy.

As First Lady, Michelle Obama has the nation's attention; she has chosen to focus it on improving children's health. In August 2013, the Center for Disease Control (CDC) reported that the obesity rate for low-income preschool-age children declined between 2008 and 2011 in 19 of 43 states and territories measured. The news announcement from the CDC included a remark from Mrs. Obama: "I am thrilled at the progress we've made over the last few years in obesity rates among our youngest Americans."*

Retweeted by Let's Move!
The First Lady @FLOTUS · Apr 4
"A big part of reaching your full potential is making sure you're putting the right fuel in your body." —The First Lady #WHTeamUSA
Expand   Reply   Retweet Favorite ··· More

Have various interviews, Tweets, and discussion of First Lady Michelle Obama's Let's Move! campaign worked in capturing your attention about diet and exercise?

* Sabrina Tavernise, "Obesity Rate for Young Children Plummets 43% in a Decade." *The New York Times.* February 25, 2014. Accessed at http://www.nytimes.com/2014/02/26/health/obesity-rate-for-young-children-plummets-43-in-a-decade.html

functions of government. By high school, students have a more complex understanding of the political system, may identify with a political party, and may take positions on issues. Students may gain some experience in political participation: first, through student elections and activities, and second, through their introduction to registration and voting while still in school.

The more formal education a person receives, the more likely it is that he or she will be interested in politics, be confident in his or her ability to understand political issues, and be an active participant in the political process.

Peers and Peer Group Influence. Once a child enters school, the child's friends become an important influence on behavior and attitudes. Friendships and associations in **peer groups** affect political attitudes. We must, however, separate the effects of peer group pressure on opinions and attitudes in general from the effects of peer group pressure on political opinions. For the most part, associations among peers are nonpolitical. Political attitudes are more likely to be shaped by peer groups when peer groups are involved directly in political activities. If you join an interest group based on your passion for the environment, you are more likely to be influenced by your organizational peers than you are by classmates.

Opinion Leaders' Influence. We are all influenced by friends at school, family members and other relatives, and teachers. In a sense, these people are **opinion leaders**, but on an *informal* level; their influence on our political views is not necessarily intentional or deliberate. When President Obama announced a change in his position on gay marriage, a similar positive change in public opinion among African Americans was detected by pollsters. We are also influenced by *formal* opinion leaders, such as presidents, lobbyists, congresspersons, media figures, and religious leaders, who have as part of their jobs the task of shaping people's views. Nicholas Kristof, a prominent *New York Times* reporter and author, has characterized empowerment of women and girls as the twenty-first century's moral imperative.[6] Former Secretary of State Hillary Clinton rarely missed an opportunity to urge nations, including the United States, to invest resources to empower women and girls: "[W]ithout providing more rights and responsibilities for women, many of the goals we claim to pursue in our foreign policy are either unachievable or much harder to achieve....Democracy means nothing if half the people can't vote, or if their vote doesn't count, or if their literacy rate is so low that the exercise of their vote is in question. Which is why when I travel, I do events with women, I talk about women's rights, I meet with women activists, I raise women's concerns with the leaders I'm talking to."[7] She continues to work for the global human rights of women and girls through the "No Ceilings: The Full Participation Project," the newest initiative of the Clinton Foundation. The project focuses on advancing women's full participation in the economy, leadership, and the use of technology. Politicians acting as opinion leaders hope to define the political agenda in such a way that discussions about policy options will take place on their terms.

Peer Groups
Groups consisting of members sharing common social characteristics. These groups play an important part in the socialization process, helping to shape attitudes and beliefs.

Opinion Leaders
People who are able to influence the opinions of others because of position, expertise, or personality.

JStone/Shutterstock.com

As First Lady, as a U.S. senator, and as secretary of state, Hillary Rodham Clinton urged nations to invest in girls and women. She now works on behalf of global human rights for women through "No Ceilings: The Full Participation Project," an initiative of the Clinton Foundation.

6. Nicholas Kristof and Sheryl WuDunn, "The Women's Crusade," *New York Times Magazine*, August 17, 2009.
7. Mark Landler, "A New Gender Agenda," *The New York Times*, August 18, 2009.

Beyond Our Borders

World Opinion of the United States

■ **LO6.4:** Assess the impact that world opinion of the United States has on the government's domestic and foreign policy decisions.

In the immediate aftermath of the September 11, 2001, terrorist attacks, most of the world expressed sympathy toward the United States. Few nations objected to the subsequent American invasion of Afghanistan in 2001 to oust the Taliban government or to the Bush administration's vow to hunt down the terrorists responsible for the attacks. When the United States announced plans to invade Iraq in 2003, however, world opinion was not supportive. By 2006, world opinion had become decidedly anti-American, as the United States' ongoing "war on terrorism" continued to offend other nations. There was a brief resurgence attributed to the "Obama Effect" in 2010, but that has largely disappeared. As the United States concludes two increasingly unpopular wars, what is the world's opinion of the United States?

NEGATIVE VIEWS OF AMERICAN UNILATERALISM

The invasion of Iraq in 2003 marked a turning point in world public opinion toward the United States. Most nations were supportive of continuing inspections by the United Nations and did not agree that Iraq was a sponsor of terrorism. The willingness of American leaders to ignore world opinion led to charges of arrogance on the part of the U.S. administration.

The Pew Global Attitudes Project regularly monitors public opinion toward the United States in more than 40 nations. Attitudes toward the United States have declined in many regions of the world. The percentage of Canadians who had a favorable view of the United States fell from 68 percent in 2009 to 64 percent in 2013. Declines in favorable views were also found in Western Europe and in some South American countries. Drone strikes, in particular, are very unpopular. Popular support for the unmanned airstrikes surpass 50 percent only in Israel and Kenya. The president's foreign policy is most popular in Germany and France—two long-time allies—and least popular in the Middle East.

ARAB AND MUSLIM OPINION TOWARD AMERICA AND ITS IDEALS

Among the majority of Middle Eastern states, approval of the United States is especially low among Muslims. This is true in such states as Egypt, Jordan, Pakistan, and Malaysia. However, divisions exist even among Muslims based on religious views. Sunni Muslims in Lebanon are much more favorably inclined toward the United States than are their Shia countrymen and women. Many Muslim nations and their peoples are opposed to the U.S.

action in Iraq and continued aggressive stance toward Iran. While those nations may not support the current regimes, they are more worried that the United States has destabilized the region, and they continue to see the United States as too supportive of the state of Israel. It is worth noting, however, that most Muslim states in Africa have favorable opinions of the United States.*

Many Arabs and Muslims resent U.S. interventionism in the Middle East. They do not, however, reject all aspects of the United States or its ideals. The majority of Muslims do not support religious extremism or terrorism in their own nations. Nor are Arabs and Muslims dismissive of democracy. There has also been broad support for democracy in the Middle East. Many individuals believe that democracy is a real possibility in their own country. However, many are still suspicious of American motives in the region.

YOUNG PEOPLE VIEW UNITED STATES MOST POSITIVELY

In many of the nations surveyed by the Global Attitudes Project, people under age 30 are especially likely to have a

Muslim women examining a mosaic of stamps depicting the image of Barack Obama during the Asian International Stamp Exhibition held in Jakarta, Indonesia, in 2008.

positive view of America. This is particularly true in Turkey, where 38 percent of 18- to 29-year-olds give the U.S. a favorable rating, compared with just 8 percent of Turks age 50 and older (a gap of 30 points). Half those under 30 in China have a favorable view, compared with just 27 percent among people 50 and older. People with a college education hold more favorable views toward America than those without a college degree—a double-digit gap in China, Russia, Pakistan, Venezuela, and Tunisia.

* The Pew Global Attitudes Project, 2013 Survey, www.pewglobal.org.

For Critical Analysis

1. *Should the U.S. government keep world opinion in mind when making decisions? Why or why not?*

2. *Some polls have shown that younger Muslims and Arabs have a more positive opinion about the United States. Why might that be the case?*

Political Change and Political Socialization. The political system is relatively stable in the United States. But what influences might the upheavals and revolutions around the world in recent years have on the political socialization of young people experiencing and witnessing those dramatic changes?[8] How will people who have learned to live under an oppressive regime such as that of Muammar Gaddafi in Libya develop and learn to live in a new regime? The 2014 presidential and provincial council elections in Afghanistan represented only the second time in the nation's history that power has changed hands through popular election. "On behalf of the American people, I congratulate the millions of Afghans who enthusiastically participated in today's historic elections, which promise to usher in the first democratic transfer of power in Afghanistan's history and which represent another important milestone in Afghans taking full responsibility for their country," President Obama declared.[9] Americans are sometimes puzzled by the slow pace of democratization once a dictator has been removed, but try to imagine the difficulty of building civil society and creating new day-to-day political norms and practices when politics has always meant capriciousness and brutality. New regimes must help people establish important political dispositions such as trust and political efficacy (the belief that your engagement will yield results) —a difficult task when the agents of socialization (education, media, religion) are associated with the old regime. The United Nations Children's Fund estimates that some Syrian children have missed out on as much as two years of education in the midst of their country's ongoing civil struggle.

The Impact of the Media

Media
Channels of mass communication.

Agenda-Setting
Determining which public policy questions will be debated or considered.

Clearly, the **media**—newspapers, television, radio, and the Internet—strongly influence public opinion. The media inform the public about the issues and events of our times and thus have an **agenda-setting** effect. To borrow from Bernard Cohen's classic statement about the media and public opinion, the media may not

8. Virginia Sapiro, "Not Your Parents' Political Socialization: Introduction for a New Generation," *Annual Review of Political Science,* Vol. 7, 2004, pp. 1–23.
9. "Obama Hails Afghan Election as Milestone Toward Democracy," FOXNews, April 5, 2014. Accessed at http://www.foxnews.com/politics/2014/04/05/obama-hails-afghan-elections-as-milestone-toward-democracy/

be successful in telling people what to think, but they are "stunningly successful in telling their audience what to think about."[10] Late-night comedian Jon Stewart mocked CNN for what he considered to be over-the-top, conspiracy-laced coverage of events in the news, such as the tragic disappearance of Malaysia Airlines Flight 370 in the spring of 2014.

The media also provide a political forum for leaders and the public. Candidates for office use news reporting to sustain interest in their campaigns, while officeholders use the media to gain support for policies or to present an image of leadership. Presidential trips abroad are an outstanding way for the chief executive to get positive and exciting news coverage that makes the president look "presidential." The media also offer ways for citizens to participate in public debate, be it through letters to the editor, televised editorials, or through social media. Americans may cherish the idea of an unbiased press, but in the early years of the nation's history, the number of politically sponsored newspapers was significant. The sole reason for the existence of such periodicals was to further the interests of the politicians who paid for their publication. As chief executive of our government during this period, George Washington has been called a "firm believer" in **managed news**. Although acknowledging that the public had a right to be informed, he believed that some matters should be kept secret and that news that might damage the image of the United States should be censored (not published). China recently announced that it will train and certify "online public opinion management specialists." These specialists, China argues, will be better equipped to meet the challenges of controlling information amid "mass incidents."[11] The Chinese government issued new rules in 2012 requiring internet users to provide their real names to service providers, while assigning internet companies greater responsibility for deleting forbidden postings and reporting them to the authorities.

> **Managed News**
> Information generated and distributed by the government in such a way as to give government interests priority over candor.

Today, many contend that the media's influence on public opinion has grown to equal that of the family. In her analysis of the role played by the media in American politics, media scholar Doris A. Graber points out that high school students, when asked where they obtain the information on which they base their attitudes, mention the mass media far more than they mention their families, friends, and teachers.[12] Of registered voters who own a cell phone, roughly half used a smart device as a tool for political participation on social networking sites and as a way to fact check campaign statements in real time. Over 70 percent of Americans have a broadband connection at home, providing high-speed access to the Internet. In 2000, even though about half of all adults reported being online at home, only 3 percent of American households had broadband access.[13] These trends, combined with the increasing popularity of cable satires such as *The Daily Show*, talk radio, blogs, social networking sites, and the Internet as information sources, may significantly alter the nature of the media's influence on public opinion. A significant difference between this form of media influence and that of the past is that today people are actively creating content through social media rather than simply consuming information produced by others.

> **did you know?**
> The average American spends 5.11 hours a day watching television; that adds up to 9 years over a lifetime.

10. Bernard C. Cohen, *The Press and Foreign Policy* (Princeton, NJ: Princeton University Press, 1963), p. 81.
11. Jonathan Kaiman, "China to Train Leaders to Manage Online Public Opinion." *The Guardian*, March 10, 2014. Accessed at http://www.theguardian.com/world/2014/mar/10/china-online-opinion-training-programme-sina-weibo
12. See Doris A. Graber, *Mass Media and American Politics*, 7th ed. (Chicago: University of Chicago Press, 2005).
13. Pew Research Internet Project, "Broadband Technology Fact Sheet." September 2013. Accessed at http://www.pewinternet.org/fact-sheets/broadband-technology-fact-sheet/

Everyday Politics

 ## Programming Public Opinion

The Wire, House of Cards, Orange Is the New Black, Homeland… all of these popular series have one thing in common—they do not air on network television. It is hard to imagine finding a network television series about a high school chemistry teacher battling lung cancer who turns to producing and selling methamphetamine to provide for his family after his death. Yet, by the end of its run in 2013 *Breaking Bad* was identified as the highest-rated television show of all time by Guinness World Records. Lesbians in prison, polygamy, single women's sex lives, mafia violence, and drug trafficking are not exactly traditional plot lines for American television—yet more American adults are watching original programming on premium cable networks than ever before. Netflix, an on-demand Internet streaming provider, broke into original content programming with the political drama, *House of Cards* and quickly followed that success with *Orange Is the New Black*. Netflix's innovation was to release the entire season at one time, which has led to the new practice of binge viewing—watching several episodes of a series at one time.

These programs are a form of socialization that shapes public opinion about current events and issues. Through programming, viewers are introduced to new ideas; values and shared norms are either reinforced or challenged. Changes in society play out on the television screen and become the content of discussions at work and school the next day. *All in the Family*, a sitcom that aired in the early 1970s, explored issues of racial integration, women's rights, homosexuality, rape, abortion, breast cancer, and the Vietnam War. Today, *Modern Family* presents viewers with alternatives to the traditional family structure in a comedic setting. By situating these controversial issues as debates within a family, viewers were introduced to competing perspectives on the most important issues of the time. Who decides what is too controversial to be aired at any given time?

The Federal Commission on Communication (FCC) is charged by Congress with regulating the public airwaves and has historically set the standard for public decency in broadcast television. The FCC has not applied the same standards to cable and satellite services (e.g. Dish Satellite TV) arguing that viewers of subscription-based services have greater control over the programming content that comes into their homes—in other words, the consumer is the regulator. The FCC's regulatory powers extend only to over-the-air broadcasters, who transmit their programs via the publicly owned spectrum. These programs are available to any member of the public with a radio or television, meaning that the FCC has greater regulatory control over content—particularly between the hours of 6 a.m. and 10 p.m., when children are more likely to be in the audience.

Critical Thinking

1. *What social or political messages are found in your favorite programs? Thinking back to when you were younger, did your parents limit what you could watch on television? Did your family talk about the programs you watched together?*

2. *Given the explosion of cable and Internet access, is there a need for government to regulate the "public airwaves" anymore? Why or why not?*

The Influence of Political Events

Older Americans tend to be somewhat more conservative than younger Americans, particularly on social issues and, to some extent, on economic issues. This is known as the **life cycle effect**. People change as they grow older as a result of age-specific experiences like employment, marriage, children, and other responsibilities. Likewise, as new generations of citizens are socialized within a particular social, economic, and political context, it in turn affects individual members' more specific opinions and actions. In other words, political events and

Life Cycle Effect
Concept that people change as they grow older because of age-specific experiences and thus are likely to hold age-specific attitudes.

environmental conditions have the power to shape the political attitudes of an entire generation. Perhaps you recall what you were doing and where you were when the September 11, 2001 terrorist attacks happened or the night the country elected the first African American president. Although you and your parents witnessed these events, the ways that they have influenced your attitudes about increased airport security measures or progress on civil rights might differ. When events produce such a long-lasting result, we refer to it as a **generational effect** (or *cohort effect*).[14]

Voters who grew up in the 1930s during the Great Depression were likely to form lifelong attachments to the Democratic Party, the party of Franklin D. Roosevelt. In the 1960s and 1970s, the war in Vietnam and the Watergate scandal and subsequent presidential cover-up fostered widespread cynicism toward government. Evidence indicates that the years of economic prosperity under President Reagan during the 1980s led many young people to identify with the Republican Party. More recently, the increase in non-party-affiliated Independents may mean that although young people heavily supported Democrat Barack Obama over Republican John McCain in the 2008 election, Democrats should not count on a lifelong attachment. After a strong showing in the 2008 presidential contest, young voters were largely absent in the 2010 midterm elections, with those under 30 indicating less interest (31 percent compared to 53 percent) and little likelihood of voting (45 percent compared to 76 percent) compared to those over 30 years of age.[15]

Young people returned to the polls in the 2012 election, however, in numbers nearly identical to 2008. Their share of the electorate increased from 18 to 19 percent, and roughly 51 percent of those under 30 cast a ballot. The majority of votes went to President Obama, although he pulled a lower share of the youth vote in 2012 than in 2008 (60 percent compared to 68 percent). Researchers characterize this as the "new normal" and expect the positive turnout trend to continue in future elections as young people begin to identify voting as an expression of power.

> **Generational Effect**
> A long-lasting effect of the events of a particular time on the political opinions of those who came of political age at that time.

Political Preferences and Voting Behavior

■ **LO6.3:** Describe three forms of social media and explain how social media can shape political decisions or events.

Various socioeconomic and demographic factors appear to influence political preferences. These factors include education, income and **socioeconomic status**, religion, race, gender, geographic region, and similar traits. People who share the same religion, occupation, or any other demographic trait are likely to influence one another and may also have common political concerns that follow from the common characteristic. Other factors, such as party identification, perception of the candidates, and issue preferences, are closely connected to the electoral process.

> **Socioeconomic Status**
> The value assigned to a person due to occupation or income. An upper-class person, for example, has high socioeconomic status.

Demographic Influences

Demographic influences reflect the individual's personal background and place in society. Some factors have to do with the family into which a person was born: race and (for most people) religion. Others may be the result of choices

---

14. Cliff Zukin, Scott Keeter, Molly Andolina, Krista Jenkins, and Michael X. Delli Carpini, *A New Engagement? Political Participation, Civic Life, and the Changing American Citizen* (New York: Oxford University Press, 2006).
15. "Lagging Youth Enthusiasm Could Hurt Democrats in 2010," Pew Research Center for the People and the Press, October 7, 2010.

made throughout an individual's life: place of residence, educational achievement, and occupation.

Many of these factors are interrelated. People who have more education are likely to have higher incomes and to hold professional jobs. Similarly, children born into wealthier families are far more likely to complete college than children from poor families. Many other interrelationships are not so immediately obvious; many people might not know that 88 percent of African Americans report that religion is very important in their lives, compared with only 57 percent of whites.[16]

Education. In the past, having a college education was associated with voting for Republicans. In recent years, however, this correlation has become weaker. In particular, individuals with a postgraduate education (professors, doctors, lawyers, other managers) have become increasingly Democratic. Also, a higher percentage of voters with only a high school education, who were likely to be blue-collar workers, voted Republican in 2000 and 2004, compared with the pattern in many previous elections, in which that group of voters tended to favor Democrats. In 2012, voters with a college degree slightly favored Republican Mitt Romney over President Obama (51 percent to 47 percent). People with a high school education or less, and those with post-graduate or professional degrees, favored Obama by much larger margins. Latino voters overwhelmingly supported the reelection of President Obama by a margin of 48 percent. Support was highest among voters with a high school education or less, even though 67 percent of those with some college or a degree also supported the president.

The Influence of Economic Status. Family income is a strong predictor of economic liberalism or conservatism. Those with low incomes tend to favor government action to benefit the poor or to promote economic equality. Historically, voters in union households have voted for the Democratic candidate. Those with high incomes tend to oppose government intervention in the economy or support it only when it benefits business. On economic issues, therefore, the traditional economic spectrum described in Chapter 1 is a useful tool. The rich trend toward the right; the poor trend toward the left.

There are no hard-and-fast rules, however. Some very poor individuals are devoted Republicans, just as some extremely wealthy people support the Democratic Party. Indeed, research indicates that a realignment is occurring among those of higher economic status: professionals now tend to vote Democratic, while small-business owners, managers, and corporate executives tend to vote Republican.[17]

The combination of the prolonged economic recession and involvement in multiple conflicts overseas has reshaped the political typology, according to new research by the Pew Research Center.[18] The public's political mood is "fractious" and more unpredictable. Pew's typology divides Republicans into "Staunch Republicans" who are conservative on both economic and social issues and "Main Street Republicans"—also conservative, but less so. On the left, Pew identifies "Solid Liberals," predominantly white, who are diametrically opposed to Staunch Republicans on nearly every issue. "New Coalition Democrats" are made up of nearly equal numbers of whites, African Americans, and Hispanics and "Hard-Pressed Democrats" are highly religious and more socially conservative than Solid

16. "A Look at Americans and Religion Today," The Gallup Poll, March 23, 2004.
17. Thomas B. Edsall, "Voters Thinking Less with Their Wallets," *International Herald Tribune*, March 27, 2001, p. 3.
18. Andrew Kohut, "Beyond Red vs. Blue Political Typology," Pew Research Center for the People and the Press, May 4, 2011.

Liberals. In the center of the new political typology are the Independents, divided into three categories with little to no overlap: Libertarians, Post-Moderns, and Disaffecteds. The first two are largely white, well-educated, and affluent. Those in the Disaffected group are financially stressed and cynical about politics. Groups on the right side of the spectrum prefer elected officials who stick to their positions rather than those who compromise, while Solid Liberals overwhelmingly prefer officials who compromise. In short, the political landscape is dynamic and makes establishing electoral coalitions based on partisanship and economic status nearly impossible today.

The 2012 campaign themes emphasized the struggling economy and job creation. Republicans believed they could win votes from Independents who had been negatively impacted by the long recession. Even though 45 percent of voters labeled the state of the national economy as "not so good" in exit polls, President Obama won 55 percent of those votes. The president did even better among the 39 percent of the electorate who believed the economy was getting better (88 percent compared to 9 percent for Governor Romney). Although the economy was important to voters, their ultimate decision was based on a far more complex array of issues and factors.

Religious Influence: Denomination. Scholars have examined the impact of religion on political attitudes by dividing the population into such categories as Protestant, Catholic, and Jewish. In recent decades, however, such a breakdown has become less valuable as a means of predicting someone's political preferences. It is true that in the past, Jewish voters were notably more liberal than members of other groups on both economic and cultural issues, and they continue to be more liberal today. Persons reporting no religion are likely to be liberal on social issues but have mixed economic views. Northern Protestants and Catholics do not differ that greatly from each other, and neither do Southern Protestants and Catholics. This represents something of a change—in the late 1800s and early 1900s, Northern Protestants were distinctly more likely to vote Republican, and Northern Catholics were more likely to vote Democratic.[19] Between 2004 and 2008, nearly all religious groups moved toward the Democratic candidate Barack Obama, with the largest shifts occurring among Catholics (+7 percentage points) and those unaffiliated with any religion (+8 percentage points).[20] Support among Catholics has remained strong even in the face of controversy over contraception coverage and insurer mandates for coverage. Catholic voters favored the president by a margin of 50 to 48 percent. Although some observers speculated that white fundamentalist Protestants would not support a Mormon candidate for president, 79 percent of self-identified born-again Christians supported Governor Romney, compared to only 20 percent for Barack Obama.

Religious Influence: Religiosity and Evangelicals. Nevertheless, two factors do turn out to be major predictors of political attitudes among members of the various Christian denominations. One is the degree of *religiosity*, or intensity in practice of beliefs, and the other is whether the person holds fundamentalist or evangelical views. A high degree of religiosity is usually manifested by frequent attendance at church services

Voters who are more devout, regardless of their church affiliation, tend to vote Republican, whereas voters who are less devout are more often Democrats.

CONNECT WITH YOUR CLASSMATES
MindTap™ for American Government

Access the Public Opinion and Political Socialization Forum: Discussion—How Religion Shapes Public Opinion.

19. John C. Green, *The Faith Factor: How Religion Influences American Elections* (New York: Praeger, 2007).
20. "How the Faithful Voted," The Pew Forum on Religion and Public Life, November 5, 2008.

In 2008, people who regularly attended church, regardless of denomination, were more likely to support John McCain than Barack Obama (55 percent to 43 percent) compared with those who attended church less often (57 percent voted for Obama, while 42 percent voted for McCain). The exception to this trend is that African Americans of all religious backgrounds have been and continue to be strongly supportive of Democrats.

Another distinctive group of voters likely to be very religious are those Americans who hold fundamentalist beliefs or consider themselves part of an evangelical group. They are usually members of a Protestant church, which may be part of a mainstream denomination or of an independent congregation. In election studies, these individuals may describe themselves as "born again" and believe in the literal word of the Bible, among other characteristics. As voters, these Christians tend to be cultural conservatives but not necessarily economic conservatives.

The Influence of Race and Ethnicity. Although African Americans are, on average, somewhat conservative on certain cultural issues such as same-sex marriage and abortion, they tend to be more liberal than whites on social welfare matters, civil liberties, and even foreign policy. African Americans voted principally for Republicans (the party of Lincoln) until Democrat Franklin Roosevelt's New Deal in the 1930s. Since then, they have strongly supported the Democratic Party. Indeed, Democratic presidential candidates have received, on average, more than 80 percent of the African American vote since 1956. President Obama won 93 percent of the African American vote in 2012. Latinos also favor the Democrats. Latinos of Cuban ancestry, however, are predominantly Republican. Most Asian American groups lean toward the Democrats, although often by narrow margins. Muslim American immigrants and their descendants are an interesting category.[21] In 2000, a majority of Muslim Americans of Middle Eastern ancestry voted for Republican George W. Bush because they shared his cultural conservatism. In the 2004 and 2008 election campaigns, however, the civil liberties issue propelled many of these voters toward the Democrats.[22] In 2012, the emergence of the Latino vote, particularly in swing states, was the big story. Making up 10 percent of the national electorate, Latino voters overwhelmingly supported Barack Obama (71 percent). As the fastest growing population in the country, Latino voters can be expected to exercise greater political influence in future elections. Some experts predict that growing Latino populations will turn a traditionally red state like Texas into a battleground state. That proposition will be tested in the 2014 midterm elections prior to the next presidential race in 2016. White voters' share of the electorate continues to decline, dropping to 72 percent in 2012.

The Gender Gap. Until the 1980s, there was little evidence that men's and women's political attitudes were very different. Following the election of Ronald Reagan in 1980, however, scholars began to detect a **gender gap**. The gender gap has reappeared in subsequent presidential elections, with women being more likely than men to support the Democratic candidate (see Figure 6–4). In the 2000 elections, 54 percent of women voted for Democrat Al Gore, compared with 42 percent of men. In 2012, Barack Obama attracted 55 percent of women's votes and 45 percent of men's votes. In many ways, 2014 resembled the 2010 midterm

---

did you know?

Great Britain had a major gender gap for much of the 20th century—because women were much more likely than men to support the Conservative Party rather than the more left-wing Labour Party.

Gender Gap

The difference between the percentage of women who vote for a particular candidate and the percentage of men who vote for the candidate.

---

21. At least one-third of U.S. Muslims are actually African Americans whose ancestors have been in this country for a long time. In terms of political preferences, African American Muslims are more likely to resemble other African Americans than Muslim immigrants from the Middle East.
22. For up-to-date information on Muslim American issues, see the Web site of the Council on American-Islamic Relations at www.cair.com.

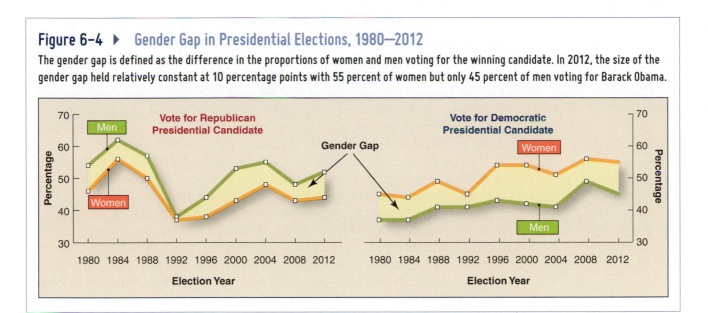

Figure 6-4 ▶ Gender Gap in Presidential Elections, 1980–2012

The gender gap is defined as the difference in the proportions of women and men voting for the winning candidate. In 2012, the size of the gender gap held relatively constant at 10 percentage points with 55 percent of women but only 45 percent of men voting for Barack Obama.

election in terms of the gender gap with men preferring Republicans by a wide margin over Democrats. In 2014, according to the exit polls, men favored Republicans by a 16-point margin (57 percent voted Republican, 41 percent for Democrats), while women voted for Democrats by a 4-point margin (51 percent to 47 percent).

Women also appear to hold different attitudes from their male counterparts on a range of issues other than presidential preferences. They are much more likely than men to oppose capital punishment and the use of force abroad. Studies also have shown that women are more concerned about risks to the environment, more supportive of social welfare, and more amenable to extending civil rights to gays and lesbians than are men. The contemporary gender gap ranges from about 7 to 12 percent. Obama won about the same proportion of women voters in 2012 as he did in 2008 (55 percent versus 54 percent), but Governor Romney fared much better among men in 2012 (52 percent) than did Senator McCain in 2008 (48 percent). Exit poll data shows some variation in the size of the gender gap in battleground states. In Iowa, the gender gap in 2012 was 15 points, whereas in Colorado there was no evidence of a gender gap. Because more women are registered to vote and more women vote than men, as a result of the gender gap, female voters can reasonably claim to have delivered victories in many electoral contests.

Reasons for the Gender Gap. What is the cause of the gender gap? A number of explanations have been offered, including the increase in the number of working women, feminism, women's concerns over abortion rights and other social issues, and the changing political attitudes of men. Researchers Lena Edlund and Rohini Pande of Columbia University, however, have identified another factor leading to the gender gap—the disparate economic impact on men and women of not being married. In the last three decades, men and women have tended to marry later in life or stay single even after having children. The divorce rate has also risen dramatically. Edlund and Pande argue that, particularly for those in the middle class, this decline in marriage has tended to make men richer and women relatively poorer. Consequently, support for Democrats is higher among single or divorced women.[23]

In 2004, observers noted that women seemed more concerned about homeland security and terrorism than men, so much so that the media coined a new

23. Lena Edlund and Rohini Pande, "Why Have Women Become Left-Wing? The Political Gender Gap and the Decline in Marriage," *The Quarterly Journal of Economics*, Vol. 117, No. 3, August 2002, pp. 917–961.

term: *security moms*. The label's origins have been traced to a poll reporting that while only 17 percent of men were personally concerned that a member of their family would be the victim of a terrorist attack, 43 percent of women and 53 percent of mothers with children under 18 expressed the same concern. Further analysis, however, found that although the Democratic candidate, John Kerry, was underperforming among female voters relative to past Democrats, "security moms" did not result in George W. Bush's victory. Researchers Laurel Elder and Steven Greene found that parenthood does not move men or women in a more conservative direction.[24] These studies suggest that labels applied to groups of voters based on demographic characteristics may not always be accurate explanations of voting behavior or political attitudes.

During the Republican presidential primaries in 2012, several issues and candidate statements became known as the "GOP War on Women." Moves to adopt increasingly severe restrictions on abortion services in several Republican-controlled states, initiatives to limit contraception insurance coverage and access, congressional budget cuts to women's health programs, and proposals to weaken the Violence Against Women Act drew lots of media attention. Sandra Fluke, then a Georgetown University law school student, was barred from testifying at a Republican congressional hearing on the Obama administration's policy requiring religiously affiliated institutions to provide free contraception in student health insurance plans. When she appeared before a House Democratic panel and testified to the difficulties female students have when reproductive services are curtailed, conservative talk-radio host Rush Limbaugh accused her of "having so much sex she can't afford the contraception," and called her a slut. Many advertisers immediately dropped his radio show, but he stayed on the air. Senate contests in Indiana and Missouri that had looked like certain wins for Republicans turned into Democratic victories over remarks about pregnancy resulting from rape. Missouri Rep. Todd Aiken claimed that "if it's a legitimate rape, the female body has ways to shut that whole thing down." In a late October debate, Republican candidate Richard Mourdock said that if a woman becomes pregnant from rape it is "something God intended to happen." Although the Romney campaign disavowed both comments, the damage compounded the Republican's image with women voters.

Geographic Region. Finally, where you live can influence your political attitudes. In one way, regional differences are less important today than just a few decades ago. The formerly solid (Democratic) South has steadily moved toward the Republican Party in national elections. Only 43 percent of the votes from the southern states went to Democrat Al Gore in 2000, while 55 percent went to Republican George W. Bush. However, Gallup poll data collected from 2008 suggest that, across all regions, the country is becoming more Democratic. In 29 states and the District of Columbia, Democrats have a 10-point or greater advantage in party affiliation. The top 10 Republican states in affiliation include only two from the South (South Carolina and Alabama), with the heaviest concentration of Republican affiliation found in Utah, Wyoming, and Idaho.[25] Because so much variability exists in political attitudes and partisan affiliation within a single state, a map constructed at the county level looks purple rather than distinctly red (representing Republicans) or blue (representing Democrats). (See Figure 6–5.)

24. Laurel Elder and Steven Greene, "The Myth of 'Security Moms' and 'NASCAR Dads'": Parenthood, Political Stereotypes, and the 2004 Election," *Social Science Quarterly*, Vol. 88, No. 1, March 2007, pp. 1–19.
25. Jeffrey M. Jones, "State of the State: Party Affiliation," Gallup, January 28, 2009.

Figure 6-5 ▶ **The Purple Election Map**

We have grown used to seeing the national vote portrayed using the electoral college map (see, for example, Figure 8-2 on page 279). Because the states are colored red or blue depending on which party's candidate receives the majority of votes, it appears as if all voters in the state are either Republicans (red) or Democrats (blue). Of course, we know that this is not true. Republican and Democratic voters are in every state, and states are broken down into smaller counties, where the diversity is even more apparent. One way to reveal more accurately the nuance in the vote is to use red, blue, and shades of purple to indicate percentages of votes that each party's candidate receives at the county level. In this way, the diversity of political affiliation within states is more visible. Areas that appear purple represent more balance between Republicans and Democrats.

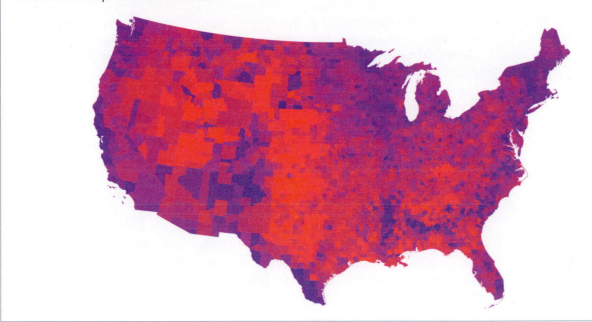

Measuring Public Opinion

■ **LO6.5:** Identify three factors that might distort public opinion results collected through opinion polling.

In a democracy, people express their opinions in a variety of ways. One of the most common means of gathering and measuring public opinion on specific issues is, of course, through the use of **opinion polls**.

The History of Opinion Polls

During the 1800s, certain American newspapers and magazines spiced up their political coverage by doing face-to-face straw polls (unofficial polls indicating the trend of political opinion) or mail surveys of their readers' opinions. In the early twentieth century, the magazine *Literary Digest* further developed the technique of opinion polling by mailing large numbers of questionnaires to individuals, many of whom were subscribers, to determine their political opinions. From 1916 to 1936, more than 70 percent of the magazine's election predictions were accurate.

Literary Digest's polling activities suffered a setback in 1936, however, when the magazine predicted, based on more than 2 million returned questionnaires, that Republican candidate Alfred Landon would win over Democratic candidate Franklin D. Roosevelt. Landon won in only two states. A major problem with the *Digest*'s polling technique was its use of nonrepresentative respondents. In 1936, at possibly the worst point of the Great Depression, the magazine's subscribers were considerably more affluent than the average American. In other words, they did not accurately represent all of the voters in the U.S. population.

Opinion Polls
A method of systematically questioning a small, selected sample of respondents who are deemed representative of the total population.

Several newcomers to the public opinion poll industry accurately predicted Roosevelt's landslide victory. The Gallup poll founded by George Gallup and the Roper poll founded by Elmo Roper are still active today. Gallup and Roper, along with Archibald Crossley, developed the modern polling techniques of market research. Using personal interviews with small samples of selected voters (fewer than 2,000), they showed that they could predict with accuracy the behavior of the total voting population.

By the 1950s, improved methods of sampling and a new science of survey research had been developed. Survey research centers sprang up throughout the United States, particularly at universities. Some of these survey groups are the American Institute of Public Opinion at Princeton, in New Jersey; the National Opinion Research Center at the University of Chicago; and the Survey Research Center at the University of Michigan.

Sampling Techniques

How can interviewing fewer than 2,000 voters tell us what tens of millions of voters will do? Clearly, it is necessary that the sample of individuals be representative of all voters in the population. Consider an analogy: Let's say we have a large jar containing 10,000 pennies of various dates, and we want to know how many pennies were minted within certain decades (1960–1969, 1970–1979, and so on).

Representative Sampling. One way to estimate the distribution of the dates on the pennies—without examining all 10,000—is to take a representative sample. This sample would be obtained by mixing the pennies up well and then removing a handful of them—perhaps 100 pennies. The distribution of dates might be as follows:

> 1960–1969: 5 percent
> 1970–1979: 5 percent
> 1980–1989: 20 percent
> 1990–1999: 30 percent
> 2000–present: 40 percent

If the pennies are very well mixed within the jar, and if you take a large enough sample, the resulting distribution will probably approach the actual distribution of the dates of all 10,000 coins.

The Principle of Randomness. The most important principle in sampling, or poll taking, is randomness. Every penny or every person should have a known chance, and especially an *equal chance*, of being sampled. If this happens, then a small sample should be representative of the whole group, both in demographic characteristics (age, religion, race, region, and the like) and in opinions. The ideal way to sample the voting population of the United States would be to put all voter names into a jar—or a computer—and randomly sample, say, 2,000 of them. Because this is too costly and inefficient, pollsters have developed other ways to obtain good samples. One technique is simply to choose a random selection of telephone numbers and interview the respective households. Prior to expanded cell phone use, this technique produced a relatively accurate sample at a low cost. In 2013, however, the proportion of people living in households without a landline grew to two in five (40 percent).[26] While you might hypothesize that the highest

---

26. National Health Statistics Reports, "Wireless Substitution: State-Level Estimates From the National Health Interview Survey, 2012." December 18, 2013. Accessed at http://www.cdc.gov/nchs/data/nhsr/nhsr070.pdf

number of cell-only households would be found in large cities, it is actually the opposite. The prevalence of cell-only households is highest in Idaho (52.3 percent) and lowest in New Jersey (19.4 percent). For certain subgroups within the population the proportions are even higher; 60 percent of Latinos are cell-only, as are 54 percent of adults ages 18 to 24 and 66 percent of adults between the ages of 25 and 29. The percentage of households with only a landline continues to decrease but is estimated at about 8 percent. Only 2 percent of the U.S. population cannot be reached by a phone of any kind.

These rapid changes in use of phone technology increase the risk for "coverage error;" that is, the bias introduced when some portion of the population is not covered by the sample. If those missed in the sample differ substantially from those covered, the bias can lead to errors in reporting the results (similar to the *Literary Digest* example). Whereas research in 2006 found that the likelihood of coverage bias in landline phone surveys was very small, a new study released by the Pew Research Center indicates that the size of the bias effect is increasing, as well as the likelihood of substantive consequences for social and political research reports.[27] Researchers continue to examine these issues as they develop new techniques such as address-based sampling frames to ensure that every person has a known and equal chance at being sampled. Yet, a majority of households now use either caller ID or some other form of call screening. This has greatly reduced the number of households that polling organizations can reach. Calls may be automatically rejected, or the respondent may not take the call. Even when reached, researchers face additional challenges as fewer adults agree to be interviewed. According to the Pew Research Center, the percentage of households in a sample that are successfully interviewed has fallen dramatically.[28]

To ensure that the random samples include respondents from relevant segments of the population—rural, urban, northeastern, southern, and so on—most survey organizations randomly choose, say, urban areas that they will consider as representative of all urban areas. Then they randomly select their respondents within those areas. A generally less accurate technique is known as *quota sampling*. Here, survey researchers decide how many persons of certain types they need in the survey—such as minorities, women, or farmers—and then send out interviewers to find the necessary number of these types. Not only is this method often less accurate, but it also may be biased if, say, the interviewer refuses to go into certain neighborhoods or will not interview after dark.

Generally, the national survey organizations take great care to select their samples randomly, because their reputations rest on the accuracy of their results. The Gallup and Roper polls usually interview about 1,500 individuals, and their results have a very high probability of being correct—within a margin of 3 percentage points.

Problems with Polls

Public opinion polls are snapshots of the opinions and preferences of the people at a specific moment in time and as expressed in response to a specific question. Given that definition, it is fairly easy to imagine situations in which the polls are wrong.

did you know?

In 2014, response rates for landline telephone surveys fell to 10 percent—only 3 points higher than for cell phone surveys.

COMPARE WITH YOUR PEERS

MindTap for American Government

Access the Public Opinion and Political Socialization Forum: Polling Activity—New York Times Instant Polls.

---

27. "Assessing the Cell Phone Challenge to Survey Research in 2010," Pew Research Center for the People and the Press, May 20, 2010.
28. "Assessing the Representativeness of Public Opinion Surveys." Pew Research Center for the People and the Press, May 15, 2012. Accessed at: http://www.people-press.org/2012/05/15/assessing-the-representativeness-of-public-opinion-surveys/

did you know?

Because of scientific sampling techniques, public opinion pollsters can typically measure national sentiment among the roughly 315 million adult Americans by interviewing only about 1,500 people.

Sampling Error
The difference between a sample's results and the true result if the entire population had been interviewed.

Sampling Errors. Polls may also report erroneous results because the pool of respondents was not chosen in a scientific manner; that is, the form of sampling and the number of people sampled may be too small to overcome **sampling error**, the difference between the sample result and the true result if the entire population had been interviewed. The sample would be biased, for example, if the poll interviewed people by telephone and did not correct for the fact that more women than men answer the telephone and that some populations (college students and very poor individuals, for example) cannot be found so easily by telephone. Unscientific mail-in polls, telephone call-in polls, Internet polls, and polls completed by the workers in a campaign office are not scientific and do not give an accurate picture of the public's views.

As pollsters get close to election day, they become even more concerned about their sample of respondents. Some continue to interview eligible voters (those over age 18 and registered to vote). Many others use a series of questions and other weighting methods to try to identify "likely voters" so that they can be more accurate in their election predictions. When a poll changes its method from reporting the views of eligible voters to reporting those of likely voters, the results tend to change dramatically.

Poll Questions. It makes sense to expect that the results of a poll will depend on the questions asked. One problem with many polls is the yes/no answer format. Suppose the poll question asks, "Do you favor or oppose the war in Iraq?" Respondents might wish to answer that they favored the war at the beginning but not as it wore on for several years, or that they favor fighting terrorism but not a military occupation. They have no way of indicating their true position with a yes or no answer. Respondents also are sometimes swayed by the inclusion of certain words in a question: More respondents will answer in the affirmative if the

President Harry Truman holds up the front page of the Chicago Daily Tribune issue that predicted his defeat on the basis of a Gallup poll. The poll had indicated that Truman would lose the 1948 contest for his reelection by a margin of 55.5 to 44.5 percent. The Gallup poll was completed more than a week before the election, so it missed a shift by undecided voters to Truman.

question asks, "Do you favor or oppose the war in Iraq as a means of fighting terrorism?" Respondents' answers are also influenced by the order in which questions are asked, by the possible answers from which they are allowed to choose, and, in some cases, by their interaction with the interviewer. To a certain extent, people try to please the interviewer. They answer questions about which they have no information and avoid some answers to try to measure up to the interviewer's expectations.

Push Polls. Some campaigns have begun using "push polls," in which the respondents are given misleading information in the questions asked in order to persuade them to vote against a candidate. The interviewer might ask, "Do you approve or disapprove of Congressman Smith, who voted to raise your taxes 22 times?" Obviously, the answers given are likely to be influenced by such techniques. Push polls have been condemned by the polling industry and are considered to be unethical, but they are still used. In the 2000 Republican Party primary in South Carolina, for example, voters were asked, "Would you be more likely or less likely to vote for John McCain for president if you knew he had fathered an illegitimate black child?" Although no basis existed for the substance of the question, and George W. Bush's campaign disavowed any connection to the calls, thousands of Republican primary voters heard a message obviously designed to *push* them away from candidate McCain. In 2008, Jewish voters in Florida and Pennsylvania were targets of a push poll linking Barack Obama to the Palestine Liberation Organization. Other than complaining to the media about such efforts, candidates are largely defenseless against this abuse of polling. Because of these problems with polls, you need to be especially careful when evaluating poll results.

Technology, Public Opinion, and the Political Process

■ **LO6.5:** Identify three factors that might distort public opinion results collected through opinion polling.

Ironically, technological advances in communication have made gathering public opinion data more difficult in some ways. Federal law prohibits any sort of unsolicited calls to cell phones using "automated dialing devices" and because virtually all pollsters now conduct surveys using computerized systems, this presents a problem. Yet while cell phones make it easier for people to decline to be interviewed, they may also open new avenues to political participation.

Public Opinion and the Political Process

Public opinion affects the political process in many ways. Whether in office or in the midst of a campaign, politicians see public opinion as important to their success. The president, members of Congress, governors, and other elected officials realize that strong public support as expressed in opinion polls is a source of power in dealing with other politicians. It is far more difficult for a senator to say no to the president if the president is immensely popular and if polls show approval of the president's policies. Public opinion also helps candidates identify the most important concerns among the people and may help them shape their campaigns successfully.

During the presidential primary contests, polling becomes extremely important. Individuals who would like to make a campaign contribution to their favorite candidate may decide not to if the polls show that the candidate is unlikely to win. Voters do not want to waste their votes on the primary candidates who are doing poorly in the polls. In 2008, the two leading Democratic candidates, Senators Barack Obama and Hillary Clinton, used poll results to try to convince convention delegates of their respective strengths as the party nominee, hoping to influence primaries late in the calendar prior to heading into the party convention. Polls indicating strong voter support are also helpful in attracting financial contributions to a campaign.

Nevertheless, surveys of public opinion are not equivalent to elections in the United States. Although opinion polls may influence political candidates or elected officials, elections are the major vehicle through which Americans express preferences that can bring about change.

Political Culture and Public Opinion

Given the diversity of American society and the wide range of opinions contained within it, how is it that the political process continues to function without being stalemated by conflict and dissension? One explanation is rooted in the concept of the American political culture, which can be described as a set of attitudes and ideas about the nation and the government. Our political culture is widely shared by Americans of many different backgrounds. The elements of our political culture include certain shared beliefs about the most important values in the American political system, including (1) liberty, equality, and property; (2) support for religious freedom; and (3) community service and personal achievement. The structure of the government—particularly federalism, separation of powers, and popular rule—is also an important value. When people share certain beliefs about the system and a reservoir of good feeling exists toward the institutions of government, the nation will be better able to weather periods of crisis. Such was the case after the 2000 presidential elections when, for several weeks, it was not certain who the next president would be and how that determination would be made. At the time, some argued that the nation was facing a true constitutional crisis. In fact, however, the broad majority of Americans did not believe that the uncertain outcome of the elections had created a constitutional crisis. Polls taken during this time found that, on the contrary, most Americans were confident in our political system's ability to decide the issue peaceably and in a lawful manner.[29]

Political Trust and Support for the Political System.

The political culture also helps Americans evaluate their government's performance. At times in our history, **political trust** in government has reached relatively high levels. At other times, political trust in government has fallen to low levels. For example, in the 1960s and 1970s, during the Vietnam War and the Watergate scandals, surveys showed that the overall level of political trust in government had declined steeply. Today people are expressing historically high levels of mistrust in government.[30] Americans' satisfaction with the way the nation is being governed has reached an all-time low (see Figure 6–6). Anger over the government shutdown in October 2013, the repeated trips to the fiscal cliff as lawmakers in Congress argue over raising the debt ceiling, and the botched roll-out of healthcare.gov are all contributing

Political Trust

The degree to which individuals express trust in the government and political institutions, usually measured through a specific series of survey questions.

29. As reported in *Public Perspective*, March/April 2002, p. 11, summarizing the results of Gallup/CNN/*USA Today* polls conducted between November 11 and December 10, 2000.
30. Gallup's annual Governance survey, updated Sept.2013. . Accessed at http://www.gallup.com/poll/5392/trust-government.aspx

Figure 6-6 ▶ Reaction to How the Nation Is Being Governed

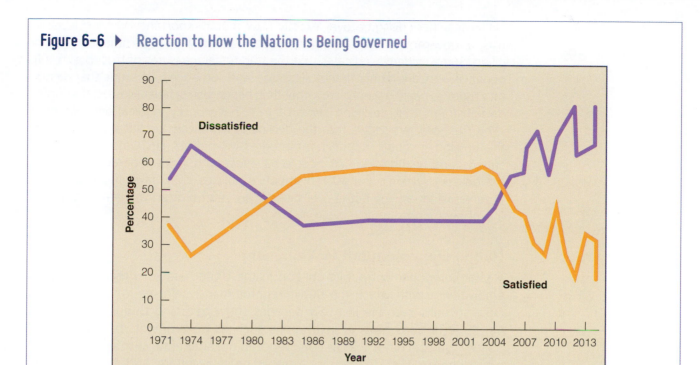

http://www.gallup.com/poll/165371/americans-satisfaction-gov-drops-new-low.aspx

factors. Civic frustration might also be attributed to divided power in Washington—with Democrats controlling the White House and U.S. Senate and Republicans controlling the House of Representatives, very little policy has been accomplished. The 113th Congress (2013–2014) is likely to be the least productive in decades. In the first half of the session (2013), Congress enacted only 55 substantive bills and met for the fewest number of hours since 2005, when such records were first filed. Polls show record or near-record criticism of Congress, elected officials, government handling of domestic problems, the scope of government power, and government waste of tax dollars. Fifty-three percent of Americans believe the federal government has become so large and powerful that it poses an immediate threat to the rights and freedoms of ordinary citizens. In May 1995, a little more than a third (36 percent) of the American public expressed this belief.[31] What does this indicate about the strength and viability of our shared political culture?

How much confidence should we have in the opinions expressed by the public? This cartoonist believes that the public is gullible and not to be trusted. What about you? Do you trust the information reported in polls? Should policymakers rely on polls when deciding the direction of the country?

31. "Majority Says the Federal Government Threatens Their Personal Rights," Pew Research Center for the People and the Press, January 31, 2013. Accessed at http://www.people-press.org/2013/01/31/majority-says-the-federal-government-threatens-their-personal-rights/

Researchers disagree over exactly how much importance varying levels of trust in government and generalized dissatisfaction with government should be given. Some evidence indicates that the traditional measures of trust bias results negatively (trust is higher than polls show), and some scholars argue that democracy requires healthy skepticism rather than blind trust. Scholar Marc Hetherington demonstrates that declining levels of trust have policy implications. His book *Why Trust Matters* shows that the decline in Americans' political trust explains the erosion in public support for progressive policies such as welfare, food stamps, and health care.[32] As people have lost faith in the federal government, the delivery system for most redistributive policies, they have also lost faith in progressive ideas. The battle over health-care reform offers a recent example of this phenomenon.

Public Opinion about Government

A vital component of public opinion in the United States is the considerable ambivalence with which the public regards many major national institutions. Opinion polls over the last few decades show declining trends in the confidence Americans have in institutions such as government, banks, and the police. The concern is that as confidence in government institutions falls, people will be less likely to embrace a shared political culture, adopt shared norms of political behavior, and as a consequence feel less constrained by government decisions. It also means that fewer people will feel compelled to serve in public office. A July 2013 Gallup poll found that 64 percent of Americans would not like their child to go into politics as a career. Unfortunately, young people express little interest in a career in politics. As Richard Fox and Jennifer Lawless noted in a *Washington Post* opinion essay, "Our political system is built on the premise that running for office is something that a broad group of citizens should want to do. . . . if the best and brightest of future generations neither hear nor heed the call to public service, then the quality of U.S. democracy may be compromised."[33] In their survey of high school and college students conducted during the 2012 presidential election, only 11 percent said that they might consider running for political office someday. When presented with choices of careers in business, law, education, sales, and government—government came in last every time. Being a member of Congress was deemed least desirable of all.

Polling organizations regularly ask Americans to name the most important problem facing the country. Figure 6–7 reflects Gallup polls conducted from the years 2001 to 2014. It shows the relative importance Americans place on the economy versus other problems like dissatisfaction with government, health care, and education, among others. In 2014 (March), noneconomic problems had a slight edge over economic problems reflecting the overall improvement in the economy. The public emphasizes problems that are immediate and that have been the subject of many stories in the media. When coverage of a particular problem increases suddenly, the public is more likely to see that as the most important problem. Note the dramatic increase in attention to the economy and economic issues and corresponding decrease in attention to

32. Marc J. Hetherington, *Why Trust Matters: Declining Political Trust and the Demise of American Liberalism* (Princeton, NJ: Princeton University Press, 2006).

33. Richard L. Fox and Jennifer L. Lawless, "Turning Off the Next Generation of Politicians" *The Washington Post*, November 22, 2013. Accessed at http://www.washingtonpost.com/opinions/turning-off-the-next-generation-of-politicians/2013/11/22/b98d1b80-52db-11e3-9e2c-e1d01116fd98_story.html

Figure 6-7 ▶ **Perceived Most Important Problem Facing the U.S**

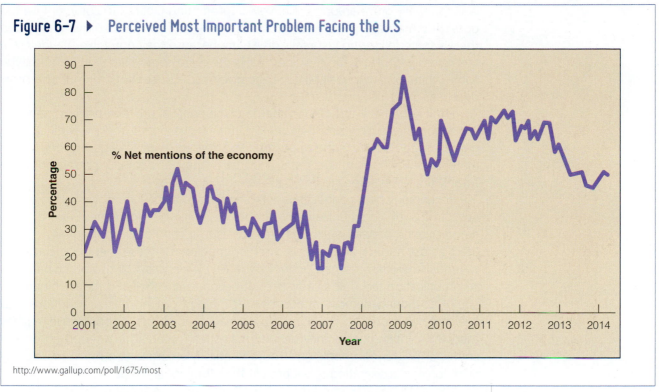

http://www.gallup.com/poll/1675/most

noneconomic issues that correlates directly with the onset of the global recession in 2008 and 2009.

When government does not respond adequately to a crisis, public reaction is swift and negative. President George W. Bush's approval rating dropped precipitously following Hurricane Katrina because the majority of the public lacked confidence in the government's response to the devastating Gulf Coast hurricane. African Americans, in particular, believed the government would have responded more quickly if those affected by the storm had been wealthy and primarily white.[34] Similarly, as the economy faltered in the latest recession, individuals, businesses, and even the states looked to the federal government for answers and assistance. When an explosion at an offshore drilling rig operated by British Petroleum (BP) dumped unprecedented amounts of oil into the Gulf, the Obama administration took action to coordinate relief and cleanup efforts, but still received criticism because it could not plug the leak. While Congress is best suited to investigate the nature of the problem, the president is best able to take action by mobilizing the resources of the federal bureaucracy. The implementation of the Affordable Care Act got off to a very rocky start in October 2013 when the central website designed to connect Americans with health insurance options crashed repeatedly. The president had promised people that if they were happy with their current health-care plans they would be able to keep them, but in many cases that turned out not to be the case because the plans did not meet the minimum coverage criteria in the new law. In November 2013, a majority of Americans (54 percent) told pollsters at Quinnipiac University that the president is not honest and trustworthy—a first for President Obama.[35] Obama's drop in the polls in 2013

34. Michael A. Fletcher and Richard Morin, "Bush's Approval Rating Drops to New Low in Wake of Storm," *The Washington Post*, September 13, 2005.
35. Ashley Killough, "Poll: Obama Approval Ratings Drop, Americans Say He's Not Trustworthy." CNN Politics, November 12, 2013. Accessed at http://politicalticker.blogs.cnn.com/2013/11/12/poll-obama-approval-ratings-drop-americans-say-hes-not-trustworthy/

was especially grave among white voters, prompting Obama to comment on the possibility that race plays a role in his approval ratings: "There's no doubt that there's some folks who just really dislike me because they don't like the idea of a black president. Now the flip side of it is there are some black folks and maybe some white folks who really like me and give me the benefit of the doubt precisely because I'm a black president."[36]

How individuals and groups approach the political process has a tremendous impact on the country's ability to deal with new challenges, resolve conflicts, and guarantee to all citizens the opportunities afforded by peace and prosperity. The material reviewed in this chapter provides some basis for optimism about the future, but raises some caution flags as well.

Technology now connects us as a people in powerful new ways. Harnessing new forms of communication to promote political engagement, particularly among young people, is exciting. Yet access to technology is not equally distributed across society and, if not carefully monitored, these inequities have the potential to widen the gap between the two Americas. On the other hand, as communication technology advances, it becomes cheaper and more ubiquitous. The Arab Spring demonstrated how technology can advance revolutions and coalesce public opinion in support of new leaders and ideas. As oppressive regimes tried to maintain power, they banned mainstream media from reporting on the conflicts. Twitter, Facebook, and YouTube quickly emerged as a much more powerful force in accelerating social protest than traditional media.

Closer to home we find that lots of Americans use social networks and that participants in social networking sites mirror the active and inactive political public in several ways. Those most likely to use social networks to urge political action are found at the farthest ends of the liberal and conservative spectrum—those most activated by their political ideologies. In this respect, they are no different from partisan activists. Political candidates, campaigns, and political organizations are actively reaching out to supporters and likely voters using all of the newest forms of communication technology. Campaign 2012 demonstrated that comfort with social media is key to reaching voters who do not watch television or read newspapers, particularly young voters. Twitter reported that people sent 31 million election-related Tweets on Election Day 2012 alone (a 94 percent increase over Election Day 2008). President Obama announced his victory with a Tweet that was re-tweeted over 714,000 times. Traditional network media outlets cited people's Tweets as evidence of voting trends on live television. Facebook was joined by tumblr, Spotify, Pinterest, and Instagram in extending the candidates' messages and images to voters. As these technologies mature and become more integrated into our daily lives, it remains important to carefully assess their impact on our political culture, shared values, and identity as a nation.

36. David Remnick, "Going the Distance: On and Off the Road with Barack Obama." *The New Yorker*, January 27, 2014. Accessed at http://www.newyorker.com/reporting/2014/01/27/140127fa_fact_remnick?currentPage=all

What Would You Do?

Can America's Social Contract Survive the Strain?

English social contract theorists such as Thomas Hobbes (1588–1679) and John Locke (1632–1704) were influential in shaping the political culture of America. Social contract theory posits that political communities are formed by a process of mutual consent whereby individuals agree to relinquish a degree of personal liberty in order to gain the protections inherent in solidarity with others. Governments are formed in support of this mutual pledge. Individuals enter the social contract on an equal footing because "all Men are created equal" and "endowed by their Creator with certain unalienable rights…" Thus equality, liberty, and opportunity are fundamental to the American Creed and to our shared understanding of the social contract.

In the 1930s and again in the 1960s the social contract was tested by circumstances beyond an individual's ability to prevail. At the height of the Great Depression unemployment rates reached 25 percent—11 million people were looking for work. Franklin D. Roosevelt's administration created a number of public works projects to put people to work (e.g., Civilian Conservation Corps, Tennessee Valley Authority, Federal Emergency Relief Administration, and the Works Progress Administration). Social insurance through the Social Security Act of 1935 provided a start to the social safety net that remains today—unemployment insurance, a pension for the elderly, aid to dependent children, death benefits, and so on. Roosevelt called the initiative a "safeguard against misfortunes which cannot be wholly eliminated in this manmade world of ours."* In the 1960s a modest health insurance program was added to America's social insurance portfolio in the form of Medicare and Medicaid.

Why Should You Care?

Americans believe that the U.S. economic system favors the wealthy (by a margin of 55 to 39 percent) and that the rich are getting richer (76 percent). Yet people remain unsure whether or not their personal fate will be any worse as a result of the poor economy. A strong belief that opportunity will prevail in the face of adversity limits American support for greater government involvement in shrinking income inequality.** This attitude stands in stark contrast to that of many Europeans, who enjoy more generous social support but believe it should be even greater. By large margins, Americans believe programs like Medicare, Social Security, Medicaid, and unemployment insurance should be maintained. However, partisan differences are widening when it comes to government's responsibility to care for the poor and about whether government should help the poor even if doing so adds to the national debt. Majorities of Republicans now say they disagree that the government should guarantee every citizen enough to eat and a place to sleep (63 percent disagree) while three-fourths of Democrats believe it is important for government to do so. This divergent opinion might stem from an overwhelming sense that government does an ineffective job at helping poor and middle class Americans—a view held by four in five Americans. Just 35 percent of Americans today believe that government should play an active role in society, while 58 percent say that everyone should be free to pursue their life's goals without interference from the state.

What Would You Do?

As president, how would you begin to restore faith in the bond between citizens and the government?

What You *Can* Do

As a result of the Great Recession of 2008, roughly 8.7 million Americans lost their jobs. Those who found new jobs quickly did so at a price—on average they earned 17 percent less than in their previous job. A decline in median earnings since 1970 means that the median earner in 2010 earned as much as the median earner in 1964.

These questions are important for you to consider and discuss with your family and friends.

- For more information, visit the Next Social Contract Initiative, a project of the New America Foundation: www.newamerica.net. Learn more about the attitudes of the Millennial Generation through "The Next America" series sponsored by the Pew Research Center: www.pewsocialtrends.org/2014/03/07/millennials-in-adulthood/.

---

* Jo Anne B. Ross, "Fifty Years of Service to Children and Their Families." Social Security Bulletin, October 1985. Accessed at http://www.ssa.gov/policy/docs/ssb/v48n10/v48n10p5.pdf.
** Leslie McCall, *The Undeserving Rich: American Beliefs about Inequality, Opportunity, and Redistribution."* New York: Cambridge University Press, 2013.

Key Terms

Chapter Summary

■ **LO6.1:** Public opinion is defined as the aggregate of individual attitudes or beliefs shared by some portion of the adult population. A consensus exists when a large proportion of the public appears to express the same view on an issue. Divisive opinion exists when the public holds widely different attitudes on an issue. Sometimes, a poll shows a distribution of opinion, indicating that most people either have no information about an issue or are not interested enough in the issue to form a position on it. Public opinion impacts government actions by providing support for elected officials to adopt or fail to adopt policies. Public opinion can limit government activity if officials are unclear about the direction a majority of Americans support or if opinion is divided and the safest course of action is no action at all.

■ **LO6.2:** People's opinions are formed through the political socialization process. Important factors in this process are the family, educational experiences, peer groups, opinion leaders, the media, and political events. The influence of the media as a socialization factor may be growing relative to the family. Voting behavior is influenced by demographic factors such as education, economic status, religion, race and ethnicity, gender, and region. It is also influenced by election-specific factors such as party identification, perception of the candidates, and issue preferences.

■ **LO6.3:** Technology is changing the way we communicate with one another. YouTube, Twitter, Instagram, and Facebook make it possible to share information with millions of people instantly. Social media have the power to shape political events (such as the Arab Spring uprisings) and influence support for or opposition to a political candidate. Candidates may learn too late that gaffes last in perpetuity because of new media. Republican presidential hopeful Rick Perry never recovered from his debate performances that were shared via Facebook and repeated endlessly on late-night comedy shows and on YouTube.

■ **LO6.4:** Public opinion also plays an important role in domestic and foreign policymaking. Although polling data show that a majority of Americans would like policy leaders to be influenced to a great extent by public opinion, politicians cannot always be guided by opinion polls. This is because the respondents often do not understand the costs and consequences of policy decisions or the trade-offs involved in making such decisions. Similarly, the actions of U.S. government officials can be encouraged or constrained by world opinion.

■ **LO6.5:** Most descriptions of public opinion are based on the results of opinion polls. The accuracy of polls depends on sampling techniques that include a representative sample of the population being polled and ensure randomness in the selection of respondents. Problems with polls include sampling errors (which may occur when the pool of respondents is not chosen in a scientific manner), the difficulty of knowing the degree to which responses are influenced by the type and order of questions asked, the use of a yes/no format for answers, and the interviewer's techniques. Many are concerned about the use of "push polls" (in which the questions "push" the respondent toward a particular candidate).

■ Selected Print, Media, and Online Resources

PRINT RESOURCES

Dalton, Russell J. *The Good Citizen: How a Younger Generation Is Reshaping American Politics.* Washington, DC: CQ Press, 2009. Despite the conventional wisdom that young people are politically disengaged, this book argues that in many ways today's youth are more engaged than those of previous generations, although the forms of engagement differ. Using public opinion surveys and other empirical research, Dalton analyzes modern citizenship norms that move away from duty-based engagement toward a more encompassing version of civic engagement.

Newsom, Gavin with Lisa Dickey. *Citizenville: How to Take the Town Square Digital and Reinvent Government.* New York: Penguin Books, 2013. Newsom, the Lt. Governor of California argues that it is imperative to bring government into the digital age so that citizens can engage and enact change to improve communities.

Sapiro, Virginia. "Not Your Parents' Political Socialization: Introduction for a New Generation." *Annual Review of Political Science.* 2004: 7: 1–23. This article reviews the newest research and research questions related to political socialization.

Smith, Christian. *Lost In Transition: The Dark Side of Emerging Adulthood.* New York: Oxford University Press, 2011. Based on over 200 in-depth interviews, this research explores the newest trends in the transition from adolescence to adulthood in the United States. Young people are waiting longer to marry, to have children, and to choose a career direction. The civic and social consequences for these trends are also addressed.

MEDIA RESOURCES

56 Up—The "Up Series" is a British documentary project that in 1964 began chronicling the lives of several 7-year-olds from a variety of economic backgrounds and has re-interviewed them every seven years since. 56 Up was released in 2013.

Blame It on Fidel—A 2007 French film in which Anna, a nine-year-old girl, must figure out her own beliefs in the confusion created as her parents become increasingly radicalized. This coming of age film explores themes of stereotyping, misinformation, the power of ideologies, and idealism.

Wag the Dog—A 1997 film that provides a very cynical look at the importance of public opinion. The film, which features Dustin Hoffman and Robert De Niro, follows the efforts of a presidential political consultant, who stages a foreign policy crisis to divert public opinion from a sex scandal in the White House.

ONLINE RESOURCES

Corporation for National and Community Service—a federal agency that engages more than 5 million Americans in service through its AmeriCorps, Senior Corps, Social Innovation Fund, and Volunteer Generation Fund programs, and leads the President's national call to service initiative, United We Serve: www.NationalService.gov.

Gallup—a polling organization that has studied human attitudes and behavior for over 75 years. Although some of the data is only available by subscription, the Gallup Daily News regularly provides information and statistics on a variety of issues and current events: www.gallup.com.

Latino Decisions—conducts state-level polls, primarily in states with high Latino populations, to inform candidates and policymakers about concerns in the Latino community: www.latinodecisions.wordpress.com/.

Pew Forum on Religion and Public Life—part of the Pew Research Center, this forum conducts surveys, demographic analyses, and other social science research on important aspects of religion and public life in the United States and around the world, in addition to providing a neutral venue for discussions of timely issues through round-tables and briefings: www.pewforum.org/.

Real Clear Politics (RCP)—daily digest of poll results, election analysis, and political commentary as well as an archive of past political polls: www.realclearpolitics.com.

Master the concept of Public Opinion and Political Socialization with MindTap for American Government

REVIEW MindTap for American Government
Access Key Term Flashcards for Chapter 6.

TEST YOURSELF MindTap for American Government
Take the Wrap It Up Quiz for Chapter 6.

STAY CURRENT MindTap for American Government
Access the KnowNow blog and customized RSS for updates on current events.

STAY FOCUSED MindTap for American Government
Complete the Focus Activities for Public Opinion and Political Socialization.

7 Interest Groups

LEARNING OUTCOMES

After reading this chapter, students will be able to:

- **LO7.1:** Define an interest group and explain the constitutional and political reasons why so many groups are found in the United States.

- **LO7.2:** Explain why an individual may or may not decide to join an interest group and the benefits that membership can confer.

- **LO7.3:** Describe different types of interest groups and the sources of their political power.

- **LO7.4:** Identify the direct and indirect techniques that interest groups use to influence government decisions.

- **LO7.5:** Describe the legislation which regulates the reporting of lobbying efforts at the federal level and discuss why it is relatively ineffective.

WATCH & LEARN MindTap™ for American Government

Watch a brief "What Do You Know?" video summarizing Interest Groups.

All Interest Groups Were Regulated by the Government?

BACKGROUND

All it takes to start an interest group is inviting other people who share a common concern to join you to study a given problem or to take action to influence the government on a particular issue. You can meet in your home or at a coffee shop or the public library. You can write letters to your congressperson or the president, or you can start a website promoting your interests. You can collect money for the effort or ask people to donate their time to the cause. All of these activities are protected by the First Amendment to the Constitution and need not involve any level of governmental oversight.

WHAT IF THE GOVERNMENT REGULATED ALL INTEREST GROUPS?

What if, when you started your group, you needed to get a license and report your group to the government? What if, when you contacted the public library to reserve a room, the librarian said, "What is your group's ID number? Do you have a license?" Americans currently join more interest groups than citizens of any other country. Would federal regulations such as these discourage Americans from forming groups and limit their right to express themselves?

Currently, some aspects of interest groups are regulated, primarily through the Internal Revenue Service (IRS) code and the limits placed on campaign contributions. If an interest group wants to accept donations to be tax deductible for the donor, it must prove that it is a nonprofit group. In that case, the group is severely restricted in its ability to take political action. Such a nonprofit group must file a specific form with the IRS every year, indicating its financial status and how it meets other requirements. Currently, groups that own property are permitted to seek nonprofit status to avoid paying local property taxes. Most religious institutions have this status.

Today, if your new interest group wants to hold a protest, some laws do apply. If your university or local government has a designated free speech zone, you may be able to speak and hold a protest without permissions needed. Anti-abortion interest groups have regularly protested outside of Planned Parenthood centers. While the institutions and local governments have tried to restrain such protests, generally the Supreme Court has held that only restrictions based on safety concerns can be enforced. On the other hand, if you want to march down the street or pitch your tents on a public plaza, you will most likely need a permit.

Most interest groups in the United States, whether nonprofit or for profit, exist without much government supervision. What would happen, though, if every interest group with 25 or more members were required to register with the government and report every contribution? Such regulations would require reporting the names of all group members and, most likely, their Social Security numbers, so that the IRS could make sure they were not avoiding taxes on their income. Once the group was registered, it could have access to public spaces for meetings and other public services, much like student groups that form on a campus.

WHAT WOULD BE THE IMPACT ON DEMOCRACY?

Regulating interest groups would be a huge, but not impossible, task for the government. Such regulation would have a chilling effect on free speech and the right to assembly in the United States. Individuals whose views are out of the mainstream or who are simply in the minority would be less likely to join groups and to take public action. Fewer groups would form, and there would be a great advantage for the larger, highly organized interest groups in society. James Madison's fear that the majority could override the interests of minorities (Federalist #10), might come true. Social scientists have long known that the voices of elites in government and in interest groups get more attention than do the voices of minorities, the poor, and new grassroots groups. As existing groups dominated political decision making, new views would have a difficult time finding a forum, and democratic debate would be diminished.

For Critical Analysis

1. *Could the government regulate groups more closely without violating the Constitution and the Bill of Rights?*

2. *Would you be more or less likely to join a group if your name would be supplied to local or federal government authorities?*

LISTEN & LEARN

MindTap for American Government

Access Read Speaker to listen to Chapter 7.

Interest Groups

An organized group of individuals sharing common objectives who actively attempt to influence policymakers.

Lobbyist

An organization or individual who attempts to influence legislation and the administrative decisions of government.

DOCTORS, INSURANCE COMPANIES, college students, oil companies, environmentalists, the elderly, African American organizations, Native American tribes, small businesses, unions, gay and lesbian groups, and foreign governments all try to influence the political leaders and policymaking processes of the United States. The structure of American government and the freedoms guaranteed in the Bill of Rights invite the participation of **interest groups** at all stages of the policymaking process. One reason why so many interest groups and other organized institutions attempt to influence our government is the many opportunities for them to do so. Interest groups can hire **lobbyists** to try to influence members of the House of Representatives, the Senate or any of its committees, or the president or any presidential officials. They can file briefs at the Supreme Court or challenge regulations issued by federal agencies. This ease of access to the government is sometimes known as the "multiple cracks" view of our political system. Interest groups can penetrate the political system through many, many entry points, and, as we will note, their right to do so is protected by the Constitution.

Interest Groups: A Natural Phenomenon

■ **LO7.1:** Define an interest group and explain the constitutional and political reasons why so many groups are found in the United States.

Alexis de Tocqueville observed in 1834 that "in no country of the world has the principle of association been more successfully used or applied to a greater multitude of objectives than in America."[1] The French traveler was amazed at the degree to which Americans formed groups to solve civic problems, establish social relationships, and speak for their economic or political interests. James Madison foresaw the importance of having multiple organizations in the political system (see Appendix C). He supported the creation of a large republic with many states to encourage the formation of multiple interests. The multitude of interests, in Madison's view, would protect minority views against the formation of an oppressive majority interest. Madison's belief in the power of groups to protect a democracy was echoed centuries later by the work of Robert A. Dahl, a contributor to the pluralist theory of politics.[2] Pluralism views the political struggle pitting different groups against each other to reach a compromise as vital to the public interest.

Surely, neither Madison nor de Tocqueville foresaw the formation of more than 100,000 associations in the United States or the spending of millions of dollars to influence legislation. Poll data show that more than two-thirds of all Americans belong to at least one group or association. Although the majority of these affiliations could not be classified as interest groups in the political sense, Americans do understand the principles of working in groups.

Today, interest groups range from the small groups such as local environmental organizations and national groups such as the American Civil Liberties Union, and the National Education Association. The continuing increase in the number of groups that lobby governments and the multiple ways in which they are involved in the political process have been seen by some scholars as a detriment to an effective government. Sometimes called *hyperpluralism,* the ability of interest

1. Alexis de Tocqueville, *Democracy in America*, Vol. 1, edited by Phillips Bradley (New York: Knopf, 1980), p. 191.
2. Robert A. Dahl, *Who Governs? Democracy and Power in an American City* (New Haven, CT: Yale University Press, 1961).

groups to mandate policy or to defeat policies needed by the nation may work against the public good.[3]

Interest Groups and Social Movements

Interest groups are often spawned by mass **social movements**. Such movements represent demands by a large segment of the population for change in the political, economic, or social system. Social movements are often the first expression of discontent with the existing system. They may be the authentic voice of weaker or oppressed groups in society that do not have the means or standing to organize as interest groups. For example, most mainstream political and social leaders disapproved of the women's movement of the 1800s. Because women were unable to vote or take an active part in the political system, it was difficult for women who desired greater freedoms to organize formal groups. After the Civil War, when more women became active in professional life, the first real women's rights group, the National Woman Suffrage Association, came into being. One of the best-known groups speaking for the rights of women is NOW, the National Organization for Women. Its website encourages blog postings and donations in order to support women's rights.

> **Social Movement**
> A movement that represents the demands of a large segment of the public for political, economic, or social change.

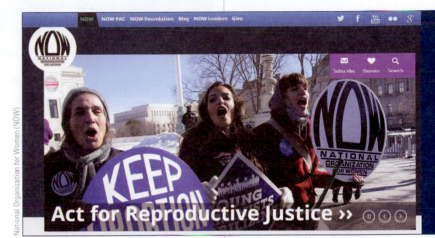

National Organization for Women (NOW)

African Americans found themselves in an even more disadvantaged situation after the end of the Reconstruction period. They were unable to exercise their political rights in many southern and border states, and their participation in any form of organization could lead to economic ruin, physical harassment, or even death. The civil rights movement of the 1950s and 1960s was clearly a social movement. Although the movement received support from several formal organizations—including the Southern Christian Leadership Conference, the National Association for the Advancement of Colored People, and the Urban League—only a social movement could generate the kinds of civil disobedience that took place in hundreds of towns and cities across the country.

In the mid-twentieth century, Hispanic or Latino Americans became part of a social movement to improve the treatment of immigrant workers. Cesar Chavez, a farmworker, organized the Mexican farm laborers in California and other western states to demand better working conditions, better treatment, and the right to form a union. At one point, the National Farm Workers Association initiated a strike against the grape growers in California and led a successful national boycott of table grapes for six years. Chavez became a national figure, and his work led to improved conditions for all farmworkers. By the 1960s, other leaders within the Hispanic American community founded the National Council of La Raza to improve educational and employment opportunities for their community. Chavez's social movement became a nationally recognized union, the United Farm Workers, while "La Raza" became recognized as an advocacy group that spoke for Hispanic Americans.

---

3. Theodore Lowi, *The End of Liberalism* (New York: W. W. Norton, 1979).

In February 2013, activists gathered in front of the White House to convince the president to deny the permits for the Keystone XL Pipeline and to show their support for other environmental issues.

Cesar Estrada Chavez, leader of the farmworker rights movement. He founded the National Farm Workers Association to secure the rights of migrant farmworkers to better wages and living conditions. One of the tactics he used was a consumer boycott against food producers.

The Stonewall riots in New York City were the beginning of the drive for greater rights and protections for gays and lesbians in the United States. This social movement began in New York City and San Francisco and then spread to gay communities throughout the nation. There is no doubt that lesbian, gay, bisexual, and transgender (LGBT) Americans have become a well-recognized interest group. At the present time, the Human Rights Campaign is the largest lobbying group, with more than 1 million members. The work of LGBT groups has been complicated by the reality that many issues of interest fall under the purview of state law. Thus, many LGBT alliances work at the state and local level. Such groups frequently have chapters on college campuses and, in some areas, within high schools.

Social movements are often precursors of interest groups, some of which are listed in Table 7–1. It is too soon to know whether the nascent social movements targeting income inequality in the United States will become more like an interest group. Social movements, including those that support sustainable farming and making high-quality food more accessible to poorer Americans may yet become interest groups if they find a need to recruit members through group incentives.

Why So Many?

Whether based in a social movement or created to meet an immediate crisis, interest groups continue to form and act in American society. One reason for the multitude of interest groups is that the right to join a group is protected by the First Amendment to the U.S. Constitution (see Chapter 4). Not only are all people guaranteed the right

Table 7-1 ▶ **Social Movement Interest Groups**

NAACP	www.naacp.org
Human Rights Campaign	www.hrc.org
The Urban League	www.nul.org
NOW	www.now.org
League of United Latin American Citizens	www.lulac.org
National Gay and Lesbian Task Force	www.ngltf.org

"peaceably to assemble," but they are also guaranteed the right "to petition the Government for a redress of grievances." This constitutional provision encourages Americans to form groups and to express their opinions to the government or to their elected representatives as members of a group.

In addition, our federal system of government provides thousands of "pressure points" for interest group activity. Interest groups and their representatives can lobby legislators for policy changes or attempt to influence the president directly. They can also contact the officials who write regulations and policies. When attempts to influence government through the executive and legislative branches fail, interest groups turn to the courts, filing suit in state or federal courts to achieve their objectives. The Boy Scouts of America has been sued by gay groups because gay men are not allowed to be troop leaders. Pluralist theorists point to the openness of the American political structure as a major factor in the power of groups in American politics.

did you know?

On average, there are now 23 lobbyists for each member of Congress.

Human Rights Campaign

Why Do Americans Join Interest Groups?

■ **LO7.2:** Explain why an individual may or may not decide to join an interest group and the benefits that membership can confer.

Why do some people join interest groups, whereas many others do not? Everyone has some interest that could benefit from government action. For many individuals, however, those concerns remain unorganized interests, or **latent interests**.

According to political theorist Mancur Olson, it simply may not be rational for individuals to join most groups.[4] In his classic work on this topic, Olson introduced the idea of the "collective good." This concept refers to any public benefit that, if available to any member of the community, cannot be denied to any other member, whether or not he or she participated in the effort to gain the good.

Although collective benefits are usually thought of as coming from such public goods as clean air or national defense, benefits are also bestowed by the government on subsets of the public. Price subsidies to dairy farmers and loans to college students are examples. Olson used economic theory to propose that it is

Latent Interests
Public-policy interests that are not recognized or addressed by a group at a particular time.

CONNECT WITH YOUR CLASSMATES
MindTap for American Government

Access the Interest Groups Forum: Discussion—Participation in Interest Groups.

---

4. Mancur Olson, *The Logic of Collective Action* (Cambridge, MA: Harvard University Press, 1965).

Free Rider Problem
The difficulty interest groups face in recruiting members when the benefits they achieve can be gained without joining the group.

Incentives
A reason or motive for supporting or participating in the activities of a group based on the desire to associate with others and to share with others a particular interest or hobby.

Material Incentives
A reason or motive for supporting or participating in the activities of a group based on economic benefits or opportunities.

not rational for interested individuals to join groups that work for group benefits. In fact, it is often more rational for the individual to wait for others to procure the benefits and then share them. How many college students, for example, even are aware of the United States Student Association, an organization that lobbies the government for increased financial aid to students? The difficulty interest groups face in recruiting members when the benefits can be obtained without joining is referred to as the **free rider problem**.

Incentives

If so little incentive exists for individuals to join together, why are there thousands of interest groups lobbying in Washington? According to the logic of collective action, if the contribution of an individual *will* make a difference to the effort, then it is worth it to the individual to join. Thus, smaller groups, which seek benefits for only a small proportion of the population, are more likely to enroll members who will give time and funds to the cause. Larger groups, which represent general public interests (the women's movement or the American Civil Liberties Union, for example), will find it relatively more difficult to get individuals to join. People need an incentive—material or otherwise—to participate.

Solidary Incentives. Interest groups offer **incentives** for their members. Solidary incentives include companionship, a sense of belonging, and the pleasure of associating with others. Although the National Audubon Society was originally founded to save the snowy egret from extinction, today most members join to learn more about birds and to meet and share their pleasure with other bird-watchers. The advent of social media has made the creation of solidary incentives much easier. An individual can make friends and exchange ideas with other members through Facebook or Twitter. Such exchanges make the connection to the organization even more worthwhile to the individual. Even though an individual may "join" a group for free through social media, the interest group benefits from the attention garnered by these "fans." For example, the World Wildlife Fund has almost 900,000 friends on Facebook. When the time comes to ask for a financial donation or to take local action, these social media participants will feel an enhanced loyalty to the group and may be willing to take action.

Material Incentives. For other individuals, interest groups offer direct **material incentives**. A case in point is AARP (formerly the American Association of Retired Persons), which provides discounts, automobile insurance, and organized travel opportunities for its members. The organization even offers free access to a range of computer games on its webpage. After Congress created the prescription drug benefit program supported by AARP, it became one of the larger insurers under that program. Because of its exceptionally low dues ($16 annually) and the benefits gained through membership, AARP has become the largest interest group in the United States, claiming more than 38 million members.

Many other interest groups offer indirect material incentives for their members. Such groups as the American Dairy Association and the National Association of Automobile Dealers do not give discounts or freebies to their members, but they do offer indirect benefits and rewards by, for example, protecting the material interests of their members from government policymaking that is injurious to their industry or business.

Purposive Incentives. Interest groups also offer the opportunity for individuals to pursue political, economic, or social goals through joint action.

Purposive incentives offer individuals the satisfaction of taking action when the goals of a group correspond to their beliefs or principles. While the Occupy movement is a new and fairly unformed interest, the individuals who took part in the tent camps and protests expressed very strong feelings about the economic imbalance in American life. The individuals who belong to a group focusing on the abortion issue, gun control, or environmental causes, for example, do so because they feel strongly enough about the issues to support the group's work with money and time.

Some scholars have argued that many people join interest groups simply for the discounts, magazine subscriptions, and other tangible benefits and are not really interested in the political positions taken by the groups. According to William P. Browne, however, research shows that people really do care about the policy stance of an interest group. Members of a group seek people who share the group's views and then ask them to join. As one group leader put it, "Getting members is about scaring the hell out of people."[5] People join the group and then feel that they are doing something about a cause that is important to them. Today, the use of social media makes sharing of views and goals even easier for a group.

> **Purposive Incentives**
> A reason for supporting or participating in the activities of a group based on agreement with the goals of the group. For example, someone with a strong interest in human rights might have a purposive incentive to join Amnesty International.

Types of Interest Groups

■ **LO7.3:** Describe different types of interest groups and the sources of their political power.

Thousands of groups exist to influence government. Among the major types of interest groups are those that represent the main sectors of the economy. Many public-interest organizations have been formed to represent the needs of the general citizenry, including some single-issue groups. The interests of foreign governments and foreign businesses are also represented in the American political arena.

Economic Interest Groups

More interest groups are formed to represent economic interests than any other set of interests. The variety of economic interest groups mirrors the complexity of the American economy. The major sectors that seek influence in Washington, DC, include business, agriculture, labor unions and their members, government workers, and professionals.

Business Interest Groups. Thousands of business groups and trade associations work to influence government policies that affect their respective industries. Umbrella groups represent certain types of businesses or companies that deal in a particular type of product. The U.S. Chamber of Commerce, for example, is an umbrella group that represents businesses, and the National Association of Manufacturers is an umbrella group that represents only manufacturing concerns. These are two of the larger groups listed in Table 7–2.

Table 7-2 ▶ Economic Interest Groups——Business

U.S. Chamber of Commerce	www.uschamber.com
Better Business Bureau	www.bbb.org
National Association of Manufacturers	www.nam.com
National Federation of Independent Business	www.nifbonline.com

---

5. William P. Browne, *Groups, Interests, and U.S. Public Policy* (Washington, DC: Georgetown University Press, 1998), p. 23.

Everyday Politics

 ## *Syriana*: Oil, Guns, and Money

Saudi Arabia and other oil-rich nations in the Middle East have been the subject of many feature films and documentaries. From the founding of the Saudi Kingdom portrayed in *Lawrence of Arabia* in 1962 to *Three Kings*, a 1999 movie about the First Gulf War, Hollywood has found intrigue and violence in the Middle East.

Syriana, released in 2005, is a scathing look at the petroleum industry, global corporations, the intelligence community, and influence-peddling in Washington, DC. In the film, U.S. energy giant Connex merges with Killen, a smaller oil company with drilling rights in Kazakhstan, after fearing the loss of its monopoly in a fictional Middle Eastern country. To gain approval from the U.S. government for its maneuver, the corporation hires a lobbying firm in Washington, DC. Subplots involve a stolen missile, laid-off oil workers who become terrorists, and bribery and corruption in the oil business. By the end of the film, cynicism triumphs, with the oil company getting its merger, the corruption charges buried, and America's energy industry stronger than ever.

Written by Stephen Gaghan and executive produced by George Clooney (who also starred), the film was a commercial and artistic success. Clooney won the Oscar for Best Supporting Actor while Gaghan was nominated for Best Original Screenplay. The screenplay was adapted from Robert Baer's 2003 memoir, *See No Evil*.* Baer, a former CIA operative, wrote of his time posted in the Middle East, claiming that Washington politics (oil politics) kept the United States from containing the growing terrorist movements in the Middle East and led to the rise of Osama bin Laden as the leader of al-Qaeda.

* Robert Baer, *See No Evil*, New York: Broadway Books, 2003.

For Critical Analysis

1. *How could legislation limit the influence of global corporations on the United States government?*

2. *Should all contacts on behalf of global corporations—formal and informal—be reported and made public?*

Some business groups are decidedly more powerful than others. The U.S. Chamber of Commerce, which has more than 300,000 member companies, can bring constituent influence to bear on every member of Congress. Another powerful lobbying organization is the National Association of Manufacturers. With a staff of more than 60 people in Washington, DC, the organization can mobilize dozens of well-educated, articulate lobbyists to work the corridors of Congress on issues of concern to its members.

Although business interest groups such as those listed in Table 7–3 are likely to agree on anything that reduces government regulation or taxation, they often do not concur on the specifics of policy, and the sector has been troubled by disagreement and fragmentation within its ranks. Large corporations have been far more concerned with federal regulation of

Table 7–3 ▶ Economic Interest Groups—Industries

American Bankers Association	www.aba.com
National Association of Home Builders	www.nahb.org
National Association of Realtors	www.realtor.com
National Beer Wholesalers Association	www.nbwa.org
National Restaurant Association	www.restaurant.org
America's Health Insurance Plans	www.ahip.org
Pharmaceutical Research and Manufacturers of America	www.phrma.org
American Hospital Association	www.aha.org

their corporate boards and insider financial arrangements, whereas small businesses lobby for tax breaks for new equipment or new employees. One of the key issues on which businesses have not agreed in the past is immigration reform. Large corporations have found the current visa regulations for bringing in highly skilled employees to be burdensome while small businesses find the government database for checking immigration status unwieldy. By 2013, however, a majority of small and large businesses supported immigration reform, seeing the economic power of immigrants as customers and employees.[6] Furthermore, in January 2014, the American Federation of Labor and Congress of Industrial Organizations (AFL-CIO), which has feared that immigrants might be hired in place of union workers, and the U.S. Chamber of Commerce agreed on common principles for immigration reform. The powerful coalition of unions now sees legal immigration and a path to legal residency for workers as an opportunity to provide themselves with new union members.[7]

Agricultural Interest Groups.

American farmers and their employees represent less than 2 percent of the U.S. population. Nevertheless, farmers' influence on legislation beneficial to their interests has been significant. Farmers have succeeded in their aims because they have very strong interest groups. Two of the largest are listed in Table 7–4. These interest groups are geographically dispersed and therefore have many representatives and senators to speak for them.

The American Farm Bureau Federation, established in 1919, has several million members (many of whom are not actually farmers) and is usually considered conservative. It was instrumental in getting government guarantees of "fair" prices during the Great Depression in the 1930s.[8] Another important agricultural interest organization is the National Farmers Union (NFU), which represents smaller family farms. Generally, the NFU holds more progressive policy positions than does the Farm Bureau. As farms have become larger and agribusiness has become a way of life, single-issue farm groups have emerged. The American Dairy Association, the Peanut Growers Group, and the National Cattleman's Association, for example, work to support their respective farmers and associated businesses. In recent years, agricultural interest groups have become active on many new issues. Among other things, they have opposed immigration restrictions and are very involved in international trade matters as they seek new markets. One of the newest agricultural groups is the American Farmland Trust, which supports policies to conserve farmland and protect natural resources.

Labor Interest Groups.

Interest groups representing the **labor movement** date back to at least 1886, when the American Federation of Labor (AFL) was formed. The largest American unions are listed in Table 7–5. In 1955, the AFL joined forces with the Congress of Industrial Organizations (CIO). Today, the combined AFL-CIO

Labor Movement
Generally, the economic and political expression of working-class interests; politically, the organization of working-class interests.

Table 7-4 ▶   Economic Interest Groups—Agriculture

American Farm Bureau Federation	www.fb.org
National Farmers Union	www.nfu.org

---

6. Kent Hoover, "What business groups like about House Republican immigration reform principles," *The Business Journals*, January 30, 2014. http://www.bizjournals.com/bizjournals/washingtonbureau/2014-01-30-business-groups-welcome-house.html
7. Steven Greenhouse, "Business and Labor Unite to Try to Alter Immigration Laws," *The New York Times*, February 7, 2014: 1.
8. The Agricultural Adjustment Act of 1933 (declared unconstitutional) was replaced by the 1938 Agricultural Adjustment Act and was later changed and amended several times.

Table 7-5 ▶ Economic Interest Groups—Labor

Change to Win Federation	www.changetowin.org
AFL-CIO	www.aflcio.org
SEIU	www.seiu.org
National Education Association	www.nea.org
International Brotherhood of Teamsters	www.teamster.org

Service Sector
The sector of the economy that provides services—such as health care, banking, and education—in contrast to the sector that produces goods.

is a large union with a membership of nearly 9 million workers and an active political arm called the Committee on Political Education. In a sense, the AFL-CIO is a union of unions.

The AFL-CIO experienced severe discord within its ranks during 2005, however, when four key unions left the federation and formed the Change to Win Coalition. The new Change to Win Coalition represents about one-third of the 13 million workers who formerly belonged to the AFL-CIO, including the SEIU, or Service Employees International Union. Formed by unions that were growing, especially in the public sector, the coalition believed that the AFL-CIO was too easily cowed by old line manufacturing unions and not aggressive enough about organizing new industries. The role of unions in American society has declined in recent decades, as witnessed by the decrease in union membership (see Figure 7–1). In the age of automation and with the rise of the **service sector**, blue-collar workers in basic industries (autos, steel, and the like) represent an increasingly smaller percentage of the total working population. Although there was some growth in union membership in the early 2000s, the economic recession that began in 2008 took its toll on union workers as employees lost their jobs. At the end of 2013, total union membership in the United States stood at 14.5 million workers, or 11.3 percent of the workforce.

Figure 7-1 ▶ Decline in Union Membership, 1948 to Present

As shown in this figure, the percentage of the total workforce that is represented by labor unions has declined precipitously over the last 40 years. Note, however, that in contrast to the decline in union representation in the private sector, the percentage of government workers who are unionized has increased significantly since about 1960.

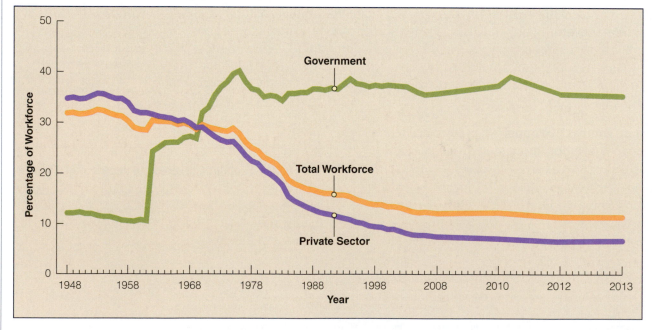

Source: Bureau of Labor Statistics, 2013.

With the steady decline in employment in the industrial sector of the economy, national unions are looking to nontraditional areas for their membership, including migrant farmworkers, service workers, and, most recently, public employees—such as police officers, firefighting personnel, and teachers, including college professors and graduate assistants. By 2012, the number of individuals who belonged to public-sector unions outnumbered those in private-sector unions.

Although the proportion of the workforce that belongs to a union has declined over the years, American labor unions have not given up their efforts to support sympathetic candidates for Congress or for state office. Currently, the AFL-CIO has a large political budget that it uses to help Democratic candidates nationwide. Although interest groups that favor Republicans continue to assist their candidates, the efforts of labor are more sustained and more targeted. Labor offers a candidate (such as President Obama) a corps of volunteers in addition to campaign contributions. A massive turnout by labor union members in critical elections can significantly increase the final vote totals for Democratic candidates.

Public-Employee Unions.

The degree of unionization in the private sector has declined since 1965, but this has been partially offset by growth in the unionization of public employees. Figure 7–1 displays the growth in public-sector unionization. With a total membership of more than 7.1 million, public-sector unions are likely to continue expanding.

The American Federation of State, County, and Municipal Employees as well as the American Federation of Teachers are members of the AFL-CIO's Public Employee Department. Over the years, public-employee unions have become quite militant and are often involved in strikes or protests.

In 2011, the Republican governor and legislature in Wisconsin passed legislation limiting the ability of public-sector union members, including teachers, to bargain for benefits. Teachers, students, and their supporters occupied the Wisconsin statehouse for many weeks, but the law stood. An effort to recall the governor of the state was mounted in 2012. After an intense and expensive campaign, Governor Scott Walker defeated the Democratic challenger in the June 2012 recall election and remained in office.

A powerful interest group lobbying on behalf of public employees is the National Education Association (NEA), a nationwide organization of about 2.8 million teachers and others connected with education. Many NEA locals function as labor unions. The NEA lobbies intensively for increased public funding of education.

Interest Groups of Professionals.

Numerous professional organizations exist, including the Association of General Contractors of America and the Institute of Electrical and Electronic Engineers. Some professional groups (see Table 7–6), are more influential than others because of their members' social status. Lawyers have a unique advantage, because many members of Congress share their profession. Interest groups that represent lawyers include both the American Bar Association and the Association of Trial Lawyers of America, which has recently renamed itself the Association for Justice. The trial lawyers have been very

Table 7-6 ▶ **Professional Interest Groups**

American Medical Association	www.ama-assm.org
American Dental Association	www.ada.org
American Bar Association	www.americanbar.org
American Library Association	www.ala.org
American Association for Justice	www.justice.org

In July 2013, the Bay Area Rapid Transit System was shut down by striking union members who opposed proposed changes in their health care and pension plans. Thousands of commuters were forced to find other types of transportation during the strike.

active in political campaigns and are usually one of the larger donors to Democratic candidates. In terms of money spent on lobbying, however, one professional organization stands head and shoulders above the rest—the American Medical Association (AMA). Founded in 1847, it is now affiliated with more than 2,000 local and state medical societies and has a total membership of about 300,000.

The Unorganized Poor. Some have argued that the system of interest group politics leaves out poor Americans or those without access to information. Americans who are disadvantaged economically cannot afford to join interest groups; if they are members of the working poor, they may hold two or more jobs just to survive, leaving them no time to participate in interest groups. Other groups in the population—including non-English-speaking groups, resident aliens, single parents, disabled Americans, and younger voters—probably do not have the time or expertise even to find out what group might represent them. Similarly, the millions of Americans affected by the mortgage default crisis, some poor and some middle class, have fought their battles against the banks and mortgage companies alone—no interest group exists or has formed to lobby for more effective policies to help these people.

R. Allen Hays examined the plight of poor Americans in his book *Who Speaks for the Poor?*[9] Hays studied groups and individuals who have lobbied for public housing and other issues related to the poor and concluded that the poor depend largely on indirect representation. Most efforts on behalf of the poor come from a policy network of groups—including public housing officials, welfare workers and officials, religious groups, public-interest groups, and some liberal general-interest groups—that speak loudly and persistently for the poor. More recent studies update this work by suggesting that community-based organizations can survive with a combination of local legitimacy and connections to regional or national organizations.[10] Schlozman, Verba and Brady completed a comprehensive

9. R. Allen Hays, *Who Speaks for the Poor?* (New York: Routledge, 2001).
10. Edward T. Walker and John D. McCarthy, "Legitimacy, Strategy, and Resources in the Survival of Community-Based Organizations," *Social Problems* (2010) 57 (3): 315–340.

Politics with a Purpose

How to Organize a Group

Within the last decade, two very different groups have organized to challenge the political status quo: the Tea Party and the Occupy movement. Although neither of these two groups can be said to have established itself as a true interest group, both have attracted a great deal of attention in the media and many supporters and critics. Both groups have formed and acted using twenty-first-century techniques for organizing.

The Tea Party is a political group that is fairly decentralized and has no top-down administration or bureaucracy. Critics suggest that it is really a faction of the Republican Party that is extremely conservative in its views. Members of Tea Party groups generally dispute that charge, although most of the candidates they back are Republicans. Survey data suggest that some of the members are, in fact, Independent voters rather than Republicans.

The Occupy movement arose in the fall of 2011 as a protest movement against the distribution of wealth in the United States and an expression of alienation from corporate values and the current distribution of benefits in society. Occupy camps sprang up across American cities and in European capitals as well. Supporters tended to be young and well educated or current students who were unemployed or underemployed, meaning that they could not find work in the field for which they had trained. The movement challenged local governments by using public spaces for its encampments and accepting the tickets issued by local police. Most camps were eventually disbanded due to public safety concerns, but then warmer weather encouraged them to sprout again.

How could you organize a group to change society or improve your university? First, define your message. Work with a group of like-minded friends to identify your goals. Figure out what kind of a group structure will work and what tasks need to be done. Now, use the Internet to organize: Set up your website, blog, or Facebook page. Generate publicity so that others who agree with you can join your group. You might decide to demonstrate or post signs, or take some symbolic action to get on the news. Maximize the news exposure by posting a video on YouTube. Use any email list available to you. Ask people to join your group by "liking" you on Facebook, following you on Twitter, and perhaps donating to the cause. Use all social media to attract followers, and inform them of your mission. Then use the media to let supporters know about your events.

Many organizing methods that seem so obvious to most Americans under 30, such as texting and using social media, did not exist 10 years ago. Of course, getting a group started is one thing, but keeping it going and actually having an impact on public policy require building a more permanent structure and establishing a solid presence in the political arena. It will not be known for some years whether the Occupy movement or the Tea Party has such a future.

For an excellent source of ideas for starting a group, see the website: http://movements.org/how-to/

Radu Bercan/Shutterstock

iStockphoto.com/GlobalStock

study of organized interests in 2012 and affirmed the findings of Hays: affluent and upper-middle-class Americans can have their voice heard while poor Americans face tremendous obstacles to participating in the political system and having their interests considered by it.[11]

Environmental Groups

Environmental interest groups are not new. We have already mentioned the National Audubon Society, which was founded in 1905 to protect the snowy egret from the commercial demand for hat decorations. The patron of the Sierra Club, John Muir, worked for the creation of national parks more than a century ago. But the blossoming of national environmental groups with mass memberships did not occur until the 1970s. Since the first Earth Day, organized in 1970, many interest groups have sprung up to protect the environment or to save unique ecological

11. Kay Lehman Schlozman, Sidney Verba, and Henry Brady, *The Unheavenly Chorus: Unequal Political Voice and the Broken Promise of American Democracy* (Princeton, NJ: Princeton University Press, 2012).

Table 7-7 ▶ **Environmental Interest Groups**

Sierra Club	www.sierraclub.org
The Nature Conservancy	www.nature.org
National Resources Defense Council	www.nrdc.org
Clean Water Action	www.cleanwateraction.org/
The World Wildlife Fund	www.wwf.org
The Audubon Society	www.audubon.org
National Wildlife Federation	www.nwf.org

CLEAN WATER ACTION

40 *years of action for clean water*
1972 through 2012

Do you feel that social media can help champion a cause that might otherwise go unnoticed?

Clean Water Action

niches. The groups, many of which are listed in Table 7–7, range from the National Wildlife Federation, with a membership of more than 5 million and an emphasis on education, to the more elite Environmental Defense Fund, with a membership of 300,000 and a focus on influencing federal policy. The National Resources Defense Council is another very powerful environmental organization, one that has often used the law and lawsuits as part of its strategy. Other groups include the Nature Conservancy, which uses members' contributions to buy up threatened natural areas and either give them to state or local governments or manage them itself, and the more radical Greenpeace Society and Earth First. A more recent entry into the field of environmental groups is the Clean Water Network, which spun off from the National Resources Defense Council in 2008 (see the screen capture). The Clean Water Action is an alliance of local, state-level, and national groups that works to stop dangerous runoff and protect streams, lakes, and rivers. Many local groups engage in activities such as water sampling and stream monitoring to make sure that water protection standards are followed.

Public-Interest Groups

Public Interest
The best interests of the overall community; the national good, rather than the narrow interests of a particular group.

Public interest is a difficult term to define because there are many publics in our nation of about 320 million. It is almost impossible for one particular public policy to benefit everybody, which makes it practically impossible to define the public interest. Nonetheless, over the past few decades, a variety of lobbying organizations listed in Table 7–8 have been formed "in the public interest."

Nader Organizations. The best-known and perhaps the most effective public-interest groups are those organized under the leadership of consumer activist Ralph Nader. Nader's rise to the top began in 1965 with the publication of his book *Unsafe at Any Speed*, a lambasting critique of General Motors. GM made a clumsy attempt to discredit Nader's background. Nader sued the company, the media exploited the story, and when GM settled out of court for $425,000, Nader became a recognized champion of consumer interests. Since then, Nader has turned over much of his income to the more than 60 public-interest groups that he has formed or sponsored. Nader ran for president in 2000 on the Green Party ticket and again in 2004 and 2008 as an independent.

Table 7-8 ▶ **Public-Interest Groups**

American Civil Liberties Union	www.aclu.org
League of Women Voters	www.lwv.org
Common Cause	www.commoncause.org
Consumer Federation of America	www.consumerfed.org
Amnesty International	www.amnesty.org

Other Public-Interest Groups. One over-arching public interest is an effective political system. One of the first groups seeking political reform was Common Cause, founded in 1970. Its goals are moving national priorities toward "the public" and making governmental institutions more responsive to the needs of the public. Anyone willing to pay dues of

Jim West/Alamy

Young people work together to clean up a creek that has been polluted by run-off and flooding.

$40 per year can become a member (student dues are only $15). Members are polled regularly to obtain information about local and national issues requiring reassessment. Some of the activities of Common Cause have been (1) helping to ensure the passage of the Twenty-sixth Amendment (giving 18-year-olds the right to vote), (2) achieving greater voter registration in all states, (3) supporting the complete withdrawal of all U.S. forces from South Vietnam in the 1970s, and (4) succeeding in passing campaign finance reform legislation.

While Common Cause has about 400,000 members and is still working for political reforms at the national and state level, it is not as well known today as MoveOn.org. Founded in 1998 by two entrepreneurs from California, the group's original purpose was to get millions of people to demand that President Clinton be censured instead of impeached and that the country should "move on" to deal with more important problems. What was strikingly different about this organization is that it was—and continues to be—an online interest group. MoveOn (www.moveon.org) has more than 5 million members and is now a family of organizations that are politically active in national campaigns and in pressuring government on specific issues.

The American Civil Liberties Union (ACLU) dates back to World War I (1914–1918), when, under a different name, it defended draft resisters. It generally enters into legal disputes related to Bill of Rights issues. The ACLU website has an excellent discussion of individuals' and groups' rights to express themselves and protest within the law. An international interest group with a strong presence on U.S. college campuses is Amnesty International. This organization, founded in 1961, spans the globe. The mission is to end human rights abuses wherever they are found. Sometimes under fire for unconventional methods, Amnesty International has compiled an outstanding record of documenting human rights abuses and was awarded the Nobel Prize in 1977.

Other Interest Groups

Single-interest groups, being narrowly focused, may be able to call attention to their causes because they have simple, straightforward goals and because their members tend to care intensely about the issues. Thus, such groups can easily

Table 7–9 ▶ **"One Issue" Interest Groups**

National Right to Life Committee	www.nrlc.org
NARAL Pro-Choice America	www.naral.org
National Rifle Association	www.nra.org
Brady Campaign (handgun control)	www.bradycampaign.org
American Society for the Prevention of Cruelty to Animals	www.aspca.org
People for the Ethical Treatment of Animals	www.peta.org
Mothers Against Drunk Driving	www.madd.org
AARP	www.aarp.org

motivate their members to contact legislators or to organize demonstrations in support of their policy goals.

A number of interest groups focus on just one issue. The abortion debate has created various groups opposed to abortion, such as the National Right to Life Committee, and groups in favor of abortion rights, such as NARAL Pro-Choice America (see Table 7–9). Other single-issue groups are the National Rifle Association, the Right to Work Committee (an anti-union group), and the American Israel Public Affairs Committee (a pro-Israel group).

Foreign Governments

Homegrown interests are not the only players in the game. Washington, DC, is also the center for lobbying by foreign governments as well as private foreign interests. The governments of the largest U.S. trading partners, such as Canada, European Union (EU) countries, Japan, and South Korea, maintain substantial research and lobbying staffs. Even smaller nations, such as those in the Caribbean, engage lobbyists when vital legislation affecting their trade interests is considered. Frequently, these foreign interests hire former representatives or former senators to promote their positions on Capitol Hill. To learn more about how foreign interests lobby the U.S. government, see this chapter's Beyond Our Borders feature.

What Makes an Interest Group Powerful?

At any time, thousands of interest groups are attempting to influence state legislatures, governors, Congress, and members of the executive branch of the U.S. government. What characteristics make some of those groups more powerful than others and more likely to have influence over government policy? Generally, interest groups attain a reputation for being powerful through their membership size, financial resources, leadership, cohesiveness, and increasingly, their ability to rally public support behind their cause, whether through in-person demonstrations or via social media. Grossmann suggests that certain groups become more powerful than others and more well known through a combination of successful tactics or behaviors and their ability to form an organization that continues these strategies.[12]

---

12. Matt Grossmann, *The Not-So-Special Interests: Interest Groups, Public Representation, and American Governance* (Berkeley, CA: Stanford University Press, 2012).

Figure 7-2 ▶ Profiles of Power—Four Influential Interest Groups

AARP, formerly the American Association of Retired People

Membership: 40 million Americans, mostly over 50

Location: Washington, DC

Web site: www.aarp.org

AARP began as an organization of retired teachers and has grown in the last three decades to a mass organization serving more than 40 million members. With a membership fee of only $16 per year, members are entitled to magazines and information, lobbying on their behalf, and access to purchase medical insurance, automobile insurance and travel services. AARP's political power derives from its huge membership, its ability to communicate to its members, and its mission to serve the needs of seniors. The group is now one of the best financed in Washington with an annual revenue base of $1.1 billion. Critics point out that AARP doesn't really offer insurance but lends its name and membership to other corporations, which pay royalties of $700 million a year to AARP. In 2013, AARP spent $9.6 million on lobbying Congress.

Source: Center for Responsive Politics, www.opensecrets.org.

The Nature Conservancy

Membership: 1 million through subscriptions to the magazine

Location: Fairfax, Virginia

Web site: www.nature.org

The Nature Conservancy is one of the largest and most successful environmental groups in the world, with total lobbying expenditures for 2012 of $900 million. The Conservancy is often criticized by other environmental groups because it is very willing to partner with private property owners, corporations and the states to purchase and save specific tracts of land. It is seen as being more favorable to private ownership and capitalism than many other environmental interest groups. However, it has successfully purchased and preserved millions of acres of land, reefs, and seabed around the world. The organization has net assets of more than $5.2 billion.

Source: The Nature Conservancy 2012 Annual report, Charity Navigator, www.charitynavigator.org.

Pharmaceutical Research and Manufacturers of America (PhRMA)

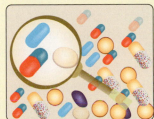

Membership: Only about 50, including all of the major drug-makers in the world. The list is available on PhRMA's website.

Location: Washington, D.C.

Web site: PhRMA.org

During the debate over the Patient Protection and Affordabilty Act (the Obama health care plan), PhRMA was considered one of the most influential players, working on the behalf of its corporate members to keep the government from regulating the cost of drugs. While the overall finances of the association are not public, the not-for-profit arm, PhRMA Foundation distributes hundreds of thousands of dollars to scholarship and research each year, and the interest group itself spent more than $17.8 million on lobbying in 2013.

Source: Center for Responsive Politics, www.opensecrets.org.

Service Employees International Union (SEIU)

Membership: 2.1 million

Location: Washington, DC

Web site: www.seiu.org

One of the fastest growing unions in the country, the SEIU played an important role in the election of President Barack Obama. With its growth concentrated among public workers, the union saw the election of a progressive president as essential to the welfare of its members. SEIU has been a major campaign contributor for Democratic party candidates. In the 2012 election cycle, the organization donated $18 million to candidates and outside organizations. In addition, the union spent about 23 million on "independent" expenditures for advertising and other forms of communication in 2012. The organization reported that it spent about $900,000 on lobbying in 2013.

Source: Center for Responsive Politics, www.opensecrets.org.

Size and Resources

No legislator can deny the power of an interest group that includes thousands of his or her own constituents among its members. Labor unions and organizations such as AARP and the American Automobile Association (AAA) are able to claim voters in every congressional district. Having a large membership—nearly 11 million in the case of the AFL-CIO—carries a great deal of weight with government officials. AARP now has about 38 million members and a budget of approximately $1 billion for its operations. In addition, AARP claims to represent all older Americans, who constitute close to 20 percent of the population, whether they join the organization or not.

Having a large number of members, even if the individual membership dues are relatively small, provides an organization with a strong financial base. Those funds pay for lobbyists, television advertisements, mailings to members, websites, and many other resources that help an interest group make its point to politicians. The business organization with the largest membership is probably the U.S. Chamber of Commerce, which has more than 300,000 members. The Chamber uses its members' dues to pay for staff and lobbyists, as well as a sophisticated communications network: all members can receive email, use Facebook and Twitter, and check the website to get updates on the latest legislative proposals.

Other organizations may have fewer members but nonetheless be able to muster significant financial resources. The pharmaceutical industry is represented in Washington, DC, by the Pharmaceutical Research Manufacturers of America (PhRMA), sometimes called Big Pharma. In 2009, this lobby poured resources into the fight over health reform legislation, seeking and getting limits on how much the new legislation would cost the pharmaceutical industry. According to Wendell Potter, a former insurance executive turned activist, Big Pharma spent more than $2.6 billion between 1998 and 2012, far more the gas and oil industry or defense contractors. What do they want for their money? Potter claims that lobbying effort is meant to keep legislators from interfering with the companies' "predatory pricing practices" while they enjoy many years of patent protection.[13]

did you know?

The industry that spends the most on lobbying each year is the pharmaceutical/health industry.

Leadership

Money is not the only resource that interest groups need to have. Strong leaders who can develop effective strategies are also important. The National Resources Defense Council, formed in 1970 by a group of lawyers and law students who saw the need for a legal approach to environmental problems, is often cited as an outstanding environmental group. The leadership of the NRDC has led strong lobbying efforts for congressional action and planned superb strategies for bringing legal action against polluters and government agencies. Another example is the American Israel Public Affairs Committee (AIPAC), which has long benefited from strong leadership. AIPAC lobbies Congress and the executive branch on issues related to U.S.–Israeli relations, as well as general foreign policy in the Middle East. AIPAC has been successful in facilitating a close relationship between the two nations, which includes the $6 billion to $8 billion in foreign aid that the United States annually bestows on Israel. Despite its modest membership size, AIPAC has won bipartisan support for its agenda and is consistently ranked among the most influential interest groups in America.

Other interest groups, including some with few financial resources, succeed in part because they are led by individuals with charisma and access to power, such as Jesse Jackson of the Rainbow Coalition. Sometimes, choosing a leader with a particular image can be an effective strategy for an organization. The National Rifle Association (NRA) had more than organizational skills in mind when it elected the late Charlton Heston as its president. The strategy of using an actor who is identified with powerful roles as the spokesperson for the organization worked to improve its national image.

---

13. Wendall Potter, "Big Pharmas' Stranglehold on Washington," Center for Public Integrity, September 13, 2013. http://www.publicintegrity.org/2013/02/11/12175/opinion-big-pharmas-stranglehold-washington

Beyond Our Borders

Lobbying and Foreign Interests

Domestic groups are not alone in lobbying the federal government. Many foreign entities hire lobbyists to influence policy and spending decisions in the United States. American lobbying firms are often utilized by foreign groups seeking to advance their agendas. The use of American lobbyists ensures greater access and increases the possibility of success. In 2010, more than 130 countries spent about $460 billion lobbying the United States government and promoting their nations through public relations campaigns. With the United States holding such a dominant position in the global economy and world affairs, it is hardly surprising that foreign entities regularly attempt to influence the U.S. government.

FOREIGN CORPORATIONS AND THE GLOBAL ECONOMY

Economic globalization has had an incalculable impact on public policy worldwide. Given the United States' prominence in the global economy, international and multinational corporations have taken a keen interest in influencing the U.S. government. Foreign corporations spend millions of dollars each year on lobbying in an effort to create favorable business and trade conditions.

Consider several examples: In the list of top spenders for lobbying in 2013 is Royal Dutch Shell, the largest oil company in the world. Based in the Netherlands, Shell Oil spent almost $9 million on lobbying in 2013. British Petroleum spent about $8 million, down considerably from the year of the gulf oil spill, when they spent more than $15 million to assure a settlement in that case. GlaxoSmithKline, one of the world's leading pharmaceutical firms, spent extensively on lobbying in the United States to influence health-care legislation. Toyota Motors, by comparison, spent only about $5 million on lobbying in 2013.*

INFLUENCE FROM OTHER NATIONS

Foreign nations also hire firms to represent their interests before Congress and with the executive branch of government. As Congress considers an immigration reform law, many nations will be lobbying to gain higher numbers of visas for their citizens to come to the United States. Ireland, South Korea, Poland, and Canada have already spent millions on this effort.

Poor nations spend some their budget to lobby Congress for an increase in economic aid, while some corrupt regimes hire lobbyists to pursue their interests in Washington rather than using their own diplomats. For example, Qorvis, a major lobbying firm, has been representing Equatorial Guinea, a very small nation in West Africa. There, the ruling family takes in most of its oil money while the majority of its people are impoverished. The

The world headquarters of Royal Dutch Shell in The Hague, The Netherlands. The company spends millions of dollars annually to influence U.S. policy.

nation spent about $70,000 for the U.S. public relations campaign to improve its image in Washington, DC.**

Individuals and firms that lobby as agents of foreign principals must register with the Department of Justice (DOJ). Each year the DOJ sends a report to Congress on the registrants and their clients, data which is available through the Foreign Agents Registration Act (FARA) online list. In recent years, legislation has been introduced to ban lobbying by foreign firms and foreign nations, but it has not become law.

For Critical Analysis

1. *Should foreign governments and foreign corporations be permitted to lobby the members of Congress in the same way as American interest groups?*

2. *Should members of Congress and the executive branch have to report any contacts from a foreign nation or corporation?*

* For reports on the expenditures of countries on lobbying efforts, go to the database at http://foreignlobbying.org, which is sustained by ProPublica and the Sunlight Foundation, two not-for-profit organizations dedicated to making information about government more public. You can also go directly to the database maintained by the Department of Justice at www.fara.gov/.

** Kessler, Aaron and Wanjohi Kabukuru. "Shadow Diplomacy: African Nations Bypass Embassies, Tap Lobbyists." Huffington Post, July 30, 2013. http://www.huffingtonpost.com/2013/07/30/african-lobbyists_n_3676489.html

Cohesiveness

Regardless of an interest group's size or the amount of funds in its coffers, the motivation of its members is a key factor in determining how powerful it is. If the members of a group are committed to their beliefs strongly enough to email or tweet their representatives, join a march on Washington, or work together to defeat a candidate, that group is considered powerful.

In contrast, although groups that oppose abortion rights have had little success in influencing policy, they are considered powerful because their members are vocal and highly motivated. Other measures of cohesion include the ability of a group to get its members to contact Washington quickly or to give extra money when needed. The NRA can generate hundreds of thousands of messages from its members when gun control legislation is under consideration.

Interest Group Strategies

■ **LO7.4:** Identify the direct and indirect techniques that interest groups use to influence government decisions.

Interest groups employ a wide range of techniques and strategies to promote their policy goals. Although few groups are successful at persuading Congress and the president to completely endorse their programs, many are able to block—or at least weaken—legislation that is injurious to their members. The key to success for interest groups is access to government officials. To gain such access, interest groups and their representatives try to cultivate long-term relationships with legislators and government officials. The best of these relationships are based on mutual respect and cooperation. The interest group provides the officials with excellent sources of information and assistance, and the officials in turn give the group opportunities to express its views.

The techniques used by interest groups can be divided into direct and indirect techniques. With **direct techniques**, the interest group and its lobbyists approach the officials personally to present their case. With **indirect techniques**, in contrast, the interest group uses the general public or individual constituents to influence the government on its behalf.

Direct Techniques

Lobbying, publicizing ratings of legislative behavior, building coalitions, and providing campaign assistance are the four main direct techniques used by interest groups.

Lobbying Techniques. The term *lobbying* comes from the activities of private citizens regularly congregating in the lobbies of legislative chambers before a session to petition legislators. In the latter part of the 1800s, railroad and industrial groups openly bribed state legislators to pass legislation beneficial to their interests, giving lobbying a well-deserved bad name. Most lobbyists today are professionals. They are either consultants to a company or interest group or members of one of the Washington, DC, law firms that specialize in providing such services. Specialized law firms based in the capital region provide specialists in every sector of government policy to meet their clients' needs. One of the most successful firms is Patton Boggs, LLP, which received more than $39 million in fees for its efforts in

Direct Techniques
An interest group activity that involves interaction with government officials to further the group's goals.

Indirect Techniques
A strategy employed by interest groups that uses third parties to influence government officials.

did you know?
The lobbying business totals more than $3.3 billion annually.

2013. AT&T, the City of San Diego, Nissan North America, and the Waterways Council are all using Patton Boggs, LLP, to do their lobbying. Amazon spent more than $600,000 on Patton Boggs.[14] Additionally, the law firm represented 13 foreign entities, billing more than $1.9 million for those efforts. Among the firm's representatives are former congressman Thomas Boggs, Jr., and former senator Trent Lott.

Lobbyists engage in an array of activities to influence legislation and government policy. These include the following:

1. Engaging in private meetings with public officials, including the president's advisers, to make known the interests of the lobbyists' clients. Although acting on behalf of their clients, lobbyists often furnish needed information to senators and representatives (and government agency appointees) that these officials could not easily obtain on their own. It is to the lobbyists' advantage to provide accurate information so that policymakers will rely on them as a source in the future.
2. Testifying before congressional committees for or against proposed legislation.
3. Testifying before executive rule-making agencies—such as the Federal Trade Commission (FTC) or the Consumer Product Safety Commission—for or against proposed rules.
4. Assisting legislators or bureaucrats in drafting legislation or prospective regulations. Often, lobbyists furnish advice on the specific details of legislation.
5. Inviting legislators to social occasions, such as cocktail parties, boating expeditions, and other events, including conferences at exotic locations. Most lobbyists believe that meeting legislators in a relaxed social setting is effective.
6. Providing political information to legislators and other government officials. Often, the lobbyists have better information than the party leadership about how other legislators are going to vote. In this case, the political information they furnish may be a key to legislative success.
7. Supplying nominations for federal appointments to the executive branch.

The Ratings Game. Many interest groups attempt to influence the overall behavior of legislators through their rating systems. Each year, the interest group selects legislation that it believes is most important to its goals and then monitors how legislators vote on it. Each legislator is given a score based on the percentage of times that he or she voted in favor of the group's position. The usual scheme ranges from 0 to 100 percent. In the ratings scheme of the liberal Americans for Democratic Action, for example, a rating of 100 means that a member of Congress voted with the group on every issue and is, by that measure, very liberal.

Ratings are a shorthand way of describing members' voting records for interested citizens. They can also be used to embarrass members. For example, an environmental group identifies the 12 representatives it believes have the worst voting records on environmental issues and labels them "the Dirty Dozen," and a watchdog group describes those representatives who took home the most "pork" for their districts or states as the biggest "pigs."

---

14. "Patton Boggs earns 1.9 million for Foreign Lobbying," The BLT: The Blog of Legal Times. http://www.legaltimes.typepad.com/blt/2013/07/patton-boogs-earns-1.9-million-for-foreign-lobbying.html

Building Alliances.   Another direct technique used by interest groups is to form a coalition with other groups that are concerned about the same legislation. Often, these groups will set up a paper organization with an innocuous name to represent their joint concerns.

Members of such a coalition share expenses and multiply the influence of their individual groups by combining their efforts. Other advantages of forming a coalition are that it blurs the specific interests of the individual groups involved and makes it appear that larger public interests are at stake. These alliances also are efficient devices for keeping like-minded groups from duplicating one another's lobbying efforts.

Campaign Assistance.   Interest groups have additional strategies to use in their attempts to influence government policies. Groups recognize that the greatest concern of legislators is to be reelected, so they focus on the legislators' campaign needs. Associations with large memberships, such as labor unions, are able to provide workers for political campaigns, including precinct workers to get out the vote, volunteers to put up posters and pass out literature, and people to staff telephone banks for campaign headquarters.

In many states where certain interest groups have large memberships, candidates vie for the groups' endorsements in the campaign. Gaining those endorsements may be automatic, or it may require that the candidates participate in debates or interviews with the interest groups. Endorsements are important, because an interest group usually publicizes its choices in its membership publication and because the candidate can use the endorsement in her or his campaign literature. Traditionally, labor unions have endorsed Democratic Party candidates. Republican candidates, however, often try to persuade union locals at least to refrain from any endorsement. Making no endorsement can then be perceived as disapproval of the Democratic Party candidate.

Despite the passage of the Bipartisan Campaign Finance Act in 2002, the 2012 election boasted record campaign spending. The usual array of interest groups—labor unions, professional groups, and business associations—gathered contributions to their political action committees and distributed them to the candidates. Most labor contributions went to Democratic candidates, while a majority of business contributions went to Republicans. Some groups, such as real estate agents, gave evenly to both parties. At the same time, the newer campaign groups, the so-called 527 organizations—tax-exempt associations focused on influencing political elections—raised more than $350 million in unregulated contributions to support

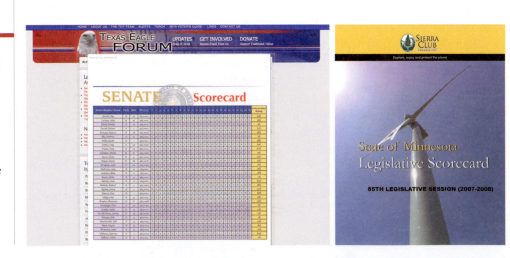

Interest groups from every imaginable ideological point of view issue scorecards of individual legislators' voting records as they relate to the organization's agenda. Shown here are two such scorecards. How much value can voters place on these kinds of ratings?

(Left: Courtesy of Pat Carlson, Texas Eagle Forum, http://www.texaseagle.org; Right: Courtesy of Sierra Club Minnesota North Star Chapter, http://minnesota.sierraclub.org)

campaign activities, registration drives, and advertising. After seeing the success of these groups in raising and spending funds, hundreds of interest groups, private and nonprofit, have founded their own 527 organizations to spend funds for advertising and other political activities. The 2009 decision of the Supreme Court in *Citizens United v. FEC* makes it possible for unions, interest groups, and corporations to spend money directly on advertising for and against candidates in every election.

Indirect Techniques

Interest groups can also try to influence government policy by working through others, who may be constituents or the general public. Indirect techniques mask the interest group's own activities and make the effort appear to be spontaneous. Furthermore, legislators and government officials are often more impressed by contacts from constituents than from an interest group's lobbyist.

Generating Public Pressure. In some instances, interest groups try to produce a groundswell of public pressure to influence the government. Such efforts may include advertisements in national magazines and newspapers, mass mailings, television publicity, and demonstrations. The Internet, YouTube, Twitter, and Facebook make communication efforts even more effective. "Like" Change to Win Federation or the Sierra Club or Occupy California on Facebook, and you will receive a constant set of Tweets, blogs, and links to videos. The Occupy movement gathered almost all of its strength and organizing power through the use of social networks.

Interest groups also may commission polls to find out what the public's sentiments are and then publicize the results. Of course, the questions in the polls are worded to get public responses that support the group's own position. The intent of this activity is to convince policymakers that public opinion overwhelmingly supports the group's position.

Some corporations and interest groups also engage in a practice that might be called **climate control**. With this strategy, public relations efforts are aimed at improving the public image of the industry or group and are not necessarily related to any specific political issue. Contributions by corporations and groups in support

Climate Control
The use of public relations techniques to create favorable public opinion toward an interest group, industry, or corporation.

To protest SOPA, a proposed law that would have placed new regulations on the Internet, Wikipedia shut its site down for one day. This screen shot captures the thank you message posted by Wikipedia after the blackout concluded.

Dusit/Shutterstock.com

of public television programs, sponsorship of special events, and commercials extolling the virtues of corporate research are some ways of achieving climate control. For example, to improve its image in the wake of the 2010 Deepwater Horizon oil spill in the Gulf of Mexico, British Petroleum (BP) launched a set of advertisements featuring individuals who work for the corporation talking about the cleanup, the good work done by BP, and their own pride in working for the corporation. Procter and Gamble (P&G) conceived its "Thank You, Mom" campaign for the 2014 Sochi Winter Olympics to build a warm image in addition to selling products. By building a reservoir of favorable public opinion, groups believe that their legislative goals will be less likely to encounter opposition from the public.

Using Constituents as Lobbyists. Interest groups also use constituents to lobby for their goals. In the "shotgun" approach, the interest group tries to mobilize large numbers of constituents to email, tweet, write, or phone their legislators or the president. These efforts are effective on Capitol Hill only with a very large number of responses, however, because legislators know that the voters did not initiate the communications on their own. Artificially manufactured grassroots activity has been aptly labeled *Astroturf lobbying.*

A more powerful variation of this technique uses only important constituents. With this approach, known as the "rifle" technique or the "Utah plant manager theory," the interest group might, for example, ask the manager of a local plant in Utah to contact the senator from Utah. Because the constituent is seen as responsible for many jobs or other resources, the legislator is more likely to listen carefully to the constituent's concerns about legislation than to a paid lobbyist.[15]

The importance of the electronic media cannot be understated for indirect lobbying. Whether Yoko Ono is speaking against allowing fracking in her home state, New York, or Beyoncé and a host of other media personalities are organizing for gun control, people recognize these individuals and want to see them, and thus receive a message about a public policy issue.[16]

Singer Jennifer Hudson joins the Sandy Hook Elementary School chorus at the Super Bowl to sing "America the Beautiful." Hudson's appearance with the children demonstrated her support for stronger gun control legislation.

Al Pereira/WireImage/Getty Images

15. Tim Hyson, "Contrary to Popular Belief, Constituents Trump Lobbyists," Congressional Management Foundation, January 25, 2011. http://www.congressionalfoundation.org/news/blog/866
16. "Demand a Plan PSA: Beyonce, Jessica Alba, Jamie Foxx, Rashida Jones and More Rally for Gun Control (video)" *Huffington Post*, December 21, 2012. www.huffingtonpost.com

Unconventional Forms of Pressure. Sometimes, interest groups may employ forms of pressure that fall outside the ordinary political process. These can include marches, rallies, civil disobedience, or demonstrations. Such assemblies, as long as they are peaceful, are protected by the First Amendment. Chapter 5 described the civil disobedience techniques of the African American civil rights movement in the 1950s and 1960s. The 1963 March on Washington in support of civil rights was one of the most effective demonstrations ever organized. The women's suffrage movement of the early 1900s also employed marches and demonstrations to great effect.

Demonstrations, however, are not always peaceable. Violent demonstrations have a long history in America, dating back to the anti-tax Boston Tea Party described in Chapter 2. The Vietnam War (1964–1975) provoked many demonstrations, some of which were violent. In 2014, protests against the police and city officials broke out in Albuquerque, New Mexico. The demonstrators were expressing their anger at a number of incidents of police shootings, including one of a homeless man who appeared to be surrendering when he was killed. Still, violent demonstrations can be counterproductive—instead of putting pressure on the authorities, they may simply alienate the public. For example, historians continue to debate whether the demonstrations against the Vietnam War were effective or counterproductive.

Another unconventional form of pressure is the **boycott**—a refusal to buy a particular product or deal with a particular business. To be effective, boycotts must command widespread support. One example was the African American boycott of buses in Montgomery, Alabama, during 1955. Another was the boycott of California grapes that were picked by nonunion workers, as part of a campaign to organize Mexican American farmworkers. The first grape boycott lasted from 1965 to 1970; a series of later boycotts was less effective. More recently, the Girl Scouts of America faced a cookie boycott from some pastors of the Christian right, who called the scouts pro-abortion and pro-lesbian, while gay and lesbian groups called for a boycott of Russian vodka because of that nation's laws restricting protests or public comment supporting homosexuals.

Boycott
A form of pressure or protest—an organized refusal to purchase a particular product or deal with a particular business.

Regulating Lobbyists

■ **LO7.5:** Describe the legislation which regulates the reporting of lobbying efforts at the federal level and discuss why it is relatively ineffective.

Congress made its first attempt to control lobbyists and lobbying activities through Title III of the Legislative Reorganization Act of 1946, otherwise known as the Federal Regulation of Lobbying Act. The act actually provided for public disclosure more than for regulation, and it neglected to specify which agency would enforce its provisions. The 1946 legislation defined a *lobbyist* as any person or organization that received money to be used principally to influence legislation before Congress. Such persons and individuals were supposed to register their clients and the purposes of their efforts and report quarterly on their activities.

The legislation was tested in a 1954 Supreme Court case, *United States v. Harriss*, and was found to be constitutional.[17] The Court agreed that the lobbying law did not violate due process, freedom of speech or of the press, or the freedom to petition. The Court narrowly construed the act, however, holding that it applied only to lobbyists who were influencing federal legislation *directly*.

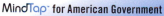

COMPARE WITH YOUR PEERS
MindTap™ for American Government

Access the Interest Group Forum: Polling Activity—Regulating Interest Groups.

---

17. 347 U.S. 612 (1954).

The Results of the 1946 Act

The immediate result of the act was that a minimal number of individuals registered as lobbyists. National interest groups, such as the NRA and the American Petroleum Institute, could employ hundreds of staff members who were, of course, working on legislation, but only register one or two lobbyists who were engaged *principally* in influencing Congress. There were no reporting requirements for lobbying the executive branch, federal agencies, the courts, or congressional staff.

According to the Center for Responsive Politics, approximately 12,278 individuals and organizations registered in 2013 as lobbyists, although most experts estimated that 10 times that number were actually employed in Washington to exert influence on the government.

While lobbying firms and individuals who represent foreign corporations must register with Congress, lobbyists who represent foreign governments must register with the Department of Justice under the Foreign Agent Registration Act of 1938. The Department of Justice publishes an annual report listing the lobbyists and the nations that have reported their activities. That report is available online at the Department of Justice website (www.fara.gov).

The Reforms of 1995

The reform-minded Congress of 1995–1996 overhauled the lobbying legislation, fundamentally changing the ground rules for those who seek to influence the federal government. Lobbying legislation passed in 1995 included the following provisions:

1. A *lobbyist* is defined as anyone who spends at least 20 percent of his or her time lobbying members of Congress, their staffs, or executive branch officials.
2. Lobbyists must register with the clerk of the House and the secretary of the Senate within 45 days of being hired or of making their first contacts. The registration requirement applies to organizations that spend more than $20,000 in one year or to individuals who are paid more than $5,000 annually for lobbying work.
3. Semiannual (now quarterly and electronic) reports must disclose the general nature of the lobbying effort, specific issues and bill numbers, the estimated cost of the campaign, and a list of the branches of government contacted. The names of the individuals contacted need not be reported.
4. Representatives of U.S.-owned subsidiaries of foreign-owned firms and lawyers who represent foreign entities also are required to register.
5. The requirements exempt grassroots lobbying efforts and those of tax-exempt organizations, such as religious groups.

Both the House and the Senate adopted new rules on gifts and travel expenses: The House adopted a flat ban on gifts, and the Senate limited gifts to $50 in value and to no more than $100 in total value from a single source in a year. There are exceptions for gifts from family members and for home-state products and souvenirs, such as T-shirts and coffee mugs. Both chambers banned all-expenses-paid trips, golf outings, and other such junkets. An exception applies for "widely attended" events, however, or if the member is a primary speaker at an event. These gift rules stopped the broad practice of taking members of Congress to lunch or dinner, but the various exemptions and exceptions have caused much controversy as the Senate and House Ethics Committees have considered individual cases.

Recent Lobbying Scandals

The regulation of lobbying activity again surfaced in 2005, when several scandals came to light. At the center of some publicized incidents was a highly influential and corrupt lobbyist, Jack Abramoff. Using his ties with numerous Republican (and a handful of Democratic) lawmakers, Abramoff brokered many deals for the special-interest clients that he represented in return for campaign donations, gifts, and various perks. In January 2006, Abramoff pled guilty to three criminal felony counts related to the defrauding of American Indian tribes and the corruption of public officials.

In 2007, both parties claimed that they wanted to reform lobbying legislation and the ethics rules in Congress. The House Democrats tightened the rules in that body early in the year, as did the Senate. The aptly named Honest Leadership and Open Government Act of 2007 was signed by President Bush in September 2007. The law tightened reporting requirements for lobbyists, extended the time period before ex-members can accept lobbying jobs (to two years for senators and one year for House members), set up rules for lobbying by members' spouses, and changed some campaign contribution rules for interest groups. The new rules adopted by the respective houses bar all members from receiving gifts or trips paid for by lobbyists unless preapproved by the Ethics Committee. Within three months after the bill took effect, a loophole was discovered that allows lobbyists to make a campaign contribution to a senator's campaign, for example, and then go to a fancy dinner where the campaign is allowed to pay the bill.[18] As with most other pieces of lobbying legislation, additional loopholes will be discovered and utilized by members and interest groups.

Interest Groups and Representative Democracy

The role played by interest groups in shaping national policy has caused many to question whether we really have a democracy at all. Most interest groups have a middle-class or upper-class bias. Members of interest groups can afford to pay the membership fees, are generally well educated, and normally participate in the political process to a greater extent than the "average" American. Furthermore, the majority of Americans do not actually join a group outside of their religious congregation or a recreational group. They allow others who do join to represent them.

Furthermore, leaders of some interest groups may constitute an "elite within an elite," in the sense that they usually are from a different economic or social class than most of their members. Certainly, association executives are highly paid individuals who live in Washington, DC, and associate regularly with the political elites of the country. The most powerful interest groups—those with the most resources and political influence—are primarily business, union, trade, or professional groups. In contrast, public-interest groups or civil rights groups make up only a small percentage of the interest groups lobbying Congress and may struggle to gain enough funds to continue to exist.

Thinking about the relatively low number of Americans who join them and their status as middle class or better leads one to conclude that interest groups are really an elitist phenomenon rather than, as discussed in Chapter 1, a manifestation of pluralism. Pluralist theory proposes that these many groups will try to influence the government and struggle to reach a compromise that will be advantageous to all sides. If most Americans are not represented by a group, say, on the

---

18. Robert Pear, "Ethics Law Isn't Without Its Loopholes," *The New York Times*, April 8, 2008.

question of farm subsidies or energy imports, however, is there any evidence that the final legislation improves life for ordinary Americans?

Interest Group Influence

The results of lobbying efforts—congressional legislation—do not always favor the interests of the most powerful groups, however. In part, this is because not all interest groups have an equal influence on government. Each group has a different combination of resources to use in the policymaking process. While some groups are composed of members who have high social status and significant economic resources, such as the National Association of Manufacturers, other groups derive influence from their large memberships. AARP's large membership allows it to wield significant power over legislators. Still other groups, such as environmentalist groups, have causes that can claim strong public support even from people who have no direct stake in the issue. Groups such as the NRA are well organized and have highly motivated members. This enables them to channel a stream of mail or electronic messages toward Congress with a few days' effort.

Even the most powerful interest groups do not always succeed in their demands. Whereas the U.S. Chamber of Commerce may understandably have a justified interest in the question of business taxes, many legislators might feel that the group should not engage in the debate over the future of Social Security. In other words, groups are seen as having a legitimate concern about the issues closest to their interests but not necessarily about broader issues. This may explain why some of the most successful groups are those that focus on very specific issues—such as tobacco farming, funding of abortions, or handgun control—and do not get involved in larger conflicts.

What Would You Do?

The Gun Control Issue

One of the issues on which Americans are clearly divided is gun control. The long-running debate over the right to own firearms has spawned numerous interest groups with a "single-issue" focus. Their passion is fueled by the 1 million gun incidents occurring in the United States each year—murders, suicides, assaults, accidents, and robberies in which guns are involved.

Why Should You Care?

Research conducted by the National School Safety Center shows that more than 300 students have died in school shootings in the past 15 years. The massacre of students at Sandy Hook Elementary School in 2012 serves as a traumatic reminder that students are increasingly vulnerable to gun violence at the hands of mentally unstable young people. In addition, hundreds of young people are killed by gun violence in urban areas and many more in accidental shootings.

On December 14, 2012, 20 children and six adult staff members were fatally shot in a mass murder at Sandy Hook Elementary School in Newtown, Connecticut. The shooter was a 20-year-old male who fatally shot his mother before driving to the school. He then fatally shot himself after carrying out the killings. It was the second deadliest mass shooting by a single person in American history, after the 2007 Virginia Tech massacre.

In response to the horrific crime, President Obama called for a renewed national debate on gun control. He formed a Gun Violence Task Force to be led by Vice President Joe Biden, with the goal of addressing the causes of gun violence in the United States. His administration called for universal background checks on firearms purchases, an assault weapons ban, and a limit on magazine capacity. The National Rifle Association (NRA) called on the United States Congress to appropriate funds for the hiring of armed police officers in every American school in order to protect students.

In April 2013, the Manchin-Toomey Background Checks Bill, a bill that would have imposed restrictions on gun control, failed to pass the U.S. Senate by six votes. President Obama called the failing of the bill "shameful." The NRA critiqued the bill, stating that expanded background checks will not reduce violent crime or keep children safe in schools.

What Would You Do?

If you were a member of Congress, presented with the request for universal background checks on firearms purchases, an assault weapons ban, and a limit on magazine capacity, would you agree that those restrictions could help prevent future shootings like the Sandy Hook Elementary School massacre?

What You *Can* Do

Most importantly, you can be extremely alert to the safety of your friends, family, and classmates. On campus, all students, staff, and faculty need to take responsibility for identifying and redirecting the energies of problematic people. Students can take advantage of training offered by the university to identify individuals with problems and pay attention to information about personal safety. Most experts believe that the majority of these violent events can be prevented by behavioral awareness.

You could consider joining an organization like the Brady Center or the Center to Prevent Youth Violence. After his brother was shot in the back of the head on the observation deck of the Empire State Building in 1997, Dan Gross quit his job to start the Center to Prevent Youth Violence (CPYV, initially called PAX). The center offers programs for young people and parents aimed at reducing gun violence. You can become part of a local group supporting this program. One of the programs sponsored by CPYV is the SPEAK UP hotline. Students who believe that someone is carrying a weapon, or has a gun available to them illegally, can call the SPEAK UP hotline and report their fear anonymously. The center also encourages young people to ask their friends' parents if there is a gun in their home when they visit and to not visit homes where guns are available to children and adults.

In direct contrast to these efforts to keep firearms and those who carry them far from young people, some Americans believe that students and educators should have the right to defend themselves, and that weapons on campus should be part of the plan. A nonprofit organization called Students for Concealed Carry on Campus has 42,000 members nationwide that include college students, faculty, and parents. This group advocates legislation that would allow licensed gun owners to carry concealed weapons on campus, believing that a well-trained citizen could stop a deranged shooter from committing mass murder. Thirteen states are currently considering a form of "concealed carry" legislation for college campuses. Gun control advocates oppose such laws and express great concern that having guns on campus or in any social situation may increase the possibility of gun violence.

- To learn about the position of a gun control advocate, contact the Brady Center to Prevent Gun Violence:
  1225 Eye St. N.W., Suite 1100
  Washington, DC 20005
  Brady Center: 202-289-7319
  Brady Campaign: 202-898-0792
  www.bradycampaign.org

- To learn about its efforts to stop gun violence, contact the Center to Prevent Youth Violence:100 Wall Street, 2nd Floor
  New York, NY 10005
  212-269-5100
  www.cpyv.org

- To find out more about its positions, contact the National Rifle Association:11250 Waples Mill Rd.
  Fairfax, VA 22030
  703-267-1000
  www.nra.org

- For more information about the rights of college students to carry weapons, contact Students for Concealed Carry on Campus:
  www.concealedcampus.org

Purestock/Getty Images

Key Terms

Chapter Summary

■ **LO7.1:** An interest group is an organization whose members share common objectives and actively attempt to influence government policy. Interest groups proliferate in the United States, because they can influence government at many points in the political structure and because their efforts are protected by the First Amendment to the Constitution. Madison believed that having many opportunities for groups to flourish would protect minority rights.

■ **LO7.2:** People join interest groups for solidary or emotional benefits, for material or financial reasons, or for purposive reasons. However, many individuals join no interest groups yet are able to benefit from the work of their members. This reality is called the "free rider" problem. Interest groups often grow from the participation of individuals in social movements.

■ **LO7.3:** Major types of interest groups include business, agricultural, labor, public employee, professional, and environmental groups. Other important groups may be considered public-interest groups. In addition, special-interest groups and foreign governments lobby the government. The relative power of interest groups can be estimated based on the size of their membership, their financial resources, leadership, cohesion, and support among the public

■ **LO7.4:** Interest groups use direct and indirect techniques to influence government. Direct techniques include testifying before committees and rule-making agencies, providing information to legislators, rating legislators' voting records, aiding political campaigns, and building alliances. Indirect techniques to influence government include campaigns to rally public sentiment, use of social media to generate public pressure, efforts to influence the climate of opinion, and the use of constituents to lobby for the group's interests. Unconventional methods of applying pressure include demonstrations and boycotts.

■ **LO7.5:** The 1946 Legislative Reorganization Act was the first attempt to control lobbyists and their activities through registration requirements. The United States Supreme Court narrowly construed the act as applying only to lobbyists who directly seek to influence federal legislation.

■ **LO7.5:** In 1995, Congress approved new legislation requiring anyone who spends 20 percent of his or her time influencing legislation to register. Also, any organization spending $20,000 or more and any individual who is paid more than $5,000 annually for his or her work must register. Quarterly reports must include the names of clients, the bills in which they are interested, and the branches of government contacted. The 2007 lobbying reform law tightened the regulations on lobbyists and imposed other rules on members who wish to become lobbyists after leaving office.

Selected Print, Media, and Online Resources

PRINT RESOURCES

Baumgartner, Frank R., Jeffrey M. Berry, Marie Hojnacki, David C. Kimball, and Beth L. Leech. *Lobbying and Policy Change: Who Wins, Who Loses, and Why.* Chicago: University of Chicago Press, 2009. The authors explore the degree to which lobbying campaigns and intense interest group effort truly change public policy. Their somewhat surprising finding is that the majority of lobbying efforts fail in the face of the strong Washington bias toward the status quo.

Grossmann, Matt. *The Not-So-Special Interests: Interest Groups, Public Representation, and American Governance,* Berkeley, CA: Stanford University Press, 2012. The author provides a new framework for analyzing interest groups. His goal is to understand why some groups seem to have a more powerful voice than others.

Leech, Beth. *Lobbyists at Work.* New York: Apress Media LLC, 2013. This volume examines how lobbyists actually assist members of congress in fund raising and examines how this relationship impacts politics in Washington, DC.

Schlozman, Kay Lehman, Sidney Verba, and Henry Brady. *The Unheavenly Chorus: Unequal Political Voice and the Broken Promise of American Democracy.* Princeton, NJ: Princeton University Press, 2012. This superb academic book examines hundreds of organization and interest groups as well as public polls to point out the continuing inequality in political participation in the United States.

Spitzer, Robert. *The Politics of Gun Control,* 5th edition. New York: Paradigm Publishers, 2011. In this updated volume, Spitzer provides an nonpartisan policy analysis of American gun laws and the opposing forces of the NRA and the anti-gun organizations.

MEDIA RESOURCES

Casino Jack and the U.S. of Money—This 2010 documentary takes a scathing look at the machinations of Jack Abramoff and his colleagues. Beginning with Abramoff's days as a College Republican, producer Alex Gibney traces his rise to fame and the tremendous corruption that money brings to Congress.

Gasland—In this 2010 documentary, a Pennsylvanian traces his community's reaction to being offered leases for fracking natural gas. The film looks at the effects of these operations on communities across the country.

Inside Job—Winner of the 2010 Oscar for best feature-length documentary, the film reveals the inside influence that kept Congress from regulating the financial industry, thus, leading to the housing crash and recession of 2008.

Norma Rae—A 1979 Hollywood movie about an attempt by a northern union organizer to unionize workers in the southern textile industry; stars Sally Field, who won an Academy Award for her performance.

Promised Land—This 2012 film stars Matt Damon as an employee of an energy company that specializes in fracking. He is sent to a Pennsylvania farming town to persuade land owners to sign mineral rights leases to allow drilling, where he encounters John Krasinski's character, who is an environmental advocate who starts a grassroots campaign against Damon's company in hopes of preventing drilling.

Syriana—Released in 2005, the thriller follows the trail of a global petroleum corporation and its executives as they use violence abroad and lobbyists at home to get their future assured.

ONLINE RESOURCES

AFL-CIO (American Federation of Labor and Congress of Industrial Organizations)—a voluntary federation of 56 national and international labor union s: www.aflcio.org

The Center for Public Integrity—a nonprofit organization dedicated to producing original, responsible investigative journalism on issues of public concern; tracks lobbyists and their expenditures: www.publicintegrity.org/lobby

Center for Responsive Politics—a nonpartisan guide to money's influence on U.S. elections and public policy with data derived from Federal Election Commission reports: www.opensecrets.org

National Rifle Association—America's foremost defender of Second Amendment rights and firearms education organization in the world; provides information on the gun control issue: www.nra.org

Sunlight Foundation—A nonpartisan organization that collects and makes available all of the data recorded at the Department of Justice for foreign lobbying registrations. www.sunlightfoundation.org.

Master the concept of Interest Groups with MindTap™ for American Government

REVIEW MindTap™ for American Government

Access Key Term Flashcards for Chapter 7.

STAY CURRENT MindTap™ for American Government

Access the KnowNow blog and customized RSS for updates on current events.

TEST YOURSELF MindTap™ for American Government

Take the Wrap It Up Quiz for Chapter 7.

STAY FOCUSED MindTap™ for American Government

Complete the Focus Activities for Interest Groups.

8 Political Parties

LEARNING OUTCOMES

After reading this chapter, students will be able to:

- **LO8.1:** Define the role political parties play in the U.S. political system.

- **LO8.2:** Identify the three major components of the political party and describe how each contributes to overall party coherence.

- **LO8.3:** Explain why political parties formed in the United States and evaluate how their strength and importance has changed over time.

- **LO8.4:** Compare and contrast the demographics of people who identify as Democrats and Republicans; explain how party positions differ on economic and social issues.

- **LO8.5:** Summarize the factors that reinforce a two-party system and explain why third parties are rarely successful at winning national elections.

- **LO8.6:** Discuss the rise of political independents and evaluate how this change might impact American politics.

 WATCH & LEARN MindTap for American Government

Watch a brief "What Do You Know?" video summarizing Political Parties.

Political Parties Ended Nominating Conventions?

BACKGROUND

The question of how to identify qualified candidates for president and vice president was not settled in the U.S. Constitution. Wary of disruptive factions emerging, the Founders did not provide any guidance on the mechanisms for nomination. In the first two national elections following ratification this omission did not matter—George Washington was a consensus candidate and was followed into office by his vice president, John Adams. By 1800, however, nascent political parties were emerging within Congress and the nominating function naturally fell to these groups. As the country grew and expanded west, congressional caucuses were less likely to naturally agree on a single candidate. In 1831, the Anti-Masonic Party met in Baltimore, Maryland to select a presidential candidate that would appeal to the entire party in the election of 1832, beginning the tradition of nominating conventions.

Today, the two major parties' quadrennial events are the Democratic National Convention and the Republican National Convention. Each party selects delegates to attend the national meeting and chooses the party's nominee by ballot. Delegates also meet to create the party platform (a statement of principles and policy positions) and determine the rules and procedures that will govern the next election cycle. Speeches allow the parties to audition future candidates. President Barack Obama, for example, was the keynote speaker at the Democratic National Convention in 2004. New Jersey Governor Chris Christie delivered the keynote address for Republicans in 2012.

Prior to direct primaries, presidential nominating conventions were exciting events with choice of the party nominee entirely in the hands of delegates (and the political bosses who influenced their votes). Primaries began in just a handful of states, but spread quickly following the chaotic 1968 Democratic National Convention in Chicago. Democrats adopted the direct primary based on the recommendation of the McGovern-Fraser Commission and Republicans followed suit in 1972. This effectively transferred the power to choose the party's nominee from party delegates to individual voters who may or may not be party loyalists. By the time the primary season is over in June, the nominee has been determined. A pro forma vote by convention delegates makes it official and the successful nominee announces his or her choice of running mate. Delegates once again endorse that decision with a vote. The presidential nominee's acceptance speech on the last night of the convention marks the first campaign speech on the road to the White House.

WHY CANCEL THE PARTY? EVERYONE IS HAVING SO MUCH FUN!

Even though the nominee might not be in question going into the national convention, the party uses the mass meeting as an opportunity to celebrate and rally supporters. In 2012, 50,000 people played a role in the Republican National Convention held in Tampa, Florida, and another 35,000 convened in Charlotte, North Carolina, for the Democrats. In each case, about a third of those involved were representatives of the media. Network television used to provide "gavel-to-gavel" coverage of the conventions but has dropped back to an hour of highlights aired each evening.

Nominating conventions are expensive affairs—$55 million was spent by Democrats and $73 million by Republicans in 2012. The Federal Election Commission gave each party $18.3 million in public campaign funds (raised with the $3 check-off on federal tax returns), and Congress gave each party another $50 million to pay for convention security costs incurred by local and state agencies. Each party covers the shortfall by raising private donations from individuals and corporations. In April 2014, President Obama signed a bill redirecting public campaign funds earmarked for conventions to the National Institute for Health and pediatric medical research. This likely spells the end for Watergate-era public financing, especially as it comes on the heels of the U.S. Supreme Court's decision in *McCutcheon v. Federal Election Commission* that struck down the cap on total giving to national candidates and political parties. Candidates Obama and Romney each declined to accept public funds in 2012 and each raised more than a billion dollars.

WOULD ANYBODY MISS THE CONVENTIONS?

Each national party must select a nominee for president, but today this important choice is accomplished through primaries and party caucuses held in all fifty states, not at the national nominating convention. There is some value to directing the nation's attention to the presidential selection process when the political parties convene, but the business of conventions could be accomplished another way.

For Critical Analysis

1. Delegates to the presidential nominating conventions are regular people who are hyper-engaged with their political party. What might be lost for those people if political parties ended the convention?

2. Conventions, campaigns, and elections are very expensive. Without public money, private donors will play a bigger role in conventions. Will this change who is nominated or the quality of candidates who choose to seek the party's nomination?

Factions
A subgroup or bloc within a legislature or political party acting in pursuit of some special interest or position.

DURING NATIONAL ELECTION YEARS, whether for congressional seats, such as 2014, or the presidency, as in 2012 and 2016, political parties are an important feature of the political landscape in the United States. Political parties are made up of people who use the organization, resources, and access to power that the parties provide in order to influence the outcomes of government. Parties play an important coordinating role across institutions and between the local, state, and national levels. The nation's founders worried that political **factions** would destroy the Republic, but in reality political parties are absolutely necessary to make our system function. Identification with a political party links individuals with a group of like-minded people who together recruit candidates for public office, conduct elections, inform voters on issues and policy choices, and organize government. Thus, while it has always been popular in America to speak of parties with disdain and the number of political independents has never been higher, to quote E. E. Schattschneider—"modern democracy is unthinkable save in terms of political parties."[1]

Interestingly, as important as parties are to American politics, affiliation is entirely voluntary and remarkably fluid. To become a "member" of a political party, you do not have to pay dues or swear an oath of allegiance. Individuals and groups switch their allegiance from one party to another between elections; within a single election cycle, an individual might select candidates from different parties for various offices. Also, not everyone within a party agrees on the best path forward, so intra-party debates are common and public. Party soul-searching typically follows electoral defeat. Having lost the White House in 2008 and 2012, Republicans are reviewing their message and evaluating the demographic changes among voters in preparation for the 2016 contest. President Obama warned Democrats not to be complacent, "During presidential elections, young people vote, women are more likely to vote, blacks, Hispanics more likely to vote. And suddenly a more representative cross-section of America gets out there and we do pretty well in presidential elections. But in midterms we get clobbered. . . . I'm just hoping you all feel the same sense of urgency that I do."[2]

What Is a Political Party and What Do Parties Do?

■ **LO8.1:** Define the role political parties play in the U.S. political system.

A **political party** is a group of political activists who organize to win elections, operate the government, and determine public policy. This definition highlights the difference between an interest group and a political party. Interest groups do not want to operate the government, and they do not put forth political candidates—even though they support candidates who will promote their interests if elected or reelected. Interest groups also tend to be exclusive, attracting people who share their set of interest positions. American political parties, because of our electoral structure where majorities determine most victories, tend to be as inclusive as possible in order to attract every possible voter, while still maintaining their unique "brand."

Political Party
A group of political activists who organize to win elections, operate the government, and determine public policy.

did you know?
Delegates to the 2004 Republican National Convention celebrated the nomination of George W. Bush by dropping 100,000 balloons.

1. E. E. Schattschneider, *Party Government* (New York: Farrar & Rinehart, 1942).
2. Tal Kopan, "President Obama: 'In midterms we get clobbered,'" *Politico*, March 21, 2014. Accessed at www.politico.com/story/2014/03/obama-democrats-midterm-elections-clobbered-104885.html#ixzz2ylovxAhF

A California Tea Party supporter holds her sign at the annual tax day rally on April 15, 2012. Why does the Tea Party claim that it is *not* a political party although it endorses candidates and works for their election?

Political parties in the United States engage in a wide variety of activities, many of which are discussed in this chapter. Through these activities, parties perform several functions in the political system. These functions include the following:

- *Recruiting candidates to run for public office under their party label.* Because a primary goal of parties is to gain control of government, they must work to recruit candidates for all elective offices. If parties did not search out and encourage political hopefuls, far more offices would be uncontested, and voters would have limited choices.
- *Organizing and running elections.* Although elections are a government activity, political parties actually organize the voter-registration drives, recruit the volunteers to work at the polls, provide most of the campaign activity to stimulate interest in the election, and work to increase voter participation.
- *Presenting alternative policies to the electorate.* Political parties are focused on a broad set of issues with specific positions on each. Because political parties are large and complex organizations, there may be smaller constituencies within the party that hold different opinions, but each party reflects a set of principles. The Democrats or Republicans in Congress who vote together do so because they represent constituencies that have similar expectations and demands.
- *Accepting responsibility for operating the government.* When a party elects the president or governor and members of the legislature, it accepts the responsibility for running the government based on the principles it espouses. This includes staffing the executive branch with loyal party supporters and developing linkages among the elected officials to gain support for policies and their implementation.
- *Acting as the organized opposition to the party in power.* The "out" party, or the one not in control, is expected to articulate its own policies and stand in opposition to the winning party when appropriate for the nation. By presenting alternative perspectives to the party in power, the opposition party forces debate on the policy alternatives and ensures that careful scrutiny is paid to policies enacted.

The major functions of American political parties are carried out by a small nucleus of party activists operating at the local, state, and national levels. This arrangement is quite different from the more highly structured, mass-membership party organization typical of many European parties. American parties concentrate on winning elections rather than on signing up large numbers of deeply committed, dues-paying members who believe passionately in the party's program.

Getting Organized: The Three Components of a Party

■ **LO8.2:** Identify the three major components of the political party and describe how each contributes to overall party coherence.

Although American parties are known by a single name each party really has three major components: party-in-the-electorate, party organization, and party-in-government.

Party-in-the-Electorate

Those members of the general public who identify with a political party or who express a preference for one party over another.

The first component, the **party-in-the-electorate**, is made up of all of the people who affiliate and identify with the political party. Although they are not required to participate in every election, they are the most likely to do so because they feel a sense of loyalty to the party and use their partisanship as a cue to decide who will earn their vote. Party membership might be a rational calculation of which party is most likely to advance their material interest, but for most people identifying with a party is more analogous to identifying with a geographic region or a major sports team. In this sense, the attachment is emotional and the affiliation helps us find and make connections with others who share our interests and passions. Some states require you to specify your party affiliation when you register to vote, while others do not. In some places, you only have two formal choices when declaring your party—Democrat or Republican—while in others, you might be allowed to choose from among many minor parties. Even then, your party preference might not always match your vote choice in a general election. Perhaps you think of yourself as a Libertarian, but because there are few Libertarian candidates standing for election in each race, you select candidates from other parties that match your preferences most closely for a given office. Party leaders pay close attention to the affiliation of their members in the electorate because winning a majority of contests is the way to gain control of government and enact the party's policies. The national Republican Party, for example, would like to win back the White House in 2016. To do that they know they need to attract more women, minorities, and young people to their party.

Party Organization

Party Organization

The formal structure and leadership of a political party, including election committees; local, state, and national executives; and paid professional staff.

The second component, the **party organization**, provides the structural framework for the political party by recruiting volunteers to become party leaders, identifying potential candidates, and organizing caucuses, conventions, and election campaigns for its candidates. The party organization and its active workers keep the party functioning between elections, as well as make sure that the party puts forth electable candidates and articulates clear positions in the elections. If the party-in-the-electorate declines in numbers and loyalty, the party organization must try to find a strategy to rebuild the grassroots following.

Each of the American political parties has a parallel structure at the national, state, and local levels. This often leads people to believe that the national party dictates to the state and local parties, but in reality the political parties have a confederal structure in which each unit has significant autonomy and is linked only loosely to the other units. State and local organizations are essential to the party's overall functions but their influence varies by state. In some states, parties receive significant contributions from individuals and interest groups for their operations, whereas in other states and localities political parties are very weak organizations with very little funding. This is particularly true of the minority party in a state or district where it has little chance to win a seat.

The National Convention. The national organization is responsible for the **national convention**, held every four years and attended by thousands of **convention delegates** from around the country. The convention is where the presidential and vice presidential candidates are officially nominated and where delegates adopt the **party platform**. The platform is a set of guiding principles and policy positions intended to bring coherence to the party brand. However, the platform is drafted by a committee of loyal party activists who may have supported different candidates for the party's nomination prior to the convention. Compromises are required to reach an agreement on the platform, and the positions articulated in the document are likely to reflect the beliefs of the strongest partisans rather than the average party voter. Republican delegates are more ideologically conservative than the likely Republican voter, just as delegates to the Democratic convention are more liberal than the majority of their party's voters. So, while it is important that the parties detail their core principles for members and voters, the platform is not binding on candidates, officeholders, or even the party itself.

Each of the parties chooses a **national committee**, elected by the individual state parties, to direct and coordinate party activities during the following four years. The Democrats include at least two members (a man and a woman) from each state, from the District of Columbia, and from the several territories. Governors, members of Congress, mayors, and other officials may be included as at-large members of the national committee. The Republicans also include state chairpersons from every state carried by the Republican Party in the preceding presidential, gubernatorial, or congressional elections. The selections of national committee members are ratified by the delegates in attendance. The national committee ratifies the presidential nominee's choice of a national chairperson, who acts as the spokesperson for the party. The national chairperson and the national committee plan the next campaign as well as the next convention, raise financial contributions, and publicize the national party. The national chairperson is an important face for the party, but his or her power today is less than party leaders enjoyed four decades ago. Robert S. Strauss, former head of the Democratic National Party, died in March 2014. Tributes to his life inevitably commented on the diminished power of political parties and their national leaders and the rise of candidate campaign operations and independent groups "aided by transforming technology that has changed the character of politics."[3]

The State Party Organization. The Union has 50 states, plus the District of Columbia and the U.S. territories, and an equal number of party organizations for each major party. Thus, there are more than 100 state parties (and even more, including local parties and minor parties). Because every state party is unique, it is impossible to describe what an "average" state political party is like. Nonetheless, state parties have several organizational features in common. Each

---

did you know?

Franklin D. Roosevelt was the first person to accept his party's nomination in person, appearing at the 1932 Democratic National Convention in Chicago.

National Convention
The meeting held every four years by each major party to select presidential and vice presidential candidates, to write a platform, to choose a national committee, and to conduct party business.

Convention Delegates
Delegates are individuals chosen to represent their states at their party conventions prior to a presidential election.

Party Platform
A document drawn up at each national convention outlining the policies, positions, and principles of the party.

National Committee
A standing committee of a national political party established to direct and coordinate party activities between national party conventions.

did you know?

The Democrats and Republicans each had exactly one woman delegate at their conventions in 1900.

---

3. Jonathan Weisman and Jennifer Steinhauer, "Kingmaker's Death Lays Bare Erosion of Parties' Authority," *The New York Times*, March 20, 2014. Accessed at www.nytimes.com/2014/03/21/us/politics/political-parties-have-seen-shift-in-center-of-power.html

Two convention delegates from Colorado cheer as their governor, John Hickenlooper, addresses the convention. The Party conventions are intended to build enthusiasm among party members and supporters and to show off their political leaders, such as Governor Hickenlooper, to the American public.

State Central Committee
The principal organized structure of each political party within each state. This committee is responsible for carrying out policy decisions of the party's state convention.

state party has a chairperson, a committee, and local organizations. In theory, the role of the **state central committee**—the principal organized structure of each political party within each state—is similar in the various states. The committee, usually composed of members who represent congressional districts, state legislative districts, or counties, has responsibility for carrying out the policy decisions of the party's state convention. In some states, the state committee can issue directives to the state chairperson.

Republican convention delegates wave flags on the last day of the 2012 Republican National Convention in Tampa, Florida. They await the arrival of nominee Mitt Romney, who will give his acceptance speech that night.

Similar to the national committee, the state central committee controls the use of party campaign funds during political campaigns. State parties are also important in national politics because of the **unit rule**, which awards electoral votes in presidential elections as an indivisible bloc (except in Maine and Nebraska). Presidential candidates concentrate their efforts in states in which voter preferences seem to be evenly divided or in which large numbers of electoral votes are at stake.

Local Party Organizations.   The lowest level of party machinery is the local organization, supported by district leaders, precinct or ward captains, and party workers. Much of the work is coordinated by county committees and their chairpersons. In the 1800s, the institution of **patronage**—rewarding the party faithful with government jobs or contracts—held the local organization together. For immigrants and the poor, the political machine often furnished important services and protections. The big-city machine was the archetypal example. Tammany Hall, or the Tammany Society, which dominated New York City government for nearly two centuries, was perhaps the most notorious example of this political form.

Today, local political organizations still can contribute a great deal to local election campaigns. These organizations are able to provide the foot soldiers of politics—individuals who pass out literature and get out the vote on election day, which can be crucial in local elections. In many regions, local Democratic and Republican organizations still exercise some patronage, such as awarding courthouse jobs, contracts for street repair, and other lucrative construction contracts. Local party organizations are also the most important vehicles for recruiting young adults into political work, because political involvement at the local level offers activists many opportunities to gain experience.

The Party-in-Government

The **party-in-government** is the third component of American political parties. The party-in-government consists of elected and appointed officials who identify with a political party. After the election is over and the winners are announced, the focus of party activity shifts to organizing and controlling the government. Partisanship plays an important role in the day-to-day operations of Congress, with party membership determining everything from office space to committee assignments. The political party furnishes to the president the pool of qualified applicants for political appointments to run the government, although the president is free to appointment individuals from any party and presidential appointment power is limited by the permanent bureaucracy. Judicial appointments, especially nominations to the U.S. Supreme Court, offer the winning party a way to extend their influence far into the future.

Divided Government.   All of these party appointments suggest that the winning political party at any level has a great deal of control in the American system. Because of the checks and balances and the relative lack of cohesion in American parties, however, such control is an illusion. One reason is that for some time, many Americans have seemed to prefer a **divided government**, with the executive and legislative branches controlled by different parties. The trend toward **ticket splitting**—voting for a president and congressperson of different parties—has increased sharply since 1952. This practice may indicate a lack of trust in government or the relative weakness of party identification

Unit Rule
A rule by which all of a state's electoral votes are cast for the presidential candidate receiving a plurality of the popular vote in that state.

Patronage
Rewarding faithful party workers and followers with government employment and contracts.

Party-in-Government
All of the elected and appointed officials who identify with a political party.

Divided Government
A situation in which one major political party controls the presidency and the other controls the chambers of Congress, or in which one party controls a state governorship and the other controls the state legislature.

Ticket Splitting
Voting for candidates of two or more parties for different offices. For example, a voter splits her ticket if she votes for a Republican presidential candidate and a Democratic congressional candidate.

among many voters. Voters seem comfortable with having a president affiliated with one party and a Congress controlled by the other.

The Limits of Party Unity. The power of the parties is limited in other ways. Consider how major laws are passed in Congress. Traditionally, legislation has rarely been passed by a vote strictly along party lines. Although most Democrats may oppose a bill, for example, some Democrats may vote for it. Their votes, combined with the votes of Republicans, may be enough to pass the bill. Similarly, support from some Republicans may enable a bill sponsored by the Democrats to pass. U.S. elections are "candidate centered," meaning that candidates may choose to run, raise their own funds, build their own organizations, and win elections largely on their own, without significant help from a political party. Since the midterm victories in 2010, Republican Speaker of the House John Boehner has had a difficult time getting Tea Party-affiliated members to follow the Republican Party line.

Party Polarization. When parties in Congress adhere to party loyalty in their votes, the institution becomes polarized. When that happens, little is accomplished and members dig in and refuse to work across the aisle to reach a compromise. Without the ability to work together, legislative action stalls and the public grows increasingly dissatisfied. One cause of polarization is the ability of the parties to create House districts that are **safe seats** in the redistricting process.[4] In 1992 roughly one-fourth of the House of Representatives was elected from competitive districts (also known as swing districts because the seat could feasibly be won by either party), but today only 32 competitive districts remain— only 7 percent of the institution. Landslide districts, places where one party regularly wins by more than 20 percentage points, have doubled since 1992 and today make up nearly 56 percent of the House. Scholars and pundits differ on whether the polarization cemented in the House through redistricting is a true reflection of divisions within the electorate. Some contend that a majority of Americans are strongly committed to tolerance of opposing political views. Political scientist Morris Fiorina argues that the American people are no more divided over their policy preferences today than they have ever been.[5] Political parties serve to channel the publics' energy and divergent opinions into political solutions enacted by government. Parties have played this role in American since the founding.

A History of Political Parties in the United States

■ **LO8.3:** Explain why political parties formed in the United States and evaluate how their strength and importance has changed over time.

Although it is difficult to imagine more than two major political parties in the United States, multiparty systems are quite common in other democracies. Sometimes parties are tied to ideological positions—such as Marxist, socialist, liberal, conservative, and ultraconservative parties. Some nations have political parties representing regional interests born of separate cultural identities, such as the French-speaking and Flemish-speaking regions of Belgium. Some parties are

CONNECT WITH YOUR CLASSMATES
MindTap® for American Government

Access the Political Parties Forum: Discussion—Working Together After Elections

Safe Seat
A district that returns the legislator with 55 percent of the vote or more.

4. Nate Silver, "As Swing Districts Dwindle, Can a Divided House Stand?" *The New York Times*, December 27, 2012. Accessed at http://fivethirtyeight.blogs.nytimes.com/2012/12/27/as-swing-districts-dwindle-can-a-divided-house-stand/?_php=true&_type=blogs&_r=0
5. Morris Fiorina, *Culture War? The Myth of a Polarized America* (New York: Longman, 2005).

Politics with a Purpose

Securing the House of Representatives One State Legislature at a Time

Our constitution is unique in that it gives state legislatures substantial control over how we elect the president and Congress. In many other democracies, the national government runs elections—usually through an impartial commission. In the United States, the party in control of the state legislature draws the lines establishing congressional districts and determines the rules by which national elections are conducted in the state. (Will there be voter ID laws? Early voting? Same-day registration?)

Following the 2008 election, Republicans created the Redistricting Majority Project (REDMAP) aimed at winning seats in state legislative contests. Republican strategist Karl Rove said, "Some of the most important contests [in 2010] will be way down the ballot in . . . state legislative races that will determine who redraws congressional district lines after this year's census, a process that could determine which party controls upwards of 20 seats [in the House of Representatives] and whether many other seats will be competitive."* As Herman Schwartz, constitutional law professor at American University observes, REDMAP succeeded brilliantly.

Republicans focused on 107 state legislative seats in 16 states where Republican pick-ups of just four or five seats from Democrats would enable the GOP to reshape over 190 congressional districts. They succeeded in increasing their share of state house and senate seats by 10 percent, took both legislative chambers in 25 states, and won the legislature and governorship in 21 states. These victories allowed Republicans to remap congressional districts in their favor to great effect in the 2012 elections.

The Republican State Leadership Committee (RSLC) has been largely responsible for carrying out this strategy. By focusing laser-like attention on the states, Republicans have been able to make significant gains in the *national* House of Representatives—gains many describe as "lasting." The Republican State Leadership Committee is described as the largest caucus of Republican state leaders in the country and the only national organization whose mission is to elect down-ballot, state-level Republican officeholders—working since 2002 to elect candidates to the office of lieutenant governor, attorney general, secretary of state and state legislator.** In the 2012 election cycle, the RSLC raised over $39 million to invest in races in 42 states. This organization is classified as a "527 group"—a tax-exempt political organization created to influence elections.

The RSLC is not a part of the Republican Party, but the direct benefit to the party is very clear in this example. In Virginia and Ohio, the vote for House of Representatives narrowly favored Republicans (50-48 in Virginia; 51-47 in Ohio), but because of the way the district lines had been drawn, the outcomes in terms of seats was not close—8-3 in Virginia and 12-4 in Ohio.

The Democratic Party counterpart is the Democratic Legislative Campaign Committee (DLCC), established in 1994.*** Focused on policy coherence at the state level in support of national party action, this group has not strategically focused on winning state elections.

The REDMAP example is an illustration of the significant influence exercised by organizations outside of the formal political party structure.

---

* Herman Schwartz, "Democrats: It's the States, Stupid!" Reuters, July 14, 2013. Accessed at http://blogs.reuters.com/great-debate/2013/07/14/democrats-its-the-states-stupid/
** Republican State Leadership Committee, www.rslc.com/
*** Democratic Legislative Campaign Committee, www.dlcc.org

rooted in religious differences. Parties also exist that represent specific economic interests—agricultural, maritime, or industrial—and some, such as monarchist parties, speak for alternative political systems.

The United States has had a **two-party system** since about 1800. The function and character of the political parties, as well as the persistence of the two-party system, are largely the result of unique historical forces operating from our country's beginning as an independent nation. James Madison (1751–1836) linked the emergence of political parties to the form of government created by the Constitution. Recall that he attributed factions to human nature—in other words, as long as people are free to form their own opinions, there will always

Two-Party System
A political system in which only two parties have a reasonable chance of winning.

be competing ideas. Federalists and Anti-Federalists differed as to the size and functions of government and ultimately over whether the constitutions should be ratified. Thus, they represent the first signs that American would be shaped by political parties. To understand the evolution of political parties, scholars organize periods of time into party systems. Party systems reflect the number of parties active at a point in time and which party or parties are gaining power and influence, or conversely, losing power or perhaps even disappearing altogether. The change from one system to another is often signaled by a critical election—one in which a significant transfer of power takes place.

The First Party System: The Development of Parties, 1789–1828

In September 1796, George Washington, who had served as president for almost two full terms, decided not to run again. In his farewell address, Washington warned that the country might be destroyed by the "baneful effects of the spirit of party." He viewed parties as a threat to both national unity and the concept of popular government. Early in his career, Thomas Jefferson agreed, stating in 1789, "[i]f I could not go to heaven but with a party, I would not go there at all."[6]

Nevertheless, in the years after the ratification of the Constitution, Americans realized that something more permanent than a faction would be necessary to identify candidates for office and represent competing political ideas among the people. The result was two political parties formed around the ideas represented by the Federalists and the Anti-Federalists. One party was called the Federalists and included John Adams, the second president (served 1797–1801). They represented commercial interests such as merchants and large planters and supported a strong national government.

Thomas Jefferson led the other party, which emerged from the thought tradition of the Anti-Federalists and came to be called the Republicans, or Jeffersonian Republicans. (These Republicans should not be confused with the later Republican Party of Abraham Lincoln. To avoid confusion, some scholars refer to Jefferson's party as the Democratic-Republicans, but this name was never used during the time that the party existed.) Jefferson's Republicans represented artisans and farmers. They strongly supported states' rights. In 1800, when Jefferson defeated Adams in the presidential contest, one of the world's first peaceful transfers of power from one party to another was achieved.

Library of Congress Prints and Photographs Division Washington, D.C.[LC-USZ62-8195]

Thomas Jefferson, founder of the first Republican Party. His election to the presidency in 1800 was one of the world's first transfers of power through a free election.

The Era of Good Feelings

From 1800 to 1820, a majority of U.S. voters regularly elected Republicans to the presidency and to Congress. By 1816, the Federalist Party had virtually collapsed, and two-party competition did not really exist. Even though the Republicans

---

6. Letter to Francis Hopkinson written from Paris while Jefferson was minister to France. In John P. Foley, ed., *The Jeffersonian Cyclopedia* (New York: Russell & Russell, 1967), p. 677.

opposed the Federalists' call for a stronger, more active central government, they undertook active government policies such as acquiring the Louisiana Territory and Florida and establishing a national bank. Because the Republicans faced no real political opposition and little political debate was stirred, the administration of James Monroe (served 1817–1825) came to be known as the **era of good feelings**. Because political competition took place among individual Republican aspirants, this period can also be called the *era of personal politics*.

The Second Party System: Democrats and Whigs, 1828–1860

Organized two-party politics returned in 1824. With the election of John Quincy Adams as president, the Democratic-Republican Party split into two entities. The followers of Adams called themselves National Republicans. The followers of Andrew Jackson, who defeated Adams in 1828, formed the **Democratic Party**. Later, the National Republicans took the name **Whig Party**, which had been a traditional name for British liberals. The Whigs stood for federal spending on internal improvements such as roads. The Democrats, the stronger of the two parties, favored personal liberty and opportunity for the "common man." It was understood implicitly that the common man was a white man—the small number of free blacks who could vote identified overwhelmingly as Whigs.[7] Women began to organize during this time period as well. Recall that the Seneca Falls Convention for women's rights was held in 1848 and issued a call for universal suffrage.

The Jacksonian Democrats' success was linked to superior efforts to involve common citizens in the political process, a philosophy known as populism. Mass participation in politics and elections was a new phenomenon in the 1820s, as the political parties began to appeal to popular enthusiasm and themes. The parties adopted the techniques of mass campaigns, including rallies and parades. Lavishing food and drink on voters at polling places also became a common practice. Perhaps of greatest importance, however, was the push to cultivate party identity and loyalty. In large part, the spirit that motivated the new mass politics was democratic pride in participation. By making citizens feel that they were part of the political process, the parties hoped to win lasting party loyalty at the ballot box.

The Third Party System: Republican's Rise to Power and The Civil War, 1860–1896

In the 1850s, hostility between the North and South over slavery divided both parties. The Whigs were the first party to split apart. They had been the party of an active federal government, but Southerners had come to believe that a strong central government might use its power to free their slaves. Southern Whigs therefore ceased to exist as an organized party. Northern Whigs united with anti-slavery Democrats and members of the radical antislavery Free Soil Party to form the modern **Republican Party**.

After the Civil War, the Democratic Party was able to heal its divisions. Southern resentment of the Republicans' role in defeating the South and fears that the federal government would intervene on behalf of African Americans ensured that the Democrats would dominate the white South for the next century.

Era of Good Feelings
The years from 1817 to 1825, when James Monroe was president and had, in effect, no political opposition.

Democratic Party
One of the two major American political parties evolving out of the Republican Party of Thomas Jefferson.

Whig Party
A major party in the United States during the first half of the 19th century, formally established in 1836. The Whig Party was anti-Jackson and represented a variety of regional interests.

Republican Party
One of the two major American political parties. It emerged in the 1850s as an antislavery party and consisted of former northern Whigs and antislavery Democrats.

---

7. Edward Pessen, *Jacksonian America: Society, Personality, and Politics* (Homewood, IL: Dorsey Press, 1969). See especially pages 246–247.

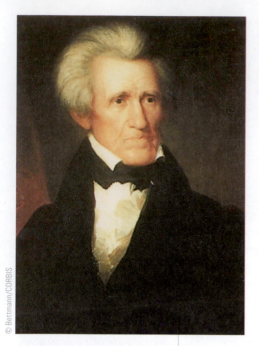

Andrew Jackson, the seventh president of the United States, was known by the name, "Old Hickory," for his victories in the War of 1812. This is a painting done by Asher Brown Durand in 1835, during the last years of Jackson's second term.

"Rum, Romanism, and Rebellion." Northern Democrats feared a strong government for other reasons. The Republicans thought that the government should promote business and economic growth, but many also wanted to use the power of government to impose evangelical Protestant moral values on society. Democrats opposed what they saw as culturally coercive measures. Many Republicans wanted to limit or even prohibit the sale of alcohol. They favored the establishment of public schools—with a Protestant curriculum. As a result, Catholics were strongly Democratic. In 1884, Protestant minister Samuel Burchard described the Democrats as the party of "rum, Romanism, and rebellion." This remark was offensive to Catholics, but as offensive as it may have been, Burchard's characterization of the Democrats contained an element of truth.

The Triumph of the Republicans. In this period, the parties were evenly matched in strength. The abolition of the three-fifths rule meant that African Americans would be counted fully when allocating House seats and electoral votes to the South. The Republicans therefore had to carry almost every northern state to win, and this was not always possible. In the 1890s, however, the Republicans gained a decisive edge. In that decade, the populist movement emerged in the West and South to champion the interests of small farmers, who were often heavily in debt. Populists supported inflation, which benefited debtors by reducing the real value of outstanding debts. In 1896, when William Jennings Bryan became the Democratic candidate for president, the Democrats embraced populism.

As it turned out, the few western farmers who were drawn to the Democrats by this step were greatly outnumbered by urban working-class voters who believed that inflation would reduce the purchasing power of their paychecks and who therefore became Republicans. William McKinley, the Republican candidate, was elected with a solid majority of the votes. Figure 8–1 shows the states taken by Bryan and McKinley. This pattern of regional support persisted for many years.

Figure 8–1 ▶ The 1896 Presidential Election

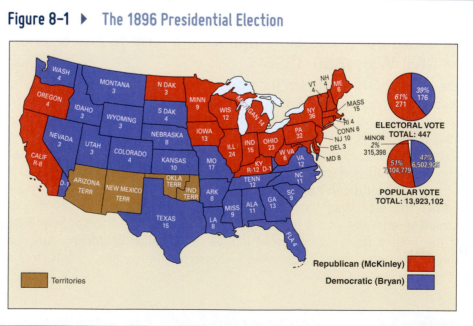

From 1896 until 1932, the Republicans were successfully able to present themselves as the party that knew how to manage the economy.

The Fourth Party System: The Progressive Interlude and Republican Dominance, 1896–1932

In the early 1900s, a spirit of political reform arose in both major parties. Called *progressivism*, this spirit was compounded by a fear of the growing power of great corporations and a belief that honest, impartial government could regulate the economy effectively. In 1912, the Republican Party temporarily split as former Republican president Theodore Roosevelt campaigned for the presidency on a third-party Progressive, or "Bull Moose," ticket. The Republican split permitted the election of Woodrow Wilson, the Democratic candidate, along with a Democratic Congress.

Like Roosevelt, Wilson considered himself a progressive, although he and Roosevelt did not agree on how progressivism ought to be implemented. Wilson's progressivism marked the beginning of a radical change in Democratic policies. Dating back to its foundation, the Democratic Party had been the party of limited government. Under Wilson, the Democrats became for the first time at least as receptive as the Republicans to government action in the economy.

The Fifth Party System: The New Deal and Democratic Dominance, 1932–1968

The Republican ascendancy ended with the election of 1932, in the depths of the Great Depression. Republican Herbert Hoover was president when the Depression began in 1929. Although Hoover took some measures to fight the Depression, they fell far short of what the public demanded. Significantly, Hoover opposed federal relief for the unemployed and the destitute. In 1932, Democrat Franklin D. Roosevelt was elected president by an overwhelming margin.

The Great Depression shattered the working-class belief in Republican economic competence. Under Roosevelt, the Democrats began to make major interventions in the economy in an attempt to combat the Depression and to relieve the suffering of the unemployed. Roosevelt's New Deal relief programs were open to all citizens, both black and white. As a result, African Americans began to support the Democratic Party in large numbers—a development that would have stunned any American politician of the 1800s. Women were also actively courted to join the electoral coalition.

© Bettmann/CORBIS

In 1912, Theodore Roosevelt campaigned for the presidency on a third-party Progressive, or Bull Moose, ticket. Here, you see a charter membership certificate showing Roosevelt and his vice-presidential candidate, Hiram W. Johnson. What was the main result of Roosevelt's formation of this third party?

Roosevelt's political coalition (the New Deal coalition) was broad enough to establish the Democrats as the new majority party and reelect Franklin D. Roosevelt. (He served an unprecedented four terms as president.) Vice President Harry Truman assumed the presidency upon Roosevelt's death and was elected to a full term in 1948. In the 1950s, Republican Dwight D. Eisenhower, the leading U.S. general during World War II, won two terms as president. Otherwise, with minor interruptions, the Democratic ascendancy lasted until 1968.

The New Deal coalition managed the unlikely feat of including both African Americans and southern whites who were hostile to African American advancement. This balancing act came to an end in the 1960s, a decade marked by the civil rights movement, several years of race riots in major cities, and increasingly heated protests against the Vietnam War. For many economically liberal, socially conservative voters (especially in the South), social issues had become more important than economic ones, and these voters left the Democrats. These voters outnumbered the new voters who joined the Democrats—newly enfranchised African Americans and former liberal Republicans in New England and the upper Midwest.

The result, since 1968, has been an era in which neither party dominates. In presidential elections, the Republicans have had more success than the Democrats. Until 1994, Congress remained Democratic, but official party labels can be misleading. Some of the Democrats were southern conservatives who normally voted with the Republicans on issues. As these conservative Democrats retired, they were largely replaced by Republicans.

A Post-Party System Era, 1968–Present?

Between the elections of 1968 and 2014, the presidency, the House of Representatives, and the Senate were simultaneously controlled by a single party only about one-third of the time. The Democrats controlled all three institutions during the presidency of Jimmy Carter (1977–1981), the first two years of Bill Clinton's presidency (1992–1994), and the first two years of Barack Obama's presidency (2008–2010). The Republicans controlled all three institutions during the third through sixth years of George W. Bush's presidency.[8] Before the 1992 elections, the electorate seemed to prefer, in most circumstances, to match a Republican president with a Democratic Congress. Under Bill Clinton, that state of affairs was reversed, with a Democratic president serving alongside a Republican Congress. After the 2006 elections, a Republican president again faced a Democratic Congress. In 2008, Americans elected Democrat Barack Obama as president, and gave the Democratic Party majorities in both houses of Congress, but the Democrats lost their majority in the House in the 2010 midterm elections.

Red State, Blue State. The pattern of a Republican Congress and a Democratic president would have continued after the election of 2000 if Democratic presidential candidate Al Gore had prevailed. Gore won the popular vote, but he lost the electoral college by a narrow margin. Despite the closeness of the result, most states had voted in favor of either Bush or Gore by a fairly wide margin. To many observers, America had become divided between states that were solidly Republican or Democratic in their leanings, with a handful of "swing states." States that had shown strong support for a Republican candidate were deemed

---

8. The Republicans also were in control of all three institutions for the first four months after Bush's inauguration. This initial period of control ended when Senator James Jeffords of Vermont left the Republican Party, giving the Democrats control of the Senate.

"red states" and so-called Democratic states were labeled "blue states." These labels have now become part of our political culture, and the outcome of any presidential race is portrayed in red and blue.

The outcome of the Bush-Gore contest in 2000 produced lingering bitterness in the political scene and may have increased general distrust of the electoral process. Although President Bush was reelected over his Democratic opponent (John Kerry) in 2004, a combination of Republican scandals, war-weariness, and anti-Bush sentiment cost the Republicans their majority in the House in 2006.

In 2008, the nation watched an unprecedented Democratic primary fight between Hillary Rodham Clinton and Barack Obama—each representing a first for the nation with the contest promising a woman or an African American nominee. Although many commentators felt that the party would be weakened by the intense primary fight, Barack Obama easily won the election over Republican John McCain and the Democrats carried both houses of Congress. Analysts began to talk about a realignment of voters to form a progressive coalition that might last well into the future. However, the economic collapse of the banks and onset of the economic recession that began during the end of the 2008 campaign lingered through much of President Obama's first term. By 2010, opponents of government debt and fears of the economic recession led to the Republicans recapturing the House of Representatives. Republicans coalesced around opposition to the Affordable Care Act and targeted Democrats who helped to pass the law in 2010.

Partisan Trends in the 2012 Elections

By the time the votes were all counted, it appeared that there was remarkably little change in the alignment of the voters following the 2012 elections. Perhaps the only real effect of the economic recession on voters was an even split of

COMPARE WITH YOUR PEERS

MindTap™ for American Government

Access the Political Parties Forum: Polling Activity—Hurricane Sandy and Politics

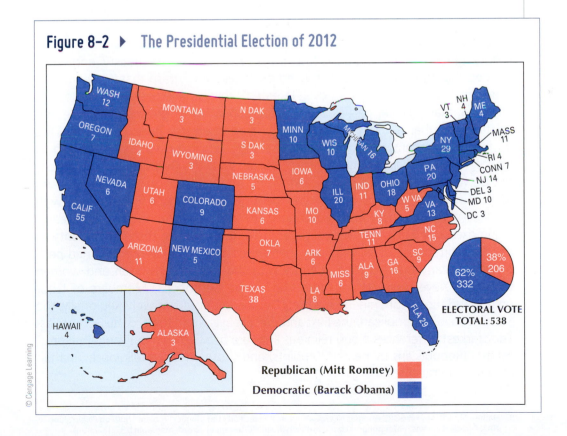

Figure 8-2 ▶ The Presidential Election of 2012

Republican (Mitt Romney)
Democratic (Barack Obama)

ELECTORAL VOTE TOTAL: 538

© Cengage Learning

independent voters for the Republicans. The coalition that came together to elect President Obama in 2008 reappeared in 2012: African American voters, women, lower income voters, union voters, and Latino voters gave the president more than a majority of their votes. These groups reflect changes in the United States population that will determine the direction of the nation. The Republican coalition also remained unchanged: better-educated voters, high-income voters, older voters, white men, and evangelical voters were more likely to vote for the Republicans. In some states, the Libertarian candidate earned 1 percent of the vote, ballots that might have been cast for Mitt Romney. The results of the Congressional elections were close to those of 2010: Republicans maintained a solid majority in the House of Representatives, and the Democrats gained two seats in the Senate to have a solid 53-45 majority in that chamber. Whether the Democratic Party has put together a coalition that will last for decades is yet to be seen, but the main groups in that coalition have been fairly consistent for the last two decades.

The Two Major U.S. Parties Today

■ **LO8.4:** Compare and contrast the demographics of people who identify as Democrats and Republicans; explain how party positions differ on economic and social issues.

Sometimes American political parties are likened to Tweedledee and Tweedledum, the twins in Lewis Carroll's *Through the Looking-Glass*. Third-party advocates have an interest in claiming that no difference exists between the two major parties—their chances of gaining support are much greater if the major parties are seen as indistinguishable. Despite such allegations, the major parties do have substantial differences, both in who belongs to each party and in their policy priorities.

Who Belongs to Each Political Party?

Following the Republican's 2012 loss of the White House, columnist George Will warned that the party was endangered by its failure to grasp that "demography is destiny."[9] While perhaps an overstatement, this is nevertheless an important reminder that political parties are built by appealing to groups of people and knitting together a coalition based on shared interests. Table 8–1 shows the profiles of partisans and independents among registered voters. Men tend to identify as Republicans, while women affiliate with the Democrats. Young people, between the ages of 18–29, lean toward Democrats; people over age 65 tend to identify as Republicans. Non-whites identify with Democrats, as do those with the least and the most formal education. The wealthiest Americans, those earning in excess of $150,000, typically identify as Republicans; those at the bottom of the income scale usually identify themselves as the Democrats. Married people, particularly married men, identify with the Republicans; men and women who have never married are more likely to be Democrats. Members of labor unions and those not working are likely Democratic voters as well. Regionally, the South is solidly Republican; the East and West coasts trend toward the Democrats. The starkest differences along religious lines are between white Evangelical protestants (Republicans by nearly 30 points) and those who are religiously unaffiliated (Democrats by a margin of 12 points).

---

9. Mathew Shoenfeld, "For GOP Demographics Are a Concern, But the Party Has a Bigger Problem." *HuffPost Politics*, June 30, 2013. Accessed atwww.huffingtonpost.com/matthew-schoenfeld/to-republicans-demographi b 3521827.html

Table 8-1 ▶ Who Belongs to Each Political Party

| | | PARTY IDENTIFICATION | | |
	ALL VOTERS %	REP %	DEM %	IND %
GENDER				
Men	47	49	39	54
Women	53	51	61	46
AGE				
18—29	15	12	15	17
30—49	32	31	30	37
50—64	31	31	32	29
65+	20	25	21	16
RACE				
White, Non-Hispanic	73	89	58	76
Black, Non-Hispanic	12	2	25	5
Hispanic	8	4	9	9
Other/Mixed, Non-Hispanic	6	3	6	7
EDUCATION				
Postgraduate	15	13	17	15
College graduate	19	20	18	21
Some college	30	31	28	30
HS graduate	29	30	28	27
Less than HS	7	5	9	6
INCOME				
$150,000+	8	10	7	7
$100,000—$149,999	11	11	10	11
$75,000—$99,999	13	13	12	13
$50,000—$74,999	14	16	14	14
$30,000—$49,999	18	19	18	18
$20,000—$29,999	10	8	11	10
Less than $20,000	15	11	18	15
Don't know	12	13	10	11

Source: www.people-press.org

* Whites and blacks include only those who are Non-Hispanic; Hispanics are of any race. Race reported only for polls conducted in both English and Spanish.

Partisans identifying with each political party differ in their positions on issues as well. For example, 52 percent of Republican registered voters think our present federal tax system is fair while 58 percent of Democrats think that our present system is not fair. Democrats (73 percent) believe the wealthy do not pay their fair share, while Republicans (45 percent) are concerned with the overall complexity of the system. Historically, one of the defining differences between the parties is a difference in vision over the size and role of government. Eighty-two percent of Republicans prefer a smaller government providing fewer services (compared to

29 percent of Democrats), while a majority (59 percent) of Democrats would choose a bigger government that provided more services (a choice of only 14 percent of Republicans). Registered Republicans favor gun ownership (71 percent), while Democrats are more likely to support controls on guns (75 percent). Democrats are more likely to favor gay marriage and allowing gays and lesbians to adopt children, and favor legal abortion in all cases. By a significant margin, Republicans disapprove of the Affordable Care Act (87 percent) but favor stricter enforcement of immigration laws.

Differences in Party Policy Priorities

Although everyone in 2014 agreed that the economy was the most important issue for government to deal with, Democrats and Republicans differ on which priorities should come next. Figure 8–3 depicts the top ten issues that partisans believe the president and Congress should deal with in the next year. As you can see, the issue priorities of the parties differ; Democrats' priorities are in the areas of education, poverty, and homelessness, health care, and Social Security and Medicaid, whereas Republicans favor policies related to terrorism, the military and national defense, and health care. Although Republicans and Democrats share seven of ten issues in common, the magnitude of importance differs across the parties. Differences exist between the parties in the importance of the distribution

Figure 8–3 ▶ Top 10 Priority Issues, by Party Identification

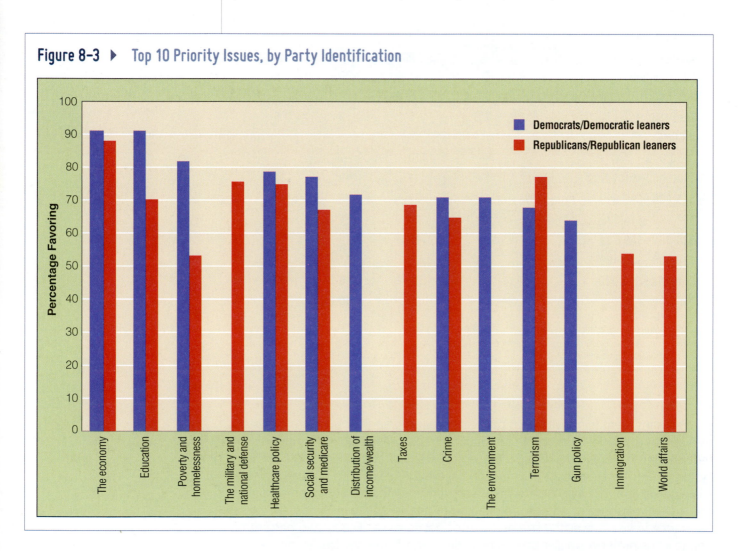

THE PARTY of the RICH

THE PARTY of the MIDDLE CLASS

THE PARTY of the POOR

Pat Bagley/Cagle Cartoons

of wealth, the environment, and gun policy (Democrats) and military, taxes, immigration, and world affairs (Republicans).

The 2012 Elections—Shaping the Parties for 2014 and 2016

In addition to the economy, social issues, specifically, reproductive rights and abortion issues, were very important in races for the U.S. Senate and persuaded many women to vote for the Democratic ticket at the presidential level.

Although economic indicators suggested a very slow and less than robust recovery from the major recession of 2008–2009, unemployment rates fell to below 8 percent by October 2012, and there was evidence of growth in the construction of housing. While the majority of voters still said that the country was going in the wrong direction, the Democratic campaign emphasized the progress that had been made towards recovery. In contrast, the Republican campaign focused on the administration's record and promised a better approach. The Republican position appealed to small business owners, to Americans who were college-educated, and to many independent voters. The Democratic vote was certainly strengthened by the recovery of the automobile industry as a result of the Obama administration's policies, and blue-collar voters kept their loyalty to the Democratic Party.

On issues important to women, the Democratic Party championed reproductive rights for women, health-care initiatives for women, and their support for the right of women to choose an abortion. The Republican Party continued its stance as the party opposed to a woman's right to choose. Their message, which officially allowed abortions under certain conditions, was completely undercut by Senate candidates who would not allow abortion in the case of rape and who made very peculiar statements about rape-caused pregnancies. The publicity

did you know?
Most historians credit Thomas Nast, political cartoonist for Harper's Weekly, with pinning the symbols of a donkey and an elephant to the Democratic and Republican Parties, respectively.

accorded to these statements and the Democratic support for women secured a majority of votes for the ticket from women.

While the politics of immigration was rarely directly addressed in the campaign, it was clear that Latino voters saw the Democratic Party as more likely to pass immigration reform than the Republicans. The Republican ticket moved to the right on this issue, and Latino voters noted this. In 2012, President Obama announced a policy which allows undocumented young people brought to this country before the age of 16 to stay for two years if they meet educational, work, or military service requirements. Undoubtedly Latino voters viewed this action as proof of the Democratic Party's openness.

Because of these electoral outcomes and the reaction of voters to positions and policies adopted by party candidates and the parties, the 2014 midterm elections gained in importance for both parties. The party of the White House typically loses congressional seats in midterm elections, but in 2014 Republicans surged to victories that both increased the size of the GOP majority in the House and gave the party control of the U.S. Senate for the first time since 2006. Republicans were successful in making the elections a national referendum on government competence by raising questions about the U.S. response to international threats such as the Islamic State in Iraq and Syria (ISIS) and Ebola in West Africa and by reminding voters about unresolved issues at home like immigration. As president, Mr. Obama is the embodiment of national government. The 2014 midterms set records for spending (an estimated $4 billion in all) and for low turnout (around 36 percent). The demographics of those who stayed home—young people, minority voters, and women—were keys to Democratic victories in 2012. Both parties will now turn their strategic attention to 2016.

Why Has the Two-Party System Endured?

■ **LO8.5:** Summarize the factors that reinforce a two-party system and explain why third parties are rarely successful at winning national elections.

There are several reasons why two major parties have dominated the political landscape in the United States for almost two centuries: (1) the historical foundations of the system, (2) political socialization and practical considerations, (3) the winner-take-all electoral system, and (4) state and federal laws favoring the two-party system.

The Historical Foundations of the Two-Party System

As we have seen, many times, one preeminent issue or dispute has divided the nation politically. In the beginning, Americans were at odds over ratifying the Constitution. After the Constitution went into effect, the power of the federal government became the major national issue. Thereafter, the dispute over slavery divided the nation by section, North versus South. At times, cultural differences have been important, with advocates of government-sponsored morality (such as banning alcoholic beverages) pitted against advocates of personal liberty.

During much of the 1900s, economic differences were paramount. In the New Deal period, the Democrats became known as the party of the working class, while the Republicans became known as the party of the middle and upper classes and commercial interests. When politics is based on an argument between just two opposing points of view, advocates of each viewpoint can mobilize most effectively by forming a single, unified party. The dualist nature of conflict is challenged in conditions of uncertainty or issue complexity when just two positions don't seem to cover the issue. The nature and causes of climate change

Everyday Politics

 The Colbert Report

The April 1, 2014 episode of Comedy Central's *The Colbert Report* opened with news that 7.1 million Americans had signed up for private health-care coverage under the Affordable Care Act (ACA) by the March 31deadline, owing largely to a last minute surge in enrollments. More than 4.8 million visits were made to HealthCare.gov on the last day alone. Many of those enrolling at the last minute were young people.

President Obama celebrated the victory with a White House Rose Garden announce-ment, even while acknowledging a rocky start with the website roll-out and continuing challenges ahead with implementation. He chided Republicans for continuing to work against healthcare for all Americans. "I don't get it. Why are folks working so hard for people not to have health insurance? Why are they so mad about the idea of people having health insurance?" the president asked. "The debate over repealing this law is over. The Affordable Care Act is here to stay."

Colbert followed clips of the president with a parade of conservative pundits who had assured him that there was no way that the Affordable Care Act would meet its goal. John Sununu predicted that enrollments would top out at 4.5 million. Karl Rove used a small whiteboard to demonstrate how it was impossible for the ACA to reach its goal. "Folks, they were never supposed to make it to 7 million…," said Colbert, "It was only logical—if no one had signed up, no one would sign up, because everyone knows past performance always indicates future results. That's why I always play yesterday's winning Lotto and let me point out that I have never lost yesterday's Lotto." Colbert bemoaned the need to cancel his "Obamacare = Failure" parade and his "Stephen Colbert's Rockin' Enrollment Failure Eve." Much of the late surge in enrollment was attributed to young adults. "No one could have foreseen that college kids could have put something off to the last minute," he noted with his usual sarcasm. The White House said that the overall effort surpassed their expectations in terms of last-minute sign-ups.

Colbert concluded the sketch by claiming that this was all a big April Fool's Day joke four years in the making because, "[s]eri-ously folks, do you really think conservatives wanted America to be the only Western industrialized country without heath care?" he asked.

Partisanship can sometimes lead people to oppose seemingly reasonable propositions like health care for all Americans. Michael Steel, a spokesman for House Speaker and Ohio Republican John Boehner, said in a statement that the law "continues to harm the American people" despite Obama's "victory lap."* Colbert, continuing the April Fool's Day theme as shown in the screen capture, said that Republican opponents will turn their loss into a victory by claiming that they have supported the Affordable Care Act all along.

* Jim Acosta, Tom Watkins, and Kevin Liptak. "Obamacare hits enrollment goal with 7.1 million sign-ups, President says." CNN Politics, April 1, 2014. Accessed at www.cnn.com/2014/04/01/politics/obamacare-signups-target/

For Critical Analysis

1. *The Colbert Report is political satire and therefore requires that viewers know something about current issues to appreciate the humor. In this case, have Republicans really been rooting for "Obamacare" to fail? Why would they do that?*

2. *The Affordable Care Act's viability depends on healthy young people signing up for health insurance. The White House used social media, celebrities, and popular athletes like LeBron James to make the pitch. Are you receptive to political or policy messages from figures like these? Why or why not?*

might be one such issue. The Affordable Care Act is another—nobody really disagrees with the goal of ensuring access to health care for all Americans, but the U.S. health-care system is incredibly complex. Congress adopted one approach to fixing the problem when it passed the ACA, but continuing opposition to the legislation leaves Republicans in the unenviable position of appearing to oppose expanded health insurance coverage. Also, when a two-party system has been in existence for almost two centuries, it becomes difficult to imagine an alternative.

Political Socialization and Practical Considerations

Given that the majority of Americans identify with one of the two major political parties, it is not surprising that most children learn at a fairly young age to think of themselves as either Democrats or Republicans. This generates a built-in mechanism to perpetuate a two-party system. Also, many politically oriented people who aspire to work for social change consider that the only realistic way to capture political power in this country is to be either a Republican or a Democrat. However, the increase in political independents today, particularly among young people, may call into question the continuing power of socialization to maintain the two-party system.

The Winner-Take-All Electoral System

Plurality
A number of votes cast for a candidate that is greater than the number of votes for any other candidate, but not necessarily a majority.

At virtually every level of government in the United States, the outcome of elections is based on the **plurality**, winner-take-all principle. The winner is the person who obtains the most votes, even if that person does not receive a majority (more than 50 percent) of the votes. Whoever gets the most votes gets everything. Most legislators in the United States are elected from single-member districts in which only one person represents the constituency. The candidate who finishes second in receives nothing for the effort and neither do their supporters. The winner-take-all system also operates in the election of the U.S president. Recall that the voters in each state do not vote for a president directly but vote for **electoral college** delegates who are committed to the various presidential candidates. These delegates are called *electors*.

Electoral College
A group of persons, called electors, who are selected by the voters in each state. This group officially elects the president and the vice president of the United States.

If the electors pledged to a particular presidential candidate receive a plurality of 40 percent of the votes in a state, that presidential candidate will receive all of the state's votes in the electoral college. Minor parties have a difficult time competing under such a system. As shown in Table 8–2, American history has seen a number of national third-party campaigns. Only Teddy Roosevelt, who ran on a third-party ticket, received more than 88 electoral votes. In 1968, George Wallace, the segregationist former governor of Alabama, received 46 electoral votes, all from Deep South states. In recent decades, Ross Perot ran the most successful third-party campaign, garnering 18.9 percent of the popular vote, but no electoral votes at all. Because voters know such candidacies are doomed by the system, it is difficult to convince them to cast their vote for such candidates. Third-party candidate Ralph Nader was accused of siphoning votes away from Democratic candidate Al Gore in 2000, leaving George W. Bush the victor.

Proportional Representation. Many other nations use a system of proportional representation with multimember districts. If, during the national election, party X obtains 12 percent of the vote, party Y gets 43 percent of the vote, and party Z gets the remaining 45 percent of the vote, then party X gets

Table 8-2 ▶ The Most Successful Third-Party Presidential Campaigns since 1864

The following list includes all third-party candidates winning more than 2 percent of the popular vote or any electoral votes since 1864. (We ignore isolated "unfaithful electors" in the electoral college who failed to vote for the candidate to whom they were pledged.)

YEAR	MAJOR THIRD PARTY	THIRD-PARTY PRESIDENTIAL CANDIDATE	PERCENT OF THE POPULAR VOTE	ELECTORAL COLLEGE VOTES	WINNING PRESIDENTIAL CANDIDATE
1892	Populist	James Weaver	8.5	22	Grover Cleveland (D)
1904	Socialist	Eugene Debs	3.0	—	Theodore Roosevelt (R)
1908	Socialist	Eugene Debs	2.8	—	William Howard Taft (R)
1912	Progressive	Theodore Roosevelt	27.4	88	Woodrow Wilson (D)
1912	Socialist	Eugene Debs	6.0	—	Woodrow Wilson (D)
1920	Socialist	Eugene Debs	3.4	—	Warren G. Harding (R)
1924	Progressive	Robert LaFollette	16.6	13	Calvin Coolidge (R)
1948	States' Rights	Strom Thurmond	2.4	39	Harry Truman (D)
1960	Independent Democrat	Harry Byrd	0.4	15*	John Kennedy (D)
1968	American Independent	George Wallace	13.5	46	Richard Nixon (R)
1980	National Union	John Anderson	6.6		Ronald Reagan (R)
1992	Independent	Ross Perot	18.9	0	Bill Clinton (D)
1996	Reform	Ross Perot	8.4	0	Bill Clinton (D)
2000	Green	RalphNader	2.74	0	George W. Bush (R)

Source: *Dave Leip's Atlas of U.S. Presidential Elections*, www.uselectionatlas.org.

* Byrd received 15 electoral votes from unpledged electors in Alabama and Mississippi.

12 percent of the seats in the legislature, party Y gets 43 percent of the seats, and party Z gets 45 percent of the seats. Because even a minor party may still obtain at least a few seats in the legislature, the smaller parties have a greater incentive to organize under such electoral systems than they do in the United States.

The relative effects of proportional representation versus our system of single-member districts are so strong that many scholars have made them one of the few "laws" of political science. Duverger's Law, named after French political scientist Maurice Duverger, states that electoral systems based on single-member districts tend to produce two parties, while systems of proportional representation produce multiple parties.[10] Still, many countries with single-member districts have more than two political parties—Britain and Canada are examples.

State and Federal Laws Favoring the Two Parties

Many state and federal election laws offer a clear advantage to the two major parties. In some states, the established major parties need to gather

10. As cited in Todd Landman, *Issues and Methods in Comparative Politics* (New York: Routledge, 2003), p. 14.

fewer signatures to place their candidates on the ballot than do minor parties or independent candidates. The criterion for determining how many signatures will be required is often based on the total party vote in the last general election, thus penalizing a new political party that did not compete in that election.

At the national level, minor parties face different obstacles. The rules and procedures of both houses of Congress divide committee seats, staff members, and other privileges on the basis of party membership. A legislator who is elected on a minor-party ticket, such as the Conservative Party of New York, must choose to be counted with one of the major parties to obtain a committee assignment. The Federal Election Commission (FEC) rules for campaign financing also place restrictions on minor-party candidates. Such candidates are not eligible for federal matching funds in either the primary or the general election. In the 1980 election, John Anderson, running for president as an independent, sued the FEC for campaign funds. The commission finally agreed to repay part of his campaign costs after the election, in proportion to the votes he received. Giving funds to a candidate when the campaign is over is, of course, much less helpful than providing funds while the campaign is still under way.

The Role of Minor Parties in U.S. Politics

Minor parties have a difficult (if not impossible) time competing within the American two-party political system. Nonetheless, minor parties have played an important role in our political life. Parties other than the Republicans or Democrats are usually called **third parties**. (Technically, of course, there could be fourth, fifth, or sixth parties as well, but we use the term *third party* because it has endured.) Third parties can come into existence in three ways: (1) They may be founded from scratch by individuals or groups who are committed to a particular interest, issue, or ideology; (2) they can split off from one of the major parties when a group becomes dissatisfied with the major party's policies; or (3) they can be organized around a particular charismatic leader and serve as that person's vehicle for contesting elections.

Third Parties
A political party other than the two major political parties (Republican and Democratic).

Third parties have forced the major parties to recognize new issues or trends in the thinking of Americans. Political scientists believe that third parties have acted as safety valves for dissident groups, preventing major confrontations and political unrest. In some instances, third parties have functioned as way stations for voters en route from one of the major parties to the other. Table 8–2 lists significant third-party presidential campaigns in American history; Table 8–3 provides a brief description of third-party beliefs. No third-party candidate received more than 1 percent of the vote in the 2008 or 2012 election, highlighting the strength of the two main parties.

Ideological Third Parties

The longest-lived third parties have been those with strong ideological foundations that are typically at odds with the majority mindset. The Socialist Party is an example. The party was founded in 1901 and lasted until 1972, when it was finally dissolved. (A smaller party later took up the name.)

Members of a minor party regard themselves as outsiders and look to one another for support; ideology provides great psychological cohesiveness. Second, because the rewards of ideological commitment are partly psychological, these minor

Table 8-3 ▶ Policies of Selected American Third Parties Since 1864

Populist: This pro-farmer party of the 1890s advocated progressive reforms. It also advocated replacing gold with silver as the basis of the currency in hopes of creating a mild inflation in prices. (It was believed by many that inflation would help debtors and stimulate the economy.)

Socialist: This party advocated a "cooperative commonwealth" based on government ownership of industry. It was pro-labor, often antiwar, and in later years, anti-communist. It was dissolved in 1972 and replaced by nonparty advocacy groups (Democratic Socialists of America and Social Democrats USA).

Communist: This left-wing breakaway from the socialists was the U.S. branch of the worldwide communist movement. The party was pro-labor and advocated full equality for African Americans. It was also closely aligned with the Communist Party—led Soviet Union, which provoked great hostility among most Americans.

Progressive: This name was given to several successive splinter parties built around individual political leaders. Theodore Roosevelt, who ran in 1912, advocated federal regulation of industry to protect consumers, workers, and small businesses. Robert LaFollette, who ran in 1924, held similar viewpoints.

American Independent: Built around George Wallace, this party opposed any further promotion of civil rights and advocated a militant foreign policy. Wallace's supporters were mostly former Democrats who were soon to be Republicans.

Libertarian: This party believes that the individual and private marketplace will produce the best policies. The national government has a role in defending the nation and little else.

Reform: The Reform Party was initially built around businessman Ross Perot but later was taken over by others. Under Perot, the party was a middle-of the-road group opposed to federal budget deficits. Under Patrick Buchan

Green: The Greens are a left-of-center pro-environmental party; they are also generally hostile to globalization.

parties do not think in terms of immediate electoral success. A poor showing at the polls therefore does not dissuade either the leadership or the grassroots participants from continuing their quest for change in American government (and, ultimately, American society).

Currently active ideological parties include the Libertarian Party and the Green Party. The Libertarian Party supports a *laissez-faire* ("let it be") capitalist economic program, together with a hands-off policy on regulating matters of moral conduct. The Green Party began as a grassroots environmentalist organization with affiliated political parties across North America and Western Europe. It was established in

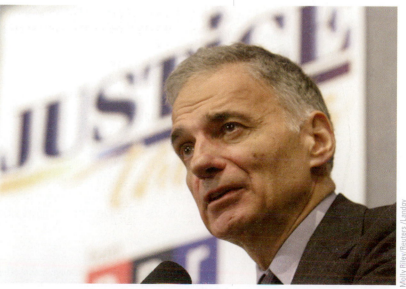

Ralph Nader, a leader of the consumer protection movement, has run for president six times, once for the New Party, three times as the Green Party candidate, and twice as an independent.

Molly Riley/Reuters /Landov

Green Party
@GPUS
The Green Party of the United States is a federation of state Green Parties.
Check us out at gp.org & facebook.com/GreenPartyUS
gp.org

Green Party

Is the Green Party active in your state?

the United States as a national party in 1996 and nominated Ralph Nader to run for president in 2000. Nader campaigned against what he called "corporate greed," advocated universal health insurance, and promoted environmental concerns.[11] He ran again for president as an independent in 2004 and in 2008. The Green Party's Twitter feed (shown in the screen capture) posts regular videos that champion key themes to the party's platform and encourages fundraising activities.

Splinter Parties

Some of the most successful minor parties have been those that split from major parties. The impetus for these **splinter parties**, or factions, has usually been a situation in which a particular personality was at odds with the major party. The most successful of these splinter parties was the Bull Moose Progressive Party, formed in 1912 to support Theodore Roosevelt for president. The Republican National Convention of that year denied Roosevelt the nomination, although he had won most of the primaries. He therefore left the Republicans and ran against Republican "regular" William Howard Taft in the general election. Although Roosevelt did not win the election, he did split the Republican vote, enabling Democrat Woodrow Wilson to become president.

Third parties have also been formed to back individual candidates who were not rebelling against a particular party. Ross Perot, for example, who challenged Republican George H. W. Bush and Democrat Bill Clinton in 1992, had not previously been active in a major party. Perot's supporters, likewise, probably would have split their votes between Bush and Clinton had Perot not been in the race. In theory, Perot ran in 1992 as a nonparty independent; in practice, he had to create a campaign organization. By 1996, Perot's organization was formalized as the Reform Party.

The Impact of Minor Parties

Third parties have rarely been able to affect American politics by actually winning elections. (One exception: third-party and independent candidates have occasionally won races for state governorships—for example, Jesse Ventura was elected governor of Minnesota on the Reform Party ticket in 1998.) Instead, the impact of third parties has taken two forms. First, third parties can influence one of the major parties to take up one or more issues. Second, third parties can determine the outcome of a particular election by pulling votes from one of the major-party candidates in what is called the "spoiler effect."

Influencing the Major Parties. One of the most clear-cut examples of a major party adopting the issues of a minor party took place in 1896, when the Democratic Party co-opted the Populist demand for "free silver"—that is, a policy of coining enough new money to create inflation. Absorbing the Populists' demands cost the Democrats votes overall.

Splinter Parties
A new party formed by a dissident faction within a major political party. Often, splinter parties have emerged when a particular personality was at odds with the major party.

---

11. Ralph Nader offers his own entertaining account of his run for the presidency in 2000 in *Crashing the Party: How to Tell the Truth and Still Run for President* (New York: St. Martin's Press, 2002).

Affecting the Outcome of an Election. The presidential election of 2000 was one instance in which a minor party may have altered the outcome. Green candidate Ralph Nader received almost 100,000 votes in Florida, a majority of which would probably have gone to Democrat Al Gore if Nader had not been in the race. The real question is whether the effect was important.

The problem is that in an election as close as the presidential election of 2000, *any* factor with an impact on the outcome can be said to have determined the results of the election. Discussing his landslide loss to Democrat Lyndon B. Johnson in 1964, Republican Barry Goldwater wrote: "When you've lost an election by that much, it isn't the case of whether you made the wrong speech or wore the wrong necktie. It was just the wrong time."[12] Given that Nader garnered almost 3 million votes nationwide, many people believe that the Nader campaign was an important reason for Gore's loss. Should voters ignore third parties to avoid spoiling the chances of a preferred major-party candidate?

H. Ross Perot, third-party candidate for president in 1992 and 1996, speaks before a California Senate committee in 2002.

Mechanisms of Political Change

Support for the two major parties is roughly balanced today. In the future, could one of the two parties decisively overtake the other and become the "natural party of government"? The Republicans held this status from 1896 until 1932, and the Democrats enjoyed it for many years after the election of Franklin D. Roosevelt in 1932. Not surprisingly, political advisers in both parties dream of circumstances that could grant them lasting political dominance.

Realignment

One mechanism by which a party might gain dominance is called **realignment**. Major constituencies shift their allegiance from one party to another, creating a long-term alteration in the political environment. Realignment has often been associated with particular elections, called *realigning elections*. The election of 1896, which established a Republican ascendancy, was clearly a realigning election. So was the election of 1932, which made the Democrats the leading party.

Realignment: The Myth of Dominance. Several myths have grown up around the concept of realignment. One is that in realignment, a newly dominant party must replace the previously dominant party. Realignment could easily strengthen an already dominant party. Alternatively, realignment could result in a tie. This has happened—twice. One example was the realignment of the 1850s, which resulted in Abraham Lincoln's election as president in 1860. After the Civil War, the Republicans and the Democrats were almost evenly matched nationally.

Realignment
A process in which a substantial group of voters switches party allegiance, producing a long-term change in the political landscape.

---

12. Barry Goldwater, *With No Apologies* (New York: William Morrow, 1979).

Beyond Our Borders

Multiparty Systems: The Rule Rather than the Exception

The United States has a two-party system. Occasionally, a third-party candidate enters the race, but has little chance of winning at the national level. Throughout the world, though, most democracies have multiparty systems.

SOME EXAMPLES

In its first legislative elections ever, Afghanistan saw the emergence of six major parties and seven minor parties. The 2013 Iraqi provincial council elections had a total of 50 political alliances plus hundreds of other parties competing. India's general election takes place in nine phases across 534 constituencies. India has 6 national parties, another 36 state parties, and more than 100 regional parties.

The latest elections in Germany resulted in a "grand coalition," bringing together two main center-right and center-left parties within a system of five parties. Any given presidential election in France has even more parties. They include several representing the left, center-left, right, and center-right. The National Front represents the extreme right, anti-immigrant part of the electorate. The Socialist Party represents the left.

After the Egyptian popular uprising, which overthrew the authoritarian government of Hosni Mubarak, the leaders of the movement quickly moved to establish an election system. Within weeks, dozens of political parties formed and, as the first presidential election approached, at least 10 of these parties had candidates for that office. Parties ranged from conservative groups that had supported Mubarak to radical leftists to democratic liberals and Islamist groups who wanted a religious-based government.

PROPORTIONAL REPRESENTATION AND COALITIONS

Great Britain has often been described as having a two and one-half party system: The major parties, the Labour and Conservative parties, have alternated governing the nation for most of the time since World War II. The Liberal Democrat party, which has a long and distinguished history, usually comes in third, not securing enough votes to make a difference.

In the 2010 parliamentary elections, neither major party won enough seats in Parliament to claim the right to form a government. As soon as the election results were announced, each of the two major parties began to "court" the Liberal Democrats, who had won enough seats to create a coalition. Within a week, Queen Elizabeth asked the head of the Conservative Party to become prime minister and to negotiate a coalition with the Liberal Democrats. In a surprising move, the two parties announced that while David Cameron, head of the Conservative Party, would be prime minister, Nick Clegg, head of the Liberal Democrat Party, would be named deputy prime minister. In the next election, 2012, the relative balance of power between the three parties did

Polling officials count ballots in January 2014. Egypt's political transition has included a revision to the constitution subject to public referendum.

not change, although Conservatives lost about 4 percent of their previous vote and a corresponding number of seats—largely due to voter dissatisfaction over the national budget.

Coalitions are almost a certainty in a multiparty system because the leading party usually does not have a majority of votes in the legislature. The leading party has to make compromises to obtain votes from other parties. These coalitions are subject to change due to the pressures of lawmaking. Often, a minor partner in a coalition finds itself unable to support the laws or policies proposed by its larger partners. Either a compromise will be found, or the coalition will be ended and new partners may be sought to form a government coalition. If we had a multiparty system in the United States, we might have a green party reflecting environmental interests, a Latino party, a western party, a labor party, and others. To gain support for her or his program, a president would have to build a coalition of several parties by persuading each that its members would benefit from the coalition. The major difficulty in a multiparty system is, of course, that the parties will withdraw from the coalition when they fail to benefit from it. Holding a coalition together for more than one issue is sometimes impossible. Creating such a system in the United States would require significant structural change to our constitutional system.

For Critical Analysis

1. *In your view, are multiparty systems more representative than the two-party system in the United States? Why or why not?*

2. *Could you imagine a coalition of minor parties forming in the United States? Who might be included and what would the common interests be?*

Mohamed Hossam/Anadolu Agency/Getty Images

Leroy Francis/hemis.fr/Getty Images

iStockphoto.com/kyoshino iStockphoto.com/martijeacock

The most recent realignment has sometimes been linked to the elections of 1968. The realignment was a gradual process that took place over many years. It is sometimes referred to as a "rolling realignment." In 1968, Democrat Hubert Humphrey, Republican Richard Nixon, and third-party candidate George Wallace of Alabama all vied for the presidency. Following the Republican victory in that election, Nixon adopted a "southern strategy" aimed at drawing dissatisfied southern Democrats into the Republican Party.[13] At the presidential level, the strategy was an immediate success, although years would pass before the Republicans could gain dominance in the South's delegation to Congress or in state legislatures. Nixon's southern strategy helped create the political environment in which we live today. Another milestone in the progress of the Republicans was Ronald Reagan's sweeping victory in the presidential election of 1980.

Realignment: The Myth of Predictability. A second myth concerning realignments is that they take place every 36 years. Supposedly, there were realigning elections in 1860, 1896, 1932, and 1968, and therefore 2004 must have been a year for realignment. No such event took place. In fact, no force could cause political realignments at precise 36-year intervals. Further, realignments are not always tied to particular elections. The most recent realignment, in which conservative southern Democrats became conservative southern Republicans, was not closely linked to a particular election. The realignment of the 1850s, following the creation of the modern Republican Party, also took place over a period of years.

Is Realignment Still Possible?. The nature of American political parties created the pattern of realignment in American history. The sheer size of the country, combined with the inexorable pressure toward a two-party system, resulted in parties made up of voters with conflicting interests or values. The pre–Civil War party system involved two parties—Whigs and Democrats—with support in both the North and the South. This system could survive only by burying, as deeply as possible, the issue of slavery. We should not be surprised that the structure eventually collapsed. The Republican ascendancy of 1896–1932 united capitalists and industrial workers under the Republican banner, despite serious economic conflicts between the two. The New Deal Democratic coalition after 1932 brought African Americans and ardent segregationists into the same party.

For realignment to occur, a substantial body of citizens must come to believe that their party can no longer represent their interests or values. The problem must be fundamental and not attributable to the behavior of an individual politician. Given the increasing cohesion of each of the parties today, it is unlikely that a realignment is in the offing. The values that unite each party are relatively coherent, and their constituents are reasonably compatible. Therefore, the current party system should be more stable than in the past, and a major realignment is not likely to take place in the foreseeable future. It appears that instead of moving from one major political party to another, voters have simply moved away from both parties choosing instead to identify as political independents.

---

13. The classic work on Nixon's southern strategy is Kirkpatrick Sales, *The Emerging Republican Majority* (New Rochelle, NY: Arlington House, 1969).

Dealignment

Dealignment
A decline in party loyalties that reduces long-term party commitment.

Party Identification
Linking oneself to a particular political party.

Straight-Ticket Voting
Voting exclusively for the candidates of one party.

■ **LO8.6:** Discuss the rise of political independents and evaluate how this change might impact American politics.

Among political scientists, one common argument has been that realignment is no longer likely because voters are not as committed to the two major parties as they were in the 1800s and early 1900s. In this view, called **dealignment** theory, large numbers of independent voters may result in political volatility, but the absence of strong partisan attachments means that it is no longer easy to "lock in" political preferences for decades.

Independent Voters.   Figure 8–4 shows trends in **party identification**, as measured by standard polling techniques from 1937 to the present. The chart displays a rise in the number of independent voters throughout the period, combined with a fall in support for the Democrats from the mid-1960s on. The decline in Democratic identification may be due to the consolidation of Republican support in the South since 1968, a process that by now may be substantially complete. In any event, the traditional Democratic advantage in party identification has vanished.

Not only has the number of independents grown over the last half-century, but voters are also less willing to vote a straight ticket—that is, to vote for all the candidates of one party. In the early 1900s, **straight-ticket voting** was nearly universal. By midcentury, 12 percent of voters engaged in ticket splitting. In recent presidential elections, between 20 and 40 percent of the voters engaged in split-ticket voting. This trend, along with the increase in the number of voters who call themselves independents, suggests that parties have lost much of their hold on the loyalty of the voters.

Not-So-Independent Voters.   A problem with dealignment theory is that many "independent" voters are not all that independent. Polling organizations estimate

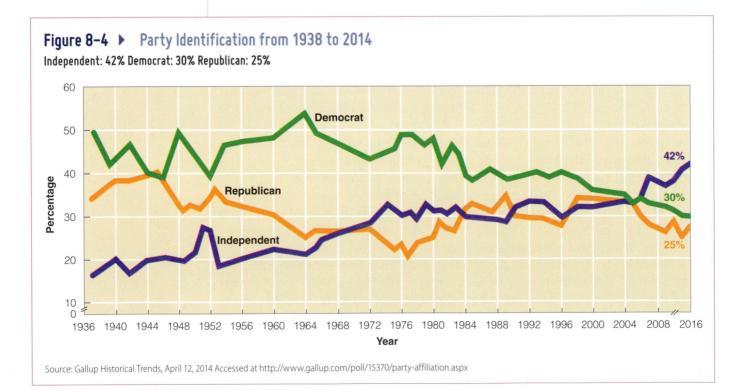

Figure 8–4 ▶ Party Identification from 1938 to 2014

Independent: 42% Democrat: 30% Republican: 25%

Source: Gallup Historical Trends, April 12, 2014 Accessed at http://www.gallup.com/poll/15370/party-affiliation.aspx

that of the 31 percent of voters who identify themselves as independents and another 18 percent who do not adhere to any political identity. If "pushed" to pick a party label, Democrats pick up another 18 percent in support but Republicans nearly match it with a 17 percent gain. The people who are willing to identify if pushed are called "leaners" and sometimes these leaners act like ardent partisans. If these "leaners" are deducted from the independent category, only 10 percent of the voters remain. These true independents are **swing voters** they can swing back and forth between the parties. These voters are important in deciding elections. Some analysts believe, however, that swing voters are far less numerous today than they were two or three decades ago. Swing voters are only relevant if the district or contest itself is competitive.

Swing Voters
Voters who frequently swing their support from one party to another.

Tipping

Political transformation can also result from changes in the composition of the electorate. Even when groups of voters never change their party preferences, if one group becomes more numerous over time, it can become dominant for that reason alone. We call this kind of demographically-based change **tipping**. Immigration is one cause of this phenomenon.

Tipping
A phenomenon that occurs when a group that is becoming more numerous over time grows large enough to change the political balance in a district, state, or country.

Tipping in Massachusetts. Consider Massachusetts, where for generations Irish Catholics confronted Protestant Yankees in the political arena. Most of the Yankees were Republican; most of the Irish were Democrats. The Yankees were numerically dominant from the founding of the state until 1928. In that year, for the first time, Democratic Irish voters came to outnumber the Republican Yankees. Massachusetts, which previously had been one of the most solidly Republican states, cast its presidential vote for Democrat Al Smith. Within a few years, Massachusetts became one of the most reliably Democratic states in the nation.

Tipping in California. California may have experienced a tipping effect during the 1990s. From 1952 until 1992, California consistently supported Republican presidential candidates, turning Democratic only in the landslide election of Lyndon Johnson in 1964. In 1992, however, the California electorate gave Democrat Bill Clinton a larger percentage of its votes than he received in the country as a whole. Since then, no Republican presidential candidate has managed to carry California.

The improved performance of the Democrats in California is almost certainly a function of demography. In 1999, California became the third state, after Hawaii and New Mexico, in which non-Latino whites do *not* make up a majority of the population. Latinos and African Americans both give most of their votes to the Democrats, but sometimes even though the eligible voting population is more diverse, voters remain older and predominantly white. For the first time, California Latinos, Asian Americans, and African Americans voted in the 2012 election numbers roughly equivalent to their share of registered voters in 2012. About 40 percent of California's electorate is now non-white, and ethnic voters made up about 40 percent of those who mailed in their ballots or went to the polls. Mitt Romney won the white vote in California by 8 percentage points while losing the state in a landslide, by 22 points. President Obama won among Latinos by 45 points, Asian Americans by 58 points and African Americans by 93 points, according to the exit poll data.[14]

---

14. Daniel Weintraub, "November election was a tipping point for ethnic voters," *California Health Report*, December 9, 2012. Accessed at www.healthycal.org/archives/10392

Political Parties of the Future

Despite the erosion of support for Republicans and Democrats, political parties perform vital functions in the American political system. Change is inevitable, but the direction of change is never entirely predictable. Technology, the rise of non-party organizational support for national candidates, and significant demographic changes in the electorate challenges the current parties.

Democratic strategists hope that the tolerant spirit of many younger voters may work to their advantage. The Democratic Party has worked hard in southwestern states and California to bring Latino voters to the fold, and the Obama administration has appealed, in particular, to female voters through its positions on health care and contraceptive coverage. If the Democrats could add a significant majority of female and Latino voters to their numbers, it could offset some losses among blue-collar workers who are concerned about jobs and the economy but persuaded by Republicans on social issues.

Republicans recognize that the current demographic trends are not working in their favor but refuse to accept that "demography is destiny." Strategists are working to hone the Republican message to women, Latinos, and young people. Republicans have created outreach initiatives designed to appeal to independents or Democratic voters. A recent example shows how difficult that can be, however. The Heritage Foundation, a conservative organization led by former Republican Senator Jim DeMint, convened a panel of conservative women during Women's History Month in hopes of shrinking the Republican's gender gap. Mona Charen, one of the panelists, advised "If we truly want women to thrive, we have to revive the marriage norm."[15] This would also have the effect of increasing Republican voters—"we do not have a sex gap here in voting. We have a marriage gap." Columnists suggested that Republicans were telling women to "lean back" (contrary to Sheryl Sandberg's message to women to "lean in" to their careers) and return to more traditional choices.[16] Given that women make up half of the full-time workforce today and are projected to reach 57 percent by 2020, the message seems unlikely to resonate with many women.

Another possibility: If the two parties continue their bitter rivalry on the campaign trail and gridlock persists in Congress such that the nation's most pressing problems go unaddressed, moderates and those who are weakly attached to a party may become true independents, deciding each election on the issues of concern to them and avoiding identification with a political party altogether. Alternatively, perhaps an issue or a charismatic candidate will capture the imagination of a new coalition of voters and a new political party will emerge, ushering in a sixth party system.

15. Dana Milbank, "Conservatives to women: Lean back." *The Washington Post*, March 31, 2014. Accessed at www.washingtonpost.com/opinions/dana-milbank-conservatives-to-women-lean-back/2014/03/31/e8b96c00-b91b-11e3-9a05c739f29ccb08_story.html?hpid=z2
16. Sheryl Sandberg, *Lean In: Women, Work, and the Will to Lead*. (New York: Knopf, 2013).

What Would You Do?

Political Parties as Engines of Diversity

Diversity in society is valued for lots of reasons, but research conducted by Scott Page demonstrates that diversity within organizations leads to better decisions and higher productivity.* Using mathematical models, he showed that diverse groups of problem solvers outperformed the groups of the best individuals at solving problems. This is because the diverse groups got stuck less often than the "smart" individuals who tended to think similarly. Professor Page explains it this way—"[d]iverse groups of people bring to organizations more and different ways of seeing a problem and, thus, faster/better ways of solving it.…The problems we face in the world are very complicated. Any one of us can get stuck. If we're in an organization where everyone thinks in the same way, everyone will get stuck in the same place."**

How does this apply to politics? Political parties are the organizations that recruit, finance, and support candidates for public office. Once elected, those public officials govern by working together to make decisions and solve problems. As political gatekeepers, political parties play a vital role in recruiting and attracting a diverse pool of political candidates at all levels of government. A recent report by FairVote, an advocacy organization dedicated to expanding voting rights, says that party leaders don't reach out and encourage women to jump into a race as often as they encourage men. Other research finds that members of underrepresented groups need to be asked and may need to be asked multiple times before they will consider a candidacy. Women and underrepresented minorities are 10 percent less likely to be asked, but when approached these potential candidates often respond positively.

Why Should You Care?

Imagine this research applied to government. The 113th Congress is the most diverse in history, but in many ways members of the House of Representatives and Senate are more like one another than different. For example, the majority in both chambers is middle-aged, white, male, Christian, and drawn predominantly from the professions of law and business.*** Although women make up roughly 20 percent of the 113th Congress, 77 percent of them are Democrats. Diversity is essential to both political parties.

Seven women in the U.S. Senate joined in a bipartisan coalition and led the effort to draft the bill that eventually ended the 16-day government shut-down. Even though women make up just 20 percent of the Senate, they made up 66 percent of the bipartisan collaborators. As Senator Susan Collins (R-Maine)

said, "Although we span the ideological spectrum, we're used to working in a collaborative way."**** Yet, at the current rate of election it will take more than two centuries for women to reach parity with men, and of course gender is not the only important facet of diversity that improves performance. Race, ethnicity, religion, military experience, education, previous occupation—all of these components shape an individual's perspective. How can political parties play a more effective role?

What Would You Do?

As the head of your political party, how can you identify strong candidates that bring a diversity of experiences to governing?

What You *Can* Do

There are several initiatives dedicated to electing women and members of underrepresented groups to political office. Some are nonpartisan or bipartisan, but many are run by the party. Republicans in particular are interested in expanding their base of voters and their candidate pool. In 2013, House Republican leaders announced Project GROW (Growing Republican Opportunities for Women) aimed at recruiting more women and providing financial support to women in competitive races. More broadly, Republicans have established the Growth and Opportunity Project to get their message out more effectively to women, African Americans, Hispanics, Asian and Pacific Islanders, and young people (groups who have traditionally supported Democrats).

You can learn more about these issues:

- GROW at www.nrcc.org/project_grow/
- National Republican Committee: www.gop.com/
- National Democratic Committee: www.democrats.org/

* Scott E. Page, *The Difference: How the Power of Diversity Creates Better Groups, Firms, Schools, and Societies.* Princeton, NJ: Princeton University Press, 2008.
** Claudia Dreifus, "In Professor's Model, Diversity=Productivity" *The New York Times,* January 8, 2008. Accessed at www.nytimes.com/2008/01/08/science/08conv.html.
*** Jennifer Manning, "Membership of the 113th Congress: A Profile." Congressional Research Service, March 14, 2014. Accessed at http://www.fas.org/sgp/crs/misc/R42964.pdf.
**** "Swanee Hunt, "20 percent women, 100 percent effective," *GlobalPost,* October 18, 2013. Accessed at www.globalpost.com/dispatches/globalpost-blogs/commentary/20-percent-women-100-percent-effective-senate-deal-shutdown

Key Terms

convention delegates 269	national convention 269	political party 266	third party 288
dealignment 294	party identification 294	realignment 291	ticket splitting 271
Democratic Party 275	party-in-government 271	Republican Party 275	tipping 295
divided government 271	party-in-the-electorate 268	safe seat 272	two-party system 273
electoral college 286	party organization 268	splinter parties 290	unit rule 271
era of good feelings 275	party platform 269	state central committee 270	Whig Party 275
faction 266	patronage 271	straight-ticket voting 294	
national committee 269	plurality 286	swing voters 295	

Chapter Summary

■ **LO8.1:** A political party is a group of political activists who organize to win elections, operate the government, and determine public policy. Political parties recruit candidates for public office, organize and run elections, present alternative policies to the voters, assume responsibility for operating the government, and act as the opposition to the party in power.

■ **LO8.2:** A political party consists of three components: the party-in-the-electorate, the party organization, and the party-in-government. The party-in-the electorate is made up of all of the people who affiliate and identify with the political party. Although they are not required to participate in every election, they are the most likely to do so because they feel a sense of loyalty to the party. The party organization provides the structural framework for the political party by recruiting volunteers to become party leaders, identifying potential candidates, and organizing caucuses, conventions, and election campaigns for its candidates. The party-in-government consists of elected and appointed officials who identify with a political party. After the election is over and the winners are announced, the focus of party activity shifts from getting out the vote to organizing and controlling the government.

■ **LO8.3:** The evolution of our nation's political parties can be divided into five party systems: (1) the development of parties, 1789–1828; (2) Democrats and Whigs, 1828–1860; (3) Republican's rise to power and the Civil War, 1860–1896; (4) the Progressive interlude and Republican dominance, 1896–1932; (5) the New Deal and Democratic dominance, 1932–1968. Political parties today differ considerably, although sometimes voters do not accurately define the differences or align predictably with a party. Weaker attachment to parties and the rising influence of non-party organizations in campaigns and elections make a sixth party system unlikely to emerge.

■ **LO8.4:** Political parties are built by appealing to groups of people and knitting together a coalition based on shared interests. The Democratic and Republican party appeal to different constituencies and embrace different issue positions. Men, people over the age of 65, the wealthy, married people, and better-educated voters tend to identify with the Republicans. Women, young people, non-whites, members of labor unions, and the unemployed affiliate with the Democrats. Regionally, the South is solidly Republican, while the East and West Coasts trend toward the Democrats. The starkest differences along religious lines are between white Evangelical protestants (Republicans) and those who are religiously unaffiliated (Democrats). Partisans identifying with each political party differ in their positions on issues as well. Historically, one of the defining differences between the parties is a difference in vision over the size and role of government. Eighty-two percent of Republicans prefer a smaller government providing fewer services (compared to 29 percent of Democrats), while a majority (59 percent) of Democrats would choose a bigger government that provided more services (a choice of only 14 percent of Republicans).

■ **LO8.5:** Two major parties have dominated the political landscape in the United States for almost two centuries. Reasons for this include (1) the historical foundations of the system, (2) political socialization and practical considerations, (3) the winner-take-all electoral system, and (4) state and federal laws favoring the two-party system. Minor parties find it extremely difficult to win elections. Yet, minor (or third) parties have emerged, sometimes as dissatisfied splinter groups from within major parties, and have acted as barometers of changes in the political mood. Third parties can affect the political process (even if they do not win) if major parties adopt their issues or if they determine which major party wins an election.

■ **LO8.6:** The share of voters who describe themselves as independents has grown steadily in each election and today represents the identity (or lack of partisan identity) of over one-third of the electorate. Many independents actually vote as if they were Democrats or Republicans, however, and we call them "leaners." Historically, realigning elections have signaled significant change in public sentiment favoring a new political direction and a new dominant political party (e.g., 1932 and the rise of the New Deal coalition of Democrats). Disaffection with both major parties leads to dealignment, resulting in unpredictable voter behavior for a period of time. Among Millennial voters, people between the ages of 18 and 33, half choose not to identify with either party and only 31 percent see a difference between the major parties. Even so, 60 percent of Millennials voted for Barack Obama in 2012. This trend toward greater independence from the major parties, particularly among the young, might signal greater instability in American elections in years to come or perhaps action by the parties to redefine their base constituencies in an effort to reclaim prior dominance.

Selected Print, Media, and Online Resources

PRINT RESOURCES

Abramowitz, Alan I. *The Disappearing Center: Engaged Citizens, Polarization, and American Democracy.* New Haven, CT: Yale University Press, 2011. Abramowitz argues that the number of moderate voters in the nation is decreasing as the two parties become more distant and more ideological, thus increasing the polarization of politics.

Purdum, Todd S. *An Idea Whose Time Has Come: Two Presidents, Two Parties, and the Battle for the Civil Rights Act of 1964.* New York: Henry Holt and Co., 2014. The political story of the creation of the landmark civil rights bill—a piece of legislation that prompted the longest filibuster in U.S. Senate history, but ultimately passed with overwhelming bipartisan support.

Skocpol, Theda, and Vanessa Williamson. *The Tea Party and the Remaking of the Republican Party.* New York: Oxford University Press, 2011. Two political scientists report on their year-long investigation into the Tea Party. By spending long periods of time talking to these supporters, they are able to describe the goals and beliefs of Tea Party voters.

MEDIA RESOURCES

The American President—A 1995 film starring Michael Douglas as a widowed president who must balance partisanship and friendship (Republicans in Congress promise to approve the president's crime bill only if he modifies an environmental plan sponsored by his liberal girlfriend).

The Best Man—A 1964 drama based on Gore Vidal's play of the same name. The film, which deals with political smear campaigns by presidential party nominees, focuses on political party power and ethics.

House of Cards—A Netflix political drama featuring Kevin Spacey as Frank Underwood, a southern Democrat in pursuit of political power at any cost.

Ides of March—A 2011 film (starring Ryan Gosling and George Clooney) about the pursuit of the Democratic nomination for president. Features intra-party intrigue and the political horse-trading that occur in national campaigns.

ONLINE RESOURCES

Democratic Party—www.democrats.org

Green Party of the United States—a federation of state Green parties committed to environmentalism, nonviolence, social justice, and grassroots organizing: www.gp.org

Libertarian Party—America's third largest and fastest-growing political party; calls itself the party of principle and supports smaller government, lower taxes, and more freedom: www.lp.org

The Pew Research Center for the People & the Press—an independent, nonpartisan public opinion research organization that studies attitudes toward politics, the press, and public policy issues and offers survey data online on how the parties fared during the most recent elections, voter typology, and numerous other issues: www.people-press.org/

Republican Party www.gop.com

Master the concept of Political Parties with MindTap™ for American Government

 REVIEW MindTap™ **for American Government**
Access Key Term Flashcards for Chapter 8.

 STAY CURRENT MindTap™ **for American Government**
Access the KnowNow blog and customized RSS for updates on current events.

 TEST YOURSELF MindTap™ **for American Government**
Take the Wrap It Up Quiz for Chapter 7.

 STAY FOCUSED MindTap™ **for American Government**
Complete the Focus Activities for Political Parties.

Campaigns, Voting, and Elections

9

Senator Debbie Stabenow, Democrat of Michigan, speaks to cherry and apple farmers about her bid for reelection in 2012.

AP Photo/John Flesher

WATCH & LEARN

Watch a brief "What Do You Know?" videos summarizing Voting and Elections.

LEARNING OUTCOMES

After reading this chapter, students will be able to:

■ **LO9.1** Explain the eligibility requirements for president, senator, and representative; discuss why an individual might choose to become a candidate for office.

■ **LO9.2** Produce a plan for a modern campaign for the United States Senate; include the strategy, staff, and finances necessary for such an endeavor.

■ **LO9.3** Demonstrate an understanding of the evolution of campaign finance regulation, the development of political action committees (PACs), and the current state of such regulation.

■ **LO9.4** Describe the general outline of today's campaign for the presidency and discuss the impact of the primary system on the outcome of the nomination process.

■ **LO9.5** Demonstrate an understanding of the electoral process in the United States and explain how it relates to democratic theory.

■ **LO9.6** Discuss the factors that influence voter turnout in the United States and compare American voter turnout to that of other nations.

■ **LO9.7** Describe historical restrictions on the vote in the United States and explain how these restrictions have been ended.

■ **LO9.8** Discuss the impact of the mechanics and technology of voting on voter turnout, vote fraud, and the ability of citizens to trust the process.

■ **LO9.9** Demonstrate an understanding of the electoral college and its impact on the presidential election campaign.

Voting on the Internet Became Universal?

BACKGROUND

Today, you can do just about anything on your smartphone. Why can't you vote using a smartphone or the Internet? This seems to be the logical extension of today's technology. Instead, almost all local governments require the voter to vote in person on a specified day or to seek an absentee ballot in advance. Some states allow advance voting in a specified place up to three weeks ahead of the vote; Oregon permits mail-in ballots.

WHAT IF INTERNET VOTING BECAME UNIVERSAL?

Many people would find it very convenient to vote over the Internet, whether via smartphone, desktop computer, or iPad. Travelers would no longer need to request an absentee ballot or to vote in advance of the election. Local governments would not have to invest millions of dollars in voting machines and cover the expense of operating polling places anymore. Even if they felt the need to honor the idea of a polling place, allowing voters to use laptops at polling places would be much less expensive and less trouble than today's voting booths.

Using today's technology for voting would likely increase voter turnout among younger Americans, the group least likely to vote. As you will read in this chapter, younger Americans are less likely to be settled in a community and less likely to have an interest in political issues. But, if they received an email alert and could vote instantly, voter turnout would likely increase in society.

Voting via the Internet would end the confusion over whether announcing the voting results of the eastern states affects turnout in the western states. A "window" for voting would open at a certain time, either in a state or across the nation, and all polls would open at the same time and close at the same time. Of course, traditional exit polling would cease to exist, as voters would no longer attend a physical location to cast their ballots. Results would be easily calculated and could be announced by a nonpartisan government agency at a specified time. The news would broadcast no more tales of hand-recounted, spoiled ballots and visual inspections of nebulous punch-card markings.

WOULD INTERNET VOTING DISENFRANCHISE SOME VOTERS?

It is important to remember that not all Americans are "connected" to the Internet. Service does not reach many rural areas of the United States and many economically disadvantaged individuals are without access to computers or to internet services. Older Americans who do not have internet services would likely be discouraged from voting, as would poorer groups. Individuals who value their privacy might prefer not to vote via the Internet because it could be traced back to their computer or smartphone.

What would be the result if older Americans, less well-off Americans, and other groups were disenfranchised by internet voting? Younger voters tend to be more liberal in their social views and, to some extent, in their views about government action. Increasing turnout among these voters would advantage Democratic Party candidates. Lowering turnout among poorer, urban voters, however, would cost those candidates votes as well. Republicans would work very hard to make sure that their older supporters had access to computers and assistance in voting, to be sure.

WHY HASN'T INTERNET VOTING BEEN ADOPTED?

The major issue with Internet voting is the security of the vote. In 2003, the U.S. Department of Defense announced that it planned to make internet voting for the 2004 election available to all members of the armed forces serving overseas. At that time, more than 100,000 members of the military were in Iraq. By early 2004, the Pentagon announced that it had cancelled that plan due to the possibility of voter fraud. Stealing voter identification, hacking into the voting system, submitting thousands of fraudulent votes using hijacked computers—all of these are possibilities. In 2010, the District of Columbia announced the trial of an internet voting system and invited hackers to try to "break into" the system. Within a few days, University of Michigan students hacked into the system, adding the Michigan fight song as a sound track for voting. The trial was cancelled.*

It is worth noting that the country of Estonia has adopted internet voting, but it is optional there. Other nations are trying to solve the security problems in various ways. The real question is this: Why do people want to tamper with the vote? The answer is because the stakes in governing are so high.

* Mike DeBonis, "Hacker infiltration ends D.C. online voting trial," Washington Post, October 12, 2010.

For Critical Analysis

1. *Which groups would be most likely to vote over the Internet and which the least?*

2. *Would Internet voting increase citizens' trust in the voting process or make them even more suspicious of vote fraud?*

FREE ELECTIONS ARE the cornerstone of the American political system. Voters choose one or more candidates from a pool of candidates by casting ballots in local, state, and federal elections. Voters are free from intimidation or coercion and able to access information about the election. Voting should be easy, with simple forms or machines, and available at convenient hours. If these conditions are met, voters can have confidence in the election process and, in turn, more confidence in their elected officials. This chapter looks at the process of campaigning for election as well as voting and elections in the American context.

LISTEN & LEARN
MindTap for American Government

Access Read Speaker to listen to Chapter 9.

Who Wants to Be a Candidate?

■ **LO9.1:** Explain the eligibility requirements for president, senator, and representative; discuss why an individual might choose to become a candidate for office.

Democratic political systems require competitive elections. If there is no competition for any office—president or local school superintendent—then the public has no ability to make a choice about its leadership or policies to be pursued. Who, then, are the people who seek to run for office?

The United States has thousands of elective offices. Political parties strive to provide a slate of candidates for every election. Recruiting candidates is easier for some offices than for others. Offices of high esteem and power have no trouble attracting candidates. In many areas of the country, however, one political party may be considerably stronger than the other. In those situations, the minority party may have more difficulty finding nominees for elections in which victory is unlikely.

Why They Run

People who run for office can be divided into two groups—the self-starters and those who are recruited. The self-starters get involved in political activities to further their careers, to carry out specific political programs, or in response to certain issues or events. Candidates for president from third parties often campaign primarily to gain publicity for their views, knowing they are unlikely to win.

Issues are important, but personal goals—status, career objectives, prestige, and income—are central in motivating some candidates to enter political life. Political office is often seen as the stepping stone to achieving certain career goals. A lawyer or an insurance agent may run for office only once or twice and then return to private life with enhanced status. Other politicians may aspire to long-term political office. Finally, we think of ambition as the desire for ever-more-important offices and higher status. Politicians who run for the state house may well desire to be elected to the U.S. House of Representatives in future years.

The Nomination Process

Individuals become official candidates through the process of nomination. Generally, nominating processes for all offices are controlled by state laws and usually favor the two major political parties. For most minor offices, individuals become candidates by submitting petitions to the local election board. Political parties often help individuals obtain the petitions, pay whatever filing fee is required, and gather signatures. In most states, a candidate from one of the two major parties faces far fewer requirements to get on the ballot than a candidate who is an independent or who represents a minor or new party.

For higher-level offices, candidates may need to petition and then be nominated by a party convention at the state level. In other jurisdictions, party caucuses are empowered to nominate candidates. Many contenders for office are nominated through a primary election in which two or more individuals contend for the party's nomination.

The American system of nominations and primary elections is one of the most complex in the world. In most European nations, the political party's choice of candidates is final, and no primary elections are ever held.

Who Is Eligible?

There are few constitutional restrictions on who can become a candidate in the United States. As set out in the Constitution, the formal requirements for national office are as follows:

1. *President.* Must be a natural-born citizen, have attained the age of 35 years, and be a resident of the country for 14 years by the time of inauguration.

2. *Vice president.* Must be a natural-born citizen, have attained the age of 35 years, and not be a resident of the same state as the candidate for president.[1]

3. *Senator.* Must be a citizen for at least nine years, have attained the age of 30 by the time of taking office, and be a resident of the state from which elected.

4. *Representative.* Must be a citizen for at least seven years, have attained the age of 25 by the time of taking office, and be a resident of the state from which elected.

The qualifications for state legislators are set by the state constitutions and likewise include age, place of residence, and citizenship. Usually, the requirements for the upper chamber of a legislature are somewhat more stringent than those for the lower chamber. The legal qualifications for running for governor or other state office are similar.

Who Runs?

Despite these minimal legal qualifications for office at both the national and state levels, a quick look at the slate of candidates in any election—or at the current members of the U.S. House of Representatives—will reveal that not all segments of the population take advantage of these opportunities. Holders of political office in the United States are overwhelmingly white and male. Until the twentieth century, presidential candidates were of northern European origin and Protestant heritage.[2] Laws that effectively denied voting rights made it impossible to elect African American public officials in many areas in which African Americans constituted a significant portion of the population. As a result of the passage of major civil rights legislation in the 1960s, however, the number of African American public officials has increased throughout the United States. By 2013, the number of African American elected officials was estimated at more than 10,500,[3] and, in

---

1. Technically, a presidential and vice presidential candidate can be from the same state, but if they are, one of the two must forfeit the electoral votes of his or her home state.
2. A number of early presidents were Unitarian. The Unitarian Church is not Protestant, but it is historically rooted in the Protestant tradition.
3. Juliet Eilperin, "What's Changed for African Americans since 1963, by the numbers," http://www.washingtonpost.com/blogs/the-fix/2013/08/22

2008, American elected Barack Obama to be the first African American president. He was reelected in 2012.

Women as Candidates. Until recently, women generally were considered to be appropriate candidates only for lower-level offices, such as state legislator or school board member. It was thought that women would be more acceptable to the voting public if they were either running for an office that allowed them to continue their family duties or were running for an office that focused on local affairs, such as city or school issues. The last 20 years have seen a tremendous increase in the number of women who run for office, not only at the state level but for the U.S. Congress as well. Figure 9–1 shows the increase in female candidates. In 2014, 182 women ran for Congress, and 81 were elected. Noteworthy in the class of women elected to the Senate in 2012 are Tammy Baldwin, the first openly gay senator, and Mazie Hirono, Hawaii's first female senator. Senator Hirono is also the first senator born in Japan and the first Buddhist senator.

In the past, women were not recruited, because they had not worked their way up through the male-dominated party organization or because they were thought to have no chance of winning. Women also had a more difficult time raising campaign funds. Since the 1970s, there has been a focused effort to increase the number of women candidates. EMILY's List, a group that raises money to recruit and support liberal women candidates, has had a strong

did you know?

EMILY's List means Early Money Is Like Yeast, referring both to needing money early in a campaign and to yeast for raising bread.

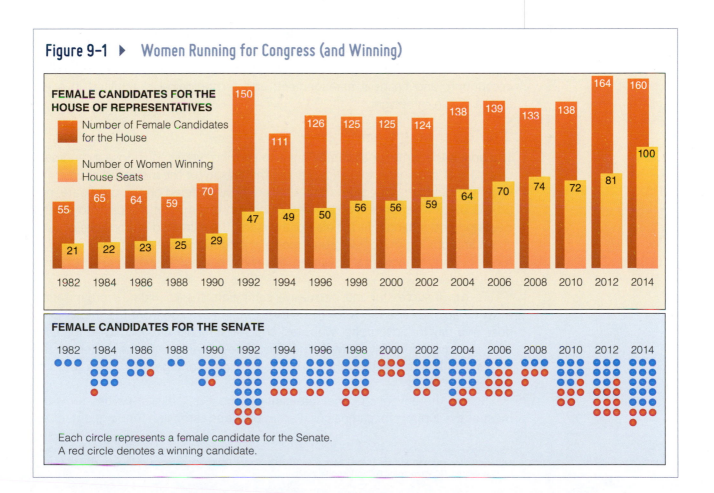

Figure 9–1 ▶ Women Running for Congress (and Winning)

FEMALE CANDIDATES FOR THE HOUSE OF REPRESENTATIVES

- Number of Female Candidates for the House
- Number of Women Winning House Seats

Year	Number of Female Candidates for the House	Number of Women Winning House Seats
1982	55	21
1984	65	22
1986	64	23
1988	59	25
1990	70	29
1992	150	47
1994	111	49
1996	126	50
1998	125	56
2000	125	56
2002	124	59
2004	138	64
2006	139	70
2008	133	74
2010	138	72
2012	164	81
2014	160	100

FEMALE CANDIDATES FOR THE SENATE

1982 1984 1986 1988 1990 1992 1994 1996 1998 2000 2002 2004 2006 2008 2010 2012 2014

Each circle represents a female candidate for the Senate.
A red circle denotes a winning candidate.

Do campaigns such as "Ban Bossy" have a greater affect on individuals when celebrity and political endorsers are involved?

impact on the situation for women candidates. Other organizations with more conservative agendas also raise money for women. Recent elections have witnessed women candidates of either party raising millions of dollars and winning office; however, women voters are more likely to perceive gender bias and a harder path for women candidates. After the 2008 election, 65 percent of women saw gender bias in the treatment of Hillary Clinton and Sarah Palin.[4] Such perceptions work to discourage other women from seeking elective office. To help fight these perceptions of women in the workplace and elected office, Condoleezza Rice, former secretary of state, has partnered with other female business leaders and politicians to start the "Ban Bossy" campaign. The goal is to ban the adjective "bossy" and to encourage young girls to speak up and participate in leadership roles.

The Twenty-First Century Campaign

■ **LO9.2:** Produce a plan for a modern campaign for the United States Senate; include the strategy, staff, and finances necessary for such an endeavor.

After the candidates have been nominated, the most exhausting and expensive part of the election process begins—the general election campaign. Even with the most appealing of candidates, today's campaigns require a strong organization; expertise in political polling and marketing; professional assistance in fundraising, accounting, and financial management; and technological capabilities in every aspect of the campaign.

The Changing Campaign

The goal is the same for all campaigns—to convince voters to choose a candidate or a slate of candidates for office. Part of the reason for the increased intensity of campaigns in the last decade is that they are now centered on the candidate, not on the party. The candidate-centered campaign emerged in response to several developments: changes in the electoral system, the increased importance of television and other forms of electronic media in campaigns, the change in campaign funding, and technological advances in ways to reach potential voters, including social media.

To run a successful and persuasive campaign, the candidate's organization must be able to raise funds for the effort; obtain coverage from the media; produce and pay for advertising, websites, and social media sites; schedule the candidate's time effectively; convey the candidate's position on the issues to the voters; conduct research on the opposing candidate; and get the voters to go to the polls.

Before the advent of candidate-centered politics, political parties provided most of the support for campaigns. Parties provided campaign funding, organized

4. Jennifer Lawless and Richard L. Fox, "Men Rule: The Continued Underrepresentation of Women in U.S. Politics," Washington, DC: Women and Politics Institute, 2012.

Everyday Politics

 Game Change: An inside look at campaign decisions

Released in 2012 on HBO, *Game Change* is a look inside the campaign decisions made by the John McCain organization in the 2008 presidential election. Faced by the charismatic Democratic candidate Barack Obama, McCain and his campaign team struggled to find a way to add excitement to his campaign. They decided on Sarah Palin, the untested governor of Alaska (a very small state in terms of voters), as the vice presidential candidate on the Republican ticket. Palin was named as the vice presidential candidate right before the Republican National Convention and completely upended the staid convention with her acceptance speech.

The movie, which stars Woody Harrelson, Ed Harris, and Julianne Moore, tells the story of Palin's rise to stardom and quick fall after some of her "gaffes." Although both Palin and McCain said that they would never see the film and that it is inaccurate, the movie was based on the book, *Game Change*, written by two veteran journalists, Mark Halperin and John Heilemann. Some of those who were insiders to the campaign and other journalists who covered the campaign say there is a lot of truth in this fictionalized account of the McCain campaign.

Like other films about political campaigns, *Game Change* underscores the intensity of a campaign and the desperate quality of the decisions that are made in the attempt to win. It also spotlights the power of the media.

For Critical Analysis

1. *Does social media such as YouTube and made-for-TV movies such as Game Change make it easier for political commentators to treat candidates as "unqualified" or as inconsequential candidates?*

2. *Does the attention given by social media have a lasting impact on campaigns and elections?*

events, registered voters and turned out the voters on election day. Prior to today's media-saturated campaigns, the party label was more important to voters than the candidate's appearance and personality.

Today, with the decline in party identification among American voters, the candidate's campaigns must provide a persuasive case for his or her election to party identifiers and to the growing class of independent voters. Consider the fact that only 20 percent of voters declared themselves independents in 1952 as compared to 45 percent in 2014.[5]

The Professional Campaign Staff

Whether a candidate is running for state legislature, the governor's office, U.S. Congress, or the presidency, every campaign has some fundamental tasks to accomplish. Today, in national elections, most of these tasks are handled by paid professionals, rather than volunteers or amateur politicians. Volunteers and amateurs are primarily used for the last-minute registration or voter turnout activities.

The most sought-after and possibly the most criticized campaign expert is the **political consultant**, who, for a large fee, devises a campaign strategy, creates a campaign theme, oversees the advertising, and possibly chooses the campaign colors and the candidate's official portrait. Political consultants began to displace

Political Consultant
A paid professional hired to devise a campaign strategy and manage a campaign.

5. Gallup Poll, February 6–9, 2014.

Finance Chairperson
The campaign professional who directs fundraising, campaign spending, and compliance with campaign finance laws and reporting requirements.

Pollster
The person or firm who conducts public opinion polls for the campaign.

Communications Director
A professional specialist who plans the communications strategy and advertising campaign for the candidate.

Press Secretary
The individual who interacts directly with the journalists covering the campaign.

Get Out the Vote (GOTV)
This phrase describes the multiple efforts expended by campaigns to get voters out to the polls on Election Day.

CONNECT WITH YOUR CLASSMATES
MindTap® for American Government

Access the Campaigning for Office Forum: Discussion—Electing Incumbents.

volunteer campaign managers in the 1960s, about the same time that television became a force in campaigns. The paid consultant and his or her staff monitors the campaign's progress, plans all media appearances, and coaches the candidate for debates. The consultants and the firms they represent are not politically neutral; most will work only for candidates from one party. Consultants are on hand constantly to plan rebuttals to the opponent's charges and to recalibrate the campaign.

Under constant pressure to raise more campaign funds and to comply with the campaign finance laws, all campaigns need a **finance chairperson** who plans the fundraising strategy and finds the legal and accounting expertise needed for the organization. Of course, campaigns will either hire an in-house **pollster** or contract with a major polling firm for the tracking polls and focus groups discussed in Chapter 6.

Candidates need to have a clear strategy to gain public attention and to respond to attacks by their opponents. The campaign's **communications director** plans appearances, the themes to be communicated by the candidate at specific points in the campaign, and the responses to any attacks. The campaign's **press secretary** is responsible for dealing directly with the press. Perhaps the most famous example of a successful communication strategy was that of Bill Clinton in his 1992 victory. The campaign organized a "War Room" to instantly respond to any attack by his opponents. Today's candidates use Twitter and other social networking sites to respond to charges instantaneously. Counterattacks, a feature of the War Room strategy, can also be launched immediately using social networking sites. At the end of the campaign is the actual election. Campaigns need to find a way to recruit and organize volunteers for the **Get Out the Vote (GOTV)** drive to persuade voters to come to the polls on election day.

The Strategy of Winning

In the United States, unlike some European countries, the candidate who comes in second gets no reward. A winner-take-all system is also known as a *plurality voting system.* In most situations, the winning candidate does not have to have a majority of the votes. Given this system, the campaign organization must plan a strategy that maximizes the candidate's chances of winning. Candidates seek to capture all of the votes of their party's supporters, to convince a majority of the independent voters to vote for them, and to gain a few votes from supporters of the other party. To accomplish these goals, candidates must consider their visibility, their message, and their campaign strategy.

Candidate Visibility and Appeal

One of the most important concerns is how well known the candidate is. If she or he is a highly visible incumbent, little campaigning may be needed except to remind the voters of the officeholder's good deeds. If, however, the candidate is an unknown challenger or a largely unfamiliar character running against a well-known public figure, the campaign must devise a strategy to get the candidate before the public.

In the case of the independent candidate or the candidate representing a minor party, the problem of name recognition is serious. Such candidates must present an overwhelming case for the voter to reject the major-party candidates.

Both Democratic and Republican candidates use the strategic ploy of labeling third-party candidates as "not serious"—and therefore not worth the voter's time.

Taking the Public Pulse

In addition to measuring name recognition and "feelings" toward a candidate, today's campaigns rely heavily on other ways to find out how the electorate views the candidate and her message. Opinion polls are a major source of information for both the media and the candidates. Dozens of public polls are reported in the news. As the election approaches, many candidates and commercial houses use **tracking polls**, which are polls taken almost every day, to find out how well they are competing for votes. Tracking polls enable consultants to fine-tune the advertising and the candidate's speeches in the last days of the campaign.

Another tactic is to use a **focus group** to gain insights into public perceptions of the candidate. Professional consultants organize a discussion of the candidate or of certain political issues among 10 to 15 ordinary citizens. The citizens are selected from specific target groups in the population—for example, working women, blue-collar men, senior citizens, or young voters. Recent campaigns have tried to reach groups such as "Millennials," "Wal-Mart shoppers," or "NASCAR dads."[6] The group discusses personality traits of the candidate, political advertising, and other candidate-related issues. The conversation is digitally video recorded (and often observed from behind a mirrored wall). Focus groups are expected to reveal more emotional responses to candidates or the deeper anxieties of voters— feelings that consultants believe often are not tapped into by more impersonal telephone surveys.

Tracking Polls
A poll taken for the candidate on a nearly daily basis as Election Day approaches.

Focus Group
A small group of individuals who are led in discussion by a professional consultant in order to gather opinions on and responses to candidates and issues.

The Media and Political Campaigns. All forms of the media—television, newspapers, radio, magazines, blogs, and podcasts—have a significant political impact on American society which is most obvious during political campaigns. With the bulk of campaign funds spent on media of one form or another, planning media strategies is one of the most important functions of a campaign. Media strategies include television news and entertainment outlets, social media and web presences, free and paid advertising, and performance in debates. The goal of this activity is for the public to accept and support the image of the candidate created by the campaign.

Financing the Campaign

For any campaign to have a chance at success, it must raise enough funds to be competitive. In a book published in 1932 entitled *Money in Elections,* Louise Overacker had the following to say about campaign financing:

> *The financing of elections in a democracy is a problem which is arousing increasing concern. Many are beginning to wonder if present-day methods of raising and spending campaign funds do not clog the wheels of our elaborately constructed mechanism of popular control, and if democracies do not inevitably become [governments ruled by small groups].[7]*

---

6. NASCAR stands for the National Association of Stock Car Auto Racing.
7. Louise Overacker, *Money in Elections* (New York: Macmillan, 1932), p. vii.

Beyond Our Borders

How Short Can a Campaign Be?

Consider the difference between U.S. presidential campaigns and the British system of elections for Parliament and prime minister. In the United States, candidates for president begin traveling the country and building up support about two years before the general election. The primary election season starts just after January 1st of the election year, and the campaigns continue nonstop for almost 11 months.

In the United Kingdom, the prime minister makes the decision to hold elections for Parliament, or the House of Commons. Parliamentary elections must be held at least every five years by law. The prime minister asks the queen to call elections either when the party's support is declining or when an advantage exists to the majority party to hold elections. In one year, there were two general elections due to the instability of the party's majority. When the queen issues the proclamation dissolving the Parliament, the date for the general election is set, and it must be held within 17 days of the proclamation. From that moment until the election is held, the parliamentary buildings are closed to the public, and government administrators may not make any announcements of new initiatives or new decisions on policy.*

In less than three weeks, the political parties assemble their candidates for each constituency, name their leaders as contenders for the prime minister's position, and do all their campaigning, both locally and nationally. With each new election in Great Britain, more American practices have come into play. American political consultants are regularly hired to help with developing party messages and planning the advertising campaign. Survey research and political polling are also well developed in Great Britain, and pre-election polls are widely read. In the 2010 election, the three major party candidates held a live debate on television, American-style, for the first time in British history.

So, how do the parties use that time, and how much money is spent during this short campaign period? British law has focused on spending limits for the campaign rather than on donation limits. Each party is limited in its expenditures during the year before the election. The spending limits are set on a constituency basis. In 2010, each major party was limited to spending about $50,000 per seat in the House of Commons. Compare that with the United States' average expenditure of more than $1 million for each seat in the House of Representatives. Altogether, the expenditures of the three contending parties in 2010 were about $52 million, far less than the billions spent in the United States over a similar period.** Finally, after the votes were counted in 2010, no party held a majority of seats in the House of Commons, meaning that none of the three contenders for prime minister would be named leader of the government. (The leader of the government in Great Britain is an elected member of Parliament and the leader of the majority party.) The Labour Party won more seats than the Conservative Party, while

British Prime Minister David Cameron meets with President Barack Obama to discuss the situation in Ukraine. Cameron, elected by Parliament, is on an equal footing with Obama, elected by the American people.

the Liberal Democratic Party won enough seats to form a coalition. Several days after the election, the Liberal Democratic Party agreed to a deal with the Conservative Party, and a government was formed. It was an interesting arrangement because the Liberal Democratic Party is actually closer to the Labour Party on many issues, but its platform insisted on electoral reform, which its new partner, the Conservative Party, agreed to.

Could the United States face a similar situation in congressional elections or even the presidential election? Yes, if a third party became strong enough. Conceivably, a third party could win enough seats in Congress to deny the majority to either the Democrats or the Republicans. It is much more difficult in America for a third party to win enough electoral votes to send the presidential election into the House of Representatives.

The larger question is whether the United States could adopt some electoral reforms to reduce the cost of our campaigns (and the possible influence of donors) and shorten the season. Most Americans would like to see a shorter election season and less campaign advertising in their lives.

For Critical Analysis

1. *Do you think American campaigns would generate more or less excitement and voter turnout if they were considerably shorter?*

2. *Is it really possible for candidates and parties to explain their platforms and present their candidates in a couple of weeks?*

* See the British Parliament website for more information: www.parliament.uk
** Library of Congress: www.loc.gov/law/help/campaign-finance/uk.php

Although writing more than 70 years ago, Overacker touched on a sensitive issue in American political campaigns—the connection between money and elections. It is difficult to comprehend how quickly spending on political campaigns has risen. Figure 9–2 shows the doubling of campaign spending over the last four presidential elections, with about $7 billion spent at all levels of campaigning during the 2011–2012 election cycle.[8] Total spending by the presidential candidates in 2012 amounted to more than $3.2 billion. In the Virginia Senate race in 2012, Tim Kane and George Allen raised about $58 million, with $30 million coming from large contributions. Ohio, Wisconsin, and Massachusetts saw senate races that cost more than $40 million. Traditionally, candidates spend much less to retain or obtain a seat in the House of Representatives, because representatives stand for seats in much smaller geographic areas; however, these races are heating up. In 2012, 10 races for the House of Representatives saw spending of more than $10 million in each respective district. That would be about $15 for every individual in the congressional district, whether or not they were registered voters. Except for the presidential campaigns, all of these funds had to be provided by the candidates and their families, borrowed, or raised by contributions from individuals, political parties, or *political action committees*, groups to be described later in this chapter. For the presidential campaigns, some of the funds could come from the federal government, but both candidates in 2012 rejected those funds to raise their own (see the screen capture).

Opensecrets.org

Regulating Campaign Financing

The way campaigns are financed has changed dramatically in the last 25 years. Today, candidates and political parties must operate within the constraints imposed by complicated laws regulating campaign financing.

A variety of federal **corrupt practices acts** have been designed to regulate campaign financing. The first, passed in 1925, limited primary and general election expenses for congressional candidates, required disclosure of election expenses and, in principle, put controls on contributions by corporations. The restrictions had many loopholes, and the acts proved to be ineffective.

The **Hatch Act** (Political Activities Act) of 1939 is best known for restricting the political activities of civil servants. It also, however, made it unlawful for a political group to spend more than $3 million in any campaign and limited individual contributions to a political group to $5,000. Of course, such restrictions were easily circumvented by creating additional political groups. In the 1970s,

Corrupt Practices Acts
A series of acts passed by Congress in an attempt to limit and regulate the size and sources of contributions and expenditures in political campaigns.

Hatch Act
An act passed in 1939 that restricted the political activities of government employees. It also prohibited a political group from spending more than $3 million in any campaign and limited individual contributions to a campaign committee to $5,000.

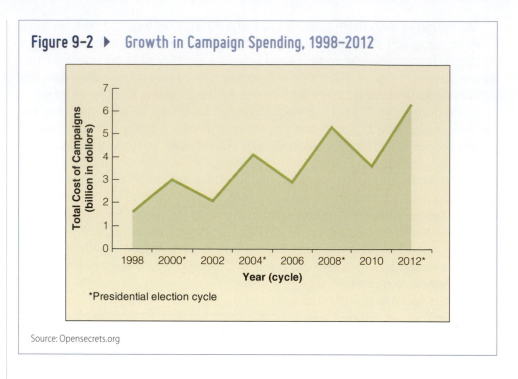

Figure 9-2 ▶ Growth in Campaign Spending, 1998–2012

*Presidential election cycle

Source: Opensecrets.org

Congress passed additional legislation to reshape the nature of campaign financing. In 1971, it passed the Federal Election Campaign Act to reform the process. Then in 1974, in the wake of the Watergate scandal, Congress enacted further reforms.

The Federal Election Campaign Act

The Federal Election Campaign Act (FECA) of 1971, which became effective in 1972, essentially replaced all past campaign finance laws. This law and all those that have followed are based on three principles: there should be limits placed on individual contributions, there needs to be a disclosure of all contributions to the public, and there should be public funding of presidential campaigns. The act placed no limit on overall spending, but restricted the total amount that could be spent on mass-media advertising, including television, if the candidate took public money. It limited the amount that candidates could contribute to their own campaigns (a limit later ruled unconstitutional) and required disclosure of all contributions and expenditures over $100. In principle, the FECA limited the role of labor unions and corporations in political campaigns. It also provided for a voluntary $1 (now $3) check-off on federal income tax returns for general campaign funds to be used by major-party presidential candidates.

Further Reforms in 1974. For many, the 1971 act did not go far enough. Amendments to the FECA passed in 1974 did the following:

1. *Created the Federal Election Commission.* This commission consists of six non-partisan administrators whose duties are to enforce compliance with the requirements of the act.

2. *Provided public financing for presidential primaries and general elections.* Any candidate running for president who is able to obtain sufficient contributions

in at least 20 states can obtain a subsidy from the U.S. Treasury to help pay for primary campaigns. The Bush-Kerry race in 2004 was the last time both general election candidates accepted public money for the general election campaign.

3. *Limited presidential campaign spending.* Any candidate accepting federal support must agree to limit campaign expenditures to the amount prescribed by federal law.

4. *Limited contributions.* Under the 1974 amendments, citizens could contribute up to $1,000 to each candidate in each federal election or primary; the total limit on all contributions from an individual to all candidates was $25,000 per year. Groups could contribute a maximum of $5,000 to a candidate in any election. (Some of these limits were changed by the 2002 campaign reform legislation.)

5. *Required disclosure.* Each candidate must file periodic reports with the FEC listing who contributed, how much was spent, and on what the funds were spent.

The 1971 and 1974 laws set in place the principles that have guided campaign finance ever since. The laws and those that have been enacted subsequently are informed by three principles: (1) set limits on what individuals and groups can give to individual candidates and within one election cycle; (2) provide some public funding for the presidential primaries, conventions, and the general election campaign; and (3) make all contributions and reports public. All contributions that are made to candidates under these laws and principles are usually called **hard money**. Individuals and groups that wish to circumvent these principles have been successful in finding ways to do so. Other kinds of campaign donations are referred to as "soft money" or "outside spending."

Hard Money
This refers to political contributions and campaign spending that is recorded under the regulations set forth in law and by the Federal Election Commission.

Buckley v. Valeo. The 1971 act had limited the amount that each individual could spend on his or her own behalf. The Supreme Court declared the provision unconstitutional in the 1976 case *Buckley v. Valeo*, stating that it was unconstitutional to restrict in any way the amount congressional candidates could spend on their own behalf: "The candidate, no less than any other person, has a First Amendment right to engage in the discussion of public issues and vigorously and tirelessly to advocate his own election."[9]

The *Buckley v. Valeo* decision, which has often been criticized, was directly countered by a 1997 Vermont law. The law, known as Act 64, imposed spending limits ranging from $2,000 to $300,000 (depending on the office sought) on candidates for state offices in Vermont. A number of groups, including the American Civil Liberties Union and the Republican Party, challenged the act, claiming that it violated the First Amendment's guarantee of free speech. In a landmark decision in August 2002, a federal appellate court disagreed and upheld the law.[10] In 2006, the U.S. Supreme Court declared that Vermont's campaign spending and donation limits were unconstitutional, thereby reaffirming the *Buckley v. Valeo* decision.

---

9. 424 U.S. 1 (1976).
10. *Randell v. Vermont Public Interest Research Group*, 300 F.3d 129 (2d Cir. 2002).

Interest Groups and Campaign Finance: Reaction to New Rules

■ **LO9.3:** Demonstrate an understanding of the evolution of campaign finance regulation, the development of political action committees (PACs), and the current state of such regulation.

In the last two decades, interest groups, individuals and corporations have worked tirelessly to find ways to support candidates through campaign donations. Candidates, in turn, have become dependent on these donations to run increasingly expensive campaigns. Interest groups and corporations funnel money to political candidates through several devices: **political action committees (PACs)**, **soft money** contributions, 527s, **issue advocacy advertising**, and, after soft money was outlawed, through "**Super PACs**." Every time legislation is passed at the federal or state level, interest groups, corporations, unions, and associations scramble to find new, legally allowable ways to influence campaigns. This activity has prompted commentators to label all campaign finance regulation as "whack the mole" law, meaning for every activity prohibited, another one pops up. Simply put, campaigns tend to net lots of money; some is regulated, some is not.

PACs and Political Campaigns

The 1974 and 1976 amendments to the Federal Election Campaign Act of 1971 allow corporations, labor unions, and other interest groups to set up political action committees or PACs to raise funds for candidates. The funds must be raised from at least 50 volunteer donors and must be given to at least five candidates in the federal election. PACs can contribute up to $5,000 to each candidate in each election. Each corporation or each union is limited to one PAC. Corporate PACs obtain contributions from executives and managers in their firms, and unions obtain PAC funds from their members.

The number of PACs has grown significantly since 1976, as has the amount they spend on elections. PACs numbered about 1,000 in 1976; today, the number is more than 4,600. Total spending by PACs grew from $19 million in 1973 to more than $1 billion in 2011–2012. About 35 percent of all campaign funds raised by House candidates in 2012 came from PACs.[11]

Political Action Committees (PACs)
A committee set up by and representing a corporation, labor union, or special-interest group. PACs raise and give campaign donations.

Soft Money
Campaign contributions unregulated by federal or state law, usually given to parties and party committees to help fund general party activities.

Issue Advocacy Advertising
Advertising paid for by interest groups that support or oppose a candidate or a candidate's position on an issue without mentioning voting or elections.

Super PAC
A political committee that can accept unlimited contributions from individuals and corporations to spend supporting a candidate as long as its efforts are not coordinated with the candidate's own campaign.

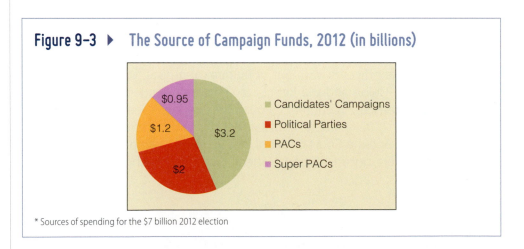

Figure 9–3 ▶ The Source of Campaign Funds, 2012 (in billions)

- $0.95
- $1.2
- $2
- $3.2

■ Candidates' Campaigns
■ Political Parties
■ PACs
■ Super PACs

* Sources of spending for the $7 billion 2012 election

---

11. Center for Responsive Politics, at www.opensecrets.org.

Interest groups funnel PAC funds to the candidates they think can do the most good for them. Frequently, they make the maximum contribution of $5,000 per election to candidates who face little or no opposition. Figure 9–4 shows that the great bulk of campaign contributions goes to incumbent candidates rather than to challengers. Table 9–1 shows the amounts contributed by the top 10 PACs during the 2011–2012 election cycle.

As Table 9–1 also shows, many PACs give most of their contributions to candidates of one party. Other PACs, particularly corporate PACs, tend to give funds to Democrats as well as to Republicans, because, with both chambers of Congress so closely divided, predicting which party will be in control after an election is almost impossible. Why would members of the National Association of Realtors give to Democrats who may be more liberal than themselves? Interest groups see PAC contributions as a way to ensure *access* to powerful legislators, even though the groups may disagree with the legislators some of the time. PAC contributions are, in a way, an investment in a relationship.

Campaign Financing beyond the Limits

Within a few years after the establishment of the tight limits on contributions, new ways to finance campaigns were developed that

did you know?
Abraham Lincoln sold pieces of fence rail that he had split as political souvenirs to finance his campaign.

Figure 9-4 ▶ **PAC Contributions to Congressional Candidates, 1991–2012**

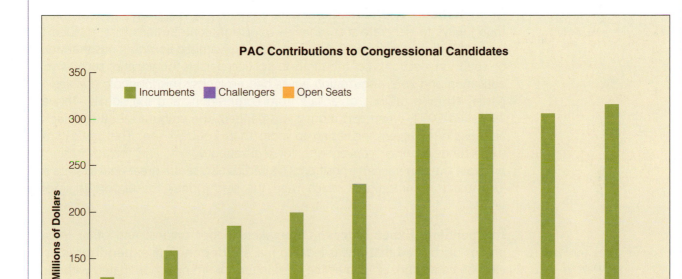

*Campaign financing regulations clearly limit the amount that a PAC can give to any one candidate, but the amount that a PAC can spend on issue advocacy is limitless, whether on behalf of a candidate or party or in opposition to one.

Source: Center for Responsive Politics, http://www.opensecrets.org

Table 9-1 ▶   The Top 10 PAC Contributors to Federal Candidates, 2011–2012 Election Cycle*

PAC NAME	TOTAL AMOUNT	DEM. (%)	REP. (%)
National Association of Realtors	$3,960,282	44	55
National Beer Wholesalers	$3,654,700	41	59
Honeywell International	$3,193,024	41	59
Operating Engineers Union	$3,186,387	84	15
National Auto Dealers Association	$3,074,000	28	72
International Brotherhood of Electrical Workers	$2,853,000	97	2
American Bankers Association	$2,736,150	20	80
AT&T	$2,543,000	35	65
American Association for Justice	$2,512,000	96	3
Credit Union National Association	$2,487,600	47	52
Blue Cross/Blue Shield	$2,401,398	35	65

*Includes subsidiaries and affiliated PACs, if any.

Source: Center for Responsive Politics, 2014.

skirted the reforms and made it possible for huge sums to be raised, especially by the major political parties.

Contributions to Political Parties. Candidates, PACs, and political parties found ways to generate *soft money*—campaign contributions that escaped the limits of federal election law. Although the FECA limited contributions that would be spent on elections, contributions to political parties for activities such as voter education and voter-registration drives had no limits. This loophole enabled the parties to raise millions of dollars from corporations and individuals. Between 1993 and 2002, when soft money was banned, the amount raised for election activities quadrupled, increasing to more than $400 million. The parties spent these funds for their conventions, for registering voters, and for advertising to promote the general party position. The parties also sent a great deal to state and local party organizations, which used the soft money to support their own tickets.

Independent Expenditures
Nonregulated contributions from PACs, organizations, and individuals. The funds may be spent on advertising or other campaign activities, so long as those expenditures are not coordinated with those of a candidate.

Independent Expenditures. Corporations, labor unions, and other interest groups discovered that it was legal to make **independent expenditures** in an election campaign, as long as the expenditures were not coordinated with those of the candidate or political party. Hundreds of unique committees and organizations blossomed to take advantage of this campaign tactic. Although a 1990 United States Supreme Court decision, *Austin v. Michigan State Chamber of Commerce,* upheld the right of the states and the federal government to limit independent, direct corporate expenditures (such as for advertisements) on behalf of *candidates*, the decision did not stop businesses and other types of groups from making independent expenditures on *issues*.[12]

Issue Advocacy. Indeed, issue advocacy—spending unregulated funds on advertising that promotes positions on issues rather than candidates—has become a common tactic in recent years. Interest groups routinely wage their own issue

---

12. 494 U.S. 652 (1990).

campaigns. Groups as varied as the AARP and the Environmental Defense Fund sponsor ads on the issues and to promote its agenda. Issue advocacy ads frequently urge voters to contact their senator or representatives and tell him or her how to vote on a specific issue of concern to the interest group sponsoring the ad.

Although promoting issue positions is very close to promoting candidates who support those positions, the courts repeatedly have held, in accordance with the *Buckley v. Valeo* decision mentioned earlier, that interest groups have a First Amendment right to advocate their positions. In a 1996 decision, the Supreme Court clarified this point, stating that political parties may also make independent expenditures on behalf of candidates—as long as the parties do so *independently* of the candidates.[13] In other words, the parties must not coordinate such expenditures with the candidates' campaigns.

The Bipartisan Campaign Reform Act of 2002

While both Democrats and Republicans argued for campaign reform legislation during the 1990s, the bill cosponsored by Senators John McCain, a Republican, and Russ Feingold, a Democrat, finally became the Bipartisan Campaign Reform Act (BCRA) in 2002. This act, which amended the 1971 FECA, took effect on the day after the congressional elections of November 5, 2002.

Key Elements of the New Law. The 2002 law banned the large, unlimited contributions to national political parties termed soft money. It placed curbs on, but did not entirely eliminate, the use of campaign ads by outside special-interest groups advocating the election or defeat of specific candidates. Limits for individual contributions directly to candidates were raised and the maximum amount that an individual can give to all federal candidates was raised from $25,000 per year to $95,000 over a two-year election cycle. It did not ban soft money contributions to state and local parties. These parties can accept such contributions, as long as they are limited to $10,000 per year per individual. Although the act was challenged by groups that viewed it as a threat to their influence in elections, the Supreme Court, in a series of decisions, upheld most of the law. Remember, however, that the law pertains to direct contributions to candidates and funds spent that are coordinated with the candidate's own campaign.

The Rise of the 527s. Interest groups that previously gave soft money to the parties responded to the 2002 BCRA by setting up new groups outside the parties: 527 organizations, so named for the section of the tax code that provides for them. These tax-exempt organizations rely on soft money contributions for their funding and generally must report their contributions and expenditures to the Internal Revenue Service. What started out as a device to circumvent the campaign finance limits on donations has now grown into a complicated web of unregulated campaign financing. The top names in Table 9–2 might look familiar. EMILY's List has been a long-standing PAC that supports women candidates, mostly Democrats. It still has a PAC that receives regulated contributions and makes direct limited donations to candidates. Yet, it also has a 527 organization that can accept unlimited donations and spend the funds on "uncoordinated advertising." The list of top 2012 groups includes labor unions, groups linked to business, groups headed by well-known politicians, and others that maintain both PACs and 527 organizations. This tactic gives the groups greater ability than a PAC to raise and spend money.

---

13. *Colorado Republican Federal Campaign Committee v. Federal Election Commission*, 518 U.S. 604 (1996).

Table 9–2 ▶ Top Ten 527 Committees in Expenditures in 2012

COMMITTEE	2010 EXPENDITURES	VIEWPOINT	AFFILIATION
ActBlue	$14.6 million	Democratic	Democratic Party
College Republican National Committee	$14.1 million	Republican	Republican Party
EMILY's List	$9.8 million	Progressive	Supports women candidates
Citizen's United	$9.3 million	Republican	Conservative
Service Employees International Union	$10.8 million	Democratic	SEIU
Int'l Brotherhood of Electrical Workers	$6.7 million	Democratic	IBEW
Plumbers/Pipefitters	$5.7 million	Democratic	Plumbers union
RightChange.com	$5.2 million	Republican	
Gay/Lesbian Victory Fund	$7.1 million	Democratic	Gay community
GOPAC	$4.4 million	Republican	Newt Gingrich

Source: OpenSecrets.org, "527 Committee Activity," Center for Responsive Politics. www.opensecrets.org/527s/

Overall, 527 groups spent more than $540 million in the 2011–2012 election cycle, with the top 10 spending more than $5 million each. Note the wholesome and patriotic titles of the 527 committees in the table. The vast majority of these groups have a partisan preference, regardless of what they call themselves.

In contrast to the 527s, charities and true not-for-profit organizations are not allowed to participate directly in any type of political activity. If they do so, they risk fines and the loss of their charitable tax-exempt status. In 2005, the IRS reviewed more than 80 churches, charities, and other tax-exempt organizations. The IRS looked for such banned activities as the distribution of printed materials encouraging members to vote for a specific candidate, contributions of cash to candidates' campaigns, and ministers' use of their pulpits to oppose or endorse specific candidates. Of the 82 churches, charities, and other tax-exempt organizations that the IRS examined, more than 75 percent engaged in prohibited political activity during the 2003–2004 election cycle. The IRS proposed to revoke the tax-exempt status of at least three of these organizations.

IRS investigations of churches and other charitable organizations have ceased, due to a 2009 federal court ruling on a case under investigation by the IRS. The court asked the IRS to clarify which level of the organization was responsible for these investigations, noting that administrative changes in the agency no longer met the requirements of the law forbidding political action by churches. The IRS has not clarified these regulations so no enforcement has occurred; in the interim, the Billy Graham ministry paid for a full page ad supporting Republican presidential candidate Mitt Romney in the 2012 election and, according to the Pew Research Center, 40 percent of black Protestants said that their pastors urged them to vote for Barack Obama in that same election.[14]

Yet another sort of organization entered the political arena in recent years. Local and statewide groups of political activists have filed to become 504 (c)(4) organizations, which are tax-exempt entities that engage in social welfare, educational, or other activities to benefit the community. Local, regional, and statewide Tea Party groups (as well as some pro-Democratic groups) have sought this status from the IRS. Beginning in 2010, such groups reported that their applications

---

14. Rachel Zoll, "Religion and Politics: IRS Not Enforcing Rules on Separation of Church and State," Associated Press, November 3, 2012, reported at www.huffingtonpost.com.

The Koch brothers, Charlies (left) and David (right), have donated millions of dollars to conservative causes and conservative candidates. Originally, the Koch brothers identified themselves as Libertarians, but they support Republicans because Libertarian candidates are unlikely to win office.

were subject to extraordinary scrutiny by the IRS and the decision on their status was delayed for years. Eventually the delay was traced to the Cincinnati office of the agency and to some specific individuals. While the agency's own investigation has found a bureaucratic problem, Republicans in Congress have continued to investigate the issue.

Citizens United, Freedom Now, and the Future of Campaign Finance Regulation

The Supreme Court decision in *Citizens United v. FEC* shook the political world like no other since *Buckley v. Valeo*.[15] In many ways, the case continued the struggle of outside groups and groups not affiliated with political parties to play a bigger role in political campaigns. Although three decades of campaign finance laws and regulation had been passed to contain the influence of groups on the political process and to limit the contributions of individuals, political action committees, and corporations, the *Citizens United* decision, on its face, lifted many of those restrictions. The decision allows corporations, unions, groups such as Citizens United, and others to spend money in campaign advertising without limit as long as it is not coordinated with a campaign. The restriction against using direct campaign language such as "vote for Mr. Smith" has been lifted as well. President Obama expressed his disagreement with the decision and most Democrats applauded his remarks. The Democratic leadership of Congress pledged to write new laws to counteract this decision, but no action has yet been taken.

George Soros, millionaire financier, has donated millions of dollars to liberal causes and candidates. He has donated funds to Moveon.org and was an initial donor to the Center for American Progress, a liberal think tank.

While public attention was focused on the *Citizens United* decision, a federal appeals court granted even more freedom to corporations, unions, individuals, and interest groups to spend money on campaigns. In the case *FreedomNow.org v. FEC*, an interest group that represents conservative economic views charged that the FEC regulations barring individuals and groups from spending as much as they want on campaigns was unconstitutional due to the decision in *Citizens United*. The appeals court agreed, and that decision has opened the doors for the creation of Super PACs, which can raise and spend unlimited amounts of money as long as their campaigns are not coordinated with those of the candidates. Individuals can give unlimited amounts of money to a Super PAC, as can corporations, unions, or other groups. In contrast to the 527 organizations, these campaign PACs must report their donors to the FEC either quarterly or monthly.

15. *Citizens United v. Federal Election Commission,* 558 U.S. (2010).

With the creation of 527s and Super PACs, what a millionaire or corporation can spend on an election has no limit, which means that campaign spending will soar until some way to regulate this spending can be implemented. Supporters of the Democratic Party claim that certain billionaires such as the Koch brothers and Sheldon Adelson have too much influence through their contributions to Super PACs. Republicans answer that billionaires such as George Soros and West Coast hedge fund manager Tom Steyer provide every bit as much money to the coffers of the Democratic Party. As noted by Jim Nicholson, a former chairman of the Republican National Committee, "The party can't coordinate with these Super PACs and neither can the campaigns so there's a lot more chaos....And the party structure clearly has a diminished role because they don't have the resources they used to have."[16]

Running for President: The Longest Campaign

■ **LO9.4:** Describe the general outline of today's campaign for the presidency and discuss the impact of the primary system on the outcome of the nomination process.

The American presidential election is the culmination of two different campaigns linked by the parties' national conventions. The **presidential primary** campaign lasts from January until June of the election year. Traditionally, the final campaign heats up around Labor Day, although if the nominees are known, it will begin even before the conventions.

Until 1968, however, there were fewer than 20 primary elections for the presidency. They were often **"beauty contests"** in which the candidates competed for popular votes, but the results had little or no impact on the selection of delegates to the national convention. National conventions were meetings of the party elite—legislators, mayors, county chairpersons, and loyal party workers—who were mostly appointed to their delegations. National conventions saw numerous trades and bargains among competing candidates, and the leaders of large blocs of delegates could direct their delegates to support a favorite candidate.

Reforming the Primaries

The character of the primary process and the makeup of the national convention have changed dramatically. The public, rather than party elites, now generally controls the nomination process. In 1968, after President Lyndon B. Johnson declined to run for another term, the Democratic Party nomination race was dominated by candidates who opposed the war in Vietnam. After Robert F. Kennedy was assassinated in June 1968, antiwar Democrats faced a convention that would nominate President Johnson's choice regardless of popular votes. After the extraordinary disruptive riots outside the doors of the 1968 Democratic Convention in Chicago, many party leaders pushed for serious reforms of the convention process. They saw the general dissatisfaction with the convention, and the riots in particular, as being caused by the inability of the average party member to influence the nomination system.

The Democratic National Committee appointed a special commission to study the problems of the primary system. Called the McGovern-Fraser Commission, the group formulated mandatory new rules on delegate selection for state Democratic parties.

Presidential Primary
A statewide primary election of delegates to a political party's national convention, held to determine a party's presidential nominee.

"Beauty Contests"
A presidential primary in which contending candidates compete for popular votes but the results do not control the selection of delegates to the national convention.

---

16. Nicholas Confessore, "Big-Money Donors Demand Larger Say in Campaign Strategy," *The New York Times*, March 1, 2014, p. 1.

The reforms instituted by the Democratic Party, which were imitated in part by the Republicans, revolutionized the nomination process for the presidency. The most important changes require that a majority of the Democratic convention delegates not be nominated by party elites; they must be elected by the voters in primary elections, in caucuses held by local parties, or at state conventions. No delegates can be awarded on a "winner-take-all" basis; all must be proportional to the votes for the contenders. Delegates are normally pledged to a particular candidate, although the pledge is not always formally binding at the convention.

The delegation from each state must also include a proportion of women, younger party members, and representatives of the minority groups within the party. At first, virtually no special privileges were given to elected party officials, such as senators and governors. After the conventions chose candidates who were not as strong as the party hoped for, the Democratic Party invented **superdelegates**, who are primarily elected Democratic officeholders and state leaders. Superdelegates comprise less than 20 percent of the delegate votes.

Front-Loading the Primaries

As soon as politicians and potential presidential candidates realized that winning as many primary elections as possible guaranteed them the party's nomination for president, their tactics changed dramatically. Candidates running in the 2012 primaries, such as former Massachusetts governor Mitt Romney, concentrated on building organizations in states that held early, important primary elections. Candidates realized that winning early contests, such as the Iowa caucuses or the New Hampshire primary election (both in January), meant that the media instantly would label the winner as the **front-runner**, thus increasing the candidate's media exposure and escalating the pace of contributions to his or her campaign fund.

The Rush to Be First States and state political parties began to see that early primaries had a much greater effect on the outcome of the presidential election and began to hold their primaries earlier in the season to secure that advantage. While New Hampshire held on to its claim to be the first primary, other states moved theirs to the following week. A group of mostly southern states decided to hold their primaries on the same date, known as Super Tuesday, setting a trend for the future. Due to this process of **front-loading** the primaries, in 2000 the presidential nominating process was over in March, with both George W. Bush and Al Gore having enough convention delegate votes to win their nominations.

The 2012 Primary Season

By early fall of 2011, many Republican voters believed that few strong candidates were available to challenge President Obama for the 2012 election. By the end of 2011, however, the Republican field was crowded with candidates who participated in multiple debates during the late fall pre-primary season. Mitt Romney began his second campaign for the nomination in 2011. Most of the candidates competed in the Iowa caucuses and, to the surprise of many, former senator Rick Santorum narrowly won the contest. Romney won the New Hampshire primary, and the race was on. One by one, the Republican candidates dropped out of the race, leaving Romney to finally clinch the nomination in late May. On the Democratic side, primaries were held and delegates selected, but because President Obama was not challenged, he received all the delegates.

Superdelegates
A party leader or elected official who is given the right to vote at the party's national convention. Superdelegates are not elected at the state level.

Front-runner
The presidential candidate who appears to be ahead at a given time in the primary season.

did you know?
David Leroy Gatchell changed his middle name to "None of the Above" but when he ran for U.S. Senate, representing Tennessee, a court ruled that he could not use his middle name on the ballot.

Front-loading
The practice of moving presidential primary elections to the early part of the campaign to maximize the impact of these primaries on the nomination.

On to the National Convention

Presidential candidates have been nominated by the convention method in every election since 1832. Delegates are sent from each state and are apportioned on the basis of state representation. Extra delegates are allowed to attend from states that had voting majorities for the party in the preceding elections. Parties also accept delegates from the District of Columbia, the territories, and certain overseas groups.

Credentials Committee
A committee used by political parties at their national conventions to determine which delegates may participate. The committee inspects the claim of each prospective delegate to be seated as a legitimate representative of his or her state.

Seating the Delegates. Each political party uses a **credentials committee** to determine which delegates may participate. The credentials committee usually prepares a roll of all delegates entitled to be seated. Controversy may arise when rival groups claim to be the official party organization for a county, district, or state. The Mississippi Democratic Party split along racial lines in 1964 at the height of the civil rights movement in the Deep South. Separate all-white and mixed white/African American sets of delegates were selected, and both factions showed up at the national convention. After much debate, the committee decided to seat the pro-civil rights delegates and exclude those who represented the traditional "white" party. While such a dispute has not occurred in recent years, there could still be controversy over who the duly elected delegates should be.

Convention Activities. The typical convention lasts only a few days. The first day consists of speech making, usually against the opposing party. During the second day, there are committee reports, and during the third day, there is presidential balloting. Because delegates generally arrive at the convention committed to presidential candidates, no convention since 1952 has required more than one ballot to choose a nominee, and since 1972, candidates have usually come into the convention with enough committed delegates to win. On the fourth day, a vice presidential candidate is usually nominated, and the presidential nominee gives the acceptance speech.

In 2012, the Democratic and Republican conventions were scheduled within one week of one another—the Republican convention right before Labor Day and the Democratic convention immediately after. The Democratic National Convention was held in Charlotte, North Carolina, and planned to increase support for the Democratic ticket in that state and neighboring Virginia.

The Republican National Convention was shortened by one day due to the possible arrival of a hurricane in Tampa, Florida, where the event was held. Events were re-scheduled, however, and the party completed the business of nominating Mitt Romney and Paul Ryan in three days. The Republicans spent much of their time showcasing young, conservative speakers who echoed their candidates' views on supporting business and the private sector of the economy. Both Romney and his wife used their speeches to provide more personal information about themselves and the nominee's accomplishments.

In contrast to the earlier Republican event, the Democratic National Convention dedicated an entire evening to supporting women's issues and concerns. Leading female office holders spoke in support of the Obama record on women's rights. Former President Bill Clinton spoke on the second night, nominating President Obama for a second term. Major networks, however, restricted their coverage of both conventions to about two to three hours per night and that few of the speeches or events drew huge numbers of viewers.

On to the General Election

Even though it may seem that the presidential election process lasts years, the general election campaign actually begins after the two party conventions, when the nominees are officially proclaimed. Candidates use media advertising, debates, social media strategies, and Get Out the Vote campaigns. In addition, campaign strategists must constantly plan in order to win enough electoral votes to receive the majority. Campaign managers quickly identify those states where their candidate will almost certainly win the popular vote. Certain states will quickly line up in the Republican or Democratic column. Those states see relatively light campaign activity and advertising. Those states that *are* likely to be close in the popular vote have been tagged **battleground states** and will see intense campaigning up to the very day of the election.

States such as Florida, Ohio, and Wisconsin, which have closely divided electorates, are often in the battleground column. It is important to note, however, that the states that will be closely fought change with every presidential election, because the issues and appeals of the two candidates determine race dynamics. In 2012, polls released just before election day suggested that the presidential election was too close to predict. Both candidates campaigned until voting started and then awaited the results. Early in the evening, Romney posted a win in North Carolina, but Obama won the electoral votes of Virginia, a key battleground state. By later in the evening, several other battleground states had swung to President Obama, and the election was almost decided. Ohio also voted for the president and although the election results in Florida were not final until days after the balloting, President Obama and Vice President Biden secured enough electoral votes to win on election night.

Voting in the United States

■ **LO9.5:** Demonstrate an understanding of the electoral process in the United States and explain how it relates to democratic theory.

In addition to voting for candidates, in some states, people can vote directly on laws. In California, often dozens of referenda are on the ballot at one time. Citizens are often asked to vote three times in one year—in a primary election to choose candidates, in elections for school taxes or other local matters, and in a general election. Americans often elect not only representatives to state and national legislatures and executive officers for the state, but also school superintendents, sheriffs, even the jailor. In addition, many states have elected judges, which can add 50 more offices in a city as large as Chicago.

Turning Out to Vote

■ **LO9.6:** Discuss the factors that influence voter turnout in the United States and compare American voter turnout to that of other nations.

In 2012, the voting-age population was more than 240 million people. Fifty-three percent of those people actually went to the polls. When only half of the voting-age population participates in elections, it means, among other things, that the winner of a close presidential election may be voted in by only about one-fourth of the voting-age population (see Table 9–3).

Figure 9–5 shows **voter turnout** for presidential and congressional elections from 1940 to 2012. According to these statistics, the last good year for voter turnout was 1960, when almost 65 percent of the voting-age population actually voted. Each of the peaks in the figure represents voter turnout in a presidential election. Thus, we can also see that turnout for congressional elections is influenced greatly by whether a presidential election occurs in the same year. Whereas voter turnout during the presidential elections of 2012 was more than 50 percent, it was only 42 percent in the midterm elections of 2014.

Battleground States
A state likely to be so closely fought that the campaigns devote exceptional effort to winning the popular and electoral vote there.

Voter Turnout
The percentage of citizens taking part in the election process; the number of eligible voters who actually "turn out" on election day to cast their ballots.

Table 9-3 ▶   **Elected by a Majority?**

Most presidents have won a majority of the votes cast in the election. We generally judge the extent of their victory by whether they have won more than 51 percent of the votes. Some presidential elections have been proclaimed landslides, meaning that the candidates won by an extraordinary majority of votes cast. As indicated below, however, no modern president has been elected by more than 38 percent of the total voting-age population.

YEAR—WINNER (PARTY)	PERCENTAGE OF TOTAL POPULAR VOTE	PERCENTAGE OF VOTING-AGE POPULATION
1932—Roosevelt (D)	57.4	30.1
1936—Roosevelt (D)	60.8	34.6
1940—Roosevelt (D)	54.7	32.2
1944—Roosevelt (D)	53.4	29.9
1948—Truman (D)	49.6	25.3
1952—Eisenhower (R)	55.1	34.0
1956—Eisenhower (R)	57.4	34.1
1960—Kennedy (D)	49.7	31.2
1964—Johnson (D)	61.1	37.8
1968—Nixon (R)	43.4	26.4
1972—Nixon (R)	60.7	33.5
1976—Carter (D)	50.1	26.8
1980—Reagan (R)	50.7	26.7
1984—Reagan (R)	58.8	31.2
1988—Bush (R)	53.4	26.8
1992—Clinton (D)	43.3	23.1
1996—Clinton (D)	49.2	23.2
2000—Bush (R)	47.8	24.5
2004—Bush (R)	51.0	27.6
2008—Obama (D)	52.6	27.5
2012—Obama (D)	51.0	25.3

Sources: Congressional Quarterly Weekly Report, January 31, 1989, p. 137; *The New York Times*, November 5, 1992; November 7, 1996; November 12, 2004; November 6, 2008; and author's update.

The same is true at the state level. When there is a race for governor, more voters participate both in the general election for governor and in the election for state representatives. Voter participation rates in gubernatorial elections are also greater in presidential election years. The average turnout in state elections is about 14 percentage points higher when a presidential election is held.

In races for mayor, city council, county auditor, and the like, it is fairly common for only 25 percent or less of the electorate to vote. Is something amiss here? It would seem that people should be more likely to vote in elections that directly affect them. At the local level, each person's vote counts more because there are fewer voters. Furthermore, the issues—crime control, school bonds, sewer bonds,

Table 9-4 ▶ **Turnout in Selected Countries, Most Recent National Election**

COUNTRY	VOTING-AGE POPULATION PERCENTAGE
Singapore	94.7
Australia	93.2
Kenya	85.9
Iceland	81.4
Argentina	79.3
Norway	78.23
United States (2012)	66.7
United Kingdom	65.8
Greece	62.5
India	58.2
France	55.4
Portugal	46.5
Romania	41.8

Source: Institute for Democracy and Electoral Assistance: http://www.idea.int/vt

and so on—touch the immediate interests of the voters. The facts, however, do not fit democratic theory. Potential voters are most interested in national elections, when a presidential choice is involved. Otherwise, voter participation in our representative government is very low (and is not stellar even in presidential elections).

The Effect of Low Voter Turnout

Some view low voter participation as a threat to representative democratic government. Too few individuals are deciding who wields political power in society.

Figure 9-5 ▶ **Voter Turnout for Presidential and Congressional Elections, 1940–2014**

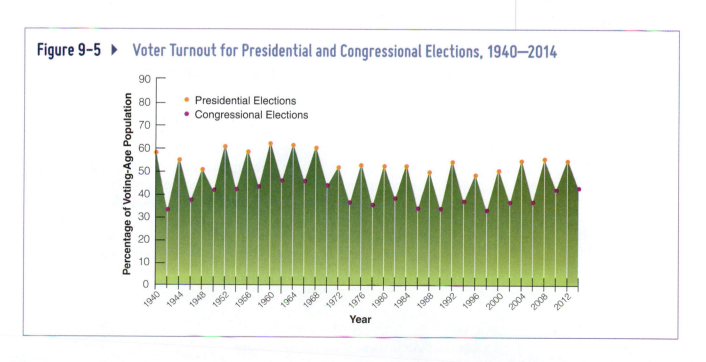

In addition, low voter participation presumably signals apathy or cynicism about the political system in general. It also may signal that potential voters simply do not want to take the time to learn about the issues or that the issues are too complicated. Some suggest that people do not vote because they do not believe that their vote will make any difference.

Others are less concerned about low voter participation. They believe that low voter participation simply indicates more satisfaction with the status quo. Also, they believe that representative democracy is a reality even if a very small percentage of eligible voters vote. If everyone who does not vote believes that the outcome of the election will accord with his or her own desires, then representative democracy is working. The nonvoters are obtaining the type of government—with the type of people running it—that they want to have anyway.

Is Voter Turnout Declining?

During many recent elections, the media have voiced concern that voter turnout is declining. Figure 9–5 appears to show somewhat lower voter turnout in recent years than during the 1960s. Pundits have blamed the low turnout on negative campaigning and broad public cynicism about the political process. But is voter turnout actually as low as it seems?

One problem with widely used measurements of voter turnout is that they compare the number of people who actually vote with the voting-age population, not the population of *eligible voters*. These figures are not the same. The figure for the voting-age population includes felons and ex-felons who have lost the right to vote. Above all, it includes new immigrants who are not yet citizens. Finally, it does not include Americans living abroad, who can cast absentee ballots.

In 2012, the measured voting-age population included 3.2 million ineligible felons and ex-felons and an estimated 20.4 million noncitizens. It did not include 4.7 million Americans abroad. In 2012, the voting-age population was 240.9 million people. The number of eligible voters, however, was only 221.9 million. That means that voter turnout in 2012 was not 53.6 percent but about 58 percent of the truly eligible voters.[17]

Factors Influencing Who Votes

A clear association exists between voter participation and the following characteristics: age, educational attainment, minority status, income level, and the existence of two-party competition.

1. *Age.* Examine Figure 9–6, which shows the breakdown of voter participation by age group for the 2012 presidential election. It is very clear that the Americans who have the highest turnout rate are those reaching retirement age. The reported turnout increases with each age group. Greater participation with age is very likely because older voters are more settled in their lives, are already registered, and have had more time to experience voting as an expected activity. Older voters may have more leisure time to learn about the campaign and the candidates; furthermore, communications, especially those from AARP, target this group.

---

17. U.S. Elections Project. http://www.gmu.edu/Turnout_2012G.html

Figure 9-6 ▶ **Voting in the 2012 Presidential Elections by Age Group**

Turnout is given as a percentage of the voting-age citizen population. The data given in this figure is from the Census Bureau. It has been gathered by polling the American public. The data from the 2012 polls indicates that turnout among older Americans remained high, although turnout among 18–24 years olds decreased more than 7 percent from the turnout in 2008.

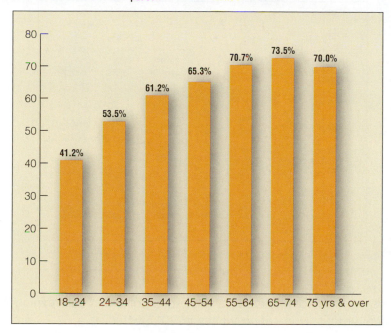

Source: U.S. Bureau of the Census, November 2012 (Accessed: February 2014). .

What is most striking about the turnout figures is that younger voters have the lowest turnout rate. Before 1971, the age of eligibility to vote was 21. Due to the prevailing sentiment that if a man was old enough to be drafted to fight in the Vietnam War, he should be old enough to vote, the U.S. Constitution was amended (via the Twenty-sixth Amendment) to lower the voting age to 18. Young Americans, however, have never exhibited a high turnout rate. In contrast to older Americans, young people are likely to change residences frequently, have fewer ties to the community, and perhaps not perceive election issues as relevant to them.

Turnout among voters aged 18 to 24 increased significantly between 2000 and 2008, from 36 percent to 48.5 percent in the presidential election. Evidence suggests that the candidates and political parties devoted much more attention to younger voters. Candidates appeared on the television shows watched by younger voters, and campaigns began to utilize the Internet and social media to reach younger voters. Younger voters greatly increased their turnout in the 2008 primary elections, with many supporting Barack Obama's campaign for the presidency, although the increase in turnout for the general election was only 1.5 percent above 2004 levels. In 2012, turnout among younger voters declined to 41.2 percent.

2. *Educational attainment.* In general, the more education you have, the more likely you are to vote. This pattern is clearly evident in the 2012 election results, as shown in Figure 9–7. Reported turnout was 27 percentage points higher for those who had some college education than for those who had never been to high school.

Figure 9-7 ▶ Voting in the 2012 Presidential Elections by Educational Level

These statistics reinforce one another. White voters are likely to be wealthier than African American voters, who are also less likely to have obtained a college education.

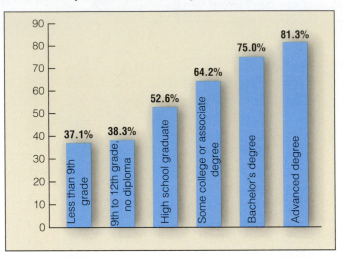

Source: U.S. Bureau of the Census, November 2012 (Accessed February 2014) http://www.census.gov

3. *Minority status.* Race and ethnicity are also important in determining the level of voter turnout. Non-Latino whites in 2012 voted at a 62.2 percent rate, whereas the non-Latino African American turnout rate was 66.2 percent, up almost 2 percent from 2008. For Latinos, the turnout rate was 48 percent, slightly down from the previous election, and for Asian Americans the rate was 47.3 percent, up slightly from the previous presidential election.[18] These low rates may occur because many Latino and Asian American immigrants are not yet citizens, or they may be attributable to language issues. The fact that the turnout increased 7 percent for African Americans may be due to the voters' pride in President Obama's identity as an African American.

4. *Income level.* Wealthier people tend to be overrepresented among voters who turn out on election day. In the 2012 presidential election, voter turnout for those with the highest annual family incomes was almost twice the turnout for those with the lowest annual family incomes.

5. *Two-party competition.* Another factor in voter turnout is the extent to which elections are competitive within a state. More competitive states generally have higher turnout rates, and turnout increases considerably in states where an extremely competitive race occurs in a particular year. In addition, turnout can be increased through targeted Get Out the Vote drives among minority voters.

Why People Do Not Vote

For many years, political scientists believed that one reason why voter turnout in the United States was so much lower than in other Western nations was that it was very difficult to register to vote. In most states, registration required a special trip to a public office far in advance of elections. Today, all states are required to

COMPARE WITH YOUR PEERS

MindTap™ for American Government

Access the Voting Forum: Polling Activity—Voter Registration.

---

18. Michael P. McDonald, "2012 Turnout: Race, Ethnicity and the Youth Vote," May 8, 2013, HYPERLINK " http://www.huffing-tonppost.com/michael-p-mcdonald/"www.huffingtonppost.com/michael-p-mcdonald/

offer voter registration at a number of sites, including the driver's license bureau. In addition, many states offer advance voting at designated places on a walk-in basis up to three weeks before the election. These two innovations have reduced barriers to registration and voting.

Uninformative Media Coverage and Negative Campaigning.

Some scholars contend that one of the reasons why some people do not vote has to do with media coverage of campaigns. Many researchers have shown that the news media tend to provide much more news about "the horse race," or which candidates are ahead in the polls, than about the actual policy positions of the candidates. Thus, voters are not given the kind of information that would provide them with an incentive to go to the polls on election day. Negative campaigning is thought to have an adverse effect on voter turnout. By the time citizens are ready to cast their ballots, most of the information they have heard about the candidates has been so negative that no candidate is appealing. Research on this issue, however, has produced no consensus: voters are able to identify ads as negative and may or may not be influenced by them depending on their own candidate preferences.[19]

The Rational Ignorance Effect.

Another explanation suggests that citizens are making a logical choice in not voting. If citizens believe that their votes will not affect the outcome of an election, then they have little incentive to seek the information needed to cast intelligent votes. The lack of incentive to obtain costly (in terms of time, attention, and so on) information about politicians and political issues has been called the **rational ignorance effect**. That term may seem contradictory, but it is not. Rational ignorance is a condition in which people purposely and rationally decide not to obtain information—to remain ignorant.[20]

Why, then, do even one-third to one-half of U.S. citizens bother to show up at the polls? One explanation is that most citizens receive personal satisfaction from the act of voting. It makes them feel that they are good citizens and that they are doing something patriotic, even though they are aware that their one vote will not change the outcome of the election. Even among voters who are registered and who plan to vote, if the cost of voting goes up (in terms of time and inconvenience), the number of registered voters who actually vote will fall. In particular, bad weather on election day means, on average, a smaller percentage of registered voters at the polls. It also appears that the greater the number of elections that are held, the smaller the turnout for primary and special elections.

Plans for Improving Voter Turnout.

Mail-in voting in Oregon and Washington and easier access to registration are ideas that have been implemented in the hope of improving voter turnout. While turnout is somewhat higher in those two states, they are also states with higher educational attainment and less economically disadvantaged populations.

Two other ideas seemed promising. The first was to allow voters to visit the polls up to three weeks before election day. The second was to allow voters to vote by absentee ballot without having to give any particular reason for doing so. The Committee for the Study of the American Electorate discovered, however, that in areas that had implemented these plans, neither plan increased voter turnout. Indeed, voter turnout actually fell in those jurisdictions. In other words, states

Rational Ignorance Effect
An effect produced when people purposely and rationally decide not to become informed on an issue because they believe that their vote on the issue is not likely to be a deciding one; a lack of incentive to seek the necessary information to cast an intelligent vote.

CONNECT WITH YOUR CLASSMATES
MindTap for American Government

Access the Voting Forum: Discussion—Election Day.

---

19. Ilya Somin, "Democracy and Political Ignorance," www.cato-unbound.org/2013/10, October 11, 2013.
20. John Wihbey, "Negative political ads, the 2012 campaign and voter effects: Research roundup," Journalists Resource, http://journalistsresource.org/studies/politics/, May 6, 2013.

that did *not* permit early voting or unrestricted absentee voting had better turnout rates than states that did. Apparently, these two innovations appeal mostly to people who already intended to vote.

What is left? One possibility is to declare election day a national holiday or to hold elections on a Sunday, as is done in many other nations. Another is to adopt a registration method that places the responsibility on the government to make sure all voters are registered. In Canada, a packet of information is mailed to each eligible voter. The citizen then returns the application to a federal office or applies

Politics with a Purpose

Let's Put It to a Vote

Have you ever heard someone say, usually in indignation, "there ought to be a law!"? Often, laws are created in state legislatures or in Congress. In some states and localities, however, average citizens (or organized groups of "average citizens") can put an idea to a popular vote.

Why would citizens want to vote on laws themselves? The answer boils down to a debate over what type of democracy a society wants: direct or representative. While representative democracy is much more common, some states explicitly have created a means by which citizens can bypass the legislative process (through an initiative), revoke the actions of legislatures (via a referendum), or even remove elected officials from office (using recall).

While all states except Delaware require that amendments to the state constitutions go before the voters for final approval,* more than half of all states do not have any initiatives or referenda. In these 26 states, no mechanism exists for citizens to legislate through initiatives (enact laws by popular vote) or to overrule legislatures through referenda. The 24 states that do give citizens the ability to affect policy changes directly have seen vigorous debates over some of the most divisive and contentious issues of the day.

For example, both gay rights laws (domestic partnership laws, antidiscrimination laws) as well as laws defining marriage as a union between a man and a woman have been put to the direct democracy test. In 2006, eight states had ballot issues to amend their constitutions to ban same-sex marriage; the amendment passed in all except one, Arizona.** In Maine, the law approving same-sex marriages was overturned by a referendum in 2009, although domestic partnerships remain legal. In 2012, advocates for same-sex marriage put another referendum on the ballot to overturn the 2009 vote. States choose the process by which a referendum, initiative, or recall effort is allowed on the ballot and the threshold of support necessary for winning. To get on the ballot, these efforts require that signatures be collected on a petition,

and the petition is allowed to circulate for a set period of time. States also choose how many signatures are necessary for the effort to get on the ballot. Usually the minimum number is a percentage of either the total number of registered voters or the total turnout in the last general election. Sometimes states specify that the effort has to have support from across the state. Wyoming, for example, mandates that the signatures have to come from at least two-thirds of its counties.*** Also, the signatures usually have to be from residents of that state who are registered voters. Often opponents of the effort use this stage to mount their attack. In the 2007 Oregon referendum effort, supporters of gay rights were able to thwart the referendum both by challenging the validity of signatures and by effectively implementing a "refuse to sign" campaign.****

Once it is on the ballot, the initiative, referendum, or recall must garner a certain percentage of votes. Often held in off-year elections, turnout for these votes may be very small. Some states go to great lengths, however, to ensure that the ballot issue has significant support not just from a majority of people voting in that election but also from the state's voting population. Massachusetts requires that the measure receive a majority of the votes during that election and that those voting on the measure (either for or against) constitute in excess of 50 percent of those who voted in the previous general election!***** States that require such a large vote or a super-majority vote to pass an initiative actually are protecting the legislature and its acts against these forms of voter lawmaking.

* M. Dane Waters, "Initiative and Referendum in the United States," a presentation to the Democracy Symposium, February 16–18, 2002, Williamsburg, VA; accessed at http://ni4d.us/library/waterspaper.pdf
** www.cnn.com/ELECTION/2006/pages/results/ballot.measures; accessed April 11, 2008.
*** Jennifer Drage, "Initiative, Referendum, and Recall: The Process," *Journal of the American Society of Legislative Clerks and Secretaries*, Vol. 5, No. 2, 2000.
**** www.basicrights.org/?p=84; accessed April 11, 2008.
***** Drage, "Initiative, Referendum, and Recall: The Process."

online to be registered. After that act, a citizen is enrolled on the National Register of Electors (or citizens may opt out). This registration activity takes place only once after the first registration—the voter simply appraises the government of any future address changes. By making sure all eligible citizens are registered and informed about the polling place, the burden of registration and voting is lightened.

Legal Restrictions on Voting

■ **LO9.7:** Describe historical restrictions on the vote in the United States and explain how these restrictions have been ended.

Legal restrictions on voter registration have existed since the founding of our nation, when the franchise was granted to free, white males and occasionally to free African Americans. Since that time, groups have struggled to gain the franchise and to overcome voting restrictions in order to be represented at all levels of government.

Historical Restrictions

In most of the American colonies, only white males who owned property with a certain minimum value were eligible to vote, leaving a far greater number of Americans ineligible than eligible to take part in the democratic process.

Property Requirements. Many government functions concern property rights and the distribution of income and wealth, and some of the founders of our nation believed it was appropriate that only people who had an interest in property should vote on these issues. The idea of extending the vote to all citizens was, according to Charles Pinckney, a South Carolina delegate to the Constitutional Convention, merely "theoretical nonsense."

The logic behind the restriction of voting rights to property owners was questioned seriously by Thomas Paine in his pamphlet *Common Sense*:

> *Here is a man who today owns a jackass, and the jackass is worth $60. Today the man is a voter and goes to the polls and deposits his vote. Tomorrow the jackass dies. The next day the man comes to vote without his jackass and cannot vote at all. Now tell me, which was the voter, the man or the jackass?* [21]

The writers of the Constitution allowed the states to decide who should vote. Thus, women were allowed to vote in Wyoming in 1870 but not in the entire nation until the Nineteenth Amendment was ratified in 1920. By about 1850, most white adult males in virtually all the states could vote without any property qualification. North Carolina was the last state to eliminate its property test for voting—in 1856.

Further Extensions of the Franchise. Extension of the franchise to black males occurred with the passage of the Fifteenth Amendment in 1870. This enfranchisement was short lived, however, as the "redemption" of the South by white racists had rolled back these gains by the end of the century. African Americans, both male and female, were not able to participate in the electoral process in all states until the 1960s. The most recent extension of the franchise occurred when the voting age was reduced to 18 by the Twenty-sixth Amendment in 1971.

did you know?
Noncitizens were allowed to vote in some states until the early 1920s.

---

21. Thomas Paine, *Common Sense* (London: H. D. Symonds, 1792), p. 28.

Is the Franchise Still Too Restrictive? Certain classes of people still do not have the right to vote. These include noncitizens and, in most states, convicted felons who have been released from prison. They also include current prison inmates, election law violators, and people who are mentally incompetent. No one under the age of 18 can vote. Some political activists have argued that some of these groups should be allowed to vote. Most other democracies do not prevent persons convicted of a crime from voting after they have completed their sentences. In the 1800s, many states let noncitizen immigrants vote. In Nicaragua, the minimum voting age is 16.

One discussion concerns the voting rights of convicted felons who have completed their sentence or who were convicted of relatively minor crimes. Some contend that voting should be a privilege, not a right, and we should not want the types of people who commit felonies participating in decision making. Others believe that it is wrong to further penalize those who have paid their debt to society. These people argue that barring felons from the polls injures minority groups because minorities make up a disproportionately large share of former prison inmates.

Current Eligibility and Registration Requirements

Registration
The entry of a person's name onto the list of registered voters for elections. To register, a person must meet certain legal requirements of age, citizenship, and residency.

Voting generally requires **registration**, and to register, a person must satisfy the following voter qualifications, or legal requirements: (1) citizenship, (2) age (18 or older), and (3) residency—the duration varies widely from state to state and with types of elections. Since 1972, states cannot impose residency requirements of more than 30 days for voting in federal elections.

Each state has different qualifications for voting and registration. In 1993, Congress passed the "motor voter" bill, which requires that states provide voter-registration materials when people receive or renew driver's licenses, that all states allow voters to register by mail, and that voter-registration forms be made available at a wider variety of public places and agencies. In general, a person must register well in advance of an election, although voters in Idaho, Maine, Minnesota, Oregon, Wisconsin, and Wyoming are allowed to register up to, and on, election day. North Dakota has no voter registration at all.

Some argue that registration requirements are responsible for much of the nonparticipation in our political process. Since their introduction in the late 1800s, registration laws have reduced the voting participation of African Americans and immigrants. The question arises as to whether registration is really necessary. If it decreases participation in the political process, perhaps it should be dropped altogether. Still, as those in favor of registration requirements argue, such requirements may prevent fraudulent voting practices, such as multiple voting or voting by noncitizens.

In recent years, a number of states have passed stronger voter identification standards, although the actual requirements vary considerably. Currently, at least eight states have strict photo-ID laws in place, requiring voters to show a government-issued photo ID to be able to vote. Another set of states requires either a photo ID or another, nonphoto ID, or that someone at the polling place vouch for the individual personally. About 15 states have lists of acceptable forms of identification and another 19 have no ID requirement to vote. The Supreme Court found Indiana's strict photo-ID law constitutional in 2008, although other states' laws have been found to be discriminatory by lower courts or by the U.S. Department of Justice.[22] A study by the Brennan Center suggested that the stricter photo-ID

---

22. *Crawford v. Marion County Election Board,* 553 U.S. 181 (2008).

laws tended to decrease voting turnout in some precincts, while they increased turnout among older voters and higher income voters.[23] The question of whether a voter should have a photo ID is highly partisan: Republicans generally support such requirements as a way to make sure only eligible voters cast ballots; Democrats suggest that strict photo-ID laws are a handicap to poorer voters, elderly voters who do not drive, immigrants, young people, and others who do not have the time to get such an identification card.

Extension of the Voting Rights Act

In the summer of 2006, President Bush signed legislation that extended the Voting Rights Act for 25 more years. As discussed in Chapter 5, the Voting Rights Act was enacted to ensure that African Americans had equal access to the polls. Most of the provisions of the 1965 Voting Rights Act became permanent law. The 2006 act extended certain temporary sections and clarified certain amendments. For example, any new voting practices or procedures in jurisdictions with a history of discrimination in voting had to be approved by the U.S. Department of Justice or the federal district court in Washington, D.C., before being implemented. Section 203 of the 2006 act ensured that American citizens with limited proficiency in English can obtain the necessary assistance to enable them to understand and cast a ballot. Further, the act authorized the U.S. attorney general to appoint federal election observers when evidence exists of attempts to intimidate minority voters at the polls.

In 2013, the United States Supreme Court struck down the core of the Voting Rights Act of 1965 and all subsequent extensions of the act. The Court voted 5-4 to end the oversight of the nine states in the South who needed to submit their voting laws to the Department of Justice. The majority of the court reasoned that, as Chief Justice Roberts wrote, "Our country has changed. While any racial discrimination in voting is too much, Congress must ensure that the legislation it passes to remedy that problem speaks to current conditions."[24] Civil rights and

Ivan Nikolov/INB WENN Photos/Newscom

Rula Jebreal, a Palestinian/Italian journalist, speaks at a 2014 United Nations rally against violence against women. Having celebrity supporters for a candidate may attract votes from younger voters or voters who are less likely to participate in the election.

23. "ID at the Polls: Assessing the Impact of Recent State Voter ID Laws on Voter Turnout," *Harvard Law and Policy Review,* Vol. 3-1, 2007.
24. Adam Liptak, "Supreme Court Invalidates Key Part of the Voting Rights Act," *The New York Times,* June 25, 2013, p. 1.

voting rights advocates were extremely disappointed in the ruling, saying that states would likely move to tighten their registration and voting laws immediately and that discrimination in voting would like increase. Indeed, Texas announced that its new identification law would go into effect immediately without Justice Department approval.

Primary Elections, General Elections, and More

One of the reasons often suggested for low voter turnout in the United States is the quantity of elections that are held. Because the United States has a federal system of government, elections are held at both the state and federal level. Additionally, most local units of government—towns, cities, counties—are staffed by officials who are elected at the local level. For the sake of convenience, the state organizes the federal elections for the House of Representatives, the Senate, and the presidency, but the county actually sets up and staffs the voting places and counts the vote.

As noted in Chapter 8, political parties in the United States do not have control over the candidates who run under their labels. Individuals who seek political office must be *nominated* in order to have their names placed on the ballot in the general election. The political party may nominate a candidate and endorse her, or another individual may submit appropriate petitions to make the nomination competitive. If two or more candidates are contesting the nomination for the party, voters will make the decision in a primary election.

Primary Elections

The purpose of a primary election is to choose a candidate who will become the party's nominee for the general election. This is true whether the primary election is for the nominee for state legislator, city council representative, or president of the United States. Primary elections were first mandated in 1903 in Wisconsin, with the intention of weakening the role of party bosses in the nomination process. Today, all states have primary elections, which, in theory, are organized so that political party members can choose their own preferred candidate for office. There are many different types of primary elections, however, and many are not restricted to party members.

Before discussing the types of primaries, we must first examine how some states use a party **caucus**. A caucus is typically a small, local meeting of party regulars who agree on a nominee. Sometimes the results of caucuses are voted on by a broader set of party members in a primary election. If the party's chosen candidates have no opponents, however, a primary election may not be necessary.

Alternatively, a slate of nominees of loyal party members may be chosen at a local or state party convention. In any event, the resulting primary elections differ from state to state.

Closed Primary   In a **closed primary**, only avowed or declared members of a party can vote in that party's primary. Voters must declare their party affiliation, either when they register to vote or at the primary election. A closed-primary system tries to make sure that registered voters cannot cross over into the other party's primary in order to nominate the weakest candidate of the opposing party or to affect the ideological direction of that party.

Caucus
A meeting of party members designed to select candidates and propose policies.

Closed Primary
A type of primary in which the voter is limited to choosing candidates of the party of which he or she is a member.

Open Primary. In an **open primary**, voters can vote in either party primary without disclosing their party affiliation. The voter makes the choice in the privacy of the voting booth. The voter must, however, choose one party's list from which to select candidates. Open primaries place no restrictions on independent voters.

Blanket Primary. In a *blanket primary,* sometimes known as "jungle primary," the voter can vote for candidates of more than one party. Louisiana and Washington have blanket primaries. Blanket-primary campaigns may be much more costly because each candidate for every office is trying to influence all of the voters, not just those in his or her party.

In 2000, the United States Supreme Court issued a decision that significantly altered the use of the blanket primary.[25] The case arose when political parties in California challenged the constitutionality of a 1996 ballot initiative authorizing the use of the blanket primary in that state. The parties contended that the blanket primary violated their First Amendment right of association. Because the nominees represent the party, they argued, party members—not the general electorate—should have the right to choose the party's nominee. The Supreme Court ruled in favor of the parties, holding that the blanket primary violated parties' First Amendment associational rights. In a more recent decision, however, the Court upheld the blanket primary approved in the state of Washington.

Runoff Primary. Some states have a two-primary system. If no candidate receives a majority of the votes in the first primary, the top two candidates must compete in another primary, called a *runoff primary.*

General and Other Elections

What we commonly think of as "the election" is the general election—the election that finally chooses the winner who will take office. In the United States, all federal general elections are held on the first Tuesday in November unless that is the first day of the month. The earliest date is thus November 2nd, and the latest is November 8th. To keep costs down, almost all states hold their elections on the same day even in years when there are no federal candidates. The interval between the primary and the general election may be more than six months or some shorter interval.

In addition to primary and general elections, states and localities often hold other types of elections. In a "special election," candidates vie for an office that has been left vacant due to death, resignation, or elevation to a higher office. Whether or not a special election is held for a representative or senator depends on state law and how much of the term remains. In some years, the nation's attention focuses on "recall elections," which are elections to remove an official from office and replace him or her with another candidate. Recall elections are held in response to petitions by the citizens, much like referenda. In 2012, Governor Scott Walker of Wisconsin, who had championed legislation to limit the bargaining rights of public employees, faced a recall election and successfully defeated the Democratic challenger.

Finally, local elections are held in many states to approve referenda or constitutional amendments, as discussed in the Politics with a Purpose in this chapter. Some state and local governments are required to seek public approval for any tax increase or bond issue beyond a constitutional limit. In a state such as Ohio, with a constitution dating back to 1803, almost all local taxes must be approved by the public.

Open Primary
A primary in which any registered voter can vote (but must vote for candidates of only one party).

---

25. *California Democratic Party v. Jones,* 530 U.S. 567 (2000).

What this means is that school districts, park districts, and other public entities are constantly going to the public to get approval for tax increases of any kind. In a less-than-perfect economy or in the face of anti-tax sentiments, it is not easy to persuade voters to increase their own taxes.

How Are Elections Conducted?

■ **LO9.8:** Discuss the impact of the mechanics and technology of voting on voter turnout, vote fraud, and the ability of citizens to trust the process.

The United States uses the **Australian ballot**—a secret ballot that is prepared, distributed, and counted by government officials at public expense. Since 1888, all states have used the Australian ballot. Before that, many states used the alternatives of oral voting and differently colored ballots prepared by the parties. Obviously, knowing which way a person was voting made it easy to apply pressure on the person to change his or her vote, and vote buying was common.

Office-Block and Party-Column Ballots

Two types of Australian ballots are used in the United States in general elections. The first, called an **office-block ballot**, or sometimes a **Massachusetts ballot**, groups all the candidates for a particular elective office under the title of that office. Parties dislike the office-block ballot because it places more emphasis on the office than on the party; it discourages straight-ticket voting and encourages split-ticket voting.

A **party-column ballot** is a form of general election ballot in which all of a party's candidates are arranged in one column under the party's label and symbol. It is also called the **Indiana ballot**. In some states, it allows voters to vote for all of a party's candidates for local, state, and national offices by simply marking a single "X" or by pulling a single lever. Most states use this type of ballot. As it encourages straight-ticket voting, the two major parties favor this form. When a party has an exceptionally strong presidential or gubernatorial candidate to head the ticket, the use of the party-column ballot increases the **coat-tail effect** (the influence of a popular candidate on the success of other candidates on the same party ticket).

Vote Fraud

Vote fraud is often suspected but seldom proved. The voting culture of the 1800s, when secret ballots were rare and people had a cavalier attitude toward the open buying of votes, was much more conducive to fraud than are modern elections. Larry J. Sabato and Glenn R. Simpson, however, claim that the potential for vote fraud is high in many states, particularly through the use of phony voter registrations and absentee ballots.[26]

The Danger of Fraud. In California, it is very difficult to remove a name from the polling list even if the person has not cast a ballot in the last two years. Thus, many persons are still on the rolls even though they no longer live in California. Enterprising political activists could use these names for absentee ballots. Other states have registration laws meant to encourage easy registration and voting. Such laws can be taken advantage of by those who seek to vote more than once.

Australian Ballot
A secret ballot prepared, distributed, and tabulated by government officials at public expense. Since 1888, all U.S. states have used the Australian ballot rather than an open, public ballot.

Office-Block or Massachusetts Ballot
A form of general-election ballot in which candidates for elective office are grouped together under the title of each office. It emphasizes voting for the office and the individual candidate, rather than for the party.

Party-Column or Indiana Ballot
A form of general-election ballot in which all of a party's candidates for elective office are arranged in one column under the party's label and symbol. It emphasizes voting for the party, rather than for the office or individual.

Coat-Tail Effect
The influence of a popular candidate on the electoral success of other candidates on the same party ticket. The effect is increased by the party-column ballot, which encourages straight-ticket voting.

---

26. Larry J. Sabato and Glenn R. Simpson, *Dirty Little Secrets: The Persistence of Corruption in American Politics* (New York: Random House, 1996).

Richard Clement/Reuters/Landov

After the 2000 elections, Larry Sabato again emphasized the problem of voting fraud. "It's a silent scandal," said Sabato, "and the problem is getting worse with increases in absentee voting, which is the easiest way to commit fraud." In 2000, one-third of Florida's counties found that more than 1,200 votes were cast illegally by felons, and in one county alone nearly 500 votes were cast by unregistered voters. In two precincts, the number of ballots cast was greater than the number of people who voted.[27]

Mistakes by Voting Officials. Some observers claim, however, that errors leading to fraud are trivial in number, and that a few mistakes are inevitable in a system involving millions of voters. These people argue that an excessive concern with vote fraud makes it harder for minorities and poor people to vote. For example, purging the rolls of thousands of names because addresses are not perfectly correct will likely remove many legitimate voters from the rolls.

The Importance of the Voting Machine

The 2000 presidential election spurred a national debate on the mechanics of how people actually cast their ballots on election day. The outcome of the 2000 presidential election hinged on Florida's electoral votes. The biggest problem lay in Florida's use of punch-card ballots. Voters slipped their card into the voting book and then "punched" the number next to the name of the candidate they preferred. Because of the layout of the printed book in 2000, names were spread across two pages, resulting in a "butterfly" ballot. Voters could accidentally punch the wrong number and cast their vote for the wrong candidate.

As the election night ended, it was clear that the votes in Florida between George W. Bush and Al Gore were "too close to call." Ballot problems abounded: Some voters invalidated their ballots by voting for both candidates; some punch

did you know?
Each new voting machine costs more than $3,000 for the equipment alone.

27. As cited in "Blind to Voter Fraud" *Wall Street Journal*, March 2, 2001, p.A10.

cards were not punched all the way through, resulting in no vote being counted; some had no vote for president at all. The Democratic Party and its candidates went to court to demand a recount of the votes. Republican political leaders in Florida tried to stop recounts in fear of losing the election. After a series of dramatic legal battles, the U.S. Supreme Court settled the election by allowing a Florida decision favoring the Republicans to stand. However, the result was a seriously flawed election process that produced tremendous cynicism about the mechanics of voting.

In 2002, Congress passed the Help America Vote Act, which established the U.S. Election Assistance Commission. The charge of the commission is to set standards for voting machines; to distribute funds to help communities acquire new, easier-to-use machines; and to act as a clearinghouse of information for the states. As expected, several companies began to create new machines for use in the voting booth. Most of these depend on digital recording of votes. Given the mistakes that occurred in Florida, many citizens wanted a record of their votes so that a mistake in tallying votes could be checked against a paper record. Election officials are deeply concerned that recording and transmitting vote counts only digitally may invite hacking and vote fraud. To date, no system, including the use of the Internet, has been devised that is totally immune to some sort of fraud, continuing concern about the security of our election system.

The Electoral College

■ **LO9.9:** Demonstrate an understanding of the electoral college and its impact on the presidential election campaign.

Many people who vote for the president and vice president think that they are voting directly for a candidate. In actuality, they are voting for **electors**, who will cast their ballots in the electoral college. Article II, Section 1, of the Constitution outlines the method of choosing electors for president and vice president. The framers of the Constitution wanted to avoid the selection of president and vice president by the "excitable masses." Rather, they wished the choice to be made by a few supposedly dispassionate, reasonable men (but not women).

The Choice of Electors

Each state's electors are selected during presidential election years, as governed by state laws. After the national party convention, the electors normally are pledged to the candidates chosen. The total number of electors today is 538, equal to 100 senators, 435 members of the House, and three electors for the District of Columbia (the Twenty-third Amendment, ratified in 1961, added electors for the District of Columbia). Each state's number of electors equals that state's number of senators (two) plus its number of representatives. Figure 9–8 shows how the electoral votes are apportioned by state.

The Electors' Commitment

When a plurality of voters in a state chooses a slate of electors—except in Maine and Nebraska, where electoral votes are based on congressional districts—those electors are pledged to cast their ballots on the first Monday after the second Wednesday in December in the state capital for the presidential and vice

THE COMPARE WITH YOUR PEERS

MindTap for American Government

Access the Elections Forum: Polling Activity—Presidential Election Process.

Electors
A member of the electoral college, which selects the president and vice president. Each state's electors are chosen in each presidential election year according to state laws.

did you know?

Forty-two states do not indicate on the ballot that the voter is casting a ballot for members of the electoral college rather than for the president or vice president directly.

Figure 9-8 ▶ Electoral Votes by State

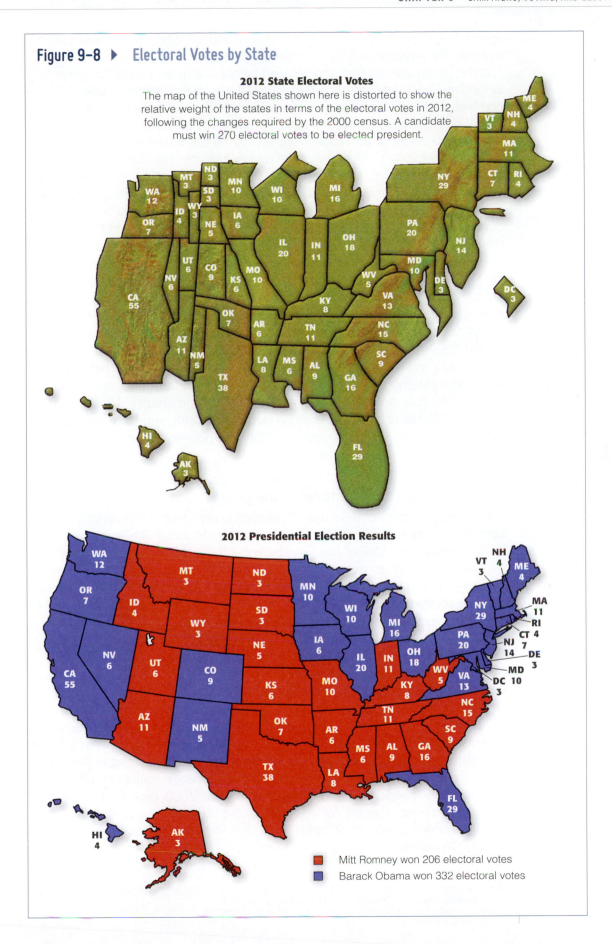

2012 State Electoral Votes

The map of the United States shown here is distorted to show the relative weight of the states in terms of the electoral votes in 2012, following the changes required by the 2000 census. A candidate must win 270 electoral votes to be elected president.

2012 Presidential Election Results

Mitt Romney won 206 electoral votes
Barack Obama won 332 electoral votes

presidential candidates of their party. The Constitution does not, however, *require* the electors to cast their ballots for the candidates of their party.

The ballots are counted and certified before a joint session of Congress early in January. The candidates who receive a majority of the electoral votes (270) are certified as president-elect and vice president–elect. According to the Constitution, if no candidate receives a majority of the electoral votes, the election of the president is decided in the House from among the candidates with the three highest numbers of votes, with each state having one vote (decided by a plurality of each state delegation). The selection of the vice president is determined by the Senate in a choice between the two candidates with the most votes, each senator having one vote. Congress was required to choose the president and vice president in 1801 (Thomas Jefferson and Aaron Burr), and the House chose the president in 1825 (John Quincy Adams).[28]

It is possible for a candidate to become president without obtaining a majority of the popular vote. Many minority presidents are found in our history, including Abraham Lincoln, Woodrow Wilson, Harry Truman, John F. Kennedy, Richard Nixon (in 1968), Bill Clinton (1992, 1996), and George W. Bush (in 2000). Such an event becomes more likely when there are important third-party candidates.

Perhaps more distressing is the possibility of a candidate's being elected when an opposing candidate receives a plurality of the popular vote. This has occurred on four occasions—in the elections of John Quincy Adams in 1824, Rutherford B. Hayes in 1876, Benjamin Harrison in 1888, and George W. Bush in 2000, all of whom won elections in which an opponent received a plurality of the popular vote.

Criticisms of the Electoral College

Besides the possibility of a candidate's becoming president even though an opponent obtains more popular votes, other complaints about the electoral college have emerged. The idea of the Constitution's framers was to have electors use their own discretion to decide who would make the best president. But electors no longer perform the selecting function envisioned by the founders, because they are committed to the candidate who has a plurality of popular votes in their state in the general election.[29]

One can also argue that the current system, which in most states gives all of the electoral votes to the candidate who has a statewide plurality, is unfair to other candidates and their supporters. The current system of voting also means that presidential campaigning will be concentrated in those states that have the largest number of electoral votes and in the battleground states. Other states may receive little attention from the campaigns. It can also be argued that the system favors states with *smaller* populations, because including Senate seats in the electoral vote total partly offsets the edge of the more populous states in the House. Wyoming (with two senators and one representative) gets an electoral vote for roughly every 164,594 inhabitants (based on the 2000 census), for example, whereas Iowa gets one vote for every 418,046 inhabitants and California has one vote for every 615,848 inhabitants. Note that many of the smallest states have Republican majorities.

---

28. For a detailed account of the process, see Michael J. Glennon, *When No Majority Rules: The Electoral College and Presidential Succession* (Washington, DC: Congressional Quarterly Press, 1993), p. 20.
29. Note, however, that there have been revolts by so-called *faithless electors*—in 1796, 1820, 1948, 1956, 1960, 1968, 1972, 1976, 1988, and 2000.

Many proposals for reform of the electoral college system have been advanced, particularly after the turmoil resulting from the 2000 elections. The most obvious proposal is to eliminate the electoral college system completely and to elect candidates on a popular-vote basis; in other words, a direct election, by the people, of the president and vice president. Because abolishing the electoral college would require a constitutional amendment, however, the chances of electing the president by a direct vote are remote. The major parties are not in favor of eliminating the electoral college, fearing that this would give minor parties a more influential role. Also, less populous states are not in favor of direct election of the president because they believe they would be overwhelmed by the large-state vote.

Efforts to improve registration systems, to make voting easier and more secure, and to make changes to the electoral college all will work to make elections in the United States more trustworthy for the voters. The explosion in campaign funding, however, especially from unregulated sources, creates new issues for the election process.

What Would You Do?

Get Out the Vote!

From the passage of the Twenty-Sixth Amendment (which extended suffrage to eighteen year-olds) in 1971 until 2008, young Americans were the group least likely to vote. President Obama's 2008 campaign energized these young voters in a way no other candidate's has. Voter turnout for 18 to 24 year-olds increased from 36 percent in 2000 to 48.5 percent in 2008. More than 60 percent of these young voters cast their ballots for the Obama-Biden ticket. Although voter turnout for this group slipped to 41 percent in 2012, the majority of young voters continued to support the president in his reelection campaign. The increased turnout among young Americans was a major factor in both of his successful presidential campaigns.

Why Should You Care?

Voting allows you to directly express your preferences about who becomes president or senator or mayor of your city. It is your voice as a citizen. If you want the country to change direction, casting your vote for the candidate of your choice is the way to do it. Although social security policy, housing policy, and care for military veterans may not interest you as a college student, national policies *will* affect your future. The decisions made on these issues will be on the national agenda for years to come and your vote can decide who will represent your issues in Washington.

Voting increases an individual's self-esteem and their confidence in expressing views to political officials. Imagine meeting a senator and having the chance to make a personal statement to her. What would say if she asks, "Did you vote in the last election?" Voting is habit-forming. Individuals who vote while they are young are most likely to continue voting throughout their lives and to feel a deep stake in their nation's well-being. People who do not vote are often hesitant about going to the polls because they do not feel competent to do so.

What Would You Do?

Suppose you are the campaign manager in your region for a very exciting candidate for senator—what would you do to get younger voters interested in your candidate and excited about the campaign?

What You *Can* Do

Register to vote! Find out where your polling place is located ahead of time so you can plan to get there. You might volunteer to be an election judge at the polling place to make sure the rules are followed and no voters are turned away due to discriminatory treatment. Consider volunteering to work for the campaign of a candidate you really like. Campaign organizations need people to make telephone calls, to walk door-to-door on election day, to post information on social media sites, and for a variety of other tasks. Being part of a campaign is an unforgettable and satisfying experience.

- For further information on candidates and their positions:
  http://www.ballotpedia.org

- For strategies for turning out the youth vote:
  http://www.rockthevote.org

- For opportunities to work in a campaign:
  College Democrats: http://www.collegedems.com
  College Republicans: http://www.crnc.org

Key Terms

Australian ballot 336
battleground state 323
"beauty contest" 320
caucus 334
closed primary 334
coat-tail effect 336
communications director 308
corrupt practices acts 311
credentials committee 322

electors 338
finance chairperson 308
focus group 309
front-loading 321
front-runner 321
Get Out the Vote (GOTV) 308
hard money 313
Hatch Act 311
independent expenditures 316

issue advocacy advertising 314
office-block, or Massachusetts, ballot 338
open primary 335
party-column, or Indiana, ballot 336
political action committee (PAC) 314
political consultant 307

pollster 308
presidential primary 320
press secretary 308
rational ignorance effect 329
registration 332
soft money 314
Super PAC 314
superdelegate 321
tracking poll 309
voter turnout 323

Chapter Summary

■ **LO9.1:** Eligibility to run for federal office is based on citizenship, residency, and age. Each office has different requirements. Only the president is to be a natural-born citizen. Candidates for senator and representative could be naturalized citizens. People run for political office to further their careers, to carry out specific political programs, or in response to certain issues or events. Legal qualifications for holding political office are minimal at state and local levels, but office holders remain predominantly white and male and are likely to be from the professional class.

■ **LO9.2:** Political campaigns are lengthy and extremely expensive. In the last decade, they have become more candidate-centered rather than party-centered due to technological innovations and decreasing party identification. Candidates have begun to rely less on the party and more on paid

professional consultants to perform the tasks necessary to wage a political campaign. The crucial task of professional political consultants is image building. The campaign organization devises a campaign strategy to maximize the candidate's chances of winning. Candidates use public opinion polls and focus groups to gauge their popularity and to test the mood of the country.

■ **LO9.3:** The amount of money spent in financing campaigns is increasing steadily. A variety of corrupt practices acts have been passed to regulate campaign finance. The Federal Election Campaign Act of 1971 and its amendments in 1974 and 1976 instituted major reforms by limiting spending and contributions; the acts allowed corporations, labor unions, and interest groups to set up political action committees (PACs) to raise money for candidates. Public matching funds were made available to primary campaigns if certain criteria were met. The intent was to help candidates be competitive in the primaries. New techniques were later developed, including "soft money" contributions to the parties and independent expenditures. The Bipartisan Campaign Reform Act (BCRA) of 2002 banned soft money contributions to the national parties, limited advertising by interest groups, and increased the limits on individual contributions. By 2008, most of the major candidates refused public funding in the primary campaigns, as did the Obama campaign in the general election, resulting in very large differences between the campaigns in financial resources. "Leveling the playing field" for candidates in either the primaries or the general election seemed to be obsolete.

■ **LO9.4:** After the Democratic Convention of 1968, the McGovern-Fraser Commission formulated new rules for primaries, adopted by all Democrats and by Republicans in many states. They opened up the presidential nomination process to all voters. It effectively removed control of the nomination process from the political party members and gave it to the voting public. Sometimes this produces a great party leader, and other years it produces a candidate who is not well supported by party loyalists and who cannot win the election.

■ **LO9.4:** A presidential primary is a statewide election to help a political party determine its presidential nominee at the national convention. Some states use the caucus method of choosing convention delegates. The primary campaign recently has been shortened to the first few months of the election year.

■ **LO9.4:** The party conventions are held to finalize the nomination of a candidate for president. Normally, the convention is used to unite the party and to introduce the winning candidate to the public. It marks the beginning of the general election campaign. Contested conventions have been rare in the last 50 years.

■ **LO9.4:** General election campaign begins after Labor Day in September. Presidential candidates and their campaign organizations use advertising, appearances, speeches, and debates to win support from voters. In recent years, attention has been lavished on battleground states where presidential contests were closely fought.

■ **LO9.5:** Free and fair elections are the basis for the continuation of a democratic form of government. Elections should be fairly administered, information about the candidates and issues must be available through a free press, and voters must be free from coercion and intimidation.

■ **LO9.6:** Voter participation in the United States is low compared with that of other countries. Some see this as a threat

to representative democracy. Others believe it simply indicates greater satisfaction with the status quo. There is an association between voting and a person's age, education, minority status, and income level. Another factor affecting voter turnout is the extent to which elections are competitive within a state. It is also true that the number of eligible voters is smaller than the number of people of voting age because of ineligible felons and immigrants who are not yet citizens.

■ **LO9.7:** In the United States, only citizens have been allowed to vote. In the early years of the republic, however, only free white male citizens who owned property were eligible to vote. Laws have excluded women, citizens under 18 years of age, felons, ex-slaves, and others. By 1971 suffrage was extended to all citizens, male and female, aged 18 or older. Questions still remain: Should felons be excluded from voting? What about resident noncitizens or people who have difficulty getting registered? Each state has somewhat different registration processes and requirements for identification at the polls. Some claim that these requirements are responsible for much of the nonparticipation in the political process in the United States.

■ **LO9.8:** Because of the federal structure of the United States, citizens vote in federal, state, and local elections. To nominate candidates for office, voters participate in primary elections, which may be restricted to party identifiers (closed), open to all (open), or allow voters to choose between both party's candidates (blanket). Candidates are elected in the general election. Voters may be asked to cast ballots on referenda, on constitutional amendments at the state level, for tax levies, or in special elections to choose candidates for a vacated office.

■ **LO9.8:** The United States uses the Australian ballot, a secret ballot that is prepared, distributed, and counted by government officials. The office-block ballot groups candidates according to office. The party-column ballot groups candidates according to their party labels and symbols.

■ **LO9.8:** Vote fraud is often charged but not often proven. After the 2000 election, states and local communities adopted new forms of voting equipment, seeking to provide secure voting systems for elections. The federal government established a commission to test new technologies and provide a clearinghouse for information.

■ **LO9.9:** The voter technically does not vote directly but chooses between slates of presidential electors. In most states, the slate that wins the most popular votes throughout the state gets to cast all the electoral votes for the state. The candidate receiving a majority (270) of the electoral votes wins. Both the mechanics and the politics of the electoral college have been sharply criticized. Proposed reforms include a proposal that the president be elected on a popular-vote basis in a direct election.

Selected Print, Media, and Online Resources

PRINT RESOURCES

Alvarez, R. Michael, and Thad E. Hall. *Electronic Elections: The Perils and Promises of igital Democracy.* Princeton, NJ: Princeton University Press, 2008. Alvarez and Hall examine all past technologies in voting and look at the new voting machines and processes that are available in the digital age. They suggest standards by which voting systems can be improved.

Karpf, David. *The MoveOn Effect:* The Unexpected Transformation of American Political Advocacy. New York: Oxford University Press, 2012. The author examines how today's organizations use the Internet and social media to gain supporters and motivate followers to join others in a common cause. His work addresses the new ways that organizations arise, organize, fundraise, and operate across the country, utilizing the capacity of the Internet to connect their followers.

Leighley, Jan and Jonathan Nagler. *Who Votes Now?: Demographics, Issues, Inequality and Turnout in the United States.* Princeton, NJ: Princeton University Press, 2013. Using data from the U.S. Census Bureau, the authors examine trends in voting turnout over four decades. They find that the voting gap between black and white Americans has disappeared but that the gap between the wealthy and the poor has not. Among the questions they tackle is whether new practices like same day registration would erase some of these inequalities in voting.

Martinez, Michael D. *Does Turnout Matter?* Boulder, CO: Westview Press, 2009. Scholars have expended much effort in examining why voter turnout is lower in the United States than in many other countries, but the question of whether low turnout actually matters has received less attention. Martinez is a professor of political science at the University of Florida.

Piven, Frances Fox, Lori Minnite, and Margaret Groarke. *Keeping Down the Black Vote: Race and Demobilization of American Voters.* New York: The New Press, 2009. The authors claim that under the banner of election reform, leading operatives in the Republican Party have sought to affect elections by suppressing the black vote.

Sides, John and Lynn Vavreck. *The Gamble: Choice and Change in the 2012 Presidential Election.* Princeton, NJ: Princeton University Press, 2013. The authors take an unusual approach to analyzing the 2012 election, Using quantitative analysis of the economy, public opinion, the media, and advertising to explain the election results from a social science approach.

MEDIA RESOURCES

American Blackout—A 2005 documentary narrated by former congresswoman Cynthia McKinney from Georgia. She investigates the ways in which African American voters can be challenged at the polls and kept from voting.

The Candidate—A 1972 film (starring Robert Redford) that effectively investigates and satirizes the decisions that a candidate for the U.S. Senate must make. It's a political classic.

Game Change—Released in 2012, this movie portrays the Republican campaign in 2008, with an emphasis on the introduction of Sarah Palin as the vice presidential candidate. It stars Ed Harris, Julianne Moore, and Woody Harrelson.

Hacking Democracy—An HBO production that follows activist Bev Harris of Seattle and others as they take on Diebold, a company that makes electronic voting machines. The documentary argues that security lapses in Diebold's machines are a threat to the democratic process.

Mississippi Burning—This 1988 film, starring Gene Hackman and Willem Dafoe, is a fictional version of the investigation of the deaths of two civil rights workers who came to Mississippi to help register African Americans to vote in 1964.

ONLINE RESOURCES

Ballotpedia—provides an online source for information about voting, state and national issues, ballot measures and election laws. www.ballotpedia.org

Center for Responsive Politics—a nonpartisan, independent, and non-profit research group that tracks money in U.S. politics and its effect on elections and public policy: www.opensecrets.org

Federal Election Commission—an independent regulatory agency created by Congress in 1975 to administer and enforce the Federal Election Campaign Act (FECA)—the statute that governs the financing of federal elections; contains detailed information about current campaign financing laws and the latest filings of finance reports: www.fec.gov

Institute for Democracy and Electoral Assistance (IDEA)—an inter-governmental organization that supports sustainable democracy worldwide. Provides information about voting and turnout around the world: www.idea.int

Project Vote Smart—investigates voting records and campaign financing information: www.vote-smart.org

Rock the Vote—provides tools to "build political power for young people." Its website provides state-level information about registration deadlines, voting requirements, and voting records for elected officials: www.rockthevote.org

Master the concepts of Voting and Elections with MindTap™ for American Government

 REVIEW MindTap™ for American Government
Access Key Term Flashcards for Chapter 9.

 STAY CURRENT MindTap™ for American Government
Access the KnowNow blog and customized RSS for updates on current events.

 TEST YOURSELF MindTap™ for American Government
Take the Wrap It Up Quiz for Chapter 9.

 STAY FOCUSED MindTap™ for American Government
Complete The Focus Activities for Voting and Elections.

10 The Media and Politics

LEARNING OUTCOMES

After reading this chapter, students will be able to:

■ **LO10.1:** Describe the evolution of American media from newspapers to the electronic and digital revolution.

■ **LO10.2:** Explain the functions of the media in American society.

■ **LO10.3:** Discuss the impact of all forms of the media on political campaigning.

■ **LO10.4:** Identify ways in which the media influence voters.

■ **LO10.5:** Demonstrate an understanding of the relationship between government and all media sources.

■ **LO10.6:** Critically analyze news stories published by any form of the media.

Egyptian protestors use their cellphones in 2011 to document the attacks on protestors by police and government security forces. Such pictures and video were quickly released to the Internet.

AP Images/DESRUS BENEDICTE

WATCH & LEARN
Watch a brief "What Do You Know?" video summarizing Media and Politics.

What if?

The Media Had to Reveal All Their Sources?

BACKGROUND

Reporters, whether they work for newspapers, newswire services, television stations, magazines, or Internet blogs, typically attempt to "protect their sources" so that they do not face penalties such as job loss. Many of these sources are willing to talk to reporters only on the condition that they remain anonymous. Consequently, untold news stories include phrases such as "informed sources said…" or "an anonymous source revealed…." Typically, these sources are confident that their names will not be disclosed because journalists are generally protected by so-called shield laws, statutes that protect reporters from being forced to disclose their sources in court or in other judicial proceedings. In 1972, the U.S. Supreme Court stated that "news gathering is not without First Amendment protections."* The majority on the Court, though, did not see those protections as absolute and held, among other things, that the First Amendment did not protect reporters from federal grand jury subpoenas seeking their confidential sources. In response to this ruling, state legislatures and courts created their own shield laws to protect reporters from being forced to reveal sources to law enforcement authorities.

WHAT IF THERE WAS NO PROTECTION FOR NEWS SOURCES?

Assume that at both the federal and state levels, shield laws were abolished. In other words, imagine a world in which reporters could continue to cite anonymous sources but would be subject to subpoenas that would legally require them to reveal their sources. News gatherers who could not guarantee confidentiality for their sources would not be provided the information they sought. In these circumstances, investigative reporting would be compromised. Fewer individuals would be willing to talk, except about minor matters that were not controversial. Public officials might be more comfortable engaging in questionable deals or dealing unfairly with public employees if they knew that their behavior could be protected by intimidating possible informants.

Many jurists have predicted the same outcome. One judge stated that compelling a reporter to disclose confidential sources "unquestionably threatens a journalist's ability to secure information that is made available to him only on a confidential basis." The judge continued by saying that the "negative effect of such disclosure on future undercover investigative reporting would be serious and threatens freedom of the press and the public's need to be informed."**

LET'S TAKE IT TO COURT

If sources were fair game without any shield-law protection, there would most likely be a significant increase in litigation. Imagine a person who is unhappy about a story suggesting that he or she was responsible for a crime. For example, after the Sandy Hook Elementary School shooting, the initial press reports accused Adam Lanza's brother of the massacre because the shooter was evidently carrying some identification that was linked to his brother. If the brother had suffered harm to his home, family, or reputation from that initial report, he could have sued the reporters who had released the false information. The sources might then face a lawsuit.

Today, most people rely on trusted news sources and dismiss what might be considered gossip. It is clear, however, from journalistic missteps made on recent important reports, such as the bombing at the Boston Marathon and the Sandy Hook massacre, that the competition to get to the news first and to release a story first does encourage the use of anonymous sources. This often results in printing "facts" that are later determined to be untrue, after greater research is conducted.

did you know?

Ninety percent of Americans between the ages of 18 and 29 use social networks.

---

* *Branzburg v. Hayes*, 408 U.S. 665 (1972).
** *Baker v. F & F Investment*, 470 F.2d 778 (1972).

For Critical Analysis

1. *Do you think it is fair that reporters can shield their sources today? If so, under what circumstances might shielding sources be considered unfair?*

2. *Why do anonymous sources wish to keep their identities secret?*

Media
The means of communication—such as radio, television, and news outlets—that reach people widely.

Barack Obama @BarackObama · Mar 1
Michael knows that being uninsured is risky—no matter where you are in life.
ofa.bo/tAn pic.twitter.com/hixY8TpeRK

I've never been sick, but no one's immune.

This is why health care reform matters to **Michael**.

12:06 PM - 1 Mar 2014 · Details   Flag media

Barack Obama/Twitter

How do partisan social media websites affect voters?

John Boehner @johnboehner · Feb 27
#hcr prices are rising. Millions of seniors are at risk of losing doctors & benefits. We need to repeal #ObamaCare & start over.
Collapse   ↩ Reply ↻ Retweet ★ Favorite ••• More

John Boehner/Twitter

Social Media
Websites and other online places where people can interact, form social contacts, and share personal or business information.

WE LIVE IN A WORLD saturated by media. Twenty-four hours a day, seven days a week, you can access news about American politics, entertainment, sports, world events, science, and the weather. From the car radio or Internet radio first thing in the morning to the opening monologue of a late-night television talk show, media surrounds us. While you watch television or check the news on the Internet, you may be receiving text messages from your friends, reading Tweets, or messaging on Instagram. This chapter explores how the media influence the political process in the United States.

The term, **media**, is defined as the means of communication—such as radio, television, and news outlets—that reach or influence people widely. True media are generally public, available to anyone who wishes to see or read coverage. They can reach millions of individuals from around the globe in a matter of seconds. Social media, such as Facebook, Twitter, and Instagram, are public websites, but individuals have discretion with regards to whether their profiles are publicly accessible. **Social media**'s major purpose is to connect individuals who want to share their personal news. As we will see in this chapter, politicians, journalists, interest groups, political parties, members of Congress and even the president have adopted social media as a way to communicate directly with citizens. Politicians use social media websites to promote policies and build support among their followers. President Obama (@BarackObama) used Twitter to promote the Affordable Care Act. Social media also allows politicians to respond to one another. Speaker of the House John Boehner responded to President Obama's Affordable Care Act with calls for repeal. The media have both changed *and* stayed the same throughout the nation's history. Newspapers still report the major news of the day; now, social media outlets allow individuals to report and interact with events in real time.

The History of the Media in the United States

■ **LO10.1:** Describe the evolution of American media from newspapers to the electronic and digital revolution.

Many years ago, Thomas Jefferson opined: "Were it left to me to decide whether we should have a government without newspapers, or newspapers without a government, I should not hesitate a moment to prefer the latter."[1] Although the media have played a significant role in politics since the founding of this nation, they were not as overwhelmingly important in the past as they are today. Political

---

1. James Madison, "Letter to W. T. Barry" (August 4, 1822), in Gaillard P. Hunt, ed., *The Writings of James Madison* 103 (1910).

discussion was controlled by a small elite who communicated personally, and before the early 1800s, news traveled slowly. If an important political event occurred in New York, it was not known until five days later in Philadelphia, and not for 10 days later in the capital cities of Connecticut, Maryland, and Virginia. Boston learned of political news 15 days later.

The Rise of the Popular Press

Roughly 3,000 newspapers were being published by 1860. Some of these, such as the *New York Tribune*, were mainly sensationalist outlets that concentrated on crimes, scandals, and social gossip. The *New York Herald* specialized in self-improvement and what today would be called "practical" news. Although sensational and biased reporting often reinforced political partisanship (this was particularly true during the Civil War), many historians believe that the growth of the print media also played an important role in unifying the country.[2]

Americans may cherish the idea of an unbiased press, but in the early years of the nation's history, the number of politically sponsored newspapers was significant. The sole reason for the existence of such periodicals was to further the interests of the politicians who paid for their publication. As chief executive of our government during this period, George Washington was a "firm believer" in **managed news**. He believed that some matters should be kept secret and that news that might damage the image of the United States should be censored. Washington, however, made no attempt to control the press.

Mass-Readership Newspapers. Two inventions in the nineteenth century led to the development of mass-readership newspapers. The first was the high-speed rotary press; the second was the telegraph. Faster presses meant lower per-unit costs and lower subscription prices. The introduction of the telegraph in 1848 allowed news of an event to reach newsrooms across the nation within hours.

Along with these technological changes came a growing population and increasing urbanization. A larger, more urban population could support daily newspapers. The burgeoning, diversified economy encouraged the growth of advertising, which meant that newspapers could obtain additional revenues from merchants who seized the opportunity to promote their wares to a larger public.

The Popular Press and Yellow Journalism. Students of the history of journalism point to a period in the latter half of the 1800s when there occurred a seismic shift—not in the amount of biased news reporting, but rather in its origin. Whereas politically-sponsored newspapers had expounded a particular political party's point of view, the post-Civil War masses-oriented newspapers expounded whatever political philosophy the owner of the newspaper happened to have.

Newspaper owners often allowed their editors to engage in sensationalism and what is known as **yellow journalism**. The questionable, or simply personal, activities of a prominent businessperson, politician, or socialite

Managed News
Information generated and distributed by the government in such a way as to give government interests priority over candor.

did you know?
The first successful daily newspaper in the United States was the *Pennsylvania Packet & General Advertiser*, which was initially published on September 21, 1784.

Yellow Journalism
A term for sensationalistic, irresponsible journalism. Reputedly, the term is an allusion to the cartoon "The Yellow Kid" in the old *New York World*, a newspaper especially noted for its sensationalism.

2. James L. Baughman, "The Fall and Rise of Partisan Journalism," Center for Journalism Ethics, The University of Wisconsin, April 15, 2011.

Hank Walker/Time Life Pictures/Getty Images

President Dwight
Eisenhower shows his
discomfort and frustration
during a news conference.
Worried about the impact of
live broadcasts, Eisenhower
allowed videotaped versions to
be shown after the event ended.

President Barack Obama
reads his prepared remarks
from a teleprompter during
an event focused on the
economic recovery in 2010.

Electronic Media
Communication channels that
involve electronic transmissions,
such as radio, television, and the
Internet.

were front-page material. Newspapers, then as now, made their economic way by maximizing readership. Whether the source is the *National Enquirer* at the grocery checkout or Tweets from Justin Bieber, sensationalism still sells.

News Comes over the Airwaves

The first scheduled radio program in the United States featured politicians. On the night of November 2, 1920, KDKA-Pittsburgh transmitted the returns of the presidential election race between Warren G. Harding and James M. Cox. The listeners were a few thousand people tuning in on primitive, homemade sets.

By 1924, there were nearly 1,400 radio stations. But it was not until 8 p.m. on November 15, 1926, that the electronic media came into its own in the United States. On that night, the National Broadcasting Company (NBC) made its debut with a four-hour program broadcast by 25 stations in 21 cities. Network broadcasting had become a reality.

Even with the advent of national radio in the 1920s and television in the late 1940s, many politicians were slow to understand the significance of the **electronic media**. The 1952 presidential campaign was the first to feature a real role for television. Television coverage of the Republican convention helped Dwight Eisenhower win over delegates and secure the nomination. President Eisenhower, however, aware of the pitfalls inherent in press conferences, insisted his be taped and replayed later. This, of course, gave his administration the chance to issue a press release before the tape was played.

Today, television dominates the campaign strategy of every would-be national politician, as well as that of every elected official. Politicians continue to innovatively draw attention to themselves because it affords them free access to the

Chip Somodevilla/Getty Images

broadcast media. All forms of media must be leveraged to run a successful campaign, including social media.

The Revolution in Electronic Media

Today, network television news competes not only with newspapers, but with cable and satellite TV, as well as the enormous number of Internet news providers. Consider this: Fifty-one years ago, President John F. Kennedy was assassinated in Dallas, Texas. The event was captured on one or two amateur videos by bystanders. News of the assassination reached Washington, DC, by landline telephone. Millions of Americans rushed to find a television to watch Walter Cronkite report the story as it unfolded on network television. Today, such an event would be recorded by hundreds of cellphone cameras, with photos, videos, and details immediately uploaded to news sources and broadcast on television news programs and the Internet within minutes as breaking news. The whole world would watch the video. Today, opposition groups in Syria fighting the government and rebels occupying buildings in Ukraine understand the power of the Internet and publish their side of the story on YouTube.

Walter Cronkite, one of the most trusted news anchors in television history, delivered the news on a live broadcast that President Kennedy had died.

In a democracy, a person's ability to gain access to the news quickly is an advantage; direct appeals can persuade the public to be more politically attentive and, in some cases, to more fully participate in public affairs. The downside to this tidal wave of news is that humans cannot process all of the information at the rate it is broadcast, so we engage in **selective information processing**. That means we only pay attention to a few news sources that we have come to prefer and, if we do not want to hear about politics, we can tailor our news sources to entertainment or sports news only. In broadcasting, **narrowcasting**, means providing news and entertainment outlets designed to cater to a small segment of the population. For example, Fox News is a traditionally conservative news source, while the Today Show focuses on popular culture and news stories that are condensed for brief updates as opposed to in-depth coverage.

A Lebanese protestor (against Syrian President Assad) photographs a demonstration in Martyrs Square in Beirut, Lebanon.

Selective Information Processing
For an individual, only thinking about the information that is really needed and disregarding the rest of the information presented.

Narrowcasting
Broadcasting that is targeted to one small sector of the population.

Talk Show Politics. When citizens depended on newspapers for political opinions, the print media provided an easy solution: the newspaper printed "news" in most of the front section of the paper, its own editorials on the editorial page, and then printed multiple essays by columnists with different points of view opposite the editorial page. Today, with the rise of thousands of "news" show on television, cable networks, and websites, the distinctions between "straight news" and opinion is very muddy. Most of the television news shows are actually "talk shows" about the news featuring an anchor or two and multiple guests who comment on the news. Networks compete heavily for audiences for the traditional 6:30 p.m. news hour, while Public Broadcasting Services (PBS) continues to have a devoted audience for its *NewsHour*. All of these shows are also available on the Internet, and many have interactive segments that

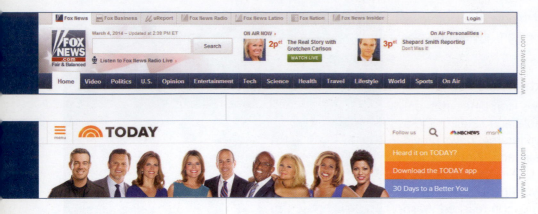

encourage their viewers to email or tweet in their own comments.

Television "news" is extended into early and late night television with Jon Stewart, Stephen Colbert, and Jimmy Fallon, among others. Stewart and Colbert have created a new form of news/talk show using humor, sarcasm and superb writing to capture young viewers with their respective shows, *The Daily Show* and *The Colbert Report*.[3] Distinguishing between news and opinion becomes extremely difficult for the viewer. For example, if President Obama appears on *The View* (with anchors of differing opinions) to announce a new program for the education of preschool children, is that "news" or is it a presidential commercial for his own initiative?

Talk Radio. "Talk" has also blossomed on radio. The number of radio stations that program only talk shows has increased from about 300 in 1989 to more than 1,200 today. The topics of talk shows range from business to sports to investment. There has been considerable criticism of the political talk shows, especially those hosted by Rush Limbaugh, Glenn Beck, and other conservatives, on the grounds that these shows focus on negative politics rather than policy issues. Recent data from the Pew Research Center show that

did you know?

Thirty-nine percent of *The Daily Show* viewers are between the ages of 18 and 29, while only 9 percent of network evening news viewers fit into that age range.

Table 10–1 ▶ Who Watches What on Television Audience by Age (N=3,003)

As the data in this table shows, younger viewers get their news from sources like Stephen Colbert and Jon Stewart, while older viewers find their news sources in more traditional and more conservative sources.

NEWS SOURCE (24 TOTAL)	18–29 YRS	30–49 YRS	50–64 YRS	65 YEARS +
Colbert	43%	37%	12%	6%
Daily Show	39%	36%	16%	7%
NY Times	32%	31%	21%	12%
WSJ	24%	40%	19%	15%
Economist	23%	41%	16%	17%
O'Reilly	12%	20%	24%	40%
Network evening	9%	31%	34%	25%
Hannity	3%	27%	24%	42%

Source: Pew Research Center, "In Changing News Landscape, Even Television News is Vulnerable." *Pew Research Center for the People and the Press.* September 27, 2012. http://www.people-press.org/files/legacy-pdf/2012 (accessed January 22, 2014)

---

3. Pew Research Center. "In Changing News Landscape, Even Television News is Vulnerable." Pew Center for the People and the Press. September 27, 2012.

Politics with a Purpose

YouTube, Jon Stewart, and Stephen Colbert: Changing Politics for the Better?

"Viral videos" and social networking have become a part of daily life. Politicians and political campaigns are scrambling to figure out how best to take advantage of new social media.

YouTube, a video-sharing site, was launched in 2005. Although many of the videos feature pets, children, and stunts gone wrong, some have tremendous political impact. The democratic uprisings in Egypt in 2012 and Ukraine in 2014 were chronicled by cell phone cameras and videos were uploaded to YouTube instantly. These videos swiftly alerted the world to the brutality of the government forces' response to the opposition.

Both Google and YouTube have easy-to-find campaign toolkits to help candidates use advertising and social networks effectively.* Although campaigns work hard to keep candidates from making memorable gaffes, viral videos and instant Twitter feeds mean missteps live longer, with greater consequences. During the primary campaign in 2012, Mitt Romney, at a private fundraising dinner, stated that about 47 percent of voters who do not pay income tax were likely to vote for President Obama. His remarks found their way to the Internet in minutes and the repercussions from them were detrimental to his presidential campaign.**

Sometimes comedians use their craft for a more serious political purpose. In 2011, Stephen Colbert and Jon Stewart teamed up to illustrate the myriad of loopholes in American election law through performance art. Colbert created "Americans for a Better Tomorrow, Tomorrow," a Super PAC, and began raising political money. In the January 2012 filing with the Federal Election Commission (FEC), Colbert's Super PAC had raised more than $1 million. In January 2012, Colbert announced that he was forming "an exploratory committee to lay the groundwork for my possible candidacy for president of the United States of America of South Carolina," requiring him to transfer control of his Super PAC. Colbert relinquished it to Jon Stewart. Stewart promptly renamed the PAC "The definitely not coordinating with Stephen Colbert Super PAC." Colbert was too late to get on the ballot in South Carolina's February Republican primary, so he mounted the "Rock Me Like a Herman Cain" campaign, in which he urged South Carolina voters to cast a vote for Cain as a proxy for Colbert. Soon after, Colbert abruptly halted his campaign.

Does this political comedy have a purpose? Yes! According to a Rasmussen survey, 30 percent of young people aged 18 to 29 say programs like Stewart's and Colbert's that feature news reports with a comic twist are replacing traditional news outlets. A university researcher found that *The Daily Show* turned the attention of apolitical viewers to political issues like the war in Afghanistan and the

presidential campaign. The most apolitical viewers were 13 percent more likely to attend to the issue very closely than were similarly inattentive nonviewers.*** Candidates at all levels will be watching the influence of new media closely in the years to come.

After giving up his own bid for the presidency in 2012, Stephen Colbert returned to South Carolina to campaign for his sister in 2013.

* "Why use YouTube," April 1, 2014, www.youtub.com/yt/politics101/index.html
**Ezra Klein, "Mitt Romney vs. the 47% and Himself," Washington Post Blog: *wonkbook*, September 18, 2012.
*** Xiaoxia Cao. (2010) "Hearing It from Jon Stewart: The Impact of *The Daily Show* on Public Attentiveness to Politics." *International Journal of Public Opinion Research*, 22(1), 26–46.

Richard Ellis/Getty Images

Radu Bercan/Shutterstock

iStockphoto.com/GlobalStock

the audience for talk radio, as well as for television "talk" shows, has sorted it out in a reasonable way. The bulk of Rush Limbaugh's listeners, for example, consider themselves conservative, while most of Rachel Maddow's audience is liberal.[4] Liberal groups have tried to counter conservative talk radio with shows that boast liberal hosts, but the most well-known effort, that of comedian Al Franken, foundered. Happily for Franken, he bounced back from his low ratings and found gainful employment in the U.S. Senate, representing the state of Minnesota.

The Impact of Social Networking, Blogging, and the Internet

The use of the Internet and other forms of electronic communication has increased beyond imagination in the last decade (see Figure 10-1). On the national level, political websites were created for the two major-party candidates for president for the first time in 1996. Since then, even the lowliest local politician feels obligated to have an occasionally updated website. Political candidates have used the Internet to raise tens of millions of dollars.[5] Howard Dean and John McCain were early adopters of the Internet to raise money, but Barack Obama became the leader in this practice in 2008. His website encouraged millions of supporters to donate small amounts to his primary campaign and to sign up for monthly charges to their credit cards. By the end of the 2012 campaign, the Obama online fundraising operation had raised $52 million[5] and had added more than 2 million new donors (who had not contributed in 2008).[6]

Figure 10-1 ▶ The Growth in Internet Use in the United States

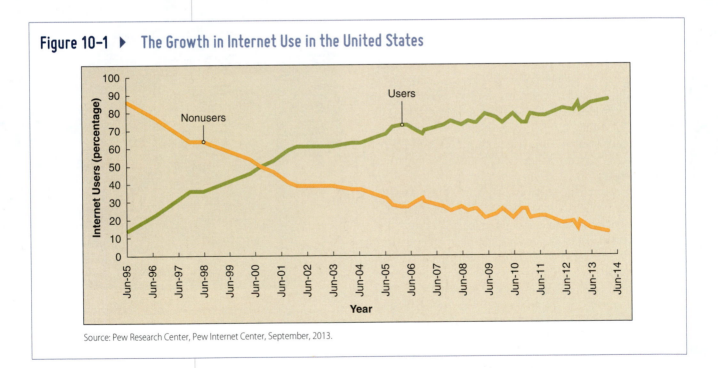

Source: Pew Research Center, Pew Internet Center, September, 2013.

4. "Demographics and Political Views of News Audiences," Pew Center for the People and the Press, September 27, 2012. http://www.people-press.org/2012/09/27/section-4-demographics-and-political-views-of-news-audiences
5. "Internet Tools in Political Campaigns," February 25, 2011. http://www.politicsandthenewmedia.commons.yale.edu/2011/02/25/internet-tools-in-political-campaigns/
6. Byron Tau, "Obama campaign final fundraising total: $1.1 billion." January 19, 2013. http://www.politico.com/story/2013/01/19

After establishing web pages, politicians took the lead from political commentators and began to add blogs to their websites. "**Blog**" comes from "web log," a regular updating of one's ideas at a specific website. Not all of the millions of blogs posted daily are political in nature, but many are, and they can have a dramatic influence on events, giving rise to the term **blogosphere politics**. Blogs can be highly specialized, highly political, and highly entertaining—and they are cheap. *The Washington Post* requires thousands of employees, many reams of paper, and tons of ink to generate its offline product and incurs delivery costs to get its papers to readers. The *Post* also hosts dozens of blogs and hires journalists to create these online columns, just as the official White House blog requires many writers and analysts from the current administration. A small blogging organization such as RealClearPolitics, however, can generate its political commentary with fewer than 10 employees.

Blogs have become well established and have expanded into the form of spoken words. Enter **podcasting**, so-called because the first online spoken blogs were downloaded onto iPods. Podcasts, though, can be heard on one's computer or downloaded onto any portable listening device and can also include videos. Hundreds of thousands of podcasts are now being generated every day. News outlets such as National Public Radio (NPR) offer dozens of options for listeners. People may express their views readily on YouTube. The protests in Ukraine could be viewed daily via cellphone videos uploaded to YouTube.

While politicians and news organizations debated how to best use the Internet and how to profit from it, young entrepreneurs were creating the applications known as social networks. Although most people thought that myspace, Facebook, and other sites were originally intended for personal use, it soon became clear to major advertisers, consumer companies, and the political world that they could have a presence on social networks as well. The Obama administration has pioneered the use of social media to keep in touch with supporters, voters, and the world. The official website for the president (http://www.whitehouse.gov) invites visitors to follow the president, his family, and the entire administration on Facebook; read his blog; to watch videos on YouTube; and to subscribe to the official Democratic National Committee Twitter feed.

Blog
A website or personal online space where an individual makes public his or her opinions, comments, or suggestions.

Blogosphere Politics
The online arena of politics where the comments of bloggers become news.

www.whitehouse.gov

Podcasting
A method of distributing multimedia files, such as audio or video files, for downloading onto mobile devices or personal computers.

did you know?
Facebook has more than 1.25 billion subscribers.

The Role of the Media in Our Society

■ **LO10.2:** Explain the functions of the media in American society.

Why does it matter if the media is practicing narrowcasting or that the circulation of major daily papers has fallen 30 percent since 1990?[7] A democracy can only exist if there are alternative sources of information for citizens. Privately owned media outlets such as *The New York Times* or *The Huffington Post* provide news reports and factual analysis for the public. Citizens must have resources available to them on which to cast an informed ballot.

---

7. State of the Media. http://wwwstateofthemedia.org/2012

Everyday Politics

 ## Facebook: How Did It Begin?

Facebook is interwoven into every aspect of life: pages are created and updated by individuals and entities from around the globe, from major companies such as General Motors and Procter and Gamble, to the president of the United States, sports stars, and local politicians and business owners. Eleven years ago, the creators of Facebook, Mark Zuckerberg, Andrew McCollum, Chris Hughes, and Dustin Moskovitz, were undergraduate students at Harvard who began a local website called "Facemash." The original website rated Harvard students on their attractiveness by comparing two student pictures side-by-side (without permission). The site was so popular that it crashed Harvard's website and the students were suspended.

The story of how Mark Zuckerberg and his partners developed the concept of Facebook was told in the Oscar-nominated film, *The Social Network*. Although the movie was criticized for its unflattering portrait of Zuckerberg and its raw portrayal of student life, it attracted wide audiences, made the "top ten" list of 2010 for many film critics, and was nominated for eight Oscars (and won three). At the heart of the movie is the claim by three of Zuckerberg's friends and fellow entrepreneurs that he stole the concept of Facebook from them and, in the process, deprived them of considerable profits. The friends and investors sue Zuckerberg in U.S. Federal Court while they are still undergraduates at Harvard. By the end of the film, all have settled with Zuckerberg (who remains CEO) for millions of dollars.

How did Facebook grow from an on-campus website to a lucrative company that could afford to buy off its partners with millions of dollars? *The Social Network* illustrates the speed at which the world of media is changing. Zuckerberg and his friends created a space where individuals could post personal updates and news, contact friends, and stay in touch with others before anyone even understood the concept of "big data" or the value that could be derived from shared information.

Similar to Facebook, news websites, bloggers, and YouTube have all flourished over the years. In most cases, these social media websites present issues that are far beyond government's policy-making abilities. Young entrepreneurs control this world. They have changed the way we shop, make friends, get news, and make news ourselves. As described in *The Social Network*, the only government involvement in the origins of Facebook took place in a courtroom. The case was settled out of court, allowing the expansion of a major media source without consideration of how individuals would share personal information with a corporation, as well as with people unknown to them.

Critical Thinking

1. *Do you think that there should be stronger protections for your personal data on social networking sites?*

2. *Most social networking sites have chosen to assist law enforcement in tracking individuals who are suspected of being sexual predators or scam artists without needing a court order to do so. Do you think this release of an individual's data is legal?*

The Media's Functions

The mass media perform several different functions in any country. In the United States, almost all of them can have political implications. Some are essential to the democratic process.

Entertainment. By far, the greatest number of radio and television hours are dedicated to entertaining the public. The battle for prime-time slots and cable ratings indicates how important successful entertainment is to the survival of networks and individual stations. In the past decade, the creation of reality shows such as *Survivor* and *The Biggest Loser*, as well as amateur talent shows including *American Idol* and *The Voice* underscores the importance of pure entertainment to the television industry.

Although there is no direct link between entertainment and politics, network dramas often introduce material that may be politically controversial and that may stimulate public discussion. Examples include the popular TV series *The West Wing* and the more recent political drama *House of Cards*, two shows that many people believe promote liberal political values. Shows such as *24* can be viewed as calls for greater use of force abroad. Made-for-TV movies have focused on many controversial topics, including AIDS, incest, and spousal abuse. In 2006, director Spike Lee produced an acclaimed four-part documentary on HBO, *When the Levees Broke: A Requiem in Four Acts*, about the destruction of New Orleans neighborhoods after Hurricane Katrina. The growing number of documentary channels on cable—Discovery, History, National Geographic, and others—often tackle topics such as global warming or other environmental issues that are on the political agenda.

Reporting the News.
A primary function of the mass media in all their forms is the reporting of news. The media provide words, pictures, sound, and video about events, facts, personalities, and ideas. The protections of the First Amendment aim to aid the free flow of news because information is an essential part of the democratic process. James Madison delivered incisive insight into the importance of the media when he stated: "A people who mean to be their own governors must arm themselves with the power knowledge gives. A popular government without popular information or the means of acquiring it is but a prologue to a farce or a tragedy or perhaps both."[8]

Identifying Public Problems.
The power of the media is important not only in revealing what the government is doing but also in determining what the government ought to do—in other words, in setting the **public agenda**. The mass media identify public issues, such as the danger posed by the shipment of oil and other inflammatory materials by rail without proper identification or safeguards. Such news stories may lead to government agencies, such as the Environmental Protection Agency (EPA), issuing new rules for such transport, or to Congress holding a hearing on the issue. American journalists have established a long tradition of uncovering and exposing public wrongdoing, corruption, and bribery.

Investigative "stories" or shows may lead to a deeper examination of policy alternatives. Public policy is often complex and difficult to make entertaining, but programs devoted to public policy are increasingly being scheduled for prime-time television. Most networks produce shows with a "news magazine" format that include segments on poverty, homelessness, disability claims, or online privacy.

Socializing New Generations.
As mentioned in Chapter 6, the media play a significant role in the political socialization of the younger generation, as well as

Public Agenda
Issues that are perceived by the political community as meriting public attention and governmental action.

---

8. James Madison, "Letter to W.T. Barry" (August 4, 1822), in Gaillard P. Hung, ed., *The Writings of James Madison* 103 (1910).

On February 13, 2014, a Norfolk Southern train derailed in Vandergrift, Pennsylvania, spilling heavy Canadian crude oil from the tanker cars and reigniting the debate over the safety of train transport versus pipeline transport of oil to American refineries.

Jason cohn/Reuters/Landov

immigrants to this country. Through the transmission of historical information (which is sometimes fictionalized), the presentation of American culture, as well as the portrayal of the diverse regions and groups found within the United States, the media teach the nation's youth and immigrants what it means to be an "American." TV talk shows, such as *The Ellen Degeneres Show*, focus on popular culture, while shows such as *Dr. Phil* sometimes focus on more controversial issues such as abortion or assisted suicide. Many children's shows are designed not only to entertain young viewers but also to instruct them in the traditional moral values of American society. Popular public television programs for children such as *Sesame Street* seek to teach the values of tolerance and respect for others.

As more young Americans turn to the Internet for entertainment, they are also finding an increasing amount of social and political information there. America's youth are the Internet generation. They download movies and music, find information for writing assignments, gather news (perhaps unknowingly), visit social networking sites, and increasingly become involved in political campaigns and interact online with those campaigns.

Providing a Political Forum. As part of their news function, the media also provide a political forum for leaders and the public. Candidates for office use news reporting to sustain interest in their campaigns, while officeholders use the media to gain support for their policies or to present an image of leadership. Today, almost all print newspapers also have an online edition where individuals can post comments on the news or on particular columns.

Making Profits. Except for the Corporation for Public Broadcasting and local public radio stations, the news media in the United States are private, for-profit corporate enterprises. One of their goals is to make profits for expansion and for dividends to the stockholders who own the companies. In general, profits are made as a result of charging for advertising.

For the most part, the media depend on advertisers to obtain revenues to make profits. Media outlets that do not succeed in generating

did you know?

Six media corporations control 90 percent of what Americans read, watch, or hear.

sufficient revenues from advertising either go bankrupt or are sold. Dwindling profits have necessitated cuts to newsroom staffs, so news organizations have fewer resources available to check the facts in the stories they report. After the disappearance of Malaysian Airlines flight MH370 in the spring of 2014, the government of Malaysia paid for positive stories to be spun from several news outlets.[9] Short-staffed newsrooms (and the pressure to report first) contribute to the airing and printing of such erroneous reports.

With the explosion in social networking websites and other Internet media, a new source of revenue has been invented for the owners of these sites. If an individual does not opt for complete privacy for his or her searches on Google, for example, the individual's personal data, including location, favorite searches, and possible personal demographics, become part of what is known is "big data." Google, Facebook, and all other similar providers tailor advertising to the user's Internet searches. In addition, they sell the data to advertisers so that the individual can be reached through email or Facebook. If you "like" a particular website on Facebook, for example, you may receive advertising for that website whenever you sign into Facebook. Numerous questions about how this data is used and sold have emerged. As yet, there are no clear answers about the ownership of personal data.

Television and Political Campaigns

■ **LO10.3:** Discuss the impact of all forms of the media on political campaigning.

Media influence on the political system is most obvious during political campaigns. News coverage of a single event, such as the results of the Iowa caucuses or the New Hampshire primary, may be the most important factor in labeling a candidate as the front-runner in a presidential campaign. Almost all national political figures, starting with the president, plan every public appearance and statement to attract media coverage.

Because television is still the primary news source for the majority of Americans, candidates and their consultants spend much of their time devising strategies that use television to their benefit. Three types of TV coverage are generally employed in campaigns for the presidency and other offices: advertising, management of news coverage, and campaign debates.

Advertising

Perhaps one of the most effective political ads of all time was a 30-second spot created by President Lyndon B. Johnson's media adviser in 1964. In this ad, a little girl stood in a field of daisies. As she held a daisy, she pulled the petals off and quietly counted to herself—when when she reached number 10, a deep bass voice cut in and began a countdown. When the voice intoned "zero," the unmistakable mushroom cloud of an atomic bomb began to fill the screen and President Johnson's voice was heard: "These are the stakes. To make a world in which all of God's children can live, or to go into the dark. We must either love each other or we must die." At the end of the commercial, the message read, "Vote for President Johnson on November 3." This ad, which was withdrawn within a few days of its original airing, put a powerful suggestion in the viewer's

---

9. Project for Excellence in Journalism, "State of the News Media, 2013: An Annual Report on American Journalism. Pew Research Center's Project for Excellence in Journalism. http://www.stateofthemedia.org/2013/overview-5/

The "Daisy Girl" ad has continued to be one of the most famous of all political advertisements. Here we see the child picking petals from the daisy while the voice-over begins the countdown to an atomic bomb explosion.

mind: Electing Barry Goldwater might bring us to nuclear war.[10] This spot is an example of negative advertising and also demonstrates how a political ad evokes strong emotions, thus influencing the voter.

Since the daisy girl advertisement, campaign advertising has blossomed. In the 2008 primary campaign, Hillary Clinton's campaign ran a television spot showing the president's red telephone ringing in the middle of the night with the voiceover asking, "When the phone rings at 3:00 a.m., who will answer it?" The ad suggested that her opponent, Barack Obama, was too inexperienced to deal with a foreign policy crisis. Negative ads are often sponsored by outside groups rather than by the candidate because the candidate's campaign does not want to appear too negative.

Political advertising can also work to inspire supporters and to encourage them to share their views with others. In 2008, a campaign ad for Barack Obama ran only on YouTube. Rapper will.i.am created an ad based on Obama's concession speech after he lost the New Hampshire primary to Hillary Clinton. The music video, filmed in black and white, became a huge hit on the Internet, with more than 22 million views within a month of its production.[11] Seen only on the Internet, it reached young voters and reaffirmed or generated their support for Obama.

Political advertising is increasingly important for the profitability of television station owners. Hearst-Argyle Television obtains well over 10 percent of its revenues from political ads during an election year. Political advertising, however, is not restricted to television. Online political advertising has proliferated. While estimates vary on total spending, the Obama and Romney campaigns reported spending at least $130 million on Internet advertising in 2012 (see the screen capture for an example).

IT'S JUST NOT GETTING BETTER

Mitt Romney and Bain Capital made millions for themselves and then closed this steel plant.

Management of News Coverage

Using political advertising to get a message across to the public is a very expensive tactic. Coverage by the news media, however, is free; it simply demands that the campaign ensure that coverage takes place. In recent years, campaign managers have shown increasing sophistication in creating newsworthy events for journalists to cover. As Doris Graber notes, "[t]o keep a favorable image of their candidates in front of the public, campaign managers arrange newsworthy events to familiarize potential voters with their candidates' best aspects."[12]

The campaign staff uses several methods to try to influence the quantity and type of coverage the campaign receives. First, the campaign staff understands the technical aspects of media coverage—camera angles, necessary equipment, timing, and deadlines—and plans political events to accommodate the press. The campaign organization is aware that political reporters and their sponsors—networks or newspapers—are in competition for the best stories

10. As quoted in, Kevin Swint, *The Mudslingers: the 25 Dirtiest Campaigns of All Time*, New York: Greenwood Press, 2008, p. 33.
11. Brian Stelter, "Finding Political News Online, the Young Pass It On," *The New York Times*, March 37, 2008.
12. Doris Graber and Johanna Duanway, *Mass Media and American Politics*, 9th ed. (Washington, DC: Congressional Quarterly Press, 2015), p. 320.

and can be manipulated through the granting of favors, such as a personal interview with the candidate. Campaign managers coordinate events in time for the evening news and work to convince reporters that the event is worth covering.

Today, the art of putting the appropriate **spin** on a story or event is highly developed. Each candidate's or elected official's press advisers, often referred to as **spin doctors**, try to convince journalists that their interpretations of political events are factual. Each political campaign, and the president's own Office of Communication, sends emails and faxes to all the major media, setting out their own version of an event virtually in real time. More recently, journalists have begun to report on the different spins used by candidates and elected officials to try to manipulate news coverage. In a recent dialogue on MSNBC's *Morning Joe* television show, executive editor Richard Wolffe and political analyst Chuck Todd discussed the Obama administration's spin on the Affordable Care Act. In regard to the difficulties in the roll-out of the health care website, Todd noted, "They were so worried about the image and the spin, that they've ended up creating their own PR problem."[13]

Campaign Debates

Debates have been a part of political campaigning in the United States for centuries, but the power of television has greatly amplified their importance, especially for presidential elections. After the first televised presidential debate in 1960, in which John F. Kennedy, a young senator from Massachusetts, took on Vice President Richard Nixon, candidates became aware of the great potential of television for changing the momentum of a campaign. In general, challengers have much more to gain from debating than do incumbents. Challengers hope that the incumbent will make a mistake in the debate and undermine a "presidential" image. Incumbent presidents are loath to debate their challengers because it puts their opponents on an equal footing with them, but the debates have become so widely anticipated that it is difficult for an incumbent to refuse.

Debates can affect the outcome of a race. In 2012, three presidential debates were held along with one vice presidential debate. Sponsored by a nonpartisan national commission, these debates attracted huge audiences. As is the rule in presidential debates, the news media emphasized the demeanor of the candidates in the debates more so than what they actually said about the issues at hand. The Republican nominee Mitt Romney used the first debate to establish himself as a strong, reassuring, yet assertive candidate, while President Obama seemed detached from the debate and uncharacteristically subdued. A Gallup poll taken after the debate showed Romney as the victor by a large margin (72 percent to 20 percent).[14] In the second debate both candidates were aggressive and often interrupted each other. President Obama was voted the winner of this debate (51 percent to 38 percent).[15] The final debate saw the president defend his policies and undermine Romney's credentials to be commander in chief. Romney remained assured, but a final Gallup poll declared President Obama the victor (56 percent to 33 percent).[16]

Spin
An interpretation of campaign events or election results that is favorable to the candidate's campaign strategy.

Spin Doctors
A political campaign advisor who tries to convince journalists of the truth of a particular interpretation of events.

---

13. Evan McMurry, "MSNBC Panel on Obama Admin.: 'So Worried about Spin, They Created Own PR Problem," October 30, 2013, http://mediaite.com/msnbc-panel-on-admin-so-worried-about–spin-they-created-own-problem/

14. The Gallup Poll, October 8, 2012. http://www.gallup.com/poll/158393/viewers-deem-obama-winner-third-debate.aspx

15. The Gallup Poll, October 12, 2012. http://www.gallup.com/poll/158237/obama-judged-winner-second-debate.aspx

16. The Gallup Poll, October 25, 2012. http://www.gallup.com/poll/158393/viewers-deem-obama-winner-third-debate.aspx.

Zuma Press, Inc/Alamy

Mitt Romney, the
Republican candidate,
listens as President Obama
makes a point during one of
the 2012 presidential
debates.

did you know?

The average length of a quote, or sound bite, for a candidate has decreased from 49 seconds in 1968 to less than nine seconds today.

After the debate, each candidate had a room where their spokespeople and surrogates could "spin" the debate and explain in great detail why his or her candidate prevailed. New polls released within a day or two measured whether either candidate had gained an advantage with his performance in the debate. The Romney-Ryan team gained momentum from the debates and benefited from being on equal footing with the president and vice president. The debates also provided extended exposure to a national television audience for the first time. The Republican gains among voters, however, were overcome by the Get Out the Vote effort conducted by the Democrats on election day.

Although debates are justified publicly as an opportunity for the voters to find out how candidates differ on the issues, candidates want to capitalize on the power of the media to project an image. They view the debate as a strategic opportunity to improve their own images or to point out their opponents' failures. Candidates also know that the morning-after interpretation of the debate by the news media may play a crucial role in how the public perceives them. In today's landscape, candidates also know that their performances will be broadcast on the Internet or posted on YouTube and that bloggers will add their own interpretations to those of the mainstream media.

Political Campaigns and the Internet

Political campaigns began using the Internet for promoting their candidates during the 2004 election campaign. At that time, when two-thirds of all American adults were using the Internet, about 7 percent of those logged onto online campaign activities. By 2008, the Obama campaign perfected the use of the campaign website to contact potential donors, streamlining the process for submitting modest donations. After donating (or merely logging on to Obama's website), supporters were subscribed to an email list; they subsequently received missives from the new president, his campaign manager, and sometimes their own senator.

The Internet was used by both presidential candidates in 2012, not only to advertise the candidates' positions, solicit donations, and offer podcasts of speeches and debates, but also to target messages. Candidates sought email lists sorted by age, gender, and other demographic variables. They then emailed messages to targeted groups to encourage support. Members of union households received, for example, messages about lowering the number of jobs going overseas. Candidates used the Internet to recruit volunteers for Get Out the Vote campaigns aimed at stimulating increased voter turnout on election day. They also used email and blogs to instruct citizens on how to participate in the political caucuses and how to persuade others to support their candidate of choice.

The 2012 Obama reelection campaign imagined new ways to find voters and encourage them to support the president's campaign. Convinced that using data from voting files could help the campaign hold on to its supporters—while also gaining new voters—the campaign funded a massive data gathering operation and hired more than 60 analysts to plan the new program. The Obama team, housed in a windowless space known as "The Cave," contracted with data processing firms, cable TV analysts, and political information brokers to create the plan for the campaign.[17] With a national list of registered voters in hand and a fairly accurate view of who had voted for the president in 2008, the team planned to **microtarget** (focus on specific individuals, types of households, or neighborhoods) voters to assure their votes.

To plan their television advertising campaign, analysts linked the TV-viewing habits of particular types of households and then bought ads only during programs popular with their chosen demographics. They ran specific types of ads microtargeted to unique groups, such as Hispanics and females, on television programs they knew from cable box data were watched in those specific households

As election day approached, both campaigns ramped up their use of the Internet to encourage support for the candidates. The Obama campaign used Facebook to rally supporters to contact their friends in swing states and remind them to vote for the president. The campaign did try to match voting records with Facebook pages to find more supporters.[18] The Internet and wireless technologies proved invaluable on election day. Get Out the Vote provided wireless communication to the "block walkers" canvassing neighborhoods to send voters to the polls. They received information from the campaign office about households before they knocked on a door and could report immediately if their visit brought out a voter.

Today, the campaign staff of every candidate running for a significant political office includes an Internet campaign component—a professional firm hired to create and maintain the campaign website, blog, Facebook page, and Twitter account(s), or else an in-house team. As the work of the Obama team has become well-known, political operatives at the highest levels of the political parties are thinking about the next campaign and how to use the Internet and advertising in new ways. The lists of voters compiled and verified by the Obama campaign are a goldmine for future Democratic candidates, but it is not clear who will gain possession of those lists or the data systems created by the campaign in 2012.

Interest groups, corporations, and political advocacy groups have watched these political uses of the Internet expand and will change their own promotional efforts as a result. Prior to elections, various groups engage in issue advocacy from their websites. At little or no cost, they can promote positions taken by favored candidates and persuade voters. It is no accident that Facebook messages from these groups end up on your own personal page—your interest in their mission has been sold as data by Facebook.

Microtarget
To use demographic and consumer data to identify individuals or small groups of people who will receive specific advertising messages.

did you know?
Half of Americans who contributed to the 2012 presidential campaigns did so online or through email.

---

17. Sasha Issenberg, "How President Obama's campaign used big data to rally individual voters, Part I," *MIT Technology Review*, December 16, 2012.
18. Lois Beckett, "Everything We Know (So Far) About Obama's Big Data Tactics," ProPublica, November 29, 2012. http://www.propublica.org/article/everyting-we-knwo-so-far-about-obamas-big-data-operation

The Media's Impact on the Voters

■ **LO10.4:** Identify ways in which the media influence voters.

The question of exactly how much influence the media have on voting behavior is difficult to answer. Generally, most individuals watch television, read newspapers, or log on to the Internet with certain preconceived ideas about political issues and candidates. These attitudes and opinions act as a kind of perceptual screen that filters out information that makes people feel uncomfortable or that does not fit with their own ideas.

Selective Attention
The tendency for individuals to only pay attention to information that reinforces their held beliefs.

Voters watch campaign commercials and news about political campaigns with "**selective attention**"—that is, they tend to watch those commercials that support the candidates that they already favor and pay more attention to news stories about these candidates. This selectivity also affects their perceptions of the content of a news story or commercial and whether it is remembered. Recent research suggests that for the highly partisan voter, watching his or her preferred political news channel does not enhance partisanship, but watching news from a channel with an opposing view *will* increase the viewer's hostility to that view.[19]

Candidates and their campaign managers have long thought that the media have the most influence on those persons who have not formed an opinion about political candidates or issues. Studies have shown that the flurry of television commercials and debates immediately before election day has the greatest impact on those voters who are truly undecided and, for the most part, are not engaged with the political system. Few voters who have already formed their opinions change their minds under the influence of the media. On the basis of these observations, campaigns increase their advertising at the last moment, often producing new advertising aimed at the undecided voter or, in the case of the 2012 Obama campaign, microtargeting specific groups and households.

The Media and Government Control

■ **LO10.5:** Demonstrate an understanding of the relationship between government and all media sources.

The mass media not only wield considerable power when it comes to political campaigns, but they also, in one way or another, can wield power over the affairs of government and over government officials. Considerable tension exists between the media and government. The influx of unaccompanied children across the Mexico/United States border in 2014 presented the media with many opportunities to discuss immigration policies and to seek information about how the undocumented children were to be processed by the government. Federal officials restricted access to the children to a few members of Congress. Protesters from both sides were showcased in the media.

Prepackaged News

In recent years, the public learned that the George W. Bush administration had spent millions of dollars on public relations, including "news" programs that were often created specifically to be rebroadcast on television. In 2005, the Bush

---

19. Kevin Arceneaux and Martin Johnson, *Changing Minds or Changing Channels? Partisan News in an Age of Choice,* Chicago: University of Chicago Press, 2013.

administration acknowledged that it paid several conservative commentators to write in support of administration-backed programs

Is the use of taxpayer dollars to create prepackaged news, such as the video created by the Bush administration, legal? Some argue that it is because the government is not forcing anyone to broadcast this "covert" propaganda. Others, however, question the ethical underpinnings of government advocacy at the expense of both unbiased journalism and taxpayers' dollars. Members of the Bush and Obama administrations, as well as the national party committees, perfected the art of sending out press releases, fact sheets, Tweets, and faxes detailing important "facts" to media outlets. Are these unbiased or are they written to support a viewpoint on the issue?

The Media and the Executive Branch

The relationship between the media and the president usually is reciprocal: each needs the other to thrive in the political arena. Because of this codependency, both the media and the president work hard to exploit one another. The media need news to report, and the president needs coverage. The political staff of the White House aims for constant and positive exposure of the president in the media. Presidential events and speeches are planned to the extent that the effort has been nicknamed, "the presidential spectacle."

In the United States, the prominence of the president is accentuated by a **White House press corps** that is assigned full-time to cover the presidency. These reporters even have a lounge in the White House where they spend their days, waiting for a story to break. Most of the time, they simply wait for the daily or twice-daily briefings conducted by the president's **press secretary**. Because of the press corps' physical proximity to the president, the chief executive cannot even take a brief stroll around the Rose Garden without it becoming news. Perhaps no other nation allows the press such access to its highest government official. Consequently, no other democratic nation has its airwaves and print media so laden with trivia regarding the personal lives of the chief executive and his or her family.

One of the first presidents to make truly effective use of the media was President Franklin D. Roosevelt. He brought new spirit to a demoralized country and led it through the Great Depression with his radio "fireside chats." In 1933, his announcement on the reorganization of the banks calmed a jittery nation and prevented the collapse of the banking industry. His famous "a day that will live in infamy" Pearl Harbor speech, following the Japanese attack on the U.S. Pacific fleet on December 7, 1941, mobilized the nation for World War II.

President Obama's White House has revolutionized the use of the media to spread the president's message. While the president is famous for his skill in rhetoric, he favors more intimate and controlled interviews with the major news anchors of virtually every network. The White House website is packed with position papers, speeches, presidential memos, and photo galleries. From the website, citizens can follow the president and his family on Twitter, Facebook, YouTube, and LinkedIn, as well as download speeches and video via iTunes.

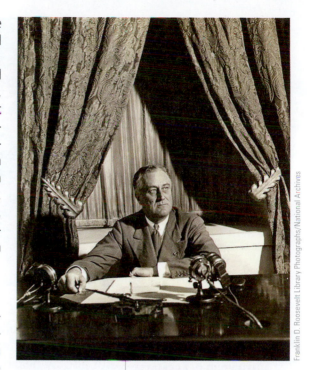

Franklin D. Roosevelt Library Photographs/National Archives

President Franklin D. Roosevelt prepares for his first "fireside chat" in 1933. In this first radio address to the nation, Roosevelt addressed the banking crisis and announced the steps he would take to end it.

White House Press Corps
The reporters assigned full-time to cover the presidency.

Press Secretary
The presidential staff member responsible for handling White House media relations and communications.

did you know?

Franklin D. Roosevelt held approximately 1,000 press conferences during his terms as president.

CBS Evening News anchor Scott Pelley interviews President Obama in the White House in September 2013. Such one-on-one interviews present the president in a more informal setting but also allow him to present his own views on policy.

AP Images/CBS News

CONNECT WITH YOUR CLASSMATES

MindTap™ for American Government

Access the Media and Politics Forum: Discussion–Influence of the Media on Policy.

Agenda Setting
The process by which the media identifies the issues the public should be concerned about.

Priming
The process by which the media suggest the importance of an issue.

Framing
The presentation of an issue by the media which influences how audiences understand it.

Setting the Public Agenda. It is clear that the media play an important part in setting the public agenda, not only by pointing out public issues to elected officials but also by helping individuals identify the most important problems facing the nation. The media raise interest in particular problems and then public officials begin investigations in order to report back to constituents and the public. **Agenda setting** may also refer to the ability of the media to influence which issues the public thinks are most important. Dozens of studies have examined just how the media makes problems and events more salient in the perception of the viewer or reader.[20]

Evidence strongly suggests that the public problems which receive the greatest media treatment will be cited by the public in contemporary surveys as the most important. Agenda setting at the individual level is closely linked with the concept of **priming**, the suggestion of standards to the viewer about the importance of an issue, especially in judging the effectiveness of political officials.[21] If a series of stories shared in various media outlets focuses on an increase in the need for food stamps, readers and viewers will likely first decide to pay more attention to the issue and then to judge whether their elected officials are doing enough to alleviate hunger in their own town. The media may also affect an individual's view of social and political issues through its **framing** of an issue. Framing refers to how the issue is actually presented to the audience: in this example, is hunger presented as a problem mostly affecting children in schools, or is the use of food stamps presented an example of fraud in government?

Although the media do not make policy decisions, they *do* influence the policy issues that will be decided—an important part of the political process. Because those who control the media are not elected representatives of the people, the agenda-setting role of the media necessarily is a controversial one. For example, when former Central Intelligence Agency (CIA) and National Security Agency

---

20. Aeron Delwiche suggests in his article, "Agenda-setting, opinion leadership, and the world of Web logs," that there have been more than 350 studies of agenda-setting. *First Monday*, December 5, 2005. http://www.firstmonday.dk/ojs/index.php/fm/article/view/1300/1220

21. See Dietram A. Scheufele and David Tewksbury, "Framing, Agenda Setting and Priming: The evolution of Three Media Effects Models," *Journal of Communication* 57 (2007): see pp. 9–20 for a review of the use of these terms in media research.

(NSA) contractor Edward Snowden decided to publicize some of the files that he had hacked from the NSA, he did not approach *The New York Times* because he feared that the *Times* would contact the government instead of publishing his releases. Instead, he found a reporter at *The Guardian* in Great Britain who was willing to run the story. Snowden's findings led a number of American news organizations to begin investigating the extent to which the NSA was recording cellphone and email messages of Americans. This put the question of such "eavesdropping" on the agenda of President Obama, who formed a blue ribbon committee to study the practice.

Because we know that the media can spotlight a political issue and has the power to stimulate the audience into concern and action, the relationship between government and media agenda setting is complex. Officials realize that media coverage can highlight difficult issues and make the officials themselves look less effective. Elected officials and their staffs may also try to control the agenda by identifying problems themselves and trying to frame the issues in a way that benefits their own agendas. Media then need to decide whether to accept a government interpretation of the issue or not.

Investigative Reporting. Most major newspapers and many television networks devote resources to investigative reporting. By finding a problem with a public policy or uncovering an official's wrongdoing, the media are alerting the public to important political information. Furthermore, the results of investigative reporting can have a very important impact on officeholders and, in the best case, bring about change for the better. Richard Nixon barely avoided impeachment and resigned from office due to the investigative reporting of Bob Woodward and Carl Bernstein of *The Washington Post*. In 2012, *The Associated Press* won a Pulitzer Prize for the investigative reporting of Matt Apuzzo, Adam Goldman, Eileen Sullivan and Chris Hawley and their reporting on the New York City Police Department's undercover surveillance of Muslim mosques and community activities.[22] The secret police program, which was aimed at exposing terrorist activities, had proceeded with neither legal authority nor warrants for its endeavors.

COMPARE WITH YOUR PEERS
MindTap™ for American Government

Access the Media and Politics Forum: Polling Activity–Fair and Balanced Media.

Government Regulation of the Media

The United States champions freedom of the press, but regulation of the media does exist, particularly regulation of electronic media.

The First Amendment does not mention electronic media, which did not exist at the time the Bill of Rights was written. The government has assumed much more control over communication via radio, television, and wireless connections than other forms of media, as those connections are made through public airspace via frequencies The Federal Communications Commission (FCC) was created to distribute and regulate the frequencies which, in a legal sense, belong to the nation as a whole. As technologies advanced from radio to broadcast television to wireless communications, the FCC has, from time to time, auctioned off more frequencies, even as they held back many frequencies for government use only.

Controlling Ownership of the Media

One of the goals of the FCC (as mandated by Congress) has been to maintain competition in the communications industry. Individuals should have the opportunity to hear or watch many different channels, read more than one

---

22. The Pulitzer Prizes, "Investigative Reporting," http://www.pulitzer.org/bycat/Investigative-reporting

newspaper, and access multiple viewpoints. In 1996, Congress passed a piece of legislation that had far-reaching implications for the communications industry: the Telecommunications Act. The act amended the Communications Act of 1934, which created the FCC and transferred regulation of interstate telephone services to the FCC. The Telecommunications Act of 1996 included the Internet within the broadcasting definition, and sought to deregulate converging broadcasting and telecommunications markets. A single corporation, such as Time Warner Cable or The Walt Disney Company (which owns ABC), can offer long-distance and local telephone services, cable television, satellite television, and Internet services, as well as libraries of films and entertainment. The Act opened the door to competition and led to greater options for consumers, who now can choose among multiple competitors for all of these services delivered to the home. At the same time, it launched a race among competing companies to control media ownership.

Increased Media Concentration

Congress and the FCC have tried to create a communications market which allows for competing voices. One measure of a conglomerate's impact is "audience reach," or the percentage of the national viewing public that has access to the conglomerate's outlets. The FCC places an upper limit on audience reach, known as the "audience-reach cap." In 2004, the FCC raised the national audience-reach cap from 35 percent to 45 percent and allowed a corporation to own a newspaper and a television station in the same market. Congress rebelled against this new rule, however, and pushed the national audience-reach cap back to 39 percent.[23] Nevertheless, a corporation can still own up to three TV stations in its largest market. There are only a few independent news operations left in the entire country.

This concentration has led to the disappearance of localism in the news. Costly locally produced news cannot be shown anywhere except in its local market. In contrast, the costs of producing a similar show for national broadcast can be amortized over millions and millions of viewers and paid for by higher revenues from national advertisers. Another concern, according to former media mogul Ted Turner, is that the rise of media conglomerates may lead to a decline in democratic debate.[24] The emergence of independent news websites, blogs, and podcasts help serve to remedy this problem. Consequently, the increased concentration of traditional media news organizations may not seem as worrisome as it did in the not-too-distant past.

Government Control of Content

The United States Supreme Court has often been slow to extend free speech and free press guarantees to new media. In 1915, the Court held that "as a matter of common sense," free-speech protections did not apply to cinema. Only in 1952 did the Court find that motion pictures were covered by the First Amendment.[25] In contrast, the Court extended full protection to the Internet almost immediately by striking down provisions of the 1996 Telecommunications Act.[26] Cable TV also received broad protection in 2000.[27] See this chapter's *Beyond Our Borders* feature for more information.

---

23. Federal Communications Commission, "Rules Adopted in the Quadrennial Review Order," http://transition.fcc.gov/ownership/rules.html
24. Ted Turner, "My Beef with Big Media," *Washington Monthly* (July–August, 2004). http://www.washingtonmonthly.com/features/2004/0407.turner.html
25. *Joseph Burstyn, Inc. v. Wilson*, 343 U.S. 495 (1952).
26. *Reno v. American Civil Liberties Union*, 521 U.S. 844 (1997).
27. *United States v. Playboy Entertainment Group*, 529 U.S. 803 (2000).

Control of Broadcasting

While the Supreme Court has held that the First Amendment is relevant to radio and television, it has never extended full protection to these media. The Court has used several arguments to justify this stance, the first of which was the scarcity of broadcast frequencies. The Court later held that the government could restrict "indecent" programming based on the "pervasive" presence of broadcasting in the home.[28] On this basis, the FCC was granted the authority to fine broadcasters for indecency or profanity.

Indecency in broadcasting became a major issue in 2004. In the first three months of that year, the FCC levied fines that exceeded those imposed in the previous nine years combined. Triggering incidents included the commentary of Howard Stern on the radio and Janet Jackson's infamous "wardrobe malfunction" at the Super Bowl. The FCC asserted its right to regulate indecency even on cable channels. In 2012, the Supreme Court heard two cases from the Fox network and, in both cases, the Court set aside the fines, holding that the FCC had not given fair notice of the change in FCC policy.[29] While the decision did not limit the power of the FCC to fine stations for indecency, neither did it enhance that power. Most observers believed that the FCC needed to rethink its policies.

Not only does the FCC enforce regulations in regard to indecent language or images in the media, but it also has the authority to issue fines for other violations of law or its regulations. In 2014, the FCC fined Viacom, ESPN, and NBCU $1.9 million for broadcasting advertisements for a movie that featured the sound of the Emergency Broadcast Alert System warning siren. FCC policy prohibits the broadcasting of that signal unless it is a test or a real emergency. Other fines have been issued in recent years for a station being silent on the air for too long, for stations failing to properly advertise job openings to their community, and for not airing sponsorship identification properly.[30]

Government Control of the Media during the Second Gulf War.

During the First Gulf War in 1991, the U.S. government was strongly criticized for not providing accurate information to the media. Stung by this criticism, the Bush administration tried a two-pronged strategy during the Second Gulf War in 2003. Every day, reporters at the central command post in Qatar were able to hear briefings from top commanders. (Reporters complained, though, that they did not hear enough about the true progress of the war.) The administration also allowed more than 500 journalists to travel with the combat forces as "embedded" journalists. Reports from the field were very favorable to the military. This was understandable, given that the journalists quickly identified with the troops and their difficulties. The Bush administration, however, was unable to control reports from foreign media.

The Government's Attempt to Control the Media after the September 11, 2001 Attacks.

Certainly, since September 11, 2001, government secrecy has increased, sometimes (apparently) with the public's acceptance. Senator Patrick Leahy (D-VT) has argued that the First Amendment would have trouble winning ratification today if it were proposed as a constitutional amendment. He based this assertion on a Knight Foundation survey which found that almost 40 percent

---

28. *FCC v. Pacifica Foundation*, 438 U.S. 230 (1978). In this case, the Court banned seven swear words (famously used by comedian George Carlin) during hours when children could hear them.
29. *FCC v. Fox Television Stations*, 132 U.S. 2307.
30. For an up-to-date report of FCC fines and penalties, take a look at the Broadcast Law Blog, http://www.broadcast lawblog.com/articles/fcc-fines

Beyond Our Borders

Government-Controlled Media Abroad

The First Amendment to the Constitution guarantees freedom of expression in the United States. While there are some restrictions on what Americans say on the radio and television, or even publish, those restrictions are few. With the growth of the Internet, and extensive use of blogs and web-based news services, there are even more opportunities for the free exchange of ideas in the United States and other democracies. This is not so in many other countries today, even though their constitutions may also guarantee freedom of expression.

CONTROLLING THE NEWS IN IRAN

In many nations, the government restricts news in order to maintain control over its population. In a nation such as Iran, there are no independent newspapers. Government censors check the content of all newspapers and broadcasts before they are made public. Independent journalists try to report the news on the Internet, but the government has technology to block the web as well if the stories are not supportive of the government's position. While there has been some improvement in journalistic freedom under President Hassan Rouhani, the government continues to arrest and detain journalists, writers, and poets. In January, 2014, Iranian poet Hashem Shaabani was executed by hanging for, in the words of the government, "waging war on God."*

THE RUSSIANS HAVE LOST MANY PRESS FREEDOMS, TOO

After the end of communism in Russia, a thriving independent press arose. Russians could read or hear all sorts of political views. Since Vladimir Putin reclaimed the office of president, most opposition journalists have been silenced, in one way or another. Privately owned television stations have been eliminated and independent radio stations are often blocked. In early 2014, as Russia began to move into Crimea, an eastern area of Ukraine, the Russian "federal media regulator" blocked several independent online news sources because, in the eyes of the government, they were violating a new law that prohibits any call for an unsanctioned mass gathering.**

The Russian government's control of their nation's media was extended quickly into Crimea in 2014. As soon as Russian troops were posted at Ukrainian military bases in that region, all Crimean television station signals were immediately replaced by Russian television broadcasts. The producers, journalists, and technical staff watched in amazement as their signal was replaced by a Russian station.***

THERE ARE OTHER EXAMPLES OF COURSE

In the present day, no government is more adept at stifling free expression than the regime of North Korea. The country's dictator, Kim Jong-un, strives to deprive North Korea's inhabitants of any knowledge of the outside world. Radios are rigged so that they can only tune in to government channels. To a much lesser degree, there are various restrictions on freedom of the press in Cuba, Egypt, Lebanon, Myanmar (formerly Burma), Saudi Arabia, Syria, Venezuela, and Yemen. In short, the government controls the media in countries in which democracy is either unknown or weak.

For Critical Analysis

1. *Has the evolution of media technology made it easier for a government to control the news or more difficult?*

2. *How could journalists continue to provide the news under a government crackdown?*

*Harriett Staff, "Iranian Poet and Activist Hashem Shaabani Executed," February 6, 2014. http://www.poetryfoundation.org/harriet/2014/02/iranian-poet-and-activits-hashem-shaabani-executed/
** "Kremlin Tightens Censorship as Tensions Over Ukraine Increase," March 14, 2014.http://www.freedomhouse.org/article/kermlin-tightens-censorship-as-tensions-over-Ukraine-Increase
*** Damien McElroy, "Russian TV swamps airwaves in Crimea propaganda war," Daily Telegraph, March13, 2014. http://www.telegraph.co.uk

Leroy Francis/hemis.fr/Getty Images

of 110,000 high school students believed that newspapers should have to get "government approval" of news articles before they are published.

The charter for the Department of Homeland Security, created soon after the September 11 terrorist attacks, includes a provision that allows certain groups to stamp "critical infrastructure information" on the top of documents when they submit information to Homeland Security. This information might include the maps of waterlines or the plans of nuclear power plants. The public has no right to see this information. Additionally, more and more government documents have been labeled "secret" so that they do not have to be revealed to the public. Despite such measures, since the war on terror and the second war in Iraq started, there have been numerous intelligence leaks to the press, chief among them Edward Snowden's revelations about NSA surveillance. The tension between needed intelligence secrecy and the public's "right to know" continues to create both legal and military problems.

The Public's Right to Media Access

Does the public have a right to **media access**? Both the FCC and the courts have gradually taken the stance that citizens do have a right of access to the media, particularly the electronic media. The argument is that because the airwaves are public, the government has the right to dictate how they are used. Congress could, for example, pass a law requiring the broadcast networks to provide free airtime to candidates, as is the case in some European nations. Senator John McCain of Arizona, a major proponent of campaign-finance reform, proposed legislation that would provide such free airtime. Broadcast networks that make bigger profits in election years quietly oppose such a law.

Regardless of the preferences of the government or broadcast corporations, technology has given citizens the tools to make their voices heard. YouTube hosts thousands of videos produced by ordinary citizens: some opine on policy problems, while others document issues such as pollution and dangerous traffic

Media Access
The public's right of access to the media. The Federal Communications Commission and the courts have gradually taken the stance that citizens do have a right to media access.

Figure 10-2 ▶ How Much Bias Do People Find in the News? (percentage)

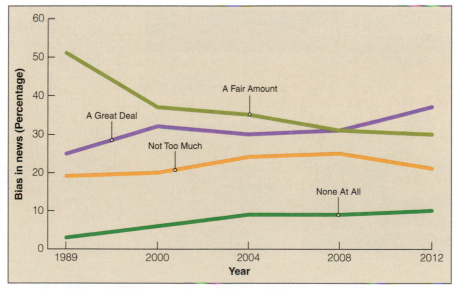

Source: Pew Research Center for the People and the Press. February 2, 2012.

conditions. Cellphone users are the photojournalists of the twenty-first century and their work is welcomed by television stations. Because cable and satellite operators do not give airtime to individuals, easy access to the Internet has made those media irrelevant for public access.

Bias in the Media

■ **LO10.6:** Critically analyze news stories published by any form of the media.

Bias
An inclination or a preference that interferes with impartial judgment.

Many studies have been undertaken to try to identify the sources and direction of **bias** in the media, and these studies have reached different conclusions. Some claim that the press exhibits a liberal bias. Others conclude that the press shows a conservative bias. Still others do not see any notable partisan bias (see Figure 10–2).

Media Matters for America

Do the Media Have a Partisan Bias?

In a classic study conducted in the 1980s, researchers found that media producers, editors, and reporters (the "media elite") exhibited a notably liberal and "left-leaning" bias in their news coverage.[31] Since then, the contention that the media have a liberal bias has been repeated time and again. In 2005, the University of Connecticut's Department of Public Policy surveyed 300 journalists nationwide about whom they voted for in the 2004 presidential election. The Democratic challenger, John Kerry, received 52 percent of their votes, while Bush received only 19 percent (27 percent of those queried either refused to disclose their vote or did not vote).[32] The results are consistent with the surveys done over the last two decades by the Pew Center for the People and the Press. However, even if more journalists held liberal beliefs, those private views should have no bearing on reporting the news.

Media Research Center

31. S. Robert Lichter, Stanley Rothman, and Linda S. Lichter, *The Media Elite* (New York: Adler and Adler, 1986).
32. University of Connecticut, "National Polls of Journalists and the American Public," May 16, 2005.

The controversy over conservatives' perception of liberal bias in the media has fostered the growth of websites and centers to track bias on the left and on the right. The Media Matters website catalogs the inflammatory statements of conservative talk show hosts and bloggers, while the Media Research Center website tracks supposedly liberal bias in the media. Generally, when surveyed, the public responds to the question of media bias as one would expect: conservatives think there is a liberal bias and liberals find a conservative bias. According to a 2012 Pew poll, there has been an increase in the percentage of people who see a great amount of bias, but a decrease in those seeing any bias at all.[33] Such data suggest that most people pay minimal attention to political news and do not see bias in the media (see the screen captures).

A Racial Bias?

Racial profiling is the act of routinely making negative assumptions about individuals based on race. The term was first used to describe the behavior of certain police officers who habitually stopped African American motorists more frequently than white ones, often on minor pretexts. African Americans have described these incidents as stops for "driving while black." Some observers have charged that the media—television in particular—engage in racial profiling in their reporting on minority group members. In 2012, for example, the news media covered the shooting of a young African American man, Trayvon Martin, by a civilian neighborhood watch volunteer, George Zimmerman. Initially, Zimmerman was not charged with a crime because he claimed the shooting was in self-defense. Although there were many accusations of bias in the news coverage on all sides, there is little doubt that Trayvon Martin was portrayed as a strong young black man walking suspiciously in a neighborhood at night.

Those who believe that the media engage in racial profiling point to common stereotypes that journalists often use when illustrating news stories or to the characters portrayed in television drama shows. Critics of racial profiling also argue that African Americans are regularly used to illustrate drug abusers or dealers, even though a majority of users are white, and that images of criminals in general are disproportionately black. A recent study compared the portrayal of African Americans, Hispanics, and whites on prime time television to a similar study conducted in 2000. By 2007, the research found that 74 percent of the actors during a two-week time period were Caucasian, 16 percent were African American and only 5 percent were Latino.[34] While these proportions underrepresent Hispanics, the more important concern lies in how these actors are characterized. Newer storylines tended to ridicule Hispanics more than those in 2000; Hispanics were often portrayed with heavy accents and as less intelligent, while African American characters were more likely to be immoral or despicable than whites or Hispanics.[35]

Greater diversity among newsroom staff members is a goal for most news outlets (see Figure 10-3). The 2012 census of newspapers conducted by the American Society of News Editors (ASNE) showed that about 12.3 percent

Racial Profiling
Making negative assumptions about a person or class of persons based on racial characteristics.

---

33. Perceptions of Bias, News Knowledge," Pew Research Center for the People and the Press, February 7, 2012. http://www.people-press.org.2012/02/07/section-3-perceptions-of-bias-news-knowledge

34. Elizabeth Monk-Turner, Mary Heiserman, Crystle Johnson, Vanity Cotton, and Manny Jackson, "The Portrayal of Racial Minorities on Prime Time Television: A Replication of the Mastro and Greenberg Study a Decade Later," *Studies in Popular Culture*, 32.2 (Spring 2010): 101–114.

35. Ibid.

(4,700 of 38,000) newspaper employees are minorities. According to the ASNE, that percentage has remained steady for about a decade. This organization strives to work until the demographics of the newsroom mirror those of the general population. It has a long way to go.

A Commercial Bias?

According to Andrew Kohut, director of the Pew Research Center in Washington, DC, the majority of those responding to Pew Research Center polls see no ideological or partisan pattern in media bias. Rather, what people mean when they say the press is biased in its political reporting is that it is biased toward its own self-interest—the need to gain higher ratings and thus more advertising revenues.

Interestingly, even though Bernard Goldberg, an Emmy-awarding-winning journalist, has argued that there is a liberal bias in the media, some of the examples he provides would indicate that the bias in the press is more toward commercialism and elitism.[36] For example, he stated that during "sweeps" months (when ratings are particularly important), the networks deliberately avoid featuring blacks, Hispanics, and poor or unattractive people on their prime-time news

Figure 10-3 ▶ **The Decline in Newsroom Staff over Time**

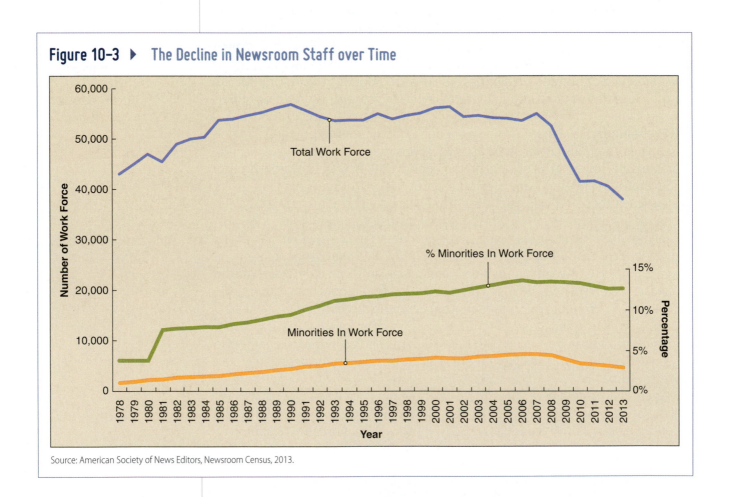

Source: American Society of News Editors, Newsroom Census, 2013.

36. Bernard Goldberg. *Bias: A CBS Insider Exposes How the Media Distort the News*. Washington, DC: Regnery, 2001.

magazine shows. This, asserts Goldberg, is because such coverage might "turn off" the white, middle-class viewers that the networks want to attract so that they can build the ratings that advertisers want.

In every election, especially at the national level, candidates charge that they are not getting fair coverage in the media. Every campaign organization has its own vision of what it would consider "fair" and "unbiased" news coverage. Studies of the opposing side's campaign and data will be produced by liberal and conservative think tanks alike and they will find some source for bias. For journalists, the first goal is to report the news, flattering or not, and to keep their viewers and readers informed.

What Would You Do?

Being a Critical Consumer of the News

Television, newspapers, and the Internet provide a wide range of choices for Americans who want to stay informed. Still, critics of the media argue that a substantial amount of programming and print is colored either by the subjectivity of editors and producers or by the demands of profit making. Additionally, so many pictures and videos are uploaded to the Internet with no substantiating material that it is difficult to know for sure if the picture that was posted is factual or, perhaps, "photoshopped." Few Americans take the time to become critical consumers of the news, nor do most electronic sources give one enough information to become a critical consumer.

Why Should You Care?

As a citizen of the United States or any democratic nation, you want to believe that you are casting your vote and participating in campaigns based on a correct interpretation of the facts about candidates and issues. You have a stake in ensuring that your beliefs are truly your own and that they represent your values and interests. If you are not a critical consumer of the media, you could find yourself voting for a candidate who is opposed to what you believe in or voting against measures that are in your interest.

The United States is in the midst of moving from an economy powered by fossil fuels (that contribute to climate change) to an economy that has a more balanced energy profile. There are many projects currently underway to produce more fuel-efficient cars and trucks, use more electric vehicles, and supply more of our energy needs from solar and wind power. Natural gas is also a clean-burning fuel. With the introduction of fracking technology, natural gas is more readily available than ever before. Energy companies advertise their view that fracking is a safe, well-controlled technology. Advocacy groups and environmental groups, on the other hand, advertise that this technology will pollute groundwater and cause earthquakes. From these conflicting reports and stories, the ordinary citizen must be able to discern the best policy to support for the future of energy in the United States.

What Would You Do?

As a member of Congress soon to be voting on legislation related to the use of fracking, how would you determine the truth about whether the process is safe for the environment or not?

What You *Can* Do

First, practice the habits of a media critic by asking: Who wrote or published a story, or who produced a given television spot, and why might they have done so? What is the motivation of the writer and who is the target audience? Realize that members of Congress, in particular, make comments on public policy based on their own or their party's vested interest in the issue at hand. When you watch television or check a news website, observe how much space is taken up by lively video, human interest stories, and entertainment news. Serious policy issues get very little coverage in comparison.

Cultivate the habit of "fact checking," and use more than one source. Some of the best fact checking websites include following: FactCheck.org (Annenberg Public Policy Center); Politifact.com (*Tampa Bay Times*); The Fact Checker (*The Washington Post*), or Snopes.com (Barbara and Michael Mikkelson, amateur sleuths). Become your own fact checker using the resources of the Internet and start your own blog. For more information about media accuracy and media literacy, visit the following websites:

- Pew Research Center for the People and the Press
  http://www.people-press.org

- "Criteria to Evaluate the Creditibility of WWW Resources," by Virginia Montecino.
  http://www.mason.gmu.edu/~montecin/web-eval-sites.htm

- "How to Analyze a Newspaper Article"
  http://www.understandmedia.com/topics/media~theory/

Purestock/Getty Images

Key Terms

agenda setting 366	**media** 348	**public agenda** 357	**spin doctor** 361
bias 372	**media access** 371	**racial profiling** 373	**white house press corps** 365
blog 355	**microtarget** 363	**selective attention** 364	**yellow journalism** 349
blogosphere politics 355	**narrowcasting** 351	**selective information processing** 351	
electronic media 350	**podcasting** 355	**social media** 348	
framing 366	**press secretary** 365	**spin** 361	
managed news 349	**priming** 366		

Chapter Summary

■ **LO10.1:** The media have always played a significant role in American politics. In the 1800s and earlier, however, news traveled slowly, and politics was controlled by small groups whose members communicated personally. The high-speed rotary press and the telegraph led to self-supported newspapers and mass readership.

■ **LO10.1:** Broadcast media (television and radio) have been important means of communication since the early twentieth century. New technologies, such as the Internet, social networking sites, and blogs offer news organizations more platforms for reaching the public. The public also has access to these platforms.

■ **LO10.2:** The media are enormously important in American politics today. They perform six main functions, including (1) entertainment, (2) news reporting, (3) identifying public problems, (4) socializing new generations, (5) providing a political forum, and (6) making profits.

■ **LO10.3:** The media exert considerable influence during political campaigns and over the affairs of government and government officials by focusing attention on political actors. Today's political campaigns use political advertising, expert management of news coverage, and social media. For presidential candidates, how they appear in presidential debates is of major importance.

■ **LO10.4:** Today's campaigns rely much more heavily on the Internet to reach potential voters and donors. Candidates and their organizations use email, podcasting, websites, blogs, and downloadable video and audio to involve people in campaigns. The use of these techniques does rely heavily on self-selection by the user, but the techniques are cheap and effective and may work to get the user to feel an attachment to the candidate or public official.

■ **LO10.5:** The relationship between the media and the president is close; each uses the other—sometimes positively, sometimes negatively. The media play an important role in investigating the government, in getting government officials to understand better the needs and desires of American society, and in setting the public agenda.

■ **LO10.5:** The electronic media are subject to government regulation. Many Federal Communications Commission

(FCC) rules pertain to ownership of TV and radio stations. Legislation has removed many rules about co-ownership of several forms of media, although the most recent steps taken by Congress have been to halt any further deregulation.

■ **LO10.6:** Studies of bias in the media have reached different conclusions. Some claim that the press has a liberal bias; others contend that the press shows a conservative bias. Still others conclude that the press is biased toward its own self-interest—the need to gain higher ratings and thus more advertising revenues. Other studies have found other types of biases, such as a bias in favor of the status quo or a bias against losers. Educated consumers of the news should avail themselves of multiple news sources, use fact-checking websites, and ask questions about the motivation for a particular news story.

Selected Print, Media, and Online Resources

PRINT RESOURCES

Arceneaux, Kevin and Martin Johnson. *Changing Minds or Changing Channels? Partisan News in an Age of Choice.* Chicago: University of Chicago Press, 2013. The authors look at the contention that increased selective viewing of television news increases polarization and find that the multiplicity of news sources actually dampens the partisanship of the electorate.

Graber, Doris. *On Media: Making Sense of Politics.* New York: Oxford University Press, 2011. Graber's research focuses on what people actually learn from the news. In this book, she contends that people make sensible decisions about politics based on information that they gain from the news and from their circle of contacts.

Ladd, Jonathan. *Why Americans Hate the Media and How it Matters.* Princeton, NJ: Princeton University Press, 2011. Ladd suggests that the increased competition between media sources has led to more sensationalism in the news. The polarization and increased partisanship of the public can be traced to the rise of the highly competitive news business.

Lehrer, Jim. *Tension City: Inside the Presidential Debates.* New York: Random House Trade Paperbacks, 2012. This volume reveals the background stories of more than forty years of presidential campaign debates as viewed by a veteran and respected PBS journalist.

McChesney, Robert Waterman, and John Nichols. *The Death and Life of American Journalism: The Media Revolution that Will Begin the World Again.* New York: Nation Books, 2011. The authors, two well-regarded journalism scholars, review the technological and social forces that have led to the decline of the print media. They believe, however, that a new future for journalism lies in hybrid forms of news media.

MEDIA RESOURCES

All the President's Men—A 1976 film produced by Warner Brothers and starring Dustin Hoffman and Robert Redford as the two *Washington Post* reporters (Bob Woodward and Carl Bernstein) who broke the story of the Watergate scandal. The film is an excellent portrayal of *The Washington Post* newsroom (at a moment when newsrooms really did set the public agenda) and the decisions that editors make in such situations.

Good Night and Good Luck—The 2005 film, which depicts Edward R. Murrow's work to discredit the communist witch hunts being conducted by Senator Joe McCarthy, is George Clooney's tribute to the early period of television journalism when news anchors like Murrow were the heroes of the media.

Shattered Glass—Released in 2003, the movie details the fall of a journalist who is found to have fabricated the stories in more than half of his articles. This film explores the importance of publishing the truth rather than sensationalism.

The Social Network—The 2010 Oscar-winning film details the founding of Facebook and the ensuing conflicts over the ownership of this blockbuster social media company.

ONLINE RESOURCES

American Journalism Review—includes features from the magazine and original content created specifically for online reading:www.ajr.org

American Review—an e-zine featuring serious columns about U.S. politics and world affairs as well as book reviews and discussions of the media:www.americanreview.us

Huffington Post—a leading source of news and opinion on subjects ranging from politics to entertainment, some of the nation's most outstanding columnists are found on the "Huffpost" website: www.huffingtonpost.com

Pew Research Center for the People and the Press—provides up-to-date research on the public and its use of the media, including an annual State of the Media report:.www.people-press.org

Slate—e-zine of politics and culture published by Microsoft:www.slate.com

Master the concepts of Media and Politics with MindTap™ for American Government

REVIEW MindTap™ **for American Government**
Access Key Term Flashcards for Chapter 10.

STAY CURRENT MindTap™ **for American Government**
Access the KnowNow blog and customized RSS for updates on current events.

TEST YOURSELF MindTap™ **for American Government**
Take the Wrap It Up Quiz for Chapter 10.

STAY FOCUSED MindTap™ **for American Government**
Complete the Focus Activities for Media and Politics.

The Congress

WATCH & LEARN MindTap™ for American Government

Watch a brief "What Do You Know?" video summarizing The Congress.

LEARNING OUTCOMES

After reading this chapter, students will be able to:

■ **LO11.1:** Describe the major powers of the Congress as granted by the U.S. Constitution.

■ **LO11.2:** Explain the differences between the House of Representatives and the Senate with regard to their constituencies, terms of office, powers, and political processes.

■ **LO11.3:** Describe the processes of reapportionment and redistricting.

■ **LO11.4:** Discuss the importance of committees to the lawmaking process and to the ability of members of Congress to do their jobs.

■ **LO11.5:** Describe the leadership structure in each house of Congress, noting the differences between the House and the Senate.

■ **LO11.6:** Demonstrate how a bill becomes a law and explain how the different processes in the House and the Senate influence legislating.

■ **LO11.7:** Explain how the federal budget is constructed and the legislative process for approving the budget.

Congress Had Time Limits?

BACKGROUND

The first year of the 1st Congress, held from 1789 to 1791, members met from March to September, passing necessary legislation and organizing the government. The next year, they met from January to August, and then reconvened from December to March. During the next five decades, Congress conducted most of its business in short sessions, with long recess periods for the members to maintain their farms and businesses back home.

Today, the U.S. Congress is still organized as two one-year sessions. The respective houses adjourn at the very end of one year and then reconvene about three weeks later. The House calendar designates the days that members can spend in their districts meeting with constituents and, in many cases, fundraising. Currently, the House works more full weeks than in the past but it has also given itself more days at home for "district work." Today's House and Senate do not want to adjourn formally because they fear the executive branch will take action while they are not in session. This work pattern allows for difficult issues (such as raising the debt ceiling) to go unresolved for many months. Other measures, such as tax relief or the extension of unemployment benefits, may persist for short periods with no attempt to resolve underlying issues. Congress may, by its own procedures, avoid such unpleasant tasks as finalizing a fiscal year budget. The government can run on a series of continuing resolutions. The low 2014 public approval ratings of Congress, along with the recent lack of congressional productivity, might make one wonder about an admittedly radical idea.

WHAT IF CONGRESS HAD TIME LIMITS?

In contrast to Congress, many state constitutions limit the days and weeks that state legislatures can meet. The Kentucky legislature may only meet for 60 "legislative days" in even-numbered years and 30 days in odd-numbered years. In Nevada, the legislature may meet for 120 calendar days. In Missouri, the legislature must conclude its business by May 30th. Additionally, most state constitutions require that the state's budget must be balanced and the government cannot continue without a budget for the fiscal year. In some states, if the legislature does not complete the work on a budget, the governor may complete the task.

If the U.S. Congress were limited by a constitutional amendment to meeting for only six months, could the body be effective? Six months to work, followed by six months to be in one's home state, would increase pressure to complete the year's business, including the budget and tax issues, before adjournment. Both political parties might feel pressure to compromise and pass legislation before going home to explain their votes to their constituents. Given the large amount of work to do, members could easily spend as much time in daily floor sessions as they do now. Communication with their constituents back home could be handled by live conferences over the Internet.

Depending on the wording of the amendment, it would be possible to consider membership in the House or Senate a part-time job, as in many state legislatures. This would mean, perhaps, paying the members a part-time or reduced salary, expecting them to maintain a career in the working world. That change alone would make individuals less likely to see election to Congress as a career. Congress might return to a legislature of citizen-legislators much as the founders envisioned. The expenses of supporting the Congress could be greatly decreased because the large amount of staff on Capitol Hill would no longer be necessary, and congresspersons would not be constantly traveling back and forth to Washington.

DISADVANTAGES OF A PART-TIME CONGRESS

Obviously, a part-time Congress would have little ability to deal with domestic or international crises. In the states, the governor has the ability to call the legislature back to the capitol in special session. The president can also call Congress into special session to deal with emergencies.

Would making membership a part-time job cost the body in terms of expertise and effectiveness? Scholars who have studied the effects of term limits on state legislatures say that having more frequent turnover of members reduces the knowledge available to make good decisions. It takes several years for a member of Congress to become well versed in public policy in any one specific area or to understand the budget, say, of the Defense Department. Making their jobs part time would make it harder to gain the expertise necessary to offset the expertise of either bureaucrats or lobbyists for special interests. Both of those groups would still be engaged in fighting for their interests full time. The executive would likely gain power if the Congress worked only six months a year. The president would be free to make more interim appointments without congressional scrutiny and to dominate the media with his or her agenda. Members of Congress would be playing "catch-up" when they returned to Washington after their six months at home.

For Critical Analysis

1. *Would forcing members of Congress to adjourn at a specified time motivate them to pass legislation or to leave decisions to the president?*

2. *Would having a part-time Congress encourage more members to retire earlier and make it possible for more individuals to serve in Congress?*

MOST AMERICANS VIEW Congress in a less-than-flattering light. In recent years, Congress has appeared to be deeply split, highly partisan in its conduct, and not very responsive to public needs. Polls show that public approval has fallen to record lows. Yet, individual members of Congress often receive much higher approval ratings from the voters in their districts. This is one of the paradoxes of the relationship between the people and Congress. Members of the public hold the institution in relatively low regard compared with the satisfaction they express with their individual representatives.

Part of the explanation for these seemingly contradictory appraisals is that congresspersons spend considerable time and effort serving their **constituents**. If the federal bureaucracy makes a mistake, the senator's or representative's office tries to resolve the issue. Members of the Congress spend considerable time and effort developing what is sometimes called a "**homestyle**" to gain the trust and appreciation of their constituents through service, local appearances, and the creation of local offices.

Congress, however, was also created to work for the nation as a whole. The representatives and senators in their Washington work are creating what might be called a "**hillstyle**," which refers to their work on legislation and in party leadership to create laws and policies for our nation.[1] This chapter describes the functions of Congress, including constituent service, representation, lawmaking, and oversight of the government; how the members of Congress are elected; how Congress organizes itself when it meets; and how bills pass through the legislative process.

The Functions of Congress

America's founders believed that the bulk of the power to be exercised by a national government should be in the hands of the legislature because the members were elected by the people, or, in the case of the Senate, by the states. The leading role envisioned for Congress is apparent from its primacy in the Constitution. Article I deals with the structure, the powers, and the operation of Congress, beginning in Section 1 with an application of the basic principle of separation of powers: "All legislative Powers herein granted shall be vested in a Congress of the United States, which shall consist of a Senate and House of Representatives." These legislative powers are spelled out in detail in Article I and elsewhere.

The **bicameralism** of Congress—its division into two legislative houses—was in part the result of the Connecticut Compromise, which tried to balance the large-state population advantage, reflected in the House, and the small-state demand for equality in policymaking, satisfied in the Senate. Beyond that, the two chambers of Congress also reflected the social-class biases of the founders. They wished to balance the interests and the numerical superiority of the common citizens with the property interests of the less numerous landowners, bankers, and merchants. They achieved this by providing in Sections 2 and 3 of Article I that members of the House of Representatives should be elected directly by "the People," whereas members of the Senate were to be chosen by the elected representatives sitting in state legislatures, who were more likely to be members of the elite. (In 1913, the passage of the Seventeenth Amendment,

Constituents
One of the persons represented by a legislator or other elected or appointed official.

Homestyle
The actions and behaviors of a member of Congress aimed at the constituents and intended to win the support and trust of the voters at home.

Hillstyle
The actions and behaviors of a member of Congress in Washington, DC, intended to promote policies and the member's own career aspirations.

Bicameralism
The division of a legislature into two separate assemblies.

did you know?
Samuel Morse demonstrated his telegraph to Congress in 1843 by stretching wire between two committee rooms.

---

1. Richard Fenno, *Home Style: House Members in Their Districts* (Boston: Little, Brown, 1978).

which provides that senators also are to be elected directly by the people, resulted in the change of the latter provision.)

The logic of separate constituencies and separate interests underlying the bicameral Congress was reinforced by differences in length of tenure. Members of the House are required to face the electorate every two years, whereas senators can serve for a much more secure term of six years—even longer than the four-year term provided for the president. Furthermore, the senators' terms are staggered so that only one-third of the senators face the electorate every two years, along with all of the House members.

The bicameral structure of Congress was designed to enable the legislative body and its members to perform certain functions for the political system. These functions include lawmaking, representation, service to constituents, oversight, public education, and conflict resolution. Of these, the two most important and the ones most often in conflict are lawmaking and representation.

The Lawmaking Function

The most obvious function of any legislature is **lawmaking**. Congress is the highest elected body in the country, charged with making binding rules for all Americans. Lawmaking requires decisions about the size of the federal budget, health care reform and gun control, and the long-term prospects for war or peace. A majority of the bills that Congress acts on originate in the executive branch, and many other bills are traceable to interest groups and political party organizations. Through the processes of compromise and **logrolling** (offering to support a fellow member's bill in exchange for that member's promise to support your bill in the future), as well as debate and discussion, backers of legislation attempt to fashion a winning majority coalition to create policies for the nation.

The Representation Function

Representation includes both representing the desires and demands of the constituents in the member's home district or state and representing larger national interests such as farmers or the environment. Because the interests of constituents in a specific district may be in conflict with the demands of national policy, the representation function is often at variance with the lawmaking function for individual lawmakers and sometimes for Congress as a whole. Although it may be in the interest of the nation to reduce defense spending by closing military bases, such closures are not in the interest of the states and districts that will lose jobs and local spending. Every legislator faces votes that set representational issues against lawmaking realities.

How should the legislators fulfill the representation function? There are several views on how this should be accomplished.

The Trustee View of Representation.
The first approach to the question of how representation should be achieved is that legislators should act as **trustees** of the broad interests of the entire society. They should vote against the narrow interests of their constituents if their conscience and their perception of national needs so dictate.

The Instructed-Delegate View of Representation.
Directly opposed to the trustee view of representation is the notion that the members of Congress should behave as **instructed delegates**; that is, they should mirror the views of the majority of the constituents who elected them to power in the first place. On the surface, this approach is plausible and rewarding. For it to work, however, we must

---

Lawmaking
The process of establishing the legal rules that govern society.

Logrolling
An arrangement in which two or more members of Congress agree in advance to support each other's bills.

CONNECT WITH YOUR CLASSMATES
MindTap° for American Government

Access The Congress Forum: Discussion—Representation in Congress

Representation
The function of members of Congress as elected officials representing the views of their constituents.

Trustees
A legislator who acts according to her or his conscience and the broad interests of the entire society.

Instructed Delegates
A legislator who is an agent of the voters who elected him or her and who votes according to the views of constituents regardless of personal beliefs.

ZUMA Press, Inc./Alamy

Congresswoman Janet Hahn visits one of her constituents, the proprietor of a small business, in her California district. This visit helps build Representative Hahn's homestyle.

assume that constituents actually have well-formed views on the issues that are decided in Congress and, further, that they have clear-cut preferences about these issues. Neither condition is likely to be satisfied very often.

Generally, most legislators hold neither a pure trustee view nor a pure instructed-delegate view. Typically, they combine both perspectives in a pragmatic mix that is often called the "politico" style.

Service to Constituents

Individual members of Congress are expected to act as brokers between private citizens and the often faceless federal government. This function usually takes the form of **casework**. Legislators make choices about their "hillstyle," deciding how much time they and their staff will spend on casework activities such as tracking down a missing Social Security check, explaining the meaning of particular bills to people who may be affected by them, promoting a local business interest, or interceding with a regulatory agency on behalf of constituents who disagree with proposed agency regulations.

Legislators and many analysts of congressional behavior regard this **ombudsperson** role as an activity that strongly benefits the members of Congress. A government characterized by a large, confusing bureaucracy and complex public programs offers innumerable opportunities for legislators to assist (usually) grateful constituents. Morris P. Fiorina once suggested, somewhat mischievously, that senators and representatives prefer to maintain bureaucratic confusion to maximize their opportunities for performing good deeds on behalf of their constituents:

> *Some poor, aggrieved constituent becomes enmeshed in the tentacles of an evil bureaucracy and calls upon Congressman St. George to do battle with the dragon. The constituent who receives aid believes that his congressman and his congressman alone got results.*[2]

did you know?

Less than half of American adults can identify the party that controls either house of Congress.

Casework
Personal work for constituents by members of Congress.

Ombudsperson
A person who hears and investigates complaints by private individuals against public officials or agencies.

---

2. Morris P. Fiorina, *Congress: Keystone of the Washington Establishment*, 2nd ed. (New Haven, CT: Yale University Press, 1989), pp. 44, 47.

General Keith Alexander, director of the National Security Agency (NSA), testifies before Congress about the agency's collection of Americans' emails and telephone calls.

Michael Reynolds/EPA/Landov

Although the political parties in Congress disagree on most issues, they find it difficult to vote against benefits for their constituents. As the economic downturn continued, the administration proposed a reduction in the percentage of wages withheld from workers' paychecks for Social Security as a way to put more money in their pockets. While Republicans pointed out the long-term consequences of the plan—setting even less money aside for Social Security—they could not vote against a tax cut. Democrats spoke to the benefit of this temporary action for ordinary workers. Both parties chose to ignore the fact that this action makes it likely that Social Security will be insolvent even earlier than has been predicted.

The Oversight Function

Oversight

The process by which Congress follows up on laws it has enacted to ensure that they are being enforced and administered in the way Congress intended.

Oversight of the bureaucracy is essential if decisions made by Congress are to have any force. **Oversight** is the process by which Congress follows up on the laws it has enacted to ensure that they are being enforced and administered in the way Congress intended. This is done by holding committee hearings and investigations, changing the size of an agency's budget, and cross-examining high-level presidential nominees to head major agencies. Sometimes Congress establishes a special commission to investigate a problem. After finding out that the National Security Agency (NSA) had been gathering and keeping records of all telephone calls and most email in the United States, Congress began a series of hearings on the work of the NSA. Congressional concern about such "eavesdropping" increased when, in 2014, it was revealed that the CIA had been reading the email of members of Congress.[3] Oversight can, of course, be partisan in nature, as when House Republicans grilled IRS administrators about their supposed targeting of some conservative political groups.

Senators and representatives increasingly see their oversight function as a critically important part of their legislative activities. In part, oversight is related to

---

3. David Horsey, "Dianne Feinstein outraged that CIA spied on her Senate staff," *LA Times*, March 13, 2014.

Everyday Politics

House of Cards

Members of Congress often refer to the House of Representatives as "the people's house." This is because voters directly choose their representatives. Netflix has upended this definition with its very popular and award-winning series, *House of Cards*.

In this political drama, the ambitions and dreams of members of Congress and the Washington press corps are shown to be as sturdy as the proverbial "house of cards." Congressman Frank Underwood, played by Kevin Spacey, is ambitious, revengeful, and capable of almost any type of underhanded dealing to get what he wants. Constituents contrive to have their interests met, journalists scheme to get the biggest stories, and Congressman Underwood plots to get a higher position.

Most members of Congress dismiss the series as being much too cynical about Congress and its members. Corruption of the sort seen in the series is very rare, but there are cases of members who have become very wealthy, quite legally, while in Washington. Members of Congress who retire from the Capitol often become extremely sought-after as lobbyists and are paid accordingly. It is clear to anyone who has spent much time with members of Congress, advisors to the president, or Washington-based bureaucrats that there are many individuals who think they could do a better job than the president living and working in the nation's capital.

For Critical Analysis

1. *Do you think that cynical portrayals of elected officials increase the public's distrust of government?*

2. *Would having more new faces in office by increasing the turnover of congressional seats make Congress more responsive to the public?*

the concept of constituency service, particularly when Congress investigates alleged arbitrariness or wrongdoing by bureaucratic agencies.

The Public-Education Function

Educating the public is a function that is performed whenever Congress holds public hearings, exercises oversight over the bureaucracy, or engages in committee and floor debate on such major issues and topics as political assassinations, aging, illegal drugs, and the concerns of small businesses. In so doing, Congress presents a range of viewpoints on pressing national questions. In recent years, members of Congress and the committees of Congress have greatly improved access to information through use of the Internet. Congress also decides what issues will come up for discussion and decision; this agenda setting is a major facet of its public-education function.

The Conflict-Resolution Function

Congress is commonly seen as an institution for resolving conflicts within American society. Organized interest groups and representatives of different racial, religious, economic, and ideological interests view Congress as an access point for airing their grievances and seeking help. This puts Congress in the position of trying to resolve the differences among competing points of view by passing laws to accommodate as many interested parties as possible. To the extent that Congress meets pluralist expectations in accommodating competing interests, it tends to build support for the entire political process.

The Powers of Congress

■ **LO11.1:** Describe the major powers of the Congress as granted by the U.S. Constitution.

The Constitution is both highly specific and extremely vague about the powers that Congress may exercise. The first 17 clauses of Article I, Section 8, specify most of the **enumerated powers** of Congress—powers expressly given to that body.

Enumerated Powers

The enumerated powers of Congress include the right to impose taxes and import tariffs; borrow funds; regulate interstate commerce and international trade; establish procedures for naturalizing citizens; make laws regulating bankruptcies; coin (and print) money and regulate its value; establish standards of weights and measures; punish counterfeiters; establish post offices and postal routes; regulate copyrights and patents; establish the federal court system; punish illegal acts on the high seas; declare war; raise and regulate an army and a navy; call up and regulate the state militias to enforce laws, to suppress insurrections, and to repel invasions; and govern the District of Columbia.

The most important of the domestic powers of Congress, listed in Article I, Section 8, are the rights to collect taxes, to spend, and to regulate commerce. The most important foreign policy power is the power to declare war. Other sections of the Constitution allow Congress to establish rules for its own members, to regulate the electoral college, and to override a presidential veto. Congress may also regulate the extent of the Supreme Court's authority to review cases decided by the lower courts, regulate relations among states, and propose amendments to the Constitution.

Powers of the Senate. Some functions are restricted to one chamber. The Senate must advise on, and consent to, the ratification of treaties and must accept or reject presidential nominations of ambassadors, Supreme Court justices, and "all other Officers of the United States." During President Obama's first term, two Supreme Court vacancies occurred through the retirements of Justices David Souter in 2009 and John Paul Stevens in 2010. The president nominated Appellate Judge Sonia Sotomayor to fill Souter's seat in 2009. Although the Republicans in the Senate would have liked to object to the appointment, Judge Sotomayor had been confirmed in her appellate seat as an appointee of George W. Bush. In 2010, President Obama made another somewhat controversial appointment, but, given the outstanding qualifications of Solicitor General Elena Kagan, she too was confirmed. In contrast, the president had more difficulty with lower judicial appointments and ambassadorial appointments.

While the Republicans in the Senate slowed the approval process for lower court judges in the first year of the Obama presidency, eventually the majority of his judicial appointments were approved. Republicans in the Senate were particularly angered by the president's decision to make recess appointments to the National Labor Relations Board and the new Consumer Protection Agency during the Christmas holiday in 2011. To prevent such appointments, the Senate did not recess but held symbolic sessions for a few moments each day. When a federal appeals court refused to stop the appointments to the National Labor Relations Board, members of the Senate appealed the case to the Supreme Court in 2014. In a unanimous opinion, the Supreme Court found the president's actions unconstitutional, stating that only the Senate can decide when it is in recess.[4]

Enumerated Powers
A power specifically granted to the national government by the Constitution. The first 17 clauses of Article I, Section 8, specify most of the enumerated powers of Congress.

COMPARE WITH YOUR PEERS

MindTap for American Government

Access The Congress Forum: Polling Activity—The Power to Declare War.

---

4. National Labor Relations Board v. Noel Canning _____U.S._____(2014).

Politics with a Purpose

Keeping Tabs on Congress

What if your instructor told you that he would decide whether your privacy on Facebook would be protected? Or how much your Internet connection costs? What if we were to tell you that for every dollar you earned, we were going to take 28 cents and decide how to spend it?* And that our actions would influence how much it cost you to fill up your gas tank? You would probably think that if you gave us all this power, you should pay attention to see if we are making the "right" choices, especially because you have a say in whether we keep our jobs.

Congress has these kinds of powers. Along with the president, Congress sets tax law—including gas taxes—and regulates interstate commerce (including the Internet). In any given week early in the legislative session, at least a hundred bills and resolutions are introduced in the U.S. Senate. How is the average citizen supposed to keep track of all of these pieces of potential legislation, any one of which may have an impact on his or her life? Substantive representation, the extent to which an elected official's actions match the interests of his or her constituency, can be assessed in a variety of ways. The Congressional Record is the official source of information on everything that has happened in Congress.** The Library of Congress provides access to the Congressional Record and provides links to other data, such as congressional committees, government reports, and presidential nominations (http://thomas.loc.gov).

A quick perusal of these sites illustrates that not only is the sheer volume of all the bills introduced overwhelming, but the legislative process is extremely complex. There are 23 House committees, 17 Senate committees, and four joint committees (where membership is shared between the chambers). These bodies all have subcommittees, where the real work of writing laws and holding hearings occurs. How can you keep track of legislation that is important to you? You can become familiar with organizations that play a vital role in the democratic process: groups that explain and track legislation. Interest groups gather all the voting records of members and then give them ratings. One nonprofit organization, Voter Information Services, hosts a website that allows users to create report cards on members of Congress by choosing from a list of advocacy groups.***

A closer examination of these report cards illustrates the differences in how particular groups assess the actions of members of Congress. For example, Americans for Democratic Action, a liberal group, describes a vote for the Domestic Energy and Jobs bill as one that would "increase oil and gas exploration, development, and production on public lands…and place roadblocks to improved air pollution and fuel efficiency standards for cars." In contrast, the American Conservative Union describes Domestic Energy Production bill as "opening up a small portion of the Alaska National Wildlife Refuge, approving the Keystone XL pipeline, and shifting authority to the Federal Energy Administration." Obviously, these two groups have very different views on protecting the environment and developing energy sources. Organizations like Voter Information Services allow you to examine these groups' assessments of members of Congress side by side.

Journalistic sources such as *Congressional Quarterly* or *The National Journal*, or specialized tracking agencies like GalleryWatch.com or CongressNow.com, the information on what our Congress does is readily available. Our role as citizens is to pay attention.

*www.irs.gov/pub/irs-pdf/n1036.pdf
**http://thomas.loc.gov/home/r110query.html
***www.vis.org/crc/groupsincrc.aspx

Constitutional Amendments. Amendments to the Constitution provide additional powers. Congress must certify the election of a president and a vice president or choose these officers if no candidate has a majority of the electoral vote (Twelfth Amendment). It may levy an income tax (Sixteenth Amendment) and determine who will be acting president in case of the death or incapacity of the president or vice president (Twentieth Amendment and Twenty-fifth Amendment).

The Necessary and Proper Clause

Congress enjoys the right under Article I, Section 8 (the "elastic" or "necessary and proper" clause), "[t]o make all Laws which shall be necessary and proper for carrying into Execution the foregoing Powers [of Article I], and all other Powers vested by this Constitution in the Government of the United States, or in any Department or Officer thereof." This vague statement of congressional responsibilities provided, over time, the basis for a greatly expanded national government. It also constituted, at least in theory, a check on the expansion of presidential powers.

Checks on Congress

When you consider all of the powers of Congress and its ability to override a presidential veto, it is undoubtedly the most powerful branch of government. However, given the diversity of interests in the nation, rarely can the Congress agree to override a presidential veto. So, one check on the Congress is the veto of the president. Another constitutional check is the power of the Supreme Court to hold a law passed by the Congress as unconstitutional. Additionally, the members of the House face election every two years. If the Congress were to exercise too much power, it is likely that many members would be voted out of office. And on the other side of Capitol Hill sits the Senate, which often curbs the House by not agreeing with proposals from the "other house."

House-Senate Differences

■ **LO11.2:** Explain the differences between the House of Representatives and the Senate with regard to their constituencies, terms of office, powers, and political processes.

Congress is composed of two markedly different—but coequal—chambers. Although the Senate and the House of Representatives exist within the same legislative institution, each has developed certain distinctive features that clearly distinguish it from the other. Table 11–1 summarizes these differences.

Table 11–1 ▶ **Differences between the House and the Senate**

HOUSE*	SENATE*
Constitutional Differences	
Members chosen from local districts	Members chosen from an entire state
Two-year term	Six-year term
Originally elected by voters	Originally (until 1913) elected by state legislatures
May impeach (indict) federal officials	May convict federal officials of impeachable offenses
Process and Culture	
Larger (435 voting members	Smaller (100 members)
More formal rules	Fewer rules and restrictions
Debate limited	Debate extended
Less prestige and less individual notice	More prestige and more media attention
More partisan	More individualistic
Specific Powers	
Originates bills for raising revenues	Has power to advise the president on, and to consent to, presidential appointments and treaties

* Some of these differences, such as the term of office, are provided for in the Constitution. Others, such as debate rules, are not.

Size and Rules

The central difference between the House and the Senate is simply that the House is much larger than the Senate. The House has 435 representatives, plus delegates from the District of Columbia, Puerto Rico, Guam, American Samoa, and the Virgin Islands; the Senate has 100 members. This size difference means that a greater number of formal rules are needed to govern activity in the House, whereas looser procedures can be observed in the less crowded Senate.

The effect of the difference in size is most obvious in the rules governing debate on the floors of the two chambers. The House employs an elaborate system to control the agenda and allot time fairly in such a large assembly. For each major bill, the **Rules Committee** normally proposes a **Rule** for debate that includes time limitations, divides the time between the majority and the minority, and specifies whether amendments can be proposed. The House debates and approves the Rule, which will govern the debate on that specific legislation. As a consequence of its stricter time limits on debate, the House, despite its greater size, often is able to act on legislation more quickly than the Senate.

Debate and Filibustering

In the Senate, the rules governing debate are much less restrictive. In fact, for legislation to reach the floor of the Senate, the body must have approved the rules of debate by a **Unanimous Consent Agreement**—the entire body agrees to the rules of debate. The Senate tradition of the **filibuster**, or the use of unlimited debate as a blocking tactic, dates back to 1790, when a proposal to move the U.S. capital from New York to Philadelphia was stalled by such time-wasting maneuvers. This unlimited-debate tradition—which also existed in the House until 1811—is hardly absolute.

Under Senate Rule 22, debate may be ended by invoking *cloture*. Cloture shuts off discussion on a bill. Amended in 1975 and 1979, Rule 22 states that debate may be closed off on a bill if 16 senators sign a petition requesting it and if, after two days have elapsed, three-fifths of the entire membership (60 votes, assuming no vacancies) vote for cloture. After cloture is invoked, each senator may speak on a bill for a maximum of one hour before a vote is taken.

Beginning in 2009, the use of the filibuster became the usual way of doing business in the Senate. At the beginning of the session, the Democratic majority plus the two independent senators (Bernie Sanders of Vermont and Joe Lieberman of Connecticut), could muster 60 votes to support President Obama's initiatives in health-care reform and financial reform. Republicans filibustered many votes but failed to stop the legislation. Beginning in 2013, Republicans controlled 45 seats, rendering their threat of the filibuster even more effective. The Democratic majority in the Senate used a parliamentary tactic to bring a change to the filibuster rule up for a vote. This "nuclear option" allowed a simple majority to change the filibuster rule. The amended rule does not allow the filibuster against any executive or judicial appointments except for Supreme Court nominees. After the vote, Republicans warned Democrats that they will not always hold a majority in the Senate and the rule will be used against them in the future.[5]

Rules Committee
A standing committee of the House of Representatives that provides special rules under which specific bills can be debated, amended, and considered by the House.

Rule
The proposal by the Rules Committee of the House that states the conditions for debate for one piece of legislation.

Unanimous Consent Agreement
An agreement on the rules of debate for proposed legislation in the Senate that is approved by all the members.

Filibuster
The use of the Senate's tradition of unlimited debate as a delaying tactic to block a bill.

---

5. Jeremy Peters, "In Landmark Vote, Senate Limits Use of the Filibuster," *The New York Times*, November 21, 2013, p. 1.

Unorthodox lawmaking
The use of out-of-the-ordinary
parliamentary tactics to pass
legislation.

The use of such tactics has increased tremendously over the last two decades, leading to the concept of **unorthodox lawmaking**, meaning the use of obscure parliamentary procedures to get laws passed in the face of strong opposition.[6] Such tactics, however, are difficult to explain to the public and certainly undercut trust in the legislative process.

Prestige

As a consequence of the greater size of the House, representatives cannot achieve as much individual recognition and public prestige as can members of the Senate. Senators can more readily gain media exposure and establish careers as spokespersons for large national constituencies. For a House member to become nationally known, he or she must be a member of the leadership or become a recognized expert on a specific policy.

Congresspersons and the Citizenry: A Comparison

Members of Congress are not typical American citizens. They are older than most Americans, partly because of constitutional age requirements and partly because a good deal of political experience normally is an advantage in running for national office. They are also disproportionately white, male, and trained in high-status occupations. Lawyers are by far the largest occupational group among congresspersons, although the proportion of lawyers in the House is lower now than it was in the past. Compared with the average American citizen, members of Congress are well paid. In 2014, annual congressional salaries were $174,000. Increasingly, members of Congress are also much wealthier than the average citizen. Whereas less than 1 percent of Americans have assets exceeding $1 million, half of the members of Congress are millionaires. Table 11–2 summarizes selected characteristics of the members of Congress.

Compared with the composition of Congress over the past 200 years, however, the House and Senate today are significantly more diverse in gender and ethnicity than ever before. In the 113th Congress (2013–2014), there were 81 women in the House of Representatives (19 percent) and 20 women in the U.S. Senate (20 percent). Minority group members filled over 20 percent of the seats in the House; they included 44 African American members, 37 Latino or Hispanic members, 13 Asian or Pacific Islander Americans, and one Native American. The Senate has two African American members, four Hispanic members and one Asian American member. The 113th Congress had significant numbers of members born in 1946 or later, the so-called baby boomers. A majority of House members and Senators belong to this postwar generation. This shift in the character of Congress may prompt consideration of the issues that will affect boomers, such as Social Security and Medicare.

Congressional Elections

Congressional elections are conducted by the individual state governments, but the states must conform to the rules established by the U.S. Constitution and by national statutes. Representatives are to be elected every second year by popular

---

6. Barbara Sinclair, *Unorthodox Lawmaking: New Legislative Processes in the U.S. Congress.* 4th ed. (Washington, DC: CQ Press, 2011).

Table 11-2 ▶ Characteristics of the 113th Congress, 2013—2015

	U.S. POPULATION, 2014	HOUSE	SENATE
Age (average)	36.8	57	62
Percent minority	28%	18%	4%
Religion			
Percent church members	60%	93%	92%
Percent Catholic	25.1%	31%	24%
Percent Protestant	51.3%	56%	55%
Percent Jewish	1.2%	7.3%	13%
Percent female	50.9%	17.5%	17%
Lawyers	0.4%	23.9%	37%
Blue-collar occupations	30%	1.6%	3%
Military veteran	7.6%	21.4%	28.9%
Percent households earning more than $50,000	42%	100%	100%
Assets more than $1 million	1%	42%	66%

Sources: E. Eric Petersen, "Representatives and Senators: Trends in Member Characteristics since 1945," Washington, DC: Congressional Research Service, 2012. Tom Shine, "47% of Congress Members Millionaires—a Status Shared by Only 1% of Americans," ABC News, November 16, 2011.

ballot, and the number of seats awarded to each state is to be determined every 10 years by the results of the census. The decennial census is viewed as crucial by members of Congress and by the states. If the census is not accurate, perhaps undercounting individuals living in a state, then that state might lose a representative in Congress. Each state has at least one representative, with most congressional districts having about 650,000 residents. Senators are elected by popular vote (the Seventeenth Amendment) every six years; approximately one-third of the seats are chosen every two years. Each state has two senators.

Only states can elect members of Congress. Therefore, territories such as Puerto Rico and Guam are not represented, though they do elect nonvoting delegates who sit in the House. The District of Columbia is also represented only by a nonvoting delegate, but is not represented in the Senate at all. Several proposals have been made to grant congressional representation to our nation's capital. In 1978, Congress approved a constitutional amendment to give the District the representation it would have if it were a state, including two senators. The amendment was not ratified, however. Democrats in Congress have generally supported more representation for the District because the majority of its citizens are African American and vote overwhelmingly Democratic. Republicans oppose the initiative for the same reason.

Candidates for Congressional Elections

Candidates for House and Senate seats may be self-selected. Members of the House must be at least 25 years old, a citizen for seven years, and live in the state they will represent. Senators must be 30 years old, a citizen for nine years, and a resident of the state they represent. In congressional districts where one party is very strong, however, there may be a shortage of candidates willing to represent the weaker party. Leaders of the weaker party must often recruit candidates. Candidates may resemble the voters of the district in ethnicity or religion, but are also likely to be very successful individuals previously active in politics. House candidates are especially likely to have local ties to their districts. Candidates usually choose to run because they believe they would enjoy the job and its accompanying status. They also may be thinking of a House seat as a steppingstone to future political office as a senator, governor, or president. Individuals who seek Senate seats may also have plans to run for governor in their home state or be considering a run for the presidency.

Congressional Campaigns and Elections. Congressional campaigns have changed considerably in the past two decades. Like all other campaigns, they are much more expensive. Today, the average cost of a winning Senate campaign is $10.2 million; a winning House campaign costs more than $1.5 million.[7] Campaign funds include direct contributions by individuals, contributions by political action committees (PACs), and "soft money" funneled through state party committees. All of these contributions are regulated by laws, including the Federal Election Campaign Act of 1971, as amended, and most recently the Bipartisan Campaign Reform Act of 2002.

Most candidates for Congress must win the nomination through a **direct primary**, in which **party identifiers** vote for the candidate who will be on the party ticket in the general election. To win the primary, candidates may take more liberal or more conservative positions to get the votes of party identifiers. In the general election, they may moderate their views to attract the votes of independents and voters from the other party.

Presidential Effects. Congressional candidates always hope that a strong presidential candidate will have "coattails" that will sweep in senators and representatives of the same party. Coattail effects have been quite limited, and in recent presidential elections have not materialized at all. One way to measure the coat-tail effect is to look at the subsequent midterm elections, held in the even-numbered years following the presidential contests—voter turnout falls sharply. In the past, the party controlling the White House normally lost seats in Congress in the midterm elections, in part because the coat-tail effect ceased to apply. Members of Congress who were from contested districts or who were in their first term were more likely not to be reelected.

Table 11–3 shows the pattern for midterm elections since 1942. The president's party lost seats in every election from 1942 to 1998. In that year, with President Clinton under the threat of impeachment, voters showed displeasure with the Republicans by voting in five more Democrats. In 2002, Republicans bucked the normal slump by winning five more Republican seats in the House. Most commentators believed that these midterm victories were based on public support for the president after the September 11, 2001, attacks. In 2006, the Republicans suffered a fairly normal midterm defeat, comparable to the midterm defeat in 1958, during the Eisenhower presidency.

Direct Primary
An intraparty election in which the voters select the candidates who will run on a party's ticket in the subsequent general election.

Party Identifiers
A person who identifies with a political party.

Table 11–3 ▶ Midterm Gains and Losses by the Party of the President, 1942–2014

SEATS GAINED OR LOST BY THE PARTY OF THE PRESIDENT IN THE HOUSE OF REPRESENTATIVES	
1942	−45 (D.)
1946	−55 (D.)
1950	−29 (D.)
1954	−18 (R.)
1958	−47 (R.)
1962	−4 (D.)
1966	−47 (D.)
1970	−12 (R.)
1974	−48 (R.)
1978	−15 (D.)
1982	−26 (R.)
1986	−5 (R.)
1990	−8 (R.)
1994	−52 (D.)
1998	+5 (D.)
2002	+5 (R.)
2006	−30 (R.)
2010	−62 (D.)
2014	−13 (D.)

7. http://www.opensecrets.org.

The 2010 midterm elections were a sweeping win by the Republicans, aided by the newly energized Tea Party movement. Republicans gained more than 60 seats in the House of Representatives, thus gaining majority control in that body. Although it is normal for the "out party" to gain seats in the midterms, the size of the Republican victory was the largest ever in modern times.

Republican candidates for the House and the Senate benefited from the unhappy mood of the electorate in 2014. Seemingly disgruntled with everyone in Washington, D.C., the voters increased the Republican majority in the House of Representatives and gave Republicans control of the Senate as well.

The Power of Incumbency

The power of incumbency in the outcome of congressional elections cannot be overemphasized. Once members are elected and survive the second election, they build considerable loyalty among constituents, and are frequently reelected as long as they wish to serve. Table 11–4 shows that more than 90 percent of representatives and a slightly smaller proportion of senators who run for reelection are successful. Several scholars contend that the pursuit of reelection is the strongest motivation behind the activities of members of Congress. Incumbents develop their homestyle, using the mass media, making personal appearances with constituents, and sending newsletters—all to produce a favorable image and to make

Table 11–4 ▶ The Power of Incumbency

| | ELECTION YEAR | | | | | | | | | | | |
	1992	1994	1996	1998	2000	2002	2004	2006	2008	2010	2012	2014
HOUSE												
Number of incumbent candidates	368	387	384	402	403	393	404	405	389	393	382	380
Reelected	325	349	361	395	394	383	397	382	372	336	345	366
Percentage of total	88.3	90.2	94.0	98.3	97.8	97.5	98.3	94.3	95.6	85.4	90.0	96.0
Defeated	43	38	23	7	9	10	7	23	17	57	37	14
In primary	19	3	2	1	3	3	1	2	3	4	5	3
In general election	24	34	21	6	6	7	6	21	17	53	32	11
Senate												
Number of incumbent candidates	28	26	21	29	29	28	26	29	32	25	22	29
Reelected	23	24	19	26	23	24	25	23	23	21	21	26
Percentage of total	82.1	92.3	90.5	89.7	79.3	85.7	96.2	79.3	81.3	84	95.0	89.7
Defeated	5	2	2	3	6	4	1	6	3	4	2	3
In primary	1	0	1	0	0	1	0	1*	0	2	1	0
In general election	4	2	1	3	6	3	1	6	3	2	1	3

* Joe Lieberman of Connecticut lost the Democratic primary but won the general election as an independent. He chose to organize with the Senate Democrats.
Sources: Norman Ornstein, Thomas E. Mann, and Michael J. Malbin, *Vital Statistics on Congress, 2001–2002* (Washington, DC: The AEI Press, 2002); and authors' update.

their name a household word. Members of Congress present themselves as informed, experienced, and responsive to their district's needs. Incumbents can demonstrate the positions that they have taken on key issues by referring to their voting records in Congress.

Party Control of Congress after the 2014 Elections

While a number of members of Congress retired before the election and a few were defeated in primaries, the majority of incumbent members ran for another term, and more than 90 percent were reelected. By the time the votes were counted, it was clear that the two houses were divided by party: The House Republicans maintained their majority, although they lost seven seats. Senate Democrats increased their margin by two, meaning the Senate is composed of 53 Democrats, 45 Republicans, and 2 Independents, Bernie Sanders of Vermont and Angus King of Maine.

Congressional Apportionment

■ **LO11.3:** Describe the processes of reapportionment and redistricting.

Two of the most complicated aspects of congressional elections are apportionment issues—**reapportionment** and **redistricting**. In a landmark 6-2 vote in 1962, the United States Supreme Court made the apportionment of state legislative districts a **justiciable question**(reviewable).[8] The Court did so by invoking the Fourteenth Amendment principle that no state can deny to any person "the equal protection of the laws." In 1964, the Court held that *both* chambers of a state legislature must be apportioned so that all districts are equal in population.[9] Later that year, the Court applied this "one person, one vote" principle to U.S. congressional districts on the basis of Article I, Section 2, of the Constitution, which requires that members of the House be chosen "by the People of the several States."[10]

Severe malapportionment of congressional districts before 1964 resulted in some districts containing two or three times the populations of other districts in the same state, thereby diluting the effect of a vote cast in the more populous districts. This system generally benefited the conservative populations of rural areas and small towns and harmed the interests of the more heavily populated and liberal cities. Suburban areas have benefited the most from the Court's rulings, as suburbs account for an increasingly larger proportion of the nation's population, while cities include a correspondingly smaller segment of the population.

Gerrymandering

Although the general issue of apportionment has been dealt with fairly successfully by the one person, one vote principle, the **gerrymandering** issue has not yet been resolved. This term refers to the legislative boundary-drawing tactics that were used under Elbridge Gerry, the governor of Massachusetts, in the 1812 elections (see Figure 11–1). A district is said to have been gerrymandered when its shape is altered substantially by the dominant party in a state legislature to maximize its electoral strength at the expense of the minority party.

Reapportionment
The allocation of seats in the House of Representatives to each state after each census.

Redistricting
The redrawing of the boundaries of the congressional districts within each state.

Justiciable Question
A question that may be raised and reviewed in court.

Gerrymandering
The drawing of legislative district boundary lines to obtain partisan or factional advantage. A district is said to be gerrymandered when its shape is manipulated by the dominant party in the state legislature to maximize electoral strength at the expense of the minority party.

8. *Baker v. Carr*, 369 U.S. 186 (1962). The term *justiciable* is pronounced "juhs-tish-a-buhl."
9. *Reynolds v. Sims*, 377 U.S. 533 (1964).
10. *Wesberry v. Sanders*, 376 U.S. 1 (1964).

Figure 11–1 ▶ The Original Gerrymander

The practice of "gerrymandering"—the excessive manipulation of the shape of a legislative district to benefit a certain incumbent or party—is probably as old as the Republic, but the name originated in 1812. In that year, the Massachusetts legislature carved out of Essex County a district that historian John Fiske said has a "dragonlike contour." When the painter Gilbert Stuart saw the misshapen district, he penciled in a head, wings, and claws and exclaimed, "That will do for a salamander!" Editor Benjamin Russell replied, "Better say a Gerrymander" (after Elbridge Gerry, then-governor of Massachusetts).

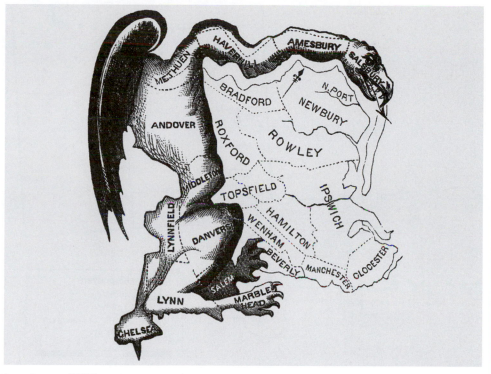

Source: Bettmann/CORBIS

In 1986, the Supreme Court heard *Davis v. Bandemer*, a case that challenged gerrymandered congressional districts in Indiana. The Court ruled for the first time that redistricting for the political benefit of one group could be challenged on constitutional grounds. In this specific case, however, the Court did not agree that the districts were drawn unfairly, because it could not be proved that a group of voters would consistently be deprived of influence at the polls as a result of the new districts.[11]

Redistricting after the 2010 Census

Republicans won a majority of seats in the House in 2010, and captured a majority of statehouses and governorships—they would have the upper hand in the drawing of new congressional districts after the release of the results of the 2010 Census. Consider Ohio: it lost enough population between 2000 and 2010 to lose two congressional seats. That meant all the districts in the state would be redrawn to adjust for the lower number of congressional districts. Through the "bipartisan" redistricting process, Ohio Republicans managed to put two sitting Democratic members of Congress—Marcy Kaptur and Dennis Kucinich—in one

11. 478 U.S. 109 (1986).

Figure 11-2 ▶ **The First Congressional District of Ohio**

Effective Beginning with the Election in 2012 for the 113th U.S. Congress

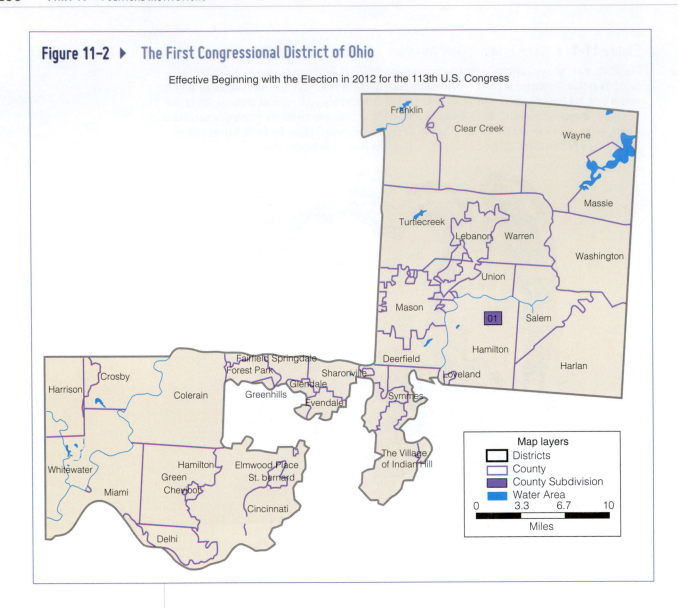

district and, through the drawing of district boundaries, enable Republicans to win 12 of the 16 districts. For an example of a Republican-leaning district, look at Figure 11–2, showing Ohio's First Congressional District. While this district included half of Hamilton County and half of the city of Cincinnati for many years, it now looks like "crossed signal flags." The district joins the traditional western Hamilton County districts with Warren County to the northeast with an odd-shaped bridge. The intent is to add enough Republican voters to the district to offset the majority Democratic vote in Cincinnati.

Redistricting decisions are often made by a small group of political leaders within a state legislature. Their goal is to shape voting districts to maximize their party's chances of winning state legislative seats as well as seats in Congress. Two of the techniques used are "packing" and "cracking." They *pack* voters supporting the opposing party into as few districts as possible or *crack* the opposing party's supporters into different districts.

Clearly, partisan redistricting aids incumbents. The party that dominates a state's legislature will be making redistricting decisions. Through gerrymandering tactics, districts can be redrawn in such a way as to ensure that party's continued strength in the state legislature or Congress. As noted earlier, some have estimated that only between 30 and 50 of the 435 seats in the House were open for any real competition in the most recent elections.

In 2004, the United States Supreme Court reviewed an obviously political redistricting scheme in Pennsylvania. The Court concluded, however, that the federal judiciary would not address purely political gerrymandering claims.[12] Two years later, the Supreme Court reached a similar conclusion with respect to most of the new congressional districts created by the Republicans in the Texas legislature in 2003. Again, the Court largely refused to intervene in what was plainly a political gerrymandering plan, although they did alter one district.[13]

Nonpartisan Redistricting

Several states, including Arizona, Iowa, and Minnesota, have adopted nonpartisan redistricting procedures. As you will see if you compare the First District of Ohio with the map of the Iowa districts (Figure 11–3), nonpartisan districts usually respect county lines and divide the state into fairly cleanly shaped districts that

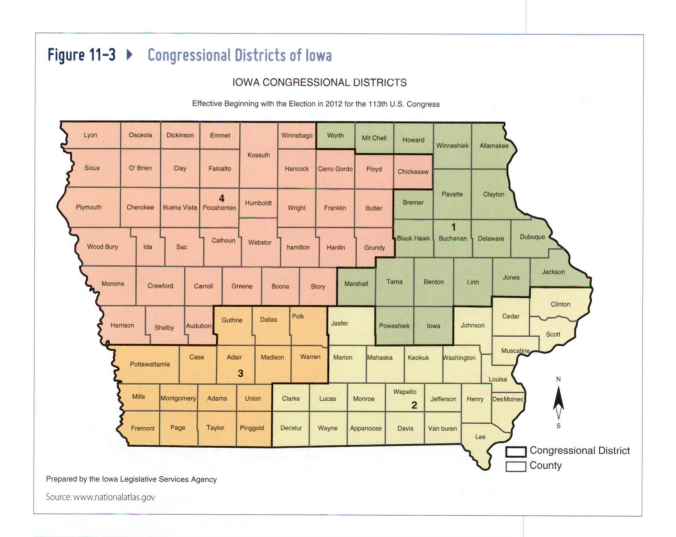

Figure 11–3 ▶ Congressional Districts of Iowa

IOWA CONGRESSIONAL DISTRICTS

Effective Beginning with the Election in 2012 for the 113th U.S. Congress

Prepared by the Iowa Legislative Services Agency

Source: www.nationalatlas.gov

12. *Vieth v. Jubelirer,* 541 U.S. 267 (2004).
13. *League of United Latin American Citizens v. Perry,* 399 F.Supp. 2nd 756 (2006).

share geographic characteristics. Research has shown that nonpartisan districts tend to be more competitive, no doubt because they have not been drawn to favor one party over the other.

"Minority-Majority" Districts

In the early 1990s, the federal government encouraged a type of gerrymandering that facilitated the election of a minority representative from a "minority-majority" area. Under the Voting Rights Act of 1965, the Justice Department issued directives to states after the 1990 census instructing them to create congressional districts that would maximize the voting power of minority groups—create districts in which minority voters were the majority. The results were several creatively drawn congressional districts—see, for example, the depiction of the Illinois Fourth Congressional District in Figure 11–4, which is commonly described as "a pair of earmuffs."

Constitutional Challenges

Many of these "minority-majority" districts were challenged in court by citizens who claimed that creating districts based on race or ethnicity alone violates the equal protection clause of the Constitution. In 1995, the Supreme Court agreed with this argument when it declared that Georgia's new Eleventh Congressional District was unconstitutional. The district stretched from Atlanta to the Atlantic,

Figure 11–4 ▶ The Fourth Congressional District of Illinois

The 4th district is outlined here in blue. It stretches from the near north side of Chicago out to the western suburbs and then turns east through the south side of Chicago. Why is the district drawn this way? The district includes a majority of Hispanic Americans and meets the criteria for a majority minority district. However, the northern portion of the district contains many Puerto Rican Americans, while many Mexican Americans live in the southern portion. The western link between the two is a superhighway where no one resides. The question is whether the people in this district have much in common other than Hispanic heritage.

Source: www.nationalatlas.gov

splitting eight counties and five municipalities along the way. The Court ruled that when a state assigns voters on the basis of race, "it engages in the offensive and demeaning assumption that voters of a particular race, because of their race, think alike, share the same political interests, and will prefer the same candidates at the polls." The Court also chastised the Justice Department for concluding that race-based districting was mandated under the Voting Rights Act of 1965: "When the Justice Department's interpretation of the Act compels race-based districting, it by definition raises a serious constitutional question."[14] In subsequent rulings, the Court affirmed its position.

Changing Directions

In the early 2000s, the Supreme Court took a new direction on racial redistricting challenges. In a 2000 case, the Court limited the federal government's authority to invalidate changes in state and local elections on the basis that the changes were discriminatory. The case involved a proposed school redistricting plan in Louisiana. The Court held that federal approval for the plan could not be withheld simply because the plan was discriminatory. Rather, the test was whether the plan left racial and ethnic minorities worse off than they were before.[15]

In 2001, the Supreme Court reviewed, for a second time, a case involving North Carolina's Twelfth District. The district was 165 miles long and largely hewed to Interstate 85. It was drawn to connect most of the urban centers where African American voters lived. In 1996, the Court had held that the district was unconstitutional because race had been the dominant factor in drawing its boundaries. Shortly thereafter, the boundaries were redrawn, but the district was again challenged as a racial gerrymander. In 2001, however, the Supreme Court held that there was insufficient evidence for the lower court's conclusion that race had been the dominant factor when the boundaries were redrawn.[16] The Twelfth District's boundaries remained as drawn.

Perks and Privileges

Legislators have many benefits that are not available to most workers. They are granted generous **franking** privileges permitting them to mail newsletters, surveys, and other correspondence to their constituents. The annual cost of congressional mail rose from $11 million in 1971 to a peak of $70 million. Congress has largely graduated to email and social networks to distribute literature. Today, the franking budget is less than $10 million.

Franking
A policy that enables members of Congress to send material through the mail by substituting their facsimile signature (frank) for postage.

Permanent Professional Staffs

More than 30,000 people are employed in the Capitol Hill bureaucracy. About half of them are personal and committee staff members. Personal staff includes office clerks and secretaries; professionals who deal with media relations, draft legislation, and satisfy constituency requests for service; and staffers who maintain local offices in the member's home district or state.

The average Senate office on Capitol Hill employs about 30 staff members, and twice that number work on the personal staffs of senators from the most populous states. House office staffs are limited to

did you know?
Members of Congress have free parking spaces at Reagan National Airport in Washington, DC.

14. *Miller v. Johnson*, 515 U.S. 900 (1995).
15. *Reno v. Bossier Parish School Board*, 528 U.S. 320 (2000).
16. *Easley v. Cromartie*, 532 U.S. 234 (2001).

18 employees. The number of staff members has increased dramatically since 1960. Most increases come in assistants to individual members—some question whether staff members are really advising on legislation or are primarily aiding constituents and gaining votes in the next election.

Congress also benefits from the expertise of the professional staffs of agencies created to produce information for members. The Congressional Research Service, the Government Accountability Office, and the Congressional Budget Office all provide reports, audits, and policy recommendations for review by members of Congress.

Privileges and Immunities under the Law

Members of Congress also benefit from some special constitutional protections. Under Article I, Section 6, of the Constitution, they "shall in all Cases, except Treason, Felony and Breach of the Peace, be privileged from Arrest during their Attendance at the Session of their respective Houses, and in going to and returning from the same; and for any Speech or Debate in either House, they shall not be questioned in any other Place." The arrest immunity clause is not really an important provision today. The "speech or debate" clause, however, means that a member may make any allegations or other statements he or she wishes in connection with official duties and normally not be sued for libel or slander or otherwise be subject to legal action.

Congressional Caucuses: Another Source of Support

All members of Congress are members of one or more caucuses. The most important caucuses are those established by the parties in each chamber. These Democratic and Republican meetings provide information and devise legislative strategy for the party. Other caucuses bring together members who have similar political views, such as the moderate Democratic Study Group, while some have a constituency focus, such as the Rust Belt Caucus or the Potato Caucus. Some of the most important and influential caucuses are those for minority and underrepresented groups in Congress.

Chair of the Congressional Black Caucus, Representative Marcia Fudge of Ohio, takes the podium to speak during a news conference on the Supreme Court's decision overturning part of the Voting Rights Act.

Bill Clark/CQ Roll Call/Getty Images

The Congressional Women's Caucus has long provided support for the women elected to the Congress and has provided a forum for discussing issues that women members find important, including the treatment of women in Afghanistan. Two of the most important minority-based caucuses are the Congressional Black Caucus and the Hispanic Congressional Caucus. Both have grown in the last two decades as the numbers of African American and Hispanic members grew. They are now funded by businesses and special interests, and provide staff assistance and information for members of Congress to help build support among specific groups of voters.

Women's Policy Inc. @WomensPolicyInc · Mar 25
2013 is the first uninterrupted year of education for girls. --The Hon. Naheed Farid discussing gains of women and girls in Afghanistan.
Expand ↩ Reply ↻ Retweet ★ Favorite ••• More

Women's Policy Inc./Twitter

did you know?
Jeannette Rankin was elected to the House of Representatives from Montana in 1916, three years before women got the right to vote.

The Committee Structure

■ **LO11.4:** Discuss the importance of committees to the lawmaking process and to the ability of members of Congress to do their jobs.

Thousands of bills are introduced in every session of Congress, and no single member can possibly be adequately informed on all the issues that arise. The committee system is a way to provide for specialization, or a division of the legislative labor. Members of a committee can concentrate on just one area or topic and develop sufficient expertise to draft appropriate legislation when needed. The flow of legislation through both the House and the Senate is determined largely by the speed with which the members of these committees act on bills and resolutions.

did you know?
Elmo of Sesame Street is the only non-human to testify before Congress.

The Power of Committees

Sometimes called "little legislatures," committees usually have the final say on pieces of legislation.[17] Committee actions may be overturned on the floor by the House or Senate, but this rarely happens. Legislators normally defer to the expertise of the chairperson and other members of the committee who speak on the floor in defense of a committee decision. Chairpersons of committees exercise control over the scheduling of hearings and formal action on a bill and decide which subcommittee will act on legislation falling within their committee's jurisdiction.

Committees only rarely are deprived of control over a bill—although this kind of action is provided for in the rules of each chamber. In the House, if a bill has been considered by a standing committee for 30 days, the signatures of a majority (218) of the House membership on a **discharge petition** can pry a bill out of an uncooperative committee's hands. From 1909 to the present, although more than 900 such petitions were initiated, only slightly more than two dozen resulted in successful discharge efforts. Of those, 20 resulted in bills that passed the House.[18]

Types of Congressional Committees

Over the past two centuries, Congress has created several different types of committees, each of which serves particular needs of the institution.

Discharge Petition
procedure by which a bill in the House of Representatives may be forced (discharged) out of a committee that has refused to report it for consideration by the House. The petition must be signed by an absolute majority (218) of representatives and is used only on rare occasions.

17. The term *little legislatures* is from Woodrow Wilson, *Congressional Government* (New York: Meridian Books, 1956 [first published in 1885]).
18. Congressional Quarterly, Inc., *Guide to Congress*, 5th ed. (Washington, DC: CQ Press, 2000); and authors' update.

AP Images/J. Scott Applewhite

Standing Committees. By far the most important committees in Congress are the **standing committees**—permanent bodies that continue from session to session. A list of the standing committees of the 113th Congress is presented in Table 11–5. In addition, most of the standing committees have created subcommittees to carry out their work. The 113th Congress had 70 subcommittees in the Senate and 104 subcommittees in the House.[19] Each standing committee is given a specific area of legislative policy jurisdiction, and almost all legislative measures are considered by the appropriate standing committees.

Representative Nydia
M. Velazquez (D-NY), the first Puerto Rican woman elected to Congress, praises the achievements of Supreme Court Justice Sonia Sotomayor, the first Latina member of the Court.

Standing Committees
A permanent committee in the House or Senate that considers bills within a certain subject area.

Table 11–5 ▸ Standing Committees of the 113th Congress, 2013–2015

HOUSE COMMITTEES	SENATE COMMITTEES
Agriculture	Agriculture, Nutrition, and Forestry
Appropriations	Appropriations
Armed Services	Armed Services
Budget	Banking, Housing, and Urban Affairs
Education and the Workforce	Budget
Energy and Commerce	Commerce, Science, and Transportation
Ethics	Energy and Natural Resources
Financial Services	Environment and Public Works
Foreign Affairs	Finance
Homeland Security	Foreign Relations
House Administration	Health, Education, Labor, and Pensions
Intelligence	Homeland Security and Governmental Affairs
Judiciary	Judiciary
Natural Resources	Rules and Administration
Oversight and Government Reform	Small Business and Entrepreneurship
Rules	Veterans Affairs
Science, Space and Technology	
Small Business	
Transportation and Infrastructure	
Veterans Affairs	
Ways and Means	

19. "The Legislature," www.whitehouse.gov.

CHAPTER 11 • THE CONGRESS

Because of the importance of their work and the traditional influence of their members in Congress, certain committees are considered to be more prestigious than others. Seats on standing committees that handle spending issues are especially desirable because members can use these positions to benefit their constituents. Committees that control spending include the Appropriations Committee in either chamber and the Ways and Means Committee in the House. Members also seek seats on committees that handle matters of special interest to their constituents. A member of the House from an agricultural district, for example, will have an interest in joining the House Agriculture Committee.

Select Committees. In principle, a **select committee** is created for a limited time and for a specific legislative purpose. For example, a select committee may be formed to investigate a public problem, such as child nutrition or aging. In practice, a select committee, such as the Select Committee on Intelligence in each chamber, may continue indefinitely. Select committees rarely create original legislation.

Joint Committees. A **joint committee** is formed by the concurrent action of both chambers of Congress and consists of members from each chamber. Joint committees, which may be permanent or temporary, have dealt with the economy, taxation, and the Library of Congress.

Conference Committees. Special joint committees—**conference committees** —are formed to achieve agreement between the House and the Senate on the exact wording of legislative acts when the two chambers pass legislative proposals in different forms. The bill is reported out of the conference committee if it is approved by the majority of members from both houses who sit on the committee and is returned to the House and Senate for final votes. No bill can be sent to the White House to be signed into law unless it first passes both chambers in identical form. Sometimes called the "third house" of Congress, conference committees are in a position to make significant alterations to legislation and frequently become the focal point of policy debates.

The House Rules Committee. Because of its special "gatekeeping" power over the terms on which legislation will reach the floor of the House of Representatives, the House Rules Committee holds a uniquely powerful position. A special committee rule sets the time limit on debate and determines whether and how a bill may be amended. This practice dates back to 1883. The Rules Committee has the unusual power to meet while the House is in session, to have its resolutions considered immediately on the floor, and to initiate legislation on its own.

The Selection of Committee Members

In both chambers, members are appointed to standing committees by the Steering Committee of their party. The majority-party member with the longest term of continuous service on a standing committee can be given preference when the leadership nominates chairpersons. Newt Gingrich, during his time as Speaker of the House, restricted chairpersons' terms to six years. Additionally, he bypassed seniority to appoint chairpersons loyal to his own platform.

Respecting seniority is an informal, traditional process, and it applies to other significant posts in Congress as well. The **seniority system**, although it deliberately treats members unequally, provides a predictable means of assigning

Select Committee
A temporary legislative committee established for a limited time period and for a special purpose.

Joint Committee
A legislative committee composed of members from both chambers of Congress.

Conference Committees
A special joint committee appointed to reconcile differences when bills pass the two chambers of Congress in different forms.

Seniority System
A custom followed in both chambers of Congress specifying that the member of the majority party with the longest term of continuous service will be given preference when a committee chairperson (or a holder of some other significant post) is selected.

Safe Seats
A district that returns a legislator with 55 percent of the vote or more.

positions of power within Congress. The most senior member of the minority party is called the *ranking committee member* for that party.

The general pattern was that members of the House or Senate who represented **safe seats** would be reelected continually and eventually would accumulate enough years of continuous committee service to enable them to become the chairpersons of their committees. In the 1970s, a number of reforms in the chairperson selection process modified the seniority system. They introduced the use of a secret ballot in electing House committee chairpersons and allowed for the possibility of choosing a chairperson on a basis other than seniority. The Democrats immediately replaced three senior chairpersons who were out of step with the rest of their party. The Republican leadership in the House has also taken more control over the selection of committee chairpersons.

The Formal Leadership

■ **LO11.5:** Describe the leadership structure in each house of Congress, noting the differences between the House and the Senate.

The limited amount of centralized power that exists in Congress is exercised through party-based mechanisms. Congress is organized by party. When the Democratic Party wins a majority of seats in either the House or the Senate, Democrats control the official positions of power in that chamber, and every important committee has a Democratic chairperson and a majority of Democratic members. The same process holds when Republicans are in the majority. For a complete list of the current leadership of both parties in the House of Representatives, go to www.house.gov.

Generally speaking, the leadership organizations in the House and the Senate look alike on paper. Leaders in the House of Representatives, however, have more control over the agenda of the body and, often, over their own party's members. Senate leaders, due to the power of individual members, must work closely with the other party's leaders to achieve success. Although the party leaders in both the House and the Senate are considered to be the most powerful members of the Congress, their powers pale compared to those given to the leaders in true "party government" legislatures. The differences between those legislatures and the U.S. Congress are detailed in the Beyond Our Borders feature.

Leadership in the House

The House leadership is made up of the Speaker, the majority and minority leaders, and the party whips.

Speaker of the House
The presiding officer in the House of Representatives. The Speaker is always a member of the majority party and is the most powerful and influential member of the House.

The Speaker. The foremost power holder in the House of Representatives is the **Speaker of the House**. The Speaker's position is a nonpartisan one, but for the better part of two centuries, has been the official leader of the majority party in the House. When a new Congress convenes, each party nominates a candidate for Speaker. All Democratic members of the House are expected to vote for their party's nominee, and all Republicans are expected to support their candidate. The vote to organize the House is the one vote in which representatives must vote with their party. In a sense, this vote defines a member's partisan status.

The influence of modern-day Speakers is based primarily on their personal prestige, persuasive ability, and knowledge of the legislative process—plus the acquiescence or active support of other representatives. In recent years, both the

Republican and Democratic parties in the House have given their leaders more power in making appointments and controlling the agenda. The major formal powers of the Speaker include the following:

1. Presiding over meetings of the House.

2. Appointing members of joint committees and conference committees.

3. Scheduling legislation for floor action.

4. Deciding points of order and interpreting the rules with the advice of the House parliamentarian.

5. Referring bills and resolutions to the appropriate standing committees of the House.

A Speaker may take part in floor debate and vote, as can any other member of Congress, but recent Speakers usually have voted only to break a tie. Since 1975, the Speaker, when a Democrat, has also had the power to appoint the Democratic Steering Committee, which determines new committee assignments for House party members.

The powers of the Speaker are related to his or her control over information and communications channels in the House and the degree of support received from members. This is a significant power in a large, decentralized institution in which information is a very important resource. Since the Speakership of Newt Gingrich (R-GA) in 1994, the leadership of the House has held significant power to control the agenda and provide rewards to the members. During the same time period, the degree of polarization between the majority and minority parties has increased, and cohesion within each party has grown stronger. Scholars suggest that this is the result of increased ideological makeup within the congressional delegation of both parties and the election of fewer moderate or centrist members to the House.

The Majority Leader. The **majority leader of the House** is elected by a caucus of the majority party to foster cohesion among party members and to act as a spokesperson for the party. The majority leader cooperates with the Speaker and other party leaders to formulate the party's legislative program and to guide it through the legislative process in the House. The Democrats often recruit future Speakers from those who hold that position.

The Minority Leader. The **minority leader of the House** is the candidate nominated for Speaker by a caucus of the minority party. Like the majority leader, the leader of the minority party has as her or his primary responsibility the maintaining of cohesion within the party's ranks. The minority leader works for cohesion among the party's members and speaks on behalf of the president if the minority party controls the White House. In relations with the majority party, the minority leader consults with both the Speaker and the majority leader on recognizing members who wish to speak on the floor, on House rules and procedures, and on the scheduling of legislation. Minority leaders have no actual power in these areas, however.

Whips. The leadership of each party includes assistants to the majority and minority leaders. **Whips** are members of Congress who assist the party leaders by passing information down from the leadership to party members and by ensuring that members show up for floor debate and cast their votes on important issues. Whips conduct polls among party members about the members' views on legislation, inform the leaders about whose vote is doubtful and whose is certain, and exert pressure on members to support the leaders' positions. In the House, serving as a whip is the first step toward positions of higher leadership.

Majority Leader of the House
A legislative position held by an important party member in the House of Representatives. The majority leader is selected by the majority party in caucus or conference to foster cohesion among party members and to act as spokesperson for the majority party in the House.

Minority Leader of the House
The party leader elected by the minority party in the House.

Whips
A member of Congress who aids the majority or minority leader of the House or the Senate.

Beyond Our Borders

Should Parties Control Legislatures (and Governments)?

The Congress of the United States is a bicameral legislature. The American-style legislature differs from most of the legislatures in the world in several significant ways. Because it is composed of three branches, separate structures sharing powers, we frequently have "divided" government, meaning that the party that controls one or both houses of Congress does not control the presidency. Does this mean that the government is hopelessly deadlocked? Not usually. Members of Congress, especially in the House, frequently support their party leaders, but on many other votes, "cross the aisle" to vote with members of the other side, thinking it best for their constituency or reelection hopes.

Most Americans think that our legislature is modeled on the British parliament. However, the parliament of Great Britain, as well as that of many other Western nations, is based on the idea of "party government." No separation of powers exists between the legislature and the executive branch. When a political party wins a majority of seats in the House of Parliament (the lower and only powerful house), that party then selects the prime minister, who is also the party leader. The prime minister and cabinet members sit in Parliament during debates, playing an active role. The party, which may have promised a better welfare system or to eliminate the armed services, votes the new law into effect, and the prime minister implements the policy.*

Another variation on this type of party government occurs when a nation (Germany, Italy, and Israel are examples) has a multiparty system. In that case, no party wins a majority of seats. The party with the plurality of seats chooses the leader and then negotiates with other parties to form a coalition to constitute a government and pass new legislation. Governing as part of a coalition is much more difficult, however, because if one partner does not agree with the proposed policy, the coalition may fall apart, and new elections may be necessary.

Consider the important relationship between the executive (prime minister or president) and the legislature. In the U.S. system, even if Congress and the president are of the same party, this does not guarantee that the president's agenda will be implemented in full. President Obama, who came into office with a majority in the House, received speedy and cohesive support for his initiatives in his first year, but legislation often bogged down in the Senate due to its procedural rules. Both the Democrats and the Republicans in the House were so cohesive throughout much of those years that some scholars believed it was a form of "conditional party government."** In a true party

Deputy Prime Minister Nick Clegg (fifth from right) and Prime Minister David Cameron of Great Britain respond to members of Parliament during the Question Hour in May, 2010.

government system, everything on the Democrats' agenda would become law, and the president would be selected by the Congress.

Although Americans complain bitterly about ineffective Congresses, they generally prefer divided government due to fear that one party will have too much power.

For Critical Analysis

1. *Would the United States ever grant the degree of power to the president to achieve his or her agenda that is afforded to the prime minister of Great Britain?*

2. *What is more important—controlling government power or having a more effective legislature?*

3. *How would the United States Congress be different if three or four parties were represented there?*

*For information on the world's legislatures, go to the Web site of the Inter-Parliamentary Union at www.ipu.org.
**The "conditional party government" thesis has been developed by David Rohde, *Parties and Leaders in the Postreform House* (Chicago: University of Chicago Press, 1991).

Leadership in the Senate

The Senate is less than one-fourth the size of the House. This fact alone explains why a formal, complex, and centralized leadership structure is not as necessary in the Senate as it is in the House. For a list of the current leaders of both parties in the U.S. Senate, go to www.senate.gov.

The two highest-ranking formal leadership positions in the Senate are essentially ceremonial in nature. Under the Constitution, the vice president of the United States is the president of the Senate and may vote to break a tie. The vice president, however, is only rarely present for a meeting of the Senate. The Senate elects instead a **president pro tempore** ("pro tem") to preside over the Senate in the vice president's absence. Ordinarily, the president pro tem is the member of the majority party with the longest continuous term of service in the Senate. The president pro tem is mostly a ceremonial position. Junior senators take turns actually presiding over the sessions of the Senate.

The real leadership power in the Senate rests in the hands of the **Senate majority leader**, the **Senate minority leader**, and their respective whips. The Senate majority and minority leaders have the right to be recognized first in debate on the floor and generally exercise the same powers available to the House majority and minority leaders. They control the scheduling of debate on the floor in conjunction with the majority party's Policy Committee, influence the allocation of committee assignments for new members or for senators attempting to transfer to a new committee, influence the selection of other party officials, and participate in selecting members of conference committees. They are expected to mobilize support for partisan legislative initiatives or for the proposals of a president who belongs to their party. The leaders act as liaisons with the White House when the president is of their party, try to obtain the cooperation of committee chairpersons, and seek to facilitate the smooth functioning of the Senate through the senators' unanimous consent. The majority and minority leaders are elected by their respective party caucuses.

Senate party whips, like their House counterparts, maintain communication within the party on platform positions and try to ensure that party colleagues

President Pro Tempore
The temporary presiding officer of the Senate in the absence of the vice president.

Senate Majority Leader
The chief spokesperson of the majority party in the Senate, who directs the legislative program and party strategy.

Senate Minority Leader
The party officer in the Senate who commands the minority party's opposition to the policies of the majority party and directs the legislative program and strategy of his or her party.

In December 2013, Senator Patty Murray (D-WA) and Representative Paul Ryan (R-WI 1st District) announce their successful negotiation of a budget bill covering two years.

T.J. Kirkpatrick/Getty Images

are present for floor debate and important votes. The Senate whip system is far less elaborate than its counterpart in the House, simply because there are fewer members to track.

How Members of Congress Decide

■ **LO11.6:** Demonstrate how a bill becomes a law and explain how the different processes in the House and the Senate influence legislating.

Each member of Congress casts hundreds of votes in each session and compiles a record of votes during the years that he or she spends in the national legislature. Research shows that the best predictor of a member's vote is party affiliation. Party leadership in each house works hard to build cohesion and agreement among the members through the activities of the party caucuses and conferences.

The Conservative Coalition

Conservative Coalition
An alliance of Republicans and southern Democrats that can form in the House or the Senate to oppose liberal legislation and support conservative legislation.

Blue Dog Democrats
Members of Congress from more moderate states or districts who sometimes "cross over" to vote with Republicans on legislation.

Political parties are not always unified. In the 1950s and 1960s, the Democrats in Congress were often split between northern liberals and southern conservatives, which gave rise to the **conservative coalition**, a voting bloc made up of conservative Democrats and conservative Republicans. This coalition was able to win many votes over the years. Today, however, most southern conservatives are Republicans, so the coalition has almost disappeared. Some Democrats in Congress, however, represent more moderate states or districts. The votes of these members, who are known as **Blue Dog Democrats**, are frequently courted by Republican leaders.

did you know?

The term "Blue Dog Democrat" was coined by a Texas Democratic congressman who said that liberal members were choking some Democrats until they turned blue.

Polarization and Gridlock

Over the last two decades, both parties have become more cohesive, both within the halls of Congress and at the state and local level. Almost all of the Democratic members of Congress would now consider themselves to be liberals, while almost all Republican members of Congress could be considered conservatives. Numerous voting studies have concluded that both houses of Congress are more polarized than at any time in the last 50 years.[20] This is due, in part, to the ability of the parties to draw congressional districts that are more heavily Democratic or Republican. To win a nomination in such a district, the candidate must gain the votes of the most liberal or most conservative voters. The majority of Democratic representatives are very likely to vote against the majority of Republicans.

Polarization
Strong divisions between groups of people over beliefs.

Divided Government
The situation when the presidency and one or more houses of Congress are controlled by different political parties.

Add to this increasing **polarization**—the strong division between groups of people over beliefs. This situation is often termed **divided government**. Divided government can be effective if the parties agree to compromise. When there is a foreign policy crisis, parties typically work well together. Divided government can also lead to a situation where neither side is willing to compromise on public policy, resulting in what is popularly known as gridlock. When this happens, major legislation stalls and the only laws that are passed are those which are noncontroversial. Polling over the years shows that the American public is strongly in favor of a productive Congress, regardless of which party is in the majority in either house.[21]

---

20. Lynda Saad, "Gridlock is Top Reason Americans are Critical of Congress," The Gallup Poll, June 12, 2013.
21. See the summary of the polarization studies in Thomas Mann and Norman Ornstein, *It's Even Worse Than It Looks: How the American Constitutional System Collided with the New Politics of Extremism* (New York: Basic Books, 2012): 51–58.).

"Crossing Over"

On some votes, individual representatives and senators vote against their party, "crossing over to the other side" because the interests of their states or districts differ from the interests that prevail within the rest of their party. Democratic senators from western states normally vote with Republicans on agricultural bills. Other voting decisions are based on the members' religious or ideological beliefs. Votes on issues such as abortion or gay rights may be motivated by a member's ideology or personal beliefs.

With so many voting decisions, every member cannot be fully informed on each issue. Research suggests that many voting decisions are based on cues provided by trusted colleagues or the party leadership. A member who sits on the committee that wrote a law may become a reliable source of information about that law. Alternatively, a member may turn to a colleague who represents a district in the same state or one who represents a similar district for cues on voting. Cues may also come from fellow committee members, leaders, and the administration.

Logrolling, Earmarks, and "Pork"

Sometimes, leaders on either side of the aisle will offer incentives to get needed votes for the passage of legislation. Even the president has been known to offer opportunities for the member to better serve his or her district by "bringing home the bacon." When a member "trades" his or her vote on a particular bill with another member in exchange for his or her vote on other legislation, the practice is known as logrolling. Often, members request that special appropriations for projects back home are attached to a bill to gain their votes. If the actual project is named, this is referred to as an **earmark**. The term comes from the V-shaped mark that is cut in a pig's ear to identify the animal. These special projects are often referred to as **pork**, as in "bringing home the bacon." Although the practice of special appropriations has a long history, earmarks now total more than $30 billion in most years. Efforts have been made to force lawmakers to reveal all of their special projects, but new methods have emerged to hide these special appropriations from the public eye.

Politicians and reformers often rail against the practice of earmarks, and some projects seem ridiculous to everyone except those who will benefit. In some cases, earmarks truly are needed; in others, they are seen as the key to keeping a member of Congress in office. As the late Senator Robert Byrd of West Virginia was known to remark, "One man's pork is another man's job."[22]

Earmark
Funding appropriations that are specifically designated for a named project in a member's state or district.

Pork
Special projects or appropriations that are intended to benefit a member's district or state; slang term for earmarks.

How a Bill Becomes Law

Each year, Congress and the president propose and approve many laws. As detailed in Figure 11–5, each law begins as a bill, which must be introduced in either the House or the Senate. Often, similar bills are introduced in both chambers. A "money bill," however, must start in the House. In each chamber, the bill follows similar steps. It is referred to a committee and its subcommittees for study, discussion, hearings, and rewriting ("markup"). When the bill is reported out to

22. "Just Say No to Earmarks," *Wall Street Journal*, editorial, October 4, 2006.

Figure 11–5 ▶ How a Bill Becomes a Law

This illustration shows the most typical way in which proposed legislation is enacted into law. Most legislation begins as similar bills introduced into the House and the Senate. The process is illustrated here with two hypothetical bills, House bill No. 100 (HR 100) and Senate bill No.200 (S 200). The path of HR 100 is shown on the left, and that of S 200, on the right

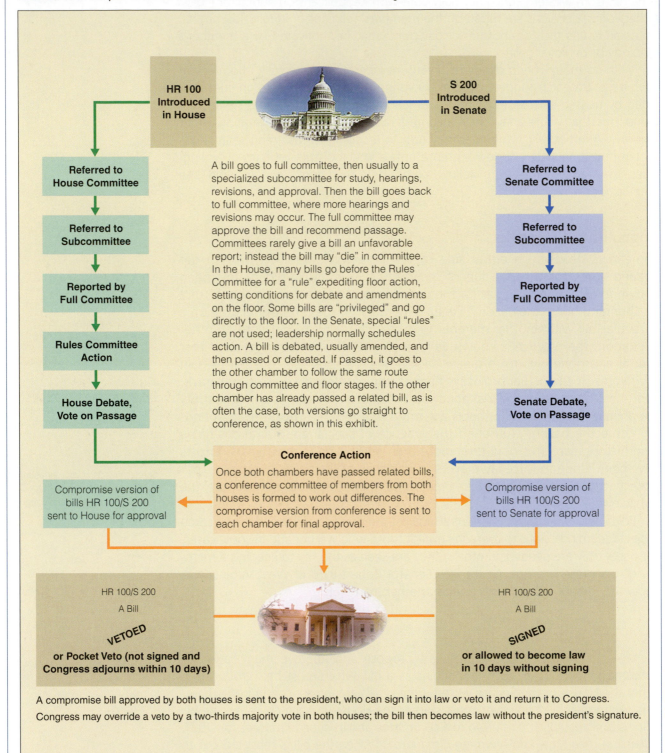

A bill goes to full committee, then usually to a specialized subcommittee for study, hearings, revisions, and approval. Then the bill goes back to full committee, where more hearings and revisions may occur. The full committee may approve the bill and recommend passage. Committees rarely give a bill an unfavorable report; instead the bill may "die" in committee. In the House, many bills go before the Rules Committee for a "rule" expediting floor action, setting conditions for debate and amendments on the floor. Some bills are "privileged" and go directly to the floor. In the Senate, special "rules" are not used; leadership normally schedules action. A bill is debated, usually amended, and then passed or defeated. If passed, it goes to the other chamber to follow the same route through committee and floor stages. If the other chamber has already passed a related bill, as is often the case, both versions go straight to conference, as shown in this exhibit.

Conference Action
Once both chambers have passed related bills, a conference committee of members from both houses is formed to work out differences. The compromise version from conference is sent to each chamber for final approval.

A compromise bill approved by both houses is sent to the president, who can sign it into law or veto it and return it to Congress.

Congress may override a veto by a two-thirds majority vote in both houses; the bill then becomes law without the president's signature.

© shutterstock.com

the full chamber, it must be scheduled for debate (by the Rules Committee in the House and by the leadership in the Senate). After the bill has been passed in each chamber, if it contains different provisions, a conference committee is formed to write a compromise bill, which must be approved by both chambers before it is sent to the president to sign or veto.

Another form of congressional action, the *joint resolution*, differs little from a bill in how it is proposed or debated. Once it is approved by both chambers and signed by the president, it has the force of law.[23] A joint resolution to amend the Constitution, however, after it is approved by two-thirds of both chambers, is sent not to the president but to the states for ratification.

How Much Will the Government Spend?

■ **LO11.7:** Explain how the federal budget is constructed and the legislative process for approving the budget.

The Constitution is very clear about where the power of the purse lies in the national government: All taxing or spending bills must originate in the House of Representatives. Today, much of the business of Congress is concerned with approving government expenditures through the budget process and raising the revenues to pay for government programs.

From 1922, when Congress required the president to prepare and present to the legislature an **executive budget**, until 1974, the congressional budget process was so disjointed that it was difficult to visualize the total picture of government finances. The president presented the executive budget to Congress in January. It was broken down into 13 or more appropriations bills. After all of the bills had been debated, amended, and passed, it was more or less possible to estimate total government spending for the next year.

Executive Budget
The budget prepared and submitted by the president to Congress.

Frustrated by the president's ability to impound (withhold) funds and dissatisfied with the entire budget process, Congress passed the Budget and Impoundment Control Act of 1974 to regain some control over the nation's spending. The act required the president to spend the funds that Congress had appropriated, ending the president's ability to kill programs by withholding funds. The other major accomplishment was to force Congress to examine total national taxing and spending at least twice in each budget cycle. See Figure 11–6 for a graphic illustration of the budget cycle.

Preparing the Budget

The federal government operates on a **fiscal year (FY)** cycle. The fiscal year runs from October through September, so that fiscal 2016, or FY16, runs from October 1, 2015, through September 30, 2016. Eighteen months before a fiscal year starts, the executive branch begins preparing the budget. The Office of Management and Budget (OMB) outlines the budget and then sends it to the various departments and agencies. Bargaining follows, in which, for example, the Department

Fiscal Year (FY)
A 12-month period that is used for bookkeeping, or accounting, purposes. Usually, the fiscal year does not coincide with the calendar year. For example, the federal government's fiscal year runs from October 1 through September 30.

---

23. In contrast, *simple resolutions* and *concurrent resolutions* do not carry the force of law, but rather are used by one or both chambers of Congress, respectively, to express facts, principles, or opinions. For example, a concurrent resolution is used to set the time when Congress will adjourn.

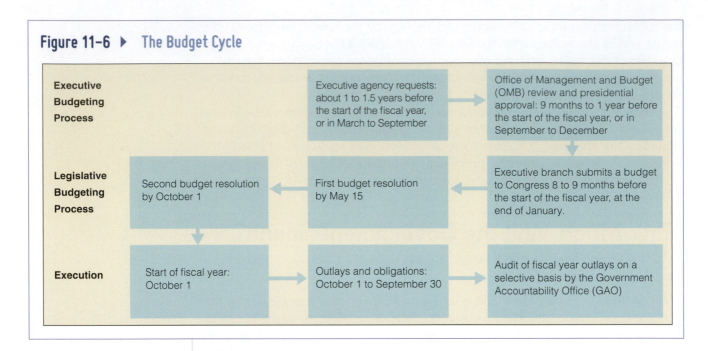

Figure 11-6 ▶ The Budget Cycle

| Executive Budgeting Process | | Executive agency requests: about 1 to 1.5 years before the start of the fiscal year, or in March to September | Office of Management and Budget (OMB) review and presidential approval: 9 months to 1 year before the start of the fiscal year, or in September to December |

| Legislative Budgeting Process | Second budget resolution by October 1 | First budget resolution by May 15 | Executive branch submits a budget to Congress 8 to 9 months before the start of the fiscal year, at the end of January. |

| Execution | Start of fiscal year: October 1 | Outlays and obligations: October 1 to September 30 | Audit of fiscal year outlays on a selective basis by the Government Accountability Office (GAO) |

How important is it that U.S. citizens are aware of where to find the federal budget and other federal documents for reference?

of Health and Human Services argues for more welfare spending, and the armed forces argue for more defense spending. You can find the federal budget on the official OMB website.

Even though the OMB has only 600 employees, it is one of the most powerful agencies in Washington. It assembles the budget documents and monitors federal agencies throughout each year. Every year, it begins the budget process with a **spring review**, in which it requires all of the agencies to review their programs, activities, and goals. Several months later, the OMB begins the **fall review**. At this time, the OMB looks at budget requests and, in almost all cases, pares them back. Although the OMB works within guidelines established by the president, specific decisions often are left to the OMB director and the director's associates. The budget must be completed by January so that it can be included in the *Economic Report of the President.*

Congress Faces the Budget

In January, nine months before the fiscal year starts, the president takes the OMB's proposed budget, approves it, and submits it to Congress. Then the congressional budgeting process takes over. The **first budget resolution** by Congress is scheduled to be passed in May of each year. It sets overall revenue goals and spending targets. During the summer, bargaining among all the concerned parties takes place. Spending and tax laws that are drawn up during

Spring Review
The annual process in which the Office of Management and Budget requires federal agencies to review their programs, activities, and goals and submit their requests for funding for the next fiscal year.

Fall Review
The annual process in which the Office of Management and Budget, after receiving formal federal agency requests for funding for the next fiscal year, reviews the requests, makes changes, and submits its recommendations to the president.

this period are supposed to be guided by the May congressional budget resolution. For each departmental budget, Congress must authorize funds to be spent. The **authorization** is a formal declaration by the appropriate congressional committee that a certain amount of funding may be available to an agency. After the funds are authorized, they must be appropriated by Congress. The appropriations committees of both the House and the Senate forward spending bills to their respective bodies. The **appropriation** of funds occurs when the final bill is passed.

Budget Resolutions

By September, Congress is scheduled to pass its **second budget resolution**, one that will set "binding" limits on taxes and spending for the fiscal year beginning October 1. Bills passed before that date that do not fit within the limits of the budget resolution are supposed to be changed.

In actuality, between 1978 and 1996, Congress did not pass a complete budget by October 1. Some years, the Congress has not succeeded in passing a budget at all. In other words, generally, Congress does not follow its own rules. In each fiscal year that starts without a budget, every agency operates on the basis of a **continuing resolution**, which enables the agency to continue its present function with funding equal to that of the previous year. Even continuing resolutions have not always been passed on time.

first budget resolution
A resolution passed by Congress in May that sets overall revenue and spending goals for the following fiscal year.

Authorization
A formal declaration by a legislative committee that a certain amount of funding may be available to an agency. Some authorizations terminate in a year; others are renewable automatically, without further congressional action.

Appropriation
The passage, by Congress, of a spending bill specifying the amount of authorized funds that actually will be allocated for an agency's use.

Second Budget Resolution
A resolution passed by Congress in September that sets "binding" limits on taxes and spending for the following fiscal year.

Continuing Resolution
A temporary funding law that Congress passes when an appropriations bill has not been decided by the beginning of the new fiscal year on October 1.

Dennis Brack / POOL/EPA/Newscom

President Obama meets with members of Congress in September 2013 to build an agreement on sending military assistance to the rebel forces in Syria.

What Would You Do?

Should Student Loans Be Saved?

Federally guaranteed student loans have only been an option for college students and their families for the last 20 years or so. The original direct loan program has mushroomed into at least four different loan programs run by the federal government, as well as programs offered by banks, colleges, and the states themselves. From time to time, Congress changes the structure of the program and raises interest rates or changes repayment options for these loans.

Why Should You Care?

Over a college career, student may borrow more than $100,000 and must begin paying that back within six months of graduation. There are some options for helping students who are deeply in debt, but the loans prevent students from buying homes or investing in further education.

Critics suggest that the availability of student loans has encouraged colleges and universities to build extravagant recreation centers and increase the number of employees, thus forcing increases in tuition and other costs for students in order to pay for such upgrades. The cost of college has risen at a much higher rate than the cost of living overall.

Congress and the executive branch have also been very concerned about the use of student loans by proprietary (or for-profit) colleges and institutes to entice students into a course of study without providing proper counselling or guidance. Working adults may find themselves carrying a student loan burden for a course of study that they were unable to complete for personal reasons.

Members of Congress are torn between putting more regulations on the student loan program in order to control its use and wishing to help even more students attend college and get needed skills for the workforce. And, of course, there is the expense to the government of lending money to students and not getting repayment of the principal and interest for many years. Many members of Congress suspect that loans often are inflated for many students in part because many students do not understand their future obligations.

What Would You Do?

As a member of Congress from a city that is home to multiple colleges and universities, would you vote to reduce the amount of student loans available to individuals or would you oppose such a change?

What You *Can* Do

Most importantly, educate yourself on your own financial situation. How many loans have you taken out to pay for college? Could you cut your expenses or otherwise reduce the size of your loan? Pay careful attention to the details of repayment and opportunities to have some portion of your loan erased through service.

Learn about the criticisms of the student loan program and about its achievements. There are excellent resources both from the government and from a nonprofit website, American Student Assistance. Pay attention to congressional activity on the issue of student loans, on changes to the Pell grant program for students with great financial need, and to all federal legislation dealing with colleges and universities.

If you don't already know, learn the identity of your senators and representative to the House. Finding out your House representative is very easy: go to House.gov and put in your zip code and you will be directed to the representative's website. You can go to VoteSmart.org to find your representative's voting record and, if you have concerns about an issue, contact his or her office directly and express yourself. You also have two senators from your state who can be contacted with regards to any issue. Write a personal letter to him or her. Find out when he or she is going to have a "town hall" meeting or day in the office and go visit. Post the response you get from the Washington office on Facebook or tweet it to your friends. Spread the word of your concerns on social network sites.

If you really want to know more about the job of a member of Congress, seek out an internship in a congressional office either in the home state or in Washington. You will quickly find out how much pressure most members are under to meet the concerns of constituents as well as the demands of their party. The websites for both houses of Congress have made it easy to find your representative. If you go to www.house.gov, put in your zip code and go immediately to your member's homepage. At www.senate.gov, enter your state and you will find your senators. Websites of individual members are more user friendly than ever before. Sign up for Twitter feeds or Facebook alerts to find out what your representative or senator is doing.

Project Vote Smart is supported by thousands of volunteers, conservative and liberal, who research the backgrounds and records of thousands of political candidates and elected officials to provide citizens with their voting records, campaign contributions, public statements, biographical data, and evaluations from more than 150 competing special-interest groups. www.votesmart.org

Nonpartisan, independent, and nonprofit, the Center for Responsive Politics (CRP) educates voters through research that tracks campaign contributions and lobbying data. They "count cash to make change" in government and strive to inform voters about how money in politics affects their lives. You can contact the CRP at www.opensecrets.org.

Purestock/Getty Images

Key Terms

Chapter Summary

■ **LO11.1:** The first 17 clauses of Article I, Section 8, of the Constitution specify most of the enumerated, or expressed, powers of Congress, including the right to impose taxes, to borrow money, to regulate commerce, and to declare war. Congress also enjoys the right to "make all Laws which shall be necessary and proper for carrying into Execution the foregoing Powers, and all other Powers vested by this Constitution in the Government of the United States, or in any Department or Officer thereof." This is called the elastic, or necessary and proper, clause.

■ **LO11.2:** The authors of the Constitution believed that the bulk of national power should reside in the legislature because it represents the voters most directly. All legislative power rests in the Congress. The Constitution states that Congress will consist of two chambers. A result of the Connecticut Compromise, this bicameral structure established a balanced legislature, with the membership in the House of Representatives based on population and the membership in the Senate based on the equality of states.

■ **LO11.2:** The functions of Congress include (1) lawmaking, (2) representation, (3) service to constituents, (4) oversight, (5) public education, and (6) conflict resolution. Members of the House and the Senate cultivate votes in their constituencies through representation of local interests, providing services, and bringing home federal dollars for projects. At the same time, they must participate in debate and lawmaking for the nation as a whole; this may entail casting votes for legislation that may be of no interest to their constituents or may, in fact, not be beneficial to them. They also participate in committees which allow them to oversee government departments, educate the public, and work to resolve conflicts over policy.

■ **LO11.2:** The House of Representatives has 435 members and the Senate has 100 members. Owing to its larger size, the House has more formal rules. The Senate tradition of unlimited debate (filibustering) dates back to 1790 and has been used over the years to frustrate the passage of bills. Under Senate Rule 22, cloture can be used to halt debate on a bill.

■ **LO11.2:** Members of Congress are older and wealthier than most Americans, disproportionately white and male, and more likely to be trained in professional occupations. Members of the Senate are more likely to be lawyers and to be wealthier than House members. Additionally, there is less diversity in the Senate than in the House of Representatives.

■ **LO11.3:** Congressional elections are operated by the individual state governments, which must abide by rules established by the Constitution and national statutes. Most candidates for Congress must win nomination through a direct primary. The overwhelming majority of incumbent representatives and a smaller proportion of senators who run for reelection are successful. A complicated aspect of congressional elections is apportionment—the allocation of legislative seats to constituencies. The Supreme Court's "one person, one vote" rule has been applied to equalize the populations of congressional and state legislative districts.

■ **LO11.4:** Most of the actual work of legislating is performed by committees and subcommittees within Congress. Legislation introduced into the House or Senate is assigned to the appropriate standing committees for review. Select committees are created for a limited time for a specific purpose. Joint committees are formed by the concurrent action of both chambers and consist of members from each chamber. Conference committees are special joint committees set up to achieve agreement between the House and the Senate on the exact wording of legislative acts passed by both chambers in different forms. The seniority rule, which is usually followed, specifies that the longest-serving member of the majority party will be the chairperson of a committee.

■ **LO11.5:** The foremost power holder in the House of Representatives is the Speaker of the House. Other leaders are the House majority leader, the House minority leader, and the majority and minority whips. Formally, the vice president is the presiding officer of the Senate, with the most senior member of the majority party serving as the president pro tempore to preside when the vice president is absent. Actual leadership in the Senate rests with the majority leader, the minority leader, and their whips.

■ **LO11.6:** A bill becomes law by progressing through both chambers of Congress and their appropriate standing and joint committees to the president. Members are usually most influenced in their voting decisions by their party affiliation, their constituency's interests, their own interests, and cues given by other legislators.

■ **LO11.7:** The budget process for a fiscal year begins with the preparation of an executive budget by the president. This is reviewed by the Office of Management and Budget and then sent to Congress, which is supposed to pass a final budget by the end of September. Since 1978, Congress generally has not followed its own time rules.

Selected Print, Media, and Online Resources

PRINT RESOURCES

Barone, Michael, and Grant Ujifusa. *The Almanac of American Politics, 2014*. Washington, DC: National Journal, 2014. This book, published biannually, is a comprehensive summary of current political information on each member of Congress, his or her state or congressional district, recent congressional election results, key votes, ratings by various organizations, sources of campaign contributions, and records of campaign expenditures.

Davidson, Roger H., and Walter J. Oleszek. *Congress and Its Members*, 14th ed. Washington, DC: CQ Press, 2013. This classic looks carefully at the "two Congresses," the one in Washington and the role played by congresspersons at home.

Draper, Robert. *Do Not Ask What Good We Do*. New York: The Free Press, 2012. Draper, a *New York Times* writer, reveals an insider's view of the Congress and some of its colorful members and criticizes both houses for their ineffectiveness.

Lebovich, Mark, *This Town: Two Parties and a Funeral—Plus Plenty of Valet Parking!—in America's Gilded Capital*. New York: Blue Rider Press, 2013. This outstanding book by a Washington journalist reveals what life in the capital is really like and the sources of information that everyone uses to follow the political life of Washington, DC.

Mann, Thomas B., and Norman J. Ornstein. *It's Even Worse Than It Looks: How the American Constitutional System Collided with the New Politics of Extremism*. Two noted political scientists analyze how extreme views and polarized parties have made Congress ineffective. New York: Basic Books, 2013.

MEDIA RESOURCES

Charlie Wilson's War—This hilarious film is based on the true story of how Wilson (Tom Hanks), a hard-living, hard-drinking representative from Texas, almost single-handedly won a billion dollars in funding for the Afghanis, who were fighting a Russian invasion. When equipped with heat-seeking missiles, the Afghanis prevail. Philip Seymour Hoffman steals the show, portraying a rogue CIA operative.

Lincoln—Although this superb 2012 movie is about Lincoln's political leadership, the plot focuses on his dealings with Congress.

House of Cards—This original series by Netflix is praised for its gritty and cynical view of how politics and journalism work in Washington, DC.

Mr. Smith Goes to Washington—A 1939 film in which Jimmy Stewart plays a naïve congressman who is quickly educated in Washington. A true American political classic.

Porked: Earmarks for Profit—A 2008 release from Fox News Channel that investigates congressional earmarks. Fox reporters contend that pork wastes tax dollars. Additionally, the network also claims that some members of Congress have funded projects that benefited their own bank accounts.

ONLINE RESOURCES

Congressional Budget Office—provides Congress with nonpartisan analyses for economic and budget decisions and with estimates required for the congressional budget process: www.cbo.gov

Congress—each house's websites are indispensable sources for discovering what committees are doing and the progress of bills: www.house.gov

The Hill—a congressional newspaper that publishes daily when Congress is in session, with a special focus on business and lobbying, political campaigns, and goings-on on Capitol Hill: http://thehill.com/

Roll Call—the newspaper of the Capitol that provides an inside view of developments in Washington, DC: www.rollcall.com

Voter Information Services—provides the interest group scorecards of all the members of Congress and allows you to create your own unique scorecard for candidates of interest: www.vis.org

Master the concept of The Congress with MindTap™ for American Government

REVIEW MindTap™ for American Government
Access Key Term Flashcards for Chapter 11.

TEST YOURSELF MindTap™ for American Government
Take the Wrap It Up Quiz for Chapter 11.

STAY CURRENT MindTap™ for American Government
Access the KnowNow blog and customized RSS for updates on current events.

STAY FOCUSED MindTap™ for American Government
Complete the Focus Activities for Media and Politics.

12 The President

LEARNING OUTCOMES

After reading this chapter, students will be able to:

- **LO12.1:** Explain the formal and informal roles played by the president, and discuss the constitutional or political origins of those roles.

- **LO12.2:** Demonstrate an understanding of the president's powers as commander in chief and the procedures described in the War Powers Act.

- **LO12.3:** Discuss the president's role in the legislative process; describe executive tools to initiate or block legislation.

- **LO12.4:** Explain the emergency powers of the president and the executive powers of the president.

- **LO12.5:** Explain the process by which a president could be impeached and forced to leave office.

- **LO12.6:** Describe the executive offices that support the president.

- **LO12.7:** Describe the job of the vice president and explain the circumstances under which the vice president becomes president.

President Obama meets with Chinese President Xi Jinping while both attend a G20 Summit in St. Petersburg, Russia. Much of the meeting focused on the civil war in Syria.

Jewel Samad/AFP/Getty Images

 WATCH & LEARN
Watch a brief "What Do You Know?" video summarizing The Presidency.

There Were No Executive Privilege?

BACKGROUND

Although executive privilege is not mentioned in the Constitution, all presidents have invoked this privilege in response to perceived encroachments on the executive branch by Congress and by the judiciary. Executive privilege is the claim set forth by the president that certain communications must be kept secret for the good of the nation, whether for domestic interests or national security interests. The trouble begins when other branches suspect the executive is claiming this right to save embarrassment for the president or presidential subordinates. For example, in 2006, when two congressional committees were investigating the federal government's response to Hurricane Katrina, the Bush administration cited the need for confidentiality of executive-branch communications as justification for refusing to turn over certain documents, including email correspondence involving White House staff members. The administration had previously refused to release the names of oil company executives who had advised Vice President Cheney on energy policy.

Nonetheless, Congress could try to prohibit the use of executive privilege by passing a law. Alternatively, the Supreme Court could hold that executive privilege as a right is an unconstitutional exercise of executive power.

IF EXECUTIVE PRIVILEGE WERE ELIMINATED

Without executive privilege, a president would have to be aware that all of his or her words, documents, and actions could be made public. We know from twentieth-century history that when a president does not have full executive privilege to protect information, the results can be devastating.

President Richard Nixon (served 1969–1974) tape-recorded hundreds of hours of conversations in the Oval Office. During the Watergate scandal, Congress requested those tapes. Nixon invoked executive privilege and refused to turn them over. Ultimately, the Supreme Court ordered him to comply; the tapes provided damning information about Nixon's role in the purported cover-up of illegal activities. Rather than face impeachment, Nixon resigned the presidency.

If executive privilege were eliminated, it is unlikely that conversations between the president and other members of the executive branch ever would be recorded or otherwise documented. As a result, we would have fewer records of an administration's activities.

EXECUTIVE PRIVILEGE IN A WORLD FILLED WITH TERRORISM

Following the terrorist attacks on September 11, 2001, Attorney General John Ashcroft advised federal agencies "to lean toward withholding information whenever possible." Often, the Bush administration attempted to withhold information from Congress and the courts, not just the public. In matters of national security, when the president and the president's advisers discuss attacks on terrorist leaders or foreign nuclear plants, claiming executive privilege to prevent leaks to America's enemies would likely be justified. In 2012, the Obama administration claimed executive privilege for communications in the Department of Justice operation known as "Fast and Furious," which involved illegal gun transfers with Mexican drug lords. No details were given, but the operation likely involved relationships with the Mexican government that the president felt could not be disclosed.

Congress itself can be a source of leaks. While Congress has procedures that can be used to guard sensitive information, it is unaccustomed to keeping secrets and often finds it hard to do so. The very size of Congress and its staff makes it difficult to keep secrets.

PAST, PRESENT, AND FUTURE PRESIDENTIAL PAPERS

The Bush administration attempted to control not only its own records, but also those of former presidents. Soon after September 11, 2001, President Bush signed Executive Order 13233, which provided that former presidents' private papers can be released only with the approval of both the former president in question and the current one. Upon taking office in 2009, President Obama rescinded several Bush executive orders, although he did allow former presidents to claim privilege for their own papers. Occasionally, Congress has attempted to place time limits for such claims, although no new laws have been successfully passed.

If executive privilege were eliminated, the White House would have a difficult time regulating the flow of past and present records into the public forum. The behavior of presidents and their administrations would certainly change. They might simply insist that no record of sensitive conversations may exist. If so, future Americans would lose much of the historical background for America's domestic and international actions.

For Critical Analysis

1. *The history of executive privilege dates back to 1796, when President George Washington refused a request by the House for certain documents. Given the changes that have taken place since that time, should executive privilege be eliminated—or is it even more necessary today than it was at that time?*

2. *What would be the costs to the nation if executive privilege were eliminated?*

THE WRITERS OF the Constitution created the presidency of the United States without any models to follow. Nowhere else in the world was there a democratically selected chief executive. What the founders did not want was a king. Given their previous experience with royal governors in the colonies, many Constitutional Convention delegates wanted a very weak executive who could not veto legislation. Other delegates, especially those who had witnessed the need for a strong leader in the Revolutionary army, believed a strong executive was necessary. Overall, however, the delegates did not spend much time discussing actual powers to be granted to the president, leaving those questions to the Committee on Detail. The delegates created a chief executive who had enough powers granted in the Constitution to balance those of Congress.[1]

The power exercised by each president has been scrutinized and judged by historians, political scientists, the media, and the public. The personalities and foibles of each president have also been investigated and judged by many. Indeed, it would seem that Americans are fascinated by presidential power and by the persons who hold the office. In this chapter, after looking at who can become president and at the process involved, we will examine closely the nature and extent of the constitutional powers held by the president, including whether the president can decide which records can be made public and which aides might testify before Congress, as discussed in the opening feature.

Who Can Become President?

The requirements for becoming president, as outlined in Article II, Section 1, of the Constitution, are not overwhelmingly stringent:

> No person except a natural born Citizen, or a Citizen of the United States, at the time of the Adoption of this Constitution, shall be eligible to the Office of President; neither shall any Person be eligible to that Office who shall not have attained to the Age of thirty-five Years, and been fourteen Years a Resident within the United States.

The only question that arises about these qualifications relates to the term *natural-born citizen*. Does that mean only citizens born in the United States and its territories? What about a child born to a U.S. citizen (or to a couple who are U.S. citizens) visiting or living in another country? Although the Supreme Court has never directly addressed the question, it is reasonable to expect that someone would be eligible if her or his parents were Americans. The first presidents, after all, were not American citizens at birth, and others were born in areas that did not join the United States until later. These questions were debated when George Romney, who was born in Chihuahua, Mexico, made a serious bid for the Republican presidential nomination in the 1960s.[2] Similar questions were raised about the 2008 Republican candidate, John McCain, who was born in Panama on an American military base. Those questions were quickly dismissed because it is clear that children born abroad to American citizens are considered natural-born Americans. From time to time, movements arise to allow *naturalized* citizens to be eligible to run for the presidency, but these have had no success.

did you know?

Grover Cleveland was the only president to have served as a hangman. He was once sheriff of Erie County, New York and twice had to spring the trap at a hanging.

---

1. Forrest McDonald, *The American Presidency: An Intellectual History* (Lawrence, KS: University Press of Kansas, 1994), p. 179.
2. George Romney was governor of Michigan from 1963 to 1969. Romney was not nominated for the presidency, and the issue remains unresolved. For a detailed explanation of who qualifies as a natural born citizen, see "Defining 'Natural Born Citizen,'" James Spurgeon, IVN, August 13, 2013. http://ivn.us/2013.08.13/defining-natural-born-citizen/

Harry Truman, left, is shown when he was the proprietor of a Kansas City, Missouri, men's clothing store, about 1920. Ronald Reagan, right, is shown as a frontier marshal in the movie *Law and Order*, released in 1953. Compared to members of Congress, presidents have had more varied backgrounds. How would varied life experiences benefit a president?

The American dream is symbolized by the statement that "anybody can become president of this country." It is true that in modern times, presidents have included a haberdasher (Harry Truman—for a short period of time), a peanut farmer (Jimmy Carter), and an actor (Ronald Reagan). But if you examine the list of presidents in the appendix, you will see that the most common previous occupation of presidents in this country has been that of lawyer. Out of 43 presidents, 26 have been lawyers, and many have been wealthy. (Fewer lawyers have become president in the last century, in part because senators, who are likely to be lawyers, have had a difficult time being elected president.)

Although the Constitution states that the minimum-age requirement for the presidency is 35 years, most presidents have been much older than that when they assumed office. John F. Kennedy, at the age of 43, was the youngest elected president; the oldest was Ronald Reagan, at age 69. The average age at inauguration has been 54. The selection of presidents reflects a clear demographic bias. Until 2009, all had been white, male, and from the Protestant tradition, except for John F. Kennedy, who was a Roman Catholic. The inauguration of Barack Obama, a man of mixed race—and of Kenyan and American ancestry—was an extraordinary milestone in American history. Presidents have been men of great stature (such as George Washington) and men in whom leadership qualities were not so pronounced (such as Warren Harding). A presidential candidate usually has experience as a vice president, senator, or state governor. Former governors have been especially successful at winning the presidency; they can make the legitimate claims to have executive experience and electability.

The Process of Becoming President

Major and minor political parties nominate candidates for president and vice president at national conventions every four years. The nation's voters do not elect a president and vice president directly, but cast ballots

did you know?

John F. Kennedy was the youngest elected president, taking office at the age of 43, but Theodore Roosevelt assumed office at the age of 42 after the assassination of President William McKinley.

for presidential electors, who then vote for president and vice president in the electoral college.

Twice, the electoral college has failed to give any candidate a majority. At this point, the election is decided in the House of Representatives. The president is then chosen from among the three candidates having the most electoral college votes, as noted in Chapter 9. Thomas Jefferson and Aaron Burr tied in the electoral college in 1800, because the Constitution had not been explicit in indicating which of the two electoral votes were for president and which were for vice president. In 1804, the **Twelfth Amendment** clarified the matter by requiring that the president and vice president be chosen separately. In 1824, the House again had to make a choice, this time among William H. Crawford, Andrew Jackson, and John Quincy Adams. It chose Adams, even though Jackson had more electoral and popular votes.

Twelfth Amendment
An amendment to the Constitution, adopted in 1804, that specifies the separate election of the president and vice president by the electoral college.

The Many Roles of the President

■ **LO12.1:** Explain the formal and informal roles played by the president, and discuss the constitutional or political origins of those roles.

The Constitution speaks briefly about the duties and obligations of the president. Based on this brief list of powers and on the precedents of history, the presidency has grown into a very complicated job that requires balancing at least five constitutional roles: (1) head of state, (2) chief executive, (3) commander in chief of the armed forces, (4) chief diplomat, and (5) chief legislator of the United States. It is worth noting that one person plays all these roles simultaneously and that these roles may at times come into conflict. For example, President Obama, in his role as commander in chief, has used drones to find and eliminate leaders of al-Qaeda in Pakistan. As leader of the Democratic Party, however, he is critical of former president Bush for his war against terrorists and the creation of the prison at Guantánamo Bay, Cuba.

Head of State

Every nation has at least one ceremonial head of state. In most democratic governments, the role of **head of state** is given to someone other than the chief executive, who leads the executive branch of government. In Britain, the head of state is the queen. In much of Europe, the prime minister is the chief executive, and the head of state is the president. But in the United States, the president is both chief executive and head of state. According to William Howard Taft, as head of state, the president symbolizes the "dignity and majesty" of the American people.

Head of State
The role of the president as ceremonial head of the government.

As head of state, the president engages in many activities that are largely symbolic or ceremonial, such as the following:

- Decorating war heroes
- Throwing out the first pitch to open the baseball season
- Dedicating national parks and opening new factories
- Receiving visiting heads of state at the White House
- Representing the nation at times of national mourning, such as after the terrorist attacks of September 11, 2001. After the loss of the space shuttle *Columbia* in 2003, and after the destruction from Hurricane Sandy in 2012

Some believe that having the president serve as both the chief executive and the head of state drastically limits the time available to do "real" work. Not all presidents have agreed with this conclusion, however—particularly those

President Barack Obama discusses global economic issues with other world leaders at the G8 summit held at Camp David, Maryland in May, 2012. Do you think such face-to-face meetings produce tangible results or just reinforce personal relationships?

presidents who have skillfully blended these two roles with their role as politician. Being head of state gives the president tremendous public exposure, which can be an important asset in a campaign for reelection. When that exposure is positive, it helps the president leverage Congress regarding proposed legislation and increases the chances of being relected—or getting the candidates of the president's party elected.

Chief Executive

According to the Constitution, "The executive Power shall be vested in a President of the United States of America. … [H]e may require the Opinion, in writing, of the principal Officer in each of the executive Departments, upon any Subject relating to the Duties of their respective Offices … and he shall nominate, and by and with the Advice and Consent of the Senate, shall appoint … Officers of the United States. … [H]e shall take Care that the Laws be faithfully executed."

As **chief executive**, the president is constitutionally bound to enforce the acts of Congress, the judgments of federal courts, and treaties signed by the United States. The duty to "faithfully execute" the laws has been a source of constitutional power for presidents. Is the president allowed to reject certain parts of legislation if he or she believes that they are unconstitutional? For at least 175 years, presidents have used **signing statements**, written declarations made by presidents that accompany legislation, to make substantive constitutional pronouncements on the bill being signed. In 1830, President Andrew Jackson created a controversy when he signed a bill and at the same time sent to Congress a message that restricted the reach of the statute. Presidents Abraham Lincoln, Andrew Johnson, Theodore Roosevelt, Woodrow Wilson, and Franklin Roosevelt all used signing statements.

As for the legality of the practice, the Department of Justice has advised the last four administrations that the Constitution provides the president with the authority to decline to enforce a clearly unconstitutional law. Four justices of the

did you know?

Thomas Jefferson was the first president to be inaugurated in Washington, DC, where he walked to the Capitol from a boardinghouse, took the oath, made a brief speech in the Senate chamber, and then walked back home.

Chief Executive
The role of the president as head of the executive branch of the government.

Signing Statements
A written declaration that a president may make when signing a bill into law. Usually, such statements point out sections of the law that the president deems unconstitutional.

Supreme Court joined in an opinion that the president may resist laws that encroach upon presidential powers by "disregarding them when they're unconstitutional."[3] After George W. Bush took office, he issued signing statements on more than 800 statutes, more than all of the previous presidents combined. He also tended to use the statements for a different purpose. When earlier presidents issued signing statements, they were used to instruct agencies on how to execute the laws or for similar purposes. Many (if not most) of President Bush's signing statements served notice that he believed parts of bills that he signed were unconstitutional or might violate national security. President Obama has continued the practice of issuing signing statements to indicate his intentions with regard to legislation.

Some members of Congress are not so concerned about presidential signing statements. Senator John Cornyn (R-TX) has predicted that federal courts would be unlikely to consider the statements when interpreting the laws with which they were issued.[4]

The Powers of Appointment and Removal.

To assist in the various tasks of the chief executive, the president has a federal bureaucracy (see Chapter 13), which consists of more than 2.7 million federal civilian employees. The president only nominally runs the executive bureaucracy. Most government positions are filled by **civil service** employees, who generally gain government employment through a merit system rather than presidential appointment.[5] Therefore, even though the president has important **appointment power**, it is limited to cabinet and subcabinet jobs, federal judgeships, agency heads, and several thousand lesser jobs. Of the more than 700,000 civilian jobs in the Department of Defense, the president may appoint fewer than 600 (less than one-tenth of 1 percent). While the president has 555 appointments available in the State Department, some are ambassadorships to important allies, usually given to major donors and supporters of the president. Soon after each presidential election, the government publishes a list of about 8,000 specific jobs in a volume titled, "The Plum Book: Policy and Supporting Positions." It is so-called because these have long been considered "plum jobs."

The president's power to remove from office those officials who are not doing a good job or who do not agree with the president is not explicitly granted by the Constitution and has been limited with regard to certain agencies. In 1926, however, a Supreme Court decision prevented Congress from interfering with the president's ability to fire those executive-branch officials whom the president had appointed with Senate approval.[6] The president can remove the heads of ten executive departments, all of the cabinet secretaries, and everyone who works in the Executive Office of the President and the White House Office. Harry Truman spoke candidly of the difficulties a president faces in trying to control the executive bureaucracy. On leaving office, he referred to the problems that Dwight Eisenhower, as a former general of the army, was going to have: "He'll sit here and he'll say do this! do that! and nothing will happen. Poor Ike—it won't be a bit like the Army. He'll find it very frustrating."[7]

Civil Service

A collective term for the body of employees working for the government. Generally, civil service is understood to apply to all those who gain government employment through a merit system.

Appointment Power

The authority vested in the president to fill a government office or position. Positions filled by presidential appointment include those in the executive branch and the federal judiciary, commissioned officers in the armed forces, and members of the independent regulatory commissions.

3. *Freytag v. C.I.R.,* 501 U.S. 868 (1991).
4. Todd Garvey, "Presidential Signing Statements: Constitutional and Institutional Implications" (Washington, DC: Congressional Research Service, January 4, 2012).
5. See Chapter 14 for a discussion of the Civil Service Reform Act.
6. *Meyers v. United States,* 272 U.S. 52 (1926).
7. Bartleby.com, Great Books Online, www.bartleby. Truman may not have considered the amount of politics involved in decision making in the upper echelon of the army.

The Power to Grant Reprieves and Pardons. Section 2 of Article II of the Constitution gives the president the power to grant **reprieves** and **pardons** for offenses against the United States, except in cases of impeachment. All pardons are administered by the Office of the Pardon Attorney in the Department of Justice. The United States Supreme Court upheld the president's power to grant reprieves and pardons in a 1925 case concerning a pardon granted by the president to an individual convicted of contempt of court. The judiciary had contended that only judges had the authority to convict individuals for contempt of court when court orders were violated and that the courts should be free from interference by the executive branch. The Court stated that the president could grant reprieves or pardons for all offenses "either before trial, during trial, or after trial, by individuals, or by classes, conditionally or absolutely, and this without modification or regulation by Congress."[8]

The power to pardon can also be used to apply to large groups of individuals who may be subject to indictment and trial. In 1977, President Jimmy Carter extended amnesty to all Vietnam War resisters who avoided the military draft by fleeing to Canada. More than 50,000 individuals were allowed to come back to the United States, free from the possibility of prosecution. The power to reprieve individuals allows the president to extend clemency to federal prisoners, usually on humanitarian grounds. However, in 1999, President Bill Clinton extended a conditional offer of clemency to a group of Puerto Rican nationalists who had been tried for planning terrorist attacks in the United States. The condition was for them to renounce the use of terrorist tactics and to not associate with other nationalists who advocate violence. Twelve accepted the offer, while two refused the conditions.

In a controversial decision, President Gerald Ford pardoned former President Nixon for his role in the Watergate affair before any charges were brought in court. President Obama pardoned 52 individuals by the fifth year of his presidency. In 2013, he pardoned eight non-violent offenders who had been convicted of using crack cocaine. The president noted that each had served more than fifteen years in prison due to a mandatory sentence that has since been changed.

Commander in Chief

■ **LO12.2:** Demonstrate an understanding of the president's powers as commander in chief and the procedures described in the War Powers Act.

The president, according to the Constitution, "shall be Commander in Chief of the Army and Navy of the United States, and of the Militia of the several States, when called into the actual Service of the United States." The armed forces are under civilian, rather than military, control.

Wartime Powers. Certainly, those who wrote the Constitution had George Washington in mind when they made the president the **commander in chief**. The founders did not, however, expect presidents to lead the country into war without congressional authorization. Remember that Congress is given the power to declare war. As the United States grew in military power and global reach, presidents became much more likely to send troops into armed combat either in crisis situations or with an authorizing resolution short of a declaration of war. The last war to be fought under a congressional declaration was World War II.

> **Reprieves**
> A formal postponement of the execution of a sentence imposed by a court of law.
>
> **Pardons**
> A release from the punishment for or legal consequences of a crime; a pardon can be granted by the president before or after a conviction.

> **did you know?**
> Four United States presidents have been awarded the Nobel Peace Prize: Theodore Roosevelt, Woodrow Wilson, Jimmy Carter, and Barack Obama.

> **Commander in Chief**
> The role of the president as supreme commander of the military forces of the United States and of the state National Guard units when they are called into federal service.

---

8. *Ex parte Grossman*, 267 U.S. 87 (1925).

Although we do not expect our president to lead the troops into battle, presidents as commanders in chief have wielded dramatic power. President Truman made the difficult decision to drop atomic bombs on Hiroshima and Nagasaki in 1945 to force Japan to surrender and thus bring World War II to an end. President Johnson ordered bombing missions against North Vietnam in the 1960s, and he personally selected some of the targets. President Nixon decided to invade Cambodia in 1970, an action widely condemned as an abuse of his power as commander in chief.

The president is the ultimate decision maker in military matters and has the final authority to launch a nuclear strike using missiles or bombs. For decades, the nuclear "football"—a briefcase filled with all the codes necessary to order a nuclear attack—accompanied the president. Today, nuclear security codes are uploaded to a website, protected by retinal scan technology, which can only accessed by the president. Only the president can order the use of nuclear force.

The use of military force by presidents has raised some very thorny issues for the balance between Congress and the presidency. President Truman sent U.S. troops to Korea under a United Nations resolution, and President Johnson escalated the U.S. involvement in Vietnam under the quickly passed Gulf of Tonkin Resolution. President Bush invaded Iraq with congressional authorization. In none of these did Congress and the public expect extended wars with many casualties.

Presidents have also used military force without any congressional authorization, particularly in emergency situations. Ronald Reagan sent troops to Grenada to stop a supposedly communist coup, and Lyndon Johnson invaded the Dominican Republic. George H. W. Bush sent troops to Panama; numerous presidents have ordered quick air strikes on perceived enemies.

The War Powers Resolution. In an attempt to gain more control over such military activities, in 1973 Congress passed the **War Powers Resolution**—over President Nixon's veto—requiring that the president consult with Congress when sending American forces into action. Once they are sent, the president must report to Congress within 48 hours. Unless Congress approves the use of troops within 60 days or extends the 60-day time limit, the forces must be withdrawn. The War Powers Resolution was tested in the fall of 1983, when Reagan requested that troops remain in Lebanon. The resulting compromise was a congressional resolution allowing troops to remain there for 18 months.

Despite the War Powers Resolution, the powers of the president as commander in chief have continued to expand. The attacks of September 11, 2001, were the first on U.S. soil since Pearl Harbor. The imminent sense of threat supported passage of legislation that gave the president and the executive branch powers that had not been seen since World War II. President Bush's use of surveillance powers and other powers granted by the PATRIOT Act have caused considerable controversy. In the face of continued terrorist threats, President Obama has signed extensions of the PATRIOT Act and continued many of the actions of the Bush administration. The Obama administration has ordered drone strikes on a number of terrorist leaders, skirting the provisions of the War Powers Resolution because no American troops are involved in a combat situation when drones are used.

Chief Diplomat

The Constitution gives the president the power to recognize foreign governments; to make treaties, with the **advice and consent** of the Senate; to make special agreements with other heads of state that do not require congressional approval;

War Powers Resolution
A law passed in 1973 spelling out the conditions under which the president can commit troops without congressional approval.

Advice and Consent
Terms in the Constitution describing the U.S. Senate's power to review and approve treaties and presidential appointments.

and to nominate ambassadors. As **chief diplomat**, the president dominates American foreign policy, a role supported many times by the Supreme Court.

Diplomatic Recognition. An important power of the president as chief diplomat is that of **diplomatic recognition**, or the power to recognize—or refuse to recognize—foreign governments. In the role of ceremonial head of state, the president has always received foreign diplomats. In modern times, the simple act of receiving a foreign diplomat has been equivalent to accrediting the diplomat and officially recognizing his or her government. Such recognition of the legitimacy of another country's government is a prerequisite to diplomatic relations or treaties between that country and the United States.

Deciding when to recognize a foreign power is not always simple. The United States did not recognize the Soviet Union until 1933—16 years after the Russian Revolution of 1917. Only after all attempts to reverse the effects of that revolution—including military invasion of Russia and diplomatic isolation—proved futile did Franklin Roosevelt extend recognition to the Soviet government. U.S. presidents faced a similar problem with the Chinese communist revolution. In December 1978, long after the communist victory in China in 1949, Jimmy Carter finally granted official recognition to the People's Republic of China.[9]

When governments are toppled by protests, the president often faces a diplomatic recognition issue. During the "Arab Spring," a new government was put in place in Egypt and recognized by the United States. In countries such as Libya, where the central government is not recognized by many regional leaders, the question becomes "who" to recognize as the official head of government.

Proposal and Ratification of Treaties. The president has the sole power to negotiate treaties with other nations. These treaties must be presented to the Senate, where they may be modified and must be approved by a two-thirds vote. After ratification, the president can approve the senatorial version of the treaty. Approval poses a problem when the Senate has added substantive amendments or reservations to a

Chief Diplomat
The role of the president in recognizing foreign governments, making treaties, and effecting executive agreements.

Diplomatic Recognition
The formal acknowledgment of a foreign government as legitimate.

President Richard Nixon and First Lady Pat Nixon lead the way as they take a tour of China's famed Great Wall, near Beijing, February 21, 1972. Why was Nixon's visit to China so historic?

9. The Nixon administration first encouraged new relations with the People's Republic of China by allowing a cultural exchange of ping-pong teams.

treaty, particularly when such changes may require reopening negotiations with the other signatory governments. A president may decide to withdraw a treaty if changes are too extensive, as Woodrow Wilson did with the Versailles Treaty in 1919. Wilson believed that the senatorial reservations would weaken the treaty so much that it would be ineffective. His refusal to accept the senatorial version of the treaty led to the eventual refusal of the United States to join the League of Nations.

President Carter was successful in lobbying for the treaties that provided for the return of the Panama Canal to Panama by the year 2000 and for neutralizing the canal. President Clinton won a major political and legislative victory in 1993 by persuading Congress to ratify the North American Free Trade Agreement (NAFTA). In so doing, he had to overcome opposition from Democrats and most of organized labor. In 1998, he worked closely with Senate Republicans to ensure Senate approval of a treaty governing the use of chemical weapons. In 2000, he won another major legislative victory when Congress voted to normalize trade relations with China permanently.

President George W. Bush indicated his intention to steer the United States in a more unilateral direction on foreign policy. He rejected the Kyoto Agreement on global warming and proposed ending the 1972 Anti-Ballistic Missile (ABM) Treaty that was part of the first Strategic Arms Limitation Treaty (SALT I). After the terrorist attacks of September 11, 2001, however, President Bush sought cooperation from U.S. allies in the war on terrorism. Bush's return to multilateralism was exemplified in the signing of a nuclear weapons reduction treaty with Russia in 2002.

The Obama administration quickly signaled a new outlook in foreign policy, with the president making multiple trips overseas, including to Egypt, in his first year in office. President Obama's stated goals in foreign policy included a more cooperative approach to world affairs and the reduction of nuclear weapons for all nations. In 2010, the president signed a treaty with Russia for a joint reduction of long-range nuclear weapons. The new START treaty was ratified by the U.S. Senate late in that year and went into force in 2011.

In late 2013, Secretary of State John Kerry signed the United Nations Arms Trade Treaty as the representative of the president. Although it has been signed, the treaty has not been sent to the Senate for ratification. Fifty-five senators have announced their opposition to this international agreement.

Executive Agreements
An international agreement made by the president, without senatorial ratification, with the head of a foreign state.

Executive Agreements. Presidential power in foreign affairs is enhanced greatly by the use of **executive agreements** made between the president and other heads of state. Such agreements do not require Senate approval, although the House and Senate may refuse to appropriate the funds necessary to implement them. Whereas treaties are binding on all succeeding administrations, executive agreements require each new president's consent to remain in effect.

Among the advantages of executive agreements are speed and secrecy. The former is essential during a crisis; the latter is important when open senatorial debate may be detrimental to the best interests of the United States or to the interests of the president.[10] Executive agreements (about 13,000) greatly outnumber treaties (about 1,300). Many executive agreements contain secret provisions calling for American military assistance or other support. Franklin Roosevelt used executive agreements to bypass congressional isolationists when he traded American destroyers for British Caribbean naval bases and when he arranged diplomatic and military affairs with Canada and Latin American nations.

10. The Case Act of 1972 requires that all executive agreements be transmitted to Congress within 60 days after the agreement takes effect. Secret agreements are transmitted to the foreign relations committees as classified information.

Everyday Politics

 Lincoln: The President as Legislator

Nominated for Best Picture in 2012, *Lincoln*, produced and directed by Steven Spielberg, examines the last four months of Lincoln's presidency. The film is based in part on Doris Kearns Goodwin's book, *Team of Rivals: The Political Genius of Abraham Lincoln*. Although set in 1865, the role of the president as chief legislator is no different than it is for President Obama; both spar with a contentious and divided Congress.

In the film, Lincoln is determined to persuade Congress to pass the Thirteenth Amendment, which eventually banned slavery in the United States. Although he had issued the Emancipation Proclamation (an executive order), at the time the film is set, he fears that the readmission of the southern states to the union at the end of the Civil War will cause the defeat of the amendment. Congress is on the verge of great turnover; many Democratic members have been defeated and are "lame ducks." The President is willing to bribe these defeated members with jobs to get their votes for the amendment. Lincoln is also willing to avoid confirming the presence of Confederate delegates who are approaching Washington to agree to peace terms, knowing that he needs the amendment to pass in order to deal with the Confederate states. The amendment passes and Lincoln makes a deal to end the war. A few days later, he is assassinated.

As in Goodwin's book, the president is portrayed as "first among equals" with his Cabinet and the leaders of Congress. He must use all of his resources to get the amendment passed and to make peace with the Confederate states. Some of the deals that are struck are less than principled, but all presidents must, at times, make deals, even with the members of their own party and with their own supporters.

For Critical Analysis

1. *Why do you think members of the president's political party in Congress require persuasion and deal-making to approve his legislation?*

2. *Although the Emancipation Proclamation was considered the document that freed the slaves, why did Lincoln feel so strongly that he needed an amendment to the Constitution?*

Chief Legislator

■ **LO12.3:** Discuss the president's role in the legislative process; describe executive tools to initiate or block legislation.

Constitutionally, presidents must recommend to Congress legislation that they judge necessary and expedient. Not all presidents have wielded their powers as **chief legislator** in the same manner. Some have been almost completely unsuccessful in getting their legislative programs implemented by Congress. Presidents Franklin Roosevelt and Lyndon Johnson, however, saw much of their proposed legislation put into effect. Each year, the *Congressional Quarterly Weekly Review* publishes an analysis of presidential success in terms of legislation passed that the president has publicly supported. As shown in Figure 12–1, presidents tend to have a high success rate at the beginning of their administration, with a steep decline toward the end of their term. George W. Bush had more than a 70 percent success rate during the years he had a Republican-controlled Congress, but it fell to 34 percent after the Democrats won control of Congress in the 2006 elections. President Obama found extraordinary support for his initiatives from the Democratic majorities in both the House and the Senate, earning the highest success score ever recorded for a president in his first year, 96.7 percent. In his second year as president, Obama's success rate remained very high at 85.8 percent, but after the Republicans won the House of Representatives in 2010, his legislative

Chief Legislator
The role of the president in influencing the making of laws.

Figure 12–1 ▶ Presidential Success Rate by Year of Presidency

The graph illustrates the president's success rate on bills on which he had taken a position. Note that presidents do very well at the beginning of their terms, especially when they have control of Congress. When the other party controls Congress, the presidential success rate falls.

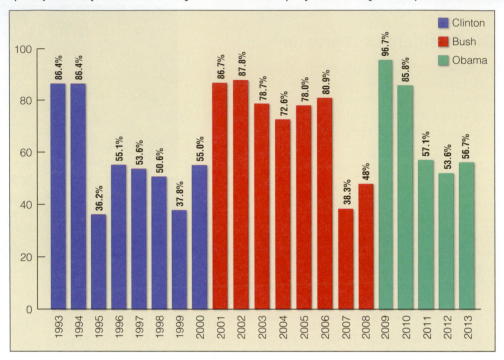

Source: *Congressional Quarterly Weekly Report*, February 4, 2014, p. 177.

State of the Union Message

An annual message to Congress in which the president proposes a legislative program. The message is addressed not only to Congress but also to the American people and to the world.

success rate for 2011 fell to 57.1 percent and remained in the mid-50 percent range throughout 2012 and 2013.

In modern times, the president has played a dominant role in creating the congressional agenda. In the president's annual **State of the Union message**, which is required by the Constitution (Article II, Section 3) and is usually given in late January, shortly after Congress reconvenes, the president, as chief legislator, presents a program. The message gives a broad, comprehensive view of what the president wishes the legislature to accomplish during its session. Originally, presidents sent a written memo to the Congress, which satisfies the constitutional requirement. In modern times, however, presidents see the State of the Union address as a tool to advance their policy agenda. The president is able to command the media stage and set out his or her goals. President Reagan began the practice of referring to ordinary citizens and bringing the subjects of those stories to sit in the balcony during the speech. Today, the president, the opposition party, and the commentators all recognize the impact of the State of the Union message on public opinion.

Legislation Passed. The president can propose legislation, but Congress is not required to pass—or even introduce—any of the administration's bills. How, then, does the president get proposals made into law? One way is by persuasion. The president writes to, telephones, and meets with various congressional leaders; makes public announcements to influence public opinion; and, as head of the party, exercises legislative leadership through the congresspersons of that party. Most presidents also have an Office of Congressional Liaison within the White

House Office. Such an office is staffed by individuals with extensive Washington experience, including former members of Congress, who lobby Congress on behalf of the president and monitor the progress of legislation on Capitol Hill. Presidents may also decide to use social events to lobby Congress, inviting the members and their spouses to parties at the White House. A more negative strategy is for the president to threaten to veto legislation if it does not correspond to his or her position.

Saying No to Legislation.   The president has the power to say no to legislation through use of the veto, by which the White House returns a bill unsigned to Congress with a **veto message** attached.[11] Because the Constitution requires that every bill passed by the House and the Senate be sent to the president before it becomes law, the president must act on each bill.

1. If the bill is signed, it becomes law.

2. If the bill is not sent back to Congress after ten congressional working days, it becomes law without the president's signature.

3. The president can reject the bill and send it back to Congress with a veto message setting forth objections. Congress then can change the bill, hoping to secure presidential approval, and pass it again. Or, Congress can simply reject the president's objections by overriding the veto with a two-thirds roll-call vote of the members present in both the House and the Senate.

4. If the president refuses to sign the bill and Congress adjourns within ten working days after the bill has been submitted to the president, the bill is killed for that session of Congress. This is called a **pocket veto**. If Congress wishes the bill to be reconsidered, the bill must be reintroduced during the following session.

Presidents employed the veto power infrequently until after the Civil War, but it has been used with increasing vigor since then (see Table 12–1). Millard Fillmore (served 1850–1853) was the last president to serve a full term in office without exercising the veto power. Only two bills have been vetoed by President Obama. While the Republican House has passed many bills that he threatened to veto, none were passed by the Senate and they did not reach his desk.

Veto Message
The president's formal explanation of a veto when legislation is returned to Congress.

Pocket Veto
A special veto exercised by the chief executive after a legislative body has adjourned. Bills not signed by the chief executive die after a specified period of time. If Congress wishes to reconsider such a bill, it must be reintroduced in the following session of Congress.

Table 12–1 ▶ Presidential Vetoes, 1789 to the Present

YEARS	PRESIDENT	REGULAR VETOES	VETOES OVERRIDDEN	POCKET VETOES	TOTAL VETOES
1789—1797	Washington	2	0	0	2
1797—1801	J. Adams	0	0	0	0
1801—1809	Jefferson	0	0	0	0
1809—1817	Madison	5	0	2	7
1817—1825	Monroe	1	0	0	1
1825—1829	J. Q. Adams	0	0	0	0
1829—1837	Jackson	5	0	7	12
1837—1841	Van Buren	0	0	1	1

(Continued)

11. *Veto* in Latin means "I forbid."

Table 12–1 (Continued)

YEARS	PRESIDENT	REGULAR VETOES	VETOES OVERRIDDEN	POCKET VETOES	TOTAL VETOES
1841–1841	W. Harrison	0	0	0	0
1841–1845	Tyler	6	1	4	10
1845–1849	Polk	2	0	1	3
1849–1850	Taylor	0	0	0	0
1850–1853	Fillmore	0	0	0	0
1853–1857	Pierce	9	5	0	9
1857–1861	Buchanan	4	0	3	7
1861–1865	Lincoln	2	0	5	7
1865–1869	A. Johnson	21	15	8	29
1869–1877	Grant	45	4	48	93
1877–1881	Hayes	12	1	1	13
1881–1881	Garfield	0	0	0	0
1881–1885	Arthur	4	1	8	12
1885–1889	Cleveland	304	2	110	414
1889–1893	B. Harrison	19	1	25	44
1893–1897	Cleveland	42	5	128	170
1897–1901	McKinley	6	0	36	42
1901–1909	T. Roosevelt	42	1	40	82
1909–1913	Taft	30	1	9	39
1913–1921	Wilson	33	6	11	44
1921–1923	Harding	5	0	1	6
1923–1929	Coolidge	20	4	30	50
1929–1933	Hoover	21	3	16	37
1933–1945	F. Roosevelt	372	9	263	635
1945–1953	Truman	180	12	70	250
1953–1961	Eisenhower	73	2	108	181
1961–1963	Kennedy	12	0	9	21
1963–1969	L. Johnson	16	0	14	30
1969–1974	Nixon	26*	7	17	43
1974–1977	Ford	48	12	18	66
1977–1981	Carter	13	2	18	31
1981–1989	Reagan	39	9	39	78
1989–1993	George H. W. Bush	29	1	15	44
1993–2001	Clinton	37**	2	1	38
2001–2008	George W. Bush	11	4	1	12
2009–2014	Obama	2	0	0	2
TOTAL		**1,497**	**110**	**1,067**	**2,565**

Source: Office of the Clerk.

*Two pocket vetoes by President Nixon, overruled in the courts, are counted here as regular vetoes.

**President Clinton's line-item vetoes are not included.

Beyond Our Borders

Do We Need a President *and* a King?

In many democratic societies, the government has a head of government, who actually guides government policy and is the political leader, and a head of state, who is the symbolic head of government. In parliamentary systems, the head of government is actually elected by his or her peers in the majority party in the legislature. In Great Britain, the queen has no political power whatsoever. She cannot refuse to name the leader of the majority party. When she opens the parliamentary session, she reads a speech written for her by the prime minister. Similar political systems with royal families and parliamentary leadership are found in Denmark, Sweden, Spain, and a few smaller European nations. The advantage of this system is that the head of state (the monarch) symbolically represents the nation. Public fascination with royalty means that the prime minister can do his or her job without the gossip and journalistic coverage that surrounds the president of the United States.

Other democracies, including Italy, France, and Germany, have no royal families. The president of the nation is separately elected for a longer term but has little political power. He or she is the head of state and may counsel the head of the government, but political and executive power rests with the prime minister or premier. In some democratic states, the president and the premier are elected, although with different terms.

Until 2008, Vladimir Putin was the president of Russia, but his two terms were limited by the 1993 constitution. After his second term, his chosen successor, Dmitry Medvedev, was elected for one term. Soon after the election, Medvedev named Putin as the premier, still leaving him with considerable power. After Medvedev served one term, Putin was elected to the presidency again because his ability to serve two more terms was constitutional. So, in the case of Russia and some other states, the head of state is the president (who is elected) and who then can name the premier and the cabinet ministers. The intent of this system is for the president to be popularly elected and to exercise political leadership, while the premier runs the everyday operations of government and leads the legislative branch. Given the recent attempt by Russia to annex Crimea and its threats to Ukraine, it appears the President Putin is not only the leader of the state but also the political leader and decision maker for the government.

For Critical Analysis

1. *Why is it important to separate the roles of head of state and head of government?*

2. *Can the existence of a symbolic head of state, such as a monarch, make the elected leader more effective?*

3. *Does the U.S. president, who is both head of state and head of government, carry too heavy a burden?*

Russian president Putin chairs a meeting on inter-ethnic relations in Moldova, a former Soviet republic. In this role, Putin is both the foreign policy leader of Russia and the symbolic head of state as he shores up relationships with the independent nation of Moldova.

President Dwight E.
Eisenhower prepares for a nationwide radio and television address in 1959 in which he called for legislation to stop corruption in labor unions.

Line-Item Veto

The power of an executive to veto individual lines or items within a piece of legislation without vetoing the entire bill.

Constitutional Powers

A power vested in the president by Article II of the Constitution.

Statutory Powers

A power created for the president through laws enacted by Congress.

Expressed Powers

A power of the president that is expressly written into the Constitution or into statutory law.

did you know?

The shortest inaugural address was George Washington's second one, which clocked in at 135 words.

The Line-Item Veto. Ronald Reagan lobbied strenuously for Congress to provide the president with the **line-item veto**, which would allow the president to veto *specific* spending provisions of legislation that was passed by Congress. In 1996, Congress passed the Line Item Veto Act. Signed by President Clinton, the law granted the president the power to rescind any item in an appropriations bill unless Congress passed a resolution of disapproval. The congressional resolution could be, in turn, vetoed by the president. The law did not take effect until after the 1996 election.

The act was soon challenged in court as an unconstitutional delegation of legislative powers to the executive branch. In 1998, by a 6-3 vote, the United States Supreme Court agreed and over-turned the act. The Court stated that "there is no provision in the Constitution that authorizes the president to enact, to amend or to repeal statutes."[12]

Congress's Power to Override Presidential Vetoes. A veto is a clear-cut indication of the president's dissatisfaction with congressional legislation. Congress, however, can override a presidential veto, although it rarely exercises this power. Two-thirds of the members of each chamber who are present must vote to override the president's veto in a roll-call vote. This means that if only one-third plus one of the members voting in the House of Senate do not agree to override the veto, the veto holds. Congress first overrode a presidential veto during the administration of John Tyler (served 1841–1845). Overall, only about 7 percent of all regular vetoes have been overridden.

Other Presidential Powers

The powers of the president just discussed are **constitutional powers**, because their basis lies in the Constitution. In addition, Congress has established by law, or statute, numerous other presidential powers, such as the ability to declare national emergencies. These are **statutory powers.** Both constitutional and statutory powers have been labeled the **expressed powers** of the president, because they are expressly written into the Constitution or into law.

Presidents also have what have come to be known as **inherent powers**. These depend on the statements in the Constitution that "the executive Power shall be vested in a President" and that the president should "take Care that the Laws be faithfully executed." The most common example of inherent powers are those emergency powers invoked by the president during wartime. Franklin Roosevelt used his inherent powers to move the Japanese and Japanese Americans living in the United States into internment camps for the duration of World War II.

Clearly, modern U.S. presidents have many powers at their disposal. According to some critics, among the powers exercised by modern presidents are certain powers that rightfully belong to Congress but that Congress has yielded to the executive branch.

---

12. *Clinton v. City of New York*, 524 U.S. 417 (1998).

The President as Party Chief and Superpolitician

Presidents are by no means above political partisanship, and one of their many roles is that of chief of party. Although the Constitution says nothing about the function of the president within a political party (the mere concept of political parties was abhorrent to most of the Constitution's authors), today presidents are the actual leaders of their parties.

The President as Chief of Party

As party leader, the president chooses the national committee chairperson and tries to discipline party members who fail to support presidential policies. One way of exerting political power is through **patronage**—appointing political supporters to government or public jobs. This power was more extensive in the past, before the establishment of the civil service in 1883 (see Chapter 13), but the president retains important patronage power. The president can appoint several thousand individuals to jobs in the cabinet, the White House, embassies, and the federal regulatory agencies.

Perhaps the most important partisan role that the president has played in recent decades is that of fundraiser. The president is able to raise large amounts for the party through appearances at dinners, speaking engagements, and other social occasions. President Clinton may have raised more than half a billion dollars for the Democratic Party during his two terms. President George W. Bush was even more successful than President Clinton. President Barack Obama continued the trend of raising money for his party, particularly in the run-up to the 2012 elections.

The president may also make it known that a particular congressperson's choice for federal judge will not be appointed unless that member of Congress is more supportive of the president's legislative program.[13] The president may agree to campaign for a particular program or for a particular candidate. Presidents also reward loyal members of Congress with support for the funding of local projects, tax breaks for local industries, invitations to fly in Air Force One, and other forms of social recognition.

The President's Power to Persuade

According to political scientist Richard E. Neustadt, without the power to persuade, no president can lead well. After all, even though the president is in the news virtually every day, the Constitution gives Congress most of the authority in the U.S. political system. The Constitution does not give the executive branch enough constitutional power to firmly establish the president in a strong leadership position. Therefore, the president must establish a "professional reputation" that will convince Congress, the bureaucracy, and the public to support the president's agenda. As Neustadt argues, "presidential power is the power to persuade."[14]

Constituencies and Public Approval

All politicians worry about their constituencies, presidents included. Presidents with high approval ratings are able to leverage those ratings with members of Congress, who would prefer not to vote against the opinions of their own constituents.

Inherent Powers
Powers of the president derived from the statements in the Constitution that "the executive Power shall be vested in a President" and that the president should "take Care that the Laws be faithfully executed;" defined through practice rather than through law.

Patronage
The practice of rewarding faithful party workers and followers with government employment and contracts.

---

13. "Senatorial courtesy" (see Chapter 15) often puts the judicial appointment in the hands of the Senate, however.
14. Richard E. Neustadt, *Presidential Power and the Modern Presidents: The Politics of Leadership from Roosevelt to Reagan*, rev. ed. (New York: Free Press, 1991).

Washington Community
Individuals regularly involved with politics in Washington, DC.

Presidential Constituencies. According to Neustadt, presidents have not just one constituency, but many. They are beholden to the entire electorate—the public of the United States—even those who did not vote. They are beholden to their party because its members helped to put them in office. The president's constituencies also include members of the opposing party, whose cooperation the president needs. Finally, the president must take into consideration a constituency that has come to be called the **Washington community**. This community consists of individuals who—whether in or out of political office—are familiar with the workings of government, thrive on gossip, and measure on a daily basis the political power of the president.

Public Approval. All of these constituencies are impressed by presidents who maintain a high level of public approval, as this is very difficult to accomplish. Presidential popularity, as measured by national polls, gives the president an extra political resource for persuading legislators or bureaucrats to pass legislation. As you will note from Figure 12–2, patterns for almost all presidents are common. Presidential approval ratings tend to be very high when a new president takes office (the honeymoon period), and decline to a low in the last two years of the second term. Spikes in public approval apart from that cycle tend to occur when the United States sends troops in harm's way. This is the "rally 'round the flag" effect. Look at George H. W. Bush's ratings. Popular approval of the president reached a new high at the beginning of the Persian Gulf War, but that approval had no staying power, and his ratings declined precipitously in the year following the victory. Bill Clinton defied all tradition by having high ratings even while he was fighting impeachment.

George W. Bush and the Public Opinion Polls. The impact of popular approval on a president's prospects was placed in sharp relief by the experiences of the second President Bush. Immediately after September 11, 2001, Bush had

Figure 12–2 ▸ Public Popularity of Modern Presidents

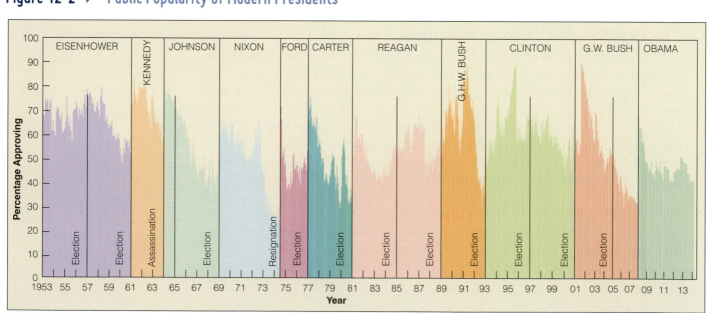

Source: Gallup Presidential Approval Center http://www.gallup.com/poll/124922/presidential-approval-center.aspx

the highest approval ratings ever recorded. His popularity then entered a steep decline that was interrupted only briefly by high ratings during the early phases of the Second Gulf War. During his second term, Bush's approval ratings reached new lows, falling to less than 30 percent by 2008. Without question, the economic crisis of fall 2008 contributed to the final low ebb of his approval ratings.

Barack Obama and Popular Approval

Like most presidents who win office with a substantial margin of victory, President Obama entered the office with very high approval ratings. Voters, as usual, were willing to give the new president high marks for his first year in office. Additionally, Obama's youth, energy, and new outlook enhanced his image. As the economic crisis deepened and various government measures failed to improve the unemployment figures, Obama began to experience some decline in his approval ratings. By the middle of his second year in office, his approval ratings had stabilized at about 50 percent, a level similar to that achieved by many other presidents in their first term in office. As Figure 12–2 shows, by the beginning of his sixth year in office, President Obama's approval rating had slipped into the low 40 percent range and seemed to stabilize at that level.

"Going Public." In the 1800s, only 7 percent of presidential speeches were addressed to the public; since 1900, 50 percent have been addressed to the public. Scholar Samuel Kernell has proposed that the style of presidential leadership has changed since World War II, owing partly to the influence of television, with a

AP Images/Bill Chaplis

President John F. Kennedy discusses the Berlin crisis at a news conference in 1961. Kennedy continues to be considered a master of such events.

resulting change in the balance of national politics.[15] Presidents frequently go over the heads of Congress and the political elites, taking their cases directly to the people.

This strategy, which Kernell dubbed "going public," gives the president additional power through the ability to persuade and manipulate public opinion. By identifying their own positions so clearly, presidents weaken the ability of Congress to modify his or her agenda. Given the increasing importance of the media as the major source of political information for citizens and elites, presidents will continue to use public opinion as part of their arsenal of weapons to gain support from Congress and to achieve their policy goals.

Special Uses of Presidential Power

■ **LO12.4:** Explain the emergency powers of the president and the executive powers of the president.

Presidents have at their disposal a variety of special powers and privileges not available in the other branches of the U.S. government: (1) emergency powers, (2) executive orders, and (3) executive privilege.

Emergency Powers

Emergency Powers
Inherent powers exercised by the president during a period of national crisis.

The Constitution does not mention additional powers that the executive office may exercise during national emergencies. The Supreme Court has indicated that an "emergency does not create power."[16] But it is clear that presidents have used their inherent powers during times of emergency, particularly concerning foreign affairs. The **emergency powers** of the president were first enunciated in *United States v. Curtiss-Wright Export Corp.*[17] In that case, President Franklin Roosevelt, without congressional authorization, ordered an embargo on the shipment of weapons to two warring South American countries. The Court recognized that the president may exercise inherent powers in foreign affairs and that the national government has primacy in these affairs.

Abraham Lincoln suspended civil liberties at the beginning of the Civil War (1861–1865) and called the state militias into national service. These actions and his subsequent governance of conquered areas and even of areas of northern states were justified by claims that they were essential to preserve the Union. President Truman authorized the federal seizure of steel plants and their operation by the national government in 1952 during the Korean War. Truman claimed that he was using his inherent emergency power as chief executive and commander in chief to safeguard the nation's security, as an ongoing strike by steelworkers threatened the supply of weapons to the armed forces. The Supreme Court did not agree, holding that the president had no authority under the Constitution to seize private property or to legislate such action.[18] This was the first time a limit was placed on the exercise of the president's emergency powers.

After September 11, 2001, the Bush administration pushed several laws through Congress that granted more power to the Department of Justice and other agencies to investigate possible terrorists. Many of these provisions of the PATRIOT Act and other laws have been reaffirmed by Congress in subsequent

15. Samuel Kernell, *Going Public: New Strategies of Presidential Leadership,* 4th ed. (Washington, DC: Congressional Quarterly Press, 2006).
16. *Home Building and Loan Association v. Blaisdell,* 290 U.S. 398 (1934).
17. 299 U.S. 304 (1936).
18. *Youngstown Sheet and Tube Co. v. Sawyer,* 343 U.S. 579 (1952).

years, while others have been revised. In 2006, it became clear that President Bush had also authorized federal agencies to eavesdrop on international telephone calls without a court order when the party overseas was suspected of having information about terrorism or might be a suspect in a terrorist plot. This eavesdropping had not been authorized under the legislation. Many scholars claimed that this exercise of presidential power was far beyond what could be claimed an emergency power.[19] The Bush administration claimed that it was entirely within the president's power to make such an authorization, although it did not claim the authorization to be within the Supreme Court's definition of "emergency power." Following these disclosures, the administration pursued an expanded law to allow such wiretapping, but provisions of that new bill proved too controversial to pass in 2008.

President Obama's administration did not attempt to pass any legislation on this matter. In 2013, however, the revelations of Edward Snowden made it clear that the eavesdropping program was still intact and, in fact, the NSA was now collecting almost all landline telephone call data both within the United States and from America to other nations.[20] The president, after appointing a commission to make recommendations, announced that some limitations on this program might be possible.

Executive Orders

Congress allows the president (and administrative agencies) to issue **executive orders** that have the force of law. These executive orders can: (1) enforce legislative statutes, (2) enforce the Constitution or treaties with foreign nations, and (3) establish or modify rules and practices of executive administrative agencies.

An executive order, then, represents the president's legislative power. The only requirement is that under the Administrative Procedure Act of 1946, all executive orders must be published in the ***Federal Register***, a daily publication of the U.S. government. Executive orders have been used to establish procedures, to implement national affirmative action regulations, to restructure the White House bureaucracy, to classify government information as secret, to establish military tribunals for suspected terrorists, and to order federal agencies to provide benefits to legally married same-sex couples.

It is important to note that executive orders can be revoked by succeeding presidents. George H. W. Bush issued an order to ban foreign aid to countries that included abortion in their family planning strategies, because that provision (the Hyde Amendment) could not make it through Congress as legislation. President Clinton revoked the order. The George W. Bush administration revoked many of the thousands of executive orders and regulations issued in the last months of the Clinton administration. Not surprisingly, the Obama administration revoked a number of the Bush orders and issued new orders in support of stronger environmental regulations, food safety, consumer safety, and many other areas.

Facing opposition to many of his legislative proposals by the Republican-controlled House of Representatives, President Obama announced in his 2013 State of the Union Address that he was willing to use executive orders to achieve his objectives if Congress did not act. One of his orders in early 2014 raised the minimum wage for all temporary workers provided to the federal government through private contracts.

Executive Orders
A rule or regulation issued by the president that has the effect of law. Executive orders can implement and give administrative effect to provisions in the Constitution, to treaties, and to statutes.

Federal Register
A publication of the U.S. government that prints executive orders, rules, and regulations.

---

19. Elizabeth Drew, "Power Grab," *New York Review of Books,* Vol. 53, No. 11, June 22, 2006.
20. See the chronology of the NSA spying program at the Electronic Frontier Foundation, "NSA Spying FAQ," www.eff.or.nsa-spying, accessed April 8, 2014.

Politics with a Purpose

"For the Record" versus "That's Privileged Information"

Do we have a right to know everything our government does? What circumstances might justify the president keeping his or her activities or those of the administration secret? These questions raise complex issues, and common sense says the answers lie somewhere in between the two extremes. How this balance is struck has been the subject of intense political debate.

After the Watergate scandal, Congress passed the Presidential Records Act of 1978 (PRA) to address control of the historical record of a presidential administration.* Immediately upon the inauguration of the successor, the National Archives physically takes control of all presidential and vice presidential records. For a period of 12 years, the National Archives is responsible for processing these papers and reviewing and examining each document for national security issues or other reasons that would preclude it from being made public. Under the PRA, after this time period, the records are released to the presidential libraries. Each library—staffed by archivists employed by the federal government—houses all of the papers of that administration.** However, current or former presidents can request that certain documents not be released, claiming executive privilege (discussed in the "Special Uses of Presidential Power" section).***

President Reagan's records were the first to be processed under the PRA. In February 2001, President Bush was notified that one of the first batches of Reagan documents was scheduled for release, as the 12-year period was set to expire. President Bush issued an executive order which significantly altered the rules on presidential documents. His order allowed current and former presidents to refuse to release any document from their administration.

A coalition of scholars, researchers, journalists, and public-interest lobby groups joined in a suit to stop the implementation of President Bush's executive order. The group won a partial victory in October 2007 when a federal court struck down the portion of E.O. 13233 allowing current and former presidents to screen the release of documents.****

Immediately after President Obama's inauguration, he signed an executive order that allowed former presidents the opportunity to claim executive privilege for any requested documents. Around the same time, the House passed another, stronger version of the 2007 bill, but the two houses have not yet agreed upon a new version of the law. The issue of executive privilege often comes into play when the Senate is considering nominations to the federal courts. In early 2010, President Obama nominated Elena Kagan for the Supreme Court. Immediately, the Senate Judiciary Committee requested access to memos that Ms. Kagan wrote as an aide in the Clinton White House. Although President Clinton's papers were not supposed to be available until 2013, the former president raised no objection to releasing the Kagan memos. In 2014, several thousand of the papers from the Clinton administration were released. More are forthcoming.

---

*www.archives.gov/presidential-libraries/laws/1978-act.html

**For a complete list of the presidential libraries, see www.archives.gov/presidential-libraries

***If someone wants access to an unreleased document, the person can file a Freedom of Information Act (FOIA) request. Archivists trained with an understanding of the PRA, FOIA, and any other governing statutes determine whether to release the documents. This process remains in place today.

****http://aaupnet.org/news/press/PRAamicus.pdf

Executive Privilege

Another inherent executive power claimed by presidents concerns the ability to withhold information from, or refuse to appear before, Congress or the courts. This is called **executive privilege** and it relies on the constitutional separation of powers for its basis.

Presidents have frequently invoked executive privilege to avoid having to disclose information to Congress on actions of the executive branch. Critics of executive privilege believe that it can be used to shield from public scrutiny executive actions that should be open to Congress and to the American citizenry.

Executive Privilege
The right of executive officials to withhold information from or refuse to appear before a legislative committee.

Limiting Executive Privilege. Limits to executive privilege went untested until the Watergate affair in the early 1970s. Five men broke into the headquarters of the Democratic National Committee and were caught searching for documents that would damage the candidacy of the Democratic nominee, George McGovern. Later investigation showed that the break-in was planned by members of Richard Nixon's campaign committee and that Nixon and his closest advisers had devised a strategy for impeding the investigation of the crime. After it became known that all of the conversations held in the Oval Office had been tape-recorded on a secret system, Nixon was ordered to turn over the tapes to the special prosecutor.

Nixon refused to do so, claiming executive privilege. He argued that "no president could function if the private papers of his office, prepared by his personal staff, were open to public scrutiny." In 1974, in one of the Supreme Court's most famous cases, *United States v. Nixon*, the justices unanimously ruled that Nixon had to hand over the tapes.[21] The Court held that executive privilege could not be used to prevent evidence from being heard in criminal proceedings.

Clinton's Attempted Use of Executive Privilege. The claim of executive privilege was also raised by the Clinton administration as a defense against the aggressive investigation of Clinton's relationship with White House intern Monica Lewinsky by Independent Counsel Kenneth Starr. The Clinton administration claimed executive privilege for several presidential aides who might have discussed the situation with the president. In addition, Clinton asserted that his White House counsel did not have to testify before the Starr grand jury due to attorney-client privilege. The Department of Justice claimed that members of the Secret Service who guard the president could not testify about his activities due to a "protective function privilege" inherent in their duties. The federal judge overseeing the case denied the claims of privilege, however, and the decision was upheld on appeal.

Abuses of Executive Power and Impeachment

■ **LO12.5:** Explain the process by which a president could be impeached and forced to leave office.

Presidents normally leave office either because their first term has expired and they have not sought (or won) reelection or because, having served two full terms, they are not allowed to be elected for a third term (owing to the Twenty-second Amendment, passed in 1951). Eight presidents have died in office. But a president may leave office in another way—**impeachment** and conviction. Articles I and II of the Constitution authorize the House and Senate to remove the president, the vice president, or other civil officers of the United States for committing "Treason, Bribery, or other high Crimes and Misdemeanors." According to the Constitution,

AP Images/Bob Daugherty

Richard Nixon says goodbye outside the White House after his resignation on August 9, 1974, as he prepares to board a helicopter for a flight to nearby Andrews Air Force Base. Nixon addressed members of his staff in the East Room prior to his departure. Was Nixon impeached?

Impeachment
An action by the House of Representatives to accuse the president, vice president, or other civil officers of the United States of committing "Treason, Bribery, or other high Crimes and Misdemeanors."

---

21. 318 U.S. 683 (1974).

the impeachment process begins in the House, which impeaches (accuses) the federal officer involved. If the House votes to impeach the officer, it draws up articles of impeachment and submits them to the Senate, which conducts the actual trial.

No president has ever actually been impeached and convicted—and thus removed from office—by means of this process. President Andrew Johnson (served 1865–1869), who succeeded to the office after the assassination of Abraham Lincoln, was impeached by the House but acquitted by the Senate. More than a century later, the House Judiciary Committee approved articles of impeachment against President Nixon for his involvement in the cover-up of the Watergate break-in of 1972. Informed by members of his own party that he would not survive the trial in the Senate, Nixon resigned on August 9, 1974, before the full House voted on the articles. Nixon is the only president to have resigned from office. The second president to be impeached by the House but not convicted by the Senate was President Clinton. In September 1998, Independent Counsel Kenneth Starr submitted the findings of his investigation of the president on the charges of perjury and obstruction of justice. The House approved two charges against Clinton: lying to the grand jury about his affair with Monica Lewinsky and obstruction of justice. The articles of impeachment were then sent to the Senate, which acquitted Clinton.

did you know?

President Richard Nixon served 56 days without a vice president, and President Gerald Ford served 132 days without a vice president.

The Executive Organization

■ **LO12.6:** Describe the executive offices that support the president.

Gone are the days when presidents answered their own mail, as George Washington did. It was not until 1857 that Congress authorized a private secretary for the president, to be paid by the federal government. Woodrow Wilson typed most of his correspondence, even though he did have several secretaries. At the beginning of Franklin Roosevelt's tenure in the White House, the entire staff consisted of 37 employees. With the New Deal and World War II, however, the presidential staff became a sizable organization.

Today, the executive organization includes a White House office staff of about 600, including part-time employees and others who are borrowed from their departments by the White House. The more than 460 employees who work in the White House Office are closest to the president. The employees who work for the numerous councils and advisory groups support the president on policy and coordinate the work of departments. The group of appointees perhaps most helpful to the president are the cabinet members, each of whom is the principal officer of a government department.

did you know?

One member of the cabinet must not attend the State of the Union speech so that someone in the line of succession to the presidency would survive in case of an attack on the Capitol.

The Cabinet

Although the Constitution does not include the word *cabinet*, it does state that the president "may require the Opinion, in writing, of the principal Officer in each of the executive Departments." All presidents have turned to an advisory group, or **cabinet**, for counsel.

Cabinet

An advisory group selected by the president to aid in making decisions. The cabinet includes the heads of 15 executive departments and others named by the president.

Members of the Cabinet. Originally, the cabinet consisted of only four officials—the secretaries of state, treasury, and war, and the attorney general. Today, the cabinet numbers 14 department secretaries and the attorney general.

The cabinet may include others as well. The president can, at his or her discretion, ascribe cabinet rank to the vice president, the head of the Office of Management and Budget, the national security adviser, the ambassador to the United Nations, or others.

Often, a president will use a **kitchen cabinet** to replace the formal cabinet as a major source of advice. The term *kitchen cabinet* originated during the presidency of Andrew Jackson, who relied on the counsel of close friends who often met with him in the kitchen of the White House. A kitchen cabinet is an informal group of advisers; usually, friends with whom the president worked before being elected.

Presidential Use of Cabinets. Because neither the Constitution nor statutory law requires the president to consult with the cabinet, its use is purely discretionary. Some presidents have relied on the counsel of their cabinets more than others. Dwight Eisenhower was used to the team approach to solving problems from his military experience, and therefore he frequently turned to his cabinet for advice on a wide range of issues. More often, presidents have solicited the opinions of their cabinets and then done what they wanted to do anyway. Lincoln supposedly said—after a cabinet meeting in which a vote was seven nays against his one aye—"Seven nays and one aye; the ayes have it." In general, few presidents have relied heavily on the advice of their cabinet members.

It is not surprising that presidents tend not to rely on their cabinet members' advice. Often, the departmental heads are more responsive to the wishes of their own staffs or to their own political ambitions than they are to the president. They may be more concerned with obtaining resources for their departments than with achieving the goals of the president. So a strong conflict of interest between presidents and their cabinet members often exists.

The Executive Office of the President

When President Franklin Roosevelt appointed a special committee on administrative management, he knew that the committee would conclude that the president needed help. The committee proposed a major reorganization of the executive branch. Congress did not approve the entire reorganization, but did create the **Executive Office of the President (EOP)** to provide staff assistance and to help coordinate the executive bureaucracy. Since then, many agencies have been created within the EOP. These agencies include the following:

- White House Office
- White House Military Office
- Office of the Vice President
- Council of Economic Advisers
- Office of National Drug Control Policy
- Office of Science and Technology Policy
- Office of the United States Trade Representative
- Council on Environmental Quality
- President's Critical Infrastructure Protection Board
- Office of Management and Budget
- National Security Council
- President's Foreign Intelligence Advisory Board
- Office of National AIDS Policy

Several of the offices within the EOP are especially important, including the White House Office, the Office of Management and Budget, and the National Security Council.

Kitchen Cabinet
The informal advisers to the president.

Executive Office of the President (EOP)
An organization established by President Franklin D. Roosevelt to assist the president in carrying out major duties.

White House Office
The personal office of the president, which tends to presidential political needs and manages the media.

Chief Of Staff
The person who is named to direct the White House Office and advise the president.

Permanent Campaign
A coordinated and planned strategy carried out by the White House to increase the president's popularity and support.

The White House Office. The **White House Office** includes most of the key personal and political advisers to the president. Among the jobs held by these aides are those of legal counsel to the president, secretary, press secretary, and appointments secretary. In all recent administrations, one member of the White House Office has been named **chief of staff**. This person, who is responsible for coordinating the office, is also one of the president's chief advisers.

Often, the individuals who hold these positions are recruited from the president's campaign staff. Their duties—mainly protecting the president's political interests—are similar to campaign functions. Most observers of the presidency agree that contemporary presidents continue their campaigning after inauguration. The **permanent campaign** is a long-term strategy planned by the White House Office of Communications with the press secretary to keep the president's approval ratings high and to improve support in Congress. The campaign includes staged events, symbolic actions, and controlled media appearances. During the Obama presidency this function rose to a new height with the adoption of all forms of electronic media. Anyone who worked in either of his campaigns or signed up for presidential updates receives emails from the president or Joe Biden or the First Lady on a weekly basis with information about the president's initiatives. The White House also sends out Tweets and posts information on all social media sites. The president's overall agenda is featured on the official White House website, with links to his policy priorities.

The president may establish special advisory units within the White House to address topics the president finds especially important. Under George W. Bush, these units also included the Office of Faith-Based and Community Initiatives and the USA Freedom Corps. The White House Office also includes the staff members who support the First Lady.

The president is also supported by a large number of military personnel, who are organized under the White House Military Office. These members of the military provide communications, transportation, medical care, and food services to the president and the White House staff.

Employees of the White House Office have been both envied and criticized. The White House Office, according to most former staffers, grants its employees access and power. They are able to use the resources of the White House to contact virtually anyone in the world by telephone, text, satellite telephone, or email, as well as to use the influence of the White House to persuade legislators and citizens. Because of this influence, staffers are often criticized for overstepping the bounds of the office. The appointments secretary is able to grant or deny senators, representatives, and cabinet secretaries access to the president. The press secretary grants the press and television journalists access to any information about the president.

What message is the president trying to send by prioritizing his policy agenda online?

White House staff members are closest to the president and may have considerable influence over the administration's decisions. When presidents are under fire for their decisions, the staff is often accused of keeping the chief executive too isolated from criticism or help. Presidents insist that they will not allow the staff to become too powerful, but, given the difficulty of the office, each president eventually turns to staff members for loyal assistance and protection.

The Office of Management and Budget.

The **Office of Management and Budget (OMB)** was originally the Bureau of the Budget, created in 1921 within the Department of the Treasury. Recognizing the importance of this agency, Franklin Roosevelt moved it into the White House Office in 1939. Richard Nixon reorganized the Bureau of the Budget in 1970 and changed its name to reflect its new managerial function. It is headed by a director, who must create the annual federal budget that the president presents to Congress each January for approval. In principle, the director of the OMB has broad fiscal powers in planning and estimating various parts of the federal budget, because all agencies must submit their proposed budget to the OMB for approval. In reality, it is not so evident that the OMB truly can affect the greater scope of the federal budget. Rather, the OMB may be more important as a clearinghouse for legislative proposals initiated in the executive agencies.

The National Security Council.

The **National Security Council (NSC)** is a link between the president's key foreign and military advisers and the president. Its members consist of the president, the vice president, and the secretaries of state and defense, plus other informal members. Included in the NSC is the president's special assistant for national security affairs. In 2001, Condoleezza Rice became the first woman to serve as a president's national security adviser. In 2013, former Ambassador to the United Nations, Susan Rice, became the national security advisor.

"Policy Czars."

For many decades presidents have created positions within the Executive Office of the President that were focused on one special policy area. Many have been titled "senior policy coordinator" or "senior adviser," and most of them have been appointments that do not require Senate confirmation. In general, these positions last only as long as the president. Each new president decides which domestic or foreign policy issues need special attention from an individual who can report directly to the chief executive. In recent administrations, the nickname "**policy czar**" has been attached to these positions.

If the president has special councils on problems such as drugs or the environment and cabinet departments or independent agencies designated to handle an area of government policy, why does the president need yet another individual to supervise government action? Presidents expect a policy czar to focus on the problem, along with coordinating the efforts of all the other government agencies that have authority in that policy area. The individuals named to these positions are often well-regarded experts who can bring an outsider's point of view both to the president and to the agencies involved in dealing with an issue. George W. Bush, over the two terms of his presidency, appointed more than 30 individuals to these positions.

President Obama created more than 40 positions in the Executive Office of the President to advise him on specific issue areas and to coordinate the work of

Office of Management and Budget (OMB)
A division of the Executive Office of the President. The OMB assists the president in preparing the annual budget, clearing and coordinating departmental agency budgets, and supervising the administration of the federal budget.

National Security Council (NSC)
An agency in the Executive Office of the President that advises the president on national security.

Policy Czar
A high-ranking member of the Executive Office of the President appointed to coordinate action in one specific policy area.

cabinet departments on such topics as health-care reform, climate change, and urban initiatives. Criticism of his decision to create so many special advisers ranged from the cost to the effectiveness of having people in place to oversee the work of cabinet secretaries, but his authority to do so was unquestionable.[22] When Congress managed to defund four of these positions in 2011, Obama noted that he could bypass that provision and appoint the advisors that he needed. Sometimes, an individual who has held one of these positions is then appointed to a regular administrative position.[23]

The Vice Presidency

■ **LO12.7:** Describe the job of the vice president and explain the circumstances under which the vice president becomes president.

The Constitution does not give much power to the vice president. The only formal duty is to preside over the Senate, which is rarely necessary. This obligation is fulfilled when the Senate organizes and adopts its rules and when the vice president is needed to decide a tie vote. In all other cases, the president pro tem manages parliamentary procedures in the Senate. The vice president is expected to participate only informally in senatorial deliberations, if at all.

The Vice President's Job

Vice presidents have traditionally been chosen to balance the ticket to attract groups of voters or appease party factions. If a presidential nominee is from the North, it is not a bad idea to have a vice presidential nominee who is from the South. If the presidential nominee is from a rural state, perhaps someone with an urban background would be most suitable as a running mate. Presidential nominees who are strongly conservative or strongly liberal would do well to have vice presidential nominees who are more in the middle of the political road.

Strengthening the Ticket.   In recent presidential elections, vice presidents have often been selected for other reasons. Bill Clinton picked Al Gore to be his running mate in 1992, even though both were southerners and moderates. The ticket appealed to southerners and moderates, both of whom were crucial to the election. In 2000, George W. Bush, who was subject to criticism for his lack of federal government experience and his "lightweight" personality, chose Dick Cheney, a former member of Congress who had also served as secretary of defense. Both presidential candidates in 2008 sought to balance their perceived weaknesses with their vice presidential choices. Barack Obama chose Senator Joseph Biden to add experience and foreign policy knowledge to his ticket, and John McCain chose Sarah Palin to add youth and an appeal to the Christian right to his ticket. In 2012, Republican nominee Mitt Romney selected Representative Paul Ryan of Wisconsin to be his running mate. Ryan, a well-known fiscal conservative, was selected to persuade Tea Party members and conservative Republicans to support the ticket.

22. Aaron J. Saiger, "Obama's "Czar's" for Domestic Policy and the Law of the White House Staff," *Fordham Law Review* 79 (2011): 2576–2616.
23. Bill Piper, "New Drug Czar a Chance to Do Things Right," *HuffPost Politics*, March 24, 2014. http://www.huffingtonpost.com/bill-piper/new-drug-czar_b_5022801.html

Vice President Joe
Biden poses with the Israeli Defense Minister, Ehud Barak, and U.S. and Israeli military personnel in Israel. The goal of Biden's trip was to show the U.S. commitment to the security of the state of Israel.

Supporting the President. The job of vice president is not extremely demanding, even when the president gives some specific task to the vice president. Typically, vice presidents spend their time supporting the president's activities. During the Clinton administration (1993–2001), however, Vice President Al Gore did much to strengthen the position by his aggressive support for environmental protection policies on a global basis. He also took a special interest in areas of emerging technology and lobbied Congress to provide subsidies to public schools for Internet use.

Vice President Dick Cheney was clearly was an influential figure in the Bush administration. Although many of the Washington elite were happy to see Dick Cheney as vice president because of his intelligence and wide range of experience, he quickly became a controversial figure due to his outspoken support for a tough foreign and military policy and for having encouraged Bush to attack Iraq.

Vice President Joe Biden, former senator from Delaware, was a popular choice for vice president among Democrats and voters. He had many years of experience in the Senate, thus balancing President's Obama's relative lack of experience on Capitol Hill. Once the Obama administration took office, Biden's role became

somewhat clearer. His experiences in the Senate prepared him to be a senior adviser to the president on foreign policy issues, although he was not as controversial a figure as Cheney had been. Of course, the vice presidency takes on more significance if the president becomes disabled or dies in office and the vice president becomes president.

Vice presidents sometimes have become elected presidents in their own right. John Adams and Thomas Jefferson were the first two vice presidents to win the office of president. Richard Nixon was elected president in 1968 after he had served as Dwight D. Eisenhower's vice president from 1953 to 1961. In 1988, George H. W. Bush was elected to the presidency after eight years as Ronald Reagan's vice president.

Presidential Succession

Eight vice presidents have become president upon the death of the president. John Tyler, the first to do so, took over William Henry Harrison's position after only one month. No one knew whether Tyler should simply be a caretaker until a new president could be elected three and a half years later or whether he actually should be president. Tyler assumed that he was supposed to be the chief executive and he acted as such, although he was commonly referred to as "His Accidency." Since then, vice presidents taking over the position of the presidency because of the incumbent's death have assumed the presidential powers.

But what should a vice president do if a president becomes incapable of carrying out necessary duties while in office? When James Garfield was shot in 1881, he survived for two and a half months. What was Vice President Chester Arthur's role? This question was not addressed in the original Constitution. Article II, Section 1, says only that "[i]n Case of the Removal of the President from Office, or of his Death, Resignation, or Inability to discharge the Powers and Duties of the said Office, the same shall devolve on [the same powers shall be exercised by] the Vice President." Many instances of presidential disability have occurred. When Dwight Eisenhower became ill a second time in 1958, he entered into a pact with Richard Nixon specifying that the vice president could determine whether the president was incapable of carrying out his duties if the president could not communicate. John F. Kennedy and Lyndon Johnson entered into similar agreements with their vice presidents. In 1967, the **Twenty-fifth Amendment** was ratified, establishing procedures in case of presidential incapacity.

The Twenty-Fifth Amendment

According to the Twenty-Fifth Amendment, when a president believes that he or she is incapable of performing the duties of office, the president must inform Congress in writing. Then the vice president serves as acting president until the president can resume normal duties. When the president is unable to communicate, a majority of the cabinet, including the vice president, can declare that fact to Congress. Then the vice president serves as acting president until the president resumes normal duties. If a dispute arises over the return of the president's ability, a two-thirds vote of Congress is required to decide whether the vice president shall remain acting president or whether the president shall resume normal duties.

Twenty-fifth Amendment
A 1967 amendment to the Constitution that establishes procedures for filling presidential and vice presidential vacancies and makes provisions for presidential disability.

AP Images/Ron Edmonds

An attempted assassination of Ronald Reagan occurred on March 31, 1981. In the foreground, two men bend over Press Secretary James Brady, who lies seriously wounded. In the background, President Reagan is watched over by a U.S. Secret Service agent with an automatic weapon. A Washington, DC, police officer, Thomas Delahanty, lies to the left after also being shot.

In 2002, President George W. Bush formally invoked the Twenty-Fifth Amendment for the first time by officially transferring presidential power to Vice President Dick Cheney while the president underwent a colonoscopy, a 20-minute procedure. He commented that he undertook this transfer of power "because we're at war," referring to the war on terrorism. The only other time the provisions of the Twenty-Fifth Amendment have been used was during President Reagan's colon surgery in 1985, although Reagan did not formally invoke the amendment.

When the Vice Presidency Becomes Vacant

The Twenty-fifth Amendment also addresses the issue of how the president should fill a vacant vice presidency. Section 2 of the amendment simply states, "Whenever there is a vacancy in the office of the Vice President, the President shall nominate a Vice President who shall take office upon confirmation by a majority vote of both Houses of Congress." This occurred when Richard Nixon's vice president, Spiro Agnew, resigned in 1973 because of his alleged receipt of construction contract kickbacks during his tenure as governor of Maryland. Nixon turned to Gerald Ford as his choice for vice president. After extensive hearings, both chambers of Congress confirmed the appointment. When Nixon resigned on August 9, 1974, Ford automatically became president and nominated Nelson Rockefeller as his vice president, which Congress confirmed. For the first time, neither the president nor the vice president had been elected to either position.

The question of who shall be president if both the president and vice president die is answered by the Succession Act of 1947. If the president and vice president die, resign, or are disabled, the Speaker of the House will become president, after resigning from Congress. Next in line is the president pro tem of the Senate, followed by the cabinet officers in the order of the creation of their departments (see Table 12–2).

did you know?
Gerald Ford was the first person to be both vice president and president without being elected by the people. He was appointed vice president when Spiro Agnew resigned and he succeeded to the presidency when Nixon resigned.

Table 12–2 ▶   Line of Succession to the Presidency of the United States

1.	Vice President
2.	Speaker of the House of Representatives
3.	Senate President Pro Tempore
4.	Secretary of State
5.	Secretary of the Treasury
6.	Secretary of Defense
7.	Attorney General (head of the Justice Department)
8.	Secretary of the Interior
9.	Secretary of Agriculture
10.	Secretary of Commerce
11.	Secretary of Labor
12.	Secretary of Health and Human Services
13.	Secretary of Housing and Urban Development
14.	Secretary of Transportation
15.	Secretary of Energy
16.	Secretary of Education
17.	Secretary of Veterans Affairs
18.	Secretary of Homeland Security

What Would You Do?

Presidential Decision Making

Presidents rarely get everything they want in legislation. Presidents use the first years of the first term of office to get as much of their agenda enacted into law as possible because their support in Congress might be weakened in the midterm elections. Even members of the president's own party, however, have ideas about what would be good for constituents and for the interest groups that provide their campaign funds. Often, when legislation is considered for domestic policy, compromises are necessary to get the legislation passed.

Why Should You Care?

Voters have strong feelings about presidential candidates and give their time and money to get their favorite candidate elected. At the time of the inauguration, millions of Americans have their hopes vested in the new president and they have high expectations. On a more personal note, many supporters are hopeful that his agenda will improve their own situation.

President Obama was elected by a powerful coalition of voters: 60 percent of young voters chose him, more than 95 percent of

African American voters voted for him, a majority of women voted for him, and a large majority of Latino voters supported him. As his first term in office came to an end, some of those voters expressed disappointment in his presidency. Women voters were very happy with the new health benefits available under the Affordable Care Act but were still concerned with issues of equal pay. African American voters were still enormously supportive of the president, but the Congressional Black Caucus did seek more support from the president in his second term. Latino voters had hoped for immigration reform in the first term, but that legislation was stalled. Support among young voters remained strong, although many were concerned about the economy and future job prospects.

It is important to know that the president must constantly make decisions about which bills to sign, which to veto, which members of Congress need to be cajoled, and about shoring up support among voters through speeches, initiatives, and public events.

What Would You Do?

As the domestic policy advisor to the president of the United States, would you advise the president to sign a budget bill that is close to his or her proposed budget but leaves out funding for important initiatives?

What You *Can* Do

Most importantly, you should become well-informed on pending legislation and the president's choices. The White House website has a wealth of information about Obama's priorities and includes his statements about every piece of legislation that he receives from Congress. Follow the White House on Facebook and Twitter to quickly receive information.

If the members of Congress are debating legislation that you feel is harmful to the nation, contact them directly. Sign a petition on the web that will go directly to Congress and the White House. Contact the office of your senator or representative by telephone or email and make sure you know with whom you are communicating. Staff members should be named on the representative's website.

Join a group to advocate for your views: There are vocal and well-respected interest groups and think tanks for every viewpoint and for all interests. Follow their research and read their explanations for legislation. If you really want to participate in policy discussions, seek an internship at one of these research institutes or in the office of a member of Congress.

- To follow the policy debates in Washington, try the following sources:
  The White House: www.whitehouse.gov
  The Senate Majority Leader: www.democrats.senate.gov/news
  The Speaker of the House: www.speaker.gov

- For a conservative viewpoint on economic issues:
  American Enterprise Institute: www.aei.org
  For a liberal position on domestic issues: The Brookings Institution: www.brookings.edu

Purestock/Getty Images

Key Terms

advice and consent 426
appointment power 424
cabinet 442
chief diplomat 427
chief executive 423
chief legislator 429
chief of staff 444
civil service 424
commander in chief 425
constitutional powers 434
diplomatic recognition 427

emergency powers 438
executive agreements 428
Executive Office of the President (EOP) 443
executive orders 439
executive privilege 440
expressed powers 434
Federal Register 439
head of state 422
impeachment 441
inherent powers 435

kitchen cabinet 443
line-item veto 434
National Security Council (NSC) 445
Office of Management and Budget (OMB) 445
pardons 425
patronage 435
permanent campaign 444
pocket veto 431
policy czar 445
reprieves 425

signing statement 423
State of the Union Message 430
statutory powers 434
Twelfth Amendment 422
Twenty-Fifth Amendment 448
veto message 431
War Powers Resolution 426
Washington community 436
White House Office 444

Chapter Summary

■ **LO12.1:** The office of the presidency in the United States, combining as it does the functions of head of state and chief executive, was unique when it was created. The framers of the Constitution were divided over whether the president should be a weak or a strong executive.

■ **LO12.1:** The requirements for the office of the presidency are outlined in Article II, Section 1, of the Constitution and include both formal and informal duties. The roles of the president include head of state, chief executive, commander in chief, chief diplomat, chief legislator, and party chief.

■ **LO12.1:** As head of state, the president is ceremonial leader of the government. As chief executive, the president is bound to enforce the acts of Congress, the judgments of the federal courts, and treaties. The chief executive has the power of appointment and the power to grant reprieves and pardons.

■ **LO12.1:** Presidents are also the political leaders of their party, naming the leadership of the party and being the chief fundraiser for future elections. To become effective leaders and to gain support for their policies, presidents try to maintain strong approval ratings from the public, as measured by frequent polls. The White House Office works to improve the president's image and reputation through its relationship with the media. Presidents who maintain their popularity are likely to have more success in their legislative programs.

■ **LO12.2:** As commander in chief, the president is the ultimate decision maker in military matters. As chief diplomat, the president recognizes foreign governments, negotiates treaties, signs agreements, and nominates and receives ambassadors.

■ **LO12.3:** The role of chief legislator includes recommending legislation to Congress, lobbying for the legislation, approving laws, and exercising the veto power. The president also has statutory powers written into law by Congress.

■ **LO12.4:** Presidents have a variety of special powers not available to other branches of the government. These include emergency power, most frequently used during war or a national crisis, and the power to issue executive orders and invoke executive privilege.

■ **LO12.5:** Abuses of executive power are addressed by Articles I and II of the Constitution, which authorize the House and Senate to impeach and remove the president, vice president, or other officers of the federal government for committing "Treason, Bribery, or other high Crimes and Misdemeanors."

■ **LO12.6:** The president fulfills the role of chief executive by appointing individuals of his or her choice to positions in the departments and agencies of government, as well as various advisers in the White House Office and the Executive Office of the President. Some of the offices within the EOP were established by law, while others are appointed as the president desires. All appointees are supposed to be working for the president's initiatives and making sure that the larger bureaucracy is also supportive of the president's programs.

■ **LO12.7:** The vice president is the constitutional officer assigned to preside over the Senate and to assume the presidency in the event of the death, resignation, removal, or disability of the president. The Twenty-Fifth Amendment, passed in 1967, established procedures to be followed in case of presidential incapacity and when filling a vacant vice presidency.

Selected Print, Media, and Online Resources

PRINT RESOURCES

Goldsmith, Jack. *Power and Constraint: the Accountable Presidency After 9/11.* New York: W.W. Norton and Company, 2012. The author takes the position that, even though presidents have exercised emergency powers and war powers since September 11, 2001, they are actually more constrained in this era than ever before by courts, congress, and the media.

Goodwin, Doris Kearns. *The Bully Pulpit: Theodore Roosevelt, William Howard Taft, and the Golden Age of Journalism.* New York: Simon and Shuster, 2013. Goodwin details the presidencies of two men, once friends, but eventually competitors for the White House, at the height of the Progressive era.

Howell, William. *Thinking about the Presidency: The Primacy of Power.* Princeton, NJ: Princeton University Press, 2013. Following on the work of Richard Neustadt, Howell examines how presidents make decisions and finds that the decision making always takes into account presidential power.

Rockman, Bert A., Andrew Rudalevige, and Colin Campbell. *The Obama Presidency: Appraisals and Prospects.* Washington, DC: CQ Press College, 2011. Three of the leading scholars of the presidency examine the successes and failures of the first two years of the Obama presidency.

Skowronek, Stephen. *Presidential Leadership in Political Time: Reprise and Reappraisal.* Lawrence, KS: University Press of Kansas, 2008. In this update of a well-known book, the author expands on his thesis that presidents' successes are, in part, constrained by the political events of the day. He includes both Bill Clinton and George W. Bush in his analysis.

MEDIA RESOURCES

Bush's War—PBS Frontline's documentary delves into the impact of 9/11 on the Bush presidency. It is free to watch at www.pbs.org/wgbh/pages/frontline/bushswar/view/.

The Butler—This 2013 award-winning movie follows the life of an African American butler in the White House through the terms of eight presidents and through the battles of the civil rights movement.

Fahrenheit 9/11—Michael Moore's scathing 2004 critique of the Bush administration has been called "one long political attack ad." It is also the highest-grossing documentary ever made. While the film takes a strong position, it is—like all of Moore's productions—entertaining.

The Guns of October—This film explores the Cuban Missile Crisis of 1962. It portrays the Kennedy decision-making process in deciding against attacking Cuba.

Veep—This comedy, starring Julia Louis-Dreyfus as the vice president of the United States, centers around the White House staff and their arguments, gossip, and interpersonal relationships. The series parodies the seriousness of much of the Washington, DC, world, but in an affectionate way.

ONLINE RESOURCES

The American Presidency Project at the University of California at Santa Barbara—a wonderful collection of presidential photographs, documents, audio, and video: www.presidency.ucsb.edu

Bartleby.com—Internet publisher of literature, reference, and verse providing unlimited access to books and information, including the inaugural addresses of American presidents from George Washington to Barack Obama: www.bartleby.com/124

Dave Leip's Atlas of U.S. Presidential Elections—offers an excellent collection of data and maps describing all U.S. presidential elections: www.uselectionatlas.org

The White House—extensive information on the White House and the presidency:www.whitehouse.gov

Master the Concept of the Presidency with MindTap™ for American Government

 REVIEW MindTap™ for American Government
Access Key Term Flashcards for Chapter 12.

 TEST YOURSELF MindTap™ for American Government
Take the Wrap It Up Quiz for Chapter 12.

 STAY CURRENT MindTap™ for American Government
Access the KnowNow blog and customized RSS for updates on current events.

 STAY FOCUSED MindTap™ for American Government
Complete the Focus Activities for The Presidency.

13 The Bureaucracy

LEARNING OUTCOMES

After reading this chapter, students will be able to:

- **LO13.1:** Define the concept of the bureaucracy, explain why such an organization is necessary, and discuss the various theories of how bureaucracies act.

- **LO13.2:** Compare the structure and function of executive departments, executive agencies, independent regulatory agencies, and government corporations.

- **LO13.3:** Explain how individuals get positions in the federal bureaucracy and discuss the history of attempts to reform that process.

- **LO13.4:** Discuss some of the critiques of large bureaucracies and describe several types of bureaucratic reform.

- **LO13.5:** Describe the tools and powers that bureaucratic agencies have to shape policies and regulations.

- **LO13.6:** Analyze the relationship between Congress, its committees, interest groups and the bureaucracy.

Internal Revenue Service workers sort individual returns at the IRS center in Covington, Kentucky. Similar centers operate in different regions of the country.

Newhouse News Service /Landov

 WATCH & LEARN MindTap for American Government
Watch a brief "What Do You Know?" video summarizing The Bureaucracy.

Every Federal Agency Reported to the People?

BACKGROUND

Each year, every federal department, commission, and agency meets with the Office of Management and Budget (OMB) to propose a budget. The General Accountability Office (GAO) may investigate an agency for wrongdoing or simply audit its financial statements. Although Congress approves the budget for every agency, appropriations committees do not have time to look at the work of the entire federal government. Many federal agencies post a great deal of work on the Internet, so why not have every federal agency report directly to the people?

WHAT IF EVERY FEDERAL AGENCY REPORTED TO THE PEOPLE?

While most agencies must produce some sort of report to Congress or to the GAO or OMB, no simple report exists showing what the federal government is doing for the people of the United States. Some agencies post their annual reports on the Internet for all to see, but they are glossy presentations that highlight their accomplishments and gloss over their less-successful ventures. Other agencies post detailed statistical reports, one example is the Agriculture Department's monthly corn production prediction. The results of other agencies' work turn up in the censuses conducted by the Department of Commerce—the Census of Farm Owners, the Census of Hospitals, or the Census of Small Business, for instance.

What if agencies had to produce, on a specified day, a five-page report of its work? The contents would be specified by law: What were its revenues and expenses? How many people did it serve? What exactly are its programs and how were its services delivered? In the case of the U.S. Postal Service, what did it cost to deliver a first-class letter or a heavy catalogue, and did the postal service make or lose money on each? The reports could be downloaded and printed from the Internet and each agency's website would be easily navigated, simplifying access to the annual report.

WHAT WOULD THE REPORTS ACCOMPLISH?

Annual reports could make citizens more aware of what their tax dollars purchase in goods and services. Citizens might find that they approve of the services being provided. While it is likely to become clear that some services provided by the government are pretty expensive, it is likely they will be deemed essential. Consider medical care and rehabilitation for wounded veterans returning from Afghanistan. The extreme cost should surprise no one. On the other hand, public awareness of some of the fraudulent schemes to get Medicare dollars might help citizens stop waste.

Annual reports, produced in very consistent ways, would make agencies more accountable to the president, to the Congress, and to the citizens. Currently, government agencies seek either equal or increased funding each year on the basis that their work is stellar and important. However, most agencies do not need to explain what they do—they assume continued existence. Short, fact-based reports would be nonpolitical, unlike the current glossy brochures. It might be a good idea for a panel of citizens and journalists to draw up the format for the Web report and occasionally check that agencies are complying with the reporting requirements.

ANNUAL REPORTS COULD BE A WASTE OF TIME AND MONEY

Few Americans would likely read annual agency reports. Most citizens do not think about government or the political process unless a presidential election looms. Reading through dry bureaucratic reports demands a high interest in government. For the agencies, these new reports would be yet another requirement consuming time and money. Currently Congress requires all sorts of reports from agencies, which tend to produce only controversy, such as the annual report on terrorist groups. Many government workers would likely find it futile to produce an annual report that few would read.

For Critical Analysis

1. *What specific items should be included in the annual report of each agency?*

2. *Name several government organizations that you might be interested in knowing about. Do you think others would have a similar list?*

LISTEN & LEARN

MindTap for American Government

Access Read Speaker to listen to Chapter 13.

FACELESS BUREAUCRATS—this image provokes a negative reaction from many, if not most, Americans. Polls consistently report that the majority of Americans support "less government." The same polls, however, report that the majority of Americans support almost every specific program that the government undertakes. The conflict between the desire for small government and the benefits that only a large government can provide has been a staple of American politics. For example, the goal of preserving endangered species has widespread support. Many people believe that restrictions imposed under the Endangered Species Act violate the rights of landowners. Helping the elderly pay their medical bills is a popular objective, but hardly anyone enjoys paying the Medicare tax that supports this effort.

Many complain about the inefficiency and wastefulness of government at all levels. The media regularly uncover examples of failures in governmental programs. Inadequate, slow, or bungled responses to a crisis such as Hurricane Sandy or the bungled website for the Affordable Care Act become the "face" of government through the news media. This chapter describes the size, organization, and staffing of the federal bureaucracy. We review modern attempts at bureaucratic reform and the process by which Congress exerts ultimate control over the bureaucracy and the bureaucracy's role in making rules and setting policy.

The Nature of Bureaucracy

■ **LO13.1:** Define the concept of the bureaucracy, explain why such an organization is necessary, and discuss the various theories of how bureaucracies act.

Every modern president, at one time or another, has proclaimed that his administration was going to "fix the government." All modern presidents also have put forth plans to end government waste and inefficiency. President Clinton's plan was Reinventing Government, followed by Performance-Based Budgeting under George W. Bush. Within a few months of his inauguration, President Obama issued a call to his departments to "cut what doesn't work."[1] The success of plans such as these has been underwhelming. Presidents generally have been powerless to affect the structure and operation of the federal bureaucracy significantly.

A **bureaucracy** is the name given to a large organization that is structured hierarchically to carry out specific functions. Most bureaucracies are characterized by an organization chart. The units of the organization are divided according to the specialization and expertise of the employees.

Public and Private Bureaucracies

Any large corporation or university can be considered a bureaucratic organization. The handling of complex problems requires a division of labor. Individuals must concentrate their skills on specific, well-defined aspects of a problem and depend on others to solve the rest of it.

Public or government bureaucracies differ from private organizations in some important ways. A private corporation, such as Microsoft, has a board of directors. Public bureaucracies, in contrast, do not have a single set of leaders. Although the president is the chief administrator of the federal system, all bureaucratic agencies are beholden to Congress for their funding, staffing, and continued existence. Furthermore, public bureaucracies purportedly serve the citizenry.

Bureaucracy
A large organization that is structured hierarchically to carry out specific functions.

---

1. President Barack Obama, Weekly Radio Address, April 25, 2009. http://www.whitehouse.gov

LUKE SHARRETT/The New York Times/Redux

The Affordable Care Act provided funding for health care "navigators," individuals who could assist people in understanding their options for health nsurance. This navigator is working with an applicant in Louisville, Kentucky, on the first day of open enrollment in October 2013.

Government bureaucracies are also not organized to make a profit. They are intended to perform their functions as efficiently as possible to conserve the taxpayers' dollars. Perhaps this ideal makes citizens hostile toward government bureaucracy when they experience inefficiency and red tape.

Models of Bureaucracy

Several theories exist to better understand the ways in which bureaucracies function. Each of these theories focuses on specific features of bureaucracies.

Weberian Model. The classic model, or **Weberian model**, of the modern bureaucracy was proposed by German sociologist Max Weber.[2] He argued that the increasingly complex nature of modern life, coupled with the steadily growing demands placed on governments by their citizens, made the formation of bureaucracies inevitable. According to Weber, most bureaucracies—whether public or private—are organized hierarchically and governed by formal procedures. The power flows from the top downward. Decision-making processes are shaped by detailed technical rules that promote similar decisions in similar situations. Bureaucrats are specialists who attempt to resolve problems through logical reasoning and data analysis instead of instinct and guesswork. Individual advancement in bureaucracies is supposed to be based on merit rather than political connections. The modern bureaucracy, according to Weber, should be an apolitical organization.

Acquisitive Model. Other theorists do not view bureaucracies in terms as benign as Weber's. Some believe that bureaucracies are acquisitive in nature. Proponents of the **acquisitive model** argue that top-level bureaucrats will always try to expand, or at least to avoid any reductions in, the size of their budgets. Even though public bureaucracies try to be efficient, they have an inevitable desire to

Weberian Model
A model of bureaucracy developed by the German sociologist Max Weber, who viewed bureaucracies as rational, hierarchical organizations in which decisions are based on logical reasoning.

Acquisitive Model
A model of bureaucracy that views top-level bureaucrats as seeking to expand the size of their budgets and staffs to gain greater power.

2. Max Weber, *Theory of Social and Economic Organization*, Talcott Parsons, ed. (New York: Oxford University Press, 1974).

expand their mission, adding staff and funding to address policy issues. In the view of most government agencies, if your budget is not increased, your organization is in decline.

Monopolistic Model. Because government bureaucracies seldom have competitors, some have suggested that these organizations may be explained best by a **monopolistic model**. The analysis is similar to that used by economists to examine the behavior of monopolistic firms. Monopolistic bureaucracies—like monopolistic firms—essentially have no competitors and act accordingly. Because monopolistic bureaucracies usually are not penalized for chronic inefficiency, they have little reason to adopt cost-saving measures or to use their resources more productively. Some have argued that such problems can be cured only by privatizing certain bureaucratic functions.

Bureaucracies Compared

The federal bureaucracy in the United States enjoys a greater degree of autonomy than do federal or national bureaucracies in many other nations. Much of the insularity that characterizes the U.S. bureaucracy may stem from the sheer size of the government organizations needed to implement an annual budget that is about $3.7 trillion.

The federal nature of the U.S. government also means that national bureaucracies regularly provide financial assistance to their state counterparts. The Department of Education and the Department of Housing and Urban Development distribute funds to their counterparts at the state level. In contrast, most bureaucracies in European countries have a top-down command structure so that national programs may be implemented directly at the lower level. This is due not only to the unitary government of most European countries but also to the fact that public ownership of such businesses as telephone companies, airlines, railroads, and utilities is far more common in Europe than in the United States.

The fact that the U.S. government owns relatively few enterprises does not mean that its bureaucracies are without resources. Many **administrative agencies** in the federal bureaucracy—such as the Environmental Protection Agency, the Nuclear Regulatory Commission, and the Securities and Exchange Commission—regulate private companies.

The Size of the Bureaucracy

In 1789, the new government's bureaucracy was minuscule. There were three departments—State (nine employees), War (two employees), and Treasury (39 employees)—and the Office of the Attorney General (later, the Department of Justice). The bureaucracy was still small in 1798. At that time, the secretary of state had seven clerks and spent a total of $500 ($8,545 in 2008 dollars) on stationery and printing. That same year, the Appropriations Act allocated $1.4 million to the War Department (or $36 million in 2013 dollars).[3]

Times have changed, as shown in Figure 13–1, which lists the various federal agencies and the number of civilian employees in each. Excluding the military, the federal bureaucracy includes

Monopolistic Model
A model of bureaucracy that compares bureaucracies to monopolistic business firms. Lack of competition in either circumstance leads to inefficient and costly operations.

Administrative Agencies
A federal, state, or local government unit established to perform a specific function. Administrative agencies are created and authorized by legislative bodies to administer and enforce specific laws.

did you know?
The federal government spends more than $1 billion every five hours, every day of the year.

---

3. Leonard D. White, *The Federalists: A Study in Administrative History, 1789–1801* (New York: Free Press, 1948).

Figure 13-1 ▶ Federal Agencies and Their Respective Numbers of Civilian Employees

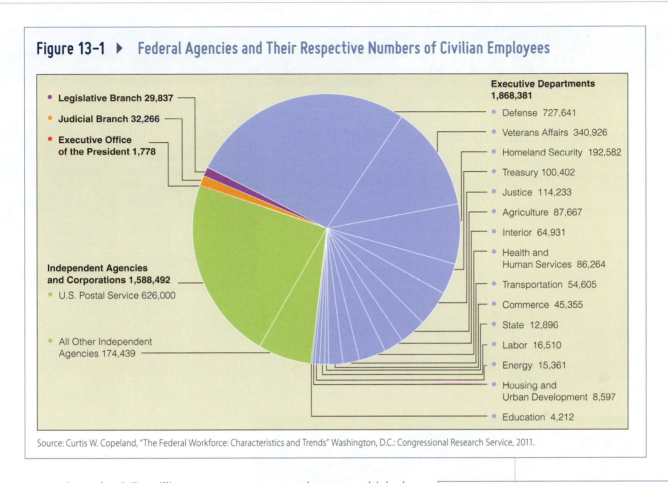

- Legislative Branch 29,837
- Judicial Branch 32,266
- Executive Office of the President 1,778

Independent Agencies and Corporations 1,588,492
- U.S. Postal Service 626,000
- All Other Independent Agencies 174,439

Executive Departments 1,868,381
- Defense 727,641
- Veterans Affairs 340,926
- Homeland Security 192,582
- Treasury 100,402
- Justice 114,233
- Agriculture 87,667
- Interior 64,931
- Health and Human Services 86,264
- Transportation 54,605
- Commerce 45,355
- State 12,896
- Labor 16,510
- Energy 15,361
- Housing and Urban Development 8,597
- Education 4,212

Source: Curtis W. Copeland, "The Federal Workforce: Characteristics and Trends" Washington, D.C.: Congressional Research Service, 2011.

approximately 2.7 million government employees, which has remained relatively stable for the last several decades. Many other individuals work directly or indirectly for the federal government as subcontractors or consultants and in other capacities. Experts estimate that the number of individuals employed through private contractors for the federal government grew from 4.4 million in 1999 to more than 7.6 million in 2005. During the Obama administration, the number of defense contracted employees declined as the U.S. role in Iraq diminished. The federal government still contracts out work, with some suggesting that contracted employees are actually more costly than regular civilian government employees.[4]

The figures for federal government employment are only part of the story. Figure 13–2 shows the growth in government employment at the federal, state, and local levels. Since 1970, this growth has occurred mostly at the state and local levels. If all government employees are included, more than 16 percent of all civilian employment is accounted for by government. The costs of the bureaucracy are commensurately high. The share of the gross domestic product accounted for by all government spending was only 8.5 percent in 1929. Today, it exceeds 40 percent. Whether government spending can be reduced without giving up services that citizens desire is an ongoing debate.

Figure 13-2 ▶ Government-Employment at the Federal, State, and Local Levels

There are more local government employees than federal or state employees combined.

- Local — 13.961
- State — 5.286
- Federal — 2.761

Number of Employees (in millions) vs *Year* (1980, 1985, 1990, 1995, 2000, 2005, 2010)

Source: U.S. Bureau of the Census, 2012.

4. Scott H. Amey, "Feds vs. Contractors: Federal Employees Often Save Money, but an Advisory Panel is Needed to Create A Cost Comparison Model," POGO (Project on Government Oversight), April 15, 2013. www.pogo.org/our-work/letters/2013/20130515-feds-vs-contractors-cost-com-arison.html

Everyday Politics

 Parks and Rec: Bureaucracy on the Small Scale

The NBC comedy *Parks and Rec* is, in fact, a show about bureaucracy. Illustrating the principle that bureaucracies exist within many organizations and at all levels of government, *Parks and Rec*, starring Emmy-winner Amy Poehler, frequently demonstrates the relationship between a civil service employee, Leslie Knope, and the political officials of her beloved (fictional) town of Pawnee, Indiana. The show begins with Poehler's character, a mid-level bureaucrat in the parks department, striving to create a park in place of an eyesore. She meets with opposition from her colleagues in city government, but continues her fight against government red tape for seasons to come (as shown in the screen capture).

The series centers on Knope's repeated attempts to save or improve her town, while confronting the politics of local government. *Parks and Rec* delves into campaigns, elections, elected office, and collaborations with government officials. The situations portrayed in the show are obviously written to parody governments, bureaucracies, and politics in general, but the underlying theme is the desire to improve the community in which they all live.

For Critical Analysis

1. *How much influence do bureaucrats have over elected officials and how is it exercised?*

2. *Does a comedy about bureaucrats and government increase or decrease the public's trust in government institutions?*

NBC

The Organization of the Federal Bureaucracy

■ **LO13.2:** Compare the structure and function of executive departments, executive agencies, independent regulatory agencies, and government corporations.

Within the federal bureaucracy are several different types of government agencies and organizations. Figure 13–3 outlines the several bodies within the executive branch, as well as the separate organizations that provide services to Congress, to the courts, and directly to the president.

The executive branch employs most of the government's staff with four major structures: (1) cabinet departments, (2) independent executive agencies, (3) independent regulatory agencies, and (4) government corporations. Each has a distinctive relationship to the president, and some have unusual internal structures, overall goals, and grants of power.

CONNECT WITH YOUR CLASSMATES
MindTap for American Government

Access The Bureaucracy Forum: Discussion—Bureaucracy at Work.

Figure 13-3 ▶ Organization Chart of the Federal Government

THE GOVERNMENT OF THE UNITED STATES

THE CONSTITUTION

LEGISLATIVE BRANCH

THE CONGRESS
SENATE   HOUSE

Architect of the Capitol
United States Botanic Garden
Government Accountability Office
Government Printing Office
Library of Congress
Congressional Budget Office

EXECUTIVE BRANCH

THE PRESIDENT
THE VICE PRESIDENT

Executive Office of the President

White House Office
Office of the Vice President
Council of Economic Advisers
Council on Environmental Quality
National Security Council
Office of Administration
Office of the Director of
    National Intelligence

Office of Management and Budget
Office of National Drug Control Policy
Office of Policy Development
Office of Science and Technology Policy
Office of the U.S. Trade Representative

JUDICIAL BRANCH

The Supreme Court of the United States

United States Courts of Appeals
United States District Courts
Territorial Courts
United States Court of International Trade
United States Court of Federal Claims
United States Court of Appeals
    for the Armed Forces
United States Tax Court
United States Court of Appeals for
    Veterans Claims
Administrative Office of the
    United States Courts
Federal Judicial Center
United States Sentencing Commission

DEPARTMENT OF AGRICULTURE	DEPARTMENT OF COMMERCE	DEPARTMENT OF DEFENSE	DEPARTMENT OF EDUCATION	DEPARTMENT OF ENERGY	DEPARTMENT OF HEALTH AND HUMAN SERVICES	DEPARTMENT OF HOMELAND SECURITY	DEPARTMENT OF HOUSING AND URBAN DEVELOPMENT

DEPARTMENT OF THE INTERIOR	DEPARTMENT OF JUSTICE	DEPARTMENT OF LABOR	DEPARTMENT OF STATE	DEPARTMENT OF TRANSPORTATION	DEPARTMENT OF THE TREASURY	DEPARTMENT OF VETERANS AFFAIRS

INDEPENDENT ESTABLISHMENTS AND GOVERNMENT CORPORATIONS

African Development Foundation
Central Intelligence Agency
Commodity Futures Trading Commission
Consumer Product Safety Commission
Corporation for National and
    Community Service
Defense Nuclear Facilities Safety Board
Environmental Protection Agency
Equal Employment Opportunity
    Commission
Export-Import Bank of the U.S.
Farm Credit Administration
Federal Communications Commission
Federal Deposit Insurance Corporation
Federal Election Commission
Federal Housing Finance Board

Federal Labor Relations Authority
Federal Maritime Commission
Federal Mediation and Conciliation Service
Federal Mine Safety and Health Review
    Commission
Federal Reserve System
Federal Retirement Thrift Investment Board
Federal Trade Commission
General Services Administration
Inter-American Foundation
Merit Systems Protection Board
National Aeronautics and Space
    Administration
National Archives and Records Administration
National Capital Planning Commission
National Credit Union Administration
National Foundation on the Arts and the
    Humanities

National Labor Relations Board
National Mediation Board
National Railroad Passenger Corporation
    (AMTRAK)
National Science Foundation
National Transportation Safety Board
Nuclear Regulatory Commission
Occupational Safety and Health
    Review Commission
Office of Government Ethics
Office of Personnel Management
Office of Special Counsel
Overseas Private Investment Corporation
Panama Canal Commission
Peace Corps
Pension Benefit Guaranty Corporation
Postal Rate Commission

Railroad Retirement Board
Securities and Exchange Commission
Selective Service System
Small Business Administration
Social Security Administration
Tennessee Valley Authority
Trade and Development Agency
U.S. Agency for International Development
U.S. Commission on Civil Rights
U.S. International Trade Commission
U.S. Postal Service

Source: United States Government Manual, 2007–2008 (Washington, DC: U.S. Government Printing Office, 2007).

Cabinet Departments
One of the 15 departments of the executive branch (State, Treasury, Defense, Justice, Interior, Agriculture, Commerce, Labor, Health and Human Services, Homeland Security, Housing and Urban Development, Education, Energy, Transportation, and Veterans Affairs).

Line Organizations
In the federal government, an administrative unit that is directly accountable to the president.

Independent Executive Agencies
A federal agency that is not part of a Cabinet department that reports directly to the president.

Attorney General Eric Holder responds to questions during a hearing. He is the nation's chief prosecutor and the chief executive of the Department of Justice and a member of the president's cabinet.

Cabinet Departments

The 15 **cabinet departments** are the major service organizations of the federal government. They can also be described in management terms as **line organizations**. They are directly accountable to the president and perform government functions, such as printing money and securing the border. These departments were created by Congress when the need for each department arose. The first to be created was State, and the most recent was Homeland Security, established in 2003. The difficulties faced in creating that new department are discussed in the "Reorganizing to Stop Terrorism" section. A president might ask that a new department be created or an old one abolished, but the president has no power to do so without legislative approval from Congress.

Each department is headed by a secretary (except for the Justice Department, headed by the attorney general). Each also has several levels of undersecretaries, assistant secretaries, and so on.

Presidents theoretically have considerable control over the cabinet departments, because presidents are able to appoint or fire all of the top officials, as listed in the Plum Book. Even cabinet departments do not always respond to the president's wishes, though. Presidents are frequently unhappy with their departments because the entire bureaucratic structure below the top political levels is staffed by permanent employees, many of whom are committed to established programs or procedures and who resist change. Table 13–1 shows that each cabinet department employs thousands of individuals, only a handful of whom are under the control of the president. The table also describes some of the functions of each department.

Independent Executive Agencies

Independent executive agencies are bureaucratic organizations that report directly to the president, who appoints their chief officials. When a new federal agency is created—the Environmental Protection Agency (EPA), for example—Congress decides where it will be located in the bureaucracy. In recent decades, presidents often have asked that a new organization be kept separate or independent rather than added to an existing department, particularly if a department may be hostile to the agency's creation. One example is the Central Intelligence Agency (CIA). Formed in 1947, the CIA gathers and analyzes political and military information about foreign countries and conducts covert operations outside the United States.

The newest independent agency is the Consumer Financial Protection Bureau, established in 2010 after the financial meltdown of 2008–2009. This

Table 13–1 ▶ Executive Departments

DEPARTMENT AND YEAR ESTABLISHED	PRINCIPAL FUNCTIONS
State (1789) (12,896 employees)	Negotiates treaties; develops foreign policy; protects citizens abroad
Treasury (1789) (100,402 employees)	Pays all federal bills; borrows money; collects federal taxes; mints coins and prints paper currency; supervises national banks
Interior (1849) (64,931 employees)	Supervises federally owned lands and parks; supervises Native American affairs
Justice (1870)* (114,233 employees)	Furnishes legal advice to the president; enforces federal criminal laws; supervises federal prisons
Agriculture (1889) (87,667 employees)	Assists farmers and ranchers; conducts agricultural research; works to protect forests
Commerce (1913)** (45,355 employees)	Grants patents and trademarks; conducts national census; monitors weather; protects interests of businesses (Note: The Commerce Department houses the Census Bureau, which increased its workforce from several thousand employees to more than a half million between early 2009 and summer 2010. Most of these workers were short-term temporary employees.)
Labor (1913)** (16,510 employees)	Administers federal labor laws; promotes interests of workers
Defense (1947)*** (727,641 employees)	Manages the armed forces; operates military bases; oversees civil defense
Housing and Urban Development (1965) (8,597 employees)	Manages nation's housing needs; develops and rehabilitates urban communities; oversees resale of mortgages
Transportation (1967) (54,605 employees)	Finances improvements in mass transit; develops and administers programs for highways, railroads, and aviation
Energy (1977) (15,361 employees)	Promotes energy conservation; analyzes energy data; conducts research and development
Health and Human Services (1979)*** (86,264 employees)	Promotes public health; enforces pure food and drug laws; conducts and sponsors health-related research
Education (1979)*** (4,212 employees)	Coordinates federal education programs and policies; administers aid to education; promotes educational research
Veterans Affairs (1988) (340,926 employees)	Promotes welfare of U.S. veterans
Homeland Security (2003) (192,582 employees)	Attempts to prevent terrorist attacks within the United States; controls U.S. borders; minimizes damage from natural disasters

Source: Office of Personnel Management, FedScope database, December 2013.

*Formed from the Office of the Attorney General (created in 1789).

**Formed from the Department of Commerce and Labor (created in 1903).

***Formed from the Department of War (created in 1789) and the Department of the Navy (created in 1798).

****Formed from the Department of Health, Education, and Welfare (created in 1953). Office of Personnel Management, FedScope database, December 2013.

agency oversees mortgages, debt collection, student loan, and credit card issuers and protects the interests of ordinary citizen in these financial matters. The creation of this independent executive agency was not without controversy: many believed that this should be an independent regulatory agency with a nonpartisan board of commissioners rather than an agency reporting to the president.

Independent Regulatory Agencies
An agency outside the major executive departments charged with making and implementing rules and regulations.

Independent Regulatory Agencies

The **independent regulatory agencies** are responsible for a specific type of public policy and make and implement rules and regulations in a particular sphere of action to protect the public interest. The earliest such agency was the Interstate Commerce Commission (ICC), which was established in 1887 when Americans began to seek some form of government control over the rapidly growing business and industrial sector. This new form of organization, the independent regulatory agency, was supposed to make technical, nonpolitical decisions about rates, profits, and rules that would benefit all and that did not require congressional legislation. After the creation of the ICC, other agencies were formed to regulate communication (the Federal Communications Commission), nuclear power (the Nuclear Regulatory Commission), etc. (The ICC was abolished on December 30, 1995.)

The Purpose and Nature of Regulatory Agencies.

The regulatory agencies are administered independently of all three branches of government. They were formed because Congress felt it was unable to handle the complexities and technicalities required to carry out specific laws in the public interest. The regulatory commissions combine some functions of all three branches of government. They are legislative in that they make rules that have the force of law, executive in that they enforce those rules, and judicial in that they decide disputes involving the rules they have made.

Members of regulatory agency boards or commissions are appointed by the president with the consent of the Senate, but do not report to the president. By law, the members of regulatory agencies cannot all be from the same political party and may be removed by the president only for causes specified in the law creating the agency. Presidents can influence regulatory agency behavior by appointing people of their own parties or individuals who share their political views when vacancies occur—in particular, when the chair is vacant. President George W. Bush placed people on the Federal Communications Commission (FCC) who shared his desire to curb obscene language in the media. Not surprisingly, the FCC soon thereafter started to "crack down" on obscenities on the air. One victim of this regulatory effort was Howard Stern, a nationally syndicated radio and television personality. His response was to switch from commercial radio and TV to unregulated satellite radio.

Agency Capture.

Captured
The act by which an industry being regulated by a government agency gains direct or indirect control over agency personnel and decision makers.

In recent decades, the true independence of regulatory agencies has been called into question. Some contend that many independent regulatory agencies have been **captured** by the very industries and firms they were supposed to regulate. The results have been less competition rather than more competition, higher prices rather than lower prices, and less choice rather than more choice for consumers. One of the accusations made after the 2010 BP oil spill in the Gulf of Mexico was that the relevant regulatory agency, the Minerals and Mining Administration, had become too lax in enforcing the safety regulations on the drilling rigs because of cozy ties with the oil companies.

Deregulation and Reregulation.

During President Reagan's administration, some significant deregulation (the removal of regulatory restraints) occurred, much of which had already commenced under President Carter. President Carter appointed a chairperson of the Civil Aeronautics Board (CAB) who gradually eliminated regulation of airline fares and routes. Under Reagan, the CAB was eliminated on January 1, 1985.

During the administration of George H. W. Bush, calls for reregulation of many businesses increased. The Americans with Disabilities Act of 1990, the Civil Rights

Act of 1991, and the Clean Air Act Amendments of 1991, all of which increased or changed the regulation of many businesses, were passed. Additionally, the Cable Act of 1992, which placed further regulation on that industry, was passed.

Under President Clinton, the Interstate Commerce Commission was eliminated, and the banking and telecommunications industries, along with many other sectors of the economy, were deregulated. At the same time, extensive regulation protected the environment. In the wake of the mortgage crisis of 2007 and failure of several large investment houses in 2008, Congress passed the Dodd-Frank bill in 2010, which tightened regulations on banks and almost all financial institutions

Government Corporations

Another form of bureaucratic organization in the United States is the **government corporation**. Although the concept is borrowed from the world of business, distinct differences exist between public and private corporations.

A private corporation has shareholders (stockholders) who elect a board of directors, who in turn choose the corporate officers, such as president and vice president. When a private corporation makes a profit, it must pay taxes (unless it avoids them through various legal loopholes). It either distributes part or all of the after-tax profits to shareholders as dividends or plows the profits back into the corporation to make new investments.

A government corporation has a board of directors and managers, but it does not have any stockholders. We cannot buy shares of stock in a government corporation. If the government corporation makes a profit, it does not distribute the profit as dividends. Also, if it makes a profit, it does not have to pay taxes; the profits remain in the corporation.

Two of the best-known government corporations are the U.S. Postal Service and AMTRAK, the domestic passenger railroad corporation. Thirty-five years ago, after several private rail companies went bankrupt, Congress created a public railway system called AMTRAK. Today, AMTRAK links 500 American towns and cities in 46 states with more than 22,000 miles of rail—and has many critics.

During AMTRAK's existence, American taxpayers have subsidized it to the tune of more than $25 billion. Current subsidies typically exceed $1 billion per year—a $1.3 billion was granted in 2013 and more than $2 billion was requested for Fiscal Year 2014. The rail service, on average, loses about $400 million a year. Harold Rogers, the Republican chairman of the House Transportation Committee, has long criticized the rail service as inefficient and costly. Those in favor of the AMTRAK subsidies argue that AMTRAK provides essential transportation for the poor. However, the majority of daily passengers are middle-class commuters on the eastern corridor routes.

For many years, critics of this government corporation have said that the benefits of AMTRAK, including reducing congestion on the highways, do not outweigh the costs. Some have suggested that the passenger service be privatized—sold to a private corporation. However, as the price of gasoline rose in 2008 and the issue of the future supply of oil became critical, AMTRAK became more popular with travelers. It had its best year in decades in 2012, carrying more passengers and a smaller operating deficit.[5] Faced with skyrocketing gas prices, rail transportation may see expansion rather than contraction in the next decade.

Government Corporation
An agency of government that administers a quasi-business enterprise. These corporations are used when activities are primarily commercial.

did you know?
The U.S. Postal Service processes 563 million pieces of mail each day.

---

5. Eleanor Randolph, "AMTRAK: Not a Money Pit After all," *New York Times Editorial Blog*, October 16, 2013. http://takingnote. blogs.nytimes.com.

The U.S. Postal Service, the second largest employer in the United States (after Walmart), has more than 626,000 employees. On paper, the postal service appears to be "breaking even" in terms of costs and revenues for its primary business. However, critics note that this government corporation has the right to borrow funds from the federal government at a very low interest rate and has borrowed its statutory limit of $15 billion to support its operations. Recently, the U.S. Postal Service has proposed several strategies for cutting costs; eliminating Saturday delivery and closing large bulk-mail centers are two proposals. Additionally, the post office is collaborating with a private corporation, UPS, to deliver packages to home addresses.

Challenges to the Bureaucracy

With cabinet departments, independent executive agencies, independent regulatory agencies, and government corporations, the federal bureaucracy is both complex and very specialized. Each agency, corporation, or line department has its own mission, its own goals, and, in many cases, its own constituents either at home or, in the case of the State Department, abroad. However, some problems and crises require the attention of multiple agencies. In these cases overlapping jurisdictions can cause confusion, or problems may arise that no agency has the authority to solve.

A famous story about the Carter administration illustrates this point: President Jimmy Carter believed he smelled something dead behind his Oval Office wall—probably a mouse. His staff called the General Services Administration, which has responsibility for the White House, but those bureaucrats claimed it was not their problem. They had fumigated recently, so the mouse must have come in from outside. The Department of the Interior, which has responsibility for the gardens and grounds, refused to help because the mouse was now inside. Eventually, an interagency task force was created to remove the mouse. If solving one small problem was this complicated for the federal bureaucracy, consider larger issues such as terrorism and natural disasters.

Reorganizing to Stop Terrorism

After September 11, 2001, the nation saw that no single agency was responsible for coordinating antiterrorism efforts. Nor was one person able to muster a nationwide response to a terrorist attack. Fighting terrorism involves so many different efforts—screening baggage at airports, inspecting freight shipments, and protecting the border, to name just a few—that coordinating them would be impossible unless all of these functions were combined into one agency.

The creation of the Department of Homeland Security (DHS) in 2003 was the largest reorganization of the U.S. government since 1947. Twenty-two agencies with responsibilities for preventing terrorism were merged into a single department. Congress and the president agreed that combining the Federal Emergency Management Agency (FEMA), Customs and Border Protection, the Coast Guard, the Secret Service, and many other organizations into a single agency would promote efficiency and improve coordination. It now has more than 190,000 employees and an estimated budget of $61 billion (as of

---

did you know?

The federal fleet of non-postal vehicles totals about 450,000.

Homeland Security @DHSgov · Apr 16
#Cybersecurity is a shared responsibility. Encourage others to ensure their online properties are safe & secure. dhs.gov/cyber
Expand　　　　　　　　　　Reply　Retweet　Favorite　More

Homeland Security/Twitter

How can an individual protect his or her email when the National Security Agency is collecting massive amounts of telephone and email traffic?

2014). The department's Twitter feed and website offer helpful suggestions and tips (see the screen capture).

It proved difficult to integrate agencies whose missions were very different. Some suggested that the bureaucratic cultures of agencies focused on law enforcement, such as the Secret Service and the Border Patrol, would be difficult to mesh with the agencies that focus on problems faced by citizens in a time of natural disasters, such as the Federal Emergency Management Agency (FEMA). Indeed, when FEMA became part of the DHS, its funding was reduced and it received less attention because the focus of the DHS has been on fighting terrorism, not on responding to natural disasters. In addition, the DHS did not actually unify all U.S. antiterrorism efforts. The most important antiterrorist agencies are the Federal Bureau of Investigation (FBI) and the Central Intelligence Agency (CIA), but neither is part of the DHS. Many believe that the number one problem in addressing terrorism is the failure of the FBI and CIA to exchange information with one another. To address this problem, President Bush created a Terrorist Threat Integration Center in *addition* to the DHS, the FBI, and the CIA. In 2004, Congress established the new Office of the Director of National Intelligence to coordinate the nation's intelligence efforts, and in 2005, President Bush appointed John Negroponte to be the director of national intelligence to try once again to coordinate the nation's intelligence agencies. This position, however, has been difficult to establish. In 2010, President Obama named the fourth director in five years, General James R. Clapper. The authority of the director is often undercut by other appointees who may be closer to the president, including the director of the CIA and the national security adviser, making this a very difficult position to hold.

Dealing with Natural Disasters

As George H. W. Bush faced a tough reelection campaign in 1992, Hurricane Andrew struck southern Florida, destroying many communities south of Miami, Florida, leaving hundreds of thousands of people without power and without homes. Although the total death toll was only 65, the storm cost more than $25 billion in damage and losses. The Bush administration was widely criticized for not getting aid to the victims quickly enough, and the president was chided for not putting in a personal appearance.

Supposedly, FEMA was strengthened and improved after Hurricane Andrew. FEMA dealt competently with hundreds of natural disasters in the years that followed, including tornados, floods, and blizzards. However, in 2005, a year in which five major hurricanes made landfall in the United States, FEMA again proved unable to meet the challenges of a massive natural disaster. When Hurricane Katrina headed toward New Orleans, all authorities warned of a possible flooding situation. No one dreamed of flooding that would trap thousands of residents in their homes for a week or more and destroy whole neighborhoods in New Orleans. No one had planned to evacuate thousands of people with no transportation of their own or to house them for years after the storm. Again, FEMA was criticized for its slow response, as was President George W. Bush. The scope of this disaster was so large and the relationship between the state and federal agencies involved so complex that FEMA could not effectively coordinate the rescue and relief efforts.

David McNew/Getty Images

An airline passenger stands in a full-body scanner at the Los Angeles International Airport in 2014. Such scanners transmit an image of the passenger to a secure room where they are checked by TSA supervisors. The image cannot be seen by the TSA screeners at the security checkpoint or by other passengers.

Natural and man-made emergencies continue to test the ability of federal agencies to respond. In 2010, an oil-drilling rig in the Gulf of Mexico exploded, triggering a massive oil spill. Again, within days, the media and local government officials were calling for faster and more effective federal government assistance even though the technology for dealing with such a spill is only available in the petroleum industry. President Obama was accused of not visiting the region quickly enough and not demonstrating enough anger at the oil company.

When Hurricane Sandy formed in the Caribbean in October 2012, weather scientists predicted that the very powerful and extraordinarily large storm might come up the east coast of the United States. Mindful of earlier events, FEMA and other local, state, and federal agencies began to plan before the storm came to the United States. Although downgraded to a tropical storm or "super storm" by the time it came ashore in New York, Sandy took more than 275 lives and caused an estimated $68 billion in damage. Thousands of people lost their homes in New Jersey and New York. FEMA and the other agencies were generally praised for their actions and for warning residents before the storm hit.

Hurricanes Katrina and Sandy illustrate the huge challenge faced by bureaucracies when dealing with natural disasters. So many agencies and levels of government must be coordinated that sometimes responses are delayed and aid does not get to the victims in a timely way. Media coverage of these tragedies focuses on the struggles of citizens, while the struggles of the bureaucrats take place in back rooms as officials strive to find the right equipment and personnel to meet unique disasters. At times, no president can be successful in dealing with the public relations aspect of these events.

Staffing the Bureaucracy

■ **LO13.3:** Explain how individuals get positions in the federal bureaucracy and discuss the history of attempts to reform that process.

The two categories of bureaucrats are political appointees and civil servants. The president is able to make political appointments to most of the top jobs in the federal bureaucracy and can appoint ambassadors to foreign posts. The rest of the national government's employees belong to the civil service and obtain their jobs through a much more formal process.

Political Appointees

To fill the positions listed in the Plum Book, the president and the president's advisers solicit suggestions from politicians, businesspersons, and other prominent individuals. Appointments offer the president a way to pay off outstanding political debts. But the president must also consider such things as the candidate's work experience, intelligence, political affiliations, and personal characteristics. Presidents have differed in the importance they attach to appointing women and minorities to plum positions. Presidents often use ambassadorships to reward individuals for their campaign contributions.

Even though the president has the power to appoint a government official, this does not mean an appointment will pass muster. Every potential nominee must undergo an FBI investigation and thorough screening. Such a process takes months, and after completing it, the appointees must be confirmed by the Senate. Sometimes, individuals withdraw from the nomination process before confirmation; others prove to be political problems for the administration only after confirmation.

AP Images/Mandel Ngan, Pool

The Aristocracy of the Federal Government.

Political appointees are in some sense the aristocracy of the federal government. Their powers, although formidable on paper, are often exaggerated. Like the president, a political appointee will occupy her or his position for a comparatively brief time. They often leave office before the president's term actually ends—the average term of service for political appointees is less than two years. Additionally, the professional civil servants who make up the permanent civil service may not feel compelled to carry out their current boss's directives quickly, because they know that he or she will not be around for very long.

The Difficulty in Firing Civil Servants.

This inertia is compounded by the fact that it is very difficult to discharge civil servants. In recent years, less than one-tenth of 1 percent of federal employees have been fired for incompetence. Because discharged employees may appeal their dismissals, many months or even years can pass before the issue is resolved conclusively. This occupational rigidity helps ensure that most political appointees, no matter how competent or driven, will not be able to exert much meaningful influence over their subordinates, let alone implement dramatic changes in the bureaucracy itself.

History of the Federal Civil Service

When the federal government was formed in 1789, it boasted no career public servants. Its ranks were comprised of amateurs, almost all of them Federalists. When Thomas Jefferson took over as president, few people in his party were holding federal administrative jobs, so he fired more than 100 officials and replaced them with his own supporters. Then, for the next 25 years, as a growing body of federal administrators gained experience and expertise, they developed

did you know?

The average federal government civilian worker earns $114,436 per year in total compensation (wages plus health insurance, pension, etc.), whereas the average private-sector worker earns $87,804 a year in total compensation.

into professional public servants. These administrators stayed in office regardless of who was elected president. The bureaucracy had become a self-maintaining, long-term element within government.

To the Victor Belong the Spoils. When Andrew Jackson took over the White House in 1828, he could not believe how many appointed officials (appointed before he became president, that is) were overtly hostile toward him and his Democratic Party. Because the bureaucracy was reluctant to carry out his programs, Jackson did the obvious: He fired federal officials—more than had all his predecessors combined. The **spoils system**—an application of the principle that to the victor belong the spoils—became the standard method of filling federal positions. Whenever a new president was elected from a different party, the staffing of the federal government would almost completely turn over.

The Civil Service Reform Act of 1883. Jackson's spoils system survived for decades, but it became increasingly corrupt. Also, as the size of the bureaucracy increased by 300 percent between 1851 and 1881, the cry for civil service reform grew louder. Reformers looked to the example of several European countries, Germany in particular, which had established a professional civil service that operated under a **merit system**, in which job appointments were based on competitive examinations.

In 1883, the **Pendleton Act**—or **Civil Service Reform Act**—was passed, placing the first limits on the spoils system. The act established the principle of employment on the basis of open, competitive examinations and created the **Civil Service Commission** to administer the personnel service. Initially, only 10 percent of federal employees were covered by the merit system. Later laws, amendments, and executive orders, however, increased the coverage to more than 90 percent of federal employees. The effects of these reforms were felt at all levels of government.

Spoils System
The awarding of government jobs to political supporters and friends.

Merit System
The selection, retention, and promotion of government employees on the basis of competitive examinations.

Pendleton Act (Civil Service Reform Act)
An act that established the principle of employment on the basis of merit and created the Civil Service Commission to administer the personnel service.

Civil Service Commission
The initial central personnel agency of the national government, created in 1883.

On September 19, 1881, President James A. Garfield was assassinated by a disappointed office seeker, Charles J. Guiteau. The long-term effect of this event was to replace the spoils system with a permanent career civil service. This process began with the passage of the Pendleton Act in 1883, which established the Civil Service Commission.

WASHINGTON, D. C.—THE ATTACK ON THE PRESIDENT'S LIFE—SCENE IN THE LADIES' ROOM OF THE BALTIMORE AND OHIO RAILROAD DEPOT—THE ARREST OF THE ASSASSIN.

The Supreme Court strengthened the civil service system in *Elrod v. Burns*[6] in 1976 and *Branti v. Finkel*[7] in 1980. In these cases, the Court used the First Amendment to forbid government officials from discharging or threatening to discharge public employees solely for *not* being supporters of the political party in power unless party affiliation is an appropriate requirement for the position. Additional enhancements to the civil service system were added in *Rutan v. Republican Party of Illinois* in 1990.[8] The Court's ruling effectively prevented the use of partisan political considerations as the basis for hiring, promoting, or transferring most public employees. An exception was permitted, however, for senior policy-making positions, which usually go to officials who will support the programs of the elected leaders.

The Civil Service Reform Act of 1978. In 1978, the Civil Service Reform Act abolished the Civil Service Commission and created two new federal agencies to perform its duties. To administer the civil service laws, rules, and regulations, the act created the Office of Personnel Management (OPM), which is empowered to recruit, interview, and test potential government workers and determine who should be hired. The OPM makes recommendations to the individual agencies as to which persons meet the standards (typically, the top three applicants for a position), and the agencies then decide whom to hire. To oversee promotions, employees' rights, and other employment matters, the act created the Merit Systems Protection Board (MSPB), which evaluates charges of wrongdoing, hears employee appeals of agency decisions, and can order corrective action against agencies and employees.

Federal Employees and Political Campaigns. In 1933, when President Franklin D. Roosevelt set up his New Deal, a virtual army of civil servants was hired to staff the numerous new agencies that were created. Because the individuals who worked in these agencies owed their jobs to the Democratic Party, it seemed natural for them to campaign for Democratic candidates. The Democrats controlling Congress in the mid-1930s did not object. But in 1938, a coalition of conservative Democrats and Republicans took control of Congress and forced through the Hatch Act—or Political Activities Act—of 1939, which prohibited federal employees from actively participating in the political management of campaigns. It also forbade the use of federal authority to influence nominations and elections and outlawed the use of bureaucratic rank to pressure federal employees to make political contributions.

The Hatch Act created a controversy that lasted for decades. Many contended that the act deprived federal employees of their First Amendment freedoms of speech and association. In 1972, a federal district court declared it unconstitutional. The Supreme Court, however, reaffirmed the challenged portion of the act in 1973, stating that the government's interest in preserving a nonpartisan civil service was so great that the prohibitions should remain.[9] Twenty years later, Congress addressed the criticisms by passing the Federal Employees Political Activities Act of 1993. This act, which amended the Hatch Act, softened the 1939 act in several ways. Among other things, the 1993 act allowed federal employees to run for office in nonpartisan elections, participate in voter-registration drives, make campaign contributions to political organizations, and campaign for candidates in partisan elections.

---

6. 427 U.S. 347 (1976).
7. 445 U.S. 507 (1980).
8. 497 U.S. 62 (1990).
9. *United States Civil Service Commission v. National Association of Letter Carriers*, 413 U.S. 548 (1973).

Modern Attempts at Bureaucratic Reform

■ **LO13.4:** Discuss some of the critiques of large bureaucracies and describe several types of bureaucratic reform.

As long as the federal bureaucracy exists, attempts to make it more open, efficient, and responsive to the needs of U.S. citizens will continue. The most important actual and proposed reforms in the last several decades include sunshine and sunset laws, privatization, incentives for efficiency, and more protection for so-called whistleblowers.

Sunshine Laws before and after September 11

Government in the Sunshine Act
A law that requires all committee-directed federal agencies to conduct their business regularly in public session.

In 1976, Congress enacted the **Government in the Sunshine Act**. It required for the first time that all multiheaded federal agencies—agencies headed by a committee instead of an individual—hold their meetings regularly in public session. The bill defined *meetings* as almost any gathering, formal or informal, of agency members, including a conference telephone call. The only exceptions to this rule of openness are discussions of matters such as court proceedings or personnel problems, and these exceptions are specifically listed in the bill. Sunshine laws now exist at all levels of government.

Information Disclosure. Sunshine laws are consistent with the policy of information disclosure supported by the government for decades. Beginning in the 1960s, several consumer protection laws have required that certain information be disclosed to consumers when purchasing homes, borrowing funds, and so on. In 1966, the federal government passed the Freedom of Information Act, which required federal government agencies, with certain exceptions, to disclose to individuals, on their request, any information about them contained in government files.

Curbs on Information Disclosure. Since September 11, 2001, the trend toward government in the sunshine and information disclosure has been reversed at both the federal and state levels. Within weeks after September 11, 2001, numerous federal agencies removed hundreds, if not thousands, of documents from websites, public libraries, and reading rooms found in various federal government departments. Information contained in some of the documents included diagrams of power plants and pipelines, structural details on dams, and safety plans for chemical plants. The military also immediately started restricting information about its current and planned activities, as did the FBI. These agencies were concerned that terrorists could use this information to plan attacks.

The federal government pioneered the withdrawal of information from public view, but state and local governments were quick to jump on the bandwagon. State and local governments control and supervise police forces, dams, electricity sources, and water supplies. It is not surprising that many state and local governments followed in the footsteps of the federal government in curbing access to certain public records and information. Most local agencies, however, do involve the public in emergency planning.

Sunset Laws

Sunset Legislation
Laws requiring that existing programs be reviewed regularly for their effectiveness and be terminated unless specifically extended as a result of these reviews.

It has often been suggested that the federal government be subject to **sunset legislation**, which places government programs on a definite schedule for congressional consideration. Unless Congress specifically reauthorizes a particular federally operated program at the end of a designated period, it is automatically terminated; that is, its sun sets.

AP images/Rick Bowmer

Much of the email and telephone data intercepted by the National Security Agency is to be stored in a $1.6 billion facility in Bluffdale, Utah.

Although this idea was first championed by Franklin D. Roosevelt in the 1930s, it has not been adopted by Congress. Texas and Alabama have sunset laws that impact all agencies.

Privatization

Another approach to bureaucratic reform is **privatization**, which occurs when government services are replaced by services from the private sector. For example, the government might contract with private firms to operate prisons. Supporters of privatization argue that some services could be provided more efficiently by the private sector. Another scheme is to furnish vouchers to "clients" in lieu of services. For example, instead of supplying housing, the government could offer vouchers that recipients could use to pay for housing in privately owned buildings.

The privatization, or contracting out, strategy has been most successful at the local level. Municipalities can form contracts with private companies for such things as trash collection. This approach is not a cure-all, however, as many functions, particularly on the national level, cannot be contracted out in any meaningful way. The federal government could not contract out most of the Defense Department's functions to private firms. Nonetheless, the U.S. military has contracted out many services in Iraq and elsewhere, as discussed in Beyond Our Borders.

Incentives for Efficiency and Productivity

An increasing number of state governments are beginning to experiment with a variety of schemes to run their operations more efficiently and capably. They focus on maximizing the efficiency and productivity of government workers by providing incentives for improved performance.[10] Some of the most promising measures have included such tactics as permitting agencies that do not spend

Privatization

The replacement of government services with services provided by private firms.

---

10. See, for example, David Osborne and Ted Gaebler, *Reinventing Government: How the Entrepreneurial Spirit Is Transforming the Public Sector* (Reading, MA: Addison-Wesley, 1992); and David Osborne and Peter Plastrik, *Banishing Bureaucracy: The Five Strategies for Reinventing Government* (Reading, MA: Addison-Wesley, 1997).

Beyond Our Borders

Privatizing the U.S. Military Abroad

All levels of government have privatized at least some activities. Less well known, however, is that for more than two decades, the U.S. military has been employing private companies abroad to perform several functions previously performed by military personnel. After the American military was downsized following the fall of the Berlin Wall in 1989, it responded by outsourcing many functions to the private sector. Before the First Gulf War, the Pentagon was already spending about 8 percent of its overall budget on private companies.

PRIVATE CONTRACTORS GALORE

In the last decade, the military has been supported by private contractors in Iraq and Afghanistan. By 2006, more than 100,000 private contractors/workers were on the ground in Iraq, all employed by the U.S. government. By mid-2008, the number reached more than 160,000, a figure roughly equal to the number of U.S. military personnel. They provide food and water for the troops, transport supplies for the coalition troops and for civilians stationed in Iraq, repair equipment, and work as guards for prisoners. In addition, most major construction on American bases and air fields is done by contractors.

THE NUMBERS TELL IT ALL

One of the reasons that the U.S. military has felt obligated to hire private contractors in Iraq and elsewhere is that the army in particular has been downsized. During the First Gulf War, active-duty troops in the army numbered 711,000. Today, that number has been reduced by almost one-third, to only about 565,000. The Pentagon asserts that it has to fill ancillary jobs and programs by contracting with private companies that either send their workers abroad or hire workers on location. The Army Corps of Engineers and the Navy Seabees did a great deal of the construction in World War II, but today, neither of these forces has the manpower to do similar work in Iraq. Additionally, there are political reasons for using contractors: many of the military troops deployed in Iraq and Afghanistan are members of the reserves or National Guard. Would it be efficient and acceptable to call up family members to go to Afghanistan to cook meals for the other troops?

As the war in Iraq wound down, the American military presence was downsized, as was the volume of contractors who supported it. By 2011, there were more than 60,000 contractors in Iraq, but only 45,000 troops, and most of the military forces were to be withdrawn in 2014. By 2014, about 78,000 contractors were employed in Iraq to support just over 35,000 troops. In Afghanistan, the policy of the U.S. military was to hire as many Afghanis as possible for contract positions. In 2014, about 30 percent of all the contracted employees in Afghanistan were citizens of that nation.*

Hiring private contractors to work in a combat zone has some real complications. They are often subject to combat

conditions, which results in the risk of capture, injury, or death. Several contractors, both American and European, have been captured and held as hostages. A few of these have been murdered. More than 1,500 civilian contractors have been killed in their line of work. In addition, private contractors can commit crimes against Iraqi or Afghani civilians or against other contractors. In accordance with a recently approved amendment to the Uniform Code of Military Justice, contractors accused of crimes are tried in military courts-martial.

Large international firms, some of which are based in the United States, are the major employers. Kellogg, Brown and Root, a firm based in Houston, Texas, is the largest employer of contractors on the ground in Iraq. Booz Allen Hamilton, based in Fairfax, Virginia, also has multiple contracts with the Department of Defense as well as various intelligence agencies. These two firms are generally considered private military companies (PMCs); there are hundreds of PMCs operating on a worldwide basis.

For Critical Analysis

1. *Does using thousands of private contractors in active war zones increase or decrease the public's support for the conflict?*

2. *What are the advantages and disadvantages of hiring local people as private contractors in conflict zones?*

---

* Department of Defense, "Contractor Support of U.S. Operations in the USCENTCOM Area of Responsibility to Include Iraq and Afghanistan." January, 2014.

their entire budgets to keep some of the difference and rewarding employees with performance-based bonuses.

Government Performance and Results Act. At the federal level, the Government Performance and Results Act of 1997 was designed to improve efficiency in the federal workforce. The act required that all government agencies (except the CIA) describe their new goals and establish methods for determining whether those goals are met.

The performance-based budgeting implemented by President George W. Bush took this results-oriented approach a step further. In the Bush administration, agencies were given specific performance criteria to meet, and the Office of Management and Budget rated each agency to determine how well it performed. Additional efforts to improve efficiency have included bonus pay to employees in some departments of the federal government.

Bureaucracy Has Changed Little, Though. Observers disagree over whether the government can meet the demands of a complex economy and diverse nation. Consequently, the government must become more responsive to cope with the increasing demands placed on it. Political scientists Joel Aberbach and Bert Rockman take issue with this contention. They argue that the bureaucracy has changed significantly over time in response to the demands of various presidential administrations. In their opinion, many of the problems attributed to the bureaucracy are, in fact, a result of the political decision-making process. Therefore, attempts to reinvent government by reforming the bureaucracy are misguided.[11]

Others have suggested that the problem lies with the people who run bureaucratic organizations. According to some scholars, what needs to be reinvented is not the machinery of government, but public officials. After each election, new appointees to bureaucratic positions may find themselves managing complex, multimillion-dollar enterprises, yet they often are untrained for their jobs. According to these authors, civil service career executives who head federal agencies do a better job than the amateurs appointed by the president.[12]

Saving Costs through E-Government. Many contend that the communications revolution brought about by the Internet has not only improved the efficiency with which government agencies deliver services to the public but also reduced the cost of government. Agencies can now communicate with members of the public, as well as other agencies, via email. Additionally, every federal agency now has a website citizens can access to find information about agency services instead of calling or appearing in person at a regional agency office. Taxes and withholdings are deposited electronically and payments such as Social Security benefits are transferred electronically. Since 2003, federal agencies have also been required by the Government Paperwork Elimination Act of 1998 to use e-commerce whenever it is practical to do so and will save on costs.

Helping Out the Whistleblowers

The term **whistleblower** as applied to the federal bureaucracy has a special meaning: It is someone who blows the whistle on a gross governmental inefficiency or illegal action. Whistleblowers may be clerical workers, managers, or even specialists, such as scientists.

Whistleblower
Someone who brings to public attention gross governmental inefficiency or an illegal action.

---

11. Joel D. Aberbach and Bert A. Rockman, *In the Web of Politics: Three Decades of the U.S. Federal Executive* (Washington, DC: Brookings Institution Press, 2000).
12. Nick Gallo and David E. Lewis, "The Consequences of Presidential Patronage for Federal Agency Performance," *Journal of Public Administration Research and Theory*, (2012), 22(2),219–243.

Laws Protecting Whistleblowers. The 1978 Civil Service Reform Act prohibits reprisals against whistleblowers by their superiors, and it set up the Merit Systems Protection Board as part of this protection. Many federal agencies also have toll-free hotlines that employees can use anonymously to report bureaucratic waste and inappropriate behavior.

Further protection for whistleblowers was provided in 1989, when Congress passed the Whistle-Blower Protection Act. That act established an independent agency, the Office of Special Counsel (OSC), to investigate complaints brought by government employees who have been demoted, fired, or otherwise sanctioned for reporting government fraud or waste.

Some state and federal laws encourage employees to blow the whistle on their employers' wrongful actions by providing monetary incentives to the whistleblowers. At the federal level, the False Claims Act of 1986 allows a whistleblower who has disclosed information about a fraud against the U.S. government to receive a monetary award. If the government chooses to prosecute the case and wins, the whistleblower receives between 15 and 25 percent of the proceeds. If the government declines to intervene, the whistleblower can bring suit on behalf of the government, and if the suit is successful, will receive between 25 and 30 percent of the proceeds.

The Problem Continues. Despite these endeavors to help whistleblowers, little evidence indicates that potential whistleblowers truly have received more protection. More than 40 percent of the employees who turned to the OSC for assistance in a recent three-year period stated that they were no longer employees of the government agencies on which they blew the whistle—most have already retired.

The Supreme Court placed restrictions on lawsuits in the 2006 case, *Garcetti v. Ceballos*, which involved an assistant district attorney, Richard Ceballos, who wrote a memo asking if a county sheriff's deputy had lied in a search warrant affidavit.[13] Ceballos claimed that he was subsequently demoted and denied a promotion for trying to expose the lie. The outcome of the case turned on an interpretation of an employee's right to freedom of speech—whether it included the right to criticize an employment-related action. In a close (5-4) and controversial decision, the Supreme Court held that when public employees make statements relating to their official duties, they are not speaking as citizens for First Amendment purposes. The Court deemed that when he wrote his memo, Ceballos was speaking as an employee, not a citizen, and was thus subject to his employer's disciplinary actions. The ruling affects millions of governmental employees.

The Obama administration has been particularly concerned with the national security implications of information leaked to journalists. While some federal employees might believe that they are whistleblowers, the Obama administration has prosecuted whistleblowers under the Espionage Act of 1917, which makes it a federal crime for federal employees to give "aid to our enemies." This legislation was only used three times between 1917 and 2008, but since President Obama took office, six cases have been prosecuted against federal workers, imposing a "chill" on relationships between federal employees and the press.[14]

COMPARE WITH YOUR PEERS

MindTap for American Government

Access The Bureaucracy Forum: Polling Activity—Bureaucracy and Regulation.

---

13. 126 S. Ct. 1951 (2006).
14. David Carr, "Blurred Line Between Espionage and Truth," *The New York Times*, February 26, 2012.

Bureaucrats as Politicians and Policymakers

■ **LO13.5:** Describe the tools and powers that bureaucratic agencies have to shape policies and regulations.

Because Congress is unable to oversee the day-to-day administration of its programs, it must delegate certain powers to administrative agencies. Congress delegates the power to implement legislation to agencies through **enabling legislation**. For example, the Federal Trade Commission was created by the Federal Trade Commission Act of 1914, the Equal Employment Opportunity Commission was created by the Civil Rights Act of 1964, and the Occupational Safety and Health Administration was created by the Occupational Safety and Health Act of 1970. The enabling legislation generally specifies the name, purpose, composition, functions, and powers of the agency.

In theory, the agencies should administer laws passed by Congress. Laws are often drafted in such vague and general terms, however, that they provide relatively little guidance to agency administrators as to how the laws should be implemented. This means that the agencies must decide how best to carry out the wishes of Congress. This role requires the agency to formulate administrative rules (regulations). But it also forces the agency to become an unelected policymaker.

Enabling Legislation
A statute enacted by Congress that authorizes the creation of an administrative agency and specifies the name, purpose, composition, functions, and powers of the agency being created.

The Rule-Making Environment

Rule making does not occur in a vacuum. The Environmental Protection Agency (EPA) might decide to implement the new law through a technical regulation on factory emissions. This proposed regulation would be published in the *Federal* so that interested parties would have an opportunity to comment on it. Individuals and companies that opposed the rule (or parts of it) might then try to convince the EPA to revise or redraft the regulation. Some parties might try to persuade the agency to withdraw the proposed regulation altogether. In any event, the EPA would consider these comments in drafting the final version of the regulation following the expiration of the comment period.

did you know?
Each year, federal administrative agencies produce rules that fill 7,500 pages in the *Code of Federal Regulations*.

Waiting Periods and Court Challenges. Once the final regulation has been published in the *Federal Register*, the rule can be enforced after a 60-day waiting period. During that period, businesses, individuals, and state and local governments can ask Congress to overturn the regulation. After that 60-day period has lapsed, the regulation can still be challenged in court by a party having a direct interest in the rule, such as a company that expects to incur significant costs in complying with it. The company could argue that the rule misinterprets the applicable law or goes beyond the agency's statutory purview. An allegation by the company that the EPA made a mistake in judgment probably would not be enough to convince the court to throw out the rule. The company instead would have to demonstrate that the rule was "arbitrary and capricious."

Controversies. How agencies implement, administer, and enforce legislation has resulted in controversy. Decisions made by agencies charged with administering the Endangered Species Act have led to protests from farmers, ranchers, and others whose economic interests have been harmed. For example, the government decided to cut off the flow of irrigation water from Klamath Lake in Oregon in the summer of 2001. That action, which affected irrigation and water for more than 1,000 farmers in southern Oregon and northern California, was undertaken to save endangered suckerfish and salmon. It was believed that the lake's water level was so low that further use of the water for irrigation would harm these fish. The results of this decision were devastating for many farmers.

One of the agencies that seems to be most sensitive to a change in presidential administration is the Environmental Protection Agency, created by Congress in 1970. Congress has passed several laws to improve air quality in the United States, giving the EPA the authority to carry out this legislation. Presidents differ, however, in how they interpret these congressional mandates. During the George W. Bush administration, the EPA issued decisions that weakened the enforcement of air pollution laws. In 1999, several environmental groups petitioned the EPA to set new standards for automobiles to reduce greenhouse gas emissions. In 2003, the EPA refused to do so, claiming that it did not have the legal authority to do this. States that passed laws regulating automobiles in their own states sued the EPA. In 2007, the Supreme Court ruled that the EPA cannot refuse to assess environmental hazards and issue appropriate regulations. As Justice John Paul Stevens wrote, "This is the Congressional design. EPA has refused to comply with this clear statutory command."[15] This was an unusual situation in that the states actually challenged a regulatory agency to issue stronger regulations. Often, challenges to regulatory agencies are intended to weaken new regulations.

The Obama administration took a much firmer stand on the enforcement of air pollution regulations. While committed to the passage of a new energy bill that would reduce the United States' contribution to greenhouse gases, by spring of 2010 it seemed that major new legislation might not pass quickly. The EPA issued new gas mileage requirements and new rules regulating tailpipe emissions for cars and trucks in April 2010. A Republican-led attempt in the Senate to veto these new regulations was defeated in June of that year. The EPA also issued new regulations for coal mining and for emissions from coal-burning power plants. In all of these cases, the executive agency noted that it had the authority to issue such rules under prior legislation such as the Clean Air Act.

Negotiated Rule Making

Since 1945, companies, environmentalists, and other special-interest groups have challenged government regulations in court. In the 1980s, however, the sheer wastefulness of attempting to regulate through litigation became more and more apparent. Today, a growing number of federal agencies encourage businesses and public-interest groups to become directly involved in drafting regulations. Agencies hope that such participation may help prevent later courtroom battles over the meaning, applicability, and legal effect of the regulations.

Congress formally approved *negotiated rulemaking*, in the Negotiated Rulemaking Act of 1990. The act authorizes agencies to allow those who will be affected by a new rule to participate in the rule-drafting process. If an agency chooses to engage in negotiated rulemaking, it must publish in the *Federal Register* the subject and scope of the rule to be developed, the parties affected significantly by the rule, and other information. Representatives of the affected groups and other interested parties then may apply to be members of the negotiating committee. The agency is represented on the committee, but a neutral third party (not the agency) presides over the proceedings. Once the committee

---

15. *Commonwealth of Massachusetts v. EPA*, 127 S. Ct. 1438 (2007).

members have reached agreement on the terms of the proposed rule, a notice is published in the *Federal Register*, followed by a period for comments by any person or organization interested in the proposed rule. Negotiated rulemaking often is practiced under the condition that the participants promise not to challenge in court the outcome of any agreement to which they were a party.

Bureaucrats Are Policymakers

Theories of public administration once assumed that bureaucrats do not make policy decisions but only implement the laws and policies promulgated by the president and legislative bodies. A more realistic view, now held by most bureaucrats and elected officials, is that the agencies and departments of government play important roles in policymaking. Many government rules, regulations, and programs are in fact initiated by bureaucrats, based on their expertise and scientific studies. How a law passed by Congress eventually is translated into concrete action—from the forms to be filled out to decisions about who gets the benefits—usually is determined within each agency or department. Even the evaluation of whether a policy has achieved its purpose usually is based on studies commissioned and interpreted by the agency administering the program.

The bureaucracy's policymaking role has often been depicted by what traditionally has been called the "iron triangle." Recently, the concept of an "issue network" has been viewed as a more accurate description of the policymaking process.

Iron Triangles.

In the past, scholars often described the bureaucracy's role in the policymaking process by using the concept of an **iron triangle**—a three-way alliance among legislators in Congress, bureaucrats, and interest groups. Consider as an example the development of agricultural policy. Congress, as one component of the triangle (see Figure 13–4), includes two major committees concerned with agricultural policy, the House Committee on Agriculture and the Senate Committee on Agriculture, Nutrition, and Forestry. The Department of Agriculture, the second component of the triangle, has more than 95,000 employees, plus thousands of contractors and consultants. Agricultural interest groups, the third component of the iron triangle in agricultural policymaking, include many large and powerful associations, such as the American Farm Bureau Federation, the National Cattleman's Association, and the Corn Growers Association. These three components of the iron triangle work together, formally or informally, to create policy.

For example, the various agricultural interest groups lobby Congress to develop policies that benefit their interests. Members of Congress cannot afford to ignore the wishes of interest groups, because they are potential sources of voter support and campaign contributions. The legislators in Congress also work closely with the Department of Agriculture, which, in implementing a policy, can develop rules that benefit—or at least do not hurt—certain industries or groups. The Department of Agriculture, in turn, supports policies that enhance the department's budget and powers. In this way, according to theory, agricultural policy is created that benefits all three components of the iron triangle.

Issue Networks.

This presents a simplified picture of how the iron triangle works. With the growth in the complexity of government, policymaking also has become more complicated. The bureaucracy is larger, Congress has more committees and subcommittees, and interest groups are more powerful

Iron Triangle
The three-way alliance among legislators, bureaucrats, and interest groups to make or preserve policies that benefit their respective interests.

did you know?
The Commerce Department's U.S. Travel and Tourism Administration gave $440,000 in disaster relief to western ski resort operators because of insufficient snow.

Figure 13-4 ▶ **Iron Triangle**

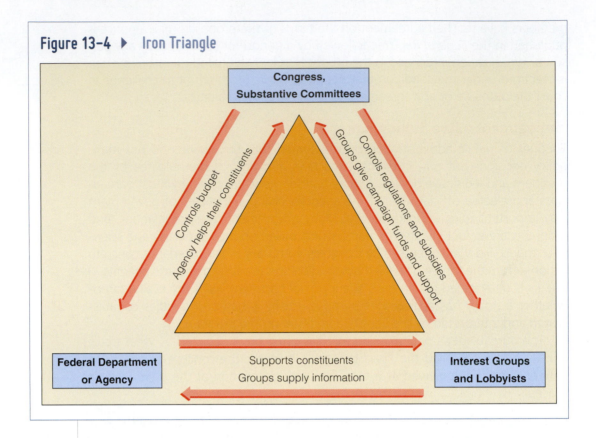

than ever. Although iron triangles still exist, often they are inadequate as descriptions of how policy is actually made. Frequently, different interest groups concerned about a certain area of policy have conflicting demands, making agency decisions difficult. Additionally, divided government in some years has meant that departments are sometimes pressured by the president to take one approach and by Congress to take another.

Many scholars now use the term *issue network* to describe the policymaking process. An **issue network** consists of individuals or organizations that support a particular policy position on the environment, taxation, consumer safety, or some other issue. Typically, it includes legislators and/or their staff members, interest groups, bureaucrats, scholars and other experts, and representatives from the media. Members of a particular issue network work together to influence the president, members of Congress, administrative agencies, and the courts to affect public policy on a specific issue. Each policy issue may involve conflicting positions taken by two or more issue networks. During the Obama administration, issue networks concerned with the health industry, the energy industry, and public education ramped up their efforts to be influential in the sweeping legislation proposed by the president.

Issue Network
A group of individuals or organizations—which may consist of legislators and legislative staff members, interest group leaders, bureaucrats, the media, scholars, and other experts—that supports a particular policy position on a given issue.

Congressional Control of the Bureaucracy

■ **LO13.6:** Analyze the relationship between Congress, its committees, interest groups and the bureaucracy.

Many political pundits doubt whether Congress can meaningfully control the federal bureaucracy. Nevertheless, Congress does have some means of exerting control.

Politics with a Purpose

Holding Government Accountable

If $17 million were stolen from the federal government, the thieves should be held accountable.* If our nation's airport security system were not keeping pace with emerging terrorist threats, policymakers in a position to act should be informed.** If sensitive U.S. military equipment such as F-13 antennae, nuclear biological chemical gear, and pieces of body armour plates could be bought freely on auction websites, an investigation should be launched to shut this practice down.*** Keeping all aspects of government accountable and investigating possible fraud, waste, and abuse are among the key responsibilities of the Government Accountability Office (GAO).

Created by Congress in 1921, the GAO (originally the General Accounting Office) was designed to audit and review executive branch agencies.**** Sometimes called Congress's watchdog, GAO is part of the legislative branch and is headed by the comptroller general, who is appointed by the president and confirmed by the Senate for a 12-year, nonrenewable term. The size, responsibilities, and reach of GAO have changed over time. In 2004, the agency's name was changed to the Government Accountability Office to reflect the way it had expanded from its original mission. With a staff of more than 3,100 people and a budget of more than $489 million, GAO conducts reviews, writes reports, and investigates (often undercover) alleged wrongdoing on the part of individuals within the federal government.*****

One of the ways GAO keeps tabs on government is to list areas within the federal government that are at high risk for "fraud, waste, abuse, and mismanagement."****** Some agencies, such as the Medicare Program and the Department of Defense Supply Chain Management, have remained on the list since 1990. An example of an agency recently removed from the list is the U.S. Postal Service, after being originally added because of concerns about its fiscal health. The GAO determined that significant changes, including retiring its debt and implementing $5 billion in cost savings, were made to justify removing it from the list.

The information the GAO provides is critical in a democracy, where citizens need to be informed about the actions of government. The GAO issues many reports each year on such topics as understanding how the government spends taxpayers' dollars, the safety of our food supply, and successful strategies for monitoring convicted sex offenders. Many reports are available online, through your college or university library, or may be ordered directly from the GAO (www.gao.gov/cgi-bin/ordtab.pl).

If this sort of investigative and analysis work sounds interesting, you might consider employment with the GAO or another similar agency among the many you will discover in this chapter. Students can intern with these organizations to gain valuable work experience.******* Those close to graduating should visit www.usajobs.opm.gov, which is a gateway to government employment opportunities. Whether you plan to be a chemist or are studying animal husbandry or criminal justice, the federal bureaucracy needs your talents.

* www.gao.gov/new.items/d07724t.pdf
** http://oversight.house.gov/documents/20071114175647.pdf
*** www.gao.gov/new.items/d08644t.pdf
****Frederick M. Kaiser, CRS Report for Congress (GAO: Government Accountability Office and General Accounting Office, 2007), updated June 22, 2007, Order Code RL30349, www.fas.org/sgp/crs/misc/RL30349.pdf, accessed May 15, 2007.
*****www.gao.gov/about/gglance.html
******www.gao.gov/new.items/d07310.pdf
*******www.studentjobs.gov/searchvol.asp

Ways Congress Does Control the Bureaucracy

These commentators forget that Congress specifies in an agency's "enabling legislation" the powers of the agency and the parameters within which it can operate. Additionally, Congress has the power of the purse and theoretically could refuse to authorize or appropriate funds for a particular agency. After allegations were made that the IRS targeted conservative political groups, funding was reduced for that agency. Congress does have the legal authority to decide whether to fund or not to fund administrative agencies. Congress can also exercise oversight over agencies through investigations and hearings.[16]

16. Walter J. Oleszek, *Congressional Oversight: An Overview*. Washington, D.C.: Congressional Research Service, 2010.

Congressional committees conduct investigations and hold hearings to oversee an agency's actions, reviewing them to ensure compliance with congressional intentions. The agency's officers and employees can be ordered to testify before a committee about the details of an action. Through these oversight activities, especially in the questions and comments of members of the House or Senate during the hearings, Congress indicates its positions on specific programs and issues.

Congress can ask the Government Accountability Office (GAO) to investigate particular agency actions as well. The Congressional Budget Office (CBO) also conducts oversight studies. The results of a GAO or CBO study may encourage Congress to hold further hearings or make changes in the law. Even if a law is not changed explicitly by Congress, however, the views expressed in any investigations and hearings are taken seriously by agency officials, who often act on those views.

In 1996, Congress passed the Congressional Review Act, which created special procedures that can be employed to express congressional disapproval of particular agency actions. Since the act's passage, the executive branch has issued more than 15,000 regulations, yet only eight resolutions of disapproval have been introduced, and none of these was passed by either chamber.

Reasons Why Congress Cannot Easily Oversee the Bureaucracy

Despite the powers just described, one theory of congressional control over the bureaucracy suggests that Congress cannot possibly oversee all of the bureaucracy. Consider two possible approaches to congressional control— (1) the "police patrol" and (2) the "fire alarm" approach. Certain congressional activities, such as annual budget hearings, fall under the police patrol approach. This regular review occasionally catches *some* deficiencies in a bureaucracy's job performance, but it usually fails to detect most problems.

In contrast, the fire alarm approach is more likely to discover gross inadequacies in a bureaucracy's job performance. In this approach, Congress and its committees react to scandal, citizen disappointment, and massive negative publicity by launching a full-scale investigation into whatever agency is suspected of wrongdoing. In 2014, newspaper reports of veterans who could not appointments or treatment at Veterans Administration Hospitals triggered special investigations and an ongoing Congressional hearing. Fire alarm investigations will not catch all problems, but they will alert bureaucracies that they need to clean up their procedures before a problem arises in their own agencies.[17]

---

17. Matthew D. McCubbins and Thomas Schwartz, "Congressional Oversight Overlooked: Police Patrols versus Fire Alarms," *American Journal of Political Science*, February 28, 1984, pp. 165–179.

What Would You Do?

Making Decisions to Keep Americans Safe

The FBI has a long-standing reputation for being an efficient and highly-trusted institution in the federal government. It is, like all federal agencies, part of the bureaucracy. The director is named by the president and the budget is approved by Congress and the president. Its mission includes investigating and prosecuting kidnappings, civil crimes, high value thefts, terrorist activities within the United States, bank theft and fraud, and civil rights violations, including hate crimes. Like all federal agencies, however, decisions about which goals should be prioritized are left to the director.

Why Should You Care?

In recent years, college campuses have seen increasing rates of gun violence and far more casualties than once seemed imaginable. The FBI maintains the system for background checks on gun purchases and works to stop illegal gun sales and the transport of illegal weapons across the nation's border. The success of the work of the FBI will result in safer campuses and communities for everyone.

In 1998, Mathew Shepard, a gay student at the University of Wyoming, was kidnapped, tortured, bound to a fence and left to die by two men. Although he was found alive, his injuries were severe and he died a week later. The two men were convicted of the assault and murder and are serving life sentences. The FBI is the primary agency in the investigation of hate crimes, the number of which continues to grow. In April, 2014, for example, a man fired at and killed two Jewish residents of Kansas while shouting Nazi slogans.

Another issue that has come to the attention of the nation and its policymakers is the kidnapping of women and children for the "sex trade." Adolescents who run away from home or who are living on their own in an urban area are at risk for becoming dependent on criminals for drugs or food or a place to live. In many cases, these relationships devolve into forced prostitution. Again, one of the major tasks of the FBI is to find individuals who have been kidnapped and prosecute the perpetrators. Often, this involves cooperation with local police, local social service providers, and with the Drug Enforcement Agency if drugs are involved.

What Would You Do?

Imagine you are the director of the FBI, working to find perpetrators of multiple kidnappings of young people in Chicago. The president reassigns you to a National Security Agency project in Texas. Will you speak up and ask to continue your work to solve possible sex trafficking occurrences or will you switch?

What You *Can* Do

There are a number of agencies that are involved in investigating human trafficking both internationally and in the United States. The FBI is deeply involved because it is responsible for solving any kidnapping case that crosses states borders. You can learn about the Bureau's long-term project, "the Innocence Lost National Initiative" and be aware of any situation that you think might involve the abuse of children. The Innocence Lost project has been in existence since 2003 and has resulted in the rescue of more than 2,700 children who were sexually exploited in the United States. In August, 2013, a special investigation named "Operation Cross Country" involved an FBI sweep of 76 cities across the country. Working in coordination with local authorities, the FBI and its partners recovered 105 children and arrested 150 pimps and other criminals involved in kidnapping the children.

If you want to be involved in the effort to assist children and adolescents who have been victimized in this way, you can get in touch with any one of a number of social service agencies that provide support to the children and their families. One of the national organizations that provides contacts to social service agencies in every state is the Polaris Project (www.polarisproject.org). Their mission is to create "a world without slavery." At their website you can find links for getting involved in this project and considerable data about the extent of sex trafficking in the United States (as shown in the screen capture).

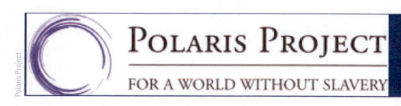

Polaris Project

Another organization that you can contact is the Global Freedom Center (www.globalfreedomcenter.org) which is focused on combating slavery throughout the world. According to the center, more than 27 million people in the world—men, women and children—have been enslaved at some point in their lives.

Finally, if you are interested in the mission of the FBI in general, you may consider joining the Bureau as an employee. Visit the website, www.FBI.gov, to find out about careers in the FBI. If you see a situation that you think merits its attention, the website direct you to an "information tip" form that you can submit electronically.

Key Terms

acquisitive model 457
administrative agency 458
bureaucracy 456
cabinet department 462
capture 464
Civil Service Commission 470
enabling legislation 477

government corporation 465
Government in the Sunshine Act 472
independent executive agency 462
independent regulatory agency 464

iron triangle 479
issue network 480
line organization 462
merit system 470
monopolistic model 458
Pendleton Act (Civil Service Reform Act) 470

privatization 473
spoils system 470
sunset legislation 472
Weberian model 457
whistleblower 475

Chapter Summary

■ **LO13.1:** Bureaucracies are hierarchical organizations characterized by a division of labor and extensive procedural rules. Bureaucracy is the primary form of organization of most major corporations and universities as well as governments. These organizations are developed to carry out complex policies and procedures or to deliver multiple services or products in a fair, consistent, and effective manner.

■ **LO13.1:** Several theories have been offered to explain bureaucracies. The Weberian model posits that bureaucracies are rational, hierarchical organizations in which decisions are based on logical reasoning. The acquisitive model views top-level bureaucrats as pressing for ever-larger budgets and staffs to augment their own sense of power and security. The monopolistic model focuses on the environment in which most government bureaucracies operate, stating that bureaucracies are inefficient and excessively costly to operate because they have no competitors.

■ **LO13.2:** Since the founding of the United States, the federal bureaucracy has grown from 50 to about 2.7 million employees (excluding the military). Federal, state, and local employees together make up more than 16 percent of the nation's civilian labor force. The federal bureaucracy consists of 15 cabinet departments, as well as a large number of independent executive agencies, independent regulatory agencies, and government corporations. These entities enjoy varying degrees of autonomy, visibility, and political support.

■ **LO13.3:** A federal bureaucracy of career civil servants was formed during Thomas Jefferson's presidency. Andrew Jackson implemented a spoils system through which he appointed his own political supporters. A civil service based on professionalism and merit was the goal of the Civil Service Reform Act of 1883. Concerns that the civil service be freed from the pressures of politics prompted the passage of the Hatch Act in 1939. Significant changes in the administration of the civil service were made by the Civil Service Reform Act of 1978.

■ **LO13.4:** Bureaucracies, due to their size and complexity, may become inefficient and slow. Presidents try to manage the bureaucracy through political appointments to top positions. Congress also becomes frustrated when it receives reports of corruption or malfeasance in the bureaucracy. To solve some of these problems, many attempts have been made to make the federal bureaucracy more open, efficient, and responsive to the needs of U.S. citizens. The most important reforms have included sunshine and sunset laws, privatization, strategies to provide incentives for increased productivity and efficiency, and protection for whistleblowers.

■ **LO13.5:** The bureaucracy has a complex relationship with the political branches of the government. While it reports to the president, the Congress oversees the bureaucracy and provides its budget. In addition, Congress delegates much of its authority to federal agencies when it creates new laws. The bureaucrats who run these agencies become important policymakers, because Congress has neither the time nor the technical expertise to oversee the administration of its laws. In the agency rulemaking process, a proposed regulation is published. A comment period follows, during which interested parties may offer suggestions for changes. Because companies and other organizations have challenged many regulations in court, federal agencies now are authorized to allow parties that will be affected by new regulations to participate in the rule-drafting process.

■ **LO13.6:** Congress exerts ultimate control over all federal agencies because it controls the federal government's purse strings. It also establishes the general guidelines by which regulatory agencies must abide. The appropriations process may provide a way to send messages of approval or disapproval to particular agencies, as do congressional hearings and investigations of agency actions.

Selected Print, Media, and Online Resources

PRINT RESOURCES

Ghattas, Kim. *The Secretary: A Journey with Hillary Clinton from Beirut to the Heart of American Power.* New York: Henry Holt and Company, 2013.
  The author, a journalist, covered Secretary of State Clinton for four years as she travelled the world. Her book is an inside account of Clinton's work and her reception in the nations she visited.

Government Jobs News, Info Tech Employment, and Partnerships for Community , editors, *Government Jobs in America: Jobs in U.S. States and Cities and U.S. Federal Agencies with Job Titles, Salaries, and Pension Estimates—Why You Want One, What Jobs are Available, How to Get One.* Washington, DC: Partnerships for Community, 2012.
  If you are interested in applying for a job with any U.S. government agency, this comprehensive guide will lead you through the process, from reviewing the qualifications necessary to the final interview.

Grisinger, Joanna. *The Unwieldy American State: Administrative Politics Since the New Deal.* New York: Cambridge University Press, 2014.
  Thinking about the size of American federal government and the vast array of policies that it implements is daunting. Grisinger traces the transformation of the federal government from the New Deal to the mid-60s, showing how administrative law has come to dominate the policy making process.

Haymann, Philip. B. *Living the Policy Process.* New York: Oxford University Press, 2008. Haymann uses case studies to examine how policymakers struggle to affect governmental decisions. His detailed accounts range from the cabinet level down to the middle tiers of the federal bureaucracy. Examples include providing support to anti-Soviet Afghan rebels and attempting to restrict smoking.

Osborne, David, and Peter Plastrik. *Banishing Bureaucracy: The Five Strategies for Reinventing Government.* San Francisco: David Osborne Publishing, 2006. In 1992, David Osborne (with Ted Gaebler) wrote a best seller entitled *Reinventing Government. Banishing Bureaucracy* is his sequel, which goes one step further—it outlines specific strategies that can help transform public systems and organizations into engines of efficiency. The book focuses on clarifying a bureaucracy's purpose, creating incentives, improving accountability, redistributing power, and nurturing the correct culture.

MEDIA RESOURCES

***Dallas Buyers Club*—**In this stark portrayal of the HIV/AIDS epidemic before widespread use of today's life-saving drugs was approved, an infected man decides to bring unapproved drugs into the country from Mexico for the people he knows. The villain of this film is the Food and Drug Administration; that agency tries to prevent the importation of the drugs (2013).

***Food Inc*—**In this startling documentary, the film-makers examine agribusiness and how corporations control food production in the United States (2008).

***Parks and Rec*—**The hit comedy series set in a small town in Indiana chronicles the efforts of a woman to improve her city and the many bureaucratic and personal obstacles she encounters along the way.

***Top Secret America*—**A decade after the September 11 attacks on the World Trade Center, Frontline produced a program tracing the efforts of the United States to protect the nation against future attacks. The program is linked to other programs that investigate the NSA and other agencies. (2011)

***When the Levees Broke: A Requiem in Four Acts*—**A strong treatment of Hurricane Katrina's impact on New Orleans by renowned director Spike Lee. We learn about the appalling performance of authorities at every level and the suffering that could have been avoided. Lee's anger at what he sees adds spice to the 2006 production.

ONLINE RESOURCES

Federal Register—the official publication for executive branch documents: www.gpoaccess.gov/fr/browse.html

The Plum Book—lists the bureaucratic positions that can be filled by presidential appointment: www.gpoaccess.gov/fr/browse.html

United States Government Manual—describes the origins, purposes, and administrators of every federal department and agency: www.gpoaccess.gov/plumbook/index.html

USA.gov—the United States government's official Web portal, which makes it easy for the public to get government information and services on the Web, such as telephone numbers for government agencies and personnel: www.USA.gov

Master the concept of Bureaucracy with MindTap™ for American Government

REVIEW MindTap™ for American Government
Access Key Term Flashcards for Chapter 13.

STAY CURRENT MindTap™ for American Government
Access the KnowNow blog and customized RSS for updates on current events.

TEST YOURSELF MindTap™ for American Government
Take the Wrap It Up Quiz for Chapter 13.

STAY FOCUSED MindTap™ for American Government
Complete the Focus Activities for The Bureaucracy.

The Courts

14

The lawyers who are members of the Supreme Court bar line up outside the lawyer's entrance to the court on the first day of the oral arguments on the constitutionality of the Affordable Health Care Act in 2012.

Jonathan Ernst/Reuters/Landov

WATCH & LEARN MindTap™ **for American Government**

Watch a brief "What Do You Know?" video summarizing The Judiciary.

LEARNING OUTCOMES

After reading this chapter, students will be able to:

- **LO14.1:** Explain how judges in the American system decide cases and define *stare decisis*.

- **LO14.2:** Define judicial review and explain the constitutional and judicial origins of this power.

- **LO14.3:** Produce a graphic illustration of the federal court system and explain how a case moves from the trial court to the highest court of appeals, the Supreme Court.

- **LO14.4:** Explain how judges are nominated and confirmed for the Supreme Court.

- **LO14.5:** Compare the concepts of judicial activism and judicial restraint; link these concepts to the decisions of the Supreme Court in the last few decades.

- **LO14.6:** Discuss the constitutional and political constraints on the Supreme Court.

What if?

Supreme Court Justices Had Term Limits?

BACKGROUND

The nine justices who sit on the Supreme Court are not elected officials. They are appointed by the president (and confirmed by the Senate). Barring gross misconduct, they hold office for life. Given the lifespan of Americans, it is common for justices to be actively serving on the court after they turn 80 years old. Would the justices be more in tune with the ideas of Americans and less likely to use their power to make policy if they did not hold permanent seats? One way to make the justices even more responsive to public opinion might be to limit their tenure in office.

WHAT IF SUPREME COURT JUSTICES HAD TERM LIMITS?

What should be the length of the term? Perhaps an appropriate one would be the average time on the bench from the founding of our nation until 1970—15 years. After confirmation by the Senate, a person could serve only 15 years on the bench and then would have to retire. The most important result of term limits would be a reduction in the rancor surrounding confirmation hearings. Today, the confirmation of a Supreme Court nominee—one chosen by the president to fit his or her views—is a major political event because that person may be on the Court for the next three decades.

Consider the current chief justice, John Roberts. When he took the Supreme Court bench at age 50, Americans could potentially anticipate that his conservative ideology would influence Supreme Court decisions for as long as 30 years. Knowing this, those who did not share his views or philosophy opposed his confirmation. If term limits had been in existence, less would have been at stake—about half as many years of his influence.

TERM LIMITS WOULD PUT THE UNITED STATES IN LINE WITH OTHER DEMOCRACIES

In having no term limits for federal judges, the United States is somewhat out of step. Not only does just one state—Rhode Island—appoint state supreme court justices for life, but virtually every other major democratic nation has age or term limits for judges. Thus, term limits in the United States for federal judges would not be an anomaly. Even with term limits, Supreme Court justices would still be independent, which is what the framers of the Constitution desired.

MORE INFUSION OF NEW BLOOD

With term limits, vacancies would be created on a more or less regular basis. Consequently, Supreme Court justices would have less temptation to time their retirements for political purposes. Thus, liberal-leaning justices would not delay their retirements until a Democratic president was in office, and conservative-leaning justices would not wait for a Republican. Fewer justices would follow the example of Justice Thurgood Marshall, who said that he was determined to hang on to his judicial power until a Democratic president was in office to appoint his successor. After many years on the bench, he joked, "I have instructed my clerks that if I should die, they should have me stuffed—and continue to cast my votes."

Virtually every president, whether he or she was a Republican or Democrat, would get a chance to fill a Supreme Court vacancy every few years. As a result, "new blood" would be infused into the Supreme Court more often. We would no longer face the risk of having Supreme Court justices who become less than enthusiastic about their work and less willing to examine new intellectual arguments. Term limits would also avoid the decrepitude that has occurred with several very old Supreme Court justices. In the last 30 years, some truly have stayed until the last possible minute. The public might prefer at least to have a mandatory retirement age.

For Critical Analysis

1. *What are the benefits of having lifetime appointments to the Supreme Court?*

2. *Just because a president can appoint whomever he or she wishes to the Supreme Court, does that necessarily mean that the successful nominee will always reflect the president's political philosophy? Explain your answer.*

AS ALEXIS DE TOCQUEVILLE, a French commentator on American society in the 1800s, noted, "scarcely any political question arises in the United States that is not resolved, sooner or later, into a judicial question."[1] Our judiciary forms part of our political process. The instant that judges interpret the law, they become actors in the political arena—policymakers working within a political institution. The most important political force within our judiciary is the United States Supreme Court.

How do courts make policy? Why do the federal courts play such an important role in American government? The answers to these questions lie, in part, in our colonial heritage. Most of American law is based on the English system, particularly the English *common-law tradition*. The decisions made by judges constitute an important source of law. The Supreme Court has extraordinary power to shape the nation's policies through the practice of **judicial review**, first explicated by Justice Marshall in the *Marbury v. Madison* case in 1803. This chapter opens with an examination of this tradition and of the various sources of American law, then looks at the federal court system.

Sources of American Law

■ **LO14.1:** Explain how judges in the American system decide cases and define *stare decisis*.

In 1066, the Normans conquered England, and William the Conqueror and his successors began the process of unifying the country under their rule, by establishing the king's courts. Before the conquest, disputes had been settled according to local custom. The king's courts sought to establish a common or uniform set of rules for the whole country. As the number of courts and cases increased, portions of the most important decisions of each year were compiled in *Year Books*. Judges settling disputes similar to ones that had been decided before used the *Year Books* as the basis for their decisions. If a case was unique, judges had to create new laws, but they based their decisions on the general principles suggested by earlier cases. The body of judge-made law that developed under this system is still used today and is known as the **common law**.

The practice of deciding new cases with reference to former decisions—according to **precedent**—became a cornerstone of the English and American judicial systems and is embodied in the doctrine of *stare decisis* (pronounced *ster-ay dih-si-ses*), a Latin phrase that means "to stand on decided cases." The doctrine of *stare decisis* obligates judges to follow the precedents set previously by their own courts or by higher courts that have authority over them.

A lower state court in California would be obligated to follow a precedent set by the California Supreme Court. That lower court, however, would not be obligated to follow a precedent set by the supreme court of another state, because each state court system is independent. When the United States Supreme Court decides an issue, all of the nation's other courts are obligated to abide by the Court's decision, because the Supreme Court is the highest court in the land.

Stare decisis provides a basis for judicial decision making in all countries that have common-law systems. Generally, those countries that were once British colonies, such as Australia, Canada, and India, have retained their English common-law heritage. An alternative legal system based on Muslim *sharia* is discussed in this chapter's Beyond Our Borders feature.

LISTEN & LEARN

MindTap™ for American Government

Access Read Speaker to listen to Chapter 14.

Judicial Review
The power of the Supreme Court or any court to hold a law or other legal action as unconstitutional.

Common Law
Judge-made law that originated in England from decisions shaped according to prevailing custom. Decisions were applied to similar situations and gradually became common to the nation.

Precedent
A court rule bearing on subsequent legal decisions in similar cases. Judges rely on precedents in deciding cases.

Stare Decisis
To stand on decided cases; the judicial policy of following precedents established by past decisions.

---

1. Alexis de Tocqueville, *Democracy in America* (New York: Harper & Row, 1966), p. 248.

The body of American law includes the federal and state constitutions, statutes passed by legislative bodies, administrative law, and case law—the legal principles expressed in court decisions.

Constitutions

The constitutions of the federal government and the states set forth the general organization, powers, and limits of government. The U.S. Constitution is the supreme law of the land. A law in violation of the Constitution, regardless of source, may be declared unconstitutional and thereafter cannot be enforced. Similarly, the state constitutions are supreme within their respective borders (unless they conflict with the U.S. Constitution or federal laws and treaties made in accordance with it). The Constitution thus defines the political playing field on which state and federal powers are reconciled. The idea that the Constitution should be supreme in certain matters stemmed from widespread dissatisfaction with the weak federal government that had existed under the Articles of Confederation adopted in 1781.

Statutes and Administrative Regulations

Although the English common law provides the basis for both our civil and criminal legal systems, statutes (laws enacted by legislatures) increasingly have become important in defining the rights and obligations of individuals. Federal statutes may relate to any subject that is a concern of the federal government and may apply to areas ranging from hazardous waste to federal taxation. State statutes include criminal codes, commercial laws, and laws covering a variety of other matters. Cities, counties, and other local political bodies also pass statutes, which are called ordinances. These ordinances may deal with such issues as zoning proposals and public safety. Rules and regulations issued by administrative agencies are another source of law. Today, much of the work of the courts consists of interpreting these laws and regulations and applying them to circumstances in cases before the courts.

Case Law

Because we have a common-law tradition, the decisions rendered by the courts also form an important body of law, collectively referred to as **case law**. Case law includes judicial interpretations of common-law principles and doctrines, as well as interpretations of the types of law just mentioned—constitutional provisions, statutes, and administrative agency regulations. It is up to the courts—and particularly the Supreme Court—to decide what a constitutional provision or a statutory phrase means. In doing so, the courts, in effect, establish law.

Judicial Review

■ **LO14.2:** Define judicial review and explain the constitutional and judicial origins of this power.

The process for deciding whether a law is contrary to the mandates of the Constitution is known as judicial review. This power is not mentioned in the U.S. Constitution. Rather, this judicial power was first established in the famous case of

Judge Tom Colbert is the first African American to be appointed to the Supreme Court of Oklahoma. Prior to that appointment, he served on the Oklahoma Court of Civil Appeals.

AP Images

Case Law
Judicial interpretations of common-law principles and doctrines, as well as interpretations of constitutional law, statutory law, and administrative law.

Beyond Our Borders

The Legal System Based on *Sharia*

Hundreds of millions of Muslims throughout the world are governed by a system of law called *sharia*. In this system, religious laws and precepts are combined with practical laws relating to common actions, such as entering into contracts and borrowing funds.

THE AUTHORITY OF *SHARIA*

It is said that *sharia*, or Islamic law, is drawn from the Quran and the specific guidelines laid down in it. The second major source, called *sunnah*, is based on the way the Prophet Muhammad lived his life. The lesser source is called *ijma*; it represents the consensus of opinion in the community of Muslims. *Sharia* law is comprehensive in nature. All possible actions of Muslims are divided into five categories: obligatory, meritorious, permissible, reprehensible, and forbidden.

THE SCOPE OF *SHARIA* LAW

Sharia law covers many aspects of daily life, including:

- Dietary rules
- Relations between married men and women
- Marriage contracts and divorces
- The role of women
- Holidays
- Dress codes, particularly for women
- Speech with respect to the Prophet Muhammad
- Crimes, including adultery, murder, and theft
- Business dealings, including the borrowing and lending of funds

WHERE *SHARIA* LAW IS APPLIED

The degree to which *sharia* is used varies throughout Muslim societies today. Several countries with the largest Muslim populations (e.g., Bangladesh, India, and Indonesia) do not have Islamic law. Other Muslim countries have dual systems of *sharia* courts and secular courts. In the nations of Western Europe and North America, *sharia* courts have been set up by local communities to deal with many issues. There are at least 85 such courts in Great Britain and the Law Society of that nation has drawn up guidelines for attorneys on some *sharia* practices that may be followed in British secular courts. As the president of the Law Society notes, "There is a wide variety of spiritual, religious and cultural beliefs within our population and the Law Society wants to support its members so they can help clients from all backgrounds."* There are other Britons who opposed this initiative, fearing that the rights of women may be weakened if there is not one law for everyone in the nation.

A *sharia* court judge in Great Britain confers with two Muslim women about their court case.

Canada, which has a *sharia* arbitration court in Ontario, is the first North American country to establish a *sharia* court. However, *sharia* courts, as such, do not exist in the United States, although the dictates of that legal system do come to play in many cases, particularly in divorce hearings. In a New Jersey divorce case, an Islamic woman asked to have her dowry returned as specified in the couples religious marriage contract. The New Jersey judge agreed, saying the contract was as valid as any other contract signed between two individuals. The fact that the contract met the conditions of *sharia* law was not at issue in the case.**

For Critical Analysis

1. *Do you think that a nation can have two different systems of law at the same time?*

2. *How should decisions about religious law be regarded by civil legal systems?*

* Sam Webb, "Sharia law to be enshrined in British legal system as lawyers get guidelines on drawing up documents according to Islamic rules," Mail online, March 23, 2014, www.dailymail.co.uk/news/article-2587215/Sharia-Law-enshrined-British-legal-lawyers-guidelines-drawing-documents-according-Islamic-rules.html

** Abed Awad, "The True Story of Sharia in American Courts," *The Nation*, July 2–9, 2012, www.thenation.com/article/168378/true-story-sharia-american-courts#

Marbury v. Madison (as discussed in the Politics with a Purpose). In that case, Chief Justice Marshall insisted that the Supreme Court had the power to decide that a law passed by Congress violated the Constitution:

> It is emphatically the province and duty of the Judicial Department to say what the law is. Those who apply the rule to a particular case must, of necessity, expound and interpret that rule. If two laws conflict with each other, the courts must decide on the operation of each.[2]

The Supreme Court has ruled parts or all of acts of Congress to be unconstitutional fewer than 200 times in its history. State laws, however, have been declared unconstitutional by the court much more often—more than 1,000 times. The court has been more active in declaring federal or state laws unconstitutional since the beginning of the twentieth century.

The Supreme Court can effectively define the separation of powers between the branches. In 1983, the Court outlawed the practice of the legislative veto by which one or both chambers of Congress could overturn decisions made by the president or by executive agencies. Then, in 2006, the Supreme Court ruled that the president had no authority to set up military tribunals at the Guantanamo Bay prison, but Congress did have the authority to create such tribunals by legislation, thus making it clear that the creation of courts is within the prerogative of Congress, not the president.

The Federal Court System

■ **LO14.3:** Produce a graphic illustration of the federal court system and explain how a case moves from the trial court to the highest court of appeals, the Supreme Court.

The United States has a dual court system with state courts and federal courts. Each of the 50 states, as well as the District of Columbia, has its own independent system of courts, for 52 court systems in total. The federal courts derive their power from the U.S. Constitution, Article III, Section 1, and are organized according to congressional legislation. State courts draw authority from state constitutions and laws. Court cases in state court systems reach the Supreme Court only after they have been appealed to the highest possible state court. Figure 14–1 shows the basic components of the state and federal court systems.

Basic Judicial Requirements

In any court system, state or federal, before a case can be brought before a court, certain requirements must be met. Two important requirements are jurisdiction and standing to sue.

Jurisdiction. A state court can exercise **jurisdiction** over the residents of a particular geographic area, such as a county or district. A state's highest court, or supreme court, has jurisdictional authority over all residents within the state. Because the Constitution established a federal government with limited powers, federal jurisdiction is also limited.

Article III, Section 1, of the U.S. Constitution limits the jurisdiction of the federal courts to cases that involve either a federal question or diversity of citizenship.

Jurisdiction
The authority of a court to decide certain cases. Not all courts have the authority to decide all cases. Two jurisdictional issues are where a case arises as well as its subject matter.

---

2. 5 U.S. (1 Cranch) 137 (1803).

Figure 14-1 ▶ **Dual Structure of the American Court System**

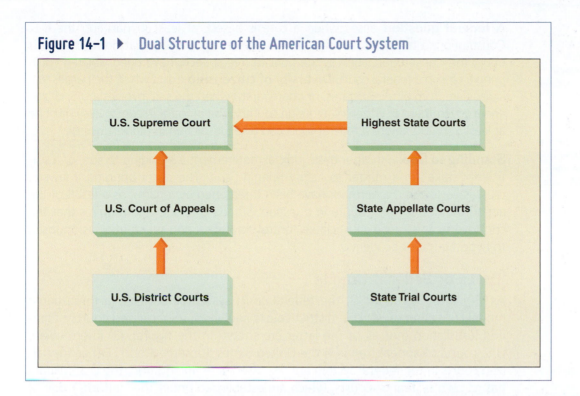

Everyday Politics

 ## The Allure of the Law In Primetime

Television audiences' appetites for crime shows and law-centered plotlines cannot be satiated. After *L.A. Law* became a hit in the 1980s, applications to law schools across the country soared. It seemed as though every undergraduate had dreams of becoming a brilliant and sharp-witted top attorney at a fast-paced law firm. Since then, television series about crime, criminal investigation, the law, and lawyers have continued to hold a captive audience, even as the demand for attorneys in the real world has declined.

Law & Order and *Law & Order: Special Victims Unit* offer an optimistic view of the American criminal justice system and focus storylines on crime dramas that combine criminal investigation with the consideration of how a trial can be prosecuted. The franchise offers a serious look at the relationship between prosecuting attorneys who work for the state and the judges who are responsible for carrying out fair trials within the law, no matter how heinous the crime.

Other series have been more closely patterned after *L.A. Law*, highlighting defense lawyers rather than the prosecution team. *The Practice* and its spinoff, *Boston Legal*, featured smart writing, complex and often eccentric characters, and plots that often reference recent political issues. *Boston Legal* was often regarded as a very witty "dramedy."

Recently, a USA network series, *Suits*, has joined the list of crime dramas. The lead character, a trial attorney, teams with a college dropout who had been selling the answers to math exams to fellow students to become a superb investigative team. The show puts the viewer in the courtroom watching trial attorneys at work.

These crime programs and a myriad of others are carefully written to make sure that the stories and the courtroom scenes are accurate. In each episode, a crime is committed, an arrest is made, the accused is questioned, and issues of criminal procedure are raised. Although it is rarely mentioned, the truth is that the Supreme Court of the United States actually regulates all police and court behavior in the United States. When the Court throws out a case or overturns a conviction because of shoddy police or legal work, its decision sets a precedent for all to follow. For example, the Court's decision in the Miranda case* created "the Miranda rule," which continues to be read or recited at every arrest in the United States. Popular television series, while they do not change the law, undoubtedly help educate the viewers about the law and the criminal process.

* Miranda v. Arizona 384 U.S. 436 (1966).

Federal Question
A question that has to do with the U.S. Constitution, acts of Congress, or treaties. A federal question provides a basis for federal jurisdiction.

Diversity of Citizenship
The condition that exists when the parties to a lawsuit are citizens of different states, or when the parties are citizens of a U.S. state and citizens or the government of a foreign country. Diversity of citizenship can provide a basis for federal jurisdiction.

Trial Court
The court in which most cases begin.

General Jurisdiction
Exists when a court's authority to hear cases is not significantly restricted. A court of general jurisdiction normally can hear a broad range of cases.

A **federal question** arises when a case is based, at least in part, on the U.S. Constitution, a treaty, or a federal law. A person who claims that her or his rights under the Constitution, such as the right to free speech, have been violated could bring a case in a federal court. **Diversity of citizenship** exists when the parties to a lawsuit are from different states, or (more rarely) when the suit involves a U.S. citizen and a government or citizen of a foreign country. The amount in controversy must be at least $75,000 before a federal court can take jurisdiction in a diversity case.

Standing to Sue.   Another basic judicial requirement is standing to sue, or a sufficient "stake" in a matter to justify bringing suit. The party bringing a lawsuit must have suffered a harm, or have been threatened by a harm, as a result of the action that led to the dispute in question. Standing to sue also requires that the controversy at issue be a justiciable controversy—real and substantial, as opposed to hypothetical or academic.

Types of Federal Courts

As shown in Figure 14–2, the federal court system is basically a three-tiered model consisting of (1) U.S. district courts and various specialized courts of limited jurisdiction (not all of the latter are shown in the figure), (2) intermediate U.S. courts of appeals, and (3) the United States Supreme Court. Other specialized courts in the federal system are discussed later. In addition, the U.S. military has its own system of courts, which are established under the Uniform Code of Military Justice. Cases from these other federal courts may also reach the Supreme Court.

U.S. District Courts.   The U.S. district courts are trial courts. A **trial court** is what the name implies—a court in which trials are held and testimony is taken. The U.S. district courts are courts of **general jurisdiction**, meaning that they can hear cases involving a broad array of issues. Federal cases involving most matters

Figure 14–2 ▶ The Federal Court System

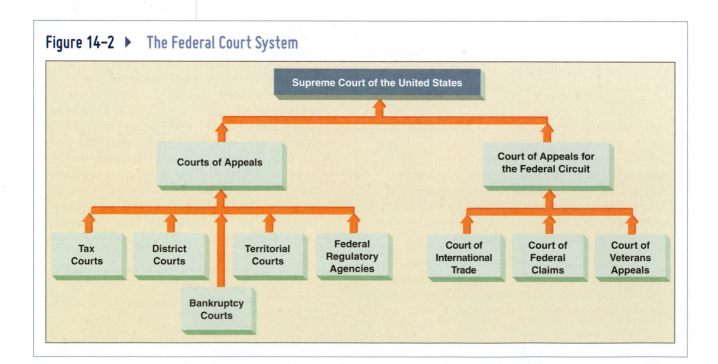

Politics with a Purpose

Political Struggles Fought in the Court

Complaints about activist judges are typical in today's political scene and might be a description of politics in the twenty-first century. This also describes the presidential election of 1800, which led to *Marbury v. Madison*, one of the most important Supreme Court cases, the influence of which is still felt today.

Marbury v. Madison established the doctrine of judicial review. It was precipitated by the presidential election of 1800, in which the incumbent president, John Adams, was defeated by his vice president, Thomas Jefferson. Not only did this event mark the first election where issues divided the emerging political parties, but it was also intensely and personally fought. President Adams was a member of the Federalist Party, which had emerged victorious in the fights over ratification of the Constitution. Jefferson was an Anti-Federalist and the leader of the ascendant Jeffersonian Republicans. These two groups disagreed on the power of the federal government. In addition, the two men bitterly disagreed with each other's politics.

Thomas Jefferson eventually won the election, but did not take office until March 1801.* Between the election and inauguration, the Federalist-controlled Congress passed a series of laws creating additional judicial positions that would be staffed with Federalist appointments. One of these positions was District of Columbia Justice of the Peace, a relatively low-level judicial appointment whose term would expire in five years. William Marbury was confirmed as an appointment. The day before inauguration, the appointment papers were signed and sealed, but not delivered. John Marshall was to deliver the appointment, but he had his own appointment to become chief justice of the Supreme Court. Upon taking office, President Jefferson ordered his secretary of state, James Madison, not to deliver the commissions. Marbury and two others brought suit to the Supreme Court, asking that the Court force Jefferson to deliver the commissions.

Some accounts argue that Marbury took this action, not because he wanted the appointment, but because he wanted to provoke a fight with Jefferson. Marbury was a committed Federalist who believed that the Jeffersonian argument to reduce federal government control and give power back to state governments was deeply flawed. These Federalists were very unhappy with the outcome of the election and were seeking mechanisms to remain influential.**

By then, the chief justice of the Supreme Court was John Marshall, a Federalist appointed by the former President Adams. Marshall knew that if he ordered Jefferson to honor the commission, the president would likely ignore the order, resulting in an unacceptably dangerous constitutional crisis for the young country, and the Supreme Court would be weakened. Marshall, writing for the Court, issued a decision that found Marbury's rights had been denied but that the law passed by Congress that would have granted the Court the power of redress was unconstitutional. In other words, Marshall said that the Supreme Court was not where Marbury should have sought a solution, arguing for the first time that the Court had the power to "say what the law is."***

John Marshall's role and the legal arguments he used in deciding the case have many interpretations.**** Without dispute, however, this case marked the formal articulation of judicial review, a power that in the twentieth century would touch Americans' most basic liberties and rights. Even more significantly, the case illustrates that the intense battles waged by groups to make a difference in contemporary politics (e.g., *Roe v. Wade* and *Bush v. Gore*) are as old as the Republic.

---

* This election was also noteworthy for illustrating the flaw in the electoral college that resulted in a tie between Jefferson and his running mate, Aaron Burr. Breaking the tie in the House of Representatives took six days and 36 ballots. www.historynow.org/09_2004/historian4b.html, accessed May 16, 2008.

** www.claremont.org/publications/crb/id.1183/article_detail.asp#, accessed May 17, 2008.

*** *Marbury v. Madison*, 5 U.S. 137 (1803).

**** See, for example, Alexander M. Bickel, *The Least Dangerous Branch: The Supreme Court at the Bar of Politics* (New Haven, CT: Yale University Press, 1986); and William E. Nelson, *Marbury v. Madison: The Origins and Legacy of Judicial Review* (Lawrence, KS: University Press of Kansas, 2000).

---

typically are heard in district courts. The courts on the lower tier of the model in Figure 14–2 are courts of **limited jurisdiction** that can try cases involving only certain types of claims, such as tax claims or bankruptcy petitions.

Every state has at least one federal district court. The number of judicial districts can vary over time due to population changes and corresponding caseloads. Currently, there are 94 federal judicial districts. A party who is dissatisfied with the decision of a district court can appeal the case to the appropriate U.S. court of

Limited Jurisdiction
Exists when a court's authority to hear cases is restricted to certain types of claims, such as tax claims or bankruptcy petitions.

Appellate Court
A court having jurisdiction to review cases and issues that were originally tried in lower courts.

appeals, or federal **appellate court**. Figure 14–3 shows the jurisdictional boundaries of the district courts (which are state boundaries, unless otherwise indicated by dotted lines within a state) and of the U.S. courts of appeals.

U.S. Courts of Appeals. The 13 U.S. courts of appeals are also referred to as U.S. circuit courts of appeals. Twelve of these courts, including the U.S. Court of Appeals for the District of Columbia, hear appeals from the federal district courts located within their respective judicial circuits (geographic areas over which they exercise jurisdiction). The Court of Appeals for the Thirteenth Circuit (the Federal Circuit) has national appellate jurisdiction over certain types of cases, such as cases involving patent law and those in which the U.S. government is a defendant. In 2013, when Republicans in the Senate were blocking President Obama's nominations for those courts, the Senate changed its rules to disallow filibusters on such appointments. When a president is able to appoint judges who share his or her viewpoint to the D.C. appellate courts, he or she is trying to ensure favorable opinions on the administration's regulations for years to come.

When an appellate court reviews a case that was decided in a district court, it does not conduct another trial. A panel of three or more judges reviews the record of the case on appeal, which includes a transcript of the trial proceedings, and determines whether the trial court committed an error. Usually, appellate courts do not look at questions of *fact* (such as whether a party did, in fact, commit a certain action, such as burning a flag) but at questions of *law* (such as whether the act of burning a flag is a form of speech protected by the First Amendment to the Constitution). An appellate court will challenge a trial court's finding of fact only when the finding is clearly contrary to the evidence presented at trial or when no evidence supports the finding.

Figure 14–3 ▶ Geographic Boundaries of Federal District Courts and Circuit Courts of Appeals

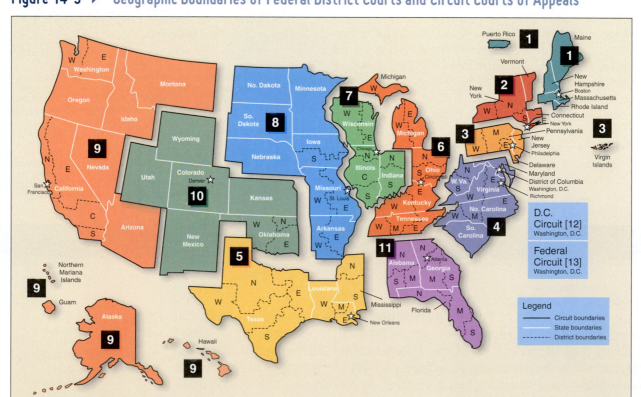

Source: Administrative Office of the United States Courts.

A party can petition the United States Supreme Court to review an appellate court's decision, but the likelihood that the Supreme Court will grant the petition is slim because the Court reviews very few of the cases decided by the appellate courts. Decisions made by appellate judges are usually final.

The United States Supreme Court. The highest level of the three-tiered model of the federal court system is the United States Supreme Court. When the Supreme Court held its first session in 1789, it had five justices. Congress passes laws that determine the number of justices and other aspects of the court. In the following years, more justices were added. Since 1869, nine justices have been on the Court at any given time.

According to Article III of the U.S. Constitution, there is only one national Supreme Court. All other courts in the federal system are considered "inferior." Congress is empowered to create other inferior courts such as the district courts, the federal courts of appeals, and the federal courts of limited jurisdiction.

Although the Supreme Court can exercise original jurisdiction (that is, act as a trial court) in certain cases, such as those affecting foreign diplomats and those in which a state is a party, most of its work is as an appellate court. The Court hears appeals not only from the federal appellate courts but also from the highest state courts. The Supreme Court can review a state supreme court decision only if a federal question is involved. Because of its importance in the federal court system, we will look more closely at the Supreme Court in a later section. Modern decisions are posted on the Supreme Court's website and Twitter feed, providing easy access to information and rulings, as shown in the screen capture.

Political analysts and political groups use social media to respond to rulings, as shown in the screen captures.

US Supreme Court/Twitter

US Supreme Court @USSupremeCourt · Apr 2
McCUTCHEON, SHAUN, ET AL. v. FEDERAL ELECTION COMMISSION. Decided 04/02/2014 j.mp/1pLtpdi
Expand   ⬑ Reply ⇄ Retweet ★ Favorite ••• More

US Supreme Court @USSupremeCourt · Apr 2
NORTHWEST, INC., ET AL. v. GINSBERG, S. BINYOMIN. Decided 04/02/2014 j.mp/1pLtpd3
Expand   ⬑ Reply ⇄ Retweet ★ Favorite ••• More

US Supreme Court @USSupremeCourt · Mar 26
UNITED STATES v. CASTLEMAN, JAMES A.. Decided 03/26/2014 j.mp/1l4eSat
Expand   ⬑ Reply ⇄ Retweet ★ Favorite ••• More

ACLU/Twitter

Walter Olson/Twitter

ACLU National @ACLU · Apr 22
BREAKING: #SCOTUS has overturned a lower court and ruled that #Michigan's Prop 2 is constitutional. Court opinion divided #affirmativeaction
Expand   ⬑ Reply ⇄ Retweet ★ Favorite ••• More

Walter Olson @walterolson · Apr 22
Sotomayor mantra "Race matters" likely to thrill some readers, but it's... imprecise (all 9 Justices agree race matters, disagree on how)
Expand   ⬑ Reply ⇄ Retweet ★ Favorite ••• More

After the Supreme Court reinstated a ban on affirmative action in admissions to Michigan's universities, many groups weighed in on the decision. Do these comments raise even more issues about discrimination for all to consider?

Specialized Federal Courts and the War on Terrorism

The federal court system includes a variety of trial courts of limited jurisdiction, dealing with matters such as tax claims, patent law, Native American claims, bankruptcy, or international trade. The government's attempts to combat terrorism have drawn attention to certain specialized courts that meet in secret.

The FISA Court. The federal government created the first secret court in 1978, when Congress passed the Foreign Intelligence Surveillance Act (FISA). This established a court to hear requests for warrants for the surveillance of suspected spies. Officials can request warrants without having to reveal to the suspect or the public the information used to justify the warrant. The FISA court has approved almost all of the thousands of requests for warrants that the U.S. attorney general's office and other officials have submitted. The seven judges on the FISA court (federal district judges from across the nation) meet in secret, with no published opinions or orders. The public has no access to the court's proceedings or records. Hence, when the court authorizes surveillance, most suspects do not even know that they are under scrutiny. Additionally, during the Clinton administration, the court was given the authority to approve physical as well as electronic searches, which means that officials may search a suspect's property without obtaining a warrant in open court and without notifying the subject.

In the aftermath of the terrorist attacks on September 11, 2001, the Bush administration expanded the powers of the FISA court. Previously, the FISA allowed secret domestic surveillance only if the target was spying as an agent of another nation. Post-September 11 amendments allow warrants if a "significant purpose" of the surveillance is to gather foreign intelligence and allow surveillance of groups who are not agents of a foreign government.

Alien "Removal Courts." The FISA court is not the only court in which suspects' rights have been reduced. In response to the Oklahoma City bombing in 1995, Congress passed the Anti-Terrorism and Effective Death Penalty Act of 1996. The act included a provision creating an alien "removal court" to hear evidence against suspected "alien terrorists." The judges rule on whether there is probable cause for deportation. If so, a public deportation proceeding is held in a U.S. district court. The prosecution does not need to follow procedures that normally apply in criminal cases and the defendant cannot see the evidence that the prosecution used to secure the hearing.

In some cases, the United States Supreme Court ruled against the George W. Bush administration's efforts to use secret legal proceedings in dealing with suspected terrorists. In 2004, it ruled that enemy combatants who are U.S. citizens and taken prisoner by the United States cannot be denied due process rights. Justice Sandra Day O'Connor wrote that "due process demands that a citizen held in the United States as an enemy combatant be given a meaningful opportunity to contest the factual basis of that detention before a neutral decision maker… [a]

The prison at
Guantánamo Bay, Cuba, where the detainees from the Afghanistan and Iraq wars were held until their military trials or their release to another country. Why did the United States create the prison at Guantánamo Bay?

AP Photo/Brennan Linsley

state of war is not a blank check for the president when it comes to the rights of the nation's citizens."[3] The Court also found that noncitizen detainees held at Guantánamo Bay in Cuba were entitled to challenge the grounds for their confinement.[4]

In response to the court rulings, the Bush administration asked Congress to enact a law establishing military tribunals to hear the prisoners' cases at Guantánamo. In 2006, the Court held that these tribunals did not meet due-process requirements for a fair hearing. The central issue in the case was whether the entire situation at the prison camp violated the prisoners' right of *habeas corpus*—the right of a detained person to challenge the legality of his or her detention before a judge or other neutral party. Congress then passed the Military Commissions Act of 2006, which eliminated federal court jurisdiction over *habeas corpus* challenges by enemy combatants. This law was also tested in court, but the Supreme Court refused to hear the case, so the law, as upheld by an appellate court, stands.[5]

Finally, in 2008, the Supreme Court, by a 5-4 majority, held that enemy combatants have the right to challenge their detention in front of a federal court if they have not been charged with a crime. This ruling essentially grants the detainees at Guantánamo Bay the right of *habeas corpus*, a right that a majority of Congress cannot constitutionally restrict.[6] After President Obama took office in 2009, he announced that the prison at Guantánamo would be closed within a year. Attorney General Eric Holder announced that several of the detainees, including Khalid Sheikh Mohammed, the self-proclaimed master-mind behind the September 11, 2001 terrorist attacks, would be transferred to the United States for trial in New York City. After public outcry about the possible trial, the president announced that military commission trials would continue to be held in Guantánamo. Furthermore, Congress has been unwilling to fund a prison in the United States to hold suspected terrorists. As of 2014, 154 prisoners remain at the Cuban facility: three are serving sentences after convictions, 76 have been cleared for release if a country will accept them, and 45 have been deemed too dangerous for release.[7] There have been less than a dozen commission verdicts given.[8]

Parties to Lawsuits

In most lawsuits, the parties are the plaintiff (the person or organization that initiates the lawsuit) and the defendant (the person or organization against whom the lawsuit is brought). Numerous plaintiffs and defendants may appear in a single lawsuit. In the last several decades, many lawsuits have been brought by interest groups (see Chapter 7). Interest groups play an important role in our judicial system, because they **litigate**—bring to trial—or assist in litigating most cases of racial or gender-based discrimination, virtually all civil liberties cases, and more than one-third of the cases involving business matters. Interest groups also file *amicus curiae* (pronounced ah-*mee*-kous *kur*-ee-eye) briefs, or "friend of the court" briefs, in more than 50 percent of these kinds of cases.

Litigate
To engage in a legal proceeding or seek relief in a court of law; to carry on a lawsuit.

3. *Hamdi v. Rumsfeld*, 542 U.S. 507 (2004).
4. Hamdi was eventually released following a settlement with the government under which he agreed to renounce his U.S. citizenship and return to Saudi Arabia.
5. *Boumediene v. Bush*, 476 F.3d 981 (D.C. Cir. 2007).
6. *Boumediene v. Bush*, 553 U.S. 723 (2008).
7. "Guantanamo by the Numbers," American Civil Liberties Union, www.aclu.org/national-security/guantanamo-numbers, April 18, 2104.
8. "The Guantanamo Trials," Human Rights Watch, www.hrw.org/features/guantanamo, 2014.

Class-Action Suit
A lawsuit filed by an individual seeking damages for "all persons similarly situated."

COMPARE WITH YOUR PEERS
MindTap™ for American Government

Access The Judiciary Forum: Polling Activity—Jury Duty.

Sometimes interest groups or other plaintiffs will bring a **class-action suit**, in which the court decision will stand for all members of a class similarly situated (such as users of a particular product manufactured by the defendant in the lawsuit). The strategy of class-action lawsuits was pioneered by such groups as the National Association for the Advancement of Colored People (NAACP), the Legal Defense Fund, and the Sierra Club, whose leaders believed that the courts would offer a more sympathetic forum for their views than would Congress.

Procedural Rules

Both the federal and the state courts have established procedural rules that shape the litigation process. These rules are designed to protect the rights and interests of the parties, to ensure that the litigation proceeds in a fair and orderly manner, and to identify the issues that must be decided by the court, thus saving court time and costs. The parties must comply with procedural rules and with any orders given by the judge during the course of the litigation. When a party does not follow a court's order, the court can cite him or her for contempt. A party who commits *civil* contempt (failing to comply with a court's order for the benefit of another party to the proceeding) can be taken into custody, fined, or both, until the party complies with the court's order. A party who commits *criminal* contempt (obstructing the administration of justice or bringing the court into disrespect) also can be taken into custody and fined but cannot avoid punishment by complying with a previous order.

The Supreme Court at Work

The Supreme Court begins its regular annual term on the first Monday in October and usually adjourns in late June or early July of the next year. Special sessions may be held after the regular term ends, but only a few cases are

A courtroom artist's rendering of the sentencing trial for Zacarias Moussaoui at the federal courthouse. The confessed September 11 conspirator testified he knew about the terrorist plot when he was arrested a month before the attacks and lied to FBI agents because he wanted the mission to go forward.

Art Lein/epa/Corbis WireCorbis

decided in this way. More commonly, cases are carried over until the next regular session.

Of the total number of cases that are decided each year, those reviewed by the Supreme Court represent less than one-half of 1 percent. Included in these, however, are decisions that profoundly affect our lives. In recent years, the United States Supreme Court has decided issues involving the Affordable Care Act, capital punishment, affirmative action programs, religious freedom, assisted suicide, abortion, property rights, sexual harassment, pornography, states' rights, limits on federal jurisdiction, and many other matters with significant consequences for the nation. Because the Supreme Court exercises a great deal of discretion over the types of cases it hears, it can influence the nation's policies both by issuing decisions in some types of cases and refusing to hear appeals in others, thereby allowing lower court decisions to stand.

Which Cases Reach the Supreme Court?

Many are surprised to learn that in a typical case, there is no absolute right of appeal to the United States Supreme Court. The Court's appellate jurisdiction is almost entirely discretionary; the Court can choose which cases it will decide. The justices never explain their reasons for hearing certain cases and not others, so it is difficult to predict which case or type of case the Court might select. Former chief justice William Rehnquist, in his description of the selection process in *The Supreme Court: How It Was, How It Is*, said that the decision of whether to accept a case "strikes me as a rather subjective decision, made up in part of intuition and in part of legal judgment."[9]

Factors That Bear on the Decision.
Factors that bear on the decision include whether a legal question has been decided differently by various lower courts and needs resolution by the highest court, whether a lower court's decision conflicts with an existing Supreme Court ruling, and whether the issue could have significance beyond the parties to the dispute.

Another factor is whether the solicitor general is pressuring the Court to take a case. The solicitor general, a high-ranking presidential appointee within the Justice Department, represents the national government before the Supreme Court and promotes presidential policies in the federal courts. He or she decides what cases the government should ask the Supreme Court to review and what position the government should take in cases before the Court.

Granting Petitions for Review.
If the Court decides to grant a petition for review, it will issue a **writ of *certiorari*** (pronounced sur-shee-uh-*rah*-ree). The writ orders a lower court to send the Supreme Court a record of the case for review. More than 90 percent of the petitions for review are denied. A denial is not a decision on the merits of a case, nor does it indicate agreement with the

AP Images/Kevin Wolf, File

Justice Ruth Bader Ginsburg being interviewed in 2008. She noted the presence of two Jewish justices on the court and that their religion plays no role in their decisions.

Writ of *Certiorari*
An order issued by a higher court to a lower court to send up the record of a case for review.

9. William H. Rehnquist, *The Supreme Court: How It Was, How It Is* (New York: Morrow, 1987).

Rule of Four
A United States Supreme Court procedure by which four justices must vote to grant a petition for review if a case is to come before the full court.

Oral Arguments
The verbal arguments presented in person by attorneys to an appellate court. Each attorney presents reasons to the court why the court should rule in her or his client's favor.

Opinion
The statement by a judge or a court of the decision reached in a case. The opinion sets forth the applicable law and details the reasoning on which the ruling was based.

Affirmed
To declare that a court ruling is valid and must stand.

Reversed
To annul or make void a court ruling on account of some error or irregularity.

Remanded
To send a case back to the court that originally heard it.

Unanimous Opinion
A court opinion or determination on which all judges agree.

Majority Opinion
A court opinion reflecting the views of the majority of the judges.

Concurring Opinion
A separate opinion prepared by a judge who supports the decision of the majority of the court but who wants to make or clarify a particular point or to voice disapproval of the grounds on which the decision was made.

Dissenting Opinions
A separate opinion in which a judge dissents from (disagrees with) the conclusion reached by the majority on the court and expounds his or her own views about the case.

lower court's opinion. (The judgment of the lower court remains in force, however.) Therefore, denial of the writ has no value as a precedent. The Court will not issue a writ unless at least four justices approve of it. This is called the **rule of four**.[10]

Deciding Cases

Once the Supreme Court grants *certiorari* in a particular case, the justices do extensive research on the legal issues and facts involved in the case. Each justice is entitled to four law clerks, who undertake much of the research and preliminary drafting necessary for the justice to form an opinion.[11]

The Court normally does not hear any evidence, as is true with all appeals courts. The Court's consideration of a case is based on the abstracts, the record, and the briefs. The attorneys are permitted to present **oral arguments**. All statements and the justices' questions are recorded during these sessions. Unlike the practice in most courts, lawyers addressing the Supreme Court can be (and often are) questioned by the justices at any time during oral argument.

The justices meet to discuss and vote on cases in conferences held throughout the term. In these conferences, in addition to deciding cases currently before the Court, the justices determine which new petitions for *certiorari* to grant. These conferences take place in the oak-paneled chamber and are strictly private—no stenographers, tape recorders, or video cameras are allowed. Two pages used to be in attendance to wait on the justices while they were in conference, but fear of information leaks caused the Court to stop this practice.[12]

Decisions and Opinions

When the Court has reached a decision, its opinion is written. The **opinion** contains the Court's ruling on the issue or issues presented, the reasons for its decision, the rules of law that apply, and other information. In many cases, the decision of the lower court is **affirmed**, resulting in the enforcement of that court's judgment or decree. If the Supreme Court believes that a reversible error was committed during the trial or that the jury was instructed improperly, however, the decision will be **reversed**. Sometimes the case will be **remanded** (sent back to the court that originally heard the case) for a new trial or other proceeding. Occasionally, the court will issue an unsigned opinion—an opinion *per curiam* (by the court).

When all justices unanimously agree on an opinion, the opinion is written for the entire Court (all the justices) and can be deemed a **unanimous opinion**. When there is not a unanimous opinion, a **majority opinion** is written, outlining the views of the majority of the justices involved in the case. Often, one or more justices who feel strongly about making or emphasizing a particular point that is not made or emphasized in the unanimous or majority written opinion will write a **concurring opinion**. That means the justice writing the concurring opinion agrees (concurs) with the conclusion given in the majority written opinion, but for different reasons. Finally, in other than unanimous opinions, one or more **dissenting opinions** are usually written by those justices who do not agree with the majority. The dissenting opinion is important because it often forms the basis

---

10. The "rule of four" is modified when seven or fewer justices participate, which occurs from time to time. When that happens, as few as three justices can grant *certiorari*.

11. A number of former clerks write about their experiences in Todd C. Peppers and Artemus Ward, eds., *In Chambers: Stories of Supreme Court Law Clerks and Their Justices*, Charlottesville, VA: University of Virginia Press, 2013.

12. It turned out that one supposed information leak came from lawyers making educated guesses.

of the arguments used years later if the Court reverses the previous decision and establishes a new precedent.

Shortly after the opinion is written, the Supreme Court announces its decision from the bench. At that time, the opinion is made available to the public at the office of the clerk of the Court. The clerk also releases the opinion for online publication. Ultimately, the opinion is published in the *United States Reports*, which is the official printed record of the Court's decisions.

Some have complained that the Court reviews too few cases each term, thus giving the lower courts less guidance on important issues. The number of signed opinions issued by the Court has dwindled notably since the 1980s. In its 1982–1983 term, the Court issued signed opinions in 141 cases. By 2013, this number dropped to less than 80. One reason that the number of opinions has dropped is the court's ability to group a number of cases into one larger case. Such was the process in the case of the Affordable Care Act challenges by the states.

The Selection of Federal Judges

■ **LO14.4:** Explain how judges are nominated and confirmed for the Supreme Court.

All federal judges are appointed. The Constitution, in Article II, Section 2, states that the president appoints the justices of the Supreme Court with the advice and consent of the Senate. Congress has provided the same procedure for staffing other federal courts. This means that the Senate and the president jointly decide who shall fill every vacant judicial position, no matter what the level.

Federal judgeships in the United States number more than 870. Once appointed to such a judgeship, a person holds that job for life. Judges serve until they resign, retire voluntarily, or die. Federal judges who engage in blatantly illegal conduct may be removed through impeachment, although such action is rare.

Judicial Appointments

Judicial candidates for federal judgeships are suggested to the president by the Department of Justice, senators, other judges, the candidates, and lawyers' associations and other interest groups. In selecting a candidate to nominate for a judgeship, the president considers not only the person's competence but also other factors, including the person's political philosophy, ethnicity, and gender.

The nomination process—no matter how the nominees are obtained—always works the same way. The president makes the actual nomination, transmitting the name to the Senate. The Senate then either confirms or rejects the nomination. To reach a conclusion, the Senate Judiciary Committee (operating through subcommittees) invites testimony, both written and oral, at its various hearings. A practice used in the Senate, called **senatorial courtesy**, is a constraint on the president's freedom to appoint federal district judges. Senatorial courtesy allows a senator of the president's political party to veto a judicial appointment in her or his state by way of a "blue slip." Traditionally, the senators from the nominee's state are sent a blue form on which to make comments. They may return the "blue slip" with comments or not return it at all. Not returning the blue slip is a veto of the nomination.[13] During much of American history,

Senatorial Courtesy
In federal district court judgeship nominations, a tradition allowing a senator to veto a judicial appointment in his or her state.

13. Charlie Savage, "Despite Filibuster Limits, a Door Remains Open to Block Judge Nominees," *The New York Times*, November 13, 2013. www.nytimes.com/2013/11/29/us/politics/despite-filibuster-limits-a-door-remains-open-to-block-judge-nominees.html. And for an historical view, see Mitchell A. Sollenberger, "The Blue Slip Process in the Senate Committee on the Judiciary: Background, Issues, and Options," Congressional Research Service, November 21, 2003.

Associate Justice Sonia
Sotomayor arrives in the
House of Representatives
for the president's State of
the Union Address in 2010.

senators from the "opposition" party (the party to which the president did not belong) also have enjoyed the right of senatorial courtesy, although their veto power has varied over time.

Federal District Court Judgeship Nominations.

Although the president officially nominates federal judges, in the past the nomination of federal district court judges actually originated with a senator or senators of the president's party from the state in which there was a vacancy. In effect, judicial appointments were a form of political patronage. President Jimmy Carter (served 1977–1981) ended this tradition by establishing independent commissions to oversee the initial nomination process. President Ronald Reagan (served 1981–1989) abolished Carter's nominating commissions and established complete presidential control of nominations.

Federal Courts of Appeals Appointments.

Appointments to the federal courts of appeals are far less numerous than federal district court appointments, but are more important. Federal appellate judges handle more important matters, at least from the point of view of the president, and therefore presidents take a keener interest in the nomination process for such judgeships. Also, the U.S. courts of appeals have become stepping stones to the Supreme Court.

Supreme Court Appointments.

The president nominates Supreme Court justices. As shown in Table 14–1, which summarizes the background of all Supreme Court justices to 2014, the most common occupational background of the justices at the time of their appointment has been private legal practice or state or federal judgeship. Those nine justices who were in federal executive posts at the time of their appointment held the high offices of secretary of state, comptroller of the treasury, secretary of the navy, postmaster general, secretary of the interior, chairman of the Securities and Exchange Commission, and secretary of labor. In the "Other" category under "Occupational Position before Appointment" in Table 14–1 are two justices who were professors of law (including William H. Taft, a former president) and one justice who was a North Carolina state employee with responsibility for organizing and revising the state's statutes.

The Special Role of the Chief Justice.

Although ideology is always important in judicial appointments, when a chief justice is selected for the Supreme Court, other considerations must also be taken into account. The chief justice is not only the head of a group of nine justices who interpret the law, but is also in essence the chief executive officer (CEO) of a large bureaucracy that includes: 1,200 judges with lifetime tenure, more than 850 magistrates and bankruptcy judges, and more than 30,000 staff members.

The chief justice is also the chair of the Judicial Conference of the United States, a policymaking body that sets priorities for the federal judiciary. That means that the chief justice also indirectly oversees the $5.5 billion budget of this group.

Finally, the chief justice appoints the director of the Administrative Office of the United States Courts. The chief justice and this director select judges who sit on judicial committees that examine international judicial relations, technology, and a variety of other topics.

Partisanship and Judicial Appointments

Ideology plays an important role in the president's choices for judicial appointments. In most circumstances, the president appoints judges or justices who belong to the president's own political party.[14] Presidents see their federal judiciary appointments as the one sure way to institutionalize their political views long after they have left office. By 1993, presidents Ronald Reagan and George H. W. Bush together had appointed nearly three-quarters of all federal court judges. This preponderance of Republican-appointed federal judges strengthened the legal moorings of the conservative social agenda on a variety of issues, ranging from abortion to civil rights. Nevertheless, President Bill Clinton had the opportunity to appoint about 200 federal judges, thereby shifting the ideological makeup of the federal judiciary.

During the first two years of his second term, President George W. Bush was able to nominate two relatively conservative justices to the Supreme Court—John Roberts, who became chief justice, and Samuel Alito. During his first term as chief justice, Roberts voted most of the time with the Court's most conservative justices, Antonin Scalia and Clarence Thomas, but was part of the majority that upheld the Affordable Care Act in 2012. Justices can shift views once on the Court. Sandra Day O'Connor, the first female justice and a conservative, gradually shifted to the left on several issues, including abortion. In 1981, during her confirmation hearing before the Senate Judiciary Committee, she said, "I am opposed to it [abortion], as a matter of birth control or otherwise." By 1992, she was part of a 5-4 majority that agreed that the Constitution protects a woman's right to an abortion.

To fill the vacancy left by the retirement of Justice John Paul Stevens, President Obama nominated

Table 14-1 ▶ Background of U.S. Supreme Court Justices to 2015 (Number of Justices = 112 Total)

OCCUPATIONAL POSITION BEFORE APPOINTMENT	
Private legal practice	25
State judgeship	21
Federal judgeship	31
U.S. attorney general	7
Deputy or assistant U.S. attorney general	2
U.S. solicitor general	3
U.S. senator	6
U.S. representative	2
State governor	3
Federal executive post	9
Other	3
RELIGIOUS BACKGROUND	
Protestant	83
Roman Catholic	14
Jewish	7
Unitarian	7
No religious affiliation	7
AGE ON APPOINTMENT	
Under 40	5
41–50	34
51–60	59
61–70	14
POLITICAL PARTY AFFILIATION	
Federalist (to 1835)	13
Jeffersonian Republican (to 1828)	7
Whig (to 1861)	1
Democrat	46
Republican	44
Independent	1
EDUCATIONAL BACKGROUND	
College graduate	96
Not a college graduate	16
GENDER	
Male	108
Female	4
RACE	
White	109
African American	2
Hispanic American	1

Source: Congressional Quarterly, Congressional Quarterly's Guide to the U.S. Supreme Court (Washington, DC: Congressional Quarterly Press, 1996); and authors' updates.

14. For a discussion of how the public regards the politics of Supreme Court appointments, see Brandon L. Bartels and Christopher D. Johnston, "Political Justice? Perceptions of Politicization and Public Preferences Toward the Supreme Court Appointment Process," *Public Opinion Quarterly* (Spring, 2012) 76 (1): 105–116.

Sipa USA/SIPA/Newscom

CONNECT WITH YOUR CLASSMATES

MindTap for American Government

Access The Judiciary Forum: Discussion—Supreme Court Confirmation Process.

Solicitor General Elena Kagan, former dean of the law school at Harvard University. His first nominee to the Court, Associate Justice Sonia Sotomayor, who replaced Justice David Souter, became the first Hispanic American to serve on the Court. Both of President Obama's appointments were to seats formerly held by relatively liberal justices, so the balance of ideology on the Supreme Court remained as it had during the George W. Bush administration.

The Senate's Role

Ideology also plays a large role in the Senate's confirmation hearings, and presidential nominees to the Supreme Court have not always been confirmed. Almost 20 percent of presidential nominations to the Supreme Court have been either rejected or not acted on by the Senate. Many acrimonious battles over Supreme Court appointments have occurred when the Senate and the president have not seen eye to eye about political matters.

The U.S. Senate had a long record of refusing to confirm the president's judicial nominations, extending from the beginning of Andrew Jackson's presidency in 1829 to the end of Ulysses Grant's presidency in 1877. From 1894 until 1968, however, only three nominees were not confirmed. Then, from 1968 through 1987, four presidential nominees to the highest court were rejected. One of the most controversial Supreme Court nominations was that of Clarence Thomas, who underwent an extremely volatile confirmation hearing in 1991, replete with charges against him of sexual harassment. He was ultimately confirmed by the Senate, however, and has been a stalwart voice for conservatism ever since.

President Bill Clinton had little trouble gaining approval for both of his nominees to the Supreme Court: Ruth Bader Ginsburg and Stephen Breyer. President George W. Bush's nominees faced hostile grilling in their confirmation hearings, and various interest groups mounted intense media advertising blitzes against them. Bush had to forgo one of his nominees, Harriet Miers, when he realized that she could not be

did you know?

Jimmy Carter is the only president who had no appointments to the Supreme Court.

confirmed by the Senate. President Obama's two nominations, Sonia Sotomayor and Elena Kagan, seen as too liberal by some senators, were eminently qualified for the Court and were approved by the Senate with little incident.

Both Clinton and Bush had trouble securing Senate approval for their judicial nominations to the lower courts. During the late 1990s and early 2000s, the duel between the Senate and the president aroused considerable concern about the consequences of the increasingly partisan and ideological tension over federal judicial appointments. On several occasions, presidents have appointed federal judges using a temporary "recess appointment." This procedure is always used for the same reason—to avoid the continuation of an acrimonious and perhaps futile Senate confirmation process.

Although the confirmation hearings on Supreme Court nominees get all of the media attention, the hearings on nominees for the lower federal courts are equally bitter, leading some to ask whether the politicization of the confirmation process has gone too far. According to Fifth Circuit Court Judge Edith Jones, judicial nominations have turned into battlegrounds because so many federal judges now view the courts as agents of social change. Jones argues that when judge-made law (as opposed to legislature-made law) enters into sensitive topics, it provokes a political reaction. Thus, the ideology and political views of the potential justices should be a matter of public concern and political debate.[15]

Policymaking and the Courts

The partisan battles over judicial appointments reflect an important reality in today's American government: the importance of the judiciary in national politics. Because appointments to the federal bench are for life, the ideology of judicial appointees can affect national policy for years to come. Although the primary function of judges in our system of government is to interpret and apply the laws, inevitably judges make policy when carrying out this task. One of the major policymaking tools of the federal courts is their power of judicial review.

Judicial Review

If a federal court declares that a federal or state law or policy is unconstitutional, the court's decision affects the application of the law or policy only within that court's jurisdiction. For this reason, the higher the level of the court, the greater the impact of the decision on society. Because of the Supreme Court's national jurisdiction, its decisions have the greatest impact. When the Supreme Court held that an Arkansas state constitutional amendment limiting the terms of congresspersons was unconstitutional, laws establishing term limits in 23 other states were also invalidated.[16]

Some claim that the power of judicial review gives judges and justices on federal court benches too much influence over national policy. Others argue that the powers exercised by the federal courts, particularly the power of judicial review, are necessary to protect our constitutional rights and liberties. Built into our federal form of government is a system of checks and balances. If the federal courts did not have the power of judicial review, no governmental body could check Congress's lawmaking authority.

15. Cited by John Leo, "A Judge with No Agenda," *Jewish World Review*, July 5, 2005.
16. *U.S. Term Limits v. Thornton*, 514 U.S. 779 (1995).

"Do you ever have one of those days when everything seems un-Constitutional?"

Judicial Activism and Judicial Restraint

■ **LO14.5:** Compare the concepts of judicial activism and judicial restraint; link these concepts to the decisions of the Supreme Court in the last few decades.

Judicial scholars like to characterize different judges and justices as being either "activist" or "restraintist." The doctrine of **judicial activism** rests on the conviction that the federal judiciary should take an active role by using its powers to check the activities of Congress, state legislatures, and administrative agencies when those governmental bodies exceed their authority. One of the Supreme Court's most activist eras was the period from 1953 to 1969, when the Court was headed by Chief Justice Earl Warren. The Warren Court propelled the civil rights movement forward by holding, among other things, that laws permitting racial segregation violated the equal protection clause.

In contrast, the doctrine of **judicial restraint** rests on the assumption that the courts should defer to the decisions made by the legislative and executive branches, because members of Congress and the president are elected by the people, whereas members of the federal judiciary are not. Because administrative agency personnel normally have more expertise than the courts do in the areas regulated by the agencies, the courts likewise should defer to agency rules and decisions. Under the doctrine of judicial restraint, the courts should not thwart the implementation of legislative acts and agency rules unless they are clearly unconstitutional.

Judicial activism sometimes is linked with liberalism, and judicial restraint with conservatism. In fact, though, a conservative judge can be activist, just as a liberal judge can be restraintist. In the 1950s and 1960s, the Supreme Court was activist and liberal. Some believe that the Rehnquist Court, with its conservative majority, became increasingly activist during the early 2000s. Some go even further and claim that the federal courts, including the Supreme Court, wield too much power in our democracy.

Judicial Activism
A doctrine holding that the Supreme Court should take an active role by using its powers to check the activities of governmental bodies when those bodies exceed their authority.

Judicial Restraint
A doctrine holding that the Supreme Court should defer to the decisions made by the elected representatives of the people in the legislative and executive branches.

Strict versus Broad Construction

Other terms that are often used to describe a justice's philosophy are *strict construction* and *broad construction*. Justices who believe in **strict construction** look to the "letter of the law" when they attempt to interpret the Constitution or a particular statute. Those who favor **broad construction** try to determine the context and purpose of the law.

As with the doctrines of judicial restraint and judicial activism, strict construction is often associated with conservative political views, whereas broad construction is often linked with liberalism. These traditional political associations sometimes appear to be reversed, however. Consider the Eleventh Amendment to the Constitution, which forbids lawsuits in federal courts "against one of the United States by Citizens of another State, or by Citizens or Subjects of any Foreign State." Nothing is said about citizens suing their *own* states, and strict construction would therefore find such suits to be constitutional. Conservative justices, however, have construed this amendment broadly to deny citizens the constitutional right to sue their own states in most circumstances. John T. Noonan, Jr., a federal appellate court judge who was appointed by a Republican president, has described these rulings as "adventurous."[17]

Broad construction is often associated with the concept of a "living constitution." As one who strongly opposed that view, Supreme Court Justice Antonin Scalia has said that the Constitution "is not a living document, it's a dead document... It's an enduring document. It is a meaningless document if its meaning changes according to whatever the Supreme Court thinks."[18]

Ideology and the Rehnquist Court

William H. Rehnquist became the 16th chief justice of the Supreme Court in 1986, after 14 years as an associate justice. He was a strong anchor of the Court's conservative wing until his death in 2005. With Rehnquist's appointment as chief justice, it seemed that the Court would necessarily become more conservative.

Indeed, that is what happened. The Court began to take a rightward shift shortly after Rehnquist became chief justice, and continued as other conservative appointments to the bench were made during the Reagan and George H. W. Bush administrations. During the late 1990s and early 2000s, three of the justices (William Rehnquist, Antonin Scalia, and Clarence Thomas) were notably conservative in their views. Four of the justices (John Paul Stevens, David Souter, Ruth Bader Ginsburg, and Stephen Breyer) held moderate-to-liberal views. The middle of the Court was occupied by two moderate-to-conservative justices, Sandra Day O'Connor and Anthony Kennedy. O'Connor and Kennedy usually provided the swing votes on the Court in controversial cases.

Although the Court seemed to become more conservative under Rehnquist's leadership, its decisions were not always predictable. Many cases were decided by very close votes, and results varied depending on the issue. The Court ruled in 1995 that Congress had overreached its powers under the commerce clause when it attempted to regulate the possession of guns in schoolyards. According to the Court, the possession of guns in school zones had nothing to do with the commerce clause.[19] Yet in 2005, the Court upheld Congress's power under the

---

Strict Construction
A judicial philosophy that looks to the "letter of the law" when interpreting the Constitution or a particular statute.

Broad Construction
A judicial philosophy that looks to the context and purpose of a law when making an interpretation.

---

17. John T. Noonan, Jr., *Narrowing the Nation's Power: The Supreme Court Sides with the States* (Berkeley, CA: University of California Press, 2002).
18. "More quotes from Justice Scalia's Speaking Tour," National Constitution Center, August 21, 2013, http://blog.constitutioncenter.org/2013/08/more-quotes-fro-justice-scalias-speaking-tour/
19. *United States v. Lopez*, 514 U.S. 549 (1995).

commerce clause to ban marijuana use even when a state's law permitted such use.[20] In other areas such as civil rights, the Court generally issued conservative opinions.

The Roberts Court

In 2006, a new chief justice was appointed to the court. John Roberts had a distinguished career as an attorney in Washington, DC, served as a clerk to the Supreme Court while in law school, and was well liked. The confirmation process had been quite smooth, and many hoped that he would be a moderate leader of the Court.

During John Roberts's first term (2005–2006) as chief justice, the Court ruled on several important issues, but no clear pattern was discernible in the decisions. In the years following his appointment, Roberts was more likely to vote with the conservative justices—Scalia, Thomas, and Alito—than with the moderate-to-liberal bloc. Thus, several important decisions were handed down with close votes. In an important case for environmentalist groups, the Court held that the Environmental Protection Agency (EPA) did have the power under the Clean Air Act to regulate greenhouse gases. The vote was 5–4, with the chief justice on the minority side.[21] Similarly, when the Court upheld the 2003 federal law banning partial-birth abortions, Roberts was on the conservative majority in a 5–4 vote.[22]

Later in 2007, the Supreme Court issued a very important opinion on school integration. By another 5-4 vote, the Court ruled that school district policies that included race as a determining factor in admission to certain schools were unconstitutional on the ground that they violated the equal protection clause of the Constitution.[23] After Justices Sonia Sotomayor and Elena Kagan joined the court, court-watchers believed that the Roberts Court would make conservative

Attorneys David Bois and Ted Olson leave the Supreme Court building after arguing for overturning California's prohibition against gay marriage. The Supreme Court ruled in their favor in 2013.

Molly Riley/ABACAUSA.COM/Newscom

20. *Gonzales v. Raich*, 545 U.S. 1 (2005).
21. *Massachusetts v. EPA*, 127 St. Ct. 1438 (2007).
22. *Gonzales v. Carhart*, 127 St. Ct. 1610 (2007).
23. *Parents Involved in Community Schools v. Seattle School District*, N. 1, 127 St. Ct. 2162 (2007).

decisions but that the majority often would be razor thin. Indeed, in 2012, the Court announced two decisions that supported this appraisal: The Court overturned four provisions of Arizona's controversial law regarding illegal immigrants but upheld the central provision allowing police officers to check the immigration status of those individuals who had been arrested or stopped on other charges. A few days later, the Supreme Court upheld the individual mandate to buy health insurance under the Affordable Care Act by a 5–4 margin, with the chief justice supporting the law as legal under the commerce clause of the Constitution.

The Roberts Court continued to issue controversial opinions in 2013 and 2014: in 2013, the court by a 5–4 vote struck down the heart of the Voting Rights Act, freeing southern states to revise voting laws without federal scrutiny. The court continued on its path to complete freedom of speech in political campaigns. In 2014, the court struck down the limits on the total amount an individual can contribute to political campaigns in each election, although it affirmed the limit per gift. Epstein and Martin have suggested that the Roberts Court is more likely to vote based on their policy preferences rather than from a consideration for judicial activism or judicial restraint.[24]

What Checks Our Courts?

■ **LO14.6:** Discuss the constitutional and political constraints on the Supreme Court.

Our judicial system is one of the most independent in the world, but the courts do not have absolute independence as part of the political process. Political checks limit the extent to which courts can exercise judicial review and engage in an activist policy. These checks are exercised by the executive branch, the legislature, the public, and the judiciary.

Executive Checks

President Andrew Jackson was once supposed to have said, after Chief Justice John Marshall made an unpopular decision, "John Marshall has made his decision; now let him enforce it."[25] This purported remark goes to the heart of **judicial implementation**— the enforcement of judicial decisions in such a way that those decisions are translated into policy. The Supreme Court simply does not have any enforcement powers, and whether a decision will be implemented depends on the cooperation of the other two branches of government. Rarely, though, will a president refuse to

Judicial Implementation
The way in which court decisions are translated into action.

Federal troops
were sent by President Eisenhower to guard Little Rock High School and to ensure the safety of the African American students who were going to attend that school.

A. Y. Owen/Time Life Pictures/Getty Images

---

24. Lee Epstein and Andrew D. Martin, "Is the Roberts Court Especially Activist—A Study of Invalidating (and Upholding) Federal, State, and Local Laws," *Emory Law Journal* 61(2011): 737.
25. The decision referred to was *Cherokee Nation v. Georgia*, 30 U.S. 1 (1831).

enforce a Supreme Court decision, as President Jackson did. To take such an action could mean a significant loss of public support because of the Supreme Court's stature in the eyes of the nation.

More commonly, presidents exercise influence over the judiciary by appointing new judges and justices as federal judicial seats become vacant. The U.S. solicitor general plays a significant role in the federal court system, and the person holding this office is a presidential appointee.

Executives at the state level may also refuse to implement court decisions with which they disagree. A notable example of such a refusal occurred in Arkansas after the Supreme Court ordered schools to desegregate "with all deliberate speed" in 1955.[26] Arkansas Governor Orval Faubus refused to cooperate with the decision and used the state's National Guard to block the integration of Central High School in Little Rock. Ultimately, President Dwight Eisenhower had to federalize the Arkansas National Guard and send federal troops to Little Rock to quell the violence that had erupted.

Legislative Checks

Courts may make rulings, but often the legislatures at local, state, and federal levels are required to appropriate funds to carry out the courts' rulings. A court, for example, may decide that prison conditions must be improved, but the legislature authorizes the funds necessary to carry out the ruling. When such funds are not appropriated, the court that made the ruling has been checked.

Constitutional Amendments. Courts' rulings can be overturned by constitutional amendments at both the federal and state levels. Many of the amendments to the U.S. Constitution (such as the Fourteenth, Fifteenth, and Twenty-sixth Amendments) check the state courts' ability to allow discrimination. Proposed constitutional amendments that were created in an effort to reverse courts' decisions on school prayer and abortion have failed.

Rewriting Laws. Finally, Congress or a state legislature can rewrite (amend) old laws or enact new ones to overturn a court's rulings if the legislature concludes that the court is interpreting laws or legislative intentions erroneously. Congress passed the Civil Rights Act of 1991 in part to overturn a series of conservative rulings in employment-discrimination cases. In 1993, Congress enacted the Religious Freedom Restoration Act (RFRA), which broadened religious liberties, after Congress concluded that a 1990 Supreme Court ruling restricted religious freedom to an unacceptable extent.[27]

According to political scientist Walter Murphy, "A permanent feature of our constitutional landscape is the ongoing tug and pull between elected government and the courts."[28] Certainly, over the last few decades, the Supreme Court has been in conflict with the other two branches of government. Congress at various times has passed laws that, among other things, made it illegal to burn the American flag and attempted to curb pornography on the Internet. In each instance, the Supreme Court ruled that those laws were unconstitutional. The Court also invalidated the RFRA.

Whenever Congress does not like what the judiciary does, it threatens to censure the judiciary for its activism. One member of the Senate Judiciary

---

26. *Brown v. Board of Education*, 349 U.S. 294 (1955) —the second *Brown* decision.
27. *Employment Division, Department of Human Resources of Oregon v. Smith*, 494 U.S. 872 (1990).
28. As quoted in Neal Devins, "The Last Word Debate: How Social and Political Forces Shape Constitutional Values," *American Bar Association Journal*, October 1997, p. 48.

Committee, John Cornyn (R-TX), claimed that judges are making "political decisions yet are unaccountable to the public." He went on to say that violence against judges in the courtroom can be explained by the public's distress at such activism.

The states can also negate or alter the effects of Supreme Court rulings, when such decisions allow it. In *Kelo v. City of New London,* the Supreme Court allowed a city to take private property for redevelopment by private businesses. Since that case was decided, a majority of states have passed legislation limiting or prohibiting such actions.[29]

Public Opinion

Public opinion plays a significant role in shaping government policy, and the judiciary is not exempt from this rule. Persons affected by a Supreme Court decision that is noticeably at odds with their views may simply ignore it. Officially sponsored prayers were banned in public schools in 1962, yet it was widely known that the ban was (and still is) ignored in many southern districts. Unless someone complains about the prayers and initiates a lawsuit, the courts can do nothing. The public can also pressure state and local government officials to refuse to enforce a certain decision. Judicial implementation requires the cooperation of government officials at all levels, and public opinion in various regions of the country will influence whether such cooperation is forthcoming.

The courts necessarily are influenced by public opinion to some extent. After all, judges are not isolated in our society; their attitudes are influenced by social trends, just as the attitudes and beliefs of all persons are. Courts generally tend to avoid issuing decisions that they know will be noticeably at odds with public opinion.[30] This is because the judiciary prefers to avoid creating divisiveness among the public. Also, a court—particularly the Supreme Court—may lose stature if it decides a case in a way that markedly diverges from public opinion. In 2002, the Supreme Court ruled that the execution of developmentally disabled criminals violates the Eighth Amendment's ban on cruel and unusual punishment. In its ruling, the Court indicated that the standards of what constitutes cruel and unusual punishment are influenced by public opinion and that there is "powerful evidence that today our society views mentally retarded offenders as categorically less culpable than the average criminal."[31]

Judicial Traditions and Doctrines

Supreme Court justices (and other federal judges) typically exercise self-restraint in fashioning decisions. In part, this restraint stems from their knowledge that the other two branches of government and the public can exercise checks on the judiciary. To a large extent, however, this restraint is mandated by various judicially-established traditions and doctrines. When reviewing a case, the Supreme Court typically narrows its focus to just one issue or one aspect of an issue involved in the case. The Court rarely makes broad, sweeping decisions on issues. The doctrine of *stare decisis* acts as a restraint because it obligates the courts, including the Supreme Court, to follow established precedents when deciding cases. Only rarely will courts overrule a precedent.

29. 545 U.S. 469 (2005).
30. One striking counterexample is the *Kelo v. City of New London* decision mentioned earlier.
31. *Atkins v. Virginia*, 536 U.S. 304 (2002).

Hypothetical and Political Questions.

Other judicial doctrines and practices also act as restraints. The courts will hear only what are called justiciable disputes, which arise out of actual cases—a court will not hear a case that involves a hypothetical issue. Additionally, if a political question is involved, the Supreme Court often will exercise judicial restraint and refuse to rule on the matter. A **political question** is one that the Supreme Court declares should be decided by the elected branches of government—the executive branch, the legislative branch, or those two branches acting together. The Supreme Court has refused to rule on the controversy regarding the rights of gays and lesbians in the military, preferring instead to defer to the executive branch's decisions on the matter. Generally, fewer questions are deemed political questions by the Supreme Court today than in the past.

Political Question
An issue that a court believes should be decided by the executive or legislative branch.

The Impact of the Lower Courts.

Higher courts can reverse the decisions of lower courts and lower courts can act as a check on higher courts. Lower courts can—and have—ignored Supreme Court decisions. Usually, this is done indirectly. A lower court might conclude, for example, that the precedent set by the Supreme Court does not apply to the exact circumstances in the case before the court; or the lower court may decide that the Supreme Court's decision was ambiguous with respect to the issue before the lower court. The fact that the Supreme Court rarely makes broad and clear-cut statements on any issue makes it easier for the lower courts to interpret the Supreme Court's decisions in a different way.

What Would You Do?

Stopping a Judicial Nomination

There are 874 federal judicial appointments currently authorized under Article III of the Constitution, plus several dozen special court appointments in Tax Court and the Court of Patent Appeals. In the last decade or so, judicial appointments have often been blocked or delayed by the filibuster in the Senate but, since 2013, the Senate has changed its rules and only a majority vote is needed except for Supreme Court appointments. However, Senators can block a nomination for a judge in their state by failing to return the "blue slip" sent to them as a courtesy by the Judiciary Committee.

Why Should You Care?

For most of the nation's history, all federal judges were white males and Protestants. Beginning in the twentieth century, Jewish judges were appointed and, at last, African American and female federal judges began to appear on the bench. Having diversity on the federal bench means that a wider variety of perspectives will be brought to bear on the cases that come before it. As the population of the United States grows increasingly diverse, federal judges should represent that diversity.

There is no requirement that each president should be able to pick a certain minimum number of judges, nor is there a maximum number of nominations for a president. Traditionally, few judgeships are filled in the last year of a president's second term to allow the new president some impact on the federal bench after he or she is inaugurated. Since the end of World War II, control of the presidency has alternated between the parties fairly frequently. Thus, both Republican and Democratic presidents have had the opportunity to appoint federal judges. Having Republican and Democratic appointees as federal district, appellate and Supreme Court judges allows for all points of view to be heard.

What Would You Do?

As a Republican Senator from a Midwestern state, you receive a "blue slip" from the Judiciary Committee with the name of the president's nominee for the Federal District Court in your state. The nominee is a well-known federal prosecutor who graduated top of his class and is a strict-crime fighter who also happens to be gay. Would you return the blue slip and let his nomination be approved?

What You *Can* Do

First, learn about the federal courts that impact your life: What is the nearest district court and who are the judges? In which appellate court circuit do you live? Follow the court cases that come before the district court. These cases will be both civil and criminal, involving patent infringement, bank fraud, corruption, drug dealing, and theft. There will also be civil cases involving civil rights violations and hate crimes. You can watch the court proceedings at federal district court by following the directions on the website of the local district court. You must contact the clerk of courts to find out when cases are being heard. The website of the Federal Judiciary Center contains information about the processes you will see in federal court.

Pay attention to the judicial nominations of the president and to the actions of your senators. The Judiciary Committee of the Senate maintains a record of upcoming nominations.

Contact your senator's office to express your concerns or your support for the nominee. Many nominees have been local judges or prosecutors and some are faculty from law schools and are prominent in the local community.

Consider getting an internship in the federal court system or with a law firm. If you are interested in a career in any aspect of law, experience as an intern or clerk will help you decide if this is the right career path for you. The Department of Justice has a very useful website listing volunteer intern opportunities for all U.S. Attorney's offices. While some of these openings are tailored for law students, others are for undergraduates.

To learn more about the federal judicial system and the nomination process for the courts, the websites below will be helpful:

- Federal Judiciary Center: www.uscourts.gov/educational-resources/federal-court-resources/visiting-courthouse.aspx
- Department of Justice Volunteer Opportunities: www.justice.gov/careers/legal/volunteer-opp-usao-summer.html
- Senate Judiciary Committee: www.judiciary.senate.gov

Purestock/Getty Images

Key Terms

affirm 502	**federal question** 494	**litigate** 499	**senatorial courtesy** 503
appellate court 496	**general jurisdiction** 494	**majority opinion** 502	*stare decisis* 489
broad construction 509	**judicial activism** 508	**opinion** 502	**strict construction** 509
case law 490	**judicial implementation** 511	**oral arguments** 502	**trial court** 494
class-action suit 500	**judicial restraint** 508	**political question** 514	**unanimous opinion** 502
common law 489	**judicial review** 489	**precedent** 489	**writ of** *certiorari* 501
concurring opinion 502	**jurisdiction** 492	**remand** 502	
dissenting opinion 502	**limited jurisdiction** 495	**reverse** 502	
diversity of citizenship 494		**rule of four** 502	

Chapter Summary

■ **LO14.1:** American law is rooted in the common-law tradition, which is part of our heritage from England. Fundamental sources of American law include the U.S. Constitution and state constitutions, statutes enacted by legislative bodies, regulations issued by administrative agencies, and case law. The common-law doctrine of *stare decisis* ("to stand on decided cases") obligates judges to follow precedents established previously by

their own courts or by higher courts that have authority over them. Precedents established by the United States Supreme Court, the highest court in the land, are binding on all lower courts

■ **LO14.2:** The most important policymaking tool of the federal courts is the power of judicial review which allows the Courts to declare unconstitutional any law or regulation in conflict with the Constitution. This power was not mentioned specifically in the Constitution, but John Marshall claimed the power for the Court in his 1803 decision in *Marbury v. Madison*.

■ **LO14.3:** Article III, Section 1, of the U.S. Constitution limits the jurisdiction of the federal courts to cases involving (1) a federal question, which is a question based, at least in part, on the U.S. Constitution, a treaty, or a federal law; or (2) diversity of citizenship, which arises when parties to a lawsuit are from different states or when the lawsuit involves a foreign citizen or government. The federal court system is a three-tiered model consisting of (1) U.S. district (trial) courts and various lower courts of limited jurisdiction, (2) U.S. courts of appeals, and (3) the United States Supreme Court. Cases may be appealed from the district courts to the appellate courts. In most cases, the decisions of the federal appellate courts are final because the Supreme Court hears relatively few cases.

■ **LO14.3:** The Supreme Court's decision to review a case is influenced by many factors, including the significance of the issues involved and whether the solicitor general is pressing the Court to take the case. After a case is accepted, the justices undertake research (with the help of their law clerks) on the issues involved in the case, hear oral arguments from the parties, meet in conference to discuss and vote on the issue, and announce the opinion, which is then released for publication.

■ **LO14.4:** Federal judges are nominated by the president and confirmed by the Senate. Once appointed, they hold office for life, barring gross misconduct. The nomination and confirmation process, particularly for Supreme Court justices, is often extremely politicized. Democrats and Republicans alike realize that justices may occupy seats on the Court for decades and naturally want to have persons appointed who share their basic views.

■ **LO14.5:** Judges who take an active role in checking the activities of the other branches of government sometimes are characterized as "activist" judges, and judges who defer to the other branches' decisions sometimes are regarded as "restraintist" judges. The Warren Court of the 1950s and 1960s was activist in a liberal direction, whereas the Rehnquist Court became increasingly activist in a conservative direction. One of the criticisms of the Court is that it should not "make law" but should defer to the legislative branch in deciding policy issues. However, in the interpretation of previously written laws, it has often fallen to the Supreme Court to make a final determination.

■ **LO14.6:** Checks on the powers of the federal courts include executive checks, legislative checks, public opinion, and judicial traditions and doctrines.

Selected Print, Media, and Online Resources

PRINT RESOURCES

Coyle, Marcia. *The Roberts Court: The Struggle for the Constitution*. New York: Simon and Schuster, 2013. In the view of this constitutional scholar, the court remains divided between liberals and conservatives. She looks at the justices and their differences in four important cases: the Affordable Care Act, money in elections, gun control, and racial integration of the schools.

Peppers, Todd C., and Artemus Ward, editors. *In Chambers: Stories of Supreme Court Law Clerks and Their Justices*. Charlottesville, VA: University of Virginia Press, 2013. Young attorneys who have completed their positions as "clerks" to the Supreme Court justices write about their experiences and about the everyday life of the court behind the scenes.

Roosevelt, Kermit. *The Myth of Judicial Activism: Making Sense of Supreme Court Decisions*. New Haven, CT: Yale University Press, 2008. Roosevelt, a University of Pennsylvania professor, defends the Court against charges of undue judicial activism. Roosevelt finds the Court's decisions to be reasonable, although he disagrees with some of them.

Stevens, John Paul. *Five Chiefs: A Supreme Court Memoir*. Boston: Little, Brown and Co., 2011. Retired Justice Stevens comments on his colleagues, the architecture of the building, and legal argument in this well-written and "gentle" memoir of his days on the high court.

Teles, Stephen. *The Rise of the Conservative Legal Movement: The Battle for Control of the Law*. Princeton, NJ: Princeton University Press, 2012. Teles provides an account of how conservative foundations and institutions fostered ways to support the education and later networking of the conservative legal scholars who have challenged liberal policies before the court.

MEDIA RESOURCES

Amistad—A 1997 movie, starring Anthony Hopkins, about a slave ship mutiny in 1839. Much of the story revolves around the prosecution, ending at the Supreme Court, of the slave who led the revolt.

Gideon's Trumpet—A 1980 film, starring Henry Fonda as the small-time criminal James Earl Gideon, which elucidates the path a case takes to the Supreme Court and the importance of cases decided there.

Marbury v. Madison—A 1987 video on the famous 1803 case that established the principle of judicial review. This is the first in a four-part series, *Equal Justice Under Law: Landmark Cases in Supreme Court History*, produced by the Judicial Conference of the United States.

The Supreme Court—A four-part PBS series that won a 2008 Parents' Choice Gold Award. The series follows the history of the Supreme Court from the first chief justice, John Marshall, to the earliest days of the Roberts Court. Some of the many topics are the Court's dismal performance in the Civil War era, its conflicts with President Franklin D. Roosevelt, its role in banning the segregation of African Americans, and the abortion controversy.

truTV—This TV channel covers high-profile trials, including those of O. J. Simpson, the Unabomber, British nanny Louise Woodward, and Timothy McVeigh. (You can learn below how to access truTV from your area via its website.)

ONLINE RESOURCES

FindLaw—searchable database of Supreme Court decisions since 1970: www.findlaw.com

Legal Information Institute at Cornell University Law School—offers an easily searchable index to Supreme Court opinions, including some important historic decisions: www.law.cornell.edu/supct/index.html

The Oyez Project—multimedia archive devoted to the Supreme Court of the United States and its work: www.oyez.org/oyez/frontpage

Supreme Court of the United States—Supreme Court decisions are available here within hours of their release: supremecourtus.gov

truTV.com—website dedicated to the television station (formerly Court TV) that focuses on real-life stories told from a first-person perspective, offering the program lineup, which features six hours of daily trial coverage; a Crime Library, which includes case histories as well as selected documents filed with the court and court transcripts; and a link to CNN Crime for trial news: www.trutv.com

United States Courts—home page of the federal courts and a good starting point for learning about the federal court system in general; follow the path of a case as it moves through the federal court system: www.uscourts.gov

Master the concept of Federalism with MindTap™ for American Government

REVIEW MindTap™ **for American Government**
Access Key Term Flashcards for Chapter 14.

STAY CURRENT MindTap™ **for American Government**
Access the KnowNow blog and customized RSS for updates on current events.

TEST YOURSELF MindTap™ **for American Government**
Take the Wrap It Up Quiz for Chapter 14.

STAY FOCUSED MindTap™ **for American Government**
Complete the Focus Activities for The Judiciary.

Appendix A

The Declaration of Independence

IN CONGRESS, JULY 4, 1776

A Declaration by the Representatives of the United States of America, in General Congress assembled. When in the Course of human Events, it becomes necessary for one People to dissolve the Political Bands which have connected them with another, and to assume among the Powers of the Earth, the separate and equal Station to which the Laws of Nature and of Nature's God entitle them, a decent Respect to the Opinions of Mankind requires that they should declare the causes which impel them to the Separation.

We hold these Truths to be self-evident, that all Men are created equal, that they are endowed by their Creator with certain unalienable Rights, that among these are Life, Liberty, and the Pursuit of Happiness—That to secure these Rights, Governments are instituted among Men, deriving their just Powers from the Consent of the Governed, that whenever any Form of Government becomes destructive of these Ends, it is the Right of the People to alter or to abolish it, and to institute new Government, laying its Foundation on such Principles, and organizing its Powers in such Forms, as to them shall seem most likely to effect their Safety and Happiness. Prudence, indeed, will dictate that Governments long established should not be changed for light and transient Causes; and accordingly all Experience hath shewn, that Mankind are more disposed to suffer, while Evils are sufferable, than to right themselves by abolishing the Forms to which they are accustomed. But when a long Train of Abuses and Usurpations, pursuing invariably the same Object, evinces a Design to reduce them under absolute Despotism, it is their Right, it is their Duty, to throw off such Government, and to provide new Guards for their future Security. Such has been the patient Sufferance of these Colonies; and such is now the Necessity which constrains them to alter their former Systems of Government. The History of the present King of Great-Britain is a History of repeated Injuries and Usurpations, all having in direct Object the Establishment of an absolute Tyranny over these States. To prove this, let Facts be submitted to a candid World.

He has refused his Assent to Laws, the most wholesome and necessary for the public Good.

He has forbidden his Governors to pass Laws of immediate and pressing Importance, unless suspended in their Operation till his Assent should be obtained; and when so suspended, he has utterly neglected to attend to them.

He has refused to pass other Laws for the Accommodation of large Districts of People, unless those People would relinquish the Right of Representation in the Legislature, a Right inestimable to them, and formidable to Tyrants only.

He has called together Legislative Bodies at Places unusual, uncomfortable, and distant from the Depository of their Public Records, for the sole Purpose of fatiguing them into Compliance with his Measures.

He has dissolved Representative Houses repeatedly, for opposing with manly Firmness his Invasions on the Rights of the People.

He has refused for a long Time, after such Dissolutions, to cause others to be elected; whereby the Legislative Powers, incapable of Annihilation, have returned to the People at large for their exercise; the State remaining in the mean time exposed to all the Dangers of Invasion from without, and Convulsions within.

He has endeavoured to prevent the Population of these States; for that Purpose obstructing the Laws for Naturalization of Foreigners; refusing to pass others to encourage their Migrations hither, and raising the Conditions of new Appropriations of Lands.

He has obstructed the Administration of Justice, by refusing his Assent to Laws for establishing Judiciary Powers.

He has made Judges dependent on his Will alone, for the Tenure of their offices, and the Amount and payment of their Salaries.

He has erected a Multitude of new Offices, and sent hither Swarms of Officers to harass our People, and eat out their Substance.

He has kept among us, in Times of Peace, Standing Armies, without the consent of our Legislatures.

He has affected to render the Military independent of, and superior to the Civil Power.

He has combined with others to subject us to a Jurisdiction foreign to our Constitution, and unacknowledged by our Laws; giving his Assent to their Acts of pretended Legislation:

For quartering large Bodies of Armed Troops among us:

For protecting them, by a mock Trial, from Punishment for any Murders which they should commit on the Inhabitants of these States:

For cutting off our Trade with all Parts of the World:

For imposing Taxes on us without our Consent:

For depriving us, in many cases, of the Benefits of Trial by Jury:

For transporting us beyond Seas to be tried for pretended Offences:

For abolishing the free System of English Laws in a neighbouring Province, establishing therein an arbitrary Government, and enlarging its Boundaries, so as to render it at once an Example and fit Instrument for introducing the same absolute Rule into these Colonies:

For taking away our Charters, abolishing our most valuable Laws, and altering fundamentally the Forms of our Governments:

For suspending our own Legislatures, and declaring themselves invested with Power to legislate for us in all Cases whatsoever.

He has abdicated Government here, by declaring us out of his Protection and waging War against us.

He has plundered our Seas, ravaged our Coasts, burnt our towns, and destroyed the Lives of our People.

He is, at this Time, transporting large Armies of foreign Mercenaries to compleat the works of Death, Desolation, and Tyranny, already begun with circumstances of Cruelty and Perfidy, scarcely paralleled in the most barbarous Ages, and totally unworthy the Head of a civilized Nation.

He has constrained our fellow Citizens taken Captive on the high Seas to bear Arms against their Country, to become the Executioners of their Friends and Brethren, or to fall themselves by their Hands.

He has excited domestic Insurrections amongst us, and has endeavoured to bring on the Inhabitants of our Frontiers, the merciless Indian Savages, whose known Rule of Warfare, is an undistinguished Destruction, of all Ages, Sexes and Conditions.

In every state of these Oppressions we have Petitioned for Redress in the most humble Terms: Our repeated Petitions have been answered only by repeated Injury. A Prince, whose Character is thus marked by every act which may define a Tyrant, is unfit to be the Ruler of a free People.

Nor have we been wanting in Attentions to our British Brethren. We have warned them from Time to Time of Attempts by their Legislature to extend an unwarrantable Jurisdiction over us.

We have reminded them of the Circumstances of our Emigration and Settlement here. We have appealed to their native Justice and Magnanimity, and we have conjured them by the Ties of our common Kindred to disavow these Usurpations, which, would inevitably interrupt our Connections and Correspondence. They too have been deaf to the Voice of Justice and of Consanguinity. We must, therefore, acquiesce in the Necessity, which denounces our Separation, and hold them, as we hold the rest of Mankind, Enemies in War, in Peace, Friends.

We, therefore, the Representatives of the UNITED STATES OF AMERICA, in General Congress Assembled, appealing to the Supreme Judge of the World for the Rectitude of our Intentions, do, in the Name, and by the Authority of the good People of these Colonies, solemnly Publish and Declare, That these United Colonies are, and of Right ought to be, Free and Independent States; that they are absolved from all Allegiance to the British Crown, and that all political Connection between them and the State of Great-Britain, is and ought to be totally dissolved; and that as Free and Independent States, they have full Power to levy War, conclude Peace, contract Alliances, establish Commerce, and to do all other Acts and Things which Independent States may of right do. And for the support of this declaration, with a firm Reliance on the Protection of divine Providence, we mutually pledge to each other our lives, our Fortunes, and our sacred Honor.

The Constitution of the United States*

THE PREAMBLE

We the People of the United States, in Order to form a more perfect Union, establish Justice, insure domestic Tranquility, provide for the common defence, promote the general Welfare, and secure the Blessings of Liberty to ourselves and our Posterity, do ordain and establish this *Constitution* for the United States of America.

The Preamble declares that "We the People" are the authority for the Constitution (unlike the Articles of Confederation, which derived their authority from the states). The Preamble also sets out the purposes of the Constitution.

ARTICLE I. *(Legislative Branch)*

The first part of the Constitution, Article I, deals with the organization and powers of the lawmaking branch of the national government, the Congress.

Section 1. *Legislative Powers*

All legislative Powers herein granted shall be vested in a Congress of the United States, which shall consist of a Senate and House of Representatives.

Section 2. *House of Representatives*

Clause 1: Composition and Election of Members. The House of Representatives shall be composed of Members chosen every second Year by the People of the several States, and the Electors in each State shall have the Qualifications requisite for Electors of the most numerous Branch of the State Legislature.

Each state has the power to decide who may vote for members of Congress. Within each state, those who may vote for state legislators may also vote for members of the House of Representatives (and, under the Seventeenth Amendment, for U.S. senators). When the Constitution was written, nearly all states limited voting rights to white male property owners or taxpayers at least 21 years old. Subsequent amendments granted voting power to African American men, all women, and everyone at least 18 years old.

Clause 2: Qualifications. No Person shall be a Representative who shall not have attained to the Age of twenty five Years, and been seven Years a Citizen of the United States, and who shall not, when elected, be an Inhabitant of that State in which he shall be chosen.

Each member of the House must be at least 25 years old, a citizen of the United States for at least seven years, and a resident of the state in which she or he is elected.

Clause 3: Apportionment of Representatives and Direct Taxes. Representatives [and direct Taxes][1] shall be apportioned among the several States which may be included within this Union, according to their respective Numbers [which shall be determined by adding to the whole Number of free Persons, including those bound to Service for a Term of Years, and excluding Indians not taxed, three fifths of all other Persons].[2] The actual Enumeration shall be made within three Years after the first Meeting of the Congress of the United States, and within every subsequent Term of ten Years, in such Manner as they shall by Law direct. The Number of Representatives shall not exceed one for every thirty Thousand, but each State shall have at Least one Representative; and until such enumeration shall be made, the State of New Hampshire shall be entitled to chuse three, Massachusetts eight, Rhode Island and Providence Plantations one, Connecticut five, New York six, New Jersey four, Pennsylvania eight, Delaware one, Maryland six, Virginia ten, North Carolina five, South Carolina five, and Georgia three.

A state's representation in the House is based on the size of its population. Population is counted in each decade's census, after which Congress reapportions House seats. Since early in the 20th century, the number of seats has been limited to 435.

Clause 4: Vacancies. When vacancies happen in the Representation from any State, the Executive Authority thereof shall issue Writs of Election to fill such Vacancies.

The "Executive Authority" is the state's governor. When a vacancy occurs in the House, the governor calls a special election to fill it.

Clause 5: Officers and Impeachment. The House of Representatives shall chuse their Speaker and other Officers; and shall have the sole Power of Impeachment.

The power to impeach is the power to accuse. In this case, it is the power to accuse members of the executive or judicial branch of wrongdoing or abuse of power. Once a bill of impeachment is issued, the Senate holds the trial.

Section 3. *The Senate*

Clause 1: Term and Number of Members. The Senate of the United States shall be composed of two Senators from each State [chosen by the Legislature thereof],[3] for six Years; and each Senator shall have one Vote.

Every state has two senators, each of whom serves for six years and has one vote in the upper chamber. Since the Seventeenth Amendment in 1913, all senators have been elected directly by voters of the state during the regular election.

---

* The spelling, capitalization, and punctuation of the original have been retained here. Brackets indicate passages that have been altered by amendments to the Constitution. We have added article titles (in parentheses), section titles, and clause designations. We have also inserted annotations in blue italic type.
1. Modified by the Sixteenth Amendment.
2. Modified by the Fourteenth Amendment.
3. Repealed by the Seventeenth Amendment.

Clause 2: Classification of Senators. Immediately after they shall be assembled in Consequence of the first Election, they shall be divided as equally as may be into three Classes. The Seats of the Senators of the first Class shall be vacated at the Expiration of the second Year, of the second Class at the Expiration of the fourth Year, and of the third Class at the Expiration of the sixth Year, so that one third may be chosen every second Year; [and if Vacancies happen by Resignation, or otherwise, during the Recess of the Legislature of any State, the Executive thereof may make temporary Appointments until the next Meeting of the Legislature, which shall then fill such Vacancies].[4]

One-third of the Senate's seats are open to election every two years (in contrast, all members of the House are elected simultaneously).

Clause 3: Qualifications. No Person shall be a Senator who shall not have attained to the Age of thirty Years, and been nine Years a Citizen of the United States, and who shall not, when elected, be an Inhabitant of that State for which he shall be chosen.

Every senator must be at least 30 years old, a citizen of the United States for a minimum of nine years, and a resident of the state in which he or she is elected.

Clause 4: The Role of the Vice President. The Vice President of the United States shall be President of the Senate, but shall have no Vote, unless they be equally divided.

The vice president presides over meetings of the Senate but cannot vote unless there is a tie. The Constitution gives no other official duties to the vice president.

Clause 5: Other Officers. The Senate shall chuse their other Officers, and also a President pro tempore, in the Absence of the Vice President, or when he shall exercise the Office of President of the United States.

The Senate votes for one of its members to preside when the vice president is absent. This person is usually called the president pro tempore because of the temporary nature of the position.

Clause 6: Impeachment Trials. The Senate shall have the sole Power to try all Impeachments. When sitting for that Purpose, they shall be on Oath or Affirmation. When the President of the United States is tried, the Chief Justice shall preside: And no Person shall be convicted without the Concurrence of two thirds of the Members present.

The Senate conducts trials of officials that the House impeaches. The Senate sits as a jury, with the vice president presiding if the president is not on trial.

Clause 7: Penalties for Conviction. Judgment in Cases of Impeachment shall not extend further than to removal from Office, and disqualification to hold and enjoy any Office of honor, Trust, or Profit under the United States: but the Party convicted shall nevertheless be liable and subject to Indictment, Trial, Judgment, and Punishment, according to Law.

On conviction of impeachment charges, the Senate can only force an official to leave office and prevent him or her from holding another office in the federal government. The individual, however, can still be tried in a regular court.

Section 4. *Congressional Elections: Times, Manner, and Places*

Clause 1: Elections. The Times, Places and Manner of holding Elections for Senators and Representatives, shall be prescribed in each State by the Legislature thereof; but the Congress may at any time by Law make or alter such Regulations, except as to the Places of chusing Senators.

Congress set the Tuesday after the first Monday in November in even-numbered years as the date for congressional elections. In states with more than one seat in the House, Congress requires that representatives be elected from districts within each state. Under the Seventeenth Amendment, senators are elected at the same places as other officials.

Clause 2: Sessions of Congress. [The Congress shall assemble at least once in every Year, and such Meeting shall be on the first Monday in December, unless they shall by Law appoint a different Day.][5]

Congress has to meet every year at least once. The regular session now begins at noon on January 3 of each year, subsequent to the Twentieth Amendment, unless Congress passes a law to fix a different date. Congress stays in session until its members vote to adjourn. Additionally, the president may call a special session.

Section 5. *Powers and Duties of the Houses*

Clause 1: Admitting Members and Quorum. Each House shall be the Judge of the Elections, Returns, and Qualifications of its own Members, and a Majority of each shall constitute a Quorum to do Business; but a smaller Number may adjourn from day to day, and may be authorized to compel the Attendance of absent Members, in such Manner, and under such Penalties as each House may provide.

Each chamber may exclude or refuse to seat a member-elect.

The quorum rule requires that 218 members of the House and 51 members of the Senate be present to conduct business. This rule normally is not enforced in the handling of routine matters.

Clause 2: Rules and Discipline of Members. Each House may determine the Rules of its Proceedings, punish its Members for disorderly Behaviour, and, with the Concurrence of two thirds, expel a Member.

The House and the Senate may adopt their own rules to guide their proceedings. Each may also discipline its members for conduct that is deemed unacceptable. No member may be expelled without a two-thirds majority vote in favor of expulsion.

Clause 3: Keeping a Record. Each House shall keep a Journal of its Proceedings, and from time to time publish the same, excepting such Parts as may in their Judgment require Secrecy; and the Yeas and Nays of the Members of either House on any question shall, at the Desire of one fifth of those Present, be entered on the Journal.

The journals of the two chambers are published at the end of each session of Congress.

---

4. Modified by the Seventeenth Amendment.
5. Changed by the Twentieth Amendment.

Clause 4: Adjournment. Neither House, during the Session of Congress, shall, without the Consent of the other, adjourn for more than three days, nor to any other Place than that in which the two Houses shall be sitting.

Congress has the power to determine when and where to meet, provided, however, that both chambers meet in the same city. Neither chamber may recess for more than three days without the consent of the other.

Section 6. *Rights of Members*

Clause 1: Compensation and Privileges. The Senators and Representatives shall receive a Compensation for their services, to be ascertained by Law, and paid out of the Treasury of the United States. They shall in all Cases, except Treason, Felony and Breach of the Peace, be privileged from Arrest during their Attendance at the Session of their respective Houses, and in going to and returning from the same; and for any Speech or Debate in either House, they shall not be questioned in any other Place.

Congressional salaries are to be paid by the U.S. Treasury rather than by the members' respective states. The original salaries were $6 per day; in 1857 they were $3,000 per year. Both representatives and senators were paid $165,200 in 2006.

Treason is defined in Article III, Section 3. A felony is any serious crime. A breach of the peace is any indictable offense less than treason or a felony. Members cannot be arrested for things they say during speeches and debates in Congress. This immunity applies to the Capitol Building itself and not to their private lives.

Clause 2: Restrictions. No Senator or Representative shall, during the Time for which he was elected, be appointed to any civil Office under the Authority of the United States, which shall have been created, or the Emoluments whereof shall have been encreased during such time; and no Person holding any Office under the United States, shall be a Member of either House during his Continuance in Office.

During the term for which a member was elected, he or she cannot concurrently accept another federal government position.

Section 7. *Legislative Powers: Bills and Resolutions*

Clause 1: Revenue Bills. All Bills for raising Revenue shall originate in the House of Representatives; but the Senate may propose or concur with Amendments as on other Bills.

All tax and appropriation bills for raising money have to originate in the House of Representatives. The Senate, though, often amends such bills and may even substitute an entirely different bill.

Clause 2: The Presidential Veto. Every Bill which shall have passed the House of Representatives and the Senate, shall, before it becomes a Law, be presented to the President of the United States; If he approve he shall sign it, but if not he shall return it, with his Objections to the House in which it shall have originated, who shall enter the Objections at large on their Journal, and proceed to reconsider it. If after such Reconsideration two thirds of that House shall agree to pass the Bill, it shall be sent together with the Objections, to the other House, by which it shall likewise be reconsidered, and if approved by two thirds of that House, it shall become a Law. But in all such Cases the Votes of both Houses shall be determined by Yeas and Nays, and the Names of the Persons voting for and against the Bill shall be entered on the Journal of each House respectively. If any Bill shall not be returned by the President within 10 Days (Sundays excepted) after it shall have been presented to him, the Same shall be a Law, in like Manner as if he had signed it, unless the Congress by their Adjournment prevent its Return in which Case it shall not be a Law.

When Congress sends the president a bill, he or she can sign it (in which case it becomes law) or send it back to the chamber in which it originated. If it is sent back, a two-thirds majority of each chamber must pass it again for it to become law. If the president neither signs it nor sends it back within 10 days, it becomes law anyway, unless Congress adjourns in the meantime.

Clause 3: Actions on Other Matters. Every Order, Resolution, or Vote to which the Concurrence of the Senate and House of Representatives may be necessary (except on a question of Adjournment) shall be presented to the President of the United States; and before the Same shall take Effect, shall be approved by him, or being disapproved by him, shall be repassed by two thirds of the Senate and House of Representatives, according to the Rules and Limitations prescribed in the Case of a Bill.

The president must have the opportunity to either sign or veto everything that Congress passes, except votes to adjourn and resolutions not having the force of law.

Section 8. *The Powers of Congress*

Clause 1: Taxing. The Congress shall have Power to lay and collect Taxes, Duties, Imposts and Excises, to pay the Debts and provide for the common Defence and general Welfare of the United States; but all Duties, Imposts and Excises shall be uniform throughout the United States;

Duties are taxes on imports and exports. Impost is a generic term for tax. Excises are taxes on the manufacture, sale, or use of goods.

Clause 2: Borrowing. To borrow Money on the credit of the United States;

Congress has the power to borrow money, which is normally carried out through the sale of U.S. treasury bonds on which interest is paid. Note that the Constitution places no limit on the amount of government borrowing.

Clause 3: Regulation of Commerce. To regulate Commerce with foreign Nations, and among the several States, and with the Indian Tribes;

This is the commerce clause, which gives to Congress the power to regulate interstate and foreign trade. Much of the activity of Congress is based on this clause.

Clause 4: Naturalization and Bankruptcy. To establish an uniform Rule of Naturalization, and uniform Laws on the subject of Bankruptcies throughout the United States;

Only Congress may determine how aliens can become citizens of the United States. Congress may make laws with respect to bankruptcy.

Clause 5: Money and Standards. To coin Money, regulate the Value thereof, and of foreign Coin, and fix the Standard of Weights and Measures;

Congress mints coins and prints and circulates paper money. Congress can establish uniform measures of time, distance, weight, and so on. In 1838, Congress adopted the English system of weights and measurements as our national standard.

Clause 6: Punishing Counterfeiters. To provide for the Punishment of counterfeiting the Securities and current Coin of the United States;

Congress has the power to punish those who copy American money and pass it off as real. Currently, the fine is up to $5,000 and/or imprisonment for up to 15 years.

Clause 7: Roads and Post Offices. To establish Post Offices and post Roads;

Post roads include all routes over which mail is carried—highways, railways, waterways, and airways.

Clause 8: Patents and Copyrights. To promote the Progress of Science and useful Arts, by securing for limited Times to Authors and Inventors the exclusive Right to their respective Writings and Discoveries;

Authors' and composers' works are protected by copyrights established by copyright law, which currently is the Copyright Act of 1976, as amended. Copyrights are valid for the life of the author or composer plus 70 years. Inventors' works are protected by patents, which vary in length of protection from 14 to 20 years. A patent gives a person the exclusive right to control the manufacture or sale of her or his invention.

Clause 9: Lower Courts. To constitute Tribunals inferior to the supreme Court;

Congress has the authority to set up all federal courts, except the Supreme Court, and to decide what cases those courts will hear.

Clause 10: Punishment for Piracy. To define and punish Piracies and Felonies committed on the high Seas, and Offences against the Law of Nations;

Congress has the authority to prohibit the commission of certain acts outside U.S. territory and to punish certain violations of international law.

Clause 11: Declaration of War. To declare War, grant Letters of Marque and Reprisal, and make Rules concerning Captures on Land and Water;

Only Congress can declare war, although the president, as commander in chief, can make war without Congress's formal declaration. Letters of marque and reprisal authorized private parties to capture and destroy enemy ships in wartime. Since the middle of the 19th century, international law has prohibited letters of marque and reprisal, and the United States has honored the ban.

Clause 12: The Army. To raise and support Armies, but no Appropriation of Money to that Use shall be for a longer Term than two Years;

Congress has the power to create an army; the money used to pay for it must be appropriated for no more than two-year

intervals. This latter restriction gives ultimate control of the army to civilians.

Clause 13: Creation of a Navy. To provide and maintain a Navy;

This clause allows for the maintenance of a navy. In 1947, Congress created the U.S. Air Force.

Clause 14: Regulation of the Armed Forces. To make Rules for the Government and Regulation of the land and naval Forces;

Congress sets the rules for the military mainly by way of the Uniform Code of Military Justice, which was enacted in 1950 by Congress.

Clause 15: The Militia. To provide for calling forth the Militia to execute the Laws of the Union, suppress Insurrections and repel Invasions;

The militia is known today as the National Guard. Both Congress and the president have the authority to call the National Guard into federal service.

Clause 16: How the Militia Is Organized. To provide for organizing, arming, and disciplining the Militia, and for governing such Part of them as may be employed in the Service of the United States, reserving to the States respectively, the Appointment of the Officers, and the Authority of training the Militia according to the discipline prescribed by Congress;

This clause gives Congress the power to "federalize" state militia (National Guard). When called into such service, the National Guard is subject to the same rules that Congress has set forth for the regular armed services.

Clause 17: Creation of the District of Columbia. To exercise exclusive Legislation in all Cases whatsoever, over such District (not exceeding ten Miles square) as may, by Cession of particular States, and the Acceptance of Congress, become the Seat of the Government of the United States, and to exercise like Authority over all Places purchased by the Consent of the Legislature of the State in which the Same shall be, for the Erection of Forts, Magazines, Arsenals, dock-Yards, and other needful Buildings;—And

Congress established the District of Columbia as the national capital in 1791. Virginia and Maryland had granted land for the District, but Virginia's grant was returned because it was believed it would not be needed. Today, the District covers 69 square miles.

Clause 18: The Elastic Clause. To make all Laws which shall be necessary and proper for carrying into Execution the foregoing Powers, and all other Powers vested by this Constitution in the Government of the United States, or in any Department or Officer thereof.

This clause—the necessary and proper clause, or the elastic clause—grants no specific powers, and thus it can be stretched to fit different circumstances. It has allowed Congress to adapt the government to changing needs and times.

Section 9. *The Powers Denied to Congress*

Clause 1: Question of Slavery. The Migration or Importation of such Persons as any of the States now existing shall think proper to admit, shall not be prohibited by the Congress prior to the Year one thousand eight hundred and eight, but a Tax or duty may be imposed on such Importation, not exceeding ten dollars for each Person.

"Persons" referred to slaves. Congress outlawed the slave trade in 1808.

Clause 2: Habeas Corpus. The privilege of the Writ of Habeas Corpus shall not be suspended, unless when in Cases of Rebellion or Invasion the public Safety may require it.

A writ of habeas corpus is a court order directing a sheriff or other public officer who is detaining another person to "produce the body" of the detainee so the court can assess the legality of the detention.

Clause 3: Special Bills. No Bill of Attainder or ex post facto Law shall be passed.

A bill of attainder is a law that inflicts punishment without a trial. An ex post facto law is a law that inflicts punishment for an act that was not illegal when it was committed.

Clause 4: Direct Taxes. [No Capitation, or other direct, Tax shall be laid, unless in Proportion to the Census or Enumeration herein before directed to be taken.][6]

A capitation is a tax on a person. A direct tax is a tax paid directly to the government, such as a property tax. This clause was intended to prevent Congress from levying a tax on slaves per person and thereby taxing slavery out of existence.

Clause 5: Export Taxes. No Tax or Duty shall be laid on Articles exported from any State.

Congress may not tax any goods sold from one state to another or from one state to a foreign country. (Congress does have the power to tax goods that are bought from other countries, however.)

Clause 6: Interstate Commerce. No Preference shall be given by any Regulation of Commerce or Revenue to the Ports of one State over those of another: nor shall Vessels bound to, or from, one State, be obliged to enter, clear, or pay Duties in another.

Congress may not treat different ports within the United States differently in terms of taxing and commerce powers. Congress may not give one state's port a legal advantage over the ports of another state.

Clause 7: Treasury Withdrawals. No Money shall be drawn from the Treasury, but in Consequence of Appropriations made by Law; and a regular Statement and Account of the Receipts and Expenditures of all public Money shall be published from time to time.

Federal funds can be spent only as Congress authorizes. This is a significant check on the president's power.

Clause 8: Titles of Nobility. No Title of Nobility shall be granted by the United States: And no Person holding any Office of Profit or Trust under them, shall, without the Consent of the Congress, accept of any present, Emolument, Office, or Title, of any kind whatever, from any King, Prince, or foreign State.

No person in the United States may hold a title of nobility, such as duke or duchess. This clause also discourages bribery of American officials by foreign governments.

Section 10. *Those Powers Denied to the States*

Clause 1: Treaties and Coinage. No State shall enter into any Treaty, Alliance, or Confederation; grant Letters of Marque and Reprisal; coin Money; emit Bills of Credit; make any Thing but gold and silver Coin a Tender in Payment of Debts; pass any Bill of Attainder, ex post facto Law, or Law impairing the Obligation of Contracts, or grant any Title of Nobility.

Prohibiting state laws "impairing the Obligation of Contracts" was intended to protect creditors. (Shayss' Rebellion—an attempt to prevent courts from giving effect to creditors' legal actions against debtors—occurred only one year before the Constitution was written.)

Clause 2: Duties and Imposts. No State shall, without the Consent of the Congress, lay any Imposts or Duties on Imports or Exports, except what may be absolutely necessary for executing its inspection Laws; and the net Produce of all Duties and Imposts, laid by any State on Imports or Exports, shall be for the Use of the Treasury of the United States; and all such Laws shall be subject to the Revision and Controul of the Congress.

Only Congress can tax imports. Further, the states cannot tax exports.

Clause 3: War. No State shall, without the Consent of Congress, lay any Duty of Tonnage, keep Troops, or Ships of War in time of Peace, enter into any Agreement or Compact with another State, or with a foreign Power or engage in War, unless actually invaded, or in such imminent Danger as will not admit of delay.

A duty of tonnage is a tax on ships according to their cargo capacity. No states may tax ships according to their cargo unless Congress agrees. Additionally, this clause forbids any state to keep troops or warships during peacetime or to make a compact with another state or foreign nation unless Congress so agrees. A state, in contrast, can maintain a militia, but its use has to be limited to disorders that occur within the state—unless, of course, the militia is called into federal service.

ARTICLE II. *(Executive Branch)*

Section 1. *The Nature and Scope of Presidential Power*

Clause 1: Four-Year Term. The executive Power shall be vested in a President of the United States of America. He shall hold his Office during the Term of four Years, and, together with the Vice President, chosen for the same Term, be elected, as follows.

The president has the power to carry out laws made by Congress, called the executive power. He or she serves in office for a four-year

---

6. Modified by the Sixteenth Amendment.

term after election. The Twenty-second Amendment limits the number of times a person may be elected president.

Clause 2: Choosing Electors from Each State. Each State shall appoint, in such Manner as the Legislature thereof may direct, a Number of Electors, equal to the whole Number of Senators and Representatives to which the State may be entitled in the Congress; but no Senator or Representative, or Person holding an Office of Trust or Profit under the United States, shall be appointed an Elector.

The "Electors" are known more commonly as the "electoral college." The president is elected by electors—that is, representatives chosen by the people—rather than by the people directly.

Clause 3: The Former System of Elections. [The Electors shall meet in their respective States, and vote by Ballot for two Persons, of whom one at least shall not be an Inhabitant of the same State with themselves. And they shall make a List of all the Persons voted for, and of the Number of Votes for each; which List they shall sign and certify, and transmit sealed to the Seat of the Government of the United States, directed to the President of the Senate. The President of the Senate shall, in the Presence of the Senate and House of Representatives, open all the Certificates, and the Votes shall then be counted. The Person having the greatest Number of Votes shall be the President, if such Number be a Majority of the whole Number of Electors appointed; and if there be more than one who have such Majority, and have an equal Number of Votes, then the House of Representatives shall immediately chuse by Ballot one of them for President; and if no Person have a Majority, then from the five highest on the List the said House shall in like Manner chuse the President. But in chusing the President, the Votes shall be taken by States, the Representation from each State having one Vote; A quorum for this Purpose shall consist of a Member or Members from two thirds of the States, and a Majority of all the States shall be necessary to a Choice. In every Case, after the Choice of the President, the Person having the greater Number of Votes of the Electors shall be the Vice President. But if there should remain two or more who have equal Votes, the Senate shall chuse from them by Ballot the Vice President.][7]

The original method of selecting the president and vice president was replaced by the Twelfth Amendment. Apparently, the framers did not anticipate the rise of political parties and the development of primaries and conventions.

Clause 4: The Time of Elections. The Congress may determine the Time of chusing the Electors, and the Day on which they shall give their Votes; which Day shall be the same throughout the United States.

Congress set the Tuesday after the first Monday in November every fourth year as the date for choosing electors. The electors cast their votes on the Monday after the second Wednesday in December of that year.

Clause 5: Qualifications for President. No person except a natural born Citizen, or a Citizen of the United States, at the time of the Adoption of this Constitution, shall be eligible to the Office of President; neither shall any Person be eligible to that Office who shall not have attained to the Age of thirty five Years, and been fourteen Years a Resident within the United States.

The president must be a natural-born citizen, be at least 35 years of age when taking office, and have been a resident within the United States for at least 14 years.

Clause 6: Succession of the Vice President. [In Case of the Removal of the President from Office, or of his Death, Resignation or Inability to discharge the Powers and Duties of the said Office, the same shall devolve on the Vice President, and the Congress may by Law provide for the Case of Removal, Death, Resignation or Inability, both of the President and Vice President, declaring what Officer shall then act as President, and such Officer shall act accordingly, until the Disability be removed, or a President shall be elected.][8]

This section provided for the method by which the vice president was to succeed to the presidency, but its wording is ambiguous. It was replaced by the Twenty-fifth Amendment.

Clause 7: The President's Salary. The President shall, at stated Times, receive for his Services, a Compensation, which shall neither be encreased nor diminished during the Period for which he shall have been elected, and he shall not receive within that Period any other Emolument from the United States, or any of them.

The president maintains the same salary during each four-year term. Moreover, she or he may not receive additional cash payments from the government. Originally set at $25,000 per year, the salary is currently $400,000 a year plus a $50,000 nontaxable expense account.

Clause 8: The Oath of Office. Before he enter on the Execution of his Office, he shall take the following Oath or Affirmation: "I do solemnly swear (or affirm) that I will faithfully execute the Office of President of the United States, and will to the best of my Ability, preserve, protect and defend the Constitution of the United States."

The president is "sworn in" prior to beginning the duties of the office. The taking of the oath of office occurs on January 20, following the November election. The ceremony is called the inauguration. The oath of office is administered by the chief justice of the United States Supreme Court.

Section 2. *Powers of the President*

Clause 1: Commander in Chief. The President shall be Commander in Chief of the Army and Navy of the United States, and of the Militia of the several States, when called into the actual Service of the United States; he may require the Opinion, in writing, of the principal Officer in each of the executive Departments, upon any Subject relating to the Duties of their respective Offices, and he shall have Power to grant Reprieves and Pardons for Offences against the United States, except in Cases of Impeachment.

The armed forces are placed under civilian control because the president is a civilian but still commander in chief of the military.

---

7. Changed by the Twelfth Amendment.
8. Modified by the Twenty-fifth Amendment.

The president may ask for the help of the head of each of the executive departments (thereby creating the Cabinet). The Cabinet members are chosen by the president with the consent of the Senate, but they can be removed without Senate approval.

The president's clemency powers extend only to federal cases. In those cases, he or she may grant a full or conditional pardon, or reduce a prison term or fine.

Clause 2: Treaties and Appointment. He shall have Power, by and with the Advice and Consent of the Senate, to make Treaties, provided two thirds of the Senators present concur; and he shall nominate, and by and with the Advice and Consent of the Senate, shall appoint Ambassadors, other public Ministers and Consuls, Judges of the supreme Court, and all other Officers of the United States, whose Appointments are not herein otherwise provided for, and which shall be established by Law; but the Congress may by Law vest the Appointment of such inferior Officers, as they think proper, in the President alone, in the Courts of Law, or in the Heads of Departments.

Many of the major powers of the president are identified in this clause, including the power to make treaties with foreign governments (with the approval of the Senate by a two-thirds vote) and the power to appoint ambassadors, Supreme Court justices, and other government officials. Most such appointments require Senate approval.

Clause 3: Vacancies. The President shall have Power to fill up all Vacancies that may happen during the Recess of the Senate, by granting Commissions which shall expire at the end of their next Session.

The president has the power to appoint temporary officials to fill vacant federal offices without Senate approval if the Congress is not in session. Such appointments expire automatically at the end of Congress's next term.

Section 3. *Duties of the President*

He shall from time to time give to the Congress Information of the State of the Union, and recommend to their Consideration such Measures as he shall judge necessary and expedient; he may, on extraordinary Occasions, convene both Houses, or either of them, and in Case of Disagreement between them, with Respect to the Time of Adjournment, he may adjourn them to such Time as he shall think proper; he shall receive Ambassadors and other public Ministers; he shall take Care that the Laws be faithfully executed, and shall Commission all the Officers of the United States.

Annually, the president reports on the state of the union to Congress, recommends legislative measures, and proposes a federal budget. The State of the Union speech is a statement not only to Congress but also to the American people. After it is given, the president proposes a federal budget and presents an economic report. At any time, the president may send special messages to Congress while it is in session. The president has the power to call special sessions, to adjourn Congress when its two chambers do not agree on when to adjourn, to receive diplomatic representatives of other governments, and to ensure the proper execution of all federal laws. The president further has the ability to empower federal officers to hold their positions and to perform their duties.

Section 4. *Impeachment*

The President, Vice President and all civil Officers of the United States, shall be removed from Office on Impeachment for, and Conviction of, Treason, Bribery, or other high Crimes and Misdemeanors.

Treason denotes giving aid to the nation's enemies. The phrase "high crimes and misdemeanors" is usually considered to mean serious abuses of political power. In either case, the president or vice president may be accused by the House (called an impeachment) and then removed from office if convicted by the Senate. (Note that impeachment does not mean removal but rather refers to an accusation of treason or high crimes and misdemeanors.)

ARTICLE III. *(Judicial Branch)*

Section 1. *Judicial Powers, Courts, and Judges*

The judicial Power of the United States, shall be vested in one supreme Court, and in such inferior Courts as the Congress may from time to time ordain and establish. The Judges, both of the supreme and inferior Courts, shall hold their Offices during good Behaviour, and shall, at stated Times, receive for their Services a Compensation, which shall not be diminished during their Continuance in Office.

The Supreme Court is vested with judicial power, as are the lower federal courts that Congress creates. Federal judges serve in their offices for life unless they are impeached and convicted by Congress. The payment of federal judges may not be reduced during their time in office.

Section 2. *Jurisdiction*

Clause 1: Cases under Federal Jurisdiction. The judicial Power shall extend to all Cases, in Law and Equity, arising under this Constitution, the Laws of the United States, and Treaties made, or which shall be made, under their Authority;—to all Cases affecting Ambassadors, other public Ministers and Consuls;—to all Cases of admiralty and maritime Jurisdiction;—to Controversies to which the United States shall be a Party;—to Controversies between two or more States; [—between a State and Citizens of another State;—][9] between Citizens of different States;—between Citizens of the same State claiming Lands under Grants of different States, [and between a State, or the Citizens thereof, and foreign States, Citizens or Subjects.][10]

The federal courts take on cases that concern the meaning of the U.S. Constitution, all federal laws, and treaties. They also can take on cases involving citizens of different states and citizens of foreign nations.

Clause 2: Cases for the Supreme Court. In all Cases affecting Ambassadors, other public Ministers and Consuls, and those in

---

which a State shall be a Party, the supreme Court shall have original Jurisdiction. In all the other Cases before mentioned, the supreme Court shall have appellate Jurisdiction, both as to Law and Fact, with such Exceptions, and under such Regulations as the Congress shall make.

In a limited number of situations, the Supreme Court acts as a trial court and has original jurisdiction. These cases involve a representative from another country or involve a state. In all other situations, the cases must first be tried in the lower courts and then can be appealed to the Supreme Court. Congress may, however, make exceptions. Today, the Supreme Court acts as a trial court of first instance on rare occasions.

Clause 3: The Conduct of Trials. The Trial of all Crimes, except in Cases of Impeachment, shall be by Jury; and such Trial shall be held in the State where the said Crimes shall have been committed; but when not committed within any State, the Trial shall be at such Place or Places as the Congress may by Law have directed.

Any person accused of a federal crime is granted the right to a trial by jury in a federal court in that state in which the crime was committed. Trials of impeachment are an exception.

Section 3. *Treason*

Clause 1: The Definition of Treason. Treason against the United States, shall consist only in levying War against them, or, in adhering to their Enemies, giving them Aid and Comfort. No Person shall be convicted of Treason unless on the Testimony of two Witnesses to the same overt Act, or on Confession in open Court.

Treason is the making of war against the United States or giving aid to its enemies.

Clause 2: Punishment. The Congress shall have Power to declare the Punishment of Treason, but no Attainder of Treason shall work Corruption of Blood, or Forfeiture except during the Life of the Person attainted.

Congress has provided that the punishment for treason ranges from a minimum of five years in prison and/or a $10,000 fine to a maximum of death. "No Attainder of Treason shall work Corruption of Blood" prohibits punishment of the traitor's heirs.

ARTICLE IV. (*Relations among the States*)

Section 1. *Full Faith and Credit*

Full Faith and Credit shall be given in each State to the public Acts, Records, and judicial Proceedings of every other State. And the Congress may by general Laws prescribe the Manner in which such Acts, Records and Proceedings shall be proved, and the Effect thereof.

All states are required to respect one another's laws, records, and lawful decisions. There are exceptions, however. A state does not have to enforce another state's criminal code. Nor does it have to recognize another state's grant of a divorce if the person obtaining the divorce did not establish legal residence in the state in which it was given.

Section 2. *Treatment of Citizens*

Clause 1: Privileges and Immunities. The Citizens of each State shall be entitled to all Privileges and Immunities of Citizens in the several States.

A citizen of a state has the same rights and privileges as the citizens of another state in which he or she happens to be.

Clause 2: Extradition. A Person charged in any State with Treason, Felony, or other Crime, who shall flee from Justice, and be found in another State, shall on Demand of the executive Authority of the State from which he fled, be delivered up, to be removed to the State having Jurisdiction of the Crime.

Any person accused of a crime who flees to another state must be returned to the state in which the crime occurred.

Clause 3: Fugitive Slaves. [No Person held to Service or Labour in one State, under the Laws thereof, escaping into another, shall, in Consequence of any Law or Regulation therein, be discharged from such Service or Labour, but shall be delivered up on Claim of the Party to whom such Service or Labour may be due.][11]

This clause was struck down by the Thirteenth Amendment, which abolished slavery in 1865.

Section 3. *Admission of States*

Clause 1: The Process. New States may be admitted by the Congress into this Union; but no new State shall be formed or erected within the Jurisdiction of any other State; nor any State be formed by the Junction of two or more States, or Parts of States, without the Consent of the Legislatures of the States concerned as well as of the Congress.

Only Congress has the power to admit new states to the union. No state may be created by taking territory from an existing state unless the state's legislature so consents.

Clause 2: Public Land. The Congress shall have Power to dispose of and make all needful Rules and Regulations respecting the Territory or other Property belonging to the United States; and nothing in this Constitution shall be so construed as to Prejudice any Claims of the United States, or of any particular State.

The federal government has the exclusive right to administer federal government public lands.

Section 4. *Republican Form of Government*

The United States shall guarantee to every State in this Union a Republican Form of Government, and shall protect each of them against Invasion; and on Application of the Legislature, or of the Executive (when the Legislature cannot be convened) against domestic Violence.

Each state is promised a republican form of government—that is, one in which the people elect their representatives. The federal government is bound to protect states against any attack by foreigners or during times of trouble within a state.

---

11. Repealed by the Thirteenth Amendment.

ARTICLE V. (*Methods of Amendment*)

The Congress, whenever two thirds of both Houses shall deem it necessary, shall propose Amendments to this Constitution, or on the Application of the Legislatures of two thirds of the several States, shall call a Convention for proposing Amendments, which, in either Case, shall be valid to all Intents and Purposes, as Part of this Constitution, when ratified by the Legislatures of three fourths of the several States, or by Conventions in three fourths thereof, as the one or the other Mode of Ratification may be proposed by the Congress; Provided that no Amendment which may be made prior to the Year One thousand eight hundred and eight shall in any Manner affect the first and fourth Clauses in the Ninth Section of the First Article; and that no State, without its Consent, shall be deprived of its equal Suffrage in the Senate.

Amendments may be proposed in either of two ways: a two-thirds vote of each chamber (Congress) or at the request of two-thirds of the states. Ratification of amendments may be carried out in two ways: by the legislatures of three-fourths of the states or by the voters in three-fourths of the states. No state may be denied equal representation in the Senate.

ARTICLE VI. (*National Supremacy*)

Clause 1: Existing Obligations. All Debts contracted and Engagements entered into, before the Adoption of this Constitution shall be as valid against the United States under this Constitution, as under the Confederation.

During the Revolutionary War and the years of the Confederation, Congress borrowed large sums. This clause pledged that the new federal government would assume those financial obligations.

Clause 2: Supreme Law of the Land. This Constitution, and the Laws of the United States which shall be made in Pursuance thereof; and all Treaties made, or which shall be made, under the Authority of the United States, shall be the supreme Law of the Land; and the Judges in every State shall be bound thereby, any Thing in the Constitution or Laws of any State to the Contrary notwithstanding.

This is typically called the supremacy clause; it declares that federal law takes precedence over all forms of state law. No government at the local or state level may make or enforce any law that conflicts with any provision of the Constitution, acts of Congress, treaties, or other rules and regulations issued by the president and his or her subordinates in the executive branch of the federal government.

Clause 3: Oath of Office. The Senators and Representatives before mentioned, and the Members of the several State Legislatures, and all executive and judicial Officers, both of the United States and of the several States, shall be bound by Oath or Affirmation, to support this Constitution; but no religious Test shall ever be required as a Qualification to any Office or public Trust under the United States.

Every federal and state official must take an oath of office promising to support the U.S. Constitution. Religion may not be used as a qualification to serve in any federal office.

ARTICLE VII. (*Ratification*)

The Ratification of the Conventions of nine States shall be sufficient for the Establishment of this Constitution between the States so ratifying the Same.

Nine states were required to ratify the Constitution. Delaware was the first and New Hampshire the ninth.

Done in Convention by the Unanimous Consent of the States present the Seventeenth Day of September in the Year of our Lord one thousand seven hundred and Eighty seven and of the Independence of the United States of America the Twelfth. In witness whereof we have hereunto subscribed our Names,
Go. WASHINGTON
Presid't.
and deputy from Virginia
Attest William Jackson Secretary

Delaware	{	Geo. Read Gunning Bedford jun John Dickinson Richard Bassett Jaco. Broom	New Hampshire	{ John Langdon Nicholas Gilman
Maryland	{	James McHenry Dan of St. Thos. Jenifer Danl. Carroll	Massachusetts	{ Nathaniel Gorham Rufus King
Virginia	{	John Blair James Madison Jr.	Connecticut	{ Wm. Saml. Johnson Roger Sherman
North Carolina	{	Wm. Blount Richd. Dobbs Spaight Hu. Williamson	New York	{ Alexander Hamilton

South Carolina	{	J. Rutledge Charles Cotesworth Pinckney Charles Pinckney Pierce Butler	New Jersey	{	Wh. Livingston David Brearley Wm. Paterson Jona. Dayton
Georgia	{	William Few Abr. Baldwin	Pennsylvania	{	B. Franklin Thomas Mifflin Robt. Morris Geo. Clymer Thos. FitzSimons Jared Ingersoll James Wilson Gouv. Morris

Amendments to the Constitution of the United States (The Bill of Rights)[12]

Articles in addition to, and amendment of, the Constitution of the United States of America, proposed by Congress and ratified by the Legislatures of the several states, pursuant to the Fifth Article of the original Constitution.

AMENDMENT I.
(Religion, Speech, Assembly, and Petition)

Congress shall make no law respecting an establishment of religion, or prohibiting the free exercise thereof; or abridging the freedom of speech, or of the press; or the right of the people peaceably to assemble, and to petition the Government for a redress of grievances.

Congress may not create an official church or enact laws limiting the freedom of religion, speech, the press, assembly, and petition. These guarantees, like the others in the Bill of Rights (the first 10 amendments), are not absolute—each may be exercised only with regard to the rights of other persons.

AMENDMENT II.
(Militia and the Right to Bear Arms)

A well regulated Militia, being necessary to the security of a free State, the right of the people to keep and bear Arms, shall not be infringed.

---

12. On September 25, 1789, Congress transmitted to the state legislatures 12 proposed amendments, two of which, having to do with congressional representation and congressional pay, were not adopted. The remaining 10 amendments became the Bill of Rights. In 1992, the amendment concerning congressional pay was adopted as the Twenty-seventh Amendment.

To protect itself, each state has the right to maintain a volunteer armed force. States and the federal government regulate the possession and use of firearms by individuals.

AMENDMENT III.
(The Quartering of Soldiers)

No Soldier shall, in time of peace be quartered in any house, without the consent of the Owner, nor in time of war, but in a manner to be prescribed by law.

Before the Revolutionary War, it had been common British practice to quarter soldiers in colonists' homes. Military troops do not have the power to take over private houses during peacetime.

AMENDMENT IV.
(Searches and Seizures)

The right of the people to be secure in their persons, houses, papers, and effects, against unreasonable searches and seizures, shall not be violated, and no Warrants shall issue, but upon probable cause, supported by Oath or affirmation, and particularly describing the place to be searched, and the persons or things to be seized.

Here the word warrant means "justification" and refers to a document issued by a magistrate or judge indicating the name, address, and possible offense committed. Anyone asking for the warrant, such as a police officer, must be able to convince the magistrate or judge that an offense probably has been committed.

AMENDMENT V.
(Grand Juries, Self-Incrimination, Double Jeopardy, Due Process, and Eminent Domain)

No person shall be held to answer for a capital, or otherwise infamous crime, unless on a presentment or indictment of a Grand Jury, except in cases arising in the land or naval forces, or in the Militia, when in actual service in time of War or public danger; nor shall any person be subject for the same offence to be twice put in jeopardy of life or limb; nor shall be compelled in any criminal case to be a witness against himself, nor be deprived of life, liberty, or property, without due process of law; nor shall private property be taken for public use, without just compensation.

There are two types of juries. A grand jury considers physical evidence and the testimony of witnesses and decides whether there is sufficient reason to bring a case to trial. A petit jury hears the case at trial and decides it. "For the same offence to be twice put in jeopardy of life or limb" means to be tried twice for the same crime. A person may not be tried for the same crime twice or forced to give evidence against herself or himself. No person's right to life, liberty, or property may be taken away except by lawful means, called the due process of law. Private property taken for use in public purposes must be paid for by the government.

AMENDMENT VI.
(Criminal Court Procedures)

In all criminal prosecutions, the accused shall enjoy the right to a speedy and public trial, by an impartial jury of the State and district wherein the crime shall have been committed, which district shall have been previously ascertained by law, and to be informed of the nature and cause of the accusation; to be confronted with the witnesses against him; to have compulsory process for obtaining witnesses in his favor, and to have the Assistance of Counsel for his defence.

Any person accused of a crime has the right to a fair and public trial by a jury in the state in which the crime took place. The charges against that person must be indicated. Any accused person has the right to a lawyer to defend him or her and to question those who testify against him or her, as well as the right to call people to speak in his or her favor at trial.

AMENDMENT VII.
(Trial by Jury in Civil Cases)

In Suits at common law, where the value in controversy shall exceed twenty dollars, the right of trial by jury shall be preserved, and no fact tried by jury, shall be otherwise re-examined in any Court of the United States, than according to the rules of the common law.

A jury trial may be requested by either party in a dispute in any case involving more than $20. If both parties agree to a trial by a judge without a jury, the right to a jury trial may be put aside.

AMENDMENT VIII.
(Bail, Cruel and Unusual Punis-hment)

Excessive bail shall not be required, nor excessive fines imposed, nor cruel and unusual punishments inflicted.

Bail is that amount of money that a person accused of a crime may be required to deposit with the court as a guaranty that she or he will appear in court when requested. The amount of bail required or the fine imposed as punishment for a crime must be reasonable compared with the seriousness of the crime involved. Any punishment judged to be too harsh or too severe for a crime shall be prohibited.

AMENDMENT IX.
(The Rights Retained by the People)

The enumeration in the Constitution, of certain rights, shall not be construed to deny or disparage others retained by the people.

Many civil rights that are not explicitly enumerated in the Constitution are still held by the people.

AMENDMENT X.
(Reserved Powers of the States)

The powers not delegated to the United States by the Constitution, nor prohibited by it to the States, are reserved to the States respectively, or to the people.

Those powers not delegated by the Constitution to the federal government or expressly denied to the states belong to the states and to the people. This amendment in essence allows the states to pass laws under their "police powers."

AMENDMENT XI.
(Ratified on February 7, 1795—Suits against States)

The Judicial power of the United States shall not be construed to extend to any suit in law or equity, commenced or prosecuted against one of the United States by Citizens of another State, or by Citizens or Subjects of any Foreign State.

This amendment has been interpreted to mean that a state cannot be sued in federal court by one of its own citizens, by a citizen of another state, or by a foreign country.

AMENDMENT XII.
(Ratified on June 15, 1804—Election of the President)

The Electors shall meet in their respective states, and vote by ballot for President and Vice-President, one of whom, at least, shall not be an inhabitant of the same State with themselves; they shall name in their ballots the person voted for as President, and in distinct ballots the person voted for as Vice-President, and they shall make distinct lists of all persons voted for as President, and of all persons voted for as Vice-President, and of the number of votes for each, which lists they shall sign and certify, and transmit sealed to the seat of the government of the United States, directed to the President of the Senate;—The President of the Senate shall, in the presence of the Senate and House of Representatives, open all the certificates and the votes shall then be counted;—The person having the greatest number of votes for President, shall be the President, if such number be a majority of the whole number of Electors appointed; and if no person have such majority, then from the persons having the highest numbers not exceeding three on the list of those voted for as President, the House of Representatives shall choose immediately, by ballot, the President. But in choosing the President, the votes shall be taken by States, the representation from each State having one vote; a quorum for this purpose shall consist of a member or members from two-thirds of the States, and a majority of all States shall be necessary to a choice. [And if the House of Representatives shall not choose a President whenever the right of choice shall devolve upon them, before the fourth day of March next following, then the Vice-President shall act as President, as in the case of the death or other constitutional disability of the President.][13]—The person having the greatest number of votes as Vice-President, shall be the Vice-President, if such number be a majority of the whole number of Electors appointed, and if no person have a majority, then from the two highest numbers on the list, the Senate shall choose the Vice-President; a quorum for the purpose shall consist of two-thirds of

the whole number of Senators, and a majority of the whole number shall be necessary to a choice. But no person constitutionally ineligible to the office of President shall be eligible to that of Vice-President of the United States.

The original procedure set out for the election of president and vice president in Article II, Section 1, resulted in a tie in 1800 between Thomas Jefferson and Aaron Burr. It was not until the next year that the House of Representatives chose Jefferson to be president. This amendment changed the procedure by providing for separate ballots for president and vice president.

AMENDMENT XIII.
(Ratified on December 6, 1865—Prohibition of Slavery)

Section 1.

Neither slavery nor involuntary servitude, except as a punishment for crime whereof the party shall have been duly convicted, shall exist within the United States, or any place subject to their jurisdiction.

Some slaves had been freed during the Civil War. This amendment freed the others and abolished slavery.

Section 2.

Congress shall have power to enforce this article by appropriate legislation.

AMENDMENT XIV.
(Ratified on July 9, 1868—Citizenship, Due Process, and Equal Protection of the Laws)

Section 1.

All persons born or naturalized in the United States, and subject to the jurisdiction thereof, are citizens of the United States and of the State wherein they reside. No State shall make or enforce any law which shall abridge the privileges or immunities of citizens of the United States; nor shall any State deprive any person of life, liberty, or property, without due process of law; nor deny to any person within its jurisdiction the equal protection of the laws.

Under this provision, states cannot make or enforce laws that take away rights given to all citizens by the federal government. States cannot act unfairly or arbitrarily toward, or discriminate against, any person.

Section 2.

Representatives shall be apportioned among the several States according to their respective numbers, counting the whole number of persons in each State, excluding Indians not taxed. But when the right to vote at any election for the choice of electors for President and Vice President of the United States, Representatives in Congress, the Executive and Judicial officers of a State, or the members of the Legislature thereof, is denied to any of the male inhabitants of such State, being [twenty-one][14] years of age, and citizens of the United States, or in any way abridged, except for

---

13. Changed by the Twentieth Amendment.
14. Changed by the Twenty-sixth Amendment.

participation in rebellion, or other crime, the basis of representation therein shall be reduced in the proportion which the number of such male citizens shall bear to the whole number of male citizens twenty-one years of age in such State.

Section 3.

No person shall be a Senator or Representative in Congress, or elector of President and Vice President, or hold any office, civil or military, under the United States, or under any State, who having previously taken an oath, as a member of Congress, or as an officer of the United States, or as a member of any State legislature, or as an executive or judicial officer of any State, to support the Constitution of the United States, shall have engaged in insurrection or rebellion against the same, or given aid or comfort to the enemies thereof. But Congress may by a vote of two-thirds of each House, remove such disability.

This provision forbade former state or federal government officials who had acted in support of the Confederacy during the Civil War to hold office again. It limited the president's power to pardon those persons. Congress removed this "disability" in 1898.

Section 4.

The validity of the public debt of the United States, authorized by law, including debts incurred for payment of pensions and bounties for services in suppressing insurrection or rebellion, shall not be questioned. But neither the United States nor any State shall assume or pay any debt or obligation incurred in aid of insurrection or rebellion against the United States, or any claim for the loss or emancipation of any slave, but all such debts, obligations and claims shall be held illegal and void.

Section 5.

The Congress shall have power to enforce, by appropriate legislation, the provisions of this article.

AMENDMENT XV.
(Ratified on February 3, 1870—The Right to Vote)

Section 1.

The right of citizens of the United States to vote shall not be denied or abridged by the United States or by any State on account of race, color, or previous condition of servitude.

No citizen can be refused the right to vote simply because of race or color or because that person was once a slave.

Section 2.

The Congress shall have power to enforce this article by appropriate legislation.

AMENDMENT XVI.
(Ratified on February 3, 1913— Income Taxes)

The Congress shall have power to lay and collect taxes on incomes, from whatever source derived, without apportionment among the several States, and without regard to any census or enumeration.

This amendment allows Congress to tax income without sharing the revenue so obtained with the states according to their population.

AMENDMENT XVII. (Ratified on April 8, 1913—The Popular Election of Senators)

Section 1.

The Senate of the United States shall be composed of two Senators from each State, elected by the people thereof, for six years; and each Senator shall have one vote. The electors in each State shall have the qualifications requisite for electors of the most numerous branch of the State legislatures.

Section 2.

When vacancies happen in the representation of any State in the Senate, the executive authority of such State shall issue writs of election to fill such vacancies: *Provided,* That the legislature of any State may empower the executive thereof to make temporary appointments until the people fill the vacancies by election as the legislature may direct.

Section 3.

This amendment shall not be so construed as to affect the election or term of any Senator chosen before it becomes valid as part of the Constitution.

This amendment modified portions of Article I, Section 3, that related to election of senators. Senators are now elected by the voters in each state directly. When a vacancy occurs, either the state may fill the vacancy by a special election, or the governor of the state involved may appoint someone to fill the seat until the next election.

AMENDMENT XVIII.
(Ratified on January 16, 1919— Prohibition)

Section 1.

After one year from the ratification of this article the manufacture, sale, or transportation of intoxicating liquors within, the importation thereof into, or the exportation thereof from the United States and all territory subject to the jurisdiction thereof for beverage purposes is hereby prohibited.

Section 2.

The Congress and the several States shall have concurrent power to enforce this article by appropriate legislation.

Section 3.

This article shall be inoperative unless it shall have been ratified as an amendment to the Constitution by the legislatures of the several States, as provided in the Constitution, within seven years from the date of the submission hereof to the States by the Congress.[15]

This amendment made it illegal to manufacture, sell, and transport alcoholic beverages in the United States. It was repealed by the Twenty-first Amendment.

---

15. The Eighteenth Amendment was repealed by the Twenty-first Amendment.

AMENDMENT XIX.
(Ratified on August 18, 1920—Women's Right to Vote)

Section 1.

The right of citizens of the United States to vote shall not be denied or abridged by the United States or by any State on account of sex.

Section 2.

Congress shall have power to enforce this article by appropriate legislation.

Women were given the right to vote by this amendment, and Congress was given the power to enforce this right.

AMENDMENT XX.
(Ratified on January 23, 1933—The Lame Duck Amendment)

Section 1.

The terms of the President and Vice President shall end at noon on the 20th day of January, and the terms of Senators and Representatives at noon on the 3d day of January, of the years in which such terms would have ended if this article had not been ratified; and the terms of their successors shall then begin.

This amendment modified Article I, Section 4, Clause 2, and other provisions relating to the president in the Twelfth Amendment. The taking of the oath of office was moved from March 4 to January 20.

Section 2.

The Congress shall assemble at least once in every year, and such meeting shall begin at noon on the 3rd day of January, unless they shall by law appoint a different day.

Congress changed the beginning of its term to January 3. The reason the Twentieth Amendment is called the Lame Duck Amendment is that it shortens the time between when a member of Congress is defeated for reelection and when he or she leaves office.

Section 3.

If, at the time fixed for the beginning of the term of the President, the President elect shall have died, the Vice President elect shall become President. If a President shall not have been chosen before the time fixed for the beginning of his term, or if the President elect shall have failed to qualify, then the Vice President elect shall act as President until a President shall have qualified; and the Congress may by law provide for the case wherein neither a President elect nor a Vice President elect shall have qualified, declaring who shall then act as President, or the manner in which one who is to act shall be selected, and such person shall act accordingly until a President or Vice President shall have qualified.

This part of the amendment deals with problem areas left ambiguous by Article II and the Twelfth Amendment. If the president dies before January 20 or fails to qualify for office, the presidency is to be filled as described in this section.

Section 4.

The Congress may by law provide for the case of the death of any of the persons from whom the House of Representatives may choose a President whenever the rights of choice shall have devolved upon them, and for the case of the death of any of the persons from whom the Senate may choose a Vice President whenever the right of choice shall have devolved upon them.

Congress has never created legislation pursuant to this section.

Section 5.

Sections 1 and 2 shall take effect on the 15th day of October following the ratification of this article.

Section 6.

This article shall be inoperative unless it shall have been ratified as an amendment to the Constitution by the legislatures of three-fourths of the several States within seven years from the date of its submission.

AMENDMENT XXI.
(Ratified on December 5, 1933—The Repeal of Prohibition)

Section 1.

The eighteenth article of amendment to the Constitution of the United States is hereby repealed.

Section 2.

The transportation or importation into any State, Territory, or possession of the United States for delivery or use therein of intoxicating liquors, in violation of the laws thereof, is hereby prohibited.

Section 3.

This article shall be inoperative unless it shall have been ratified as an amendment to the Constitution by conventions in the several States, as provided in the Constitution, within seven years from the date of the submission hereof to the States by the Congress.

The amendment repealed the Eighteenth Amendment but did not make alcoholic beverages legal everywhere. Rather, they remained illegal in any state that so designated them. Many such "dry" states existed for a number of years after 1933. Today, there are still "dry" counties within the United States, in which the sale of alcoholic beverages is illegal.

AMENDMENT XXII.
(Ratified on February 27, 1951— Limitation of Presidential Terms)

Section 1.

No person shall be elected to the office of the President more than twice, and no person who has held the office of President, or acted as President, for more than two years of a term to which some other person was elected President shall be elected to the office of President more than once. But this Article shall not apply to any person holding the office of President when this Article was proposed by the Congress, and shall not prevent any person who may be holding the office of President, or acting as President, during the term within which this Article becomes operative from holding the office of President or acting as President during the remainder of such term.

Section 2.

This article shall be inoperative unless it shall have been ratified as an amendment to the Constitution by the legislatures of three-fourths of the several States within seven years from the date of its submission to the States by the Congress.

No president may serve more than two elected terms. If, however, a president has succeeded to the office after the halfway point of a term in which another president was originally elected, then that president may serve for more than eight years, but not to exceed 10 years.

AMENDMENT XXIII.
(Ratified on March 29, 1961—Presidential Electors for the District of Columbia)

Section 1.

The District constituting the seat of Government of the United States shall appoint in such manner as the Congress may direct:

A number of electors of President and Vice President equal to the whole number of Senators and Representatives in Congress to which the District would be entitled if it were a State, but in no event more than the least populous State; they shall be in addition to those appointed by the States, but they shall be considered, for the purposes of the election of President and Vice President, to be electors appointed by a State; and they shall meet in the District and perform such duties as provided by the twelfth article of amendment.

Section 2.

The Congress shall have power to enforce this article by appropriate legislation.

Citizens living in the District of Columbia have the right to vote in elections for president and vice president. The District of Columbia has three presidential electors, whereas before this amendment it had none.

AMENDMENT XXIV.
(Ratified on January 23, 1964— The Anti–Poll Tax Amendment)

Section 1.

The right of citizens of the United States to vote in any primary or other election for President or Vice President, for electors for President or Vice President, or for Senator or Representative in Congress, shall not be denied or abridged by the United States, or any State by reason of failure to pay any poll tax or other tax.

Section 2.

The Congress shall have power to enforce this article by appropriate legislation.

No government shall require a person to pay a poll tax to vote in any federal election.

AMENDMENT XXV.
(Ratified on February 10, 1967— Presidential Disability and Vice Presidential Vacancies)

Section 1.

In case of the removal of the President from office or of his death or resignation, the Vice President shall become President.

Whenever a president dies or resigns from office, the vice president becomes president.

Section 2.

Whenever there is a vacancy in the office of the Vice President, the President shall nominate a Vice President who shall take office upon confirmation by a majority vote of both Houses of Congress.

Whenever the office of the vice presidency becomes vacant, the president may appoint someone to fill this office, provided Congress consents.

Section 3.

Whenever the President transmits to the President pro tempore of the Senate and the Speaker of the House of Representatives his written declaration that he is unable to discharge the powers and duties of his office, and until he transmits to them a written declaration to the contrary, such powers and duties shall be discharged by the Vice President as Acting President.

Whenever the president believes she or he is unable to carry out the duties of the office, she or he shall so indicate to Congress in writing. The vice president then acts as president until the president declares that she or he is again able to carry out the duties of the office.

Section 4.

Whenever the Vice President and a majority of either the principal officers of the executive departments or of such other body as Congress may by law provide, transmit to the President pro tempore of the Senate and the Speaker of the House of Representatives their written declaration that the President is unable to discharge the powers and duties of his office, the Vice President shall immediately assume the powers and duties of the office as Acting President.

Thereafter, when the President transmits to the President pro tempore of the Senate and the Speaker of the House of Representatives his written declaration that no inability exists, he shall resume the powers and duties of his office unless the Vice President and a majority of either the principal officers of the executive department or of such other body as Congress may by law provide, transmit within four days to the President pro tempore of the Senate and the Speaker of the House of Representatives their written declaration that the President is unable to discharge the powers and duties of his office. Thereupon Congress shall decide the issue, assembling within forty-eight hours for that purpose if not in session. If the Congress, within twenty-one days after receipt of the latter written declaration, or, if Congress is not in session, within twenty-one days after Congress is required to assemble, determines by two-thirds vote of both Houses that the President is unable to discharge the powers and duties of his office, the Vice President shall continue to discharge the same as Acting President; otherwise, the President shall resume the powers and duties of his office.

Whenever the vice president and a majority of the members of the Cabinet believe that the president cannot carry out her or his duties, they shall so indicate in writing to Congress. The vice president shall then act as president. When the president believes that she or he is able to carry out her or his duties again, she or he shall so indicate to the Congress. However, if the vice president and a majority of the Cabinet do not agree, Congress must decide by a two-thirds vote within three weeks who shall act as president.

AMENDMENT XXVI.
(Ratified on July 1, 1971— The 18-Year-Old Vote)

Section 1.

The right of citizens of the United States, who are eighteen years of age or older, to vote shall not be denied or abridged by the United States or by any State on account of age

.No one 18 years of age or older can be denied the right to vote in federal or state elections by virtue of age.

Section 2.

The Congress shall have power to enforce this article by appropriate legislation.

AMENDMENT XXVII.
(Ratified on May 7, 1992— Congressional Pay)

No law, varying the compensation for the services of the Senators and Representatives, shall take effect, until an election of representatives shall have intervened.

This amendment allows the voters to have some control over increases in salaries for congressional members. Originally submitted to the states for ratification in 1789, it was not ratified until 203 years later, in 1992

Appendix C

The Federalist Papers Nos. 10 and 51

In 1787, after the newly drafted U.S. Constitution was submitted to the 13 states for ratification, a major political debate ensued between the Federalists (who favored ratification) and the Anti-Federalists (who opposed ratification). Anti-Federalists in New York were particularly critical of the Constitution, and in response to their objections, Federalists Alexander Hamilton, James Madison, and John Jay wrote a series of 85 essays in defense of the Constitution. The essays were published in New York newspapers and reprinted in other newspapers throughout the country.

For students of American government, the essays, collectively known as the Federalist Papers, are particularly important because they provide a glimpse of the founders' political philosophy and intentions in designing the Constitution—and, consequently, in shaping the American philosophy of government.

We have included in this appendix two of these essays: Federalist Papers No. 10 and No. 51. Each essay has been annotated by the authors to indicate its importance in American political thought and to clarify the meaning of particular passages.

Federalist Paper No. 10

Federalist Paper No. 10, penned by James Madison, has often been singled out as a key document in American political thought. In this essay, Madison attacks the Anti-Federalists' fear that a republican form of government will inevitably give rise to "factions"—small political parties or groups united by a common interest—that will control the government. Factions will be harmful to the country because they will implement policies beneficial to their own interests but adverse to other people's rights and to the public good. In this essay, Madison attempts to lay to rest this fear by explaining how, in a large republic such as the United States, there will be so many different factions, held together by regional or local interests, that no single one of them will dominate national politics.

Madison opens his essay with a paragraph discussing how important it is to devise a plan of government that can control the "instability, injustice, and confusion" brought about by factions.

Among the numerous advantages promised by a well-constructed Union, none deserves to be more accurately developed than its tendency to break and control the violence of faction. The friend of popular governments never finds himself so much alarmed for their character and fate as when he contemplates their propensity to this dangerous vice. He will not fail, therefore, to set a due value on any plan which, without violating the principles to which he is attached, provides a proper cure for it. The instability, injustice, and confusion introduced into the public councils have, in truth, been the mortal diseases under which popular governments have everywhere perished, as they continue to be the favorite and fruitful topics from which the

adversaries to liberty derive their most specious declamations. The valuable improvements made by the American constitutions on the popular models, both ancient and modern, cannot certainly be too much admired; but it would be an unwarrantable partiality to contend that they have as effectually obviated the danger on this side, as was wished and expected. Complaints are everywhere heard from our most considerate and virtuous citizens, equally the friends of public and private faith and of public and personal liberty, that our governments are too unstable, that the public good is disregarded in the conflicts of rival parties, and that measures are too often decided, not according to the rules of justice and the rights of the minor party, but by the superior force of an interested and overbearing majority. However anxiously we may wish that these complaints had no foundation, the evidence of known facts will not permit us to deny that they are in some degree true. It will be found, indeed, on a candid review of our situation, that some of the distresses under which we labor have been erroneously charged on the operation of our governments; but it will be found, at the same time, that other causes will not alone account for many of our heaviest misfortunes; and, particularly, for that prevailing and increasing distrust of public engagements and alarm for private rights which are echoed from one end of the continent to the other. These must be chiefly, if not wholly, effects of the unsteadiness and injustice with which a factious spirit has tainted our public administration.

Madison now defines what he means by the term faction.

By a faction I understand a number of citizens, whether amounting to a majority or minority of the whole, who are united and actuated by some common impulse of passion, or of interest, adverse to the rights of other citizens, or the permanent and aggregate interests of the community.

Madison next contends that there are two methods by which the "mischiefs of faction" can be cured: by removing the causes of faction or by controlling their effects. In the following paragraphs, Madison explains how liberty itself nourishes factions. Therefore, to abolish factions would involve abolishing liberty—a cure "worse than the disease."

There are two methods of curing the mischiefs of faction: the one, by removing its causes; the other, by controlling its effects.

There are again two methods of removing the causes of faction: the one, by destroying the liberty which is essential to its existence; the other, by giving to every citizen the same opinions, the same passions, and the same interests.

It could never be more truly said than of the first remedy that it was worse than the disease. Liberty is to faction what air is to fire, an aliment without which it instantly expires. But it could not be a less folly to abolish liberty, which is essential to political life, because it nourishes faction than it would be to wish the annihilation of air, which is essential to animal life, because it imparts to fire its destructive agency.

The second expedient is as impracticable as the first would be unwise. As long as the reason of man continues fallible, and he is at liberty to exercise it, different opinions will be formed. As long as the connection subsists between his reason and his self-love, his opinions and his passions will have a reciprocal influence on each other; and the former will be objects to which the latter will attach themselves. The diversity in the faculties of men, from which the rights of property originate, is not less an insuperable obstacle to a uniformity of interests. The protection of these faculties is the first object of government. From the protection of different and unequal faculties of acquiring property, the possession of different degrees and kinds of property immediately results; and from the influence of these on the sentiments and views of the respective proprietors ensues a division of the society into different interests and parties.

The latent causes of faction are thus sown in the nature of man; and we see them everywhere brought into different degrees of activity, according to the different circumstances of civil society. A zeal for different opinions concerning religion, concerning government, and many other points, as well of speculation as of practice; an attachment to different leaders ambitiously contending for pre-eminence and power; or to persons of other descriptions whose fortunes have been interesting to the human passions, have, in turn, divided mankind into parties, inflamed them with mutual animosity, and rendered them much more disposed to vex and oppress each other than to co-operate for their common good. So strong is this propensity of mankind to fall into mutual animosities that where no substantial occasion presents itself the most frivolous and fanciful distinctions have been sufficient to kindle their unfriendly passions and excite their most violent conflicts. But the most common and durable source of factions has been the various and unequal distribution of property. Those who hold and those who are without property have ever formed distinct interests in society. Those who are creditors, and those who are debtors, fall under a like discrimination. A landed interest, a manufacturing interest, a mercantile interest, a moneyed interest, with many lesser interests, grow up of necessity in civilized nations, and divide them into different classes, actuated by different sentiments and views. The regulation of these various and interfering interests forms the principal task of modern legislation and involves the spirit of party and faction in the necessary and ordinary operations of government.

No man is allowed to be a judge in his own cause, because his interest would certainly bias his judgment, and, not improbably, corrupt his integrity. With equal, nay with greater reason, a body of men are unfit to be both judges and parties at the same time; yet what are many of the most important acts of legislation but so many judicial determinations, not indeed concerning the rights of single persons, but concerning the rights of large bodies of citizens? And what are the different classes of legislators but advocates and parties to the causes which they determine? Is a law proposed concerning private debts? It is a question to which the creditors are parties on one side and the debtors on the other. Justice ought to hold the balance between them. Yet the parties are, and must be, themselves the judges; and the most numerous party, or in other words, the most powerful faction must be expected to prevail. Shall domestic manufacturers be encouraged, and in what degree, by restrictions on foreign manufacturers? [These] are questions which would be differently decided by the landed and the manufacturing classes, and probably by neither with a sole regard to justice and the public good. The apportionment of taxes on the various descriptions of property is an act which seems to require the most exact impartiality; yet there is, perhaps, no legislative act in which greater opportunity and temptation are given to a predominant party to trample on the rules of justice. Every shilling with which they overburden the inferior number is a shilling saved to their own pockets.

It is in vain to say that enlightened statesmen will be able to adjust these clashing interests and render them all subservient to the public good. Enlightened statesmen will not always be at the helm. Nor, in many cases, can such an adjustment be made at all without taking into view indirect and remote considerations, which will rarely prevail over the immediate interest which one party may find in disregarding the rights of another or the good of the whole.

The inference to which we are brought is that the **causes** of faction cannot be removed and that relief is only to be sought in the means of controlling its **effects**.

Having concluded that "the causes of faction cannot be removed," Madison now looks in some detail at the other method by which factions can be cured—by controlling their effects. This is the heart of his essay. He begins by positing a significant question: How can you have self-government without risking the possibility that a ruling faction, particularly a majority faction, might tyrannize over the rights of others?

If a faction consists of less than a majority, relief is supplied by the republican principle, which enables the majority to defeat its sinister views by regular vote. It may clog the administration, it may convulse the society; but it will be unable to execute and mask its violence under the forms of the Constitution. When a majority is included in a faction, the form of popular government, on the other hand, enables it to sacrifice to its ruling passion or interest both the public good and the rights of other citizens. To secure the public good and private rights against the danger of such a faction, and at the same time to preserve the spirit and the form of popular government, is then the great object to which our inquiries are directed. Let me add that it is the great desideratum by which alone this form of government can be rescued from the opprobrium under which it has so long labored and be recommended to the esteem and adoption of mankind.

Madison now sets forth the idea that one way to control the effects of factions is to ensure that the majority is rendered incapable of acting in concert in order to "carry into effect schemes of oppression." He goes on to state that in a democracy, in which all citizens participate personally in government decision making, there is no way to prevent the majority from communicating with each other and, as a result, acting in concert.

By what means is this object attainable? Evidently by one of two only. Either the existence of the same passion or interest in a majority at the same time must be prevented, or the majority, having such coexistent passion or interest, must be rendered, by their number and local situation, unable to concert and carry into effect schemes of oppression. If the impulse and the opportunity be suffered to coincide, we well know that neither moral nor religious motives can be relied on as an adequate control. They are not found to be such on the injustice and violence of individuals, and lose their efficacy in proportion to the number combined together, that is, in proportion as their efficacy becomes needful.

From this view of the subject it may be concluded that a pure democracy, by which I mean a society consisting of a small number of citizens, who assemble and administer the government in person, can admit of no cure for the mischiefs of faction. A common passion or interest will, in almost every case, be felt by a majority of the whole; a communication and concert results from the form of government itself; and there is nothing to check the inducements to sacrifice the weaker party or an obnoxious individual. Hence it is that such democracies have ever been spectacles of turbulence and contention; have ever been found incompatible with personal security or the rights of property; and have in general been as short in their lives as they have been violent in their deaths. Theoretic politicians, who have patronized this species of government, have erroneously supposed that by reducing mankind to a perfect equality in their political rights, they would at the same time be perfectly equalized and assimilated in their possessions, their opinions, and their passions.

Madison now moves on to discuss the benefits of a republic with respect to controlling the effects of factions. He begins by defining a republic and then pointing out the "two great points of difference" between a republic and a democracy: a republic is governed by a small body of elected representatives, not by the people directly; and a republic can extend over a much larger territory and embrace more citizens than a democracy can.

A republic, by which I mean a government in which the scheme of representation takes place, opens a different prospect and promises the cure for which we are seeking. Let us examine the points in which it varies from pure democracy, and we shall comprehend both the nature of the cure and the efficacy which it must derive from the Union.

The two great points of difference between a democracy and a republic are: first, the delegation of the government, in the latter, to a small number of citizens elected by the rest; secondly, the greater number of citizens and greater sphere of country over which the latter may be extended.

In the following four paragraphs, Madison explains how in a republic, particularly a large republic, the delegation of authority to elected representatives will increase the likelihood that those who govern will be "fit" for their positions and that a proper balance will be achieved between local (factional) interests and national interests. Note how he stresses that the new federal Constitution, by dividing powers between state governments and the national government, provides a "happy combination in this respect."

The effect of the first difference is, on the one hand, to refine and enlarge the public views by passing them through the medium of a chosen body of citizens, whose wisdom may best discern the true interest of their country and whose patriotism

and love of justice will be least likely to sacrifice it to temporary or partial considerations. Under such a regulation it may well happen that the public voice, pronounced by the representatives of the people, will be more consonant to the public good than if pronounced by the people themselves, convened for the purpose. On the other hand, the effect may be inverted. Men of factious tempers, of local prejudices, or of sinister designs, may, by intrigue, by corruption, or by other means, first obtain the suffrages, and then betray the interests of the people. The question resulting is, whether small or extensive republics are most favorable to the election of proper guardians of the public weal; and it is clearly decided in favor of the latter by two obvious considerations.

In the first place, it is to be remarked that however small the republic may be the representatives must be raised to a certain number in order to guard against the cabals of a few; and that however large it may be, they must be limited to a certain number in order to guard against the confusion of a multitude. Hence, the number of representatives in the two cases not being in proportion to that of the constituents, and being proportionally greater in the small republic, it follows that if the proportion of fit characters be not less in the large than in the small republic, the former will present a greater option, and consequently a greater probability of a fit choice.

In the next place, as each representative will be chosen by a greater number of citizens in the large than in the small republic, it will be more difficult for unworthy candidates to practice with success the vicious arts by which elections are too often carried; and the suffrages of the people being more free, will be more likely to center on men who possess the most attractive merit and the most diffusive and established characters.

It must be confessed that in this, as in most other cases, there is a mean, on both sides of which inconveniencies will be found to lie. By enlarging too much the number of electors, you render the representative too little acquainted with all their local circumstances and lesser interests; as by reducing it too much, you render him unduly attached to these, and too little fit to comprehend and pursue great and national objects. The federal Constitution forms a happy combination in this respect; the great and aggregate interests being referred to the national, the local and particular to the State legislatures.

Madison now looks more closely at the other difference between a republic and a democracy—namely, that a republic can encompass a larger territory and more citizens than a democracy can. In the remaining paragraphs of his essay, Madison concludes that in a large republic, it will be difficult for factions to act in concert. Although a factious group—religious, political, economic, or otherwise—may control a local or regional government, it will have little chance of gathering a national following. This is because in a large republic, there will be numerous factions whose work will offset the work of any one particular faction ("sect"). As Madison phrases it, these numerous factions will "secure the national councils against any danger from that source."

The other point of difference is the greater number of citizens and extent of territory which may be brought within the compass of republican than of democratic government; and it is this circumstance principally which renders factious combinations less to be dreaded in the former than in the latter. The smaller the society, the fewer probably will be the distinct parties and interests composing it; the fewer the distinct parties and interests, the more frequently will a majority be found of the same party; and the smaller the number of individuals composing a majority, and the smaller the compass within which they are placed, the more easily will they concert and execute their plans of oppression. Extend the sphere and you take in a greater variety of parties and interests; you make it less probable that a majority of the whole will have a common motive to invade the rights of other citizens; or if such a common motive exists, it will be more difficult for all who feel it to discover their own strength and to act in unison with each other. Besides other impediments, it may be remarked that, where there is a consciousness of unjust or dishonorable purposes, communication is always checked by distrust in proportion to the number whose concurrence is necessary.

Hence, it clearly appears that the same advantage which a republic has over a democracy in controlling the effects of faction is enjoyed by a large over a small republic—is enjoyed by the Union over the States composing it. Does this advantage consist in the substitution of representatives whose enlightened views and virtuous sentiments render them superior to local prejudices and to schemes of injustice? It will not be denied that the representation of the Union will be most likely to possess these requisite endowments. Does it consist in the greater security afforded by a greater variety of parties, against the event of any one party being able to outnumber and oppress the rest? In an equal degree does the increased variety of parties comprised within the Union increase this security. Does it, in fine, consist in the greater obstacles opposed to the concert and accomplishment of the secret wishes of an unjust and interested majority? Here again the extent of the Union gives it the most palpable advantage.

The influence of factious leaders may kindle a flame within their particular States but will be unable to spread a general conflagration through the other States. A religious sect may degenerate into a political faction in a part of the Confederacy; but the variety of sects dispersed over the entire face of it must secure the national councils against any danger from that source. A rage for paper money, for an abolition of debts, for an equal division of property, or for any other improper or wicked project, will be less apt to pervade the whole body of the Union than a particular member of it, in the same proportion as such a malady is more likely to taint a particular county or district than an entire State.

In the extent and proper structure of the Union, therefore, we behold a republican remedy for the diseases most incident to republican government. And according to the degree of pleasure and pride we feel in being republicans ought to be our zeal in cherishing the spirit and supporting the character of federalists.
Publius
(James Madison)

Federalist Paper No. 51

Federalist Paper No. 51, also authored by James Madison, is another classic in American political theory. Although the Federalists wanted a strong national government, they had not abandoned the traditional American view, particularly notable during the revolutionary era, that those holding powerful government positions could not be trusted to put national interests and the common good above their own personal interests. In this essay, Madison explains why the separation of the national government's powers into three branches—executive, legislative, and judicial—and a federal structure of government offer the best protection against tyranny.

To what expedient, then, shall we finally resort, for maintaining in practice the necessary partition of power among the several departments as laid down in the Constitution? The only answer that can be given is that as all these exterior provisions are found to be inadequate the defect must be supplied, by so contriving the interior structure of the government as that its several constituent parts may, by their mutual relations, be the means of keeping each other in their proper places. Without presuming to undertake a full development of this important idea I will hazard a few general observations which may perhaps place it in a clearer light, and enable us to form a more correct judgment of the principles and structure of the government planned by the convention.

In the next two paragraphs, Madison stresses that for the powers of the different branches (departments) of government to be truly separated, the personnel in one branch should not be dependent on another branch for their appointment or for the "emoluments" (compensation) attached to their offices.

In order to lay a due foundation for that separate and distinct exercise of the different powers of government, which to a certain extent is admitted on all hands to be essential to the preservation of liberty, it is evident that each department should have a will of its own; and consequently should be so constituted that the members of each should have as little agency as possible in the appointment of the members of the others. Were this principle rigorously adhered to, it would require that all the appointments for the supreme executive, legislative, and judiciary magistracies should be drawn from the same fountain of authority, the people, through channels having no communication whatever with one another. Perhaps such a plan of constructing the several departments would be less difficult in practice than it may in contemplation appear. Some difficulties, however, and some additional expense would attend the execution of it. Some deviations, therefore, from the principle must be admitted. In the constitution of the judiciary department in particular, it might be inexpedient to insist rigorously on the principle: first, because peculiar qualifications being essential in the members, the primary consideration ought to be to select that mode of choice which best secures these qualifications; second, because the permanent tenure by which the appointments are held in that department must soon destroy all sense of dependence on the authority conferring them.

It is equally evident that the members of each department should be as little dependent as possible on those of the others for the emoluments annexed to their offices. Were the executive magistrate, or the judges, not independent of the legislature in this particular, their independence in every other would be merely nominal.

In the following passages, which are among the most widely quoted of Madison's writings, he explains how the separation of the powers of government into three branches helps to counter the effects of personal ambition on government. The separation of powers allows personal motives to be linked to the constitutional rights of a branch of government. In effect, competing personal interests in each branch will help to keep the powers of the three government branches separate and, in so doing, will help to guard the public interest.

But the great security against a gradual concentration of the several powers in the same department consists in giving to those who administer each department the necessary constitutional means and personal motives to resist encroachments of the others. The provision for defense must in this, as in all other cases, be made commensurate to the danger of attack. Ambition must be made to counteract ambition. The interest of the man must be connected with the constitutional rights of the place. It may be a reflection on human nature that such devices should be necessary to control the abuses of government. But what is government itself but the greatest of all reflections on human nature? If men were angels, no government would be necessary. If angels were to govern men, neither external nor internal controls on government would be necessary. In framing a government which is to be administered by men over men, the great difficulty lies in this: you must first enable the government to control the governed; and in the next place oblige it to control itself. A dependence on the people is, no doubt, the primary control on the government; but experience has taught mankind the necessity of auxiliary precautions.

This policy of supplying, by opposite and rival interests, the defect of better motives, might be traced through the whole system of human affairs, private as well as public. We see it particularly displayed in all the subordinate distributions of power, where the constant aim is to divide and arrange the several offices in such a manner as that each may be a check on the other—that the private interest of every individual may be a sentinel over the public rights. These inventions of prudence cannot be less requisite in the distribution of the supreme powers of the State.

Madison now addresses the issue of equality between the branches of government. The legislature will necessarily predominate, but if the executive is given an "absolute negative" (absolute veto power) over legislative actions, this also could lead to an abuse of power. Madison concludes that the division of the legislature into two "branches" (parts, or chambers) will act as a check on the legislature's powers.

But it is not possible to give to each department an equal power of self-defense. In republican government, the legislative authority necessarily predominates. The remedy for this inconveniency is to divide the legislature into different branches; and to render them, by different modes of election and different principles of action, as little connected with each other as the nature of their common functions and their common dependence on the society will admit. It may even be necessary to guard against dangerous encroachments by still further precautions. As the weight of the legislative authority requires that it should be thus divided, the weakness of the executive may require, on the other hand, that it should be fortified. An absolute negative on the legislature appears, at first view, to be the natural defense with which the executive magistrate should be armed. But perhaps it would be neither altogether safe nor alone sufficient. On ordinary occasions it might not be exerted with the requisite firmness, and on extraordinary occasions it might be perfidiously abused. May not this defect of an absolute negative be supplied by some qualified connection between this weaker department and the weaker branch of the stronger department, by which the latter may be led to support the constitutional rights of the former, without being too much detached from the rights of its own department?

If the principles on which these observations are founded be just, as I persuade myself they are, and they be applied as a criterion to the several State constitutions, and to the federal Constitution, it will be found that if the latter does not perfectly correspond with them, the former are infinitely less able to bear such a test.

In the remainder of the essay, Madison discusses how a federal system of government, in which powers are divided between the states and the national government, offers "double security" against tyranny.

There are, moreover, two considerations particularly applicable to the federal system of America, which place that system in a very interesting point of view.

First. In a single republic, all the power surrendered by the people is submitted to the administration of a single government; and the usurpations are guarded against by a division of the government into distinct and separate departments. In the compound republic of America, the power surrendered by the people is first divided between two distinct governments, and then the portion allotted to each subdivided among distinct and separate departments. Hence a double security arises to the rights of the people. The different governments will control each other, at the same time that each will be controlled by itself.

Second. It is of great importance in a republic not only to guard the society against the oppression of its rulers, but to guard one part of the society against the injustice of the other part. Different interests necessarily exist in different classes of citizens. If a majority be united by a common interest, the rights of the minority will be insecure. There are but two methods of providing against this evil: the one by creating a will in the community independent of the majority—that is, of the society itself; the other, by comprehending in the society so many separate descriptions of citizens as will render an unjust combination of a majority of the whole very improbable, if not impracticable. The first method prevails in all governments possessing an hereditary or self-appointed authority. This, at best, is but a precarious security; because a power independent of the society may as well espouse the unjust views of the major as the rightful interests of the minor party, and may possibly be turned against both parties. The second method will be exemplified in the federal republic of the United States. Whilst all authority in it will be derived from and dependent on the society, the society itself will be broken into so many parts, interests and classes of citizens, that the rights of individuals, or of the minority, will be in little danger from interested combinations of the majority.

In a free government the security for civil rights must be the same as that for religious rights. It consists in the one case in the multiplicity of interests, and in the other in the multiplicity of sects.

The degree of security in both cases will depend on the number of interests and sects; and this may be presumed to depend on the extent of country and number of people comprehended under the same government. This view of the subject must particularly recommend a proper federal system to all the sincere and considerate friends of republican government, since it shows that in exact proportion as the territory of the Union may be formed into more circumscribed Confederacies, or States, oppressive combinations of a majority will be facilitated; the best security, under the republican forms, for the rights of every class of citizen, will be diminished; and consequently the stability and independence of some member of the government, the only other security, must be proportionally increased. Justice is the end of government. It is the end of civil society. It ever has been and ever will be pursued until it be obtained, or until liberty be lost in the pursuit. In a society under the forms of which the stronger faction can readily unite and oppress the weaker, anarchy may as truly be said to reign as in a state of nature, where the weaker individual is not secured against the violence of the stronger; and as, in the latter state, even the stronger individuals are prompted, by the uncertainty of their condition, to submit to a government which may protect the weak as well as themselves; so, in the former state, will the more powerful factions or parties be gradually induced, by a like motive, to wish for a government which will protect all parties, the weaker as well as the more powerful.

It can be little doubted that if the State of Rhode Island was separated from the Confederacy and left to itself, the insecurity of rights under the popular form of government within such narrow limits would be displayed by such reiterated oppressions of factious majorities that some power altogether independent of the people would soon be called for by the voice of the very factions whose misrule had proved the necessity of it. In the extended republic of the United States, and among the great variety of interests, parties, and sects which it embraces, a coalition of a majority of the whole society could seldom take place on any other principles than those of justice and the general good; whilst there being thus less danger to a minor from the will of a major party, there must be less pretext, also, to provide for the security of the former, by introducing into the government a will not dependent on the latter, or, in other words, a will independent of the society itself. It is no less certain than it is important, notwithstanding the contrary opinions which have been entertained, that the larger the society, provided it lie within a practicable sphere, the more duly capable it will be of self-government. And happily for the republican cause, the practicable sphere may be carried to a very great extent by a judicious modification and mixture of the *federal principle*.

Publius

(James Madison)

Glossary

A

Acquisitive Model   A model of bureaucracy that view stop-level bureaucrats as seeking to expand the size of their budgets and staffs to gain greater power.

Actual Malice   Either knowledge of a defamatory statement's falsity or a reckless disregard for the truth.

Administrative Agency   A federal, state, or local government unit established to perform a specific function. Administrative agencies are created and authorized by legislative bodies to administer and enforce specific laws.

Advice and Consent   Terms in the Constitution describing the U.S. Senate's power to review and approve treaties and presidential appointments.

Affirm   To declare that a court ruling is valid and must stand.

Affirmative Action   A policy in educational admissions or job hiring that gives special attention or compensatory treatment to traditionally disadvantaged groups in an effort to overcome present effects of past discrimination.

Agenda setting   The process by which the media identifies the issues the public should be concerns about.

Anarchy   The absence of any form of government or political authority.

Anti-Federalist   An individual who opposed the ratification of the new Constitution in 1787. The Anti-Federalists were opposed to a strong central government.

Appellate Court   A court having jurisdiction to review cases and issues that were originally tried in lower courts.

Appointment Power   The authority vested in the president to fill a government office or position. Positions filled by presidential appointment include those in the executive branch and the federal judiciary, commissioned officers in the armed forces, and members of the independent regulatory commissions.

Appropriation   The passage, by Congress, of a spending bill specifying the amount of authorized funds that actually will be allocated for an agency's use.

Aristocracy   Rule by the "best"; in reality, rule by an upper class.

Attentive Public   That portion of the general public that pays attention to policy issues.

Australian Ballot   A secret ballot prepared, distributed, and tabulated by government officials at public expense. Since 1888, all U.S. states have used the Australian ballot rather than an open, public ballot.

Authoritarianism   A type of regime in which only the government is fully controlled by the ruler. Social and economic institutions exist that are not under the government's control.

Authorization   A formal declaration by a legislative committee that a certain amount of funding may be available to an agency. Some authorizations terminate in a year; others are renewable automatically, without further congressional action.

B

Balance of Trade   The difference between the value of a nation's exports of goods and the value of its imports of goods.

Battleground State   A state that is likely to be so closely fought that the campaigns devote exceptional effort to winning the popular and electoral vote there.

"Beauty Contest"   A presidential primary in which contending candidates compete for popular votes but the results do not control the selection of delegates to the national convention.

Bias   An inclination or a preference that interferes with impartial judgment.

Bicameral Legislature   A legislature made up of two parts, called chambers. The U.S. Congress, composed of the House of Representatives and the Senate, is a bicameral legislature.

Bicameralism   The division of a legislature into two separate assemblies.

Black Codes   Laws passed by Southern states immediately after the Civil war denying most legal rights to freed slaves.

Block Grants   Federal programs that provide funds to state and local governments for general functional areas, such as criminal justice or mental health programs.

blog   A website or personal online space where an individual makes public his or her opinions, comments, or suggestions.

blogosphere politics   The online arena of politics where the comments of bloggers become news.

Blue Dog Democrats   Members of Congress from more moderate states or districts who sometimes "cross over" to vote with Republicans on legislation.

Boycott   A form of pressure or protest—an organized refusal to purchase a particular product or deal with a particular business.

Broad Construction   A judicial philosophy that looks to the context and purpose of a law when making an interpretation.

Budget Deficit   Government expenditures that exceed receipts.

Bureaucracy   A large organization that is structured hierarchically to carry out specific functions.

Business Cycle   A term that describes fluctuations in the nation's economic activity including periods of economic expansion and contraction.

Busing   In the context of civil rights, the transportation of public school students from areas where they live to schools in other areas to eliminate school segregation based on residential racial patterns.

C

Cabinet   An advisory group selected by the president to aid in making decisions. The Cabinet includes the heads of 15 executive departments and others named by the president.

Cabinet Department   One of the 15 departments of the executive branch (State, Treasury, Defense, Justice, Interior, Agriculture, Commerce, Labor, Health and Human Services, Homeland Security, Housing and Urban Development, Education, Energy, Transportation, and Veterans Affairs).

Capitalism   An economic system characterized by the private ownership of wealth-creating assets, free markets, and freedom of contract.

Capture   The act by which an industry being regulated by a government agency gains direct or indirect control over agency personnel and decision makers.

Case Law   Judicial interpretations of common-law principles and doctrines, as well as interpretations of constitutional law, statutory law, and administrative law.

Casework   Personal work for constituents by members of Congress.

Categorical Grants   Federal grants to states or local governments that are for specific programs or projects.

Caucus   A meeting of party members designed to select candidates and propose policies.

Charter   A document issued by a government that grants to a person, a group of persons, or a corporation the right to carry on one or more specific activities. A state government can grant a charter to a municipality.

Checks and Balances   A major principle of the American system of government whereby each branch of the government can check the actions of the others.

Chief Diplomat   The role of the president in recognizing foreign governments, making treaties, and effecting executive agreements.

Chief Executive   The role of the president as head of the executive branch of the government.

Chief Legislator   The role of the president in influencing the making of laws.

Chief of Staff   The person who is named to direct the White House Office and advise the president.

Civil Disobedience   A nonviolent, public refusal to obey allegedly unjust laws.

Civil Liberties   Those personal freedoms that are protected for all individuals. Civil liberties typically involve restraining the government's actions against individuals.

Civil Rights   All rights rooted in the Fourteenth Amendment's guarantee of equal protection under the law.

Civil Service   A collective term for the body of employees working for the government. Generally, civil service is understood to apply to all those who gain government employment through a merit system.

Civil Service Commission   The initial central personnel agency of the national government, created in 1883.

Class-Action Suit   A lawsuit filed by an individual seeking damages for "all persons similarly situated."

Clear and Present Danger Test   The test proposed by Justice Oliver Wendell Holmes for determining when government may restrict free speech. Restrictions are permissible, he argued, only when speech creates a *clear and present danger* to the public order.

Climate Control   The use of public relations techniques to create favorable public opinion toward an interest group, industry, or corporation.

Closed Primary   A type of primary in which the voter is limited to choosing candidates of the party of which he or she is a member.

Coattail Effect   The influence of a popular candidate on the electoral success of other candidates on the same party ticket. The effect is increased by the party-column ballot, which encourages straight-ticket voting.

Cold War   The ideological, political, and economic confrontation between the United States and the Soviet Union following World War II.

Commander in Chief   The role of the president as supreme commander of the military forces of the United States and of the state National Guard units when they are called into federal service.

Commerce Clause   The section of the Constitution in which Congress is given the power to regulate trade among the states and with foreign countries.

Commercial Speech   Advertising statements, which increasingly have been given First Amendment protection.

Common Law   Judge-made law that originated in England from decisions shaped according to prevailing custom. Decisions were applied to similar situations and gradually became common to the nation.

Communications Director   A professional specialist who plans the communications strategy and advertising campaign for the candidate.

Concurrent Powers   Powers held jointly by the national and state governments.

Concurring Opinion   A separate opinion prepared by a judge who supports the decision of the majority of the court but who wants to make or clarify a particular point or to voice disapproval of the grounds on which the decision was made.

Confederal System   A system consisting of a league of independent states, each having essentially sovereign powers. The central government created by such a league has only limited powers over the states.

Confederation   A political system in which states or regional governments retain ultimate authority except for those powers they expressly delegate to a central government. A voluntary association of independent states, in which the member states agree to limited restraints on their freedom of action.

Conference Committee   A special joint committee appointed to reconcile differences when bills pass the two chambers of Congress in different forms.

Consensus   General agreement among the citizenry on an issue.

Conservatism   A set of beliefs that includes a limited role for the national government in helping individuals, support for traditional values and lifestyles, and a cautious response to change.

Conservative Coalition   An alliance of Republicans and Southern Democrats that can form in the House or the Senate to oppose liberal legislation and support conservative legislation.

Consolidation   The union of two or more governmental units to form a single unit.

Constituent   One of the persons represented by a legislator or other elected or appointed official.

Constitutional Initiative   An electoral device whereby citizens can propose a constitutional amendment through petitions signed by the required number of registered voters.

Constitutional Power   A power vested in the president by Article II of the Constitution.

Consumer Price Index (CPI)   A measure of the change in price over time of a specific group of goods and services used by the average household.

Containment   A U.S. diplomatic policy adopted by the Truman administration to contain communist power within its existing boundaries.

Continuing Resolution   A temporary funding law that Congress passes when an appropriations bill has not been decided by the beginning of the new fiscal year on October 1.

Cooley's Rule   The view that cities should be able to govern themselves, presented in an 1871 Michigan decision by Judge Thomas Cooley.

Cooperative Federalism   The theory that the states and the national government should cooperate in solving problems.

Corrupt Practices Acts   A series of acts passed by Congress in an attempt to limit and regulate the size and sources of contributions and expenditures in political campaigns.

Council of Governments (COG) A voluntary organization of counties and municipalities concerned with area-wide problems.

County The chief governmental unit set up by the state to administer state law and business at the local level. Counties are drawn up by area, rather than by rural or urban criteria.

Credentials Committee A committee used by political parties at their national conventions to determine which delegates may participate. The committee inspects the claim of each prospective delegate to be seated as a legitimate representative of his or her state

D

De Facto **Segregation** Racial segregation that occurs because of past social and economic conditions and residential racial patterns.

De Jure **Segregation** Racial segregation that occurs because of laws or administrative decisions by public agencies.

Dealignment A decline in party loyalties that reduces long-term party commitment.

Defamation of Character Wrongfully hurting a person's good reputation. The law imposes a general duty on all persons to refrain from making false, defamatory statements about others.

Defense Policy A subset of national security policies having to do with the U.S. armed forces.

Democracy A system of government in which political authority is vested in the people. Derived from the Greek words *demos* ("the people") and *kratos* ("authority").

Democratic Party One of the two major American political parties evolving out of the Republican Party of Thomas Jefferson.

Democratic Republic A republic in which representatives elected by the people make and enforce laws and policies.

Détente A French word meaning a relaxation of tensions. The term characterized U.S.-Soviet relations as they developed under President Richard Nixon and Secretary of State Henry Kissinger.

Devolution The transfer of powers from a national or central government to a state or local government.

Dillon's Rule The narrowest possible interpretation of the legal status of local governments, outlined by Judge John E. Dillon, who in 1872 stated that a municipal corporation can exercise only those powers expressly granted by state law.

Diplomacy The process by which states carry on political relations with each other; settling conflicts among nations by peaceful means.

Diplomatic Recognition The formal acknowledgment of a foreign government as legitimate.

Direct Democracy A system of government in which political decisions are made by the people directly, rather than by their elected representatives; probably attained most easily in small political communities.

Direct Primary An intraparty election in which the voters select the candidates who will run on a party's ticket in the subsequent general election.

Direct Technique An interest group activity that involves interaction with government officials to further the group's goals.

Discharge Petition A procedure by which a bill in the House of Representatives may be forced (discharged) out of a committee that has refused to report it for consideration by the House. The petition must be signed by an absolute majority (218) of representatives and is used only on rare occasions.

Dissenting Opinion A separate opinion in which a judge dissents from (disagrees with) the conclusion reached by the majority on the court and expounds his or her own views about the case.

Diversity of Citizenship The condition that exists when the parties to a lawsuit are citizens of different states, or when the parties are citizens of a U.S. state and citizens or the government of a foreign country. Diversity of citizenship can provide a basis for federal jurisdiction.

Divided Government A situation in which one major political party controls the presidency and the other controls the chambers of Congress, or in which one party controls a state governorship and the other controls the state legislature.

Divine Right of Kings A political and religious doctrine that asserts a monarchy's legitimacy is conferred directly by God and as such a king is not subject to any earthly authority, including his people or the church.

Divisive Opinion Public opinion that is polarized between two quite different positions.

Domestic Policy Public plans or courses of action that concern internal issues of national importance, such as poverty, crime, and the environment.

Dual Federalism A system in which the states and the national government each remains supreme within its own sphere. The doctrine looks on nation and state as coequal sovereign powers. Neither the state government nor the national government should interfere in the other's sphere.

E

Earmarks Funding appropriations that are specifically designated for a named project in a member's state or district.

Earned-Income Tax Credit (EITC) Program A government program that helps low-income workers by giving back part or all of their Social Security taxes.

Economic Aid Assistance to other nations in the form of grants, loans, or credits to buy the assisting nation's products.

Elastic Clause, or Necessary and Proper Clause The clause in Article I, Section 8, that grants Congress the power to do whatever is necessary to execute its specifically delegated powers.

Elector A member of the electoral college, which selects the president and vice president. Each state's electors are chosen in each presidential election year according to state laws.

Electoral College A group of persons called *electors* selected by the voters in each state and the District of Columbia; this group officially elects the president and vice president of the United States. The number of electors in each state is equal to the number of each state's representatives in both chambers of Congress.

Electronic media Communication channels that involve electronic transmissions, such as radio, television, and, to an increasing extent, the Internet.

Elite Theory A perspective holding that society is ruled by a small number of people who exercise power to further their self-interest.

Emergency Power An inherent power exercised by the president during a period of national crisis.

Eminent Domain A power set forth in the Fifth Amendment to the U.S. Constitution that allows government to take private property for public use under the condition that compensation is offered to the landowner.

Enabling Legislation A statute enacted by Congress that authorizes the creation of an administrative agency and specifies the name, purpose, composition, functions, and powers of the agency being created.

Energy Policy Laws concerned with how much energy is needed and used.

Enumerated Power   A power specifically granted to the national government by the Constitution. The first 17 clauses of Article I, Section 8, specify most of the enumerated powers of Congress.

Environmental Impact Statement (EIS)   A report that must show the costs and benefits of major federal actions that could significantly affect the quality of the environment.

Equality   As a political value, the idea that all people are of equal worth.

Era of Good Feelings   The years from 1817 to 1825, when James Monroe was president and there was, in effect, no political opposition.

Establishment Clause   The part of the First Amendment prohibiting the establishment of a church officially supported by the national government. It is applied to questions of state and local government aid to religious organizations and schools, the legality of allowing or requiring school prayers, and the teaching of evolution versus intelligent design.

Exclusionary Rule   A policy forbidding the admission at trial of illegally seized evidence.

Executive Agreement   An international agreement made by the president, without senatorial ratification, with the head of a foreign state.

Executive Budget   The budget prepared and submitted by the president to Congress.

Executive Office of the President (EOP)   An organization established by President Franklin D. Roosevelt to assist the president in carrying out major duties.

Executive Order   A rule or regulation issued by the president that has the effect of law. Executive orders can implement and give administrative effect to provisions in the Constitution, to treaties, and to statutes.

Executive Privilege   The right of executive officials to withhold information from or to refuse to appear before a legislative committee.

Expansionist Policy   A policy that embraces the extension of American borders as far as possible.

Exports   Goods and services produced domestically for sale abroad.

Expressed Power   A power of the president that is expressly written into the Constitution or into statutory law.

Extradite   To surrender an accused or convicted criminal to the authorities of the state from which he or she has fled; to return a fugitive criminal to the jurisdiction of the accusing state.

F

Faction   A group or bloc in a legislature or political party acting in pursuit of some special interest or position.

Fall Review   The annual process in which the Office of Management and Budget, after receiving formal federal agency requests for funding for the next fiscal year, reviews the requests, makes changes, and submits its recommendations to the president.

Federal Mandate   A requirement in federal legislation that forces states and municipalities to comply with certain rules.

Federal Open Market Committee   The most important body within the Federal Reserve System. The Federal Open Market Committee decides how monetary policy should be carried out.

Federal Question   A question that has to do with the U.S. Constitution, acts of Congress, or treaties. A federal question provides a basis for federal jurisdiction.

Federal Register   A publication of the U.S. government that prints executive orders, rules, and regulations.

Federal Reserve System (the Fed)   The agency created by Congress in 1913 to serve as the nation's central banking organization.

Federal System   A system of government in which power is divided between a central government and regional, or subdivisional, governments. Each level must have some domain in which its policies are dominant and some genuine political or constitutional guarantee of its authority.

Federalism   A system of government in which power is divided by a written constitution between a central government and regional or subdivisional governments. Each level must have some domain in which its policies are dominant and some genuine constitutional guarantee of its authority.

Federalist   The name given to one who was in favor of the adoption of the U.S. Constitution and the creation of a federal union with a strong central government.

Feminism   The philosophy of political, economic, and social equality for women and the gender consciousness sufficient to mobilize women for change.

Filibuster   The use of the Senate's tradition of unlimited debate as a delaying tactic to block a bill.

Finance Chairperson   The campaign professional who directs fund-raising, campaign spending, and compliance with campaign finance laws and reporting requirements.

First Budget Resolution   A resolution passed by Congress in May that sets overall revenue and spending goals for the following fiscal year.

Fiscal Policy   The federal government's use of taxation and spending policies to affect overall business activity.

Fiscal Year (FY)   A 12-month period that is used for bookkeeping, or accounting purposes. Usually, the fiscal year does not coincide with the calendar year. For example, the federal government's fiscal year runs from October 1 through September 30.

Focus Group   A small group of individuals who are led in discussion by a professional consultant in order to gather opinions on and responses to candidates and issues.

Food Stamps   Benefits issued by the federal government to low-income individuals to be used for the purchase of food; originally provided as coupons, but now typically provided electronically through a card similar to a debit card.

Foreign Policy   A nation's external goals and the techniques and strategies used to achieve them.

Foreign Policy Process   The steps by which foreign policy goals are decided and acted on.

framing   The presentation of an issue by the media which influences how audiences understand it.

Franking   A policy that enables members of Congress to send material through the mail by substituting their facsimile signature (frank) for postage.

Free Exercise Clause   The provision of the First Amendment guaranteeing the free exercise of religion.

Free Rider Problem   The difficulty interest groups face in recruiting members when the benefits they achieve can be gained without joining the group.

Front-Loading   The practice of moving presidential primary elections to the early part of the campaign to maximize the impact of these primaries on the nomination.

Front-Runner   The presidential candidate who appears to be ahead at a given time in the primary season.

Full Employment   An arbitrary level of unemployment that corresponds to "normal" friction in the labor market. In 1986, a 6.5 percent rate of unemployment was considered full employment. Today, it is assumed to be around 5 percent.

Full Faith and Credit Clause   This section of the Constitution requires states to recognize one another's laws and court decisions. It ensures that rights established under deeds, wills, contracts, and other civil matters in one state will be honored by other states.

Functional Consolidation   Cooperation by two or more units of local government in providing services to their inhabitants. This is generally done by unifying a set of departments (e.g., the police departments) into a single agency.

G

Gag Order   An order issued by a judge restricting the publication of news about a trial or a pretrial hearing to protect the accused's right to a fair trial.

Gender Discrimination   Any practice, policy, or procedure that denies equality of treatment to an individual or to a group because of gender.

Gender Gap   The difference between the percentage of women who vote for a particular candidate and the percentage of men who vote for the candidate.

General Jurisdiction   Exists when a court's authority to hear cases is not significantly restricted. A court of general jurisdiction normally can hear a broad range of cases.

General Law City   A city operating under general state laws that apply to all local governmental units of a similar type.

General Sales Tax   A tax levied as a proportion of the retail price of a commodity at the point of sale.

Generational Effect   A long-lasting effect of the events of a particular time on the political opinions of those who came of political age at that time.

Gerrymandering   The drawing of legislative district boundary lines to obtain partisan or factional advantage. A district is said to be gerrymandered when its shape is manipulated by the dominant party in the state legislature to maximize electoral strength at the expense of the minority party.

Get Out the Vote (GOTV)   This phrase describes the multiple efforts expended by campaigns to get voters out to the polls on election day.

Gini Index   A statistical measure of the distribution of income in a nation. A higher number indicates more inequality in incomes within a nation.

Glass-Steagall Act   A law passed in 1933 to regulate the banking industry which prohibited banks from engaging in speculative investments or becoming investment houses.

Government   The preeminent institution in which decisions are made that resolve conflicts or allocate benefits and privileges. It is unique because it has the ultimate authority within society.

Government Corporation   An agency of government that administers a quasi-business enterprise. These corporations are used when activities are primarily commercial.

Government in the Sunshine Act   A law that requires all committee-directed federal agencies to conduct their business regularly in public session.

Grandfather Clause   A device used by Southern states to disenfranchise African Americans. It restricted voting to those whose grandfathers had voted before 1867.

Great Compromise   The compromise between the New Jersey and Virginia plans that created one chamber of the Congress based on population and one chamber representing each state equally; also called the Connecticut Compromise.

Gross Domestic Product (GDP)   The dollar value of all final goods and services produced in a one-year period.

Gross Public Debt   The net public debt plus interagency borrowings within the government.

H

Hard Money   This refers to political contributions and campaign spending that is recorded under the regulations set forth in law and by the Federal Election Commission.

Hatch Act   An act passed in 1939 that restricted the political activities of government employees. It also prohibited a political group from spending more than $3 million in any campaign and limited individual contributions to a campaign committee to $5,000.

Hate Crime   A criminal offense committed against a person or property that is motivated, in whole or in part, by the offender's bias against a race, color, ethnicity, national origin, sex, gender identity or expression, sexual orientation, disability, age, or religion.

Head of State   The role of the president as ceremonial head of the government.

Hillstyle   The actions and behaviors of a member of Congress in Washington, D.C., intended to promote policies and the member's own career aspirations.

Hispanic   Someone who can claim a heritage from a Spanish-speaking country other than Spain. This is the term most often used by government agencies to describe this group. Citizens of Spanish-speaking countries do not use this term to describe themselves.

Home Rule City   A city permitted by the state to let local voters frame, adopt, and amend their own charter.

Homestyle   The actions and behaviors of a member of Congress aimed at the constituents and intended to win the support and trust of the voters at home.

I

Ideology   A comprehensive set of beliefs about the nature of people and about the role of an institution or government.

Impeachment   An action by the House of Representatives to accuse the president, vice president, or other civil officers of the United States of committing "Treason, Bribery, or other high Crimes and Misdemeanors."

Import Quota   A restriction imposed on the value or number of units of a particular good that can be brought into a country. Foreign suppliers are unable to sell more than the amount specified in the import quota.

Imports   Goods and services produced outside a country but sold within its borders.

Income Transfer   A transfer of income from some individuals in the economy to other individuals. This is generally done by government action.

Incorporation Theory   The view that most of the protections of the Bill of Rights apply to state governments through the Fourteenth Amendment's due process clause.

Independent   A voter or candidate who does not identify with a political party.

Independent Executive Agency   A federal agency that is not part of a Cabinet department but reports directly to the president.

Independent Expenditures   Nonregulated contributions from PACs, organizations, and individuals. The funds may be spent on advertising or other campaign activities, so long as those expenditures are not coordinated with those of a candidate.

Independent Regulatory Agency   An agency outside the major executive departments charged with making and implementing rules and regulations.

Indirect Technique   A strategy employed by interest groups that uses third parties to influence government officials.

Inflation   A sustained rise in the general price level of goods and services.

Inherent Power   A power of the president derived from the statements in the Constitution that "the executive Power shall be vested in a President" and that the president should "take Care that the Laws be faithfully executed"; defined through practice rather than through law.

Initiative   A procedure by which voters can propose a law or constitutional amendment.

In-Kind Subsidy   A good or service—such as food stamps, housing, or medical care—provided by the government to low-income groups.

Institution   An ongoing organization that performs certain functions for society.

Instructed Delegate   A legislator who is an agent of the voters who elected him or her and who votes according to the views of constituents regardless of personal beliefs.

Intelligence Community   The government agencies that gather information about the capabilities and intentions of foreign governments or that engage in covert actions.

Interest Group   An organized group of individuals sharing common objectives who actively attempt to influence policy makers.

Interstate Compact   An agreement between two or more states. Agreements on minor matters are made without congressional consent, but any compact that tends to increase the power of the contracting states relative to other states or relative to the national government generally requires the consent of Congress. Such compacts serve as a means by which states can solve regional problems.

Iron Curtain   The term used to describe the division of Europe between the Soviet bloc and the West; coined by Winston Churchill.

Iron Triangle   The three-way alliance among legislators, bureaucrats, and interest groups to make or preserve policies that benefit their respective interests.

Isolationist Foreign Policy   A policy of abstaining from an active role in international affairs or alliances, which characterized U.S. foreign policy toward Europe during most of the 1800s.

Issue Advocacy Advertising   Advertising paid for by interest groups that support or oppose a candidate or a candidate's position on an issue without mentioning voting or elections.

Issue Network   A group of individuals or organizations—which may consist of legislators and legislative staff members, interest group leaders, bureaucrats, the media, scholars, and other experts—that supports a particular policy position on a given issue.

Item Veto   The power exercised by the governors of most states to veto particular sections or items of an appropriations bill, while signing the remainder of the bill into law.

J

Jim Crow Laws   Laws enacted by Southern states that enforced segregation in schools, on transportation, and in public accommodations.

Joint Committee   A legislative committee composed of members from both chambers of Congress.

Judicial Activism   A doctrine holding that the Supreme Court should take an active role by using its powers to check the activities of governmental bodies when those bodies exceed their authority.

Judicial Implementation   The way in which court decisions are translated into action.

Judicial Restraint   A doctrine holding that the Supreme Court should defer to the decisions made by the elected representatives of the people in the legislative and executive branches.

Judicial Review   The power of the Supreme Court or any court to hold a law or other legal action as unconstitutional.

Jurisdiction   The authority of a court to decide certain cases. Not all courts have the authority to decide all cases. Two jurisdictional issues are where a case arises as well as its subject matter.

Justiciable Question   A question that may be raised and reviewed in court.

K

Keynesian Economics   A school of economic thought that tends to favor active federal government policy making to stabilize economy-wide fluctuations, usually by implementing discretionary fiscal policy.

Kitchen Cabinet   The informal advisers to the president.

L

Labor Movement   Generally, the economic and political expression of working-class interests; politically, the organization of working-class interests.

Latent Interests   Public-policy interests that are not recognized or addressed by a group at a particular time.

Latino   Preferred term for referring to individuals who claim a heritage from a Spanish-speaking country other than Spain.

Lawmaking   The process of establishing the legal rules that govern society.

Legislature   A governmental body primarily responsible for the making of laws.

Libel   A written defamation of a person's character, reputation, business, or property rights.

Liberalism   A set of beliefs that includes the advocacy of positive government action to improve the welfare of individuals, support for civil rights, and tolerance for political and social change.

Libertarianism   A political ideology based on skepticism or opposition toward almost all government activities.

Liberty   The greatest freedom of individuals that is consistent with the freedom of other individuals in the society.

Life Cycle Effect   People change as they grow older because of age-specific experiences and thus people are likely to hold age-specific attitudes.

Limited Government   The principle that the powers of government should be limited, usually by constitutional checks.

Limited Jurisdiction   Exists when a court's authority to hear cases is restricted to certain types of claims, such as tax claims or bankruptcy petitions.

Line Organization   In the federal government, an administrative unit that is directly accountable to the president.

Line-Item Veto   The power of an executive to veto individual lines or items within a piece of legislation without vetoing the entire bill.

Literacy Test   A test administered as a precondition for voting, often used to prevent African Americans from exercising their right to vote.

Litigate   To engage in a legal proceeding or seek relief in a court of law; to carry on a lawsuit.

Lobbyist   An organization or individual who attempts to influence legislation and the administrative decisions of government.

Logrolling   An arrangement in which two or more members of Congress agree in advance to support each other's bills.

Loophole   A legal method by which individuals and businesses are allowed to reduce the tax liabilities owed to the government.

Loose Monetary Policy   Monetary policy that makes credit inexpensive and abundant, possibly leading to inflation.

M

Madisonian Model   A structure of government proposed by James Madison in which the powers of the government are separated into three branches: executive, legislative, and judicial.

Majoritarianism   A political theory holding that in a democracy, the government ought to do what the majority of the people want.

Majority   More than 50 percent.

Majority Leader of the House   A legislative position held by an important party member in the House of Representatives. The majority leader is selected by the majority party in caucus or conference to foster cohesion among party members and to act as spokesperson for the majority party in the House.

Majority Opinion   A court opinion reflecting the views of the majority of the judges.

Majority Rule   A basic principle of democracy asserting that the greatest number of citizens in any political unit should select officials and determine policy.

managed news   Information generated and distributed by the government in such a way as to give government interests priority over candor.

Material Incentive   A reason or motive having to do with economic benefits or opportunities.

media   The means of communication, as radio, television, news outlets, that reach people widely.

media access   The public's right of access to the media. The Federal Communications Commission and the courts have gradually taken the stance that citizens do have a right to media access.

Medicaid   A joint state–federal program that provides medical care to the poor (including indigent elderly persons in nursing homes). The program is funded out of general government revenues.

Medicare   A federal health insurance program that covers U.S. residents age 65 and older. The costs are met by a tax on wages and salaries.

Merit System   The selection, retention, and promotion of government employees on the basis of competitive examinations.

Military-Industrial Complex   The mutually beneficial relationship between the armed forces and defense contractors.

microtarget   To use demographic and consumer data to identify individuals or small groups of people who will receive specific advertising messages.

Minority Leader of the House   The party leader elected by the minority party in the House.

Monetary Policy   The utilization of changes in the amount of money in circulation to alter credit markets, employment, and the rate of inflation.

Monopolistic Model   A model of bureaucracy that compares bureaucracies to monopolistic business firms. Lack of competition in either circumstance leads to inefficient and costly operations.

Monroe Doctrine   A policy statement made by President James Monroe in 1823, which set out three principles: (1) European nations should not establish new colonies in the Western Hemisphere; (2) European nations should not intervene in the affairs of independent nations of the Western Hemisphere; and (3) the United States would not interfere in the affairs of European nations.

Moralist Foreign Policy   A foreign policy based on values and moral beliefs.

Municipal Home Rule   The power vested in a local unit of government to draft or change its own charter and to manage its own affairs.

N

narrowcasting   Broadcasting that is targeted to one small sector of the population.

National Committee   A standing committee of a national political party established to direct and coordinate party activities between national party conventions.

National Convention   The meeting held every four years by each major party to select presidential and vice presidential candidates, to write a platform, to choose a national committee, and to conduct party business.

National Health Insurance   A plan to provide universal health insurance under which the government provides basic health care coverage to all citizens. In most such plans, the program is funded by taxes on wages or salaries.

National Security Council (NSC)   An agency in the Executive Office of the President that advises the president on national security.

National Security Policy   Foreign and domestic policy designed to protect the nation's independence and political and economic integrity; policy that is concerned with the safety and defense of the nation.

Natural Rights   Rights held to be inherent in natural law, not dependent on governments. John Locke stated that natural law, being superior to human law, specifies certain rights of "life, liberty, and property." These rights, altered to become "life, liberty, and the pursuit of happiness," are asserted in the Declaration of Independence.

Negative Constituents   Citizens who openly oppose the government's policies.

Net Public Debt   The accumulation of all past federal government deficits; the total amount owed by the federal government to individuals, businesses, and foreigners.

New England Town   A governmental unit in the New England states that combines the roles of city and county in one unit.

Nonopinion   The lack of an opinion on an issue or policy among the majority.

Normal Trade Relations (NTR) Status   A status granted through an international treaty by which each member nation must treat other members at least as well as it treats the country that receives its most favorable treatment. This status was formerly known as most-favored-nation status.

O

Office of Management and Budget (OMB)   A division of the Executive Office of the President. The OMB assists the president in preparing the annual budget, clearing and coordinating departmental agency budgets, and supervising the administration of the federal budget.

Office-Block, or Massachusetts, Ballot   A form of general-election ballot in which candidates for elective office are grouped together under the title of each office. It emphasizes voting for the office and the individual candidate, rather than for the party.

Oligarchy   Rule by the few in their own interests.

Ombudsperson A person who hears and investigates complaints by private individuals against public officials or agencies.

Open Primary A primary in which any registered voter can vote (but must vote for candidates of only one party).

Opinion Leader One who is able to influence the opinions of others because of position, expertise, or personality.

Opinion Poll A method of systematically questioning a small, selected sample of respondents who are deemed representative of the total population.

Opinion The statement by a judge or a court of the decision reached in a case. The opinion sets forth the applicable law and details the reasoning on which the ruling was based.

Oral Arguments The verbal arguments presented in person by attorneys to an appellate court. Each attorney presents reasons to the court why the court should rule in her or his client's favor.

Order A state of peace and security. Maintaining order by protecting members of society from violence and criminal activity is the oldest purpose of government.

Oversight The process by which Congress follows up on laws it has enacted to ensure that they are being enforced and administered in the way Congress intended.

P

Pardon A release from the punishment for or legal consequences of a crime; a pardon can be granted by the president before or after a conviction.

Party Identification Linking oneself to a particular political party.

Party Identifier A person who identifies with a political party.

Party Organization The formal structure and leadership of a political party, including election committees; local, state, and national executives; and paid professional staff.

Party Platform A document drawn up at each national convention outlining the policies, positions, and principles of the party.

Party-Column, or Indiana, Ballot A form of general-election ballot in which all of a party's candidates for elective office are arranged in one column under the party's label and symbol. It emphasizes voting for the party, rather than for the office or individual.

Party-in-Government All of the elected and appointed officials who identify with a political party.

Party-in-the-Electorate Those members of the general public who identify with a political party or who express a preference for one party over another.

Patronage The practice of rewarding faithful party workers and followers with government employment and contracts.

Peer Group A group consisting of members sharing common social characteristics. These groups play an important part in the socialization process, helping to shape attitudes and beliefs.

Pendleton Act (Civil Service Reform Act) An act that established the principle of employment on the basis of merit and created the Civil Service Commission to administer the personnel service.

Permanent Campaign A coordinated and planned strategy carried out by the White House to increase the president's popularity and support.

Picket-Fence Federalism A model of federalism in which specific programs and policies (depicted as vertical pickets in a picket fence) involve all levels of government—national, state, and local (depicted by the horizontal boards in a picket fence).

Pluralism A theory that views politics as a conflict among interest groups. Political decision making is characterized by bargaining and compromise.

Plurality A number of votes cast for a candidate that is greater than the number of votes for any other candidate but not necessarily a majority.

Pocket Veto A special veto exercised by the chief executive after a legislative body has adjourned. Bills not signed by the chief executive die after a specified period of time. If Congress wishes to reconsider such a bill, it must be reintroduced in the following session of Congress.

podcasting A method of distributing multimedia files, such as audio or video files, for downloading onto mobile devices or personal computers.

Police Power The authority to legislate for the protection of the health, morals, safety, and welfare of the people. In the United States, most police power is reserved to the states.

Policy Tsar A high-ranking member of the Executive Office of the President appointed to coordinate action in one specific policy area.

Political Action Committee (PAC) A committee set up by and representing a corporation, labor union, or special-interest group. PACs raise and give campaign donations.

Political Consultant A paid professional hired to devise a campaign strategy and manage a campaign.

Political Culture The set of ideals, values, and ways of thinking about government and politics that is shared by all citizens.

Political Party A group of political activists who organize to win elections, operate the government, and determine public policy.

Political Question An issue that a court believes should be decided by the executive or legislative branch.

Political Socialization The process through which individuals learn a set of political attitudes and form opinions about social issues. Families and the educational system are two of the most important forces in the political socialization process.

Political Trust The degree to which individuals express trust in the government and political institutions, usually measured through a specific series of survey questions.

Politics The process of resolving conflicts and deciding "who gets what, when, and how." More specifically, politics is the struggle over power or influence within organizations or informal groups that can grant or withhold benefits or privileges.

Poll Tax A special tax that must be paid as a qualification for voting. The Twenty-fourth Amendment to the Constitution outlawed the poll tax in national elections, and in 1966, the Supreme Court declared it unconstitutional in all elections.

Pollster The person or firm who conducts public opinion polls for the campaign.

Pork Special projects or appropriations that are intended to benefit a member's district or state; slang term for earmarks.

Precedent A court rule bearing on subsequent legal decisions in similar cases. Judges rely on precedents in deciding cases.

Preemptive War A military engagement fought to stop an enemy before that enemy attacks the United States.

President Pro Tempore The temporary presiding officer of the Senate in the absence of the vice president.

Presidential Primary A statewide primary election of delegates to a political party's national convention, held to determine a party's presidential nominee.

Press Secretary The individual who interacts directly with the journalists covering the campaign.

press secretary The presidential staff member responsible for handling White House media relations and communications.

priming   The process by which the media suggest the importance of an issue.

Prior Restraint   Restraining an action before the activity has actually occurred. When expression is involved, this means censorship.

Privatization   The replacement of government services with services provided by private firms.

Privileges and Immunities   Special rights and exceptions provided by law. States may not discriminate against one another's citizens.

Progressive Tax   A tax that rises in percentage terms as incomes rise.

Property   Anything that is or may be subject to ownership. As conceived by the political philosopher John Locke, the right to property is a natural right superior to human law (laws made by government).

Property Tax   A tax on the value of real estate. This tax is a particularly important source of revenue for local governments.

public agenda   Issues that are perceived by the political community as meriting public attention and governmental action.

Public Figure   A public official, movie star, or other person known to the public because of his or her position or activities.

Public Interest   The best interests of the overall community; the national good, rather than the narrow interests of a particular group.

Public Opinion   The aggregate of individual attitudes or beliefs shared by some portion of the adult population.

Purposive Incentive   A reason for supporting or participating in the activities of a group that is based on agreement with the goals of the group. For example, someone with a strong interest in human rights might have a purposive incentive to join Amnesty International.

R

racial profiling   Making negative assumptions about a person or class of persons based on racial characteristics.

Ratification   Formal approval.

Rational Ignorance Effect   An effect produced when people purposely and rationally decide not to become informed on an issue because they believe that their vote on the issue is not likely to be a deciding one; a lack of incentive to seek the necessary information to cast an intelligent vote.

Realignment   A process in which a substantial group of voters switches party allegiance, producing a long-term change in the political landscape.

Realist Foreign Policy   A foreign policy based on an understanding of the nation's economic and security interests.

Reapportionment   The allocation of seats in the House of Representatives to each state after each census.

Recall   A procedure allowing people to vote to dismiss an elected official from state office before his or her term has expired.

Recession   Two or more successive quarters in which the economy shrinks instead of grows.

Redistricting   The redrawing of the boundaries of the congressional districts within each state.

Referendum   An electoral device whereby legislative or constitutional measures are referred by the legislature to the voters for approval or disapproval.

Registration   The entry of a person's name onto the list of registered voters for elections. To register, a person must meet certain legal requirements of age, citizenship, and residency.

Regressive Tax   A tax that falls in percentage terms as incomes rise.

Remand   To send a case back to the court that originally heard it.

Reparation   Compensation, monetary or nonmonetary (e.g., formal apology), to make amends for a past transgression or harm.

Representation   The function of members of Congress as elected officials representing the views of their constituents.

Representative Assembly   A legislature composed of individuals who represent the population.

Representative Democracy   A form of government in which representatives elected by the people make and enforce laws and policies; may retain the monarchy in a ceremonial role.

Reprieve   A formal postponement of the execution of a sentence imposed by a court of law.

Republic   A form of government in which sovereignty rests with the people, as opposed to a king or monarch.

Republican Party   One of the two major American political parties. It emerged in the 1850s as an antislavery party and consisted of former Northern Whigs and antislavery Democrats.

Reverse Discrimination   The charge that an affirmative action program discriminates against those who do not have minority status.

Reverse   To annul or make void a court ruling on account of some error or irregularity.

Reverse-Income Effect   A tendency for wealthier states or regions to favor the Democrats and for less wealthy states or regions to favor the Republicans. The effect appears paradoxical because it reverses traditional patterns of support.

Rule of Four   A United States Supreme Court procedure by which four justices must vote to grant a petition for review if a case is to come before the full court.

Rule   The proposal by the Rules Committee of the House that states the conditions for debate for one piece of legislation.

Rules Committee   A standing committee of the House of Representatives that provides special rules under which specific bills can be debated, amended, and considered by the House.

S

Safe Seat   A district that returns the legislator with 55 percent of the vote or more.

Sampling Error   The difference between a sample's results and the true result if the entire population had been interviewed.

Second Budget Resolution   A resolution passed by Congress in September that sets "binding" limits on taxes and spending for the following fiscal year.

Select Committee   A temporary legislative committee established for a limited time period and for a special purpose.

selective attention   The tendency for individuals to only pay attention to information that reinforces their held beliefs.

selective information processing   For an individual, only thinking about the information that is really needed and disregarding the rest of the information presented.

Selectperson   A member of the governing group of a town.

Senate Majority Leader   The chief spokesperson of the majority party in the Senate, who directs the legislative program and party strategy.

Senate Minority Leader   The party officer in the Senate who commands the minority party's opposition to the policies of the majority party and directs the legislative program and strategy of his or her party.

Senatorial Courtesy   In federal district court judgeship nominations, a tradition allowing a senator to veto a judicial appointment in his or her state.

Seniority System A custom followed in both chambers of Congress specifying that the member of the majority party with the longest term of continuous service will be given preference when a committee chairperson (or a holder of some other significant post) is selected.

Separate-but-Equal Doctrine The 1896 doctrine holding that separate-but-equal facilities do not violate the equal protection clause.

Separation of Powers The principle of dividing governmental powers among different branches of government.

Service Sector The sector of the economy that provides services—such as health care, banking, and education—in contrast to the sector that produces goods.

Sexual Harassment Unwanted physical or verbal conduct or abuse of a sexual nature that interferes with a recipient's job performance, creates a hostile work environment, or carries with it an implicit or explicit threat of adverse employment consequences.

Signing Statement A written declaration that a president may make when signing a bill into law. Usually, such statements point out sections of the law that the president deems unconstitutional.

Single-Payer Plan A plan under which one entity has a monopoly on issuing a particular type of insurance. Typically, the entity is the government, and the insurance is basic health coverage.

Slander The public uttering of a false statement that harms the good reputation of another. The statement must be made to, or within the hearing of, persons other than the defamed party.

Social Contract A theory of politics that asserts that individuals form political communities by a process of mutual consent, giving up a measure of their individual liberty in order to gain the protection of government.

social media Websites and other online places where people can interact, form social contacts, and share personal or business information.

Social Movement A movement that represents the demands of a large segment of the public for political, economic, or social change.

Socialism A political ideology based on strong support for economic and social equality. Socialists traditionally envisioned a society in which major businesses were taken over by the government or by employee cooperatives

Socioeconomic Status The value assigned to a person due to occupation or income. An upper-class person, for example, has high socioeconomic status.

Soft Money Campaign contributions unregulated by federal or state law, usually given to parties and party committees to help fund general party activities.

Solidary Incentive A reason or motive having to do with the desire to associate with others and to share with others a particular interest or hobby.

Soviet Bloc The Soviet Union and the Eastern European countries that installed communist regimes after World War II and were dominated by the Soviet Union.

Speaker of the House The presiding officer in the House of Representatives. The Speaker is always a member of the majority party and is the most powerful and influential member of the House.

spin An interpretation of campaign events or election results that is favorable to the candidate's campaign strategy.

spin doctor A political campaign advisor who tries to convince journalists of the truth of a particular interpretation of events.

Splinter Party A new party formed by a dissident faction within a major political party. Often, splinter parties have emerged when a particular personality was at odds with the major party.

Spoils System The awarding of government jobs to political supporters and friends.

Spring Review The annual process in which the Office of Management and Budget requires federal agencies to review their programs, activities, and goals and submit their requests for funding for the next fiscal year.

Standing Committee A permanent committee in the House or Senate that considers bills within a certain subject area.

Stare Decisis To stand on decided cases; the judicial policy of following precedents established by past decisions.

State A group of people occupying a specific area and organized under one government; may be either a nation or a subunit of a nation.

State Central Committee The principal organized structure of each political party within each state. This committee is responsible for carrying out policy decisions of the party's state convention.

State of the Union Message An annual message to Congress in which the president proposes a legislative program. The message is addressed not only to Congress but also to the American people and to the world.

Statutory Power A power created for the president through laws enacted by Congress.

Straight-Ticket Voting Voting exclusively for the candidates of one party.

Strategic Arms Limitation Treaty (SALT I) A treaty between the United States and the Soviet Union to stabilize the nuclear arms competition between the two countries. SALT I talks began in 1969, and agreements were signed on May 26, 1972.

Strict Construction A judicial philosophy that looks to the "letter of the law" when interpreting the Constitution or a particular statute.

Subpoena A legal writ requiring a person's appearance in court to give testimony.

Suffrage The right to vote; the franchise.

Sunset Legislation Laws requiring that existing programs be reviewed regularly for their effectiveness and be terminated unless specifically extended as a result of these reviews.

Super PAC A political committee that can accept unlimited contributions from individuals and corporations to spend supporting a candidate as long as its efforts are not coordinated with the candidate's own campaign.

Superdelegate A party leader or elected official who is given the right to vote at the party's national convention. Superdelegates are not elected at the state level.

Supplemental Security Income (SSI) A federal program established to provide assistance to elderly persons and persons with disabilities.

Supremacy Clause The constitutional provision that makes the Constitution and federal laws superior to all conflicting state and local laws.

Supremacy Doctrine A doctrine that asserts the priority of national law over state laws. This principle is rooted in Article VI of the Constitution, which provides that the Constitution, the laws passed by the national government under its constitutional powers, and all treaties constitute the supreme law of the land.

Sustainability Achieving a balance between society and nature that will permit both to exist in harmony.

Swing Voters Voters who frequently swing their support from one party to another.

Symbolic Speech Nonverbal expression of beliefs, which is given substantial protection by the courts.

T

Tariffs   Taxes on imports.

Technical Assistance   The practice of sending experts in such areas as agriculture, engineering, or business to aid other nations.

Temporary Assistance to Needy Families (TANF)   A state-administered program in which grants from the national government are used to provide welfare benefits. The TANF program replaced the Aid to Families with Dependent Children (AFDC) program.

Third Party   A political party other than the two major political parties (Republican and Democratic).

Ticket Splitting   Voting for candidates of two or more parties for different offices. For example, a voter splits her ticket if she votes for a Republican presidential candidate and a Democratic congressional candidate.

Tight Monetary Policy   Monetary policy that makes credit expensive in an effort to slow the economy.

Tipping   A phenomenon that occurs when a group that is becoming more numerous over time grows large enough to change the political balance in a district, state, or country.

Totalitarian Regime   A form of government that controls all aspects of the political and social life of a nation.

Town Manager System   A form of town government in which voters elect three selectpersons, who then appoint a professional town manager, who in turn appoints other officials.

Town Meeting   The governing authority of a New England town. Qualified voters may participate in the election of officers and the passage of legislation.

Township   A rural unit of government based on federal land surveys of the American frontier in the 1780s. Townships have declined significantly in importance.

Tracking Poll   A poll taken for the candidate on a nearly daily basis as election day approaches.

Trial Court   The court in which most cases begin.

Truman Doctrine   The policy adopted by President Harry Truman in 1947 to halt communist expansion in southeastern Europe.

Trustee   A legislator who acts according to her or his conscience and the broad interests of the entire society.

Twelfth Amendment   An amendment to the Constitution, adopted in 1804, that specifies the separate election of the president and vice president by the electoral college.

Twenty-fifth Amendment   A 1967 amendment to the Constitution that establishes procedures for filling presidential and vice presidential vacancies and makes provisions for presidential disability.

Two-Party System   A political system in which only two parties have a reasonable chance of winning.

U

U.S. Treasury Bond   Debt issued by the federal government.

Unanimous Consent Agreement   An agreement on the rules of debate for proposed legislation in the Senate that is approved by all the members.

Unanimous Opinion   A court opinion or determination on which all judges agree.

Unemployment   The inability of those who are in the labor force to find a job; defined as the total number of those in the labor force actively looking for a job but unable to find one.

Unicameral Legislature   A legislature with only one legislative chamber, as opposed to a bicameral (two-chamber) legislature, such as the U.S. Congress. Today, Nebraska is the only state in the Union with a unicameral legislature.

Unincorporated Area   An area not loca-ted within the boundary of a municipality.

Unit Rule   A rule by which all of a state's electoral votes are cast for the presidential candidate receiving a plurality of the popular vote in that state.

Unitary System   A centralized governmental system in which local or subdivisional governments exercise only those powers given to them by the central government.

Universal Suffrage   The right of all adults to vote for their representative.

Unorthodox Lawmaking   The use of out-of-the-ordinary parliamentary tactics to pass legislation.

V

Veto Message   The president's formal explanation of a veto when legislation is returned to Congress.

Voter Turnout   The percentage of citizens taking part in the election process; the number of eligible voters who actually "turn out" on election day to cast their ballots.

W

War Powers Resolution   A law passed in 1973 spelling out the conditions under which the president can commit troops without congressional approval.

Washington Community   Individuals regularly involved with politics in Washington, D.C.

Watergate Break-in   The 1972 illegal entry into the Democratic National Committee offices by participants in President Richard Nixon's reelection campaign.

Weberian Model   A model of bureaucracy developed by the German sociologist Max Weber, who viewed bureaucracies as rational, hierarchical organizations in which decisions are based on logical reasoning.

Whig Party   A major party in the United States during the first half of the 19th century, formally established in 1836. The Whig Party was anti-Jackson and represented a variety of regional interests.

Whip   A member of Congress who aids the majority or minority leader of the House or the Senate.

Whistleblower   Someone who brings to public attention gross governmental inefficiency or an illegal action.

White House Office   The personal office of the president, which tends to presidential political needs and manages the media.

White House press corps   The reporters assigned full-time to cover the presidency.

White Primary   A state primary election that restricts voting to whites only; outlawed by the Supreme Court in 1944.

Writ of *Certiorari*   An order issued by a higher court to a lower court to send up the record of a case for review.

Y

yellow journalism   A term for sensationalistic, irresponsible journalism. Reputedly, the term is an allusion to the cartoon "The Yellow Kid" in the old *New York World,* a newspaper especially noted for its sensationalism.

Index